Routledge Revivals

ACCOUNTICS
APRIL 1897 TO AUGUST 1900

ACCOUNTICS APRIL 1897 TO AUGUST 1900

Part II

Volume III, Nos. 1 to 9, April 1898 to December 1898

Volume IV, Nos. 1 to 6, January 1899 to June 1899

Volume V, Nos. 1 to 6, July 1899 to December 1899

Foreword by

Gary John Previts

Routledge
Taylor & Francis Group

First published in 1992 by Garland Publishing, Inc.

This edition first published in 2018 by Routledge
2 Park Square, Milton Park, Abingdon, Oxon, OX14 4RN
and by Routledge
52 Vanderbilt Avenue, New York, NY 10017, USA

Routledge is an imprint of the Taylor & Francis Group, an informa business

Publisher's Note
The publisher has gone to great lengths to ensure the quality of this reprint but points out that some imperfections in the original copies may be apparent.

Disclaimer
The publisher has made every effort to trace copyright holders and welcomes correspondence from those they have been unable to contact.

A Library of Congress record exists under ISBN: 49029564

ISBN 13: 978-0-367-14387-9 (hbk)
ISBN 13: 978-0-429-03177-9 (ebk)

ISSN 1060-1228
Design by Marisel Tavarez

NEW WORKS IN ACCOUNTING HISTORY

Richard P. Brief, *Series Editor*

Leonard N. Stern School of Business
New York University

A Garland Series

ACCOUNTICS APRIL 1897 TO AUGUST 1900

Part II

Volume III, Nos. 1 to 9, April 1898 to December 1898
Volume IV, Nos. 1 to 6, January 1899 to June 1899
Volume V, Nos. 1 to 6, July 1899 to December 1899

Foreword by
Gary John Previts

Garland Publishing, Inc.
New York and London 1992

Library of Congress Cataloging-in-Publication Data

Accountics: A monthly magazine for Office Men. Published from April 1897 to Aug
1900.
This reprint has been classified by the Library of Congress as a serial.

ISBN 0-8153-0683-0 (pt. 2)
ISSN 1060-1228

Printed on acid-free, 250-year-life paper.
Manufactured in the United States of America.

Design by Marisel Tavarez

Contents

Volume III

Volume IV

Volume V

Volume III, Nos. 1 to 7
April 1898 to October 1898

Accountics

The Office Magazine

One Dollar a Year
Ten Cents a Copy

APRIL 1898

Volume III
Number 1

CONTENTS.

Published by the ACCOUNTICS ASSOCIATION: Wool Exchange New York

Accountics

VOL. III APRIL 1898 No. 1

The Monthly Statement

A pertinent question at this time is what effect will the Spanish-American war have upon the affairs of the accountancy profession? This question very naturally is being asked by accountants as they meet each other. The fact that the war scare to date has caused the postponement of many business enterprises is exerting a depressing influence in various directions. No definite and conclusive answer to the question, of course, can be given by any one, but it is not out of place in this connection to point out some of the more prominent facts which bear upon it.

It is becoming evident day by day that the war, which at this writing is barely begun, is likely to last longer and prove a more formidable undertaking than has been imagined by many of the hotheads who have been so eager for the fray. The antagonist with which our Government has to deal is much more likely to prolong the contest by avoiding as long as possible a decisive trial of strength on sea or land than to decide quickly the question at issue. A true estimate of strength shows the balance to be upon our side, but it may be many months before the real measure of that strength can be used against the enemy. The very preparations which our Government is making show that those in high authority appreciate the gravity of the situation, for they are putting into motion resources which will not be available for use for a considerable period of time.

The effect upon business must be to delay various new enterprises. As long as there is an uncertainty as to matters of national finance, taxation and the immediate results of the war, and as long as there is considerable popular excitement and anxiety, business must suffer. Therefore accountants will have to wait for those pieces of work upon which, otherwise, they would have been engaged before this. On the other hand, accepting as the probabilities of the case that the war will be considerably prolonged rather than quickly decided, it is very likely that the business public will ere long become so accustomed to war news that the cry of extras on the streets will cease to attract special attention, much less fan public excitement, and that the wheels of commerce and industry will very soon proceed to turn as though nothing was the matter.

As pointed out in a recent issue of Dun's Review, it is hardly to be supposed that seventy-three millions of Americans will want less food, less shoes or less clothing because of the war. The masses have got to go right on living and their wants will have to be supplied regardless. The contest, so far as battles are concerned, is likely to be one on the high seas rather than on land, and therefore only a limited number of contestants can take part at best. The drafts upon the men and general resources of the country, at the very worst, will be but a small fraction, comparatively speaking, of what the country could stand without being reduced to sore straits. These facts, and many others of a similar nature, have been cited by those who have discussed the question since war became probable.

Americans, we may add, can do business under almost any set of circumstances that can be imagined, and have often illustrated this fact. They very generally hesitate to engage in transactions, however, until conditions are measurably well established. The established conditions of war will permit certain lines of business to go forward as though no war existed. Others will be quickened by the special demand created by the war. The probabilities of the case are that with a full knowledge of, and firm faith in, the superior strength of the United States, the results of the war will be discounted by business men in general long before hostilities cease. Upon this basis various lines of business now checked in their activities will commence to go forward again as though there had been no interruption to the season of prosperity which was apparently at hand a little time since. Altogether the outlook is not without its hopeful features, so far as accountants and other professional men are concerned.

According to the announcement made in our last issue we present at this time the first of an important series of articles on Cost Accounts. There is no other subject pertaining to the accounting of manufacturing establishments that is as important as that of Cost Accounts, or "costing," as some of our English cousins put it. Selling prices are so low that nothing but the closest scrutiny of costs, in detail as well as in gross, will enable the manufacturer to manage his affairs safely. There are thousands of accountants in every part of the country who are proceeding alone in their cost records and calculations, devising schemes and inventing plans as they go along without any suggestions or assistance from those who have previously been over the same road. They are making the best applications that they are able of the principles of double entry, to a division of accounting that has never been thoroughly exploited in print, and of the fundamental principles of which a very insufficient knowledge exists among the most practical men. While many of these original investigators have succeeded in working out really excellent systems, all will be benefitted by an examination of what others have done in the same field, and a comparison of views, which our plan of investigation is to include before we are done, will therefore be extremely interesting, as well as immediately profitable.

As announced in the March number, this series of articles is to be practically exhaustive. There will be a careful review of what has preceded in this line, an indication of what is contained in various volumes that are to be bought, and a presentation of several new studies carefully wrought out in the light of actual requirements. The paper presented in another part of this issue, proceeding as it does from an accountant who views the subject of Cost Accounts from the professional point of view and who points out methods in a way to particularly interest and benefit his fellow professionals, is still of special interest to practical bookkeepers wherever engaged. The forms with which Mr. Tindall illustrates his remarks, while requiring minor modifications to adapt them to special uses, are comprehensive in character, and each will bear study in various respects outside of his description.

One point which Mr. Tindall makes in his paper is very important, and is something that will be still further developed before the series of articles has been completed. It is the proper connection between the Cost Accounts or Factory Accounts of a manufacturing business and the general books of the same business. Every double-entry bookkeeper learns early in his experience to depend upon the principle of balance for an indication of the correctness of his work. Without such a proof he feels all at sea. Manifestly there should be a balance maintained between the total Factory Accounts and the sum of charges against manufacturing, as shown in the principal books of the establishment. This feature is very frequently overlooked by those who are in charge of Manufacturing Accounts, but it is something too important to be allowed to go by default.

In another part of this issue particulars are given of the defeat of a bill before the recent Legislature of the State of New York which had for its object sweeping changes in what is known as the Accountant's Law. The bill was introduced and aggressively pushed in the interest of a single individual, who attempted, through political means, to reestablish himself in a position under the law from which he had been removed by the regents of the University for cause. The profession is to be congratulated upon the defeat of the measure. It is only proper to remark in this connection, however, that if there had been a united body of accountants in the State such a bill could not have been advanced so far as it was before being defeated. It is to the advantage of accountants throughout the State, therefore, to get closer together than they have been in the past in the management of matters which relate to their common interest. It is now certain that, for the present at least, the Accountant's Law will remain on the statute book without modification, and those who have hesitated to take advantage of it on the prospect of change should delay no longer.

Accountants' Associations

New York Chapter

The March meeting of the New York Chapter of the Institute of Accounts, held in the Waldorf-Astoria, was well attended, and those who were present, including a number of guests, were amply repaid for the trouble by the able and interesting address by Charles Dutton on "Corporations." A full report of this effort is printed in another part of this issue.

A communication from Gershom Smith, of Hartford, concerning his success in the formation of a chapter in that center, was presented, as well as a cordial invitation to his fellow-members to be present at the first meeting. A number of members signified their intention to accept the invitation.

Pennsylvania Public Accountants

The second annual meeting of the Pennsylvania Association of Public Accountants was held in Philadelphia, on Monday, April 18, and was largely attended by the members and much interest manifested. The treasurer's report showed the finances to be in excellent condition, all initiation fees and dues being paid up, and all expenses for the year paid, leaving a comfortable balance in the treasury.

The following officers were elected to serve for the ensuing year: President, John Heins, Philadelphia; vice-president, John Vaughan, Pittsburg; secretary, J. E. Sterrett, Philadelphia, and treasurer, William M. Lybrand, Philadelphia. Executive committee—C. N. Vollum, chairman, Philadelphia; John W. Francis, Philadelphia, H. B. Hayes, Philadelphia, and the president and secretary, ex-officio. The Association has in its membership practically all the leading public accountants in the State, and new members are rapidly being added.

Philadelphia Association

The Bookkeepers' Beneficial Association, of Philadelphia, held two meetings during April. The first, April 18, was addressed by Professor Robert E. Thompson, president of the Boys' High School, Philadelphia, the subject being "The History of the House." He spoke for a full hour, and was listened to with the closest attention by his audience, which consisted of both ladies and gentlemen. The speaker described the houses of the past, present and future. He combined a vast fund of information in regard to the habitations of the people in the dark ages, and the gradual progress made in each century, with many humorous incidents in connection with his description of Scotch, Irish, Dutch and Norwegian abodes. He declared that the houses of the present time had three very unnecessary industries carried on in them, which they would not have in the good time coming. These were heating, washing and cooking. He demonstrated that each community could have their heat provided by a general heat plant entirely outside of the houses themselves, and that the same thing held good in regard to the washing and cooking, and grew quite eloquent over the great advantages accruing therefrom on the score of health, economy and comfort.

On the 26th of April the members were entertained by a dramatic recital given by Mr. and Mrs. William Merriman Price. The object of this entertainment was to attract a large audience composed, so far as possible, of bookkeepers, in order to impress upon them the advantages of membership in the organization. The Philadelphia Association is in a very prosperous condition and, as usual, its leading members are energetically pushing its interests.

Hartford Chapter

As announced in our last number, steps for the organization of a Chapter of the Institute of Accounts in Hartford have been in progress for some time past. They have been entirely successful, and the Chapter has been formed. It was publicly introduced to the business world by a meeting held on the evening of March 29. The Hartford Chapter starts with twenty-six charter members. The officers selected include the following: President,

George A. Reynolds, of the Pratt & Whitney Co.; Secretary and Treasurer, Edwin Brower, Cashier of the Mercantile National Bank. The Governing Board consists of the two above mentioned and the following: Gershom Smith, of the Pope Manufacturing Co., elected for one year: Frederick Plimpton, Treasurer of Plimpton Manufacturing Co., for two years, and Jas. H. Turner, Treasurer of the Cass, Lockwood & Brainard Co., for three years. By special invitation several representatives of the New York Chapter were present at the first meeting of the Hartford Chapter, including Henry Harney, Secretary of the (National) Institute of Accounts: Chas. Dutton, President of the New York Chapter; F. W. Child, W. B. Jaudon and A. O. Kittredge.

The meeting was held in the rooms of the Y. M. C. A. Building, and there were upward of seventy accountants and bookkeepers present. Geo. A. Reynolds was chairman, and in his introductory remarks referred to the usefulness of such an organization as the Institute of Accounts and the advantage of being members of a Chapter of a National organization. He mentioned the enthusiasm with which the movement had been inaugurated in Hartford and the earnest work which the members were now prepared to do.

Chas. Dutton, President of the New York Chapter, who was then introduced, spoke upon the "Underlying Principle." Mr. Dutton's address, which was listened to with profound attention, was devoted to an analysis of business, having for its object the discovery of the vital principle without which business can neither proceed nor continue to exist. This principle, he clearly demonstrated, is accounting. He illustrated his meaning by various apt comparisons, showing how attraction and gravitation existed before the science of astronomy was formulated, and how accounting as an element of business has existed since man began to trade or barter, even though its literature and the expression of its principles in any form whatsoever are of comparatively recent date. Continuing his analysis, he showed that accounting as an element of business finds expression in accounts, the principles of which have been formulated into a science—namely, the science of accounts. Practical application of the principle of accounts to the recording of the transactions of business constitutes the art of bookkeeping. This led the speaker to the statement of element, science and art, or, otherwise expressed, element, knowledge and practice. First, he said we have accounting as an element of business; second, the science of accounts, a knowledge of the expression or manifestation of accounts; and, third, the art of bookkeeping, the practical application of the principles and methods of accounts to the records of business transactions. This triad, he asserted, is in its entirety accountics, a term originated in the Institute of Accounts, and which is a necessary addition to our vocabulary for the purpose of accurate expression. The exponent of the science, the speaker continued, is the accountant. His vocation is the profession of accountancy. The exponent of the art, he declared, is the bookkeeper. His occupation is the practice of bookkeeping. While the terms "accountant" and "bookkeeper" are commonly used interchangeably, as being one and the same, the functions of the two are, as a matter of fact, separate and distinct, and the lines of demarkation are very sharply drawn. The profession of accounts and the profession of bookkeeping are separate professions. The work of the bookkeeper is synthetical, for he compiles history or records acts performed. The work of the accountant, on the other hand, is analytical; he analyzes the record, proves its correctness, searches for causes and inquires into methods.

Referring again to the element, the speaker described the Institute of Accounts as the exponent of the element of accounting or the science of accounts. It stands, he declares, between business and its promoters and transactors as an interpreter of the elements and principles of economics. Its functions, he declared, are as follows: To secure a proper recognition of accounting as an element of business; to discover new principles of accounting and to orderly arrange them for the enlargement of the science; to originate and circulate the literature of accountics; to maintain the dignity and uphold the importance of the profession of accountancy; to broaden the scope of the science of political economy and to establish a harmonious relation of mutual dependence between itself and the business world, and to introduce able and experienced men everywhere to devote their energies in association with it to the accomplishment of its purposes.

The chairman next introduced Frederick W. Child, who spoke for a brief period upon the necessity for accurate accounting, illustrating his remarks by numerous references to the needs which have arisen in practical work, where manufacturers and others have been compelled to call in the services of expert accountants in order to determine what they could safely undertake in the production of goods, the arrangement of prices and meeting the other conditions with which they are confronted.

A. O. Kittredge, editor of ACCOUNTICS, was next introduced, who spoke on "Sustaining Interest in Institute Work." He likened a chapter of the Institute to a training school, wherein each one profits by drill and practice. He also compared it to an encyclopaedia of practical information, each page of which is a member of the organization. He referred to the New York Chapter as one in which the members have prided themselves upon being open books of knowledge and experience, to be consulted on call by their fellow members as their requirements may be. With respect to what might be done by the Hartford Chapter in the sense of sustaining interest, he pointed out first that every one should be given something to do. There should be no members without occupation in the work of the organization. By giving every one a duty all have the chance to be workers, and there will be none whose function it is to criticize and object. He then briefly referred to what may be accomplished in advancing the art of bookkeeping and promoting the science of accounts by discussions among the members, by formal papers prepared and read before the meeting, by addresses delivered by advanced accountants, both in the organization and outside, and by those who are experienced in collateral branches, referring more particularly to commercial law and to political economy. He pointed out that the fellowship is an honor conferred by the Institute, to which every member should aspire, and that properly regarded, it is an incentive to the performance of work that would go far toward maintaining interest in Chapter enterprises. He dwelt briefly upon what might be done by exhibitions, saying there was no good reason why there should not be an accountant's exhibition as well as exhibitions in other departments of intelligence and activity. He also referred to what the Hartford Chapter might do sooner or later with respect to securing proper laws upon the statute books of the State for regulating the profession of accountancy.

The chairman then introduced Henry Harney, Secretary of the National body, who expressed his pleasure at being present under such pleasant conditions. He referred to a former visit to the Connecticut capital, made many years ago, when there was a most important question to be propounded and one the answer to which he was sure at the time would affect his whole life. Fortunately she said "Yes." He was pleased to state that the partnership soon after entered into had been continued all these years with the most satisfactory results. The speaker then dwelt upon what the Institute has accomplished, upon its usefulness to its members, upon its influence in the business community and upon the high objects to which it is devoted.

The chairman next called upon Gershom Smith, whom he introduced as the one who had been especially responsible for the organization of the Hartford Chapter. Mr. Smith's remarks were brief and much to the point. We quote them in full: "I have been a member of the Institute of Accounts since June, 1895. My reason for joining the Institute was my conviction of the necessity of elevating the science and practice of accounts. I knew of no better way in which to contribute what I could do in that direction, and by which I might also obtain an advantage, than by associating myself with a society of its kind, embracing as it does in its membership the best accounting talent in every line of business. The results have been more than I anticipated, both in the way of forming desirable acquaintances and in the education derived. The latter has followed not only from the papers which have been read at the monthly meeting and published in the pages of the official journal of the Institute, but also by the discussions which the papers have drawn out. These discussions at all times have been both entertaining and instructive. While in Hartford we shall have few, if any, public accountants in the Chapter membership, we shall be well represented by the highest talent in insurance, banking, commercial and industrial lines. If the members of the Chapter will exert themselves to make the meetings interesting, either by reading papers themselves or getting others to do so, whether Institute members or not, and by taking part in the discussion which should follow the addresses, the meetings will never fail to be both interesting and beneficial. I want to appeal to every member of the Hartford Chapter not to be afraid to impart something of what he knows to his fellow-members. By so doing the benefits obtained will more than compensate for whatever may be imparted or given away. In closing, let me give you a special reason for the necessity of an association of this kind: Not long ago, in the course of a business talk on bookkeeping with a friend, he made this remark to me: It seems to me, Smith, that double-entry bookkeeping consists of opening the accounts that are really necessary for the conduct of the business, and then opening another lot of —— fool accounts to balance them." This was not an elegant way of expressing an idea which possibly finds lodgment in the heads of many business men of the day. There is need of combatting such mistaken notions. It should be the purpose of every member who has a friend of this kind to bring him to the meetings of the Chapter, so that he may in time learn that there is a reason for every account which the double-entry bookkeeper finds it expedient to open."

Remarks were also made by Clarkson N. Fowler, cashier of the Scottish Union and National and Lion Fire Insurance Company; Frank H. Bosson, of the Pope Manufacturing Company, and others. Several questions were also propounded by members and visitors present with regard to the scope and purpose of the Institute of Accounts, which were answered by President Dutton, Secretary Harney and others. In addition to the twenty-six charter members, a number of applications for membership are in the hands of the officers, showing that the Hartford Chapter starts out numerically very strong.

Chartered Accountants of Ontario

A pamphlet just issued by the Institute of Chartered Accountants of Ontario contains, in addition to the charter of the organization and its by-laws, various features which make it a most desirable addition to every accountant's literary collection. At the outset there is a table of contents, following which is a list of past presidents and vice-presidents of the Institute, giving in brief the administrative history of the organization from 1883 to date. Next follows the officers for the current year, a list of which was given in full on page 99 of our issue for February. Following the by-laws are various forms prescribed by the organization, and then comes a list of members and their addresses, showing date of election, when admitted as Associates, and when admitted as Fellows. A corresponding list of students of accounts who have passed the intermediate examination follows, after which is a list of the affiliated institutions. The latter include business colleges at Belleville, Kingston, Owen Sound, St. Thomas, Pickering and Toronto. By it the reader is informed that the business educational institutions of the Dominion and its leading organization of accountants are working together for the proper advancement of the profession.

More than half of the book is devoted to particulars which concern candidates for admission. There is a chapter on the primary examinations, another on intermediate examinations, and another on final examinations. A page is devoted to the fellowship degree, another to lectures, and then follows a list of the books recommended for study and reference. Still another list of books includes those which are in the circulating and reference departments of the library at Toronto. Then follows a reprint of the questions set for the intermediate examination of last year, and also the questions set for the final examination of last year. The reader cannot fail to be impressed in going through this pamphlet, with the thoroughness of the work performed by this organization. It argues well for the business interests of the Dominion.

St. Louis Society of Accountants

The Society of Accountants of St. Louis at a meeting, held late in March, decided to cut loose from the national organization with which it has heretofore been affiliated, and to proceed upon an independent basis. It was decided to hold meetings regularly on the third Wednesday of each month. For the present the meeting-place is in the Y. M. C. A. building. The officers elected for the ensuing year are as follows: President, Charles A. Sweetland, of the Platt & Thornburgh Paint and Glass Co.; vice-president, Charles C. Robartson, of the Woodward & Tiseman Printing Co.; secretary, William C. Manser, of the Donnewald Stephan Coal Co.; treasurer, Frank J. Davis, of the Flesh & Mook Printing Co.; librarian, Elbert E. Hickoff, of Scharff-Bernheimer Grocery Co. The organization is in a flourishing condition and has excellent prospects.

New York State Society of Certified Public Accountants

A very artistically arranged pamphlet has recently been issued by the New York State Society of Certified Public Accountants, devoted to the first annual dinner of this organization, held at the Waldorf-Astoria, December 28, last. An account of this banquet appeared in our January number (See page 93). The pamphlet before us gives the proceedings without abbreviation. The dinner was such a success and exerted such an influence of good in the affairs of the Association that this publication will no doubt be prized and preserved by all the members, as well as by many who are interested in the work of the Association, but are outside of the membership. The last pages are devoted to a list of officers and directors, as well also as a list of the members at the time the banquet was given.

At the meeting of the Board of Directors of this organization, held March 29, the following certified public accountants were elected to membership: S. Rodger Mitchell, Anson O. Kittridge, Edward W. Hooke, Capel Ellis LeJeune, R. DeWitt Mann, Alexander A. Kleborg, Anton R. Beaujon, John H. Carmlencke, James H. McKenna and John W. Francis.

A regular monthly meeting was held in the Waldorf-Astoria, Monday evening, April 11. The room was comfortably filled, although there was not so large an attendance as had been expected, since the order of business included a special report from the committee on legislation, and which has had in charge the efforts to defeat what is known as the Wray bill, and which is referred to at length in other parts of this number. President Haskins occupied the chair, and Rodney S. Dennis officiated as secretary pro tem. Routine business was conducted, the reports of various committees were submitted, including the committee on legislation. The report of this latter committee was received with evident satisfaction, and at the conclusion of the reading a vote of thanks was extended to the committee, and particularly to Mr. Dennis, who personally has been very efficient, and to whose efforts is largely due the defeat of an obnoxious piece of legislation.

The report of the committee on permanent headquarters evoked considerable discussion. It was the sentiment of the members present that headquarters should be secured without delay, and that they should be so located as to be most convenient for the members at all hours and for holding the regular meetings. The committee was continued with instructions to report still more definitely at the next meeting.

At the conclusion of the business session the chairman of the committee on entertainment introduced Francis Gottsberger, who presented a paper entitled "The Iniquity of the Legal Tender Act." At the outset the speaker explained that the paper he proposed reading had been prepared several years since as a magazine article, and had been tendered to a number of reviews, monthly magazines and daily papers, with the result in each case that it was politely declined as being untimely. The speaker's inference was that it was too radical in its denunciations of the Legal Tender Act for the constituency addressed by these several publications. The paper proved to be a historical review of the Legal Tender Act, with brief considerations of the circumstances by which the nation was surrounded at the time. Extracts from speeches in Congress and from decisions of the bench with respect to the act were presented. While admitting that the Legal Tender Act was a war measure and deemed absolutely necessary by many who were concerned in its passage, the speaker proceeded to show the injustice that it wrought, and traced to it the panic of 1873, also the panic of 1893, and the unsatisfactory condition of the national finances of the present time. At the conclusion of the paper brief discussion followed. Several of the members, while endorsing the conclusion of the speaker, yet pointed out certain inconsistencies in the train of argument.

Corporations: Their Importance and Use

By Charles Dutton, F. I. A.

Nothing is more common than for men to think that because they are familiar with words, they understand the ideas the words stand for. It is human nature to criticise, and sometimes severely so, those matters concerning which we are not familiar, and of which we have little or no knowledge. Johnson says: "Knowledge is of two kinds—we know a subject ourselves; and we know where we can get information upon it." But it is a lamentable fact that the knowledge or information that the great mass of people get is not sought; it is absorbed from the daily press and from intercourse with others; and concerning many every-day subjects that form a part of our environment but do not enter into our actual every-day life, we have only impressions and very little absolute knowledge.

The record of events and the doing in the business world which comes to us each day, more often than otherwise forms a very dark picture in the mind. Misfortune, disaster and business mismanagement are given in minutest detail, are flashed around the world between the days, reproduced, reprinted with glaring head lines, and illustrated with hideous pictures of men and situations. The function of the daily press, at least that which is read by the masses, is expressed in the lines of the poet:

—"to hunt corruption from her secret den;
And show the monster up, the gaze of wondering men."

Under such conditions it is not strange that our impressions and judgment are very much warped concerning many of the every-day transactions with which we think we are familiar, for the reason that we know so much of the ill connected with them and so little of the good. Further, it is true of very many of us, as stated by Dryden: "We think too little and we talk too much."

If these statements are not true, I cannot account for the prejudice there is in the minds of so many against corporations. A larger number of intelligent people than we imagine are of the opinion that corporations are formed simply and solely for the manipulation of some dark scheme, or that a business may be so conducted that the public shall know nothing about its composition or its purposes; that, as a matter of fact, corporations are a curse. Not long since, a gentleman, who had conducted a successful business and had accumulated a fortune, was consulting how he might leave his business and his name, and provide for his several sons and daughters. It was suggested that he form a corporation and give each of his children certain shares of stock, keeping some himself, which would be a provision for his widow. The suggestion surprised the old gentleman, who said with emphasis: "I have been in business a great many years, have made my money honestly and my name is honored in the community. Now I do not propose to allow that name to be brought into disrepute. I shall never consent to have my business conducted upon dishonest principles." His information concerning corporations had evidently been gathered from very unreliable sources.

Not long ago, and not many miles away, at a public meeting, a speaker gave utterance to these words: "Whether the world is growing better or not is a question." Among other things, in proof that it was not growing better, he said: "Look at business. Everything now is done under cover and in the dark. Legitimate business by merchants and firms is being crowded out by corporations and stock companies. If this continue, it will only be a question of time when there will be no honesty in business." Such language emanates either from compound stupidity, or from a highly cultivated or overwrought imagination.

The Sultan of Turkey has an enormous income, but it all comes from an impoverished peasantry. In the same way, many corporations are one-sided affairs, managed by those who enrich themselves at the expense of the confiding and unsuspecting stockholders; but for such I have no voice except in words of condemnation. Certainly there should be no subtraction before there is addition.

Combinations and trusts are simply corporations on a grander scale. Very little, if anything, is ever said or written in favor of them. Although they may be and undoubtedly there have been combinations which have been a curse, it does not follow that it must be so of

*An address before the New York Chapter of the Institute of Accounts, March, 1898.

necessity, for combinations may be and they have been a blessing.

There is a principle in science known as the principle of "tough or strong compounds." Two or more weak substances may be united and form a very strong substance, or two comparatively worthless substances may, by union, become valuable. For example, clorine and sodium. Each is of little value alone. The one is offensive and the other is a poison—yet when united they make our common salt, which is indispensable for manufacturing and culinary purposes. Copper, a soft metal, and zinc, not only soft, but brittle, when combined make brass, one of the toughest metals known, from which the artillery of years ago was made, because of its strength. So it may be possible to combine two or more industries, which of themselves have little reason for existence, and the result be a combination of legitimate value and importance.

I call your attention to one corporation which is a combination of corporations. I refer to the Pennsylvania Railroad Company, which controls 140 distinct corporations. It operates 8,800 miles of track, with ramifications in eleven States. It employs an army of nearly 100,000 men. With its adjuncts it represents an investment of $815,000,000 and an annual revenue of $135,000,000. It controls more wealth than any one of twenty-two States of the Union that might be named. It controls more wealth than the aggregate wealth of seven States of the Union. The United States Leather Company might also be cited, which has a dividend paying capital of $138,000,000, and which has given life to scores of helpless tanneries and utilized thousands of acres of isolated timber land. What kind of a copartnership could successfully carry on such an undertaking as either of these. Certainly there is nothing in the principle of combination detrimental to the best interest of general business. At this particular time we have nothing to do with the methods of management, whether good or bad.

It is my purpose to-night to speak as best I can in favor of and for the existence of corporations, and demonstrate their importance by showing their use. Corporations had their origin, I believe, in Rome, but they are known in almost every civilized country of the world, not all, however, existing under the same conditions or governed by the same authoritative power. But, on this occasion, we must confine ourselves to our own country, and we may do so with pride, for we can defend America's business with as much confidence as we can America's honor. In the United States, corporations are created by legitimate enactment and governed by statutory laws, differing materially in the several States, of which I shall speak hereafter.

Corporations are the natural and orderly result of the evolution and development of economics. In the days of our primitive civilization, labor was not only the original element, but the only element, and the perplexing complications of labor and capital were not known. And labor is still the original element in production. In getting something ready to sell, effort, physical or mental, or both, begins, accompanies and concludes the process. It leans on its counterpart, capital, which is not an original element. There is no natural opposition of interest between them, for capital is as dependent upon labor as labor is dependent upon capital. Each is equally interested in the prosperity of the other. Thus a deep and admirable harmony subsists in this, as in every other part of the social organism, and under no conditions can these elements be brought into more harmonious relations than through the operations of a legitimately organized corporation. And in this age of extensive commerce, the multiplication of manufactures and the extended business relations, corporations are not merely a convenience but a necessity.

What is a corporation? The dictionary informs us that a corporation is an artificial person created by law, or under authority of law, from a group or succession of natural persons, and having a continuous existence, irrespective of that of its members, and powers and liabilities different from those of its members. Stubbs in his "Constitutional History" says: "The marks of a legal corporation are the right of perpetual succession, to sue and be sued by name, to have a common seal and to make by-laws."

When two or more persons combine their property, labor or skill for the transaction of business, for their own common profit, they enter into partnership. The law merchant makes each partner an agent of the whole partnership, with full power to bind all its members. Corporations are precisely what their organic law makes them. For every function they claim to exercise they must find authority in the legislative or statutory grant. The difference between a copartnership and a corporation is this—the one may do as much as any one member pleases; the other must do as the State determines.

Let me direct your attention to some of the advantages of a corporation as contrasted with a partnership:

In most cases the principal inducement is "limited liability." To appreciate the extent of this advantage one has but to consider the position of those who engage in business without availing themselves of incorporation. A person who goes into business, whether on his own account or as a partner in a firm, is liable for all the debts incurred in the business to the full extent of his means. "If," says the law, "you are in business you must risk all you have." This is bad enough in the case of an individual, but is worse still in the case of a partner, for his entire property is at the mercy of his co-partners.

Suppose a man to have $15,000 invested in his business, and $10,000 otherwise invested. He cannot limit his liability to the $15,000, so that if the business fails the $10,000 will be safe.

Suppose a man with $50,000 to be a partner in a concern in which he has invested $5,000. He cannot limit his liability to the $5,000. If the firm fails the whole of his property may be swept away to pay the creditors, even though the failure may have been caused by the dishonesty or imprudence of his partners, or of some person in the employment of the firm, and even though the partnership agreement expressly declares that his liability is to be limited to $5,000.

Suppose three men enter into partnership upon an agreement that each shall contribute as capital $20,000, viz., $10,000 down and $10,000 when wanted, and that the liability of each to creditors shall be limited to the amount so agreed to be contributed. This attempt to limit their liability is void as to outsiders, and if debts are incurred each partner will be liable to his last dollar to pay the creditors in full. The law is well stated thus:

"As between the partners and the outside world (whatever may be their private arrangements between themselves), each partner is an unlimited agent of every other in every matter connected with the partnership business or which he represents as partnership business, and not being in its nature beyond the scope of the partnership. A partner who may not have a dollar of capital left may take money or assets of the partnership to the value of millions, may bind the partnership by contracts to any amount, may give the partnership notes for any amount, and may even—as has been shown in many painful instances—involve his innocent partners in unlimited amounts for frauds which he has craftily concealed from them. Partners may stipulate among themselves that some one of them only shall enter into particular contracts, or that, as to certain of their contracts, none shall be liable except those by whom they are actually made; but with such private arrangements third persons dealing with the firm without notice have no concern."

Such are the limited risks which the law imposes on those engaged in business.

"Business Corporations," says a late writer, "are the offspring of a great necessity—that is, that men should be entitled to engage in commercial pursuits without necessarily involving the whole of their property in that particular pursuit in which they are engaged."

The facilities which a corporation has for borrowing are much greater than those of an individual or firm engaged in business. Not only can a corporation borrow in the same way and by the same methods as an ordinary individual, but it can raise money by the issue of bonds or preferred stock. The bonds and preferred stock of a corporation are securities with which the public is familiar. They are easily enforced, and can be made readily transferable. If issued by a corporation in good repute they are a marketable security. It is by no means uncommon for a business to be organized into a corporation for the express purpose of raising money by the issue of bonds or debenture stock. In this way money may be raised on easy terms, which, but for the incorporation, it would have been impossible to raise.

Another inducement to the formation of private corporations is that persons doing business as a corporation can effectually restrict the powers of the acting partners (the directors). In the case of an ordinary partnership every partner is the unlimited agent of every other partner in every matter connected with the partnership. Thus, every partner may pledge and sell the partnership property, may buy goods on account of the partnership, may borrow money, contract debts on account of the partnership, and may make, indorse and procure to be discounted promissory notes and other negotiable paper in the name of the partnership. And these powers cannot be limited by agreement between the partners so as to bind outsiders. Accordingly a person dealing with a partner is entitled, unless he has express notice to the contrary, to assume that the partner has the usual powers. Thus, suppose the articles of partnership provide that one of the partners shall not be entitled to sign notes in the name of the firm; a note made by him in the name of the firm will nevertheless be valid unless the person taking it knew that he was not entitled to make it. A man, therefore, who is a member of a firm, is at the mercy of his partners, just as they are at his mercy. If one member of the firm proves dishonest or imprudent he has it in his power to involve his partners in liabilities unlimited in amount.

But the officers of a corporation are in a very different position. They are special agents, and have only such powers as are given to them by the Certificate of Incorporation, the By-Laws or by resolution of the Directors, and every one dealing with a corporation is ordinarily presumed to know the limitations and restrictions contained in the By-Laws and Certificate of Incorporation. If, therefore, those provisions say that the officers shall not borrow more than a specified sum without a resolution of the directors, a lender must see that they are not exceeding their power. So, if the By-Laws say that every note must be signed by at least two officers, the person dealing with the corporation must see that two officers sign, otherwise the note may be invalid. Then, too, if the officers without authority issue notes in the name of the company and apply the proceeds to their own use, the company may not be liable. The power of thus effectually limiting the authority and creating a safeguard against the unlawful acts of the acting partners is of great value, and constitutes one of the chief advantages which a corporation has over a partnership.

Another inducement to form a private corporation consists in the advantages which a corporation with perpetual existence has over an individual or partnership. A corporation is a person distinct from its members, and accordingly no change among its members by reason of death, bankruptcy, retirement or otherwise, affects the corporation's identity. It still remains and continues to exist until dissolved according to law. Some of the advantages resulting from this perpetual existence are as follows:

Where a man is engaged in business, whether alone or in partnership, he is liable to be forced into solvency. His position may be the result of mischance or of fraud or misconduct of a partner, a trusted agent or clerk, and he may be quite blameless himself; but as he has carried on business without availing himself of the advantages offered by the corporation act, he must take the consequences, and must lose every dollar he has, whether invested in the business or otherwise. He may attempt to make secure a part of his property by transferring a portion into the name of his wife, but in case of failure such transfers are generally attacked and frequently with success. He is not only ruined financially, but he cannot go into business under his own name.

But a corporation cannot make its stockholders bankrupt because of the corporation's liabilities. If the corporation gets into difficulties it will be wound up voluntarily or otherwise, and its creditors can take the corporation's property, but nothing more. The stockholders are free to go into business again, and are not put to expense of defending against insolvency proceedings or humiliated by examinations as insolvents, or by the appointment of receivers.

When one member of a firm becomes insolvent great inconvenience may be caused to the solvent members of the firm, for the share of the insolvent partner has to be ascertained and paid, and attachments and executions against the insolvent partner's interest in the firm are apt to follow, which discredit the firm and often wreck it. But in the case of a corporation the bankruptcy of a stockholder or officer does not affect the corporation; the creditor of the stockholder is not entitled to have the accounts of the corporation taken and the property sold, or to require the other shareholders to pay off the bankrupt's share; accordingly the concern goes on as before, its capital remains intact and its powers unaffected. The sheriff can never levy upon the property of the corporation under a claim against a stockholder.

A corporation has the great advantage of being able to contract with its stockholders, and to sue and be sued on such contracts. Thus, if a stockholder is indebted to a corporation for money lent or for goods purchased, the corporation can sue for the recovery without difficulty. So, too, if a stockholder lends money to the corporation he can sue for it and enforce any security given him by the corporation just as if he were not a stockholder. This a member of a firm cannot do, and great difficulties and inconveniences arise in seeking to enforce contracts between the members of a partnership in connection with the business of the firm; and a member of the firm cannot, as a rule, prove his claim in competition with the outside creditors of the firm. They must first be paid before he can get anything. This is one of the great disadvantages of a co-partnership. When a firm sees financial difficulties approaching, it is most natural that it should turn to one of its members for assistance. But this member of the firm cannot loan money and be on the same footing as a stranger. He cannot take security from the firm, nor can he be secured or made a preference creditor in case of insolvency. It is quite natural, too, that a near relative of a member of the firm should advance money to the co-partnership, but in case of insolvency preferences to relatives of members of the firm create suspicion, and the books are full of attacks upon assignments on the ground of preferences to relatives, an alleged preference to a relative often being the pretence used by dishonest firms for an attempt to convey property beyond the reach of firm creditors. All these difficulties, however, disappear in case of a corporation. Any stockholder or any other person may loan money to the corporation, may take security, may be preferred in case of insolvency, and when the fact becomes public it provokes neither adverse comment nor attack.

When a partner becomes a lunatic or of unsound mind the partnership is placed in an extremely inconvenient position, and litigation is generally inevitable, and the capital of the lunatic partner has to be determined and paid, and ofttimes the title to real and personal property becomes involved in difficulties. But the lunacy of a stockholder causes a corporation no material inconvenience. The committee retains or transfers the shares as the court directs, and there is no litigation as far as the corporation is concerned.

In the case of a partnership the property of the firm is usually vested in the partners jointly, or in one or more in trust for all, and the admission, retirement, death, bankruptcy or liquidation of a member generally involves some dealing by conveyance or otherwise with the property; this is inconvenient, and causes expense. Moreover, where partnership property is to be dealt with, by sale or mortgage, it is very common to find that by reason of some slip or omission the legal title is defective, or some release or conveyance is requisite, in order to complete the title of the partners. But in the case of a corporation the property is vested in the corporation as a body corporate, and no alteration among the members affects the title. The property remains vested in the corporation, and the directors for the time being can, in the name of the corporation, convey, assign, mortgage or deal with it regardless of any such change.

Contracts with a partnership are in law regarded as contracts with the members of it, for the partnership has not in law any separate existence; accordingly, if a partner dies, retires or becomes lunatic or bankrupt, or if a new partner is admitted, difficulties and inconveniences may ensue and releases, assignments, powers of attorney and indemnities may be requisite. But a corporation, being a body corporate, can sue and be sued on contracts made by it, notwithstanding any changes among its shareholders.

(*To be continued.*)

Test Question.—Explain the difference between single-entry and double-entry bookkeeping and the advantages to be derived from the latter system. Explain how the profit and loss for a given period is arrived at under both the single and double-entry systems. How does a single-entry balance sheet differ from one prepared under the double-entry system?

Test Question.—Explain the various ways in which a Banking Account can be recorded in one's books. What advantages and disadvantages may arise from keeping the Bank Account entitrely in the Cash Book?

Cost Accounts*

By W. B. Tindall, C. A.

Competition in the sale of manufactured goods is so keen and aggressive, and the margin of profits attainable so small, that the manufacturer who cannot tell by his accounts to a nicety what his goods cost, will probably not get what he should, or, in some cases, will ask too much and find himself out of the market. It is not my purpose to give an elaborate system for the keeping of cost accounts, but rather to discuss the principles which govern any method adopted, so as to arrive at results that will be found to be practical and, above all, accurate. In this particular branch of accounting it is generally conceded that it is not practical to get a system applicable to every branch of trade or that will give equally good results when applied to all the various kinds of goods manufactured, but rather that the accounts must be adapted to the peculiar wants of each business. The same principles, however, will be found applicable to all.

It has been urged by some business men that cost accounts, or, to use a more expressive term, "cost records," of any real practical value are not obtainable from their books of accounts, and, moreover, that even when a system has been devised that is reliable, the expense is so great as to be a question whether it would not be cheaper to stick to the method very much in use, of figuring cost of goods from data furnished by the foremen of departments, controlling the different processes the goods may pass through, together with the help of their expert workmen. It shall be my endeavor to show that this contention is not well taken; that it is possible to get the cost records of real practical value, accurate and upon a plan which will not increase the cost of the goods by reason of the expense incurred in getting the desired information. Bear in mind, I am speaking now of cost of goods composed of raw material of any kind upon which

No.	Name	Description of Work	Date required		Date delivered		Sales Book page	Cost Ledger page

FIG. 1.—FORM OF FACTORY ORDER BOOK.

No. John Smith 500 Spadina Avenue

Account Charged	Time	January 7	8	9	10	11	12	13	14	15	16	17	18	19	20	Total	Rate per hour	Cost
	Regular																	
	Overtime																	
	Regular																	
	Over																	
	Total																	

FIG. 2.—FORM OF TIME SHEET.

*A paper read before the Institute of Chartered Accountants of Ontario, February 10, 1898, by W. B. Tindall, C. A.

manual and machine labor are expended to put it in the form desired for the purposes of commerce.

The cost of any manufactured article is divided into the following component parts: First, material; second, labor, and, third, direct charge of production, which will be enumerated later on. These three items added together make the first cost of the goods or the shop cost. To these is then added the cost of selling, advertising and distributing, the total making the cost of the goods. The margin between the selling price and the cost as determined will be the gross profit to be transferred from the trading account to profit and loss account.

We have now to consider the books necessary to obtain a record. I shall only outline the principal books, for details vary with almost every business: First, the order book for entering the work required from the factory, whether the goods are for stock or are contract work. It may be of the form shown in Fig. 1. The number of the order is the number used all through the different shops to identify the particular work, and the accounts to be opened in the cost ledger are to be designated by this number, together with the name of the machine or description of goods.

Our next book will be the purchase register or invoice book, ruled as per form in Fig. 3, or in any other way that may be applicable to the particular business with which it is used. The totals of the columns 8, 9 and 10 should equal those of 5, 6 and 7; and the totals of cash-paid columns should agree with similar columns in the cash book, if there are many entries, and check with the individual entries, if few. The invoices are to be numbered consecutively with a rubber

No.	Name and Address		What for	Cre[...]	
				Invoices	Stor[...] Issu[...]
				5	6

FIG 3.—FORM OF PURCH[...]

Name	Page Cost Ledger	Labor	Material	Pro rata Expenses Production	Pro rata Expenses Selling	Total Cost	Pa[...] Sa[...]

FIG. 4.—MONTHLY S[...]

stamp, which should mark the invoice account in the cost ledger, to which the goods have been charged. This should give a tolerably complete record of the material used.

We have next the time sheet of the men, Fig 2, and the wages register, which will take care of the labor item of all costs. The books above enumerated will constitute the main posting mediums to the principal book of account—the cost ledger—which should contain spaces for material and labor. The form of cost ledger shown in Fig. 5 has been used most advantageously.

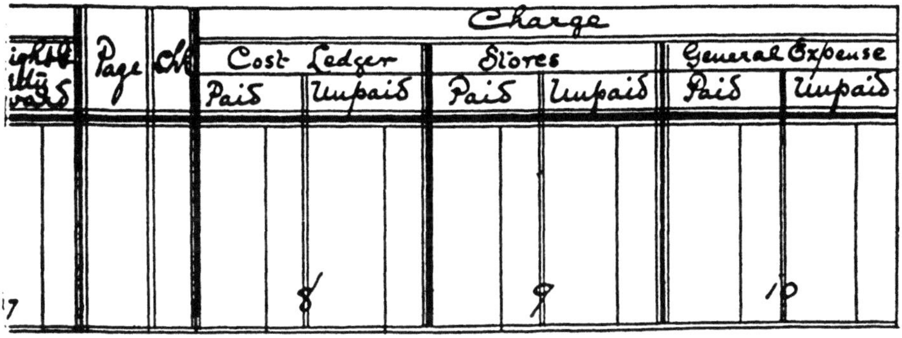

ER OR INVOICE RECORDS

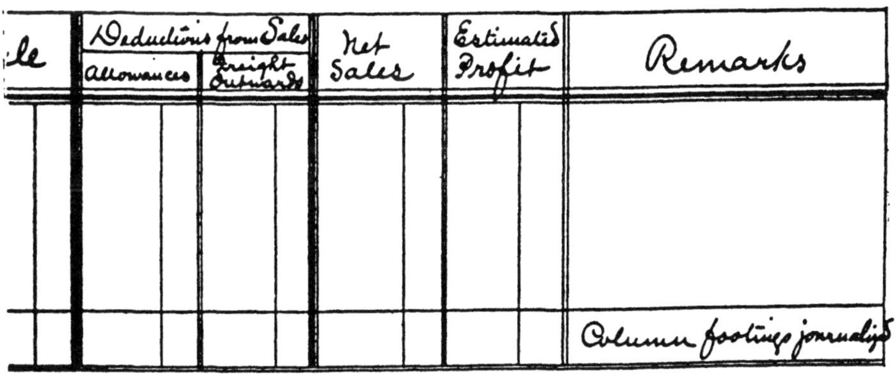

E. FROM COST LEDGER.

These are the principal books necessary for the record, and should, of course, be used in conjunction with and connected to the commercial books by means of a summary made from the cost ledger, monthly or quarterly, as desired. A form for this is presented in Fig. 4.

I shall now take up the various elements of the cost record in the order enumerated. The first principle we lay down in our costing is that material entering into cost must be taken at its invoice price laid down at the factory. This will apply to the majority of cases. In the case of a commodity that fluctuates very much in value (as, for instance, leather), and when the material used in the same line and pattern of goods is taken from stores purchased at different dates during the financial period under review, the plan is sometimes adopted of fixing upon a standard price for the material used. Then, if it is desired to get at the exact cost, say on a very marked advance in price, it is done by a simple calculation in proportion. Thus: If the material of an article cost $1 at the standard price of 15 cents per pound, what would it cost at the market price of 20 cents per pound?

In distributing material for the purpose of having labor expended upon it great care must be taken that all so distributed has been properly accounted for, and also charged to the proper account in the cost ledger. In large undertakings this is usually done through the store-room by means of warrants or orders on that department for the quantity of material required, but in small concerns which do not want to go to that expense it can be done by specially buying the material or having it invoiced separately for each particular piece of work or contract it is desired to obtain the cost of. The invoice then is charged direct to the job. Stores that cannot be handled in that way are distributed by one of the men under the superintendence of the foreman of the shop. The form of invoice register here given is designed for a business of this kind (Fig. 3).

It is well to bear in mind that the rule should be as closely followed as possible of only giving to a foreman the quantity of material necessary for the work, he having furnished an estimate of the quantity needed. Let me illustrate: Suppose the business is making furniture and it is decided to make 100 tables of the pattern to be called "A." An estimate would be made of the quantity of lumber required for tops, legs, sides, material for trimmings and fastenings, paints and oils

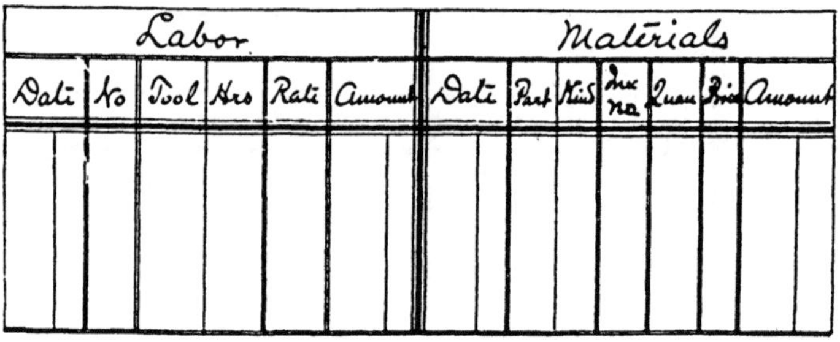

FIG. 5.—FORM OF COST LEDGER.

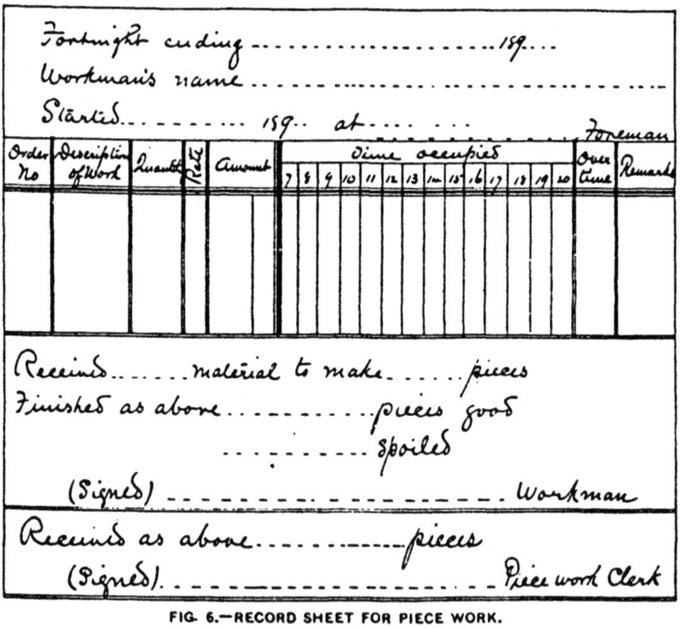

FIG. 6.—RECORD SHEET FOR PIECE WORK.

to finish, etc., allowing, of course, for waste in cutting up. Suppose that the estimate furnished was 600 feet of oak boards for tops and sides at $15, 1,200 feet of 4x4 inch oak for legs, and other material in proportion. Now, if the foreman is given or takes from store a larger quantity than the 1,800 feet specified, two evils will arise: First, the material over what is charged to this order will not be accounted for, and very probably will be used on another job, to which it is likely never charged. Second, it is liable to be wasted in the manufacture. If greater care were taken the result would be different. Should more material be asked for, the superintendent's attention would be called to it, and very often waste and loss through bad workmanship by this precaution would be avoided.

I also urge the importance, wherever practicable, of keeping track of quantities, such as tons of coal, feet of lumber, tons of pig iron and such like. Take the one important item in the expense account of any manufacturing business—namely, the supply of coal for the furnaces. If the engineer is aware that strict account is kept of the tons of coal purchased, and if he has represented that steam for the power required can be supplied on a consumption of ten tons per day, he will do all that he can to accomplish this result. If, at the end of the year, the record which shows exactly the number of tons purchased and the number of tons consumed further indicates that the daily consumption has been greater than the estimate, the superintendent will be able to fix the responsi-

No. ...... 100 Tables .... Pattern A ......

Particulars	Ripping & Cutting out	Planing and molding	Assembling	Painting & Varnishing: Material amount	Painting & Varnishing: Material cost	Painting & Varnishing: Labor	Credits (to be deducted from Costs): Particulars	Credits (to be deducted from Costs): Amount

FIG. 7.—FORM FOR SUNDRY PROCESS ACCOUNT.

Expenses apportioned to production and Selling by Manager	Total Expenses	Expense of Production	Expense of Selling and Distribution	Transfers	Expense of Production	Expense of Selling
To Sundry Shop Expenses				By transferred from est-		
as charged in Cost Ledger	500 -	500 -		imated expense a/c		
" General Expenses	300 -	300 -		charged contracts and		
" Office Salaries	300 -	150 -	150 -	work on basis of 35%		
" Repairs & Renewals	75 -	75 -		on labor paid to pro-		
" Com. & Travelling	300 -	100 -	200 -	duce $3428.57	1200 -	
" Warehouse Exp	80 -		80 -	By 5% on sales for		
" Rent & Taxes	75 -	20 -	55 -	year $12,000.		600 -
" Postage & Stationery	50 -	30 -	20 -	By charged Profit & Loss		
" Advertising	100 -		100 -	deficiency occasioned		
" Incidentals	40 -	15 -	25 -	by short output	90 -	30 -
	1920 -	1290 -	630 -		1290 -	630 -

FIG. 8.—ESTIMATED AND ACTUAL EXPENSES.

bility for the extra expense, either on the fuel or the firing. In my own experience I have found such practice very beneficial in checking profit and loss figures.

A case in point is as follows: On reviewing the year's trading in oats, the trading account showed a much smaller profit than had been anticipated, and on the test of quantities received and sold being applied, I found a large quantity had never been charged through oversight in the warehouse.

In some trades it is highly important that the record should show what portion of raw material has gone to waste in the operation of cutting up. This is particularly the case in all wood-working industries, such as sash and door factories, furniture factories and piano factories. In such lines of business it is quite possible for the manufacturer to make quite a saving by buying the dearer in price of two lots of materials that may be offered him simply because he has less waste in cutting up. If a record is kept of how each lot of materials turns out in this respect for the full season, it gives the principal just such information as he requires in order to buy economically for his purpose. In some trades the record would require to show the value of by-products, which would influence the cost very largely. The method of distributing material would not necessarily be any different whether labor is paid by the hour or on piece-work principle.

From the above we further conclude that the part of the cost consisting of material will affect the total cost in the following ways: First, as to price paid; second, as to quantities received; third, as to waste in manufacture in cutting up, and, fourth, as to material spoiled by bad workmanship. The cost record should give us information on each of these points.

For the keeping track of labor there are devices and specially ruled books without number, all of more or less merit. It is not my purpose to go into these in detail, but simply to say that whatever is used must be of such a nature as to quickly, economically and accurately give the following information: First, that all labor on the monthly pay roll has actually been performed; second, that it has been performed at the rate agreed upon, and, third, that the work upon which it has been expended is properly charged with it in two particulars—namely, number of hours and value.

To facilitate the recording of time in the cost books, each man should have a number assigned to him. In concerns where there are a number of departments each department is given a separate set of numbers. The numbers of one department run from one to three hundred; of another from three hundred and one to five hundred; of a third from five hundred and one to seven hundred, and so on. By this means the number indicates the department as well as the workman. In a great many concerns the practice is to issue a daily time slip to each workman, and insist upon his entering upon it the time that he spends upon each piece of work, and to have this slip in turn verified by the foreman of the shop and finally returned to the office. In some businesses this may work very well, and be the best way, particularly in the building trades, where men may be working outside of the factory at two or three different jobs. When the undertaking is not of this nature, and where there are from 100 to 200 men or over, the better plan seems to be to have this information collected by one of the regular office staff. If the pay day is fortnightly the time sheets may include time for that period. A good form of time sheets, which will be found applicable to a great number of businesses, is shown in Fig. 2.

The advantage claimed for the daily slip system is that the work is always kept entered up to date and available. But it must be borne in mind that while this is true it is a very expensive system. Workmen, as a general rule, do not care to use the pen or pencil any more than they can help, and if the time consumed by each man in filling up his card is taken into account it will be found to more than equal the salary of the necessary clerks to do this work. Particularly is this the case in such undertakings as may have men working in gangs of four or five, where the filling in of the card for any one man may stop the work of the whole gang. Men, in making the entries on their slips, seldom appreciate the necessity of accuracy in such matters as the quantity of material or the correct number for designating their work. Very often they will explain in a very few minutes to a clerk what they could not write down in a very much longer time. The form of time sheet referred to has the additional advantage of being the analysis of the time made by the timekeeper when it is being taken up, and the amount is posted direct from this time sheet to the several accounts in the cost ledger.

Another system advocated is to have all the time work distributed by means of a book which has columns for each piece of work or order. Under each head are entered the number of hours worked and the total number of hours charged at a fixed rate, according to the whole amount of wages paid each month, leaving out the foreman. On this point allow me to quote an article by Mr. F. W. Child:

"This plan is objectionable for at least two reasons. In all classes of shops there are some parts of the work which can be done by less expensive men in the same class of labor than others. The money value in the labor item in such cases will be too high, while the other parts, which are really more expensive to make, the value will be proportionately too low. Accordingly, results thus reached are useless as a basis for piece-work prices, or even for sales prices. Again, the identity by the average system is lost, whereas the former system enables the foreman to fix responsibility for bad workmanship."

This is a much more important matter than would at first appear, and after looking carefully into the matter, I am convinced that the best way to arrive at cost is by charging the actual time expended upon the work at the actual rate paid. When we come to consider that circumstances may arise wherein it is very desirable that work should be secured, even at small profit, in order that the output of a factory may be kept up to its full capacity, the total annual volume plays such a very important part in determining the cost of goods, as I shall show more clearly further on, that by the average system the work that could be done almost wholly by apprentice labor would apparently cost more than the purchaser was prepared or could afford to pay. By the other system a very small margin of profit could be shown and the order accepted.

I have treated the item of labor so far only on the system of paying for number of hours. We have next to consider the system of paying by piece work. Some concerns seek to get nearly all the processes through which the goods may go paid on the piece-work basis; and, when the work is continuous, this is probably the best way. It is the one generally adopted by the largest manufacturers. A record sheet—the voucher upon which the work is paid—may be of the form shown in Fig. 6. In piece work great care must be exercised as to the quality of work turned out, and also as to spoiled material. When the material is valuable this is charged back to the workman, and if not treated in this way the value of the material spoiled must be taken into account in arriving at the cost. The portion of cost consisting of labor will affect the total cost in each of the ways following: A. By the rate of wages paid. B. By the amount of efficient work received, and C, by the judicious distributing of work. By this I mean to avoid giving work to a man receiving 20 cents per hour that can just as well be done by one receiving 10 cents per hour. The record sheet should give information on all these points.

Let us next give attention to the fixed charges of production. By this I mean all charges that cannot definitely be charged against any piece of work or job, such as wages or foreman, engineer, fireman, portion of watchman's wages, wages paid for cleaning shops, etc.; coal, oil and other engine supplies used in connection with the supply of power, taxes on machinery and depreciation of machinery. The main point for consideration is how shall this expense charge be distributed over the work done so that each piece of work or contract shall bear its equitable share. Bear in mind that we are now discussing a purely manufacturing business and the fixed charges necessary to production. The fixed charges necessary to selling and distributing we will consider later on.

John Man, Jr., M. A., C. A., of Glasgow, in a paper read before the Glasgow Chartered Accountant's Debating Society and published in the Accountant for 1891, presents this subject so ably and clearly that I cannot do better than quote from his paper:

"But turning now to the expense of production proper, what I called before 'direct expenses,' mainly superintendence and up-keep of plant and buildings, to what do these vary in proportion? In other words, are such direct expenses of manufacturing greater or less, (1) as the number of men is greater or less, (2) as the wages are higher or lower, (3) as material used is greater or less in proportion, or, (4) as material used is higher or lower in price. That is, do direct expenses vary (1) with quantity of time worked, or (2) with value of time spent, or (3) with quantity of material used up, cr (4) with value of material used up.

"This is one of the most essential points in our whole inquiry, and is worth minute attention. Unless in very special cases (where cost of raw material is practically the whole cost, for example, as in a foundry), the direct expense of production has little or no appreciable relation, either to the quantity or value of the raw material used up. The expenses certainly do not rise and fall with the markets for the raw material. We may therefore dismiss the two cases indicated by three and four above.

"I now refer, remember, to the direct expenses. Part of the expenses, as I have just pointed out, do bear a relation to the value of the material used up. We are therefore reduced to the labor expended. Do the direct expenses, in theory, vary with labor? My answer is that they do, not so much with the value of the labor as with the quantity, and my conclusion is that in theory direct expenses of production bear the closest relation to the time expended, and that therefore, in determining the prime cost, such direct expense should be distributed over the work in proportion to that expended on each job.

"Consider for a moment: Take a quick, expert, efficient workman. Does he require as much instruction, control and supervision as a lazy, inefficient man? Does he waste material, gas, water, fuel and tools as much as a lazy, inefficient man? No; he does not. Of course, if two such workmen get the same rate of weekly wages for working the same time, as they frequently do, under the present trade-union principles, it is immaterial whether we charge our direct expenses in proportion to the time spent or to the wages paid for each job. The work of the inferior man will always be more costly, and will be so shown. Now, if we charge direct expenses upon wages, the higher the wages the greater the burden of direct expenses it bears, where it should really be the other way. I think it clear, then, that direct expenses vary most closely with the time occupied with each job, and can be best applied in proportion to the time, and not the value of such time as expressed in the wages paid.

"Direct expenses vary directly with the time occupied, and inversely as the wages paid. This is corroborated by the admitted fact that within certain limits it is really cheapest in the end to employ efficient and thoroughly competent hands. Now this, as I have said, is the theoretical position, but I am afraid that it is rarely, if ever, carried out in costing, probably because the records of the value of wages paid for each job are of themselves such a prominent element in costing that they are taken as the foundation for direct expenses rather than the time occupied, which lies behind these wages for nearly all practical purposes. However, the direct expenses may be safely applied in proportion to the wages paid."

(To be continued.)

The Broaker Incident

All the signs point to a conclusion of the Broaker incident. The bill introduced before the last Legislature by Senator Wray, which had for its object to compel the Board of Regents of the University of the State to appoint on the board of examiners of public accountants one man each from the American Association of Public Accountants, the National Society of Certified Public Accountants, and the New York State Society of Certified Public Accountants, failed to pass the Assembly after it had passed the Senate.

On the 23d of March the bill came up in the order of second reading. Assemblyman Greene asked for an explanation, and Assemblyman Marshall, who had assumed charge of the measure, replied that he would like to have the bill advanced and let the discussion go for third reading. Assemblyman Oliver objected, saying that it was inexpedient to advance any bill which embodies an insult to the entire Board of Regents of the State. Assemblyman Fish attacked the bill with vigor, declaring it to be a bad measure. The man behind it, he said, had had trouble with the regents and had been deposed. The worst feature of the measure was that it was mandatory in its provisions. He declared it was drawn to further mere personal and individual ends and in the interest of one man who had had differences with the regents. The bill had been killed twice and had been reported simply out of consideration to the member from Kings, Mr. Marshall. Mr. Oliver replied that he was authorized by the Regents of the University to state that the man discharged by them was discharged for good and sufficient reasons. He moved to recommit, and on that Mr. Marshall called for the yeas and nays. The motion was carried 42 to 31, and the bill went back to the committee, where it will doubtless remain.

The bill made it mandatory upon the Board of Regents to grant a certificate to any person who is a citizen of the United States, or who has declared his intention of becoming such citizen, and who shall have been, for one year or more before the 17th day of April, 1896, practising in this State on his own account or as a public accountant. The Mail and Express, of New York, in its issue of the 24th ult., commenting on this bill, said:

"The bill was introduced in January by Senator Wray, of Brooklyn, and on account of the circumstances that are alleged to have inspired it, it has aroused considerable public interest. Last November, after asking for his resignation from the Board of Examiners of Public Accounts, the State Board of Regents dropped Mr. Frank Broaker and appointed in his place Mr. James Anyon. This action resulted from the information conveyed to the Regents that Broaker was using his office for personal gain and that he was blocking the efforts of the two other members of the board. It is stated that the president of the American Association of Public Accountants admits that the bill was inaugurated for the purpose of vindicating Mr. Broaker and avenging the action taken against him. Mr. Broaker's position in the American Association of Public Accountants, which is practically identical with the National Society of Certified Public Accountants, both of which are composed largely of members residing outside of New York State, would have given him the opportunity, in case the bill was passed, to control the Board of Examiners. Possessing this power, he would be able to defeat the aim and purpose of the original accountants bill, which derived its strength from the fact that the profession of accountancy in this State is regulated by the Board of Regents, the highest educational body, and is not prescribed by those whose interests in it are purely personal."

The account in the same paper gives the following additional particulars:

"Last week a number of the members of the New York State Society of the Certified Public Accountants went before the Assembly Judiciary Committee and presented several urgent objections to the bill under consideration by that body. It was urged at that conference that there was no necessity for the changes proposed in the amendments; that the original bill was perfectly satisfactory to all the accountants of the State; that the changes would be detrimental to public interests and the profession concerned, inasmuch as the amendment permits accountants of no moral standing and of but meager proficiency to gain a certificate placing them on a level with men who have devoted years to the study of their profession and whose integrity is unquestionable. Now the regents' certificate in public repute represents that a test of moral character has been passed; also that the holder has qualified in an examination equal in severity to those imposed by the regents upon candidates for any of the professions, and that, besides, he has concluded a five-year period of apprenticeship in accountancy.

"The danger to public interests likely to engage the services of accountants from the proposed amendment lies in the fact that, under the new plan, certificates would be granted to all who had been practising as accountants one year previous to April 17, 1896. This would do away with an examination and bring into the profession a crowd of irresponsible and incompetent clerks and bookkeepers, by whom the settlement of important and complicated business matters would be unsatisfactory and with whom the charge of such affairs would be insecure.

"The New York State Society of Certified Public Accountants further opposed the amendment on the ground that it would require the regents to approve and certify to the acts of an irresponsible, irremovable body; that it placed the administration of a New York State law in the hands of persons not necessarily residents or citizens of the State; that it used the authority of the State to serve the private ends and controversies of individuals, and, finally, that it was an unwarranted expression of lack of confidence in the highest educational body in the State.

"The New York State Society of Certified Public Accountants is endeavoring to throw greater safeguards around the public requiring the services of accountants in trying to raise the standard of proficiency required of its members, and is wholly opposed to any measure which tends to lower this standard or admit men unless their moral character and efficiency is unquestioned."

Banking in Austria*

By Th. Pentlarge, C. P. A.

At a time when currency reform and banking reform is on everybody's lips, I shall not be amiss by engaging your attention for a few minutes with the banking system of a country whose experience with fiat money ought to be an object lesson for other nations. At the outset I shall endeavor to make a brief sketch of Austria's business customs. In the dual Empire a banking and credit system as we have in the United States is practically unknown. Business settlements are mostly made in actual cash and time drafts, the latter taking the place of our promissory notes. Banks of deposit (and that not in the sense of our National or State Banks) exist only in large cities and commercial centers. The check system, as practiced here and in England, is hardly known. The bank and currency system as it does exist, however, is very interesting, if for no other reason, to show what can be accomplished by honest and wise management and how it has withstood crises which hardly any other system could weather.

In 1814, at the close of the Napoleonic wars, which had taxed to the utmost the resources of all European powers, Austria found herself bankrupt, a large debt on hand, no money to run the Government with and the people so exhausted that there was really nothing to be gotten out of them. People laughed at threatened sales for taxes, because no one had money to attend to the buying. In 1816, under these conditions, with the help of a Franco-English Syndicate, the National Bank of Austria was organized with a capital of ninety millions. In consideration of a loan of eighty millions of this capital for an indefinite period (terminating with the life of the bank's charter) and without interest, the State parted with the privilege of note issue and transferred it for a period of thirty years to the new bank, which was authorized to issue notes not exceeding the sum of two hundred millions, with the proviso that the bank is to keep a coin reserve of 33 1-3 per cent. of the amount of notes issued, the balance to be covered by secured loans and good commercial paper.

*A paper read before the New York State Society of Certified Public Accountants.

This charter has since been repeatedly extended, suspended and often simply violated as the exigencies of the stormy period of over fifty years following its grant have required. Time and time again, when the Imperial treasury was empty it took the coin reserve of the bank and replaced it by fiat money issued in flagrant violation of the charter. There have been times when the Imperial treasury has owed the bank over two hundred millions on open account and has paid every cent of it with legal tender fiat money, compelling the bank to use it as a basis for a note issue of its own. So it has happened that the circulation of the bank, instead of being restricted to two hundred millions, has amounted at times to six hundred millions and over, and has existed side by side with a fiat money issue of from one to four hundred millions.

Astounding as it seems, the confidence in the management of the concern and the honesty of the managers has always been such that never, even under most adverse circumstances, have the notes of the bank depreciated below 75 per cent. By this, I mean that they were never taken for less than seventy-five cents on the dollar. The managers have justified this confidence. They have succeeded in quickly restoring their reserve, and by discounting bills on a large scale to keep the circulation as nearly equal to the demand as possible. In the year preceding the crisis of 1873, the Bank discounted over seven hundred millions' worth of commercial paper, and when that memorable crisis came, the bank not only succeeded in getting out of it with very little loss by gradually reducing its discount lines, and at the same time its circulation, but it was enabled to consummate a financial feat of the greatest magnitude. Taking advantage of a temporary rise in silver, it secretly disposed of its coin reserve in that metal and replaced it with eighty-three millions of gold, realizing a profit on the transaction. So secretly was this done that even the Bank of England did not become aware of the fact until long after it was accomplished. Whilst the banks of France and England lost millions on the silver stored in their vaults, the National Bank of Austria realized a profit, and when our own treasury was coining silver dollars under the Sherman law, the National Bank of Austria was on a gold basis and had compelled the Imperial Government to follow suit. In December, 1895, the circulation of the Bank was six hundred and fourteen millions secured by gold coin to the amount of two hundred and sixty-three millions, and the balance by good commercial paper. The balance sheet of that period showed a surplus of seventy-eight millions, and the profits for that year were $7,081.219.

The bank is allowed to pay a dividend of 7 per cent. on its stock. The surplus earnings are divided between the Imperial treasury and a surplus fund. The bank discounts paper for concerns rated over fifty thousand dollars only. The paper discounted must be approved by the Board of Examiners and by the Board of Governors. On the latter the Imperial Government is represented.

Another institution of large magnitude is the "Creditanstalt fur Handel & Gewerbe," founded somewhat on the plan of the French Credit Mobiler now long since defunct. Its charter dates from 1855 and it commenced business with one hundred millions paid-up capital. It issued a loan of one hundred millions in 1856. This loan bears interest at 6 per cent.; 5 per cent. is represented on the coupons of the bond and 1 per cent. is distributed as a prize bonus upon one-fiftieth part of the loan which is annually redeemed. This distribution is graded so that the first bond drawn for redemption receives a bonus of $250,000, the next, $150,000, and so down to $100 on each bond drawn. This ingenious scheme, reducing the indebtedness (consequently bettering the security) and the element of chance coupled with it made the bonds very attractive and the whole issue was speedily taken.

The bank owns and operates tin, iron and coal mines, railroads, sugar refineries, flour mills, breweries, machine, paper and textile factories. It does a large discount and loan business, and accepts deposits for which certificates are issued bearing 2½, 3, 3½ and 4 per cent. interest, according to their running time. These certificates are generally accepted in payment of debt. They have on their backs a printed table of their value for every day of their existence until maturity. Under the prevailing system of trade, cash is accumulating in the hands of country merchants and they make large and profitable use of this opportunity. The bank enjoys the confidence of European financiers, its stock is considered a standard security, and European bourses gauge the other Austrian securities by the fluctuations of this stock.

A very curious system of banking in vogue is that of the discount banks. They operate in large and small towns with capital from a hundred millions down to fifty thousand. Their modus operandi is about as follows: The capital is allotted to two, three or more prevailing industries. Three to five prominent firms in each of these industries are invited to form a Discount Board, and with each is opened a credit account on the books of the bank. This Discount Board passes upon applications of other parties in their respective lines of business, subject, however, to the approval of the Board of Managers. Every new borrower becomes a member of the Board, and each successful applicant deposits 10 per cent. in cash of the amount of credit opened to him, for which he draws interest and which is held in a separate fund called the guaranty fund. Any loss accruing to the bank from loans to the members of a particular branch is made good from this fund. In plain words, the borrowers guarantee each other's indebtedness to the extent of 10 per cent. of the total amount borrowed. They deposit cash and notes with the bank and make all their debts due there. The bank charges them 5 per cent. on the amount of credit actually used and allows them on the other side of the account-current from 4 to 4½ per cent.

The mortgage banks are another type of banking in Austria. They are chartered for loans of real estate only. They usually give the borrower 25 per cent. in cash and 75 per cent. their own mortgage bonds running for periods of one, six and twelve years, and bearing 4½ per cent. interest. The borrower pays 6 per cent. The borrowers at first found it difficult to dispose of these mortgage bonds at par. Since then, however, a system of surveillance and registry of the issue with the governing committee of the bourses has developed, and now the bonds are slightly above par and are readily bought for actual investment.

Within the last decade or so most of the large banks have adopted a system of opening both credit and deposit accounts with their customers. Against their deposit and credit the latter draw time drafts or have their account transferred from one bank to another. For instance, A has an account with the National Bank and B with the Credit Anstalt. He owes B a sum due April 1st. He, therefore, orders the National Bank to pay on that date to the Credit Anstalt to the account of B.

Gradually the magnitude of the business has compelled the establishment of still another type of bank of which the Wiener Giro and Cassen Verein is the largest. Practically, it is a Clearing House. The amount of business done by this bank in 1895 aggregated to $8,660,000,-000. Comparing it with the New York Clearing House this seems small, but it must be considered that the bulk of business is done outside of banks, only large concerns enjoying bank credit.

Correspondence

Banking Credits

From J. B. W., New York:

Has the reader ever compared the banking credits of London with those which exist in this country? I noticed a short time since the totals of two of the private banking institutions of that city, the aggregate deposits being $90,000,000, equal to about one-fifth of the total deposits of all the banks of New York City. No wonder that English bankers regard our banking ways almost the same as pawnbroking. We had a chance in our original bank, the United States Bank and its successor, (I mean the one chartered by the Government, not the one chartered by Pennsylvania), to get at a knowledge of banking in its large and full meaning, but Jackson killed all that, and we have been crawling and pawnbroking ever since. We have been running upon the idea that the smaller the capital and the larger the deposits the more profit—to the banker, not to the community.

Look at a recent failure. A bank with $100,000 capital had $1,200,000 to $1,500,000 deposits. Evidently this bank never banked with its own money, but, instead, with the cash of its confiding depositors, and with the usual results. The depositors now have experience in lieu of cash. It may be more profitable to some, but it is not so good to go to market with.

A Problem of Sequents

From F. W. C., New York:

The following problem was given to me a short time since for solution by a member of the Institute of Accounts. It may interest some of the Office Juniors, inasmuch as it develops two sets of sequents:

A buys some apples and distributes them among his friends. To B he gives one-quarter of the whole number and one-quarter of an apple. To C he gives one-third of the remainder and one-third of an apple, and to D he gives one-half of the number then remaining and one-half of an apple. A then takes what is left, which proves to be one-half of B's share. How many apples did A buy?

By analyzing this question I find first that the addition of one-quarter of an apple and one-third of the remainder and one-half of tne remain-ier adds exactly 1 apple to any number of apples. Thus:

¼ of 1=	¼
1—¼=¾	1-3 of ¾=¼
¾—¼=2-4	½ of 2-4=¼
2-4—¼=	¼
	—
Total....................	1

Next I find that the result of the three operations called for in the problem is ap even division of one-third each of any number large enough to divide by 3. Thus take 3:

3—1=2. 1-3 of 2=2-3+1-3=1
¼ of 3=¾+¼ =1
3—1=2. 1-3 of 2=2-3+1-3=1
2—1=1. ½ of 1=½+½=1
—
Total.................... 3
and no remainder.

As the operations each result alike and the first is ¼ of the total number, then ¼ of this will be added each time, or 1 in every four numbers progressively. Thus:

7	gives	three	2s	and	1	remainder
11	"	"	3s	"	2	"
15	"	"	4s	"	3	"
19	"	"	5s	"	4	"
23	"	"	6s	"	5	" and so on.

Since 7 is the only number where the remainder (1) is twice the even divisor (2), A must have bought 7 apples and distributed them as follows: To B he gave 2, to C he gave 2, to D he gave 2, and he had one remaining, making a total of 7.

Now, if the problem had stated that A received one-third or one-quarter or one-fifth as many as D, remaining the same in all other respects, the division of the thirds would have to be increased by 1, or the quarter of an apple, third of an apple, and half of an apple remainders would have to be again added. It would increase the division by 1 every third number progressively. Thus, divide 10:

¼ of the whole=2½+(¼+¼) or ½=3, B's share.
1-3 of the reaminder, 2 1-3+(1-3+1-3) or 2-3=3, C's share.|
½ of the remainder, 2+(½+½)or 1=3, D's share.
Remainder=1, A's share.
Total, 10.

Or, taking 13:
¼ of whole, 3¼+(½+¼) or ¾=4, B's share.
1-3 of remainder, 3+(2-3+1-3) or 1=4, C's share.
½ of remainder, 2½+(1+½) or 1½=4, D's share.
Remainder=1, A's share.
Total, 13.

Or, taking 16:
¼ of whole, 4+(¾+¼) or 1=5, B's share.
1-3 of remainder, 3 2-3+(1+1-3) or 1 1-3=5, C's share.
½ of remainder, 3+(1½+½) or 2=5, D's share.
Remainder=1, A's share.
Total, 16.

Success at first doth many times undo men at last.—Venning.

Basis of Insurance Adjustments

From Accountant, Connecticut.

I have read with much interest in the January number of ACCOUNTICS the report of Mr. Higganbotham's essay on "Insurance from a Business Man's Standpoint." Especially does the sentence "If I were an agent I would take note of the applicant's character and reputation, as well as his financial standing," appeal to me, as it is thoroughly in line with my ideas on the subject. I would, however, go further. After making a thorough investigation as to insurer's character, etc., I think it would be a boon to the insuring world if the companies would put themselves on record as to what, in their opinion, is a fair basis of settlement in case of loss. This would, I believe, tend to allay the feeling of antagonism now so often existing between the insurance companies' adjusters and the insured, when seeking to arrive at a basis of settlement after a loss. Why should this not be as definitely understood beforehand as in the case of life insurance. Unless it is that owing to ignorance of the basis on which the company will settle, some perfectly honorable concerns will over insure and thereby the agents' commissions be increased. I believe I am correct in stating that with the exception of such as have gone through the unfortunate experience of a fire, the percentage of those who have a correct idea of the companies' basis of settlement is very small.

To explain more clearly what I am seeking to demonstrate, let me say that I think it should be understood beforehand that in case of loss, settlement will be made for the cost of the goods or their market value at the time of loss, plus transportation charges, and that such other expenses as form practically a part of the cost will or will not be considered as a part of the cost.

Again, in the case of manufacturing concerns having branch houses or depots, the cost will be the cost of the material and labor plus factory or shop expense and transportation charges to the branch, and also in this case that such expenses as the necessary bookkeeping, insurance, rent or storage, and interest on investment will or will not be included as part of the cost. To sum up, I believe that the investigation now made by the adjusters after a fire should be made when the insurance is placed. Life insurance companies don't examine the corpse to see how much they shall pay. By an arrangement such as proposed, both insurer and insured would know where they stood in case of loss, and the work of the adjusters would be reduced to the matter of ascertaining the amount of stock on hand and the cause of the fire. The plan proposed would also be a guide to the insured, in the event of a co-insurance clause being included in his policies. Referring to the latter, I think the agents should explain, or, better still, the companies should give printed explanation of the nature of a co-insurance clause, which I know is not understood by a large number of those in whose policies it is incorporated. I have had experience as an accountant for the insured in the case of a large fire and I write this in view of facts which have come to my notice through such experience.

Business Schools

From E. D. Snow, Rutland, Vt.

In looking over the back numbers of ACCOUNTICS, I notice that "Free Lance" states he has been instructed to go light on business schools, since business college proprietors are somewhat touchy. I think this is decidedly a wrong impression. Business school proprietors and teachers, as a fact, do not object to honest, intelligent criticism, but they do object to being ridiculed. Every little while some jay bookkeeper, who attended a snide business school twenty-five or thirty years ago, attempts to advertise his gigantic intellect by ridiculing certain teachings of business colleges. This would-be censor of what is practical and what is impractical, places all business colleges in the same class—namely, the class represented by the one that he attended. He steadily ignores any good points which the business schools may possess and holds up to view some of the methods which he considers antiquated.

Even the best of schools have a few old-fashioned ideas, but what business man or practical accountant is not similarly afflicted? I do not make these remarks as a defence of obsolete methods or of the teachings of fake schools, but instead, to say that it is not intelligent criticism against which we protest. I wish ACCOUNTICS might maintain a special department devoted to suggestions for business-school teachers. I am sure such a department would be greatly appreciated by the progressive teachers of the country. Even if such a department is not established, ACCOUNTICS ought to be in the hands of every teacher and bookkeeper because its pages bring them into close relationship with the actual life of bookkeeping, accountancy and business itself.

Business Law Course

From A. G. S., Detroit, Mich.

Will some reader be so good as to advise a junior member of the profession what books to read as a business law course?

Test Question.—What do you consider the best system for arriving at the depreciation to be written off or provided to redeem the following assets? (a) Fixed or Permanent Machinery; (b) Loose Machinery, Utensils, Tools, Implements, etc.; (c) Office and Shop Furniture and Fittings; (d) Horses; (e) Leasehold Property, and (f) Good Will.

Test Question.—Under what circumstances do you consider "good will" or "patent rights" legitimate assets? As an auditor how would you advise dealing with such assets year by year?

Depreciation*

By H. C. McJilton

I will first take up the definition of the word Depreciation. As laid down by Webster's Unabridged Dictionary, it is as follows:

> 1st:—The act of lessening, or seeking to lessen, price, value or reputation.—
>
> 2nd:—The falling of value; reduction of worth. (Burke).

The second definition seems to most clearly define the subject to be treated, and with that in view, my next step will be to divide the subject under two heads, as follows:—First—What Should Not Be Charged to Depreciation, and Second, What Should Be Charged to Depreciation.—

For convenience, I will give, first, some of the most important items which should not be charged, under the heads of the different sub-division of accounts.—In Transportation Expenses there are renewal of Fare Registers, Punches, Etc.—Under the head of Motive Power there are repairs or renewals of Dynamos and their parts, the labor in removing and replacing; renewals or repairs of the Switch-board Equipment, and labor making such repair or renewal; the renewal of Armatures, Commutators, Bearings and Boxes, Fields, Gears, Pinions, Trolleys, Lightning Arrestors, Rheostats, Switches, Etc., the cost of labor replacing same, and making connections with those damaged or destroyed; the renewals or repairs to Steam Plant in Power Houses, including Boilers, Engines, Pumps, Shafting, Belts, Piping, Steam Fitting, Station Fixtures, Etc., and the cost of labor necessary in making such renewals or repairs; and the repairs or renewals of Tools, Machinery, Shafting, Boilers, Engines, Etc., in Shops of the Company, including labor, etc.

In Maintenance of Way renewal of Conduits (Cable or Electric), Rails, Cross-tics, Paving, Trolley Poles, Feed and Span Wires, and appliances for suspension and insulation of same; Track Bonding, Drains under Tracks, Flooring Bridges, Frogs and Switches, Joint Fastenings, Tools, Implements, Wages of Laborers engaged in this work; Repairs to Power Stations, Car Houses, Car Shops, Repair Shops, Blacksmith and Machine Shops; Coal Chutes and Bins; Pits in Car Houses and Shops; Cranes in Power Houses; Buildings, Wharves, Etc.; and under the head of Maintenance of Cars there are New Cars taking the place of old to make the number good; Repairs, including Labor, to keep Cars up to standard; Renewals of Trucks, Axles, Wheels, Brakes, Headlights, Brake Shoes, Axle Boxes, Springs, Sand Boxes, Etc.

None of the above items should be charged to Depreciation for the reason that the first cost has either been charged to Construction or Plant Account, or carried as an asset in other accounts, and to which nothing should be added, except for the first and original cost of the property; and, therefore, if not chargeable to either of the above accounts, repairs of every description and character must necessarily be chargeable to Operating Expenses —less the amounts received from sale of removed or defective parts—in order not to wrongfully increase the assets of the company. Further, inasmuch as the operating of the road receives all benefits of the cost of the first installation, Operating Expenses should stand the cost of repairs, including labor, and all renewals. This is essential, notwithstanding they all add materially to the present or future value of the property; but in order to get at the correct cost of the operation of the road, as a whole, or per car mile, you do not arrive at a proper basis for calculation until the second or third year of operation; and it is not fair to compare a newly-equipped road with one which has been in operation a number of years.

It is, no doubt, a well-understood fact that it matters not how much is spent and charged to Operating Expenses in order to keep the plant of a street railway company, or manufacturing corporation, in A1 condition, it is never, after once put in operation, considered as good as new, for the reason that more improved machinery, etc., can be purchased later on to replace the same—often at a reduced cost. This is most important in the case of loss by fire, when you are making up your schedule, preparing for settlement of your loss with the insurance companies (as those having gone through the experience of fires know), there is always a certain amount deducted by insurance companies on account of Depreciation, whether apparent or not. And the same state of affairs applies to the sale of any particular piece of machinery, etc., which has been discarded. Therefore, conceding the above to be true, that is, by charging the cost of repairs and renewals to Operating Expenses, your property is virtually in as good a condition, physically, at the end of each year, as it was in the beginning; at the same time agreeing that there is a Depreciation, it is wise and appropriate for corporations to set aside, at the end of each year, such an amount as is warranted, after a thorough and impartial inspection of the property. I further believe that it is thoroughly understood that circumstances alter cases, but by carefully following out the above method, it is the opinion of the writer that you will not go wrong, but will be protecting the assets of your Company, and I know of no better way of doing this than by charging to Operating Expenses all renewals and repairs, as I have indicated in the first part of this paper, and by the accumulation of a fund as an offset against such Depreciation as cannot be covered by charges to Operating Expenses.

---

*A Paper read at the first meeting of the Street Railway Accountants' Association by H. C. McJilton, Secretary of the Baltimore (Md.), Traction Company.

Accountics

A. O. Kittredge, F. I. A., Editor

Accountics is devoted to the Science of Accounting, to the Art of Bookkeeping and to the advocacy of Improved Office Methods.

Subscription.—One dollar a year, payable in advance.

Postage is prepaid by the publishers in the United States, Canada and Mexico. For all other countries in the Postal Union, subscribers must add 50 cents a year.

Discontinuances.—In the absence of specific orders to discontinue at the end of the subscription term the paper will be continued and a bill sent.

Remittances should be by Draft, P. O. Order or Express Order, payable to the order of the ACCOUNTICS ASSOCIATION. Money and postage-stamps are at the risk of the sender, unless sent by express or in registered letters. Add 10 cents each to checks on local banks to defray collection charges.

Advertising Rates.—The following rates prevail, whether orders are given to solicitors or sent direct to the office:—

	1 year	6 mos.	3 mos.	1 mo.
Page..........	$200.00	$120.00	$67.50	$25.60
Half page.....	125.00	77.60	39.65	14.40
Quarter page..	70.00	42.16	22.50	7.75
Three inches..	55.00	32.40	16.60	6.00
Two inches...	38.00	22.50	11.30	4.20
One inch......	20.00	11.25	6.00	2.40

Last page of cover advance 50 per cent. Facing reading matter advance 33⅓ per cent. Panel, first cover page, $30 each insertion.

Official Journal.—This publication, by resolutions duly passed, has been made the official publication of the following organizations:—

THE INSTITUTE OF ACCOUNTS.

The NEW YORK CHAPTER of the Institute of Accounts.

ACCOUNTICS is the accredited medium of intercommunication between members of the Institute of Accounts wherever located.

ACCOUNTICS ASSOCIATION, Publishers

Wool Exchange, New York

Entered at the Post Office New York as Second Class Matter.

COST ACCOUNTING IN MANUFACTURES

The following is an incomplete list of the articles on COST ACCOUNTING IN MANUFACTURES, arranged to appear in early numbers of ACCOUNTICS, commencing with the issue for April, 1898, and more particularly referred to in the announcement on the preceding page.

COST ACCOUNTS.—A carefully prepared paper, fully illustrated, read before the Ontario Institute of Chartered Accountants, February 10, 1898. By W. B. Tindall, C. A.

This article embodies an examination into cost accounting methods by a public accountant of high standing and long experience. He addresses his fellow-accountants upon plans and principles, and surveys the subject from a point of view that has seldom, if ever, before been occupied. His conclusions are exceedingly practical, and are of interest to all who have to do with manufacturing establishments.

IMPROVED METHODS IN COST ACCOUNTING.—Illustrated by numerous diagrams and examples showing recent applications of well-established principles. By Frank J. Sager.

This paper is mildly argumentative, and contains a discussion of methods from the standpoint of one who is in position to carefully weigh financial results.

BIBLIOGRAPHY OF COST ACCOUNTS.—A critical and comprehensive review and digest of the books now before the public relating to costs of manufacture and factory administration. By A. O. Kittredge, F. I. A., C. P. A., Editor of ACCOUNTICS.

Each of a considerable number of books, pamphlets and articles which have appeared upon the subject of cost accounts will be described and dissected in a way to enable the reader to draw his own conclusions as to the merits of the plans proposed and the desirability of including the volume in his library. The length of the article precludes publication in a single instalment. It will run through several numbers.

THE RELATIONSHIP OF FACTORY BOOKS AND RECORDS TO THE PRINCIPAL BOOKS OF ACCOUNT.

This article will discuss the logical and necessary relationship between the principal books of a manufacturing establishment and the cost records in the factory, whether located close to the office or at a distant point. It will describe the checks that may be established to prevent fraud, and methods of balancing that may be employed. It will also show how duplications of work may be avoided as between the general office on the one hand and the factory office on the other.

ACCOUNTS WITH STORES.

This article will indicate how materials may be charged to Stores when received and credited to Stores when used, with the resulting balance representing at all times the amount of materials on hand. It will embody a contrast between practical methods and theoretical plans.

THE MECHANICAL EQUIPMENT FOR COST ACCOUNTING.—Books and Book Rulings; Slips and Card Indexes; Orders and Requisitions; Reports, Files, and Binders.

This article is a description in careful detail of the mechanical equipment of some of the most satisfactory cost accounting systems now in practical use.

LABOR ACCOUNTS.—Methods of keeping time, and of keeping records of where the time is used. Plans of paying shop hands. Illustrated.

SPREADING FIXED CHARGES.—A symposium of theories, methods and experience from the pens of from fifty or more practical accountants connected with prominent manufacturing establishments of the United States and Canada.

Still other articles to be included in the series will be announced later on.

ACCOUNTICS ASSOCIATION, Wool Exchange Building, New York.

Accountics

The Office Magazine

ONE DOLLAR A YEAR
TEN CENTS A COPY

MAY 1898

VOLUME III
NUMBER 2

CONTENTS.

Published by the ACCOUNTICS ASSOCIATION: Wool Exchange New York

# Accountics

VOL. III MAY 1898 No. 2

The Monthly Statement

The New York Accountants' Law and the recent efforts to modify it have attracted the attention of British accountants, and of the periodicals which they support. In the last issue of the Accountants' Magazine is a general review of the situation as seen from its point of view. After referring to the original act, which has its endorsement, there is printed the following: "It would appear, however, that the accountants of New York have not yet quite reached the stage of development necessary to appreciate provisions of the stringent character contained in this act. The privilege of registration without examination was very properly limited to those who applied within one year after the passing of the act, and the examinations also very properly were under the control of the Board of Regents of the University. But no sooner has the benefit of registration under the act become apparent than those who did not apply in time and who are not prepared to undergo the examination begin to agitate the extension of the period of admission without examination. A certain section desires that the conduct of the examinations should be under the control of the accountants themselves, apparently overlooking the principle that legislative privileges can hardly be given without a certain amount of public control. Perhaps this movement may be partly due to the action of one of the examiners employed by the regents, himself a Certified Public Accountant, who, having, without the authority of the board, issued and sold a book containing answers to the questions which he himself set, was not continued in his office. Anyhow, a bill has been introduced to amend the original act in these two respects, but we hope it has little chance of passing. If the title of 'Certified Public Accountant' is to have any value in America it will only be by the safeguards originally provided for establishing and maintaining a high standard of efficiency being rigidly adhered to." A postscript is added to this to the effect that since the above was written the bill has been defeated in the Assembly by 67 to 50.

The Incorporated Accountants' Journal, commenting on the same subject, says: "The Certified Public Accountants' bill, which was passed by the United States Senate (?) a short time ago, has failed to pass through its remaining stages. The control of the profession in the State of New York, therefore, remains with the Regents of the University." We are always on the lookout for blunders of the kind in English writings indicated above, and, therefore, are ever ready to accept the will for the deed. This esteemed contemporary, as is evidenced by other paragraphs which we have not space to quote, is in deep sympathy with the movement in this country and is pleased that the amended bill failed to pass.

An eminent critic, discussing the public taste with respect to what should be printed, from time to time, in papers of general circulation, said recently that no journal can at present safely ignore the Spanish-American war, and that all periodicals, of whatever class or description, are obliged, in their own interest, to bring into view, in every issue, something about the war. Perhaps the critic is right and, therefore, has presented a plausible explanation of the presence of war items in every paper that is published. Perhaps, also, he is wrong, to the extent of overlooking the intense feeling in the matter of the war which actuates editors as well as laymen, and which would cause them to give special attention to the topic most in mind. However that may be, we are glad to read this distinguished critic's reason for and approval of what was presented in our columns last month.

The reality of war is now upon us, but up to this writing it has appeared to be a one-sided affair. The Spaniard has wofully overrated his ability to cope with the United States, and when it has come to a test of skill and strength, he has been found lacking. So much has been accomplished in the direction of showing the inferiority of Spain and the superiority of the United States, that business has already largely discounted the final result. To many persons, the war is now over, in the sense of there having come an end to the anxious forebodings with which peace-at-any-price men and various faint hearts were contending only a short time since. The victory at Manila influenced all markets. The average advance in railroad shares within a week from the first news of Commodore Dewey's achievement was $3 per share. The general condition of business has also materially improved. It would appear, therefore, that one day's work by the officers and men at Manila changed the aspect of affairs in general. It has, in fact, given employment to thousands of men who otherwise would have been held in idleness pending the close of the war. Other victories which are sure to come will have a similar effect, and before the summer is fairly upon us, as it appears now, we shall have forgotten that there was such a thing as anxiety about the war. We shall be looking ahead into those business problems which ever confront the man of affairs, and arranging to meet an active trade. Many accountants who were faced by possible inactivity a few weeks ago have, in the interval, found something to do, and in their field as well as in others, there are many signs of renewed activity.

In the April number of this magazine a very full account was presented of the organization and first meeting of the Hartford Chapter of the Institute of Accounts. The success of the effort to organize a Chapter in Hartford, and the good work that the organization thus formed is already engaged upon, raises the question why should not similar Chapters be organized in a hundred other cities? There is but one possible answer to this question and that is that such organizations are advantageous, and therefore should be formed everywhere. Mr. Gershom Smith's conspicuous success in this matter should be emulated by accountants in every city and business center of the Union. There is only necessary a leader who, rising above the small prejudices which sometimes beset and befog the minds of men of like trades or professions, is willing to devote a little time to getting acquainted with his fellow-workers, make the preliminary arrangements for a meeting and secure the co-operation of the officers of the National Institute, and particularly of the members of the New York Chapter, a number of whom are ever ready for missionary work. Incidentally ACCOUNTICS will do all that is possible to help in all these undertakings. There should be a hundred new Chapters of the Institute organized between this and next New Year's day. Who will be the first to commence in the good work?

We shall be glad to correspond with every accountant in the land who is at present engaged in public or purely professional work. We shall also be glad to correspond with every bookkeeper who aspires to the work of public accountant. We have some important suggestions to offer. The profession of accounting at the present time is in a state of rapid development. There is a greater demand for public accountants to-day of the right sort than ever before, and in the near future this demand is likely to be greatly increased. Many of those who are at present engaged in the work are not improving their real opportunities, while those who are ambitious to become public accountants are in a majority of cases proceeding without a clear conception of what the real work is.

In far-off Australia there are a number of organizations among accountants, variously called societies, institutes, etc. Recently steps have been taken looking to a federation of these organizations. Incidentally it is proposed, in case the association is formed, to follow the example of the Scottish chartered societies, by holding examinations and prescribing a high grade of accomplishments as a condition of membership. This movement in Australia is only in keeping with others that are in progress in different parts of the world looking to the elevation and advancement of the profession. It is a step highly commendable, and American accountants will wish the movement every success.

Cost Accounts

By W. B. Tindall, C. A.

(Concluded from page 13, April Number)

The opinion so well expressed in the above quotation is certainly a strong argument for distributing expenses in proportion to wages paid. Another plan advocated is to charge expenses at so much per hour for time worked. What is meant is illustrated thus: Presuming that the cost ledger for a month is charged wages for 100 men, 26,000 hours, average rate fifteen cents, equal $3,900, and that the proportionate part of the yearly expenses amount to $780, the cost of a machine might be figured as follows:

Material	$100.00	
Labor, 700 hours at 15 cents..	105.00	
		$205.00
Expenses, 700 hours at 3c.....		21.00
Total cost		$226.00

This, at first sight, would seem to be the same, but it differs in this respect, that the cheaper the labor, if it took more hours at a less price, the more heavily would it contribute to the expense charge.

Now let us suppose that in the machine just referred to, the cost was made as follows:

Material		$100.00	
Labor, 350 hours at 20c.	$70.00		
200 hours at 10c.	20.00		
300 hours at 5c.	15.00		
850 hours, costing		105.00	
Expense charge, 850 hours at 3c.		25.50	
Total cost			$230.50

This would seem to bear out Mr. Man's theoretical contention that the cheaper work should bear the largest share of these charges which would undoubtedly apply if the charges were composed only of foremen's wages, and supplies for the particular machines, but these charges include other items which would not be influenced in the same way, such as taxes: engineers', firemen's, watchmen's wages and others.

The plan generally adopted in this country, as far as I can learn, is to add a percentage to the combined value of labor and material. I do not think this method is sound, for we laid down as a principle that no profit is to be put on material in costing: neither do I think any burden should be put upon it in arriving at the cost of production. Let us compare the cost of one machine by each of these methods:

First Method.

Material	$100.00
Labor	105.00
	$205.00
Expenses, 20% on labor	21.00
	$226.00

Second Method.

Material	$100.00
850 hours	105.00
	$205.00
850 hours at 3c.	25.50
	$230.50

Third Method.

Material	$100.00
850 hours	105.00
	$205.00
10% on materials and labor	20.50
	$225.50

Now take the same machine and use material of very much greater value, with the same workmanship. In this case the labor item will not be changed except probably in the second plan, as dearer material is being used. Less or no apprentice labor would be put on, but the work would probably be done quicker and the value be not much changed. For the purposes of comparison we will presume it is the same:

First Method.

Material	$300.00
Labor	105.00
	$405.00
Expenses, 20% on labor	21.00
	$426.00

Second Method.

Material	$300.00
700 hours	105.00
	$405.00
700 hours at 3c.	21.00
	$426.00

Third Method.

Material	$300.00
700 hours	105.00
	$405.00
10% cent on labor and materials	40.50
	$445.50

Now, presuming the latter machine was sold for $450.00 by the last method, a profit of $4.50 would be shown, whereas by the other and truer method the profit indicated would be $24.00.

The next item we have to consider is fixed charges of distribution and selling the finished product. These charges will usually be represented by such accounts as advertising, office expenses, office salaries (such as do not enter into costs of production), salesmen's salaries and expenses, commission to agents, and all accounts which cannot properly be charged to production, but which are necessary to the care and distribution of the product. The volume of the output or turn-over at its selling price is the factor which regulates how much shall be added to represent this element of the cost. I am referring more particularly now to undertakings that sell the manufactured product directly from the factory. In others that have manufacturing and wholesaling combined, only such charges of distribution as are necessary to deliver to the factory will be taken into account in our cost. The question of volume of trade or turn-over for any period under review is one which presents the greatest difficulties, in determining how costs shall be represented. That is to say, should they show the cost on the actual turn-over for the year, or on the turn-over for the previous year, or on the medium standard turn-over equivalent to the ordinary capacity of the mill? It will be found that the latter method will work out and be more useful and furnish information of greater value than the others. I will endeavor to show this by comparison: Assume that the turn-over for the year under review, by reason of various disturbing causes, was only $50,000; that the turn-over for the previous year was at selling price, after deducting all rebates and allowances, $125,000; that the ordinary capacity of the factory is generally estimated to be $100,000; that the fixed charges of selling in both years was $3,000.

Now the percentage in the first case would be 6 per cent.; in the second case it would be 2.4 per cent., and in the third case, 3 per cent. If the second plan is used, it would probably show a much better profit than can ordinarily be obtained, taking one year with another, and in tendering on contract work, where competition is very keen, the manufacturer might possibly, by relying on these cost figures, fix the price too low. Again, if he took the first plan, and used the figures of the year that were too low, he might place himself out of the market; but, by taking the other or normal output at all times, he will come nearer to actual results.

In using this normal amount, my plan would be to open an account in the ledger called "Estimated Fixed Charges," and have the debit and credit sides with two money columns headed Production and Selling. Then, as the different accounts in the cost ledger were charged with determined percentages, credit the amount so charged to this account, and at the end of the year charge the actual expenses to the same account, and show the balance either as a profit or loss, by reason of the increased or decreased volume of business.

Accounting for increased profits or for losses in this way, the showing of these matters in a clear and concise manner may affect an undertaking in many ways. Take the case of an application to one's banker for increased accommodation to augment working capital. It is quite possible to conceive a revenue account made up for the first six months of a business, during which little or no selling has been done. Take, for instance, brewing, or any business whose heaviest sales are made in the latter half of the year. If the facts were presented by the actual figures of the trading for the period, it might appear as if the goods were sold at a very heavy cost, and the banker, drawing his conclusions from such a statement, might refuse the advance asked for, whereas had the cost been presented to him from a properly kept set of cost accounts, the cost of the goods sold would be in proper proportion for the small amount of goods sold to date. Therefore, the portion of cost consisting of direct charges of production and indirect charges of selling and distributing affect the total cost by the proportion they bear to the amount of wages of direct producers, and the volume of turn-over. The cost will be reduced by reduction of expenses or increase in the volume of trade.

We have now discussed the several items that go to make up the cost of any finished article and reach the following formula:

Material ....
Labor ....

  Total ....
Expenses of production: Percentage on basis they bear to wages paid to producers ....

  Total ....
Expenses of selling and distributing: Percentage on basis of output for the year..................................

  Total ....

I advocate always showing the total of labor and material, before adding the percentage of expenses of production, and also showing these three items in another total, before adding the percentage representing expenses of selling and distribution, and management, etc.

It may be very desirable in some businesses, where goods go through a great many processes, to arrive at the cost of each process for the purpose of establishing piece-work prices, or for getting information that may possibly be of benefit and lead to reduction in the cost. When this is desired, all that is necessary is to open two accounts in the cost ledger, calling one "Production Account," and the other "Sundry Process Account." The latter account is to be ruled in the ledger as shown in Fig. 7, with a series of columns representing the different processes it is desired to keep track of. Then when the work is finished, transfer the amount of this sundry process account to the production account, detailing the cost of each process. The page of the ledger can either be divided horizontally or longitudinally. If the former plan is employed, leave the upper portion for wages and the lower for material. The material I refer to in such cases would be what is used in the process under review, such as paint or varnish, in the case of painting or enamelling.

We have now to consider how the information in the cost ledger is to be used with the greatest advantage, and how incorporated with the commercial books of the business, so that the full benefit of double entry may not be lost. In adopting a cost system it would not be necessary to alter the commercial books. All that is required is first to open an account in the general or private ledger, and call it "Cost Ledger Account," or by any other suitable title. To that account charge in monthly or quarterly totals, wages and stores used in the factory, and credit the corresponding wages and purchase accounts, and when the work is completed, charge the trading account with the cost in total, and credit cost ledger account. The cost ledger then will give the details and must always balance with the amount in the private or general ledger. Such a method as outlined will not increase the work of the office to any material extent, and the information that such accounts will give will be facts.

I am well aware that many manufacturers claim that they can tell the cost of their goods without all this work and expense, and that they, therefore, see no necessity for it. Many of them, particularly if practical men of long experience, can figure very accurately, I do not

	Cost of Goods Sold				Sales		
	1896	1897	Increase	Decrease	1896	1897	Increase
Purchases	$88,264	$100,338	$12,074		$100,350	$125,423	$25,073
Interest	850	1,000	150				
General expenses	4,012	5,240	1,228				
Bad debts	800	900	100				
Profit	6,424	7,945	1,521				
	$100,350	$125,423	$25,073		$100,350	$125,423	$25,073

FIG. 9.—COMPARATIVE STATEMENT OF TRADING ACCOUNT, 1896-1897.

	Cost of Goods				Sales		
	1896	1897	Increase	Decrease	1896	1897	
Purchases	87.95	80.		7.95	100	100	
Interest	.85	.80		.05			
General expenses	4.	4.18	.18				
Bad debts	.79	.71		.08			
Profit	6.41	14.31	7.90				
	100%	100%	8.08%	8.08%	100%	100%	

FIG. 10.—SAME COMPARED BY THE PERCENTAGE THAT COST BEARS TO SALES.

doubt, but what I claim is that the figuring in a great many cases, upon this plan, is what the goods should cost under good management and favorable circumstances. The all-important point seems to me to be, Did the goods cost the amount so figured? Or did some of them cost more? If so, why? Is not the bookkeeper often greeted, upon the occasion of furnishing his principal with the usual balance sheets, with this remark: "I am sure we made more money than that. We sold so many goods and they cost us so much" (by his style of figuring) "and there is only interest and insurance to come out of that. You must have made a mistake somewhere." In some of these cases the trouble may have been in the taking of the inventory, or in the extension or calculation of it. But mainly I think the costing, or absence of it, will be the cause of not being able to reconcile the figures submitted with those anticipated. The reasoning is in this wise: The foreman is asked to figure on the cost of making some line of goods, and probably does so as follows:

Material (Enumerating all the separate parts)		$......
Labor (Number of men can do so much labor)		$......
	Add percentage for expenses	$......
Total		$......

And in this he may not have allowed enough for waste. The tendency is always to show the most that can be made from material. In regard to labor, if much of it is machine work, any one who has had experience with machinery will tell you that it is rarely possible to get ten hours' (day in and out) work out of any machine. Belts will break, knives require to be sharpened, journals to be re-babbited, and the machine oiled. Upon reviewing the year's work, eight and a half or nine hours per day will be nearer the mark. But still wages will be paid for ten hours, so that if wages are two dollars per day or twenty cents per hour, they should be taken at twenty-five cents, to be nearer the mark of actual cost.

To stock on hand at commencement	$4,318.34......			Dec. 31. By sales after deducting allowances and nets	(100%)......	$125,423.34
Purchases	99,439.75......					
	$103,758.09......					
Deduct stock now on hand	3,419.42......					
		(80%)......	$100,338.67			
Gross profit brought down		(20%)......	25,084.67			
		(100%).	$125,423.34		(100%)......	$125,423.34

Interest	(.80%)......	$1,000.00	Balance brought down	(.20%)......	$25,084.67
General expense, salesmen, etc	(4.18%)......	5,240.00			
Bad accounts	(.71%)......	900.00			
Net profit	(14.31%)......	7,944.67			
	(.20%)......	$25,084.67		(.20%)......	$25,084.67

FIG. 11.—TRADING ACCOUNT—DEPARTMENT A.—12 MONTHS ENDING DECEMBER 31, 1897.

Again, the percentage item for expenses may be either too high or too low. If the estimate made out as above is verified, as it sometimes is, by taking the week's work, or by keeping close tab on the cost of one or two machines, it is still weak, inasmuch as men generally find out that close watch is being kept on their work. In such instances, they work under pressure, and accordingly the resulting figures are likely to be lower than the actual average cost for the year. Formerly, particularly in the early days of this country and the United States, when the percentage of profit on sales was all the way from 25 per cent. to 75 per cent., there was not the necessity for close figuring as now, where the percentage profit on the sale has often shrunk to 7 per cent. or lower.

If my statement is correct, as I believe it is, is not the position of the present-day manufacturer summed up as follows: Sales prices have reached the maximum obtainable, and profits have shrunk to a mere interest on actual capital invested. Therefore the only way now to increase profits is to reduce cost of production to a minimum. What will tell you whether this can be done or not, better than an accurate cost record?

I have so far only treated cost accounts as pertaining to manufacturing. I now desire to say something in regard to cost, for a purely commercial or trading business. The question comes up first, What is meant by the cost of goods? Second, should the cost price show anything more than the invoice, freight and duty, inwards added? and third, should the expenses of selling and distributing the goods and storing them be added to the cost?

To the first question I answer, the cost is invoice price, plus freight and duty inward, cartage, and all expenses of delivering goods to the warehouse. To the second question, if the cost price is desired of goods to be sold, I answer, No, because to do so would be to mark the goods at a higher price than they could be sold to any purchaser in the same line of business who desired to buy them on the shelves, or as stored in the warehouse. Again, an inventory based on such a method would show a false asset. But if it is desired to arrive at the cost of goods that have been sold, then the item referred to, in question three, should be taken into account. Some business men confound these two portions of their stock-in-trade. I take it that the trader buys certain goods to sell at a gross profit over the prime cost, and that gross profit should be large enough to bear all the burdens and return a profitable interest for the money invested in the venture.

I know of no record that, to my mind, is so useful, as keeping yearly track of sales by percentages. The fixed charges are influenced as in manufacturing by the turn-over.

[In speaking of percentages the lecturer compared the Trading Account of a business on the usual Increase and Decrease Statement and took the same figures, leaving the values out, but taking the sales each year irrespective of volume or amount, at 100 per cent. The illustrations given are in Figs. 9, 10 and 11.]

I think I have demonstrated so far that it is practical to obtain a cost record; that the expense of obtaining it will be more than covered by the advantages of knowing to a certainty the cost of goods manufactured; and that it will furnish the manufacturer reliable figures as facts, showing whether the material has been used to the best advantage, whether he has received full value for wages paid for labor, and whether expenses are increasing or decreasing.

It appears to me that in former years too much of the accountant's work has been historical. At the present day it is not history alone that is wanted, but good, reliable information as the business progresses. The more information that can be given, as the business goes on from day to day, particularly if the information so given is verified by the historical record at the end of the year, the more that information will be appreciated.

Test Question.—Explain fully the items entering into costs account in a manufacturing business consisting of three departments, each semi-dependent on the other. Give full particulars as to the method you would pursue to arrive at the net and gross cost of production.

Test Question.—In taking stock, what valuation is a manufacturer justified in placing upon goods in the process of manufacture, finished stock unsold and finished stock sold but not delivered? Give reasons for your answer.

Test Question.—You are appointed bookkeeper to a firm whose accounts have been kept by a single entry and you are required to transfer them to the double-entry system. Explain the process and give an illustration.

The instinct of interest is the universal instinct of mankind.—Charles Macklin.

A successful career has been full of blunders.—Charles Buxton.

He that gives a portion of his time and talent to the investigation of mathematical truth will come to all other questions with a decided advantage.—Colton.

To know how to wait is the great secret of success.—De Maistre.

The Approaching Convention of the National Association of Credit Men

The date appointed for the annual convention of the National Association of Credit Men is June 22, 23 and 24. It is to be held in Detroit. The headquarters of the convention will be at the Hotel Cadillac, where, on the evening of Wednesday, the first day, a reception will be tendered to the delegates and visitors; and on the evening of Friday, the third day, there is to be a smoker, enlivened by various attractive and appropriate features of divertisement. There will also be other entertainment, including several excursions.

It is the proposition of those having the arrangements of this convention in charge to reduce the number of sessions from two a day to one, extending from 10 o'clock in the morning to 2 in the afternoon. This will undoubtedly insure a larger attendance than would be otherwise secured upon the business meetings, which bid fair to be extremely important as well as interesting. Instead of twenty-minute speeches, which has been the rule heretofore, limitation to five minutes will probably be agreed to. It is expected that there will be more debate than has characterized either of the preceding conventions, and the open parliament, as these debates are termed, will be an important feature of each day's work.

The discussion at this convention will turn largely upon specific resolutions, properly introduced, relating to the work of the credit men now in progress in different departments of activity. By this means the policy of the Association and the scope of the work to be carried forward next year will be clearly defined. From advices which have reached the committees in charge of the preparations for this gathering it is evident that there will be a very large attendance, both of delegates and visitors. Many ladies are expected, and special provision for their entertainment is being made. There is no more important business reform movement before the public to-day than that for which the Credit Men's Association stands, and it is a pleasure to state that it is receiving, as it deserves, a very large measure of approval and encouragement.

A strenuous soul hates cheap success.—Emerson.

Business Leniency

By E. S. Campbell

Those who give credit ought to know that they injure both themselves and their debtors by undue leniency. Exact fulfillment of the contract is essential to the well being of both parties. The creditor is injured by delay, for it keeps him short of cash, and makes it necessary to pay more for interest, or it causes the loss of what could be made by discounting bills. He is also injured by the increased and constantly growing risk which delay brings, and further, by the certain and costly demoralization which follows as the consequence of all wrong methods. Business demoralization is nowhere more apparent than in connection with this cause.

The debtor is injured by the false feeling of restfulness and confidence which the leniency of his creditor engenders. By this leniency he is taught to rely upon using what really belongs to another, but which has been left in his hands through a mistaken desire to accommodate. He is wronged by the demoralization which comes to him through false training. Further, he is injured by the temptation which is thus presented to be slack in pressing his own collections. Leniency upon his part toward debtors increases his business losses.

Many instances are in mind where loans and discounts have been refused simply because the banker has perceived that the applicant, instead of borrowing money, should push his collections. In some instances the would-be borrower has subsequently expressed his gratitude for the refusal because the lesson thereby taught resulted in saving of money. I recall an instance of too easy loaning by a bank to a retail butcher, which resulted in the borrower deliberately permitting customers' bills to grow until they became so large that in many instances the temptation to default was too great to be resisted. The end was what might have been expected. The butcher lost heavily and finally failed. The bank lost its claim. It had loaned thousands where hundreds would have been a reasonable limit. Had it loaned only so much as was appropriate there would have been no failure upon the part of the butcher, and no loss to the bank. A strong and firm adherence to contracts is essential to safety. Carrying leniency to extremes always means loss, and in many cases absolute ruin.

The Importance of Accounting

A proper system of books, coupled with intelligence and integrity of management, will to a large extent guide any enterprise past shoals and hidden dangers. To my mind every business enterprise of magnitude and prominence should employ a skilled accountant, whose sole province should be to establish and maintain a system of bookkeeping that cannot be manipulated, and that will at all times give to the managers a true and correct showing of the condition of the business.

I assign to accountancy still another mission. I believe the day will come when every city, county, town and school district in this State, and, in fact, throughout the whole United States, will be compelled by law to have its books examined annually by competent public accountants, and to have its statements bearing the verification of such an expert published as a matter of public record. It seems to me that large sums could be saved annually by such a system of accounting.—From an address by James G. Cannon, President of the National Association of Credit Men, before the New York State Society of Certified Public Accountants.

Annual Inventories

By Geo. L. Pender

My experience with the retail trade convinces me that there is no evil to which the average country merchant is more prone than the neglect to make a careful reckoning of his real condition from time to time. Some retail merchants will permit two or three, or even four, years to elapse between inventories, and some of them never take stock.

No merchant, however small his business, can afford to disregard this most important duty. An inventory should be taken at least once a year. Twice a year would not be too often. The advantages of inventories at frequent intervals are manifold. It is the surest way of determining the real worth of the merchant. It is the only method he can adopt of ascertaining whether or not he is conducting his business on a profitable basis. It is the best and most reliable plan of reducing stock and of finding out how much of the goods on hand is old or unsalable, and therefore needs special effort to work it off.

There is no good excuse for any merchant who neglects to follow this desirable and beneficial practice. There are at least two seasons of the year when trade is sufficiently slack to enable him to perform this most important work. These periods are those just preceding the Spring and Fall seasons, when stocks of merchandise are at their lowest. It is very desirable that a careful summing up of the previous season's results should be before the merchant at these dates, in order that he may know where he stands.

The Meaning of Co-Insurance

By J. R. Ainsley

Within a few years insurance companies have, by unanimous agreement, put into all policies covering merchandise a new condition known as the "Eighty Per Cent Co-Insurance Clause." This clause provides that in the event of a loss the adjustment shall be made on the basis of there being an insurance carried and in force equal to 80 per cent. of the value of the property insured. It is evident from various facts that very few fully understand the effect of this clause or have taken it fairly into mind in deciding on the amount of insurance that they should carry.

It may help to an understanding of this matter to say that if the merchant has an insurance equal to 80 per cent. of the value of the property insured, then the clause has absolutely no effect in case of loss. Or if the property insured is absolutely and wholly destroyed, leaving no value whatever, then the clause has no effect whatever.

On the other hand, if the merchant has a partial loss, the effect is very different. It may be illustrated as follows: Assume that the total value of the property insured is $40,000. Then 80 per cent. of its value will be $32,000, which is the amount of insurance that should be carried. Assume that the amount of insurance that is actually placed amounts to only $25,000. This, it will be seen, is $7,000 short of the proper amount. Suppose that a fire occurs, resulting in a loss of $10,000. The insurance being $7,000 short, the $32,000 proper insurance has to pay the $10,000 loss, figuring $312.50 to each $1,000. That is to say, the insurance companies pay on $25,000, which is the amount of their policies, to the extent of $7,812.50, and the merchant, who is a co-insurer on the $7,000 short insurance, pays upon that basis $2,187.50. Thus the merchant receives out of his $10,000 loss the sum of $7,812.50. He is obliged to count as additional loss the $2,187.50 on account of not being insured up to 80 per cent. of the value of his stock.

Possibly this deficiency in insurance has occurred from a desire to save the premium on $7,000. Let us examine into the real economy of the saving. Assume that the average rate paid by merchants is 1½ per cent. Then the premium on $7,000 insurance would amount to $105 a year. In twenty years it would amount to $2,100. From this it will be seen that such a loss as is illustrated in the example would more than eat up the saving in premiums of twenty years. The importance of carrying an adequate amount of fire insurance in strictly good companies and under forms of policies carefully and properly prepared is thus made apparent.

The Bookkeeping of Department Stores

By Charles F. Jones

(Continued from page 133, March number)

It may be well imagined that to separate all the sales tickets for purposes of classification, as described, would be a gigantic task, unless some adequate system is employed. A frame of the kind shown in Fig. 42 greatly facilitates the work. This frame may be a board or a trellis, so arranged as to have projecting from it a number of sharp wires or file points as designated in the sketch by PP. The frame should hang upon the wall, in front of the clerk who is assorting the

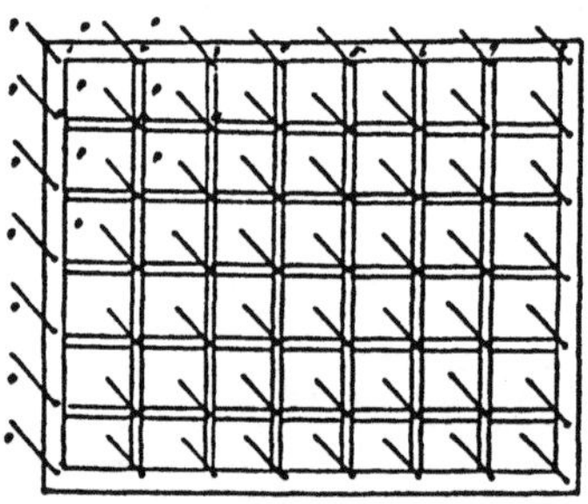

FIG. 42.—CHECK CLERK'S STICK FILE.

checks. The first thing to be done is to get all the checks arranged in departments as nearly as possible. For this purpose the points on the file may be numbered 1, 2, 3, etc. Whenever a check belonging to department No. 1 is taken up, it is stuck upon point 1; and a check that belongs to department No. 5, for example, is stuck upon point 5, and so on.

Having thus separated the checks into departments, the next step is to take them off from the files, tying them in packages, each department by itself.

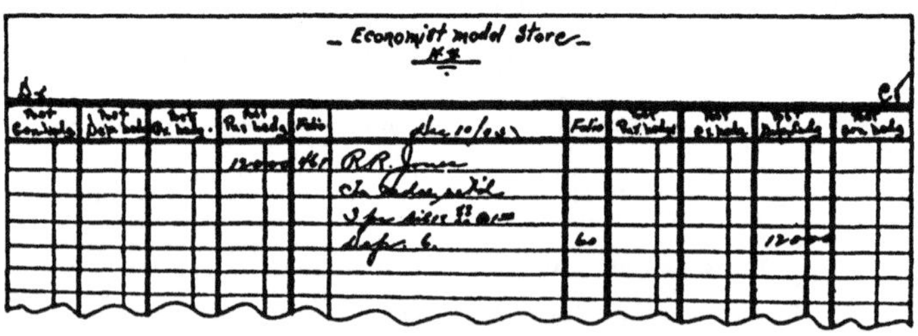

FIG. 43.—RULING OF COLUMNAR JOURNAL.

Then take these packages in turn and sort them, using the rack of points again in the same manner as described, in a way to get the tickets of each individual clerk by themselves. For this purpose a

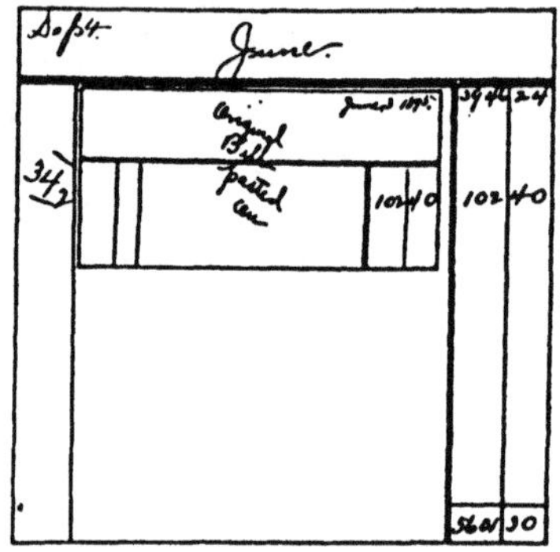

FIG. 44.—FORM OF INVOICE BOOK.

second series of numbers on the points may be necessary, calling them 101, 102, etc. All the checks made out by clerk No. 101 would be stuck upon point 101, and so on to the completion of the list.

By the use of some system similar to this, it is possible to sort the checks from ont thousand clerks working in a store divided into fifty departments in a very short space of time with the utmost accuracy. If the sharp points are objected to, a series of small pigeon-holes may be arranged against the wall in which the checks may be placed as picked up. Upon this plan each pigeon-hole will be treated the same as the wires above described. It is not necessary to have as many points or pigeon-holes as there are clerks, but it is necessary to have as many points or pigeon-holes as there are departments, and as many as the largest number of clerks in any one department.

For example, if there are fifty departments in the store, and if the department having the largest number of clerks employs seventy-five, then seventy-five points or seventy-five pigeon-holes will

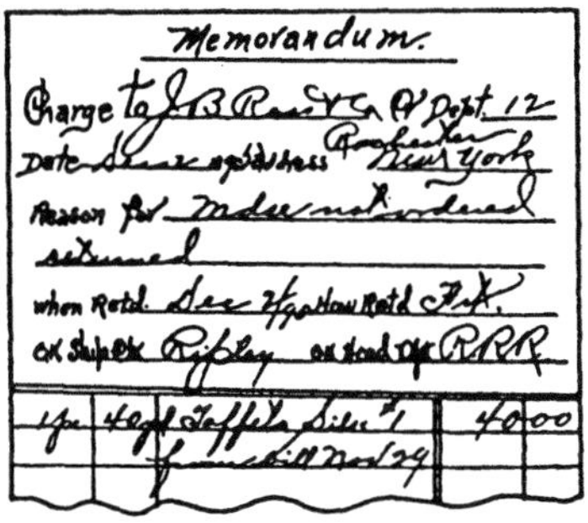

FIG. 45.—FORM FOR RECORDING GOODS RETURNED TO SHIPPER.

be sufficient for the purpose. If it is desired to have two persons to work at the same time in this sorting of checks, it is expedient to have two similar sets of wires or pigeon-holes, as the case may be, one for each person assorting.

Let us next consider the treatment of the invoices received by the firm for the goods which are purchased. There are various ways of handling bills or invoices, each of which requires its own special kind of entries in order to complete the record. The system which is found to be the most easily worked in a large department store is to require that every person supplying goods shall furnish two bills with each purchase, one marked "Original" and the other marked "Duplicate." This puts a little more labor upon the seller, but it saves a still greater amount of labor, not only for the bookkeeper in the department store, but also for each department manager who may have occasion to refer to the bill of a past purchase. It is necessary that each department manager should have access to his back bills, and it is also necessary that the head bookkeeper should have these bills as vouchers for the goods that have come into the establishment. Hence the desirability of an original for the bookkeeper and a duplicate for proper filing in the department.

Where the duplicate bill system is in use, the head bookkeeper should provide an ordinary invoice book for each department, in which all the bills may be pasted in alphebetical order, or in the order in which they are received, and then indexed in a way that any one required can be easily and speedily found. For every bill, before it is pasted in the invoice book, a journal entry will have to be made in order to get the total posted in the general ledger. This journal entry can be made in any kind of a journal which the bookkeeper may wish to provide for this purpose, or the form of journal illustrated in Fig. 43, which may be described as an eight-column journal, may be employed.

So far as the bookkeeping system that is here described is concerned, the plan of duplicate bills will be followed. Two bills, the original and the duplicate, having been received for a given purchase of goods, it is a very simple matter to allow the department manager to have the duplicate for his use, and the bookkeeper to keep the original for his use. Two invoice books then should be employed, and for this purpose the form shown in Fig. 44 is suggested. The invoice book, as it will be seen, is of a very common form, and into the one which is used in the department bills are pasted together according to the names of the sellers. All the bills of a given seller, say A. & Co., are pasted in one part, for example, from pages 1 to 10; and all those of another seller, say B & Co., in another part, as, for example, in pages 10 to 21, and so on.

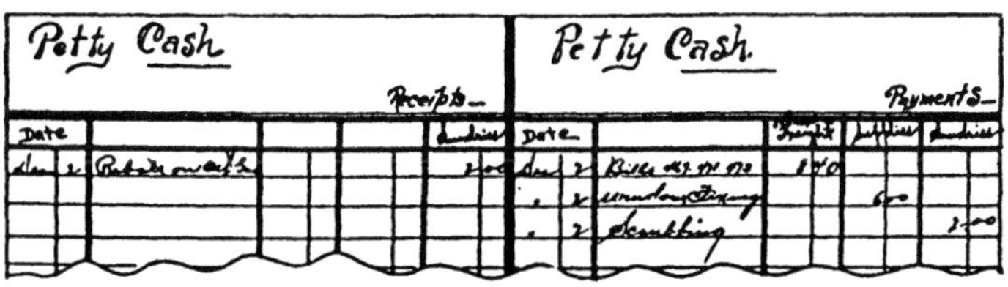

FIG. 46.—RULING OF PETTY CASH BOOK.

By this plan the bills are kept assorted according to the names of the sellers, so that any bill desired may be turned to at once without even the book being indexed, save only to show the sections of pages that are devoted to the different sellers.

The O. K.'s of department managers and bookkeepers should be made on the original bills. The original bills are to be pasted in the second of the invoice books, which is of the same general character as shown in Fig. 44. The only change is that in this book the bills are classified, not according to sellers, but according to departments receiving the goods. Referring now to Fig. 44, it will be seen that the page shown is one belonging to department No. 4, and a bill of June 3, 1895, has been extended so that its amount is included in the general footings. The total of the column at the end of the month then shows the amount of bills to this department from various sellers during the month. The manner of posting these footings will be referred to later.

When merchandise is received and subsequently returned to the seller, but too late to have the amount deducted from the original bill, the head of the department or the shipping clerk should furnish the bookkeeper in the main office a memorandum similar to that shown in Fig. 45. This memorandum is preserved by the bookkeeper, showing the full particulars of why the goods were returned, how shipped, etc. From this memorandum the bookkeeper makes a journal entry

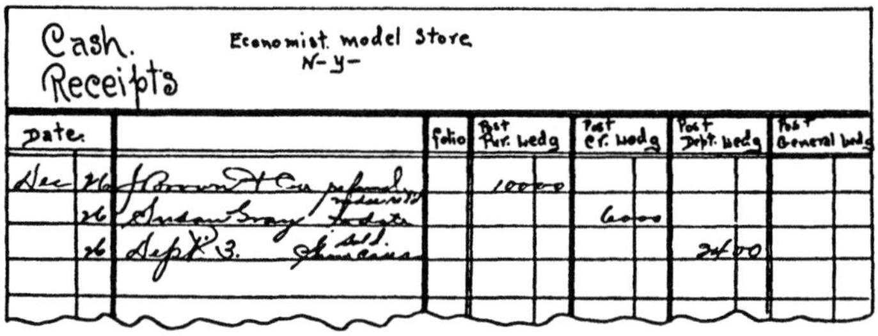

FIG. 47.—RULING OF BOOK FOR CASH RECEIPTS.

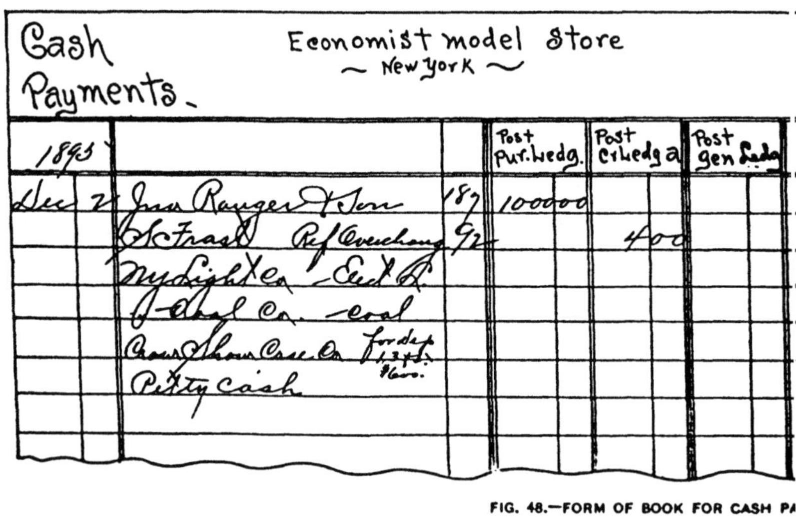

FIG. 48.—FORM OF BOOK FOR CASH PA

charging the firm with the goods returned, or the amount of the memorandum may be deducted direct from the footing of the invoice book without making a journal entry, and the memorandum, as evidence of the deduction, pasted into the invoice book in regular course. If it is thus deducted, the bookkeeper must be careful to remember, when posting up the amount of this memorandum, that exactly the opposite entry is to be made to that which is necessary in case of a purchase bill, and for which purpose the invoice book is primarily designed.

Let us next take up the cash books used by the department store. A cash book of ordinary form may be employed, if desired, but its use in a department store will make necessary so many extra entries and so many extra postings, that it is better to divide it into several parts. One of these parts would naturally be the pay-roll, another is that commonly called petty cash. In many of the department stores small cash transactions are so numerous that to record all of them in the general cash book would burden it unreasonably. Accordingly, a petty cash book, of the form shown in Fig. 46, is used for small and miscellaneous items. These petty amounts may be divided under various headings, such as Freight, Supplies, etc. Accordingly, a petty cash book with several columns is found convenient. The total of each of these general divisions is transferred into the general cash book at the end of the day. No postings are made from the petty cash book, for its use is simply that of a memorandum by which to collect the various items to make up a single entry in the general cash book. Attention has already been given to the cash sales book and it will be referred to again later on. In ad-

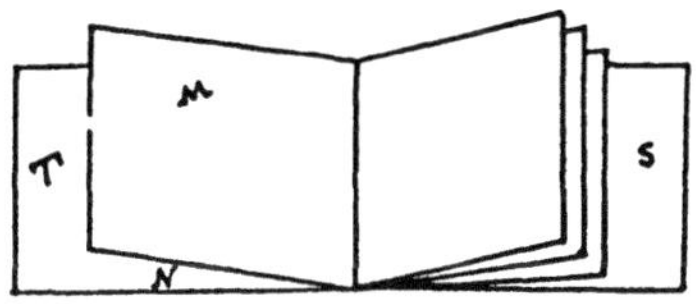

FIG. 49.—BOOK COMPOSED OF ALTERNATING WIDE AND NARROW LEAVES.

dition to these divisions of the cash book, there should be two general cash books, one for cash receipts and one for cash payments. Fig. 47 shows cash receipts. Columns are used corresponding to the ledgers in which occur the accounts to be credited with the amounts which this cash book records. The method of posting will be referred to when we reach a consideration of ledgers.

A department store doing a credit business will require at least four ledgers, a purchase ledger, a department ledger, a

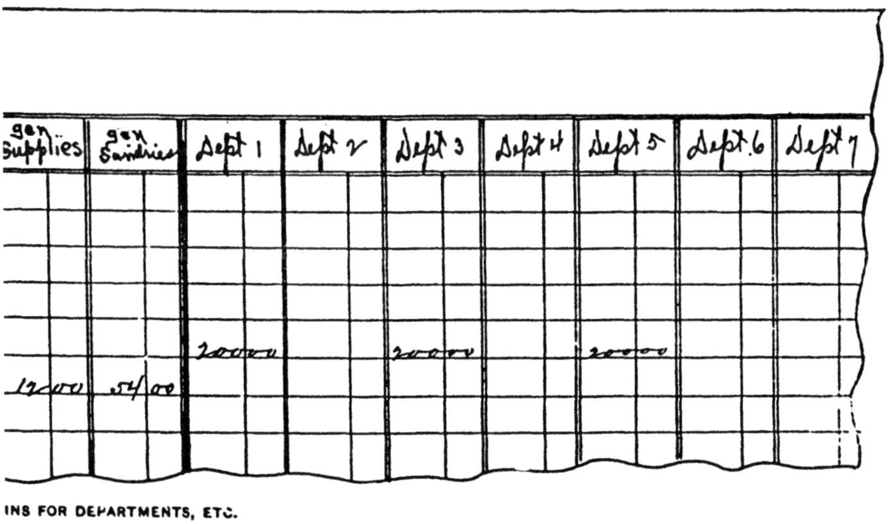

INS FOR DEPARTMENTS, ETC.

general ledger and a credit ledger. If the department store is doing a strictly cash business, the credit ledger will not be necessary. If the store is doing a very extensive credit business, so that one credit ledger is not enough to contain all the accounts, then as many volumes of the credit ledger will be required as may be determined by the number of accounts.

FIG. 50.—INVENTORY SLIP.

This is the explanation of the columns shown in the book for recording cash receipts, as indicated in Fig. 47.

Fig. 48 shows a cash book for general payments or cash disbursements. In this case not only are columns for the several ledgers provided, but also a column for each of the different departments is included in the department ledger. There are also columns for general expenses, in which a considerable number of entries are to be expected month by month. With reference to the latter it should be remarked that these are not necessary in order to keep an accurate set of books, but they are convenient and are great labor savers. Instead of posting each item to the ledger, no posting at all is made of the items falling into these columns, until the end of the month, when devoted to all the departments, and the amounts posted individually. If many entries, however, are to be charged against departments through the cash book, it will be found that the separation of the departments will materially lessen the labor of department bookkeeping. In some cases there may be so many departments in the store that it would be practically impossible to have enough columns on one sheet, or even on a double sheet, to provide space for all of them. For this purpose the construction of the book shown in Fig. 49 is suggested. It is a book made with wide and narrow leaves, with as many narrow leaves or interleaves, as they are sometimes called, as may be necessary to provide proper space for the columns. The difference in width between the narrow pages and the wide pages provides space for the entries. This entry space T appears on the side of one leaf, and when the short leaf M is closed down over N, T and M become as one page, and the entry is made thereon and posted as circumstances may require.

Referring back to Fig. 43, which illustrates an eight-column journal, it is to be remarked that four columns are used to post to the debit side of the ledger, and four columns are used to post to the credit side of the ledger. The journal is only used for extraordinary entries—in fact, such entries as cannot be made through the medium of any of the other books. The old method of keeping books

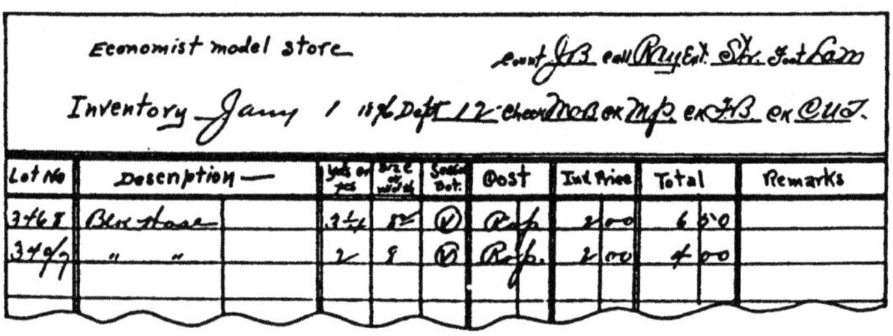

FIG. 51.—INVENTORY BOOK.

the total is posted in lump. This answers for purpose of record in the general ledger and makes one posting a month instead of possibly one hundred postings each day.

If for any reason it is not desired to keep the departments separate in the cash book, then a single column may be employed the journal for the majority of entries. The journal and cash book, in fact, were made the principal means of getting entries into the ledger. In the system here described, the journal is seldom required, and, as explained, only for those entries which cannot be made in any other way.

Before taking up the posting from the various books into the several ledgers, a moment should be spent in considering the system of inventorying; and in connection with it attention should be given to methods of marking goods. Every piece of goods received should have attached to it a tag or a pin ticket, upon which is marked the original cost, the selling price and some indication of the date of the purchase of the goods. By this plan, merely referring to the tags or tickets will show how long the goods have been in stock, and thus avoid keeping on hand too long any article of merchandise. Money is frequently saved by cleaning out old stock, even if no profit is made on that particular sale.

In taking an inventory great care is to be exercised, first to see that every item is recorded and that the exact value of every item is estimated in some parfectly fair way. For the purpose of counting stock, it is well to have the clerk go through every package and count the number of goods therein, and where goods are boxed, to use a form similar to that shown in Fig. 50. This slip of paper should have the blank end fastened under the lid of the box to which it refers, and on the other end have recorded the contents of the box. When the whole stock has thus been gone over in a preliminary way, the face of every box will show what is in it, what the goods cost, when they were purchased, what they sell for, and the lot numbers under which they were purchased. It then becomes a very easy matter to collect all these clips, or, rather, to have one of the clerks call off from them and another record them in the inventory book, the form of which is shown in Fig. 51. Goods not in boxes can be counted and the result recorded in the book direct.

The inventory book, as will be seen by reference to the form, shows the original lot number, a description of the goods, and all other necessary particulars. A single book, or as many books as may be needed, should be devoted to each department, so that the inventory of each department shall be kept entirely separate. The footings of each department book would be the total inventory for that department. It is very necessary in compiling an inventory that great care shall be taken to avoid errors. For the convenience of future reference, on each page of the inventory book as recorded and checked should appear the initials or signatures of the persons making the calculations and responsible for them. Every step should be proved by checking or balancing. Counting should be done by more than one person. For example, very box should be counted by one person, and then his counting should be gone over and checked by another. Every clip should be called out to the inventory clerk by one person, and the calling should be checked by another. The same things should be done in extending the amounts in the total column and in footing up the columns. Each bit of work should be done by one person and then verified by another.

An Auditor's Decalogue

Early in February last, Oscar M. Wihl, barrister-at-law, Manchester, England, delivered an address before the students of the Society of Incorporated Accountants, in which he submitted for consideration some general laws applicable to the conduct of an audit. He viewed the auditor's work from the standpoint of the lawyer. He said he had devoted considerable attention to the matter. From the lawyer's standpoint he declared that if an auditor obeyed the following decalogue in carrying out his duty, there would be no danger of any court of justice imparting liability to him:

1. Be a thorough accountant, even in the most trifling particulars.
2. Be acquainted with the general method of conducting a business similar to the one whose accounts you are auditing.
3. Rigidly adhere to any special regulations applicable to the particular audit you have in hand.
4. Endeavor to learn whether there be anything peculiar or special in the circumstances under which the concern in which you are interested has been carried on.
5. Whenever possible, obtain primary evidence and get down to the bare transactions.
6. Ask for and insist on full explanations, and obtain them wherever possible from persons having an adverse interest.
7. When technical details are doubtful, invoke expert assistance.
8. If specially prepared reports are to be relied upon, for example, in connection with stock, returns from branch establishments, and so forth, see that they are formally certified by responsible persons.
9. If there be anything special, frame a sufficient report directing the members' attention specifically to such matters.
10. Neither favor nor fear directors.

Mediocrity succeeds best in the world.—Colton.

Corporations: Their Importance and Use

By Charles Dutton, F. I. A.

(Concluded from page 12, April Number)

Where a man has a profitable business he ordinarily wishes to provide for its continuance in the event of his death. If he proposes to leave the business to some one person (a son) absolutely, there is little difficulty; but his sons may be under age or not fitted for the business; or he may wish the concern to be carried on for the benefit of his estate until they attain maturity or until certain provision is made for his widow and daughters or otherwise for a limited period; or he may desire to give an interest in the concern to his daughters or others who could not personally carry it on. In such cases the ordinary course (where the business is not incorporated) is to leave the business, with the capital employed in it, to trustees, who are directed to carry it on. But it is always a matter of difficulty to find competent trustees willing to undertake such trusts, for in carrying on the concern (even though acting avowedly as trustees or executors) they may become personally responsible for debts and liabilities contracted therein after the testator's death. Even if trustees are found they may die before the testator, or when upon the death of the testator they are properly advised as to their responsibilities they may decline to act or they may die before the trusts are at an end or wish to retire, and there may be difficulty in finding successors. Where, however, the business has been incorporated these difficulties disappear.

Sometimes the deceased partner authorizes his trustee or executors to carry on the business in conjunction with the surviving partners; but here again difficulties are apt to arise, for the trustees or executors may fail or refuse to qualify, or the surviving partners may be unwilling or find it impracticable to act with them, or disputes may arise. As stated in Lindley on Partnership:

"The position of the executors of a deceased partner is, in fact, one of considerable hardship and difficulty; if they insist on an immediate winding up of the firm they may ruin those whom the deceased may have been most anxious to benefit, while, if for their advantage the partnership is allowed to go on, the executors may run the risk of being ruined themselves. With a view to obviate this, it is not unusual for one partner to make his co-partner his executor; but the difficulty of the executor's position is thus rather increased than diminished, for his own personal interest as a surviving partner is brought into direct conflict with his duty as an executor. Everything, therefore, which he does is liable to question and misconstruction on the part of the persons beneficially entitled to the estate of the deceased, and he is practically much more fettered in the discharge of his duties and in the exercise of his rights than if he had not to act in the double character imposed on him."

If, however, the business has been incorporated, no such difficulties arise. The shares of the deceased partner become part of his assets, and are bequeathed in trust or otherwise dealt with as may be convenient, and his estate will be represented on the Board of Directors by his trustees or their nominees, who can act without incurring personal responsibilities.

The admission of a new partner generally involves the preparation of entirely new articles of partnership, and a general disturbance of the business. But in the case of a corporation the transaction is of the simplest character. If the new shareholder is to bring in new capital, he takes shares in the corporation to the amount agreed on, is entered in the register, and thereupon the transaction is complete. Where he is not to bring in new capital, but is to take the place of some existing member, the latter signs a transfer of his shares to the new member, who pays him the purchase money, the transfer is registered, and the transaction is complete. Where a member of a partnership retires, the concern is more or less dislocated, the capital reduced, and the rights of all the parties affected. Moreover, the retiring partner still remains liable for the existing debts and obligations of the partnership, and must rely on the agreement of the remaining partners to indemnify him; if that agreement is not performed, he may have to pay the creditors or become bankrupt, even though years may have passed since his retirement. Further, the retiring member may even become liable for the subsequent debts of the firm, unless his retirement is advertised, and existing customers notified. But in the case of a corporation the retirement of a stockholder is effected without difficulty. He signs a transfer to the person who takes his place; this is registered and the transaction is complete. There is no need to give notice by publication, or by circular or otherwise; and the retiring member is entirely freed from the debts and liabilities of the corporation.

The sale of a partner's interest in a partnership ordinarily dissolves it, and to mortgage an interest in a partnership involves very serious difficulties, and is likely to give rise to litigation and dispute. But stock in a corporation can be readily sold, mortgaged, bequeathed, or otherwise dealt with. Accordingly the incorporation of a business enhances the value of the owner's interest therein, by rendering the same more convertible and more easily dealt with.

The appropriation of some share of the profits of a concern to the employees is calculated to promote the success of the concern. But in the case of a partnership, it is not easy to grant employees the right to share profits, without the danger of having such employees declared partners, a matter open to grave objection. More than this, a right to a percentage of the profits often carries with it a right to an accounting and an examination of the partnership books and accounts, a right which an unscrupulous employee, after discharge, often attempts to enforce for ulterior purposes. In a corporation, however, there is no such difficulty or objection. The schemes commonly adopted are to give the employees a special class of "employees' shares," or to allow them to take up shares on favorable terms, or to transfer shares to trustees, who are to receive the dividends and distribute among the employees, or accumulate for their benefit. Another plan is to establish a participation fund and to notify that at the end of each year a certain percentage of the surplus profits will be carried thereto; and, in each case, the employees are given participation certificates conferring a right to equal or varying shares in the fund subject to conditions. Sometimes all the employees are admitted to participate; in other cases only those who have been employed for a term of years; in other cases only the managers or heads of departments.

In the case of a partnership, especially if the arrangements are detailed, the articles of partnership are involved and complicated, and the document is in all probability barely intelligible to the partners, and changes from time to time as occasion may require are effected and formulated with difficulty and inconvenience.

No one partner, even though he owns a major portion of the business, can govern and control his partners. He has but one vote, and he cannot effectually prevent his other partners from doing (it may be with his property) what he does not wish. He cannot withdraw his own property except by order of the court in a proceeding to dissolve the firm. Either of his partners, notwithstanding the provisions of the co-partnership articles, in case of difference, may place the co-partnership property in the hands of a receiver. Whereas, in the case of a private corporation the partner owning the larger interest can stipulate for a legitimate control, which cannot be disturbed, and in case a stockholder is dissatisfied, he has no other remedy than to sell his stock, which does not disturb the pusiness. In the case of a private corporation, the certificate of incorporation and the by-laws are short and simple and readily understood by any one. Matters which in a partnership agreement involve elaborate provisions can be easily dealt with in a certificate of incorporation and by-laws. This results from the fact that a private corporation is a separate body. The formation of a private corporation is, in many cases, the simplest mode of constituting what is in substance, though not in point of law, a partnership agreement.

And now in conclusion: It is easy for principles to be confused with methods. The principle upon which corporations are formed and upon which they have statutory existence is often confounded with the methods of applying or misapplying them. Shakespeare says: "Virtue itself turns vice, being misapplied." So that, if the principles are not clearly conceived, one cannot intelligently know from the methods whether those principles are misapplied or not. The legitimate operations of a corporation are often confounded with operations outside of the corporate body and which are separate and distinct from it; operations which cannot be controlled by the corporation, although they may be detrimental to its best interests. It is as absurd to argue against a corporation because of speculations and gambling in its stock, in which it does not participate and over which it has no control, as it is to argue against the growing of wheat and grain, because the operations of the board of trade cannot be controlled by the producers. The fact that corporations exist that are ignorantly or fraudulently managed is no argument against corporations per se.

Because there is a definite number of marriages each year, and a definite number of divorces each year, we should not cry out against the institution of marriage. Because, according to statistics, there were in the United States during the year 1897 no less than 13,522 failures in business by merchants and firms, with a total liability of $182,582,771, it could not be said that business itself was a failure. Because money in the hands of some has proved a curse; because it is squandered, wasted and even worse than wasted, does not determine that money is not a necessity. Because corporations exist, that have proved disastrous financially to their members, because they furnish a medium for purposes of speculation and gambling, does not by any manner of means prove that legitimate corporations are not a necessity.

As a matter of fact, if what has been presented is true, and I firmly believe it is, corporations are not a forced product. They have grown up spontaneously. They have arisen naturally out of economic conditions, and are not a contingency, but a necessity; and it is certain that as the principles which govern them are more clearly understood, they will be more generally and unhesitatingly accepted. It is the true position of the business community to recognize these principles as an important factor in the evolution of commercialism and to contend only against abuses.

Test Question.—How would you treat the following in the balance sheet? (a) Provision for bad and doubtful debts. (b) Contingent fund (which is the amount charged against profit and loss on account of depreciation of plant). (c) Partners' capital account, and (d) Unused premiums of fire insurance.

Success soon palls. The joyous time is when the breeze first strikes your sails, and the waters rustle under your bows.—Charles Buxton.

Wants

From time to time we receive indications of wants from our readers and the profession in general. There are lacking many things which should be in the literature of accounting, and to prepare which it is fair to suppose there are in the country many men able, if not willing. Undoubtedly, they would be willing if they knew of the need that exists. We propose, therefore, under this head, to indicate, from time to time, some of those wants which come to our knowledge. At present we call attention to the following:

A system of accounts for a receivership.

An essay on the financial operations of corporations.

A system of bookkeeping for a life insurance company.

A treatise on the capitalization of corporations in the matter of plant, patents, good-will and the like, and the issuing of different grades of stock and bonds.

A plan of bookkeeping for an assignee.

Brain vs. Muscle

Some of the daily papers have seized upon the Manila incident as a text for a sermon upon the superiority of brain as compared with muscle, and of intelligence as contrasted with unintelligence. What won at Manila, they say, and what will win whenever we fight, is a combination of brains and courage. The real fighting, it is set forth, was done in the heads of the men on our ships. Muscle is all very well, but in this case it did very little. As a fact, every man thought and worked with his head. The same text and the same conclusions might be used in various other directions. All men who succeed at the present day work with their brains rather than with their hands. The accountants who lead in the profession are not those who do the most work at the desk, measured by hours, but instead, are those who think out plans and save labor of execution by their engineering skill. It is distinctively the day of brain work, and that man, be he bookkeeper or accountant, field officer or naval commander, who would distinguish himself, must use his brain freely and keep his muscle in reserve; must think out his work in a way to save time and thereby do twice or three times as much in a given period as his rival or opponent. The expression is frequently used, "He is a brainy fellow," referring to the author, the statesman, the judge on the bench, or the successful leader of men. The business of the day demands brainy bookkeepers and brainy accountants, and ere long, even though it is not the rule at present, these men will be selected with reference to their mental equipment and discipline, rather than on account of their per diem charges.

Accountants' Associations

New York Chapter

The annual meeting of the New York Chapter of the Institute of Accounts was held at the Waldorf-Astoria Thursday evening, April 28. Charles Dutton was reelected president and W. P. Plant was reelected secretary. Thos. S. Whitbeck and A. O. Kittredge were chosen to fill vacancies in the Board of Governors.

At the regular monthly meeting of the chapter, May 20, a paper entitled "An Economic View of Using and Consuming Wealth," was presented by Thos. S. Whitbeck. It was an interesting and instructive dissertation upon the application of important economic principles and was greatly enjoyed by all who were present. Mr. Whitbeck is an original thinker and in his theories of political enonomy does not adhere strictly to any of the accepted schools. Several of those listening to the address manifested by copious note-taking their intention to argue some of the points made by the speaker when the hour of discussion should arrive When the president finally announced that the paper and the speaker were in the hands of the audience for proper consideration, the ball was opened by a few questions addressed to the essayist, ostensibly asking for information on certain points, but in reality referring to his definitions of terms. It was soon developed that there were scarcely two persons in the room who could agree upon such leading economic terms as "wealth." This effectually checked discussion of the paper, although it drew forth various remarks that added materially to the interest of the occasion. One member said that, in the light of the evening's experience, he began to realize why political economy was sometimes defined as the "dismal science." The fact that there is no substantial agreement between authors in the definitions of terms that are necessary to employ in setting forth their views, he said, may be likened to the routes through a very dark swamp which various explorers have followed in a way to reach the other side, but which no one has since been able to trace because they had neglected to blaze the trees in passing. In picking their paths, without the help of chart or compass, they had in frequent instances deviated from a straight course, and sometimes had even doubled upon themselves. Further, in some cases, they had crossed the courses of their fellow pioneers without recognizing the fact, and occasionally had traveled through certain portions of the tangle in almost identical lines, but moving in opposite directions. The explorers in the field of political ecomomy have put upon record what, comparatively speaking, are contradictory descriptions of the same pieces of ground.

We trust to find room for the whole, or at least portions, of Mr. Whitbeck's paper in subsequent issues. A special guest of the chapter on this occasion, and one who participated in the discussion, was Charles Dyer Chase, of the Massachusetts Institute of Accounts, who formerly resided in the neighborhood of Boston, but who is at present located in New York.

Brooklyn Chapter

Through the efforts of Mr. William Dillon, a number of accountants residing in Brooklyn have become much interested in the work of the Institute of Accounts and have signified their intention to cooperate at an early date in organizing a chapter in that portion of Greater New York. Whenever the date of the meeting for organization is announced a strong delegation from the New York Chapter will be found ready to take proper steps to assist in the work and give the Brooklyn men a suitable send-off. Those who desire to be enrolled as charter members of the Brooklyn Chapter should communicate with Mr. Dillon without further delay. Address him at No. 101 Moffat street, Brooklyn.

Associated Accountants of New Orleans

The subject arranged for discussion at the June meeting of the Associated Accountants of New Orleans is "The Conversion of Partnership Books into Those of a Limited Company, Under Certain Conditions." The speaker is the president of the organization, August M. Benedic. In order to lend interest to the occasion and to cause the members and visitors to come to the meeting well prepared for the discussion, the problem has been presented to them in the form of a neat circular. Those who are unable to be present in person will undoubtedly find their manuscript discussion of the problem or any part of it welcome by the meeting. For the benefit of those who have not seen the circular and who wish to consider the problem, we present it in full:

The partners A and B have agreed with C and D to form a Limited Company, with a capital of $200,000, divided into 2,000 shares of $100 each. Five hundred of these shares are preferred shares, and the balance are common shares. A subscribes for 208 shares of preferred stock and 209 shares of common; B subscribes for 292 shares of preferred and 291 shares of the common; C subscribes for 200 shares of the common, and D for 200 shares of the common. The balance of the stock is to remain in the treasury.

A and B are to pay for their stock with their respective interests in the partnership, and whatever difference there is is to be considered as payment of their good-will in the business. C agrees to pay cash for his stock. D agrees to pay for his stock $7,500 cash and give his thirty-day note secured by collateral for the balance.

The trial balance of the partnership books shows the following:

A's Capital		$15,000
B's Capital		20,000
Cash in Bank	$9,000	
Notes Receivable (including rent notes $2,500)	5,000	
Accrued interest on above $100.		
Collateral Notes Receivable	7,000	
Accrued interest on above $300.		
Book Accounts Receivable (including J. Brown's Accommodation Account, $2,000)	8,000	
Book Accounts Payable		4,300
Real Estate	52,000	
Real Estate Revenue (in the credit of this account there is $500 of rent notes not yet due)	2,400	6,200
Office and Office Fixtures	750	
Fidelity Trust Co. (a certain annuity of $2,500 and to continue for ten years)		2,500
U. S. 4 per cent. bonds, 1908 (value $12,000)	12,000	480
Orleans R. R. Co., 6 per cent. bonds, Gold (value $5,000)	5,000	300
Notes Payable (including note favor J. Brown, $2,000)		4,000
Interest accrued on above $40.		
Notes Payable (secured with $3,000 of Collateral notes receivable)		2,500
Interest accrued on above $35.		
First Mortgage Bonds Payable, 5 per cent., 10 years		35,000
Shipment to Havana, No. 1, on joint account with A, half gains and losses	2,330	
Merchandise from Livingston in Co., with A and B, each one-third gains and losses	3,350	2,000
Trading and Merchandising	165,000	194,750
Commission Account		7,000
General Expenses	1,000	
Salaries	5,000	
Insurance (Unexpired Premiums $75)	200	
Taxes and License (prepaid $120)	500	
Rolling Stock (appraised at $2,000)	2,500	
Live Stock (appraised at $2,400)	3,000	
Rolling Stock Expenses	200	
Live Stock Expenses	500	
Stable Expenses	800	
Feed (on hand $200)	2,500	
A's Withdrawals	3,500	
B's Withdrawals	2,500	
	$294,030	$294,030

The partners A and B share gains and losses in proportion to their capital invested and are to pay 6 per cent. interest on their withdrawals; A's equated time to charge interest, six months; B's equated time to charge interest, four months. Five hundred dollars is allowed on notes receivable for unforeseen losses and expenses in collecting; $1,200 of the book accounts are considered worthless. Stock in trade appraised at $10,000. The 400 bbls. flour, account Mdse. from Livingston in Company, not yet sold, the new company agrees to purchase for $2,400, which closes the consignment. Commission $110. Received from A, account sales of shipment to Havana No. 1 on joint account, net proceeds, $2,000.

The partners have also agreed as follows: To sell to the new company their $2,500 annuity on a 4 per cent. compound interest basis; to pay the interest at present due on the first mortgage bonds, $1,750; to create a first mortgage bonds fund account and deposit the cash in trust bearing 3 per cent. compound interest, so that principal and interest together will meet the bonds at maturity.

From the above trial balance and conditions presented, prepare the following: Trading and merchandising account, showing the gross and net gain percentage on trading, and loss and gain account; balance sheet of the partnership A and B; respective partner's account; entries necessary to close the partnership books; entries necessary to open a new set of books for the A and B Co.; limited, from the accounts of the partnership A and B.; C and D have paid for their stock—show what entries are necessary; make a trial balance of the books of the A and B Co., limited.

Pennsylvania Public Accountants

It will be several months before the next Legislature of the State of Pennsylvania assembles, but soon after it is organized, a bill will be introduced in the interest of the public accountants of that State, which is intended to give the profession a standing before the law not unlike that which has been accomplished in the State of New York. The Pennsylvania Association of Public Accountants is fully alive to its opportunities as well as responsibilities in this regard, and will by all proper means push the measure. In this work the Pennsylvania accountants are sure of the sympathy and moral support of their fellow-professionals in New York and throughout the country at large.

The Cartoonist's Use of Bookkeeping

We present on this and the following page two characteristic cartoons by Davenport, which are of interest to our readers because of the employment of bookkeeping as a symbol. In a sense, the suggestion conveyed by the picture is grewsome, and yet it typifies much of the thought and feeling that is current at the present time. The fundamental idea of bookkeeping, in the minds of those who have not thoroughly investigated it,

SHORTLY AFTER DEWEY'S VICTORY.

is that of a score or tally. It is something that keeps track of what is owing to us, and of what payments we receive. The bookkeeper, as the representative of business, is put in the position of exacting payment, according to the books, to the last farthing.

Here we see Uncle Sam, first with his ledger open, on which he has charged to to the account with Spain, under date of February 15, one battleship and 266 men. Next in comes Messenger Dewey with a contra statement, wherein the account is more or less balanced under a later date by eleven Spanish warships destroyed and 300 men killed.

A day or two after this cartoon was

JUST AFTER THE LOSS OF ENSIGN BAGLEY.

published in one of the daily papers thère occurred the Winslow affair off the coast of Cuba, wherein were lost Ensign Bagley and five men. The second cartoon, therefore, represents Uncle Sam as the bookkeeper charging Spain with this additional item.

Davenport always draws spirited pictures, and a better representation of Uncle Sam as an old-style office man, with quill pen and ancient inkstand, could scarcely be produced by any one. The primitive idea of bookkeeping is very happily expressed in these sketches, and yet there is something in the thought of applying a conception of bookkeeping to an illustration of or a comment upon war affairs which, at best, are horrors indescribable that causes every well-regulated mind to revolt.

REVIEWS AND CRITICISMS

The Science of Speculation

Speculation as a Science. By Geo. MacLean Irwin. Pocket Size. 68 pages, bound in cloth. Published by the Authors' Publishing Co. 1898. Price, 75 cents.

By the title of this book the reader is assured that the author believes that there is such a thing as the science of speculation. With this thought in mind, we turn the pages to discover the proof of the fact and the applications made of it. The first chapter is an inquiry entitled, "What is Speculation?" The question turns on whether it is an art or a science, and also as to the right and wrong of it. The conclusion is reached that with society, as organized, speculation is a necessity. The author then proceeds to show the difference between speculation and gambling. Speculation is declared to be an intellectual effort, while gambling is described as blind chance. Speculation is a venture based upon calculation, gambling a venture without calculation. The adroit speculator, it is asserted, has four great essential qualifications in combination—namely, experience, nerve, patience and capital. To the professional, speculation is a scientific operation based upon cold calculation. Contrasted with this is the assertion that the gambler plunges in on impulse.

The author argues that speculation can be taught and that such a term as "professor of speculation" might be borne with honor by many men. All business is declared to be more or less speculative in character, and yet speculation in its narrower sense is applied to business of exceptional uncertainty. With this introduction, Mr. Irwin proceeds to set forth what he conceives to be the underlying principles of speculation. He discusses his subject under various chapter heads, among which are The Amateur in Speculation, Brokers and Commission Merchants, Market Letters, The Investor, Exchanges, Actual and Speculative Values, Statistics in Speculation, Gauging Market Conditions, Pools, Public Sentiment, Tips, Pitfalls and Snares, Discretionary Orders and Pools, Grain and Cotton Speculation, etc. The volume concludes with a chapter entitled, Effect of War on Speculative Markets.

If fortune wishes to make a man estimable, she gives him virtues; if she wishes to make him esteemed, she gives him success.—Joubert.

Office Equipment

Postage Stamp Holder

The accompanying illustration shows a holder for postage stamps that must win instant approval in all concerns sending

THE GLOBE POSTAGE STAMP HOLDER.

out large mails. Its utility is so evident that a detailed description seems superfluous. It may be described as a book, durably and attractively bound in cloth, containing indexed parrafine - coated leaves. In size, it accommodates full sheets. The postage stamps are laid flat between the parrafine sheets, opposite the indexed pages, according to their denominations. The result is that the stamps are kept in flat form and are successfully prevented from sticking together. This device is manufactured by the Globe Company, Cincinnati, Ohio.

Automatic Order Binder

The very general use of loose sheets for orders, records of shipments, lists of names, and many other purposes, has produced a very extensive demand for what are distinctively called "post binders," and which in a more restricted sense are designated simply as order binders. Various devices have been invented for securing the proper locking or clamping of binders of this class. Clamps, springs, screws and other forms of mechanical movements are in use in different directions. Samuel C. Tatum Cc, Johnwater street, Cincinnati, Ohio, are putting upon the market what they have designated as Tatum's Automatic Order Binder, the general features of which are clearly indicated by the accompanying illustration. The covers are held in correct relative position by automatic catches, which in one position bear against the posts, and with the resistance of the contained papers form a lock to hold the cover at any point at which it may be placed. The cover is easily released and raised by grasping these catches with the finger and thumb of one hand and using them as a handle by which to lift it. In this way the cover

FIG. 1.—METHOD OF OPENING THE BINDER.

may be removed, thus opening the binder for insertion of new sheets or the removal of those already in place. When the binder has been entirely filled, as shown in the second illustration, the spring catches lie flat, thus overcoming the objection of projecting parts when putting a filled binder away for perma-

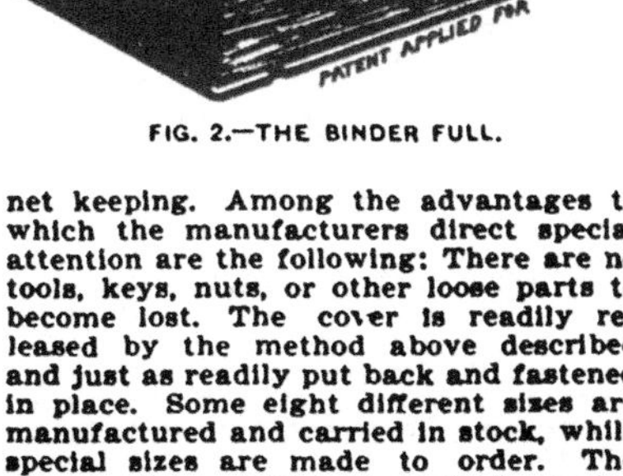

FIG. 2.—THE BINDER FULL.

net keeping. Among the advantages to which the manufacturers direct special attention are the following: There are no tools, keys, nuts, or other loose parts to become lost. The cover is readily released by the method above described and just as readily put back and fastened in place. Some eight different sizes are manufactured and carried in stock, while special sizes are made to order. The manufacturers will send a priced circular to those who write for it, mentioning this article.

Labor-Saving Error Preventers

We know from experience and from practical contact with bookkeepers and accountants in different parts of the country that there are comparatively few who have a proper conception of the saving in labor and the safeguarding against errors that may be accomplished by a judicious use of the manifold process. Thousands of office men every day laboriously copy orders or fill out stubs with the particulars of orders, whose labor would be greatly diminished, and who would have a corresponding assurance of absolute accuracy if only they were properly employing a carbon manifold process. Philip Hano & Co., 812 Greenwich Street, New York, have for many years past made a specialty of manifolding processes and carbon papers, and, as the result, are in a position to intelligently advise accountants, business men, bookkeepers and office employees with respect to the use of devices of the kind named. They have recently issued an illustrated catalogue, which contains information that is of the greatest service to all who are interested in matters of this kind.

Whenever a manifold process or carbon sheet is mentioned the average person is apt to suppose that nothing more is meant than such a commonplace duplication as is seen every day in retail stores in their sales checks. The manifolding employed by retail stores is in nowise to be despised, particularly in view of the perfected appliances for it which this firm supplies, and what the retail store finds advantageous to employ is in principle applicable in many other directions. For example, every business house sends out more or less orders, a copy of each of which should be retained. An order book with the orders numbered seriatim is accepted as a necessity. By adding the manifold feature an exact copy of the order is retained, thus overcoming the danger of mistakes in writing the order, checking bills from a stub and others, which depend upon double writing. Salesmen on the road, in transmitting the results of their calls upon customers, also find it useful to retain a copy of what they send in for their own information and to supply the buyer with a copy also. Some houses, for the sake of expediting work, require the orders to be transmitted in duplicate. By this means they save copying in the office into an order book or shipping book after the order comes to hand. It is needless to say that the carbon process for all these purposes is invaluable. All the necessary copies can be made at one writing. For certain lines of business a combination invoice and sales book is desirable; one page, being detachable, is the invoice that goes to the customer, and the other page, receiving the impression from the same writing, constitutes the sales book entry. Here also the carbon process is invaluable.

Many office men suppose that carbon paper can be advantageously used only with a pencil. As a fact, a special grade of carbon paper is supplied by this firm which is more successfully used with a pen than the ordinary grade with a pencil. We might continue this description, referring to manifold shipping receipts, to duplicate and triplicate books for buyers, to counter-check books for cash and credit stores, to duplicate bank deposit slips, to complete retail store systems, to a special grade of typewriter carbon papers, and to many other features. We might also continue it to the extent of describing special mechanical devices which have been invented for quickly operating the carbon in a way to save soiling the fingers, while at the same time getting a larger amount of wear from the carbon sheet. All this, however, can be gained by inspection of the book which Philip Hano & Co., 812 Greenwich Street, New York, will send to any reader of this notice who applies for it.

Accounting Data

Among the very live, pushing, working accountants of the country, A. O. Kittredge, F. I. A., is a prominent figure. A student of accounting in its higher forms, he is working out many new problems. We acknowledge receipt of a very neatly printed memoranda on "The Accounting Engineer," on "Accounting Specifications and Formulas" and on "I Write Books on Accounting." Mr. Kittredge's office is in the Wool Exchange Building, New York. —Financial Record.

Trade Congresses at the Credit Men's Convention.

A special feature of the approaching convention of the National Association of Credit Men, which is to be held in Detroit, June 22, 23 and 24, is special congresses of the delegates and visitors present, representing several leading lines of trade and allied branches. A prominent credit man of each line of business has been invited to act as chairman of his meeting, and, in addition, a reception committee will see that those who are present are duly introduced to all others and thus made thoroughly at home. Congresses have been arranged for the hardware, dry goods, grocery, drug, clothing and boot and shoe trades. These special meetings are to be held in the afternoon of Wednesday, June 22, after adjournment of the first day's session of the convention. In each of these conferences discussion will be in order upon such topics as "Datings," "Discounts," "Credits," "Collections" and various other subjects peculiar to the interests represented. In some of the congresses special topics outside of these general features will be taken up. The opportunity that will be afforded by these gatherings for men in the same lines of business to meet and become better acquainted with each other, together with the importance of the themes to be discussed and the practical suggestions that are likely to be offered, promise to make them very interesting as well as profitable incidents of the convention.

The "Acx" System of

Filing Invoices

Pronounced by those who are employing it, simpler, more convenient and more serviceable than any other. A new and time-saving application of elements more or less used in every up-to-date office.

Copies of orders, records of arrivals of goods, and the invoices brought together in sets, adequately indexed and permanently bound in book form. Posting may be made direct to credit of Purchase Accounts, with daily, weekly or monthly summaries for charges.

No journalizing necessary. Some of the more prominent features of the system include the following:

1. A strongly-bound book, and one of even thickness, whether holding 10 invoices or 1,000 invoices. Books may be large or small at pleasure.

2. Each record contains a copy of the order, the report of receiving clerk and the seller's invoice.

3. Copies of orders are presented seriatim according to their numbers. Leaves of book are regularly numbered.

4. Knowing the name of the seller or the number of the order or the date of the invoice, the required place in the book is found instantly.

5. No special form of order is demanded.

6. Full provision is made for recording partial shipments, shipments of a single order distributed through a considerable period of time, or several orders combined in one shipment.

7. Always up-to-date. Less labor than by any other plan.

8. Book is built up progressively. No blank pages or dead stock to lift or carry around.

9. The "Acx" System is the bookkeeper's delight, because it saves labor, keeps everything ship-shape and enables him to answer questions about invoices and prices instantly from the actual figures.

10. The "Acx" System is greatly enjoyed by the buyer as well as by the proprietor and business manager, because it instantly furnishes all required information about purchases and orders out whether examined by order numbers, by names of sellers, by date of order or by date of invoice.

11. The "Acx" System employs cheaper equipment in view of the results accomplished than any other.

Samples, together with full and complete specification for construction and management, forwarded carriage paid for **One Dollar.**

ACCOUNTICS ASSOCIATION

Publishers and Booksellers

Wool Exchange Building - - - - New York

Local checks are not acceptable unless 15 cents be added for collection costs. Remit by banker's draft on New York, post-office or express money order, or send currency by registered letter at our risk.

Accountics

The Office Magazine.

A. O. KITTREDGE, F. I. A., C. P. A., EDITOR.

Accountics is devoted to the Science of Accounting, to the Art of Bookkeeping and to the advocacy of Improved Office Methods.

Subscription.—One dollar a year, payable in advance.

Postage is prepaid by the publishers in the United States, Canada and Mexico. For all other countries in the Postal Union, subscribers must add 50 cents a year.

Discontinuances.—In the absence of specific orders to discontinue at the end of the subscription term the magazine will be continued and a bill sent.

Remittances should be by Draft, P. O. Order or Express Order, payable to the order of the ACCOUNTICS ASSOCIATION. Money and postage stamps are at the risk of the sender, unless sent by express or in registered letters. Add 10 cents each to checks on local banks to defray collection charges.

Advertising Rates will be quoted on application.

Official Journal.—This publication, by resolutions duly passed, has been made the official publication of the following organizations:—
THE INSTITUTE OF ACCOUNTS.
THE NEW YORK CHAPTER of the Institute of Accounts.
THE WASHINGTON CHAPTER of the Institute of Accounts.
THE HARTFORD CHAPTER of the Institute of Accounts.

ACCOUNTICS is the accredited medium of intercommunication between members of the Institute of Accounts wherever located.

ACCOUNTICS ASSOCIATION,
Publishers,
Wool Exchange, New York.

ınting is the Vital Element of Business

Accountics

The Office Magazine

One Dollar a Year
Ten Cents a Copy

JUNE 1898

Volume III
Number 3

CONTENTS.

Published by the ACCOUNTICS ASSOCIATION: Wool Exchange New York

The "Acx" System of

Filing Invoices

Pronounced by those who are employing it, simpler, more convenient and more serviceable than any other. A new and time-saving application of elements more or less used in every up-to-date office.

Copies of orders, records of arrivals of goods, and the invoices brought together in sets, adequately indexed and permanently bound in book form. Posting may be made direct to credit of Purchase Accounts, with daily, weekly or monthly summaries for charges.

No journalizing necessary. Some of the more prominent features of the system include the following:

1. A strongly-bound book, and one of even thickness, whether holding 10 invoices or 1,000 invoices. Books may be large or small at pleasure.

2. Each record contains a copy of the order, the report of receiving clerk and the seller's invoice.

3. Copies of orders are presented seriatim according to their numbers. Leaves of book are regularly numbered.

4. Knowing the name of the seller or the number of the order or the date of the invoice, the required place in the book is found instantly.

5. No special form of order is demanded.

6. Full provision is made for recording partial shipments, shipments of a single order distributed through a considerable period of time, or several orders combined in one shipment.

7. Always up-to-date. Less labor than by any other plan.

8. Book is built up progressively. No blank pages or dead stock to lift or carry around.

9. The "Acx" System is the bookkeeper's delight, because it saves labor, keeps everything ship-shape and enables him to answer questions about invoices and prices instantly from the actual figures.

10. The "Acx" System is greatly enjoyed by the buyer as well as by the proprietor and business manager, because it instantly furnishes all required information about purchases and orders out whether examined by order numbers, by names of sellers, by date of order or by date of invoice.

11. The "Acx" System employs cheaper equipment in view of the results accomplished than any other.

Samples, together with full and complete specification for construction and management, forwarded carriage paid for **One Dollar.**

ACCOUNTICS ASSOCIATION

Publishers and Booksellers

Wool Exchange Building - - - - New York

Local checks are not acceptable unless 15 cents be added for collection costs. Remit by banker's draft on New York, post-office or express money order, or send currency by registered letter at our risk.

Accountics

VOL. III JUNE 1898 No. 3

The Monthly Statement

The article in the series on Cost Accounts in Manufactures presented this month proceeds from the pen of a practical accountant and a very careful student of industrial and financial affairs. From one point of view the article may be regarded as an application to private shops of the system developed some years since by Captain Henry Metcalf for arsenal practice, and set forth in his well-known work entitled "Cost of Manufactures." There is enough of originality, however, brought to bear upon the application of the different methods to make the article very acceptable to managers, superintendents and accountants in manufacturing establishments, wherever situated.

At the outset the author touches upon a proper connecting link between the accounts of the factory and the general accounts that are of necessity conducted in the principal books of an establishment, representing factory operations. He takes cognizance of the necessity of proof by the method of balance and comparison between these two sets of accounts and assumes a position that will be endorsed by every practitioner of the double entry system. He also brings into use an account with manufactured stock, so adjusted and managed as to show by its balance the inventory value of the finished goods on hand. Its presence leaves the account which he calls Manufacturing, in a form to show by its balance at all times the inventory value of the materials and supplies on hand.

His provisions with respect to the Labor Account insure every dollar's cost of labor for which payment is made being charged to some of the going orders. The author also discriminates very carefully between the cost of producing a lot of goods and the incidental cost of the preparation of machinery and other facilities for turning out the order. Finally, he lays down the rule by which general expenses are to be distributed—namely, upon the basis of hours of labor. The illustrations presented with the article add interest and value to the study. Altogether, it is one that will be profitably considered by accountants wherever located.

To the shame and disgrace of the profession of accountancy in New York and other business centers for many years past, there have been various persons of foreign extraction seeking patronage whose antecedents would not bear investigation. It has been freely charged that some of these men left their own country between two days for their country's good, if not for their own safety. Others have been accused of operating in this country under assumed names, and in general the gossip concerning them, more or less of which has been based upon well-established facts, has been such as to give the business public most excellent grounds for distrust. Their presence in the ranks of the profession has served to discredit all practitioners. The passage of the Accountants' law in this State has served to check the operations of men of this kind to a certain extent, at least, and to put a distinguishing mark upon those who hold a legitimate position in the accounting profession, as opposed to those who are mere pretenders and frauds.

It will be recalled that a prosecution for violating the law limiting the use of "C. P. A." to such as have qualified for it was undertaken some time since against one Arthur C. Fenton. This man was finally convicted and fined. In the course of the prosecution the statement was made that the accused was a member of the English Society of Accountants and Auditors. This fact was widely published and came to the attention of the accounting journals published in England, and particularly to that of the Incorporated Accountants' Journal, the official organ of the Society of Accountants and Auditors. This journal, in its May issue, unconditionally repudiates Mr. Fenton's claims and says that there is not and never has been any person of the name of Fenton on the society's roll of members. It says further that the Society of Accountants and Auditors does not admit to membership accountants practising in the United States. It acknowledges, however, that one member who passed his examinations in England some time ago has since taken up his residence in this country.

We refer to the utterances of this contemporary only to show that the good work is progressing all along the line and that the conditions are being made harder and harder for those who prefer a fraudulent course to a course of strict integrity in connection with accounting work. A little while ago it seemed to be the opinion, held by at least one English paper published in the interests of accountants, that it was only a good joke on Americans that a spurious accountant from that country should be humbugging the business interests of this side of the Atlantic by printing after his name "C. A." A little later a journal of the same general class waxed very indignant over the proposition to establish by law various grades of accountants in this country, and if we remember correctly, even went so far as to propose coming over here and actively lobbying against the bill. Better counsels of late seem to be prevailing, and now the disposition is to hound the fraud and brand him, wherever he may be found. At any rate the English accountants are quickly repudiating those of shady reputations and doubtful antecedents, who, in their own defence, claim membership in their societies.

A letter published in the correspondence page of this issue and which was written by an accountant prominently identified with one of the leading bookkeepers' organizations in Chicago, discusses accounting as a profession. Contrary to the idea that might be gained from his title alone, this writer's plea is in the interest of the bookkeeper who devotes his entire time and talent to the establishment with which he is connected, rather than in the interests of the so-called public accountants. He describes in earnest and forceful terms the need of a standard by which bookkeepers and attached accountants of real ability may be distinguished from those who, without adequate qualifications, assume the name and occupy the positions of account keepers. While he reaches no conclusion that is satisfactory, even to himself, and therefore suggests no standard and advocates no remedy for the evil he has described, yet his presentation of the subject is well worth perusal. His real conclusion is that, however difficult of solution the question may be, or even though a positive solution is impossible, still organizations among bookkeepers which have education and progress as their corner-stone, confer a great benefit upon the craft and become an important force in the business world.

If we were to be specially critical of this correspondent's communication, we should take issue with what apparently is his position with respect to those who, practising as bookkeepers at present, aspire to some executive position at some future date in the business with which they are associated. In other words, those who are using bookkeeping as a mere stepping-stone to something which they esteem to be higher and better. He seems to condemn them, and inferentially his argument is, once a bookkeeper always a bookkeeper. We do not agree with him in this. Our sympathies have always gone out to the young man who aspires to the highest position that a given business may afford, and who, starting in where he can, always struggles toward the goal. With due respect for bookkeeping and accounting, we must all admit that the bookkeeper's position is seldom, if ever, the highest position that a given business affords, nor is it the most lucrative position in business at large. Therefore there is justification in aspiring to something above and beyond it. We have always felt that the more a proprietor, or executive man in any capacity, knows of bookkeeping and practical accounting, the better business man he will be. We might illustrate this by citing numerous examples of those who have used bookkeeping as a stepping-stone to something else, not only to their own advantage, but greatly to the advantage of the special industry in which they are working. True it is that a bookkeeper, to be the greatest success, should be in love with his work, but this is not in the least inconsistent with an ambition to climb as high as possible in the business scale.

A captious critic might infer from certain sentences in our correspondent's letter that his real argument is: Having entered upon a profession, never think of anything else. If at present you are a bookkeeper, strive to become a still better bookkeeper, but never let your mind be distracted by a consideration of chances to better your position or to rise to higher responsibilities. Indeed, he cites other professions — medicince, dentistry, and law—in support of this theory. In doing so, however, he seems to overlook the fact that in all these professions and in still others that he might have mentioned, many eminent specialists have been developed. Men have arisen in them who have gone far beyond the traditions; who have used the profession simply as a stepping-stone to a larger and broader career, and who, in thus doing, have called down upon their devoted heads adverse criticisms for deviating from the established routine. These same men a later generation has praised for their aggressiveness and honored for their success. The net result of their lives has been to broaden the profession.

The business man who reaches the top round in the ladder, and who in his career has employed bookkeeping as a mere stepping-stone, carries with him a very large measure of the art to which some of his earlier years were devoted. If truly in love with his profession and thoroughly grounded in its principles and applications, he is as much of an accountant when he becomes the executive head of a great firm or corporation as he was when he was in the humble position of bookkeeper, working under the direction of his business superior.

However, this line of thought, if seriously offered in criticism of our correspondent, whose letter we have referred to, is scarcely fair, for manifestly his effort is directed toward weeding out from the ranks of those who call themselves bookkeepers and accountants the pretenders and the incompetents, and the men whose personal character and professional accomplishments are of such a nature as to degrade the profession instead of elevating it. His letter is written in the light of profound conviction upon a subject in which every reader of this magazine must feel a lively interest. We therefore commend it to the careful attention of all. No one will dispute his final conclusion, that well-directed associated effort among bookkeepers, having educational features at its foundation, will ever benefit the craft. It should be the ambition of every bookkeeper to be a member of such an organization.

Various opinions have been expressed by accountants concerning what is known as the Accountants' Law in the State of New York. While the majority of the profession are greatly in favor of the measure, and many of them will be glad to see still further legislation of the same general kind, but more sweeping in its provisions, there are a few who are assertedly opposed to it and who affect to believe that the Accountants' Law is wrong in principle as well as inexpedient. Their argument is that it promotes the interests of a class, and that it puts new and uncalled-for difficulties in the way of those who are making a living in the profession; in short that to the extent of the examination fee, if no further, it is of the nature of a restriction upon trade. The fact that the community at large is benefited many times over the amount of the possible hardship that is thus wrought is of no force or effect in their minds. Nor yet do they seem to derive any help from the fact that other professions are similarly restricted by law and that in various other lines of practice a fixed standard of qualification has been established, greatly to the advantage of all concerned.

The general tendency in all matters of this kind is to raise the standard to a comparatively high plane, and to bring the practitioner's profession more and more under legal restriction, and at the same time to bar out those who are essentially disqualified. This is made evident by the new act of the Legislature of New York, which requires the registration of all attorneys-at-law in the office of the Clerk of the Court of Appeals, and which is to commence September 1 next. This law exacts an affidavit of all practitioners of the law, present and future, setting forth when and where the affiant was admitted to practice. So far as those who are now members of the bar are concerned, the affidavit must be made before January 1, 1899, and filed in the office of the Clerk of the Court of Appeals. The statute prohibits any one from practising law in this State without having taken the oath or made the affirmation thus prescribed. This law has been variously criticised, but for the most part the legal profession heartily approves of it.

Another illustration in point is the law recently passed in Illinois, which requires architects to submit their qualifications to a professional board. The object, in part at least, of this new law is to draw the line, especially in smaller towns, between architect and contractor, the profession of designing and superintending and the business of building. Certain difficulties which arose in this matter were finally overcome by defining an architect, for this special case, as one who makes plans for buildings which he does not build himself. Omitting all details, however, we may say that the examination as to qualification, in this case, is based primarily on plans submitted of some considerable building actually constructed.

This law, like others of the same general class, has been opposed by certain so-called architects, while it has also been widely approved by the best element in the profession. It may seem odd, but nevertheless it is true, that Illinois licenses for architects are actually being applied for at present by practitioners from other States, just as the certificates granted under the Accountants' Law by the regents of the University of New York have been applied for by accountants from other States.

Some of the provisions of the Illinois law with respect to architects are of interest in this connection, because they suggest certain matters that may be of advantage with respect to accountancy laws yet to be discussed. The licensed architect, for example, is required to stamp his seal upon all work leaving his office, and may be punished for neglecting to do so upon information laid by any outsider. Why would it not be a good plan for certified public accountants to have a seal, which should be similarly attached to every account, every statement, and every document of whatsoever kind that passes from their office for the use of the business public?

A prominent member of the New York State Society of Certified Public Accountants, remarking a short time since upon the really small amount of valuable accounting literature in existence, asserted that for the credit of the profession and for the benefit of the business community at large, he held it to be the bounden duty of every practising accountant to liberally contribute of his special fund of knowledge and experience to the literature of accounting. Explaining his thought still further, he called attention to the result that in a comparatively short time would follow if every accountant who has made a specialty of any division of work should contribute even a very short paper bearing upon that feature of accounting practice. The bank examiner, the insurance actuary, the expert in manufacturing accounts, the practitioner making a specialty of municipal accounts and various others particularly referred to.

The idea is certainly a good one. Put into practice, it would tend to elevate the profession and advance the practice of accounting, while also greatly benefitting the business community. That it has already been acted upon to a certain extent is evidenced by the good work done in the past by the members of the Institute of Accounts, by the members of the Institute of Chartered Accountants of Ontario, by the Associated Accountants of New Orleans, and by various other bodies that may be referred to. The work, however, has not been systematically nor exhaustively done, nor have all of the brighter minds and the more experienced men in the organizations named contributed as they might of their quota of knowledge and experience.

The paucity of works on accounting in the English language is something to be remarked by every one who investigates the subject, particularly if his object be the selection of books to constitute an accountant's library. Of works on bookkeeping there are many, mostly, however, text-books prepared by commercial teachers for class use, the contents of which are separated by a wide gulf from the actual practice existing in business offices. Of works on accounting, considering the subject broadly or as subdivided into classes and departments, there are comparatively few. The reasons for this are, perhaps, not hard to find. Accounting, from the publisher's point of view, has not been a profitable field to exploit. The number of purchasers of technical works, in whatever division of applied science they may be issued, is comparatively small, and those who are interested in higher accounting are unusually few in number. This has been particularly true in the past, but, perhaps, will prevail to a less pronounced degree in the future, for interest in accounting is constantly growing and business men everywhere of late are awakening to the fact that accounting is the vital element of business, and, therefore, are insisting upon their accounting being intelligently performed. This will have its proper effect upon the literature of accounting and in time will greatly increase the demand for all the really good books that are brought out.

Those who are called upon to pay what seem to be exorbitant prices for stenographic work and typewriting at the hands of public stenographers located in the large office buildings will perhaps be interested in knowing that prices for work of this kind are sustained by a species of the strongest kind of protection. Each typewriter or firm of typewriters that may be approached by the professional or business man for copying or dictated correspondence has paid a premium for a monopoly of the business in the building in which the office is located. Rates at large are sustained by trade agreements between operators in buildings in the same general neighborhood. Freed from all competition, and fully assured of a monopoly, the persons following this line of business feel safe in running prices up to the limit of what the public can be made to stand. When an office building is about completed in New York the owner or agent, as the case may be, invites proposals for a monopoly of the public stenographic and typewriting work which the tenants and patrons of the building may require. Bids for a building of ordinary dimensions will run from $500 to $1,000 a year in excess of the ordinary rental price of the rooms occupied. On larger buildings the figures will be from $1,500 to $2,500 per year.

It might be supposed that such arrangements, being practical restrictions of trade, would be illegal, and that proper effort would break up and destroy the monopoly, but the landlords are very careful to guard themselves in this respect. Other stenographers and typewriters are freely offered all the facilities that the building affords at the regular rental prices of the offices, but inasmuch as the landlord reserves to himself in all the leases the right to decide what character of signs may go on the office doors, he prohibits in the contracts, as a rule, all indication of the business followed. Favored tenants are allowed to tell the public what they do. Those who are not so favored are denied the privilege—that is, they are restricted to the letter of the contract. Jane Smith, for example, who has paid a heavy premium for the monopoly of the business, is allowed to put on her door, below her name, "Stenographer and Typewriter," but Matilda Jones, in the same line of business, who has also leased a room, is denied the right to indicate her business, and must content herself with simply her name upon the door. This little difference in the advertising constitutes and enforces the monopoly.

This method of protecting the typewriting business and securing maximum prices from the public has gone so far that there are at present recognized firms of stenographers who are ever on the lookout for opportunities, and who regularly bid for new and eligible buildings, thus constituting a league or circuit that greatly resembles in principle some of the larger trusts. The public would be less concerned in this matter—that is, they would more willingly pay the prices exacted—if only the quality of the service rendered was more satisfactory. Some of the best talent for securing privileges and exacting rates has the least ability to do really satisfactory work for the public. Accordingly the business and professional men are injured in two directions—first, by high prices and, second, by poor work, both of these growing out of the monopoly. The same monopolistic plan extends to hotel stenographic service and to stenographic service in connection with conventions and public meetings in general.

Improved Methods in Cost Accounting

By Frank J. Sager

Improvement is the watchword in all professions. The constant aim of progressive accountants should be to improve upon old methods. When, in obedience to this law of progress, conditions are encountered which imperatively demand attention, we are not only remiss in our duty to ourselves and to those whose interests are intrusted to our care, but we fail to command for our business that respect to which its place in the economy of production and distribution entitles it, if we fail to find or neglect to apply a method that meets requirements. The factory accounts of many of the largest manufacturing establishments present good illustrations of elementary bookkeeping, with the element left out. They are merely memorandum books which are never required to balance with the accounts in the commercial books, and from which at best only approximate systems of cost can be made.

The importance of a correct system of cost accounts or factory accounts is generally recognized. The inadequacy of present systems must be admitted by all who are in the least familiar with the results obtained from their use. Who is responsible for the continuation in use of present systems? To whom must we look for their improvement? In a large measure the accountant bears the responsibility for what is in use and it is to him to whom the manufacturing public very naturally looks for improved methods. It devolves upon the accountant, therefore, to devise and adapt to the requirements of different industries systems that shall be complete and adequate, and at the same time not too complicated nor cumbersome to be thoroughly practical.

The multiplying industries of this country, and the sharp competition in prices that is the result, are creating an imperative demand for the information so necessary to economical administration. Accountants must devise the forms and perfect the methods for the collection of this information, for analyzing it and for tabulating it in a form to render it available as an aid in directing these enterprises. The field for the exercise of the accountant's abilities is wide. Will they prove themselves equal to the opportunity?

A knowledge of the gross amount of the expense of conducting a business of any magnitude is of comparatively little practical value in assisting in an intelligent administration of its affairs. This is particularly true with reference to cost accounts, especially those relating to the production of staple goods. If these accounts show, however correctly, only the total or gross cost of producing a given number of articles, or even the component parts of these articles, they fail to accomplish that of which they are capable, and which, to be of the greatest value, they must be made to show—namely, the localization of cost to the smallest possible detail, in order that the pressure to minimize cost of production may be applied in the right direction.

Let us first consider the accounts that we require in order to connect the factory accounts with the commercial books. For this purpose we shall need Stores (for raw material), Labor, and Manufactured Stock. In addition, I shall introduce another account called Manufacturing. The Stores Account will be charged with the invoices of all purchases. The Labor Account will be charged periodically with the pay-roll. Manufacturing Account will be charged at cost with all materials withdrawn from stores to be combined with labor to form the complete product. This account will also be charged from day to day with the cost of the labor expended upon the work in process. Coincident with these charges there will be corresponding credits to Stores and to Labor Accounts. The Manufactured Stock Account will be charged at cost of production with the manufactured product as completed and delivered to the warehouse; and Manufacturing Account will be correspondingly credited. The transfers from and to these several accounts will be made through a factory journal, the arrangement of which on the columnar plan will minimize the work of posting.

It must be apparent, I think, that with the introduction of the Manufacturing Account, a connecting link is provided, which serves an important purpose, one which cannot be served by tracers or other similar records which follow the goods through the factory to completion before the transfers are made. The latter class of records are always open to the objection of providing an easy entrance for discrepancies, and thus defeating the very purpose for which they were created. Another important advantage gained in the use of the Manufacturing Account is this: The Stores Account will at any and all times show, without survey or inventory, the exact amount of material in store. The Manufacturing Account will show, without consulting any other account, the cost to date of all goods in process of manufacture. The Labor Account will be a constant check on the pay-roll. The system also establishes a check which will insure more accurate records in connection with the store-room, warehouse, time and costing accounts.

We are now ready to consider the means for collecting and recording the information from which will be made up the cost accounts proper. The items of with his shop number, name and wages per hour, half hour, quarter hour, or other time unit by which time is kept, stamped in the space indicated. He gets this book from the foreman on going to work in the morning and returns it to him on leaving work. He makes but one entry on each ticket, that is reporting the time he works on each shop order on a separate ticket. This, in many cases, necessitates the use of several tickets for a single day's work performed, but the advantages gained by this method far outweigh any imaginary disadvantages with which it may be charged. The workman fills out the charge section of the ticket, using symbols as will be explained further on, and adding further explanation, if any is needed, in the space that is provided for that purpose. In the time unit space he enters the time

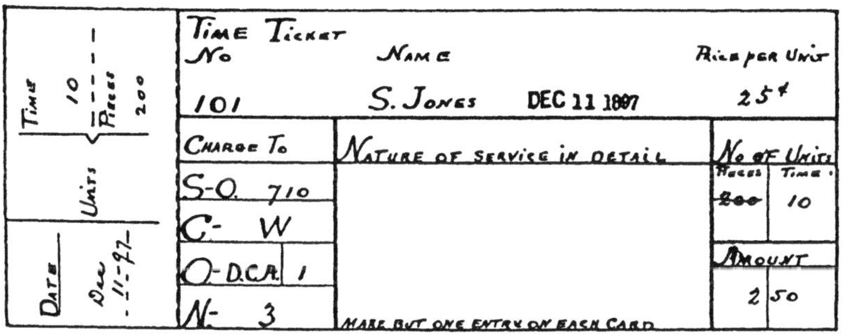

Time 10 — Pieces 200 — Units

Date Dec. 11-97

Time Ticket

No	Name		Rate per Unit
101	S. Jones	DEC 11 1897	25¢

Charge To	Nature of Service in Detail	No. of Units: Pieces	Time
S-O. 710		~~200~~	10
C- W		Amount	
O-DCA. 1		2	50
N- 3	Make but one entry on each card		

FIG. 1—FORM OF TIME TICKET.

cost may be stated under three heads—first, charges for labor; second, charges for material, and third, charges for incidental expenses, which will include wages of foremen, engineers, firemen, roustabouts, the cost of fuel, oil, lights and the factory's proportion of office expenses for clerical labor.

If all purchases, whether made for specific shop order or for current orders, together with transportation charges on same, are charged to Stores and regularly withdrawn therefrom, there will be no confusion of charges through the other books. Charges for labor are made from the time ticket (Fig. 1), the form of which is borrowed from Captain Metcalf's book entitled "Cost of Manufactures." Each workman is to be furnished with a book containing fifty or more of these tickets, he has worked upon the job indicated in the time section.

An absentee for a whole day is so reported by the foreman upon a leaf taken from his own book. This precludes any future question as to whether the man worked on that day or not. If a man comes late to work, the foreman, before giving him his book, fills out the first ticket, showing the time absent. If a workman leaves early, the foreman fills out the last page for the day to show the time lost.

The workman should be required to record his time on the completion of each job worked upon. If he is set to work upon the same job a second time in a given day, no harm is done by having two tickets for it.

The symbols that are employed can be displayed on bulletin boards, so placed throughout the shop as to be readily referred to by all the workmen, without any inconvenience and loss of time. However, the symbols will soon be learned so that reference to the lists will not be necessary. The method of using this ticket where pieceworkers are employed will readily suggest itself without special explanation.

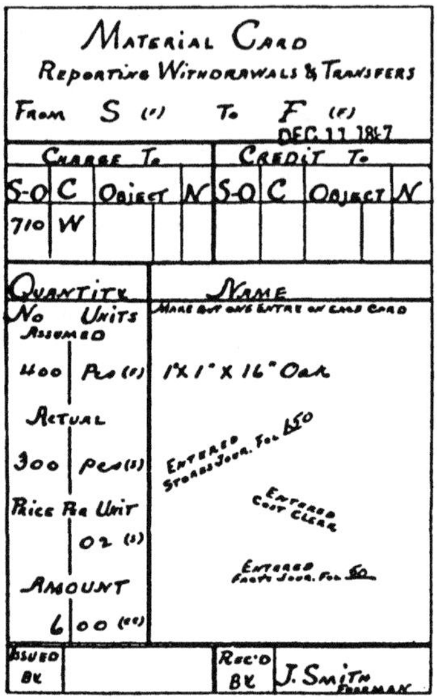

FIG. 2.

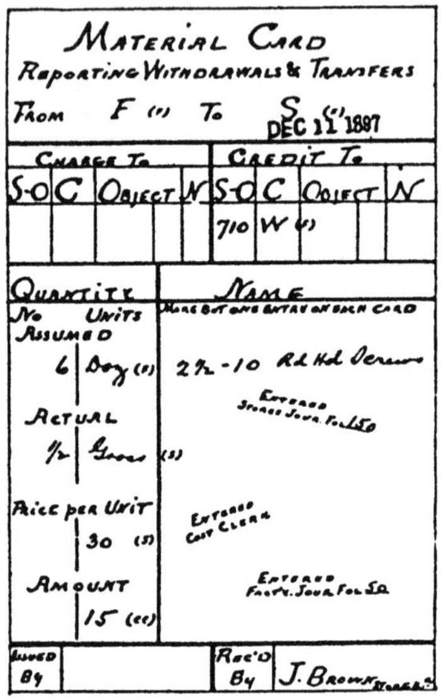

FIG. 3.

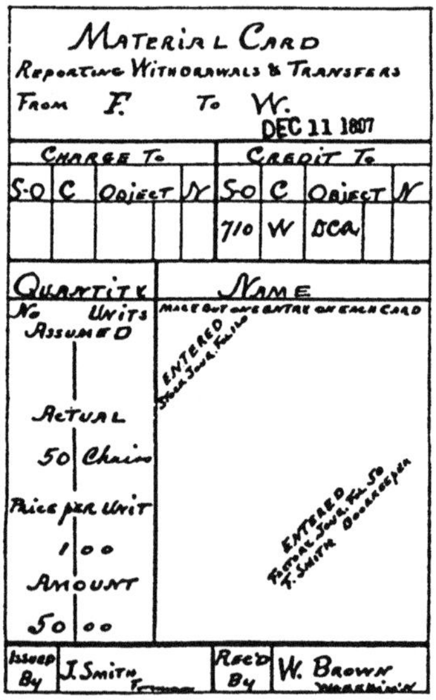

FIG. 4.

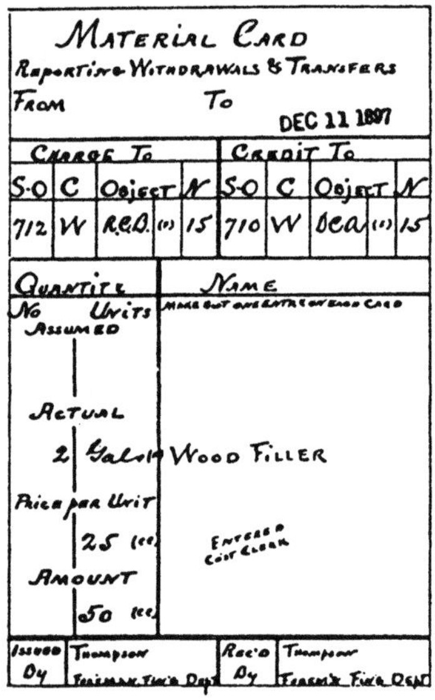

FIG. 5.

SPECIMEN MATERIAL CARDS.

When the books are turned in to the

foreman at the end of the day, he tears out the tickets used, verifies their correctness and stamps the date upon each. His dating stamp is taken as his acknowledgement of their correctness. From this it will be seen that the workman is required to write no more on each ticket than he would for each job, if all work were reported on one ticket, as is the usual custom. By this system all the operations of every workman are reported in the truest and fullest possible manner.

All transfers of materials in stock are to be reported on the material card (Figs. 2, 3, 4 and 5), which is a revised form of the card proposed by Captain Metcalf for reporting transactions of this character. The regulations of the shop or factory should require that no materials be delivered from stores or transferred from one shop order to another, except on a card properly filled out, showing the shop order to be charged, and, in the case of transfers, showing also the order to be credited. In withdrawing material from stores the card will be filled out by either the workman requiring the material or by the foreman, according to circumstances. In the former case the card will require the foreman's approval before delivery of the material. The approval or receipt of the foreman and the receipts of storekeepers or warehouse men may be indicated either by signature, by rubber stamp, or by pencil mark.

In reporting surplus material returned to stores and completed product delivered to warehouse, the card will be filled up by the foreman relinquishing the property and should be retained by him as his voucher for the property surrendered. The use of the card in transferring material from one order to another is explained in the illustration Fig. 5, except that when one of these cards is turned in to the cost clerk, he should make a duplicate of the credit entry and file the duplicate with the cards of the order number credited. The foreman should not approve transfer cards until both charge and credit sections are properly filled up.

The initials S, F and W, used in the title section of material cards refer respectively to stores, factory and warehouse, and the small letters f, s and cc enclosed in brackets denote that the entries opposite which they are placed were made by foreman, or storekeepers, or cost clerks.

It now remains to show how the information reported on the several cards is utilized. The time tickets are turned into the office by the foreman, sorted by names of workmen and the time of each man in the regular form of time book. They are next sorted by shop order numbers. All cards reporting work upon the same order number are summed up, and after the cost is copied in a cost ledger, the amount is passed through the cost journal to the debit of the order number in the ledger. If cost books are dispensed with and the cost reported is carried on daily cost sheets (Fig. 6), then the total amount reported on the tickets is entered in the ledger column of the cost sheet, opposite the shop order number. The cards are then filled with all other cards relating to the same number, in a pigeonhole labelled with the shop order number.

Cards relating to the transfer of material are similarly disposed of, being, of course, first entered in the stores book, if reporting withdrawals from or returns to store before being sent to the office.

DAILY COST SHEET — DEC 11 1907

Shop Order	Objects	Labor Time	Labor		Material		Shop Expense		Gross Cost		Credits		Net Cost		Net Cost for Last Report		Net Cost to Date		Remarks
710	100 B Ch[illegible]	45	9	00	6	00	1	35	16	35		50	15	85	35	15	51	00	[illegible]
712	500 B =					50				50				50	1.50		1.50	50	
713	1000 K =	1.50	30		25		4	50	59	50	– 2	50	57		93		1.50		

FIG. 6.—FORM OF DAILY COST SHEET.

Cards reporting stock delivered to warehouse are filed after being entered in the stock books with the other cards bearing the same number. The stock reported on these cards is charged through the factory journal at an arbitrary price to Manufactured Stock Account and credited to Manufacturing Account in the general ledger. These accounts in the general ledger are adjusted on completion of the order, when the actual cost is ascertained.

When the order is completed, the cards corresponding to it are taken out, shuffled according to C, O, N, and, if desired, an analysis made of the cost in detail, as shown in Fig. 7. They may then be filed away by order number, or they may be assorted according to C, O, N, and filed with orders bearing the same symbol under their order numbers, so that at any time definite knowledge may be obtained of the cost of performing each operation on every one of the staple products of the shop.

The symbols used will now be explained, so far as possible, by quoting from Metcalf's "Cost of Manufactures:" "S. O.," or shop order, indicates the job for which the expenditure was made. It is identified by a serial number in the order book. C. means character. The job being thus made known, evident distinction arises as to the character or purpose of the work done on it. It may be permanent in its character, done, so to speak, to last for all time, or at least for the year of the accounts with which we are engaged, or it may be transient in its nature, of a necessity recurring every time

ANALYSIS OF MATERIAL EXPENDED ON SHOP ORDER NO 710

Charged To C	Charged To O	Charged To N	Name	Quantity	Unit	Price per Unit		Cost		N		O		C		Rem.
P	F		1½"x6" Hickory	15	Ft		05		75		75		75		75	Form
W	OCR	1	1"x1"x16" Oak	400	Pcs		02	8	00	8	00					
		4	2⅞-10 R.H. Screws	1	Gro		30		30		15					½ Gross
		5	?	!	!	?		20		20						
		6						5								
		.						2		7						
		9						1.5								
		.						2		17						
		12						1	50	1	50					
		15	Wood Filler	5	Gals		25	1	25		75	54	40	54	40	[illegible]
														55	15	

RECAPITULATED ANALYSIS OF COST OF SHOP ORDER NO 71[illegible]

	Days Worked P	Days Worked W	Days Worked Total	Charged To Rent		Charged To Work		Total		Remarks
Total Labor	2.5	19.1	21.6	9	25	34	65	43	90	
Shop and Incidental Expenses @ 3¢ per Hr					75	5	73	6	48	
Material per Report					75	54	40	55	15	
Totals				10	75	94	78	105	53	

FIG. 7.—ANALYSIS OF LA

the operation is repeated. A most evident illustration of this feature is found in the relation between a working drawing and the thing made in accordance with its requirements—let us say a machine constructed by virtue of shop order No. 789. The drawing once made answers for all similar machines to be hereafter made. They will all profit by its existence, and hence should bear their share of its cost material on the drawing to S. O. 789, adding P in the second column (headed C. character), to show that the outlay belongs to the plant of the order, so that the card reads 789, P. Expenditures for patterns, gauges and special tools belong to this category, and are designated by using in the proper column the letter P, which may be taken to mean either Plant, Permanent or Preparation.

ANALYSIS OF LABOR PERFORMED ON SHOP ORDER NO 719

Charged To			Rate per Unit		No. of Units		Cost		Total Time Units			Amounts						Remarks
												N		O		C		
C	O	N	$	c	[illegible]	Time	$	c	N	O	C	$	c	$	c	$	c	
P	F	1		35		8	2	80										
		"		25		5	1	25	13			4	05					
		2		25		4	1	00	4									
		"		50	2		1	00		17		2	00	6	05			Special Forms
	B	9		40		8	3	20	8	8	25	3	20	3	20	9	25	" Bits
W	DCA	1		15		20	3	00	20			3	00					
		3		20		20	4	00										
		"		15		1		15	21			4	15					
		4		175		100	17	50	100			17	50					
		15		20		50	10		50	191	191	10		34	65	34	65	
																43	90	

AND RECAPITULATION.

instead of having the cost of the drawing go to swell unduly the charges for the first machine constructed—that is, if other machines are actually so made. If but one is made, or is likely to be made, the cost of the drawing belongs to it as much as that of any other part of the machine, and it should be so charged.

"P. means Plant. We meet the difficulty at the start by charging the work and

"W. means Work. Outlays, therefore, which are made upon the machine itself, and which would have to be repeated every time such a machine was constructed, are represented by W, standing for Work. This symbol, whether used in connection with labor or material, is to be understood as always referring to product. The difference between P and W is that between the construction and operating accounts in railroad bookkeeping. Charges for fitting, assembling, painting and possibly boxing the machine would be charged to 789, W. Now when the job is done, we may either give the cost of 789, including both P and W, or, deducting the cost of plant, be prepared to say with exactness for how much such machines could be duplicated in future, the plant being on hand.

"O means Object. Whether the third and fourth spaces yet to be discussed, which refer to the specific object worked on and to the operation performed on it, are to be filled out or not, depends entirely upon the value of the information which the filling of these spaces will give. If detailed knowledge is or may be required, there is no way of obtaining it correctly except from the data given in like detail. Where the object worked on is a stated object of manufacture, it is given a symbolic name represented by a combination of letters and figures appearing on the time tickets and material cards under the heading O or Object.

"N means Operation. Under this heading on the cards is to come the symbolic number of the operation requiring the expenditure, which the card reports. A good system of symbols is very important, for upon the exact knowledge of their comparative cost will be founded the most important economical reforms.

The entries on the different forms will perhaps be more readily understood if we assume that those shown herewith are a part of the records of a factory manufacturing chairs, of which they make several styles. D. C. A. signifies a dining chair style A, and in the time ticket the numeral 1 indicating piece No. 1 or a leg. Under N, 3 will indicate that the operation performed upon this piece was turning. The time ticket then shows that S. Jones was engaged for ten hours turning legs for a particular style of chairs under order No. 710, at a cost of $2.50. The illustration Fig. 2 shows that, while 400 leg pieces were required, only 300 were delivered to the factory on this card, and that the cost of these, in the rough, was $6. Fig. 4 shows that on December 11 fifty completed chairs manufactured under this order, were sent to the warehouse, the card bearing the evidence of the action of warehouseman and bookkeeper. Fig. 5 shows that two gallons of wood filler, prepared for and charged to order No. 710, were used on order No. 712. In the N space 15 represents the operation of filling.

In Fig. 7 there is attempted a demonstration of the utility of this system, the record shown, of course, being imaginary. In the material section the omission of a charge for steel used in making the special bits for the plant of this order is apparent. However, it was not noticed until the entries were completed. By referring to the left page of the form and reversing the order of analysis, we learn that the labor on the plant of this order (some special forms and bits) cost in the aggregate $9.25; that $6.05 of this amount was for labor performed on the forms, and $3.20 for work on the bits; that operation (N) had cost $4.05, and operation No. 2 cost $2. The gross cost of labor on the product of the order was $34.65, made up of the cost of performing four different operations, say turning, shaping, putting together and finishing. The cost of each operation is given in detail. The right hand page shows the form of an analysis of material used on this order, together with the cost in detail and a recapitulation of the complete analysis.

For the purposes of illustration, let us suppose that the maximum price at which these chairs could be sold is $1 each. Our recapitulated analysis shows that they cost practically 95 cents each. We shall not require the aid of a philosopher under these conditions to enable us to determine at once that unless the cost can be reduced, the manufacture of this particular style of chair must be discontinued. This is evident because the margin between the cost of production and the selling price would not pay the necessary selling expenses, to say nothing of a profit. It is at this point that the vaue of the detail in these records becomes apparent.

By referring to the analysis of labor we ascertained that 50 per cent. of the cost of labor on this order was charged to one operation. If means can be devised whereby this item of cost can be reduced 25 per cent., the saving on each chair will be something over 4 cents. On the other hand, a saving of 50 per cent. on operation No. 1 would result in a saving of about 1½ cents per chair. The same general remarks apply to the material section of the analysis. From the details given, it can readily be determined where a reduction of cost would prove of most advantage. In addition to giving information as to the most vulnerable and advantageous point on which an attack should be made to affect a reduction in cost, these forms are capable of furnishing ready answers to scores of questions that ought to be and would be more frequently asked if the information necessary to answer was at hand.

Shop or incidental expenses should be apportioned to the different orders on the basis of labor time. Thus, if the total labor time was 600 hours per day, and the incidental expenses were $18 per day, the charge to each order on this account would be 3 cents per hour of labor performed under it.

The ideas presented in this paper are not original with the writer. They were developed some years since by Captain Henry Metcalf, Ordinance Department U. S. A., and have been employed in the accounting departments of some of the largest arsenals of our government. The object of the present article is to illustrate their application to the requirements of private shops. In point of adaptability to the requirements of different industries and the possibilities of a thorough classification and analysis, this system possesses many advantages over other systems of cost accounting. Its strong point lies in the adoption of the loose sheet or card index system, giving it flexibility and the possibility of almost unlimited combinations of the different elements of cost. The importance of good cost accounting to the business interests of the country will justify a careful consideration of the merits of the system.

Until all managers shall have the gift of so arranging their experience that it is always ready with an answer to whatever question new conditions may propose, there will exist the necessity for a system of cost accounts, from which may be determined the cost of administration, both in gross and the remotest details by such impersonal, invariable means that their record may be looked upon as being as nearly absolutely true as that of any other similarly extended series of observations.

Accounting and Accounting Facilities

By ROLLIN JEFFRIES

The editor of ACCOUNTICS has placed before me several communications which have reached him in reply to and discussion of my article in a recent issue of the magazine, bearing the above title. I am requested to give them such consideration as seems to me to be appropriate Their number is so considerable that I am obliged to pass by many without any notice. I shall select for very brief attention two letters which may be regarded as types of classes, one fully agreeing with the views that I have expressed, and the other deploring them, although practically admitting that they are correct.

The first letter comes from one who has long been engaged in manufacturing and selling improved office appliances. He is a large advertiser and has been very successful in building up the business with which he is still connected. He has tried as many different plans of introducing his goods as almost any one who might be mentioned, and is therefore, in a position to speak authoritatively on the subject from actual experience. In the course of his letter he says:

"In my opinion the views expressed by Rollin Jeffries are entirely correct and I am glad to have read the article entitled 'Accounting and Accounting Facilities,' for it strengthens my own convictions on the subject. I can recall many an instance where we have been defeated in a sale by the perverseness of the bookkeeper, and many other where we succeeded only to the discomfiture of the bookkeeper, where I have convinced his business superior that a labor-saving device was worth the price charged. I have been greatly disappointed at the meagre results of advertising in publications directed especially to bookkeepers. One's first impression would naturally be that mediums of that class are exactly the thing for publishing the merits of labor-saving office devices, but my experience has not justified the previous expectations."

The conclusion of this letter, which so cordially endorses the opinions that I attempted to express, is worthy of special note. It is as follows: "I presume that when a man has taken the trouble to write an article and let it be published, it pleases him to know that others agree with him, and this is my only motive in writing this letter."

The other letter to which I shall refer comes from an active, progressive, wide-awake bookkeeper in Chicago, connected with a leading concern in a very important line of business, and one who is sufficiently public-spirited to associate himself with his fellow-bookkeepers in an organization which has for its object the elevation and advancement of the craft through educational means. Here is what he says:

"Under the head of 'Accounting and Accounting Facilities,' an article lately appeared in ACCOUNTICS, which fairly illustrates my contention, namely, that probably more than 50 per cent. of those constituting the rank and file of bookkeepers are not bookkeepers at all and have no idea of becoming bookkeepers, and yet they fill positions and give character or lack of character to the entire fraternity. Rollin Jeffries says in effect that bookkeepers as a class are narrow-minded, prejudiced, unprogressive, lacking in ambition and self-respect, learning nothing by experience, and are blind and deaf even to appeals to their own self-interest. He holds that the vocation itself has a tendency to produce and promote the growth of these qualities and, therefore, should be shunned except as a matter of education, or as a stepping-stone to something more worthy, or, as a last resort for those who are good for nothing else. This writer is grossly unjust. Nevertheless most of us can see in the situation by which we are surrounded that there is much to explain the various hard things which are said concerning bookkeepers."

I have referred above to the letter last quoted as one deploring my views, although practically admitting that the facts warrant them. Whether the incompetents occupying positions as bookkeepers belong rightfully to the profession or not, still they are everywhere very much in evidence. They certainly contribute their share to the character of the profession as it appears from the standpoint of the disinterested observer. The real question then is, what is to be done for them? Manufacturers undoubtedly can take care of themselves, as has been demonstrated by the success of the writer of the first letter above quoted, and many others in his class. The business community is making progress, if slowly, still surely, in spite of the opposition of the incompetent, narrow-minded, short-sighted persons who arrogate to themselves the name of bookkeeper or accountant. Bookkeepers, as a class, are progressing, at least a little, as is evidenced by the letter from which the second quotation is taken. Their advancement is also shown on every side by the fact that better men are continually coming to the front as bookkeepers, accountants and office managers, and are succeeding to the positions that in the past have been securely held by men of the other class. From all this it would seem that it is only the forlorn, discouraged, incompetent, narrow-minded "has-been" bookkeeper that is to be hurt in the least by the progress which is the order of the day.

The special thought that was in my mind when I first wrote on this subject was to show why bookkeepers and accountants get less attention from manufacturers and from specialists who have new things to introduce, in which they are supposed to be especially interested, than do superintendents of factories, foremen of shops, mechanical engineers and various others whose stated positions in the business world are more or less analagous to those of bookkeepers.

The reason has been shown to be that they are at heart unprogressive. But there still remains the question of what can be done to help men of this class who, left in their present position, will be ground to powder between the millstones of commercial progress.

Inasmuch as some men are led to exclaim, due solely to the misuse of terms and a lack of knowledge of the meaning of words: "I will drown; nobody shall save me," instead of "I shall drown; nobody will save me." It may be inferred that the victims in this case who are saying in effect, "I will be ignorant; nobody shall instruct me," really mean, "I am ignorant; who is there that will instruct me?" It is the bounden duty of every progressive bookkeeper and of every broad-minded business man to help these unfortunates by throwing to them the ropes of instruction and persuasion against their mistaken course, ere they sink to oblivion in the sea of ignorance in which they are at present struggling. No matter whether the calling of bookkeeping really narrows the man who follows it or attracts narrow-minded men to it for a livelihood, we can all unite in doing whatever is possible to throw light into dark corners and to help all narrow-minded and mistaken men by painstaking instruction and wholesome example.

Reviews and Criticisms

Improved Shorthand

20th Century Shorthand. Brevity and Simplicity reduced. Legibility and consistency exalted. Based upon a vowel scheme by means of which, independent of position, form, or dimensions, the vowel is expressed with precision and prominence within the body of the word. Suitable for all purposes and designed for universal use. By T. C. Strickland. 130 pages. Bound in cloth, gold side title. Published by the author. Price, $1.50.

The volume before us presents a system of shorthand writing arranged in 24 carefully graded lessons, with explanatory notes and references, and adapted for class use or self-instruction. The system is fundamentally unlike other systems which have preceded it. It consists of a simple method of flexible lines and flowing movements, by means of which, without resort to the prevailing positions, arbitrary word signs, or irregular methods, the motions of the voice are imitated by the pen, with brevity sufficient for the demands of speed. The author first became proficient in one of the standard systems of shorthand, but finding it unsatisfactory, according to his ideas, set speedily to work to demonstrate either the possibility or impossibility of a system that should be free from the faults that he found with that in use. His preliminary study, therefore, included an examination of all previous systems, with the result that among the hundred or more which he examined, he found none that was entirely satisfactory, and therefore he was compelled to invent something to meet his requirements. Two apparently impossible things were attempted. The first to devise a mode of expressing vowels which should be independent of the position, form or dimension of any character; and, second, to construct a consonant alphabet in imitation of the motion of the voice, and to be as flexible as the voice itself. Both these he claims have been found to be possible, and have been adopted as the basis of the new system which it is the mission of this book to expound. By examination of the plates with which the work is illustrated, the reader discovers that in the 20th Century system the strokes which in the Pitman writing represent the consonants are here allotted to the vowels. For example: The horizontal stroke "k" of the old system becomes a; the inclined stroke "p" in this system reads e, and the vertical stroke "t" stands for the diphthong oi. Consonants are added by hooks, loops and circles. Without engravings or fac similes of writing it would be impossible to carry the comparison further with advantage. The resulting outlines made up upon the plan here described are so different from those which shorthand writers are accustomed to use that a page of notes presents a very odd appearance.

The work is prefaced by an introduction devoted to a comparison of the fundamental principles of all the modern systems of shorthand writing. There is an analysis of five classes, including some sixteen or more systems, wherein leading features and number of characters are contrasted. This is something that will be examined with interest by all who take a philosophic view of shorthand. Two pages are devoted to a comparison of modern shorthand systems, in which the Graham, Cross Eclectic, Porter's Stem Vowel, Lindsley's Takigrafy, Pernin's Universal, and the 20th Century are graphically contrasted.

Shorthand Speed

The Factors of Shorthand Speed; or, How to Become a Stenographic Expert. A book of practical aids and suggestions to the student, the teacher, and the young reporter. By David Wolfe Brown, official reporter, United States House of Representatives. Small octavo. 200 pages, bound in cloth, gilt side title. Published by the The Shorthand Publication Bureau. 1897. Price, $1.00.

It has always appeared strange to the writer of this review that various books on shorthand should make their appearance with never a shorthand character displayed in their pages, and yet he is aware that the lack of a universally accepted system of shorthand makes it impossible to reach all shorthand students and shorthand writers by any other plan than the use of ordinary long hand. If Mr. Brown, for example, had attempted to give the results of his experience in acquiring speed in the shorthand which he writes; or if he had presented the advice which these pages contain in any one of the leading systems of shorthand, no matter how carefully the pages were engraved, the book would have been acceptable to only the comparatively few stenographers who read that particular system. It would have been a sealed book, the same as though it had never been written, to all others. This may or may not be an argument in support of that ideal of which many enthusiasts dream—a universal shorthand system.

The author says, in introducing his subject, that an appropriate system having been selected, it is all-important that the student should make no mistake in his methods of study and practice. He does not advise as to the system to be employed; he assumes the general principles of stenographic shorthand and confines his remarks to features obtaining in any and all of the leading phonographic systems, and yet perhaps it would be fair to say that he inclines slightly at least toward the English Pitman shorthand, in which, if we mistake not, he was originally trained for the important work which he has done as Congressional reporter.

The advice in the work is practical. The position and distinguished success of the author would make it impossible for him to write a book other than valuable in this respect. The book is extremely cheerful in the way in which it is constructed. It does not alone set forth the success attained at the extreme limits of speed, but tells as well how speed is to be increased from the very beginning. The work is divided into leading chapters with numerous subheads, and it is so happily enlivened by the presence of anecdotes and illustrations as to be interesting to read from beginning to end. The author has not wasted any pages with stated exercises, and yet he plainly tells the student how exercises are to be used and where he should turn for proper practice. Nor does he spare some of the writers of phonographic books for some of the nonsense that they contain. No student of shorthand and no amanuensis, whether aspiring to regular reportorial work or not, can fail to be benefited by a careful study of this work.

Bookkeeping and Theology

Every art and every science lends its quota of simile and metaphor to teachers, writers and orators. When two systems of bookkeeping are referred to in ordinary conversation, there is meant as a rule double entry and single entry. It has remained, however, for a correspondent of a paper published at West Newton, Pa., to contrast what he calls finite and infinite systems of bookkeeping. Without indorsing or condemning either the theology or the good sense of the following extract from this writer's work, we commend it to the consideration of the reader as a curiosity. It might perplex a finite auditor to make up a balance sheet under the conditions here described, but we presume that the reply to this would be that only an infinite auditor would be competent under the circumstances:

Sin and its attendant evils are the odds and ends left over from the creation of good and its result and happiness. The former has to be carried as stock in the profit and loss column of God's ledger in order to appear in its proper place on the daily balance sheet. The odds and ends are never forgotten by the great bookkeeper. Every man is charged with the evil he chooses to use in his business and heart life, and is credited with it when returned. What of good he chooses for use is credited to him, and charged when he returns it, thus keeping the accounts separate. God would rather, you observe, have the good stay out, bringing in two-fold, three-fold, or one hundred-fold to the borrower, than to leave it remain idle. This is the infinite system of bookkeeping. Strangely different from the finite system, under which the good is charged at a high profit, and never bought back but at another profit, called discount. The finite system also sells evil at a profit and makes money in the barter for its return.

When man changes his system to that of God's, then the millennium, when God's column for "profit and loss" will be abandoned for want of business in evil choosing, the profit and loss column will then be but a memory of a sin-cursed creation redeemed from its odds and ends of evil by the Creator.

The Office Man's Physical Condition

It is very difficult for bookkeepers and office employes in general to secure enough time apart from their business and social duties to take the exercise that is believed to be indispensable to health, and yet there are opportunities for exercise which many office men neglect, which, if improved, would tend greatly to their benefit. The trouble with office men is that they fail to discriminate between a slouchy, careless position, such as their ordinary work would suggest, and standing erect and maintaining that general carriage of body that conduces to the best physical condition.

Those who cannot find time for horseback riding, long walks, rowing, mountain climbing, wheeling, and other popular and fashionable forms of exercise, can still keep themselves in good condition by observing a few simple rules with respect to the management of the body while at their daily work. Many men burden themselves with shoulder braces when what they really require is enough backbone to stand up straight and inflate their lungs. It is needless to say that no amount of application to the outside of the body will compensate for neglect in the use of natural functions.

An erect carriage is one of the best indications of health. Exercise that will improve a man's physical condition will tend to give him an erect carriage. A few simple exercises, taken at various times in the day as opportunity presents, will tend to this result, and will overcome the necessity of those more difficult undertakings which require vacation seasons, expenditure of more or less money, and special preparations. Some of the habits and exercises on which special stress may be laid for the purpose are included in the following simple rules:

1. Make it a rule to keep the back of the neck close to the back of the collar.

2. Roll the shoulders backward and downward.

3. Try to squeeze the shoulder blades together many times a day.

4. Stand erect at short intervals during the day—"head up, chin in, chest out, shoulders back."

5. Walk or stand with the hands clasped behind the head and the elbows wide apart.

6. Walk about, or even run up stairs, with from ten to forty pounds on the top of your head.

7. Try to look at the top of your high-cut vest or your necktie.

8. Practice the arm movements of breast stroke swimming while standing or walking.

9. Hold the arms behind the back.

10. Carry a cane or umbrella behind the small part of the back or behind the neck.

11. Put the hands on the hips with elbows back and fingers forward.

12. Walk with the thumbs in the arm-holes of vest.

13. When walking swing the arms and shoulders strongly backward.

14. Stand now and then during the day with all the posterior parts of the body, as far as possible, touching a vertical wall.

15. Look upward as you walk on the sunny side of the street.

The greater part performed achieves the less.—Dryden.

The Use of Postal Cards

By Walton Day

While speaking of postal cards, allusion may be made to a report which was in circulation a short time since to the effect that at an early date the Government proposed to permit the issuance of private postal cards, by which was meant that individual firms and persons could get up their own postal cards, either having them printed by the Government with the regulation stamp or affixing a one-cent stamp the same as stamps are affixed to regular mail matter. This has been authoritatively denied by the department, and accordingly the postal card stands at present just as it has stood heretofore. Any person may get up a postal card at the present time to suit himself, but he may not put any writing thereon while paying postage at the rate of one cent per card. Private postal cards for advertising purposes are very largely employed, and are found exceedingly useful.

If in the reduction of first-class postage to one cent postal-card rates should be lowered, it is probable that the use of postal cards for advertising purposes would be very largely increased, perhaps in a way to diminish the revenues of certain advertising mediums now largely employed. When advertising is considered, it is primarily a question of circulation. Where can the largest measure of the circulation that is desired, class and quality being considered, be obtained for the least sum? By postal cards specifically addressed, by advertisements in the magazines, or where? The postal card at the present time receives a large share of attention, and at a lower price would be still more generally employed for the purpose.

Every man takes care that his neighbor shall not cheat him. But a day comes when he begins to care that he does not cheat his neighbor. Then all goes well. He has changed his market cart into a chariot of the sun.—Emerson.

The mould of a man's fortune is in his own hands.—Bacon.

Neither irony nor sarcasm is argument. —Rufus Choate.

Correspondence

Accounting as a Profession

From R. H. Moore, Chicago.

Those who have made accounting the business of their lives, who have always regarded it as a worthy and honorable calling, are very frequently reminded of the need of some standard by which its status as a profession may be fixed and the ability of its followers judged. The feeling that there is need of such a standard does not necessarily indicate any spirit of exclusiveness, nor the disposition to restrict the number of those engaged in the calling. Instead, it indicates a desire to give character to the profession and to place it on a higher plane in the esteem of the business public. Accountants collectively are aware of the vast differences in ability to be found in the ranks of those who profess to be experts, differences bounded on the one extreme by the man, who, having mastered the various theories, has also a practical knowledge of their application, and on the other, by the man whose ignorance of everything save simple routine gives him the confidence to call himself an accountant.

These extremes suggest two classes, the first of which, while constituting but a small part of the whole, comprises those who regard accounting as the business of their lives in the sense that it is a permanency, not a mere stepping-stone to something outside of the profession. Men of this class, possessing the pride of their calling, are the ones to properly uphold its dignity and importance. On the other hand, these man are the ones to accept the responsibility for whatever shortcomings the profession may properly be charged with.

The second class undoubtedly comprises the larger number of those at present in the ranks. Its members regard themselves as accountants merely for the time being and feel no other interest in their work than that of a temporary source of livelihood. Followers of other professions, for example, lawyers, doctors, dentists, first select their life work and then fit themselves for it. With commendable ambition each makes up his mind to be a success in his chosen calling. He turns his back on other pursuits and devotes himself unreservedly to his work and energetically follows it up to the end. It is true that men at times give a certain amount of attention to professions which are intended to be merely auxiliary to their main purpose. For example, a man may study medicine or law with this end in view—but it seldom happens that thereby he becomes a good doctor or an able lawyer. In the same way a man may study accounting as part of his business education, but thereby he would not become an efficient bookkeeper.

The point that I wish to make is just this: Probably 50 per cent., and possibly more of those constituting the rank and file of the profession are not bookkeepers at all. They have no idea of becoming good bookkeepers and yet they fill positions and give character or lack of character to the entire fraternity. The profession is over-crowded with transients who are not accountants, and most of whom never expect to be accountants. They stumble along and hold their places because there is so little real appreciation of competent men. In these days any old thing is called a bookkeeper. It is no exaggeration to say that perhaps half of the business houses really have no bookkeepers or accountants in their employ, but instead hire clerks, mere machine men, to carry out the orders of the proprietor, superintendent or manager.

Theoretically, a business man, in selecting a bookkeeper employs one whom he deems competent to fill all the requirements of the position. He then places in his charge the accounting of the business, feeling that inasmuch as he has selected an able man, the accounts will be properly conducted. Under these circumstances, having the confidence of his employer and having full charge in his particular department, the bookkeeper would deserve all blame if his system was not good, and if in the discharge of his duties he failed to measure up to what is xpected of the ideal.

Practically, the business man who, perhaps, has mastered the rudiments of bookkeeping, preparatory to business, while selecting a man whom he considers able to fill the position, does so with no idea of allowing him any more latitude than he thinks is absolutely necessary. The bookkeeper so engaged is placed pretty much on the same plane as an unskilled employee. His system and methods must, of necessity, conform in a large degree to the ideas of his employer.

Just as there are many grades of bookkeepers, so there are also many kinds of positions to be filled. Every business requires some bookkeeping. From the simplest up to the most complex there are many grades of requirements making necessary different grades of proficiency. No objection can be raised to the course of the proprietor of a small and simple business, who selects an ordinary bookkeeper at a small salary instead of engaging an expert accountant at a large salary. The latter man, of course, is not necessary, and it would be poor management to employ him. On the other hand there are numerous positions requiring the highest order of talent, worthy of the best salaries and often commanding them. It is not uncommon to find in these top notches of the profession, that the accountant is estimated at his real value, not only in the matter of salary, but in the regard in which he is held by his employers, and by every one who knows his character and ability. But between these extremes there is sufficient latitude to satisfy a modest and worthy ambition. It is no disparagement of an accountant in such a position to say that he has no ambition to become the head of some other department of the business, for which he may have neither talent nor inclination. It is no reflection on him to say that he has no ambition to become President of the United States. Of course, it may be inconceivable to some people that a bookkeeper should like his profession, that he should find pleasure in doing accounting work above any other kind of work, and yet such is the rule among those who reach the highest ranks in the profession.

The profession of accountant has held an honorable place for many years. It had recognition in a business way in England and Scotland two centuries ago. Soule speaks of accounting as "a queenly science, a science which governs the thrones of commercial empires and guides the financial affairs of the world." Andrew Carnegie has said, "There is not a science or class of men on whom the business world is more dependent than the science of accounts and accountants." The accountant, outside of England and Scotland, has never been able to obtain the honorable place to which he is entitled, save through organization and regulation, which effectually separates incompetence from ability and provides some badge or some test whereby the distinction may be known of all men.

This is the problem which confronts us, the solution of which offers the most weighty plea for organization. Public accountants may effect their organizations and induce legislation to promote their interests, but bookkeepers at large cannot hope thereby to read any benefit. It is questionable, indeed, if the problem admits of any reasonable solution. Even if this is so, we still have the assurance that all organizations based upon education and progress are steps in the right direction.

Bank Balances

From T. P., New York.

Permit me to say a few words in regard to the article "Bank Balances and Charges for Banking Facilities," contained in your March number, and to correct some of the impressions V. D. C.'s rather peculiar assertions may have created. I fully agree with V. D. C. that the banks should charge a small commission on the volume of business of accounts not carrying a paying balance in bank. The present system of requiring a certain minimum amount of balance is wrong because it discriminates against the small merchant, who has use for his money and only uses the bank as collector of the checks he receives, in favor of the rich man who can afford to keep a large balance in bank. The small man needs this facility, as otherwise he is put to great inconvenience, and he ought to pay for it. One-eighth to one-quarter per cent. on the amount of his deposit is a reasonable charge for the trouble on the part of the bank, and the corresponding benefit to the customer. But V. D. C. starts out from premises and reaches conclusions which ought not to remain unchallenged.

A comparison between the Continental and American banking system is almost impossible, as they have originated under different conditions and are based on different principles. To say that a bank should be confined to loaning its own capital to its customers is a fallacy, which would place the banking business in the hands of large monopolies working with hundreds of millions of capital; otherwise it would not pay. It is not true that the National Banks use their depositors' money only and allow their capital and undivided profits to lie idle. The National Bank receives 90 or 95 per cent. of its capital in bank notes under government guarantee. These bank notes are not counted as reserve which must consist of gold coins and legal tender. Consequently, the capital of the bank is loaned out and the reserve consists of 25 per cent. of the depositors' balances, and 25 per cent. of the bank's circulation converted into legal tender.

I will further show that this reserve is not lying idle, but circulates in the shape of checks drawn against the largest portion of it. It may be that a few "merchants and manufacturers, wishing to stand well at the bank, keep a large deposit all the time—useless to them except as outward show," but they generally are well-known to the bank officers, and end in due time in the bankruptcy court, if not in jail. The large majority of merchants keep a substantial balance because they need it for eventualities in their business, such as unexpected drafts, maturing paper, duties and a thousand other things.

V. D. C. forgets that the balance on a merchant's check-book is considerably smaller than his balance on the bank's books by reason of the number of checks that are out and not yet presented for payment. To say that the balance in bank is fictitious, because the depositor owes the bank for borrowed money at the same time, discloses an equal amount of unacquaintance with facts. The merchant receiving promissory notes from his correspondents in payment of debt avails himself of the opportunity of being able to turn them into cash by the bank discounting them. He pays his own debt with their proceeds, and in many cases profitably anticipates his debts by the accommodation of the bank. But once the note is discounted he is not indebted to the bank except in the remote contingency of an endorser's liability. His bank balance may be the result of this transaction, but it is there because it is needed there and for no other reason. I fully agree with V. D. C. that this proposition may, at first, appear absurd and ridiculous. I go even a little further and say it is so from beginning to end.

Continental banks generally do business with their own capital plus a circulation which is twice to three or four times as large as this capital, undivided profits and a reserve fund regulated according to their respective charters. The deposit business is a secondary consideration with them and the charging of a commission on deposits has developed from the times when the banks were used as means for safekeeping only. Our National Banks have to secure their circulation by legal tender, coin or United States bonds, and receive only 90 per cent. of the face value of their security. They naturally use a certain portion of the depositor's money above the legal reserve to make loans, each loan representing another business transaction either in merchandise, stocks, bonds or other values.

What is said against stock gambling is only true as far as it is gambling, and I do not believe that there is a reputable bank in this city encouraging any kind of gambling. They may stimulate speculation, but that is the life of business, and is not only legitimate, but necessary. Let us look at the transactions complained of by V. D. C. and compare them with merchandise transactions, but eliminating the absurd charge that any bank would accept a security which has not an intrinsic value.

I. A buys $50,000 worth of stock, deposits it with a bank who lends him $30,000 (on demand) on the same, with which he discharges the balance of his indebtedness incurred in this or other transactions; he sells the stock either as a whole or in small parcels and pays for it as he withdraws it from the bank.

II. B buys $50,000 worth of tea in a warehouse, deposits the warehouse receipt with a banker who lends him $30,000, on the same with which he discharges his indebtedness incurred either in this or other transactions. He sells the tea and pays the bank as he makes his withdrawals.

III. C buys $50,000 worth of tea and gives in payment his three months' note, which, in turn, is discounted by the vendor's bank. He sells the tea for $51,000, receives for it a sixty days' note, and discounts the same in his own bank. He uses the money so received less profit to pay his note at maturity—his bank also collecting from maker of second note.

The third example is the most frequent occurrence. In this case the banks had no security except the standing of the respective firms. They loaned collectively $101,000 on transactions involving $50,000 worth of tea. The second example makes the bank the custodian of the tea, and it only lent three-fifths of its value, but in case of failure of borrower it would be compelled to find a market for the tea and to enter into a business transaction foreign to its regular line. In the first example, the bank also holds the security, but in case of failure of the borrower, or if the security has weakened in price, it has it in its power to sell it and reimburse itself. I will leave it to the readers to follow these transactions to their ultimate consequences and draw their own conclusions.

However, the most preposterous assertion that V. D. C. makes is "Not only are the funds of New York merchants and manufacturers deposited in the banks of New York, but also the funds of the whole United States, for the country banks keep large balances in New York, thereby depriving their own depositors of the use of the money on the plea that in their neighborhoods there are no legitimate enterprises, etc." Does V. D. C. not know that New York is also a trade center buying of the whole United States and selling to the whole United States? That the whole United States, therefore, keep large balances in New York because of necessary liquidations? Has V. D. C. never heard of Chicago or other cities paying a premium on New York Exchange so as to be able to cover drafts made in favor of their customers for purposes of liquidation and vice versa? Of course, the amount of drafts in transit swell these balances in proportion to the distance of the depositing banks.

New York State Society of Certified Public Accountants.

Very comfortable headquarters in the Johnston Building, No. 30 Broad street, have been secured by the New York State Society of Certified Public Accountants. E. E. Schmitt has been chosen as librarian, and will be in charge of the rooms. The location is central to a considerable number of the offices of the active accountants in the society, and the library, which it is proposed to accumulate and sustain at this place, as well as the stenographic and typewriting facilities provided which are a part of the general plan, will make the rooms the equivalent of an accountants' exchange.

The place will be very acceptable for business appointments by out-of-town members, meetings of committees, etc. It is also proposed to maintain at these headquarters a register of accountants' assistants. All those who are out of employment, and who register, will be carefully investigated and their credentials placed on file, so that members in need of help will be able to secure it at a minimum of trouble, and in the shortest possible time.

That talent confers an inequality of a much higher order than rank would appear from various views of the subject, and most particularly from this—many a man may justly thank his talent for his rank; but no man has ever yet been able to return the compliment, by thanking his rank for his talent. When Leonardo da Vinci died, his sovereign exclaimed: "I can make a thousands lords, but not one Leonardo."—Colton.

Talent, lying in the understanding, is often inherited; genius, being the action of reason or imagination, rarely or never. —Coleridge.

Character the Basis of Credit.

The following extract from an address before the students of Packard's Business College, delivered a short time since by James G. Cannon, vice-president of the Fourth National Bank, New York, and president of the National Credit Men's Association, presents in a forceful manner the relationship of credit to character:

The three component parts of credit are character, capacity and capital, and the greatest of these is character. Character counts continually for credit, and I intend to speak to you for a moment upon the question of character in its relation to credit. George Washington, whose birthday we have just celebrated, in his first inaugural address said: "The foundation of our national policy will be laid in the pure and immutable principles of private morality," and in reply to this address of Washington by the Senate of the United States these words were used: "We feel, sir, the force and acknowledge the justice of the observation, that the foundation of our national policy should be laid in private morality. If individuals be not influenced by moral principles, it is vain to look for public virtue." A well-known writer says: "What we are sooner or later shows itself in what we seem. Our character, unconsciously but inevitably, expresses itself in our actions, our speech, our manner, our looks, and finally it is seen by our fellows as they observe us."

What is character? It is an individual matter. You cannot have another's character. You may try to imitate, perhaps, the character of some great man; but to the man himself who is his own master, his character standeth or falleth. Character is that something within you which receives and impresses upon your mind and writes in indelible letters on your heart your thoughts, words and deeds. Character is the fine tone of your heart strings, or else it is the dull thud of life which seems to chill you through and through. Character is that something which points you onward and upward in life's work, or else drags you down to lower and lower depths as it becomes foul with the heavier material of life's dregs. Some one has well said that "Character is not something that is added to your life, but it is life itself." Character building is not the work of a moment or a day. You cannot jump into a character as you would into a suit of clothes, unless it be an assumed character. The man with an assumed character is a hypocrite, whom we all despise. Character building is a slow process. It must be worked at continually, and we are building even when we are not conscious of it.

Mutual Dependence in Business.

By Walton Day.

There is a mutual dependence in business of the greatest importance—namely, that of jobber upon retailer and retailer upon jobber. The retail merchant depends upon the jobber for his supply of goods to sell, and very naturally demands that the goods shall be forthcoming promptly when they are needed, according to the orders placed for them. On the other hand the jobber depends upon the retailer for such remittances of money in payment for the goods as shall replenish his coffers and enable him to continue in business.

The jobber has therefore the right to demand of the retailer the same promptness in remitting for goods purchased as the retailer has to demand of the jobber in shipping the goods. The retailer, before placing orders, examines into the resources of the jobber, sometimes in a perfunctory way, but nevertheless in such a manner as to satisfy himself that he is depending upon no uncertain support. He places his orders with a given jobber only when he has the assurance that the goods will be forthcoming. The jobber surely has the same right to investigate the retailer, in order to know that the corresponding payments will be forthcoming when due.

The only plan which the jobber has for his investigation of the retailer that is competent to secure such a statement of his affairs as is appropriate under the circumstances is to frankly ask the retailer to tell him the whole truth about himself. This is the foundation of the request for a property statement now so common.

A recent writer, treating upon this subjec, has said: "The giving of a statement by one who asks credit at the hands of another is simply exchanging an honest confession for the influence of the good opinion, the confidence and the esteem to be derived therefrom. To extend credit does not alone imply the trusting out of a sum of money. It embraces that closer communion wherein men seek to know each other to that degree of confidence upon which implicit trust is built. Giving a statement of one's condition implies honesty of purpose. Giving it readily, in response to the request of the credit man, lays the initial foundation for confidence, and always promotes a healthy condition and mutual interest which can be secured only through the channel of honor."

Certified Public Accountants

The following is an alphabetical list of the C. P. A.'s of the State of New York, with their addresses. The numbers prefixed to the names correspond to the numbers of their certificates. Those designated by the asterisk are members of the New York State Society of Certified Public Accountants:

66 *Abrahams, John W., 62 William Street, New York.

67 *Adams, Edward, 69 Wall Street, New York.

68 Allen, Franklin, 371 Fulton Street, Brooklyn.

87 *Angelo, William, 237 Broadway, New York.

31 Anyon, James T., 27 Pine Street, New York.

32 Arnold, Thomas E., 206 Broadway, New York.

45 *Bagot, Thomas, 62 William Street New York.

33 *Beaujou, Anton R., 140 Nassau Street, New York.

69 *Bierck, Albert B., 392 Lafayette Avenue, Brooklyn.

34 *Both, Charles, 27 Pine Street, New York.

109 *Bragg, Henry T., 253 Broadway, New York.

1 Broaker, Frank, 150 Nassau Street, New York.

88 *Brummer, Leon, 7 Pine Street, New York.

123 Cady, Charles E., 280 Broadway, New York.

89 *Caesar, William J., 54 Wall Street, New York.

70 Campbell, Hudson, 97 Cedar Street, New York.

120 *Carmiencke, John B., 320 Broadway, New York.

46 Carson, William, 112 Wall Street, New York.

2 Chapman, Richard M., 150 Nassau Street, New York.

119 Charles, Edward, Wingate Sanitarium, Asheville, N. C.

15 Clarke, Andrew Allen, 62 Wall Street, New York.

90 *Clerihew, Alexander C., 11 Broadway, New York.

91 *Cockey, Edward T., 25 West Twenty-third Street, New York.

3 *Conant, Leonard H., 141 Broadway, New York.

107 *Cook, Henry R. M., 7 Pine Street, New York.

56 *Corwin, Hamilton S., 30 Broad Street, New York.

58 *Cowell, Lewis Philip, 80 Broadway, New York.

35 *Cowles, Walter C., 103 White Building, Buffalo.

16 *Cuthbert, Robert L., 25 Pine Street, New York.

17 *Davidson, Arnold, 49 Exchange Place, New York.

4 Davies, William S., 45 Broadway, New York.

71 *Davis, Henry Clark, 44 Pine Street, New York.

125 Dawson, James H., 189 Montague Street, Brooklyn.

116 Dean, Thomas B., 150 Nassau Street, New York.

5 *Dennis, Rodney Strong, 30 Broad Street, New York.

92 *Dixon, Hiram Robert, 61 Broadway, New York.

114 Dodd, Frank N., 55 West Thirty-third Street, New York.

93 *Edmonds, David J., 45 Exchange Place, New York.

72 *Ewen, William A. C., 2 Wall Street, New York.

73 *Farrington, Wesley, 203 Broadway, New York.

47 Fischer, August, Times Building, New York.

74 *Francis, John W., 120 Broadway, New York.

36 *Gottsberger, Francis, 156 Broadway, New York.

118 Gunnell, William J., 317 Main Street, Buffalo.

37 Hamilton, James A., Austin Building, Buffalo.

104 *Hardcastle, Joseph, 1193 Broadway, New York.

18 *Harney, Henry, 88 Wall Street, New York.

6 *Haskins, Charles W., 30 Broad Street, New York.

126 Herington, P. R., 68 Broad Street, New York.

38 *Hooke, Edward W., 63 Wall Street, New York.

106 *Horley, Thomas R., 7 Pine Street, New York.

19 *Hourigan, John, 31 N. Pearl Street, Buffalo.

94 How, Francis W., 11 William Street, New York.

75 Howard, Thomas P., 50 Stone Street, New York.

47 Hutchison, Richard N., 32 Nassau Street, New York.

105 Jasper, William Henry, 68 Broad Street, New York.

95 *Jaudon, William B., 40 Broadway, New York.

96 Kavanagh, John B., 280 Broadway, New York.

49 *Kelly, James Nicholas, 30 Broad Street, New York.

50 Kerr, James Cameron, 256 Broadway, New York.

110 *Ketchum, Nelson V., 132 Nassau Street, New York.

121 *Kittredge, Anson O., 1003 Wool Exchange, New York.

117 *Kleberg, Alexander A., 428 Clinton Street, Brooklyn.
76 Koehler, Theodore C. C., 1215 Broadway, New York.
97 Kuhns, Maurice S., 192 West Broadway, New York.
20 Lafrentz, Ferdinand W., 100 Broadway, New York.
21 Lamb, Fergus, 253 Broadway, New York.
39 *Le Jeune, Capel E., 23 Pine Street, New York.
40 Lever, Samuel, 27 Pine Street, New York.
111 *Lewis, Richard, 115 Broadway, New York.
51 *Loomis, John Rice, 30 Broad Street, New York.
115 *Ludlam, Charles S., 30 Broad Street, New York.
127 *Lingley, Richard T., 30 Broad Street, New York.
98 *McClement, John H., 15 Broad Street, New York
7 McGibbon, Brownell, 44 Pearl Street, New York.
22 *McKenna, James A., 43 Cedar Street, New York.
23 *MacRae, Farquhar J., 16 Exchange Place, New York.
77 *Mann, Richard D., 328 Kirk Building, Syracuse.
8 Manvel, Frederick C., 32 Liberty Street, New York.
124 *Marin, John C., 253 Broadway, New York.
24 *Martin, Andrew B., 75 Times Building, New York.
25 *Martin, Clarence A., 75 Times Building, New York.
122 Mason, John D., Jr., 186 Broadway, New York.
9 *Mercer, Charles J., 52 Wall Street, New York.
128 *Mitchell, S. Roger, 31 Nassau Street, New York.
78 Morton, Oscar E., 56 Pine Street, New York.
64 Mowat, William C., 702 D. S. Morgan Building, Buffalo.
99 Niles, Charles E., 50 Broadway, New York.
59 Niles, Henry A., 50 Broadway, New York.
79 Nield, Charles F., 45 Broadway, New York.
41 *Patterson, Andrew S., 30 Broad Street, New York.
100 *Penney, John, 83 Beaver Street, New York.
129 *Pentlarge, Theodore, 203 Broadway, New York.
42 Perrenoud, Gustavus, 56 New Street, New York.
43 Phelps, Charles D., 143 Liberty Street, New York.
80 Pladwell, John E., Albany.
108 Reckitt, Charles Coleby, 169 Jackson Street, Chicago.
61 Reckitt, Ernest, 62 Wall Street, New York.
26 Roberts, Thomas E. C., 56-58 Pine Street, New York.
57 *Robinson, Charles Palmer, 31 Nassau Street, New York.
27 Rollo, David, 62 Wall Street, New York.
60 Rose, Alfred, 150 Nassau Street, New York.
63 *Ryan, Thomas P., 725 Broadway, New York.
101 *Salway, William Sargent, 280 Broadway, New York.
28 *Sargent, Sidney Eugene, 1971 Seventh Avenue, New York.
52 *Self, Edward, 814 Bennett Building, New York.
10 *Sells, Elijah Watt, 30 Broad Street, New York.
62 Shaible, William George, Comptroller's Office, Albany.
112 *Shankland, James A., 280 Broadway, New York.
81 Sheridan, Frank J., 45-49 Cedar Street, New York.
44 Smith, Arthur William, 62 Wall Street, New York.
53 Smith, Charles Peck, 45 Broadway, New York.
54 *Sparrow, John R., 99 Nassau Street, New York.
11 *Sprague, Charles Ezra, 54 West Thirty-second Street, New York.
29 Stevens, Richard Fowler, 56-58 Pine Street, New York.
102 Stocking, Charles Henry, 27 Thames Street, New York.
124 *Stott, Frank Irving, 68 Broad Street, New York.
82 *Strickland, Sylvester R., 45 Pine Street, New York.
65 *Suffern, Edward L., 30 Broad Street, New York.
83 Sullivan, Thomas J., 280 Broadway, New York.
30 *Tate, Daniel Camp, 66 Broadway, New York.
113 *Taylor, Samuel M., 195 Broadway, New York.
13 *Teele, Arthur W., 30 Broad Street, New York.
84 Tipson, Frederick Samson, 441 Pearl Street, New York.
55 Townsend, Ferdinand Charles, 44 Pine Street, New York.
14 Walker, Alfred Percy, 32 Nassau Street, New York.
85 *Warren, Haynes W., 125 Pearl Street, New York.
103 *Whitehead, John W., 11 Broadway, New York.
86 Wicks, Alfred B., 280 Broadway, New York.

How, without clothes, could we possess the master organ, soul's seat and true pineal gland of the body social—I mean a purse?—Carlyle.

Buying From Numerous Houses

Many merchants, greatly to their surprise when the crisis comes, find themselves embarrassed, not alone because their liabilities are large, but more particularly because they are held by many different houses and frequently by houses situated remote from the debtor and from each other. In the best managed enterprises, conditions occasionally arise when leniency upon the part of creditors, if not an out-and-out extension, is absolutely necessary. With liabilities in the hands of many creditors, the merchant is at a disadvantage in obtaining what would be readily granted at the hands of a few. It is expedient for the merchant, therefore, so far as possible, to confine his purchases to a comparatively small number of jobbers. Then, if he needs a favor, however small or however large, there is comparatively little difficulty in getting before those in interest a statement of what he really requires, accompanied also by a statement of his actual financial condition. With scattered liabilities, whenever it is necessary to ask a favor, those holding odd amounts and knowing comparatively little of the debtor, feel that with their small stake they can afford to crowd for payment. Underlying this, of course, is the thought that the debtor out of his own resources or through some help from friends, or under the direction of the larger creditors, will settle rather than have any trouble.

There is nothing in the advice herein offered that should restrict the merchant from judicious buying in all the markets that are open to him to the extent of keeping his stock properly assorted. But with the multitude of salesmen that wait upon him, each urging the special advantages of his own particular firm, and with the flood of advertising literature that reaches him, all calling attention to bargains, the temptation is to buy small lots in very many different directions. Frequently it is hard to perceive the absence of real advantage in what is so temptingly displayed until the aggregate of many little bills has made a large amount. If care is not exercised, all the advantages of the bargains offered will be swallowed up in the direction named.

Public Business and Public Accounts

The machinery of government generally, says the New York "Sun," is run on business methods, though not on the business principles of private enterprises, whatever those may be. The business principles extolled by the Chamber of Commerce, and followed by its members, are merely rules of conduct, which are not fixed and definite. They vary according to varying circumstances and conditions, and their value is not intrinsic and determined by a scientific law, but depends on their practical application and the discretion used by those who apply them. Business is not a science; it has not even any settled principles of universal application. Its successful results as obtained by some members of the Chamber of Commerce are due to individual shrewdness and sagacity, with a large element of mere chance added, and not to obedience to any principles which can be laid down as general. Many books have been written by successful men of affairs to show other people the road to the wealth which is the end of business, but they do not point it out. They can only show how their authors themselves got there, though the mass of men pursuing the same general path never reach the prize.

Public business, however, is controlled by definite principles, though as to them there is the disagreement that divides the people into political parties. If a party does not represent distinctive principles of public business there is no reason for its existence; and if its success at an election does not imply the establishment of its definite business principles in practical government, the people throw away their votes. That is, the people determine the principles on which the Government is to be run, and the men they elect to office are simply servants chosen to apply them practically, and with no discretion in the premises.

As to the practical methods of conducting the public business, they are the conventional methods of business generally, except that public officers are held to a stricter accountability than private employees. In all the departments of the Government there is a system of keeping accounts which is the same as that prevailing in private business, except that the checks and safeguards to prevent dishonesty are more numerous and more complicated; there is more red tape; and the books are open for public examination. There can be no secrecy. Accordingly, the protection against dishonesty is greater in public business than in private affairs, where the management is within the discretion of an individual.

Hence the much-talked-about business principles, or business methods as they really are, do not need to be introduced into the public business, for they are already there. The city accounts are kept as systematically as the accounts of a bank, and there is no private corporation whose management is more businesslike in its details than that of the public corporation of New York.

Accountics

The Office Magazine

ONE DOLLAR A YEAR } JULY 1898 { VOLUME III
TEN CENTS A COPY } { NUMBER 4

CONTENTS.

Published by the ACCOUNTICS ASSOCIATION: Wool Exchange New York

The Self-Proving Accounting System

A Manual on Higher Accounting With Many Original Features.

By A. O. KITTREDGE, F.I.A., C.P.A., and J. F. BROWN, Merchant.

Large Octavo. 328 Pages. 4 Fac-simile Insets and Numerous Other Illustrations. Good Paper, Excellent Typography and Substantial Binding.

This work describes and illustrates a system of accounts adapted to all lines of business, which has for its foundation a Perpetual Balance Sheet. This balance sheet, in place of being made up at intervals, is an integral and going part of the system and keeps the net results of the business constantly before the eye of the manager. It introduces no new elements, but makes various new applications of old principles. A rigid classification of accounts upon balance sheet principles is enforced, and the columnar method of condensation and summarizing is intelligently applied. A given business is represented by the smallest possible number of accounts, and each class of accounts is furnished with books adapted to its special requirements.

The ledgers used with the SELF-PROVING ACCOUNTING SYSTEM are so constructed as to be readily sectionalized for purposes of proof. The system subdivides to any extent required by the character and amount of help employed, but always with the work of each clerk and ledger-keeper so arranged as to be capable of proof by itself.

All the secrets of the business are in the Balance Sheet Ledger. This book, which is the central feature of the system, always shows the condition of the business in regard to resources and liabilities, and, in addition, in regard to profits and losses, the same as a balance sheet of ordinary form. It is not necessary to stop the business in order to close or balance the books. The results are always shown. Profits or losses to date may be instantly ascertained at any time and as often as desired.

Postings are from original entries. There is no copying. Modern facilities are used throughout. Several new features of account-book construction and various new ideas in rulings are employed.

By the SELF-PROVING ACCOUNTING SYSTEM all the terrors of the trial balance are fully overcome.

The examples for illustrative purposes used in the MANUAL of the SELF-PROVING ACCOUNTING SYSTEM are taken from the Installment Business, a line of commercial enterprise heretofore sadly neglected by accountants. The Manual, in addition to general features, contains complete exposition of the SELF-PROVING ACCOUNTING SYSTEM applied to the Installment Business, thus making it a hand-book for instant use in that line of trade.

The SELF-PROVING ACCOUNTING SYSTEM makes use of every known satisfactory method of proving ledger-work. At the same time, it is not a secret system, but is explained in full in this volume.

The Self-Proving Accounting System, while double entry in principle, is more than double entry in detail by reason of the methods employed for summarizing and condensing. It is a careful application of the most advanced principles of accounting brought down to date.

The *Accountant's Magazine*, Edinburgh and London, says: "The system is a development of the device of keeping in the general or private ledger, accounts representing the various subsidiary or departmental ledgers. The accounts are classified in separate ledgers corresponding with the form in which they ultimately appear in the Balance Sheet, and an account is opened in the private ledger with each class."

Extracts From Press Notices and Opinions of Practical Accountants:

From Maurice S. Kuhns, C.P.A., Secretary of the Safeguard Account Co., Chicago:

The authors of the Self-Proving Accounting System are not likely to be accused of plagiarism, for the book bristles with originality on every page.

From The Dry Goods Economist, New York:

The reader's attention is at once drawn to certain new applications that may be made of double-entry principles.

From A. T. S., Boston:

The work explains in careful detail what a number of specialists have tried to keep secret for their own commercial advantage.

From E. R. Baker, Accountant for the Chicago Union Lime Works, Chicago:

It took but a second of my time to perceive that the volume is a valuable contribution to accountancy literature. It is the most unique thing I have seen in accounting in a special branch of mercantile business.

From George Soule, New Orleans, Author of "Soule's New Science and Practice of Accounts," and various other works:

I have given the Manual of the Self-Proving Accounting System careful examination. I am pleased with it. It contains many new points of merit in the line of higher and progressive accounting, and of summarizing and systematizing accounts to save labor and to supply the information that is needed in the safe administration of business. It is a valuable acquisition to the literature of accounts and should be in the library of every bookkeeper who would occupy a position in the front line of his profession.

From The Financial Record, New York:

The Manual of the Self-Proving Accounting System is an admirable work.

From The Dry Goods Chronicle, New York:

It is good accounting, and while there is nothing new in principle about it, it is novel in the specific results achieved.

From Business, Toronto:

The work treats first of accounting and second of bookkeeping. It commences the discussion to which it is devoted where the ordinary volume ends. It will be welcomed by accountants everywhere.

From Chas. Dutton, Public Accountant, New York:

I am pleased with the Self-Proving Accounting System. It is original in conception, complete in detail and just what many accountants have long been wishing for.

From Stoves and Hardware, St. Louis:

The work has been prepared by skilled accountants who understand both theory and practice; it simplifies bookkeeping, yet renders its figures conclusive.

From Hide and Leather, Chicago:

The work is written in a style to recommend it to the business man, as well as to the skilled bookkeeper and accountant. The practical results which are ever kept in view appeal to business managers very forcibly.

From The Mississippi Valley Lumberman, Minneapolis:

It is a double-entry system brought down to date and adapted to modern requirements. It is self-proving in that it affords a means of verification of each and every part, as well as of all the parts taken collectively. The one book in the system that is always in balance is the Private Ledger. The other ledgers, while not in balance themselves, prove by comparison with the balances in the Private Ledger.

From Outing, New York:

The work appeals to us because by the general adoption of the system expounded our readers will be freer from distraction in camp and field. The subject is too technical for cursory review. It is good accounting.

From The Boot and Shoe Recorder, Boston:

The volume is readable, whether the chapters are taken in course or it is opened at random. It bristles with practical suggestions on every page.

From M. F. A., New York:

It is the only book I have ever seen which illustrates what are called Line-Account, or Boston Ledgers.

From Farm Machinery, St. Louis, Mo.

The system is adapted to all lines of business and is worthy of the attention of every accountant.

From The Manufacturers' Record, Baltimore, Md.

The essential feature of the system is the accounts so classified, according to kind, and the resulting classes so arranged as to make of the Private Ledger, which contains the boiled-down facts of the business, a Perpetual Balance Sheet.

From The Scientific American, New York:

The Private Ledger contains the condensed facts of the business and is a perpetual balance sheet as to resources and liabilities, and also an exhibit of profits and losses. The business man may thus at all times have a knowledge of his exact financial condition and the rate of his profits and losses.

From The Inland Printer, Chicago:

The work is well printed and neatly bound. It treats of a tried and tested system, not of theories.

From The American Carpet and Upholstery Journal, Philadelphia:

We heartily indorse the idea set forth. The work will be found of great value to concerns which at present are troubled with defective or faulty systems.

From The American Cabinet Maker and Upholsterer, New York:

The authors of the system are both practical men. Mr. Kittredge has been prominent in accounting circles for many years past. Mr. Brown is a successful merchant. By reason of the joint authorship, the volume presents a completeness of detail which would otherwise be impossible.

From Domestic Engineering, Chicago:

There is nothing of mere theory about the methods outlined. Every detail has been subjected to the severe test of actual trial. The system in complete form is in use in leading business houses.

From Hardware, New York:

The work differs from various books on accounting which have preceded it in that it treats first of accounting and second of bookkeeping, and that it commences the inquiry and discussion to which it is devoted where the ordinary volume ends.

From T. O. R., Philadelphia:

It explains the only Plan of Private Ledger that deserves the name.

From The Bookkeeper, Detroit:

The ledgers used are so constructed as to be readily sectionalized for purposes of proof. The system sub-divides to any extent required by the character and amount of help employed, but always with the work of each clerk and ledger-keeper so arranged as to be capable of proof by itself.

From A. J. F., Cincinnati:

The only work on accounting I have found that is strictly up-to-date.

The Self-Proving Accounting System is adapted to any line of business. It is in use in prominent establishments throughout the country covering almost every branch of commerce. The Manual gives complete description of the system so that its application to any required business may readily be made.

Price, $5 carriage paid. Make remittances to the order of

SELF-PROVING ACCOUNT-BOOK COMPANY

3-5-7 Queen St., East, Toronto, Ont. 260 West Broadway, New York

116 Bedford Street, Boston, Mass.

Accountics

VOL. III JULY 1898

The Monthly Statement

The meeting of the National Educational Association at Washington, occurring in the first and second weeks of July, was more largely attended, so far as mere presence in the city was concerned, than perhaps any other gathering of this organization. Some 23,000 people availed themselves of the special rates made by the railway companies, and of these it was estimated that upwards of 18,000 were really engaged in the profession of teaching. The discrepancy, however, between the number of people nominally attending the convention and those who found it worth while to be present at the various sessions which were held, was very marked. In the general gathering or initial meeting, to which every one was invited, irrespective of the special field in which he was working, and which usually proves to be the largest meeting of the occasion, less than 1,000 persons put in an appearance. The different sessions of the various sections were similarly disregarded. Secretary of the Treasury Lyman P. Gage had been extensively advertised as the star feature of the Business Section, but when he came to address the meeting at the Academy of Music on Friday afternoon, July 8, less than fifty persons composed his audience. It was the rule throughout that the meetings were sparsely attended. Sight-seeing and pleasure-seeking occupied all the time of most of the delegates. Many of the men prominent in the sessions of different departments of this organization in years gone by, notwithstanding the fact that their names appeared upon the programme the present year, were conspicuous by their absence. The general managers of the enterprise have been put in a quandary to account for this apparent lack of interest in the work of the organization, and yet their question is easily answered. The reply was furnished by thousands who, being expostulated with for not attending the sessions, gave as their excuse, "It does not matter, for all that is done will appear in the proceedings."

It would seem for a fact that the day of conventions, of which the leading features, as the reading of papers and the delivery of set speeches, is passing by, if, indeed, it has not already passed by. To a certain extent the day of the political speech has also passed by, and even the sermon appears to be in its decadence. The present day is pre-eminently a reading day and not a listening day. Few there are who are able writers that can read what they have written in a way to command attention and to entertain an audience. Almost every one, and with very good reasons for the choice, prefers to read amid the congenial surroundings of his own office or library what has been prepared for his instruction, rather than to spend hours in an uncomfortable position, in listening to it when read by an indifferent orator. When one reads he has the opportunity of making selection and of skipping uninteresting details; but when he listens he is obliged to take whatever is offered, and in full measure. This is another reason for preferring to read.

The programme of the Business Section of the National Educational Association included a number of attractive features, which were distributed through three days—Friday, July 8; Monday, July 11, and Tuesday, July 12. Following the address of the president of the Section, T. W. Springer, of Ann Arbor, Mich. was the address by Hon. Lyman P. Gage, Secretary of the Treasury, entitled "Reasonable Expectations in Business Education." J. M. Mehan, of Des Moines, Iowa, in behalf of the Committee of Nine, presented the outline of "A Model Business Course," and Professor Emory E. Johnson, of the University of Pennsylvania, Philadelphia, addressed the section on "Business Education in the High School." The session of Monday was devoted to round table discussion of the papers and addresses delivered on Friday and to the election of officers. At the session on Tuesday, Geo. M. Coffin, Deputy Comptroller of the Treasury Department, Washington, addressed the section on "The Administration and Bookkeeping of a National Bank." At the same session A. O. Kittredge, Editor of Accountics, read a paper on "The Accounting and Bookkeeping of the Periodical Publishing Business," which was fully illustrated. David Wolfe Brown, Chief Reporter of the United States House of Representatives, spoke on "The Qualifications and Training of the Congressional Reporter," and J. O. Crissey, Inspector of Business Schools, University of the State of New York, presented a most interesting paper, recounting the work of the University in connection with business education, and referring particularly to the accountancy law of New York, and what has been accomplished under it. Professor Weaver, of Paris, Ky., addressed the session on "The Business College and the High School," contrasting the work of the two and pointing out wherein they could co-operate to the material advantage of the business public.

It is understood that preliminary to his address in Washington, before the Business Section of the National Educational Association, Mr. Kittredge said that no up-to-date business man and no first-class business enterprise, no matter in what line of business engaged, or how small or how large, would dare keep books at the present time as bookkeeping is taught by the schools and as set forth in the ordinary text books. If this remark was made, it went unchallenged, due, perhaps, to the absence from the meeting in question of the various war horses of the organization, and likewise of a number of gentlemen engaged in business school work, who are ever on the lookout for aspersions of this character. Something that the speaker really did present and which likewise passed without comment was an impeachment of the authors of bookkeeping treatises, whom he accused of copying from each other, even to the perpetuation of radical mistakes and omissions. His arraignment of the Merchandise Account as commonly conducted commanded particular attention, but no one ventured a remark in defence. The speaker's theory was that in the earliest English treatises upon double-entry bookkeeping a link in the system had been left out or a cog slipped, and that the mistakes there made had been copied unthinkingly by all who have come after, without ever any one noticing the error. He contended that in view of the two sets of values, cost and selling, pertaining to all merchandise, two accounts should have been placed where only one now appears. The title of Mr. Kittredge's address was "The Bookkeeping and Accounting of the Periodical Publishing Business." He explained that he had chosen so complicated an example for the purpose of better illustrating the principles of analysis involved and of pointing out some of the shortcomings of bookkeeping as ordinarily taught.

In another part of this issue is presented a very important contribution to the literature of accounting, being a paper by the president of the leading society of accountants in the Dominion of Canada, Harry Vigeon, F.C.A., who treats of trustees' and executors' accounts. This paper, while read before an audience of fellow accountants, was yet in part addressed to the students of accounting preparing for final examinations for admission to the Institute of Chartered Accountants of Ontario. Accordingly, it has interest for beginners as well as experts. Few authors of treatises and essays on accounting succeed as well in investing their subject with interest as has Mr. Vigeon in this case. Not only has he made the subject entertaining to the general reader, but he has also shown in a pleasing way the importance that attaches to adequate and proper accounting. The paper is one that may be studied advantageously by students of accounting practice everywhere. Taken in connection with the paper on Surrogates' Accounts, by W. B. Jaudon, F. I. A., C. P. A., presented in these columns several months since, the student is afforded a comprehensive view of the general requirements of dealing with estates of deceased persons.

The laws governing the accounts to be rendered by executors, trustees and others in a similar capacity, differ as between this country and Canada and as between the various States in the Union. In view of the fact that we have upwards of forty States, it may be held that such an article as either of those above referred to is of comparatively little value outside of the particular commonwealth in the light of the laws of which it was written. To a certain extent this is true, but irrespective of special provisions of the law, the fundamental principles are the same. There remains, therefore, only adaptations in view of the laws of the State in which the work is to be done. As contributions to the literature of accounting, therefore, papers of this kind are very valuable, not only to accountants and students living in the community whose laws are especially referred to, but also for the investigators of accounting practice wherever situated. Practicing accountants, who may be assumed to be experts in the fundamental principles, enjoy a comparison of such articles one with the other for the purpose of acquainting themselves with the difference in practice in different parts of the country.

Some leading accountants met some time since in the capacity of a committee to consider a standard system for use in the industry with which they are connected. The occasion referred to was not their first meeting. They had been at the work for almost two years, and in that time had formulated a report embodying their recommendations of changes so far as the expense accounts of the industry are concerned. A considerable number of those connected with the association of which this committee is an important instrument have already adapted for use the modifications recommended. Preliminary to the special occasion referred to, letters were addressed to those who had put the system into operation, and to many others in the same line of industry, saying that the committee would be glad to hear from them with respect to criticisms on what had so far been done, if criticisms were to be offered, or asking questions, if doubt upon any point existed, which answers would serve to clear away. The result was no criticisms and a very small number of inquiries—practically none of importance. Thereupon the members of the committee had the feeling that their efforts were not being appreciated, and that for some reason they were failing to command that attention of accountants engaged in the industry in connection with which they were working, which they supposed they were to receive. Their conclusions in this regard were reached by comparing the results of their letters of suggestion with respect to a technical topic of great importance, and what would follow upon letters of inquiry sent out concerning some everyday detail of business.

In discussing this matter, a public accountant who was present pointed out that such a comparison by way of results was altogether unreasonable, and further made the point that the number who were able to ask questions, much less present criticisms, was very small indeed. He likened the committee to pioneers who had penetrated a virgin forest far beyond the limits of the explorations of others. Few were able to follow them, but, nevertheless, as explorers, they had the confidence of those who sent them forth. He argued, therefore, that of those who had manifested interest in this accounting, comparatively few were able to offer criticism and comment, while all, by reason of their position and their acquaintance with the men immediately upon the committee, were fully persuaded that the work was being well done by competent investigators. His conclusion was that it was not at all strange that the circular letters of inquiry had failed to call out a larger response.

The same principles, we take it, will hold good in various other directions. There are thousands of men quietly interested in the work of investigators and pioneers, whether in science or other divisions of human activity, who have never ventured to offer so much as a word of approval to those who are doing the work, much less to criticise that upon which they are engaged, and yet who expect ultimately to take an active part in the work when it has reached a stage that will permit their co-operation. Their silence now is no evidence of indifference to the results that are being worked out.

In more or less of the discussion in this country which has occurred in the past with respect to laws regulating the accountant's profession, reference has been made to British laws and to the very satisfactory condition of the profession under those laws which it was assumed is prevailing. This has occurred notwithstanding that well informed persons have frequently pointed out that British laws on this subject are not entirely satisfactory to the profession in that country, and in spite of the fact also that English accounting journals, commenting upon what has been pending in New York, for example, and the law that recently has been put upon the statute books of that State have indicated that the accountants of this country were securing for themselves far better conditions than prevail in Great Britain. The idea still obtains in many directions that our British cousins are well established before the law. That this is not true is evident from the efforts that are being made from time to time to correct and advance British legislation upon this point. For example, there is at present a bill before the House of Commons known as the Accountants' (Scotland) Bill, which is exciting considerable attention. It has for its object to prohibit the use of the title "accountant" by unqualified persons, and it follows mainly on the lines of what are known as the Medical Acts. It provides that a register is to be established, which is to be kept by a general council to be nominated in the first instance by the Lord President of the Court of Sessions, and thereafter elected by the persons registered. The court has also power to control the entries in the register on appeal taken by any person aggrieved, and a similar right as to the professional training and examinations prescribed by the council.

It will no doubt interest American accountants to know something with respect to the provisions of the bill. The section describing the persons who are entitled to be registered under the act is as follows: "All present members of the Chartered Societies who shall pay the prescribed fee for registration, and all persons who, although not members of any of the Chartered Societies, were in professional practice as accountants in Scotland at the date of the passing of this act, and who shall apply, before the first day of January next thereafter, to be registered, and shall produce evidence reasonably satisfactory to the General Council of their having been in practice as aforesaid, and shall pay the prescribed fee for registration. All persons who shall apply on or after the first day of January next after the passing of this act to be registered, and shall produce evidence satisfactory to the General Council of their having undergone such professional education and training and passed such examinations as shall, for the time, be prescribed by the General Council as conditions of registration, and shall pay the prescribed fee for registration, due regard being had by the General Council to the cases of those who, prior to the passing of this act, had entered upon their professional education and training."

It is not to be supposed that a bill of this kind could be passed without calling out discussion and opposition from certain quarters of a very lively character. Objections to it have been urged by an organization known as the Corporation of Accountants, Limited. One of the contentions is that there is no provision for the registration of the members of the other two bodies of accountants in Scotland, as such, in the same way as the members of the three chartered societies. The editor of the Accountant's Magazine (Edinburgh), commenting on this objection, says:

"Were the promoters of the bill satisfied that the members of these bodies, as such, had the necessary qualifications, there would be no objection to their admission to the register as members of these bodies, but we do not think that either the promoters of the bill or the general public are so satisfied. Any individual members who are qualified, will, in terms of the bill, at once be placed on the register, but it is hardly surprising, nor do we think it is an 'objection, that those who are not qualified should be excluded. Another objection offered by the same organization is that there is no provision for future entrance to the chartered societies, but only to the register. The same authority, as quoted above, answers this by saying that there is no reason why there should be any such provision, and points out that the bill seeks to establish a register of accountants, and that it is not apparent why it should deal with the admission of members either to the Chartered Societies or to the Corporation of Accountants, Limited.

Still other objections urged turn upon the question of English and Irish accountants' privileges to employment in Scotland, and the privilege of Scottish accountants to employment in England and Ireland, and the point is also made as an objection that the members of the chartered societies will have a legal monopoly of the designation "Chartered Accountant" and the letters "C. A." To this point our contemporary replies as follows: "The chief grievance appears to be that the bill will restrict the meaning of the initials 'C. A.' to what the public at large naturally take them to represent, namely, 'Chartered Accountant,' whereas, the Corporation of Accountants contends that they should also be allowed to signify 'Corporate Accountant.' No advantage that we can see would follow the acceptation of a double meaning for one form of contraction, except the doubtful one of leading people to take a man to be that which he is not. Moreover, the clause in question only seeks to make statutory the legal right at present possessed by Chartered Accountants in Scotland the exclusive use of the designation 'Chartered Accountant' and the initials 'C. A.' "

From all this it would appear that within the ranks of the profession in Great Britain, as well as in other parts of the world, there are some who desire to acquire, by one means if they are not able to secure it by another, the use of titles which are well known to the public and which are accepted by the business public as evidence of competency and good character. After all, human nature is very much alike whether manifested in one part of the world or another. The Accountants' Magazine concludes its comments upon this bill, which, as the reader may have noticed, applies to Scotland only, with the following sentence: "It is earnestly to be hoped, both in the interests of the profession and of the public, that the bill may soon become law, and that it will be followed by similar bills for England and Ireland, or, preferably, by a bill for the whole United Kingdom."

After an improvement has been made and introduced, and after we become accustomed to the new order of things, we wonder how it was possible that we ever succeeded in getting along with that which has been superseded. Using gas for illumination, we wonder how any one ever endured the tallow dip, or, with the modern cook stove in daily request, how any one got along with an open fire and brick oven and the very crude appliances of two or three generations back. With a typewriting machine at command, we wonder how it was possible to conduct business correspondence before this useful article came into use. With fountain pens, we wonder how business was done when quills were the sole dependence for writing instruments. All these things served their purpose well and passed away, and in the same manner many of those things which are serving useful purposes to-day will in their turn pass away, being superseded by something better.

But there are other questions of wonder and curiosity to which attention may be well devoted. How is it that with all the inventiveness for which the American public is credited we permit certain very valuable contrivances to remain in an imperfect condition? For example, why is it that the individual does not appear who is to make the typewriting machine less of a fierce and abominable institution than it, is at present? Its noise should be overcome and its capacity should be increased; we should be able to write continuously without changing the machine for each new line. Why does not some inventor come forward, able to make the phonograph of practical value? Why must one who wishes to dictate to a machine sit gazing at a whirring wheel which disjoints his thoughts, or be compelled at frequent intervals to stimulate the machine by turning a crank? Where is the man who will give us a phonograph able to take matters deliberately and permit of talk less frantic than that of a howling savage? This list by no means exhausts what might be discussed in the same strain. Those things that we have to-day we put up with because they are the best that is offered, but there is none of them that we would not be glad to dispense with if better could be had.

Voucher Record

The accompanying cut is a reproduction of a Voucher Record and Distribution Sheet designed by Frank J. Sager, of White Oaks, N. M., for a manufacturing company. The necessary reduction in photo-engraving has made the writing, as well also as the printed heads of the form, somewhat difficult to decipher unless one is blessed with unusually keen eyesight. The interposition of a reading glass, an ordinary magnifying glass, or even the lens of a pair of spectacles will help in this regard.

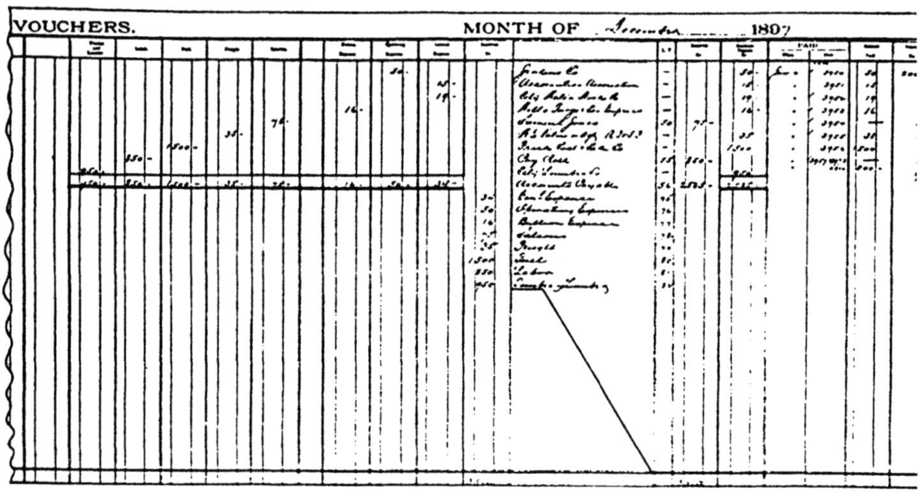
VOUCHERS.

MONTH OF

FORM OF VOUCHER RECORD SUBMITTED BY F. J. SAGER.

It will be seen that the columnar plan is made use of to a very liberal degree; that the postings to the ledger are by totals, and that there is a complete record of the number of the voucher, the date of payment and the number of the check employed in making payment. Finally, there is a proof balance at the bottom of the page. The form will bear study, and will be found to contain various useful features.

I can get no remedy against this consumption of the purse; borrowing only lingers and lingers it out, but the disease is incurable.—Shakespeare.

As the interest of man, so his God; as his God, so he.—Lavater.

What Constitutes a Compromise

The doctrine that debt is not discharged by the receipt, even ostensibly in satisfaction, of a smaller amount, is based on the fact that there is in such case no consideration for the compromise. It does not apply to the case of a disputed claim. In some of the States the courts have stated the old rule to apply to liquidated claims, and the distinction is made between those that are liquidated and those which are not. The term "liquidated," when used in this connection, means one where the amount due has been ascertained and agreed upon between the parties, or is fixed by operation of law. But it is now generally held that where a certain sum of money is tendered to a creditor by a debtor on the condition that he accept it in full satisfaction of his demand, the sum due being in dispute, the creditor must either refuse the tender or accept it as made subject to the condition. If he accept it he accepts the condition also, notwithstanding any protest he may make to the contrary.

As to great and commanding talents, they are the gift of Providence in some way unknown to us. They rise where they are least expected. They fail when everything seems disposed to produce them, or at least to call them forth.—Burke.

Accounts of Executors and Trustees*

By HARRY VIGEON, F.C.A.

The subject to be discussed this evening is an important one, and one that you, as accountants, will have to be prepared to handle intelligently whenever you practice as public accountants. First let us have an idea of what an executor is and of the meaning of one or two other terms which are also of importance.

Personal property or personalty consisted formerly of moveable things of pretty much everything which is not land. Money, goods, stocks, shares and leases for years are all personalty. Realty, which is opposed to personalty, is land, houses or leases for a life or lives. A trustee is the person intrusted with realty for the benefit of another. Generally speaking, the executor is only concerned with the personal property. When the executor has administered the estate as far as he has the power to do so, and has passed his residuary account, he may be directed by the testator to stand possessed of the residue on certain trusts. In that case he ceases to be an executor and becomes a trustee.

A legacy is a gift of personality by will. A beneficiary is a person for whose benefit the executor administers the testator's estate. A will is an instrument, not necessarily in any particular form, but one which is to take effect after the death of the maker of it or testator, as he is called. A will must be signed by the testator and attested by two witnesses, who ought to be two persons not taking any benefit under the will. They ought to sign the attestation clause in the presence of the testator and of each other. If there is a will, the testator generally appoints one or more persons, who are to carry out the provisions of it after his death. Such a person is called the executor.

It is almost a matter of necessity that the services of the skilled accountant should be employed to aid the executor and other solicitor in the preparation of the accounts and administration. Doubtless, in time, this branch of an accountant's business will so develop as to render it of much more importance than has hitherto been. In fact the same may be said of this as of other branches of the profession. As trade and commerce increase and bring with them the accumulation of property and wealth, and large undertakings, with their accompanying responsbilities, so will the utility of a professional accountant and the distinctive duties attaching to his calling become more widely recognized.

With reference more particularly to the duties attaching to them in connection with executors' and trustees' accounts, it has frequently been a matter of doubt as to where those of an accountant end and those of a solicitor begin. I think, however, there need be no difficulty on this point, and to my mind their respective duties may be clearly defined, and, where carefully and judiciously managed, the two professions may work together in the most perfect harmony. Of course, when accounts are placed in our hands, we must remember that we are held responsible for their accuracy. The solicitor does not feel called upon to exercise that supervision which he would if the accountant had not been employed. It is therefore our duty to our client, when occasion requires, to consult the solicitor in the preparation of the accounts.

When once the accounts have been prepared and the estate disposed of, it is too late to make corrections. Any error of principle upon our part discovered at that time may not only lead to a serious complication, but be very damaging to our professional reputation as well. It therefore behooves us to devote much care and attention to the preparation of the accounts, and to thoroughly clear up at once every point upon which there may be even a shadow of doubt. In this, as in all branches of our profession, it is necessary for us to be equipped with some legal knowledge. It should not be necessary for us to run to the solicitors' office for guidance in every little matter, for the various duties we are called upon to perform are so subservient to the law that without it we are unable to conduct the various matters intrusted to our care to any practical and reliable issue. For these reasons the Institute of Chartered Accountants require candidates for examination to possess legal as well as practical knowledge of those subjects

*Executors' and Trustees' Accounts. A paper read at the monthly meeting of the Institute of Chartered Accountants of Ontario, at Toronto, March 17, 1898, by Harry Vigeon, F.C.A., President of the Institute.

which directly bear upon the duties of our profession.

* * * * * *

A man dies, leaving behind him considerable property. He has left a will stating how that property is to be disposed of and intrusting the disposition of it to one or more individuals, who are styled his executors and trustees. These are usually friends or relatives, and, perhaps, are persons of some standing and business capacity, in whom he has implicit confidence. He may or he may not have bequeathed them a legacy as a token of his esteem and as a compliment for the trouble and attention they will be required to devote to the performance of the duties of the office. Invariably the sum so bequeathed is a mere compliment and totally inadequate to the time and responsibilities usually attending such duties. In fact, the responsibilities are perhaps greater than those of any other capacity in which one may be placed. They are seldom realized at the outset.

A man can do what he likes with his own. He can enter into engagements and contracts. He can speculate and embark capital in anything he chooses. He can buy and sell and hold shares in both limited and unlimited joint stock companies, banks and the like, and if he suffers loss thereby he has no one to account to but himself. Not so with the executor and trustee. He can only make such investments as are admissible by law or by specific declaration of the will of the testator. If he enters into an engagement or contract, or carries on a business, even with specific authority for so doing, he runs a risk. He must account strictly to the estate for all profits made. If a loss is incurred, he is liable to be required to make it good out of his own private resources. If he holds shares in public companies or banks, or in any undertaking upon which there are implied calls, even where such investments are part of the trust estate which comes to his hands at the death of the testator, he had better realize as soon as possible, for in the event of the estate being insufficient to meet the calls when made, he is personally liable.

The executor and trustee can claim no remuneration for his services, however onerous or complicated the estate may be, but he may claim expenses out of pocket incurred in performance of the duties. He can employ the services of a solicitor and an accountant or agent, where the need of the case justifies such employment, but he will not be allowed the costs of either in respect of work which he should have performed himself. If he refuses or is unwilling to act in the capacity to which he is appointed he must be careful not to interfere or intermeddle in the slightest degree with the testator's affairs, for having in any way done so and then refusing to continue, he is liable to be committed for contempt of court. Having acted, he must not purchase for himself, either directly or indirectly, any part of the testator's assets, even in the most perfect good faith.

It is therefore clear that the office of an executor or trustee is by no means a sinecure. It is one involving serious responsibility, and when attended with the annoyance and worry not infrequently experienced with dissatisfied and needy legatees, it may well be said to be a thankless office.

So far I have named a few of the grave responsibilities of executor and trustee, but there are still more which I have not touched upon, as the student will readily see if he goes into the subject. I think I have, however, said sufficient to show that it is a matter of infinite importance that executors and trustees should have their accounts accurately and faithfully kept, and in a manner clear and straightforward and strictly in accordance with law. It follows, therefore, that if we, as professional accountants, are to be of any real service to our clients in these matters, we must be thorough masters of the subject, and when accounts are placed in our hands we must be able to do all that is required of us by seeing that the accounts are established on a basis at once in conformity with the law and with the specific provisions of the will.

We should be in a position to produce a clean and perfect account of the executors' stewardship, showing the estate which has come into their hands, the realization, management and disposition thereof from the death of the testator to the date upon which the account may be required. The powers usually delegated to us are not restricted, and full and perfect protection is expected. In a word, when the accounts are placed in our hands, as already stated, we are held responsible for their accuracy, not merely as to the accounting for actual receipts and payments, but as to the adjustment of capital and income and the proper appropriation and distribution thereof.

The first duty of an executor, after the interment of the deceased is to prove the will—that is to say, obtain a grant of probate to show evidence of his rights, although his actual right in the will begins at the date of the decease. In order to obtain this grant he must ascertain the total amount of personal estate of which the testator died possessed. In England it is the custom for the solicitor to attend the funeral and read the will in the presence of the various relatives and friends who are present.

By personal estate is meant all the estate except real property. It includes that which is subject to probate, embracing the following items: Cash in house, household furniture and effects, stocks or funds, rents of real or leasehold property due at death, rents of leasehold property accrued since death, life assurance policies, proprietary shares in public companies with dividends, money out on mortgage and interest, book debts, bonds and bills, notes and interest thereon, good will, stock in trade, farming stock and all other personal property.

In the case of items upon which a value has to be affixed, a valuation is usually obtained from competent valuers. In that of stock and shares which may be taken at the assumed selling price of the day, it is well to have the values vouched for by a broker's certificate. When the whole of the personalty and its value has been ascertained, an account with particulars should be furnished to the solicitor acting for the executor, who at once will prepare the necessary forms and apply for the grant of probate and pay the fees chargeable thereon. I will assume for my purpose this evening that probate has been granted before the accountant has been called in.

It will be found, perhaps, that few books have been kept by the executor—possibly only a cash book, showing actual receipts and payments, so as to have some record of the transactions, but no ledger containing an account of the estate which he has to deal with or in which the entries of the cash book have been classified in a way to show the necessary particulars required to make up the residue accounts. There will also be discovered, perhaps, a bank pass book, a check book and a batch of papers and receipts, among which will doubtless be found the solicitor's bill. I mention the latter because it is usually one of the most useful documents in the parcel. A perusal of it will invariably give you a history of the transactions of the trust and throw much light upon entries and matters with which you will personally have to deal.

Here comes the question, What books are necessary to be kept so as to show a clear and concise account of the estate which has come into the hands of the executor, and the manner in which it has been dealt with? What is the best method to adopt so as to present the accounts in a clear and simple form in a way at once to meet the requirements of the residuary accounts and be such that executors who are not professional accountants may be able to refer to and understand it for themselves without having to ask for explanations? It seems to me that this is what is required, and that the simpler the accounts are the better, whether we are dealing with trust accounts or other accounts, provided they contain all that is necessary.

The books required are two in number—cash book and ledger—both combining the journal features of full details. In some cases the word "journal" describes the first of these, although it will be found convenient to keep it in the form of a cash book. Executors rarely keep cash in hand. If they are wise, most of their receipts will be paid directly into bank and most of their payments will be made by check. This means crediting the account from which the receipt is derived and debiting the bank or debiting an account on which the payment is made and crediting the bank, as the case may be.

The advantages of dispensing with the journal are that it is particularly desirable in these accounts that the ledger should contain the fullest particulars of all the entries, so that the facts of the various transactions may be readily traced without having recourse to any other book. It is an advantage to be able to see in the most concise form possible all the transactions of the estate, and if the ledger and the cash book can be made with a little extra detail to show the particulars usually given in the journal, I think it is advisable to manage in that way. It saves at least one book of reference, and gives every particular required without the necessity of constantly turning to the journal.

At the outset it will be found advantageous to prepare a preliminary draft of the arrangement of the accounts. In the process of your work you are almost sure to meet with items requiring explanation before you can decide to what particular account they should be placed or what proportion of them is capital and what income. If you do not find it necessary as you proceed to make alterations and corrections in entries which you have already made you will indeed be fortunate. It will indicate that you have had a trust committed to your care in which the information in your possession is unusually complete and straightforward. For your preliminary draft two ordinary, cheap books, paper binding, both ruled alike, namely, in the form of an ordinary cash book, with double cash columns, will be found most convenient. Use one for the cash book and the other for the ledger. The form of ruling described will be found suitable for the ledger, since it affords ample space to detail full descriptive particulars of the entries, which in trust books are indispensable, and the form also provides separate cash columns for income and capital. This plan, in the case of investments and personal accounts of settled legacies enables the capital and income to be dealt with separately in one account and so obviates the necessity of having two accounts. It secures the convenience of having the whole matter in respect to an investment or settled legacy before you at one opening.

With these books in hand you will find it of great service, as well as a saving of time and trouble afterwards, if you carefully peruse the will and enter a short abstract of its provisions and dispositions on the fly leaf of one of them. Enter, in addition, such particulars as the date of the will, date of death, date of grant of probate, the amount sworn to, the names and addresses of the executors and trustees, and where there are legatees under age, not coming into the full benefit of the full legacies until they have attained their majority, the dates of their respective births. By this plan, in case of a long trust, in which, in all probability, you will be charged with the usual audit of the accounts, you will not lose sight of these matters, but always have the information required ready at hand without the necessity of wading time after time through the legal phraseology of somewhat lengthy documents. When you have done this and have carefully read through all of the batch of papers to which I have already alluded, you will find yourself tolerably well acquainted with the leading points of the matters in hand. You will have a very fair idea of the framework of your task, and will be ready to commence arranging the necessary entries for the basis of your account.

You will first ascertain if the various items of the estate returned in the form for probate are accurate, and in case any difference should arise in consequence of information which lapse of time may have revealed or from any other cause, you make a note of it. You then commence your cash book and journal, with entries of the personal estate, first crediting capital and debiting the various accounts of which it is composed, in such order as you propose to open them in the ledger, Capital Account being the first.

Here it may be pointed out that by recent enactments of the legislature the executors or trustees are required to deal with the whole of the estate, whether real or personal. A separate account should be opened with each parcel of real estate, and on the opposite folio an account of the incumbrance, if any, existing against it. The whole transaction relating to that particular item of capital can then be seen at a glance. The account will show the parcel of real estate, the incumbrance on same, the revenue derivable from the rental, lease or use of property, and the cost of carrying the mortgage.

When the ledger entries setting forth the personal estate have been made and posted to the respective accounts in the order referred to, you will then have got a fair start. The Capital Account will show the total personal estate of which the testator died possessed. If this agrees with the amount sworn to for probate or at any rate does not exceed to such an extent as to render the executor liable to payment for further duty, very well. If, on the contrary, it exceeds the amount so much as to show that insufficient duty has been paid, you should at once communicate with your client in order that he may give you definite instructions thereon.

Having so far proceeded, it is then necessary to complete Capital Account by making the entries through the ledger of real estate and any other estate not already included. Although the real estate may be specially bequeathed, it is always well to pass it through the books by debiting Real Estate and crediting Capital. When you appropriate the estate debit Capital and credit the legatee, and debit the legatee by a transfer from Real Estate Account. This closes the transaction. By adopting this course, the books will show the disposition of the whole estate of which the testator died possessed, whether personal or real.

I now assume that the whole estate, real and personal, of which the testator died possessed has been entered, with full descriptive particulars in the cash book and the ledger, and that the values inserted are either the amounts actually realized or vouched for by valuation and certificate of competent authorities, that the entries have been duly classified and posted to accounts opened in the ledger, with the several investments, in the order that I have indicated, and that all the entries of capital as distinct from income have been entered in the other, or capital column. I assume that the date which has been given to these entries is the date of the death and that all further items of rents and income due and accrued at death have been apportioned in the ledger and those of income entered in the inner or income column, and that they have been treated as part of the capital in accordance with the law. In short, I assume that the books now contain an account of the whole of the assets of the testator, and show exactly the estate with which the executors have to deal.

The next thing to proceed with is the dealings with the estate, which, of course, comprise the transactions of the executors. As these consist entirely of receipts and payments, they appear in the form of a cash account, the entries being made in the order of date on which the transactions occur. The first entry will be Cash in the House, and which is brought from the previous ledger entries. Then, following on the debit or receipt side, will come the sum received in payment of the back debts, proceeds of shares and other investments realized, also rents and dividends, interest, etc., received. These are income. Checks drawn on the bank are also receipts from the bank, being money drawn out to discharge debts. These entries will be balanced by corresponding entries on the credit or payment side. On the credit side will appear all payments and disbursements made by the executor in discharge of debts due by the deceased, his funeral and testamentary expenses, dues and payment into bank. Vouchers should be produced for all of these payments, and where they contain items incurred previous to death, as well as those incurred subsequently, the items should be carefully separated and classified, so as to insure their ultimate entry in the proper account.

The payments will be found to comprise the following: 1. Probate and administration, which includes fees payable on the grant of probate. 2. Funeral expenses, which include coffin, hearse and coaches, interment fees, gravestone and monument, family mourning, etc. 3. Executorship expenses, including valuation fees, law costs, accountant's charges, traveling expenses, check book and the numerous expenses incident to the execution of the trust. 4. Debts on simple contract, comprising debts owing by the testator, rent, taxes and wages. 5. Debts on mortgage, if any, with interest due at death. 6. Debts on bonds and other securities. 7. Pecuniary legacies. Accounts should be opened in the ledger under these headings, following those already opened, and the various payments previously and correctly classified in the cash book fully posted to them respectively.

In posting the various entries from the cash book to the ledger, I would here observe that care must be taken to post all the sums received on account of income, such as dividends on shares, interest on mortgages, rents of properties, etc., to the respective accounts opened with these investments in the ledger in the inner or income column, as well as all payments for repairs, insurance, etc., that may be made on account of the properties which, with very few exceptions, are chargeable against income.

It will now be necessary to make closing entries transferring the several accounts under the head of Payments already referred to, namely, probate duty, funeral expenses, expenses of executorship, debts, etc., to the debit of capital account. It will also be necessary to transfer to the debit of this account any deficiency that may have arisen in the realization of investments, etc., or property previously taken at valuation, as well as to place to the credit of the same account any excess that may have been realized over and above such valuations.

When all these entries have been made a balance should be struck and brought down, which, in the event of all the debts having been paid, liabilities discharged or provided for and assets realized, will be the net amount of the sum applicable to legacies and bequests. In all cases where there is still a portion of the estate unrealized and debts outstanding, a reserve should be made, equal to the amount at which such items have been valued in the accounts. This may be carried forward as a balance, only to be divided when realized. In the event also of an annuity of life being bequeathed, either a sum should be specially invested to produce the amount of such annuity, or, if paid out of the income of the estate, a sufficient portion of the capital should be reserved out of the residue to cover it before division. Matters of this description and any special matter of the nature of a contingent liability, which often happens, having been duly provided for so as to protect the executors from parting with any estate not absolutely ascertained by realization, you may proceed to apply the balance as directed by will.

First will come pecuniary legatees, if any, for which an entry should be made through the journal, debiting and crediting legatees in a separate account, which account or accounts will be closed when actual payment is made by posting the cash to the debit. When the pecuniary and specific bequests have been duly provided for, the rest will be the residue of the capital. It now remains to close those accounts relating to income, which are sums placed to the credit of the various investments for dividends, interest, rents, etc., less the proportion accrued at death, which has already been posted to the debit in the first entries made in the ledger of the testator's estate. The balance is transferred by debiting these accounts respectively and crediting Income Account. The books now contain in a concise form all the information required to complete the residuary account.

It will be necessary to show what property has been converted into money and the date of such conversion and the value of property not converted into money. In the latter case the value of the property at the time the account is rendered is required. Inventories and proper valuations must be produced, and care must be taken to ascertain wherein variation has arisen since the accounts were opened, and to adjust them accordingly. Shares not converted into money are to be valued at the asumed price at the date on which the account is dated. If there be shares in many companies, it may be convenient to insert the total amount or value in this account, and then annex a schedule of the particular shares. When the various amounts have been credited in the account under the respective headings therein required, the total of the first column in which all property converted into money has been entered is carried out into column No. 2 and cast up with it, the total being the total of property.

We now come to the deductions of payments, which include the probate duty, funeral expenses, executorship expenses, debts under three distinct headings, namely, simple contract debts, mortgage debts and debts on bonds and other securities, and finally pecuniary legatees. A schedule of the debts signed by the executor or administrator is to be annexed, and the particulars of any other lawful payments and of the fund and other securities purchased, prepared and inserted with the date of such purchase. These deductions are entered in an inner column, and the total written out and deducted from the total property, leaving the net amount of property to be carried forward to the next page of the amount in column No. 3, in which must be inserted and added the accumulation of interest, dividends, rents, etc., from date of death to date of account classified in a manner therein described. From this total should be deducted payments out of interest on mortgages, bonds, legatees, etc., payments on account of annuities and other payments comprising the expenses incurred in the management of the trust estate and chargeable against income and a balance again shown. Then any deductions from residue should be taken, including debts still due from the estate, if any, and money retained to pay outstanding legacies.

I have thus far endeavored to give you a brief sketch of what is required to be done in the preparation of executors' and trustees' accounts. I have not by any means exhausted the subject. It would be futile to attempt to do so in the short space of a single hour. I hope, however, that I have succeeded in giving you some idea of the broad principles that should govern, and by illustrating a simple, straigthforward case and referring to some of the duties and responsibilities attaching to this branch of the profession, prove that this meeting has been an instructive one.

You will, however, in the course of experience meet with many problems presenting special features and matters requiring special treatment. You will rarely find two trusts alike. You may be well acquainted with the law relating to the general particulars of the duties of trustees and the accounts to be kept by them, but in all cases the will is paramount and its directions must be closely complied with. It may be truthfully said of wills, as of faces, that there are no two alike. It requires much judgment, therefore, and common sense, in addition to a knowledge of figures, to work out to an equitable and successful issue the various crotchets and dispositions which are often evidenced in these interesting documents.

Why Should He Fail?

The fact that the general press has got into a position to discuss business details intelligently and in a way to make an impression upon the community is a sign of real business progress. It is rare indeed at the present time to take up a trade or industrial paper in which there is not found either a stated article upon some subject intimately associated with accounting and business management, or an anecdote in the same general line or a joke which is calculated to impress a bit of business science. A recent issue of the Michigan Tradesman may be referred to in this connection by way of example. An old-fashioned merchant, according to the story, who had done business in one of the interior towns for many years past had failed. When one of the creditors reached the place it was to find the merchant working hard to figure it all out:

"Lands! but I don't see why I should fail," he kept on saying. "Mebbe, though, I didn't collect sharp enough."

"You have a heap of goods here," said the agent, as he looked around.

"Yes, more or less."

"When did you take the last inventory?"

"Inventory? Take everything down?"

"Yes."

"And make out a list?"

"Yes."

"And dust off the shelves and mop the floor?"

"That's it."

"And clean the windows and paint the front of the store?"

"Yes."

"I never went into that. I was going to one day about fifteen years ago, but they had a wrestling match in town, and I left the inventory. Mercy on me, but I can't understand why I should fail!"

Memoranda

In the list of certified public accountants, published in the June number of Accountics, the number of certificate placed opposite the name of Frank I. Stott was 124. It should have been No. 12.

We are indebted to Fred A. Moss, Secretary of the Chamber of Commerce, Idaho Springs, Col., for one of the most attractive advertising pamphlets that has come to us in a long time. It is descriptive of Idaho Springs, Col., and treats of it as a mountain resort, and also a gold mining region. It shows it to be a place that may be visited for health, wealth and recreation. The book is most attractively printed and profusely and appropriately illustrated with carefully prepared engravings.

Every office man should possess himself of the neat little sample book of carbon papers which is being sent out by Philip Hano & Co., 812 Greenwich street, New York City. The sample book contains certain novelties in carbon, as well as standards, among which may be mentioned a green and red carbon—if carbon can be green or red. Perhaps it were better to have said "impression" papers. The high quality of the Hano goods is recognized everywhere, and the attractive manner in which the goods are put up makes them very acceptable. In writing for this sample book mention Accountics.

Talent of the highest order, and such as is calculated to command admiration, may exist apart from wisdom.—Robert Hall.

Talent is a docile creature; it bows its head meekly while the world slips the collar over it; it backs into the shafts like a lamb.—O. W. Holmes.

The most fertile soil does not necessarily produce the most abundant harvest. It is the use we make of our faculties which renders them valuable. Talent, like other things, may lie fallow.—T. W. Higginson.

Convention of the National Association of Credit Men

The annual convention of the National Association of Credit Men was held in Detroit June 22, 23 and 24, and was in many respects a model business meeting and one which the managers of various business organizations may study with advantage. It was an up-to-date meeting, not only in the subjects discussed and in the plans which had been arranged in advance for the convention, but also by reason of the manner in which the delegates made known their views and enforced their sentiments.

The work of this organization between conventions is largely in the hands of a number of standing committees, and very naturally a considerable portion of the work of the convention is the reception of the reports of officers and committees and action thereon. In this case the several committees had formulated resolutions, which, from their point of view, seemed appropriate expressions of sentiment and outlines of future work. These resolutions had been printed in full in the programme, and an outsider who inspected this document might have thought that there was little for the delegates to do except to approve of the cut and dried measures submitted for their inspection. The convention, however, showed in the sessions that it had a will of its own, and that it would only approve of that which in the estimation of the majority was expedient. The time schedule of the programme, which was a most remarkable feature, was closely adhered to. Some of the resolutions proposed were snowed under unanimously; others were temporarily tabled pending further inquiry, and still others were essentially modified. New resolutions were also brought forward, and quite enough was done in a number of directions to show that the convention, while thoroughly approving of the preliminary work done by its officers and committees in the way of a programme, and willing to accept the programme so far as it coincided with their ideas, still had a will of its own. The delegates did not shirk their proper responsibilities.

Allusion has already been made to the time-table feature of the programme. The time to be devoted to various matters of business had been calculated to a nicety, and the presiding officer, who has had wide experience in managing meetings, was able to hold very closely to the schedule during each of the sessions. The result was that an immense amount of business was transacted in a remarkably short period of time. The sessions of the convention were limited to one per day, greatly to the advantage of all concerned.

A special feature of the occasion was getting men of like interests together in separate congresses. Gatherings of this kind were held of representatives of the boot and shoe trade, the dry goods trade, the grocery trade, the hardware trade, the drug trade and the clothing trade. Another feature of the convention and one which also marks the up-to-date character of the Credit Men's movement was the publication of an abstract of the proceedings, including an outline of the work of each of the congresses above referred to, within a few hours after adjournment. Business Topics, a clipping sheet for the use of editors of the trade and commercial papers, was the medium by which the proceedings were distributed. A special edition of the clipping sheet, several times larger than usual, was employed. The convention adjourned at two o'clock on Friday, and in the course of the afternoon of Saturday this issue of Business Topics was in the post-office, addressed not only to the trade and commercial papers of the country, but also to every member of the Credit Men's Association, and a considerable list of selected names in addition.

The net results of the convention were to thoroughly indorse the policy adopted by the general officers of the preceding year and to make provision for continuing the work upon the lines already established. Jas. G. Cannon, Vice-President of the Fourth National Bank, New York, was re-elected to the presidency; T. Homer Green, of Sioux City, Iowa, was re-elected treasurer, and F. R. Boocock, of New York, was re-elected secretary.

In announcing the new year of the Ad Book, of which Fred. Vail Owen, 1043 Call Building, San Francisco, Cal., is editor, reference is made to a new department to be added, which is that of out-door advertising. It is explained that heretofore this phase of advertising has been neglected because, in the nature of things, the limits of the Ad Book precluded covering the entire field adequately. A way, however, has been found to meet the demand, and, accordingly, the readers of this enterprising journal are promised for the future various illustrations of what in recent years has become the most artistic form of display advertising.

Accountants' Associations

Illinois Institute of Accountants

At a special meeting of this organization, held in the office of the Illinois Steel Company, Chicago, Thursday evening, July 7, there was present by invitation A. O. Kittredge, Editor of ACCOUNTICS, who addressed the meeting on "Organization," the subject which had been nominated for the occasion. At the outset the speaker pointed out the objects to be attained by organizations among accountants and bookkeepers, the benefits which are likely to flow from efforts of this kind, and very briefly referred to the means which may be employed for sustaining interest in the work. Rapidly reviewing the history of the different organizations in this country among the craft, the speaker said that so far as he had been able to ascertain, no organization among bookkeepers, as such, exists outside of the United States. Numerous associations among accountants are to be found in various parts of the civilized world, but none of those engaged in routine bookkeeping outside of our own country. In this country mixed organizations abound, composed in part of bookkeepers and in part of accountants.

The special point made by the speaker was embodied in his explanation of why the bookkeeper, as a rule, is an overworked, underpaid, unappreciated and usually discouraged individual. He declared that it was due not alone to the temperament and personal peculiarities of the individuals, but more especially to the dual duties which are demanded of bookkeepers. They are called upon for both accounting and bookkeeping results.

He contrasted bookkeeping and accounting by pointing out that the latter is the scientific plan or scheme, while the former is the art or practice. The bookkeeper, as ordinarily situated, is called upon to perform the functions of both accountant and bookkeeper—that is, to design and install the system of accounts required in the business, maintain it in correct operation, and at the same time to attend to all the details of routine bookkeeping. However good a bookkeeper he may be, he frequently fails of being an accountant, and however good an executive man he may be at the desk, he frequently fails in the work of planning and engineering.

The remedy for this state of affairs, the speaker pointed out, is largely to be secured by bringing the business man to a realizing sense of the difference between accounting and bookkeeping. Whenever the employer realizes that there are two functions and two lines of duties he will discriminate between them to the material advantage of his employes. The speaker for this reason urged upon bookkeepers to favor independent audits and to welcome the occasional presence in the office of competent public accountants. He pointed out that through the work of public auditors and accountants employers will be led to perceive the difference between routine bookkeeping and the scientific plan upon which the bookkeeping is based. Whenever the bookkeeper is enabled to stand upon his own merits without having demanded of him that for which he has no qualifications nor technical equipment, he is likely to be appreciated for his real worth and be afforded an opportunity to secure recognition for special industry and devotion to duty. At the conclusion of the address a round table discussion followed, in which many interesting points and narratives of experiences were brought out.

American Railway Accounting Officers' Association

The tenth annual session of the American Railway Accounting Officers' Association was held in Atlantic City, N. J., May 25 and 26. It was largely attended. In fact, it is reported that there was the largest number of members present that has ever answered to the roll-call. Upwards of 200 members were registered and there were some seventy-five ladies in the gathering. The sessions were held in the music room of the Hotel Dennis. President Koscherberger, in his annual address, reviewed the work that would occupy the attention of the meeting, and referred especially to the organization and its annual gatherings as a school of instruction. He emphasized the need of railway accounting officers keeping more in touch with the equipment and materials that their companies have in service and on hand. He believed that by employing everything to the best advantage, a great economy in operating expenses would result to the advantage of the corporations. Due entirely to carelessness and oversight, much material, he said, which had cost money, was lost sight of, and allowed to accumulate. In course of time it deteriorated in value to such a degree as to be useless, thus making a loss of its total cost.

A report was submitted by the Executive Committee relating to matters of conference with the Interstate Commerce Commission and with the Railway Commissioners of various States. The report as read was adopted.

A report was submitted by the standing committee on freight. The report, which was carefully debated in various details, embodied a plan for the settlement of freight accounts of junction stations, and also a plan for auditing office settlements of interline freight accounts. Other features of the report of this committee included changes in the association's form of freight bill; changes in the association form of card way bill; revision upon present lines of what is commonly termed the Niagara Falls plan of auditing office settlements; the lightweighting and stencilling of freight cars from a revenue and accounting standpoint; whether the use of side cards on loaded cars cannot be dispensed with; whether it is necessary and advisable that regular tariff numbers, as well as special rate numbers, special contract numbers, and percentage division numbers, be quoted on way bills; formulating a plan for the settling between junction agents of prepaid accounts upon fast freight lines and other interline way bills; through billing for transcontinental freight, East and West, between the Atlantic and Pacific coast, and standard way bills.

The report of the standing committee on disbursements embodied among other features suggestions of local clearing houses for the settlement of car mileage balances, standard forms and methods of the Association, standard form of draft voucher, payment of sight drafts, etc.

The report of the special committee on nomenclature included among others definitions of such terms as "through," "way," "competitive" and "non-competitive."

The report of the standing committee on passengers covered such points as settlement of omnibus freight charges; efforts to promote the general adoption by members, of the recommendations of the association, and errors in interline reports. Among the general subjects discussed were the following: Classification of operating expenses; classification of construction and operating expenses for electrical railways; to what account should street lights prescribed by municipal ordnance, maintained at highway crossings, be charged? To what should the wages of general and local storekeepers be charged? and the minimum amount for which one road may make a bill against another on account of overcharge, and loss and damaged claims.

A paper was read by Marshall N. Kirkman, vice-president of the Chicago and Northwestern Railway, on the "Profit and Loss Accounts of a Railway."

Various features of entertainment were provided for this gathering by the citizens of Atlantic City, and in spite of inclement weather which prevailed a part of the time, the visitors and delegates had a very enjoyable time.

The officers elected for the ensuing year are as follows: President, P. A. Hewitt, of the C. C. C. & St. L. R. R.; first vice-president, H. D. Bulkley, of the B. & O. R. R.; second vice-president, Daniel Jones, of the P. & R. R. R.; secretary and treasurer, C. G. Phillips, of Chicago. The executive committee is composed as follows: William Nicholson, of the F. B. R. R.; H. A. Rubridge, of the C. & E. I. R. R.; G. J. Pollock, of the M. & T. R. R., and W. B. Bend, of the C. & G. W. R. R. Among the honorary members elected at this meeting was A. D. Penfold, late auditor of the Merchants' Dispatch Transportation Co., New York, and for many years past a member of the Institute of Accounts. The next convention is to be held in June, 1899, at Montreal.

Words of Commendation

From Preston H. Grover:

I acknowledge with much pleasure the receipt of copies of ACCOUNTICS from its first issue to date. I have had an extremely pleasant time examining the same. I presume you have received so many compliments from many who stand higher in the accounting profession than myself, that you will scarcely appreciate the testimony of one of the lesser lights, but I want, nevertheless, to send most hearty congratulations upon the extremely instructive monthly which you are issuing. I anticipate many pleasant hours in reviewing the articles which the numbers contain.

COST ACCOUNTS

Methods of Distributing General Expenses and Fixed Charges. A Symposium of Views by Prominent Manufacturers. Compiled by the Editor.

When we announced our series of articles on Cost Accounts in Manufactures, we included in the programme a symposium of views by accountants and experienced manufacturers with respect to methods of distributing general expenses and fixed charges—in other words, as to plans of loading the total of the apparent costs of the articles produced with those costs which are general and not specific. In carrying out the scheme, we addressed a considerable number of letters to leading manufacturers in different lines of business in all parts of the country. A very generous response has been made to our inquiries, and all who have written to us have indicated special interest in the general subject. Not a few have expressed themselves as being quite willing to contribute of their store of experience to the common fund, to an extent far beyond the scope of our questions.

It would be impossible, in the space that can be devoted to this subject, even though the article were to be extended through several numbers, to present in full all the interesting communications that we have received. We must content ourselves, therefore, with selections from the material at hand. In making the selection we shall attempt to cover as many different lines of trade and as many different sections of country as our space will permit.

The manager of a manufacturing concern, located in the central belt, which is very prominent in a line of business furniture, including filing cabinets, office desks and stationers' goods, and maintains various departments, more or less of which make goods to order, writes a letter, from which we take the following:

Office Specialties

We do not believe that the expense incurred by the office of a manufacturing concern is properly a part of the cost of the goods manufactured. We treat all items of expense, except salaries of officers, clerks, salesmen and the like, advertising, commissions, interest, bad debts and miscellaneous office expenses, as a part of factory expenses, and therefore as a part of the cost of manufacture. Our factory expenses include all such items as rent, taxes, insurance, fuel, heating and depreciation. In order to include this latter expense in our cost, we wipe out all such accounts monthly against the several departments of our business, subdivided on an arbitrary basis. A manufacturing concern conducting only one department would simply charge this cost to factory. We have various departments, each of which is credited with the goods that it turns out, at cost, as nearly as the same can be determined. This cost consists of labor and material, plus the amount which has been charged to the departments for general factory expenses, as above.

In order to enable the departments to determine what percentage they should add to their labor, to cover the amount charged to them for general expenses as above, we compare the average amount of payroll in the department for the preceding year (or, if the business happens to be growing rapidly, for the preceding half year or quarter year), with the average amount of fixed charges so debited to them. In the light of this comparison the rate of percentage is determined. If, at the end of the year, the records show that the department has made a considerable profit on this basis, we reduce the percentage for the new year. On the other hand, if the department has fallen behind, we increase the percentage, the intention being to bring the departments out as nearly even as possible.

It will be noticed that we apply this percentage to labor only. We carry our material at cost. We are particular not to fall short on this item, and on many kinds of material we have a standing value, as, for example, lumber. We figure lumber always to cost the same, at least until there is a very decided advance or decline in the market. However, if we pick up an exceedingly good bargain, the department that uses the material gets the benefit of it. The material is charged to the department at actual cost, while it is frequently credited to a department at an agreed cost. The result of this plan is that the percentage, which we apply to labor only, is very much higher than it would be if applied to the aggregate of labor and material. The reason for this, and it is a logical one, is that the percentage for fixed charges is not disturbed by fluctuations or differences in materials. As a fact, material does fluctuate, but in contrast labor does not change in rate to any great extent.

We are of the opinion that fixed charges are no more on a desk made of mahogany than on a desk made of plain sawed oak, although mahogany costs five times as much as the oak. Of course, this is on the assumption that the time that the article takes in going through the shop is the same. The cost of superintendence is the same, and there is no reason why the fixed charges on the mahogany desk should be any more than on the oak desk. We are of the opinion that this is contrary to usual methods. Nevertheless, we think it is right.

As we can only account for the time of our producers, we carry the non-producers, such as foremen, etc., by scaling upward the actual wages of the producers enough to cover the non-producers. This also we do by percentage method based on actual payrolls. If, for example, the non-producers of a department draw 20 per cent. of the payroll, then we figure each producer in that department at 25 per cent. more than we pay him.

On goods which we make in quantities for stock, when we find after two or more trials that the factory cost comes out about the same, we fix an arbitrary figure as the factory cost price, and this figure remains until it is materially changed, or until some good reason presents itself for making a new investigation of the cost. On special orders—that is, work made to order, of which we have a good deal—we allow the departments about one-fifth more for fixed charges than on stock work. This is to cover contingencies which are very well understood by all manufacturers who do order work.

In fixing our selling price, we advance it over our cost prices sufficient, first, to cover our office or administration expenses. This is easily arrived at by comparing the aggregate of such expenses with the output of our departments, or, as it might be called, our purchases from them. This is virtually the debit side of our Merchandise Account, and, of course, includes both material and labor, as well as the assessments for fixed charges on Factory Account. Second, we advance it enough to afford a profit.

Our experience convinces us that our method of providing for our factory fixed charges on labor alone is very much safer, more uniform and more satisfactory than adding a percentage to the aggregate of labor and materials, although in such factories as use only one kind of material all the time, such as iron or brass, the result would be pretty nearly right, simply by reason of the uniformity in value of the material used. In the case of a foundry, for instance, using nothing but pig iron as material, the result would be about the same. But if pig iron were to double in price, and the foundry could succeed in selling its goods at prices made up on the same basis, it would find itself making so much money that it would not know what to do with it. On the other hand, if the case were reversed, and pig iron declined one-half, the foundry managers who depended upon this system would wonder why they were not making money.

From a very carefully prepared letter, written by a prominent manufacturing firm in Connecticut, we take the following summary:

MACHINE TOOLS'

All known charges are added into the cost of the product. Unknown expenses are estimated as per statistics and other records, which we have carefully kept for a good many years, and by this plan are also added to the cost.

The secretary of a manufacturing corporation producing specialties in the machinery line that are used throughout the United States, writes as follows:

Although I have been in business for the past twenty-five years, I still find it a hard matter to place the fixed charges and general expenses of products. We have different methods of making quotations on work, and in connection therewith, we have a method special to ourselves for getting at the fixed charges and expenses for purposes of quotations. Our general expenses are, in most cases, pro rated on the cost of each man's labor. In quoting prices, we estimate the cost of production by the labor of the mechanics who will be most likely to do the work on the article quoted.

A manufacturing company producing a line of goods grading far above the ordinary and requiring high technical skill upon the part of many mechanics, submits the following:

Our system of computing the cost of goods is in most cases as follows: We take the payroll of a given department and divide it into two classes, known as the active class and the auxiliary class. The first class embraces all the operatives who work directly on the article itself. In the auxiliary class are such men as foremen, elevator men, sweepers, oilers, carriers and the like. We ascertain what proportion of the whole wages in this department on an average is paid to the auxiliary class, and we add to the labor done by the active class on any given line of goods a percentage to cover the ascertained proportion of auxiliary labor in that department. To this we add the material, and to the sum of both we add a further percentage to cover the general expense account.

The proportion which the general expense account bears to the material and labor consumed in our manufactures can be easily ascertained by reference to our expense account. This expense account covers salesmen, administrative force, bookkeepers, rent, steam, coal, light, repairs to buildings, taxes, etc. The average from year to year seldom varies more than one per cent. The percentage is smallest when the business is the largest.

A company manufacturing machinery and tools that is known throughout the world, and whose product holds the very highest rank, writes as follows:

It is our custom to add to the cost of material and cost of labor a percentage of the cost of labor, the said percentage being based upon our calculation of what we call general shop expenses, and those expenses which are not included in the labor expended directly upon the products. Our shop expenses include such items as salaries, etc.

One of the oldest and best-known manufacturers of special machinery in the

United States answers our inquiry as follows:

It is our practice to add to our costs certain rates per hour for all machine tool time charged, the rates being dependent upon the value of the machine on which the work is done. The balance of expenses is distributed in proportion to the wages entering into the cost.

A shoe manufacturing concern in the West writes as follows:

BOOTS AND SHOES.

The best way we have found of distributing general expenses and fixed charges against our shoes in figuring costs is by the percentage plan. The records of our business for past years give us the necessary data, and in our estimates for selling purposes we pursue the plan here outlined.

A large manufacturing concern producing a special article in iron, and whose works are in the Pittsburgh district, send a more detailed account of their cost methods than they are willing to have published. A summary is as follows:

PLATE IRON.

Materials and labor are carefully accounted for, as are also all direct charges, depreciation of plant, etc. Great care is taken to get as large a proportion of the costs of manufacture distributed in this manner as possible, leaving to be spread by way of fixed charges and general expenses just as small an amount as possible. Our sales employ the ton as the unit, and while the selling prices per ton vary somewhat, the difference in cost of product between the highest and lowest markets depends upon labor rather than upon material. Accordingly, the ton prices are to each other as the cost of the labor consumed in producing them.

The fixed charges and general expenses of the current year are estimated in the light of years in the recent past. The tonnage sales for the present year are likewise estimated in the light of past years. The amount of expenses to be spread, divided by the estimated tonnage to be made, gives the amount per ton to be added to other items of cost, in order to make the cost price cover general expenses. As the months of the current year pass by, watchful attention is given to the development of the business. If the production stated in tons is running very much above that of recent years, with no corresponding increase in the general expenses to be pro rated, the management realizes that the cost estimates are above actual figures. In turn, if the tonnage falls below the estimate and the fixed charges or general expenses remain the same, the management perceives that the cost price has been figured too low. In the light of the development of the business, then, the cost estimates are varied from time to time. This plan has been pursued for a number of years with detailed records carefully maintained, and thereby its accuracy and efficiency have been fully indicated.

A manufacturing concern operating in the New England States and having a very extended system of branch houses for the distribution of its goods, which, on account of their high standard of excellence, are known throughout the world, replies to our questions with respect to the distribution of general expenses, fixed charges, etc., as follows:

BICYCLES.

Our present method of loading the total figures, which consist of the cost of materials and the direct or producing labor, with their proper share of general factory expenses and fixed charges, is that of dividing the sum of such expenses and fixed charges by the total number of hours of direct or producing labor consumed. For instance, should the expenses for a given period amount to $5,000 and the hours of direct labor for the same period amount to 25,000, the constant to be used would be 20 cents per hour. On an order costing for stock $250 and for labor 1,000 hours at 25 cents = $250, the factory expenses would be figured 1,000 hours at 20 cents = $200, making the total cost $700. This plan, after a very careful investigation and consideration, seems to us to be a far more equitable manner of estimating than that which, until recently, we used. Our old plan, briefly, was ascertaining the percentage that the factory expenses and fixed charges bear to the direct labor for the same period, and then loading cost figures accordingly. This method was, of course, correct collectively, but was manifestly unfair in many individual cases. The objection to it was that it tended to burden skilled labor more heavily than the unskilled. In the majority of cases the reverse of this should be the rule.

Suppose, for example, a boy is employed at 10 cents an hour, who takes twice as long to do a given job as would a man at 25 cents an hour. The boy also requires more superintendence than the man, and is inclined to be more wasteful of supplies and harder on the tools. He is, of necessity, less skillful in the use of machinery. Figured upon the percentage method, on the basis of the figures above given, the boy's time would cost us for two hours 20 cents, and the factory expense, say at 80 per cent., 16 cents additional, making a total of 36 cents. The man's time, on the other hand, would cost for one hour 25 cents, and the factory expense at 80 per cent., 20 cents, making a total of 45 cents.

Contrast with this the plan of figuring with the hour constant, as is our present plan. The boy's time cost 20 cents. Two hours factory expenses at 20 cents or 40 cents makes a total of 60 cents. On the other hand, the man's time cost 25 cents, plus one hour's factory expense, 20 cents, making a total of 45 cents. This latter seems to us to be more nearly correct as a result.

We also use this plan of figuring upon piece work, the hours of piece workers being kept, as well as those of the day workers.

It should not be lost sight of, of course, that to arrive at a correct hour constant, a period of time covering all conditions of business should be taken. Were the busiest season alone to be figured, the constant would be too low, and the reverse would be the case if a slack season were taken. We think a year's experience is the best for this purpose, taking that of the previous year for the basis to use the present year, unless, indeed, the conditions of the present year are greatly changed as compared with the former year. However the figures are taken, they are to be corrected from time to time as changes occur.

We are the present year keeping track of our factory expenses by departments, and while this is a new plan for us, we have already gone far enough to discover that by doing so we are enabled to get at very much closer figures for the cost of the units of our production than we were able to establish before, when we loaded the whole of such expense on our direct labor for the complete factory. While the old way was satisfactory, so far as related to the cost of our completed product, it did not enable us to arrive at the correct cost of the individual units nor of the various operations applied to those units. For instance, some of our departments are full of expensive machinery, on which the annual depreciation is considerable, while others have no machinery at all. Certainly the latter should not be be charged with any portion of such depreciation, and yet these departments were so charged when we followed the plan of loading evenly on to all direct labor.

A prominent stove concern writes as follows:

STOVES AND RANGES.

It would be pretty hard for us to answer intelligently, in any sort of reasonable space, the question raised with reference to our method of distributing cost. We can only reply in a general sort of way. There are really two kinds of costs, one of which includes what are known as fixed costs, which are charged to certain items, as they are known to belong to those particular items. The other includes what are called diffused costs, and these are spread over the entire product.

Our method of figuring costs is that adopted by the National Association of Stove Manufacturers—in other words, it is that which is known as the "National Association of Stove Manufacturers' Cost Formula." In arriving at costs by this method, we reach what we consider to be absolute cost, because our cost ledger balances the same as our regular ledgers. In a line of goods made up of various kinds, such as steel ranges, high and low finish goods, etc., there is, of course, with the use of any formula, a question as to whether the cost of a certain article is accurately arrived at, owing to the fact that there are certain things which are not common to every article. However, as stated at the outset, it is a very large subject that we are discussing, and one that would be almost impossible to do justice to in correspondence. It would be useless to go into detail, for it would be impossible in that case to treat the subject in a letter of anything like a reasonable length.

The president of one of the leading stove manufacturing concerns of the East writes us as follows:

We use the formula of the National Association of Stove Manufacturers in computing the cost of our productions. Our plan, therefore, for loading the general manufacturing and selling cost of goods upon the specific cost of the goods is by the percentage method. What the percentage is for general manufacturing expense and for selling expense, we determine by our actual experience. For instance, if we pay for pig iron, electroplating, molding, mounting and trimmings the sum of $300,000 in our whole business during one year, and if we find that the costs grouped under general manufacturing expense amount to $120,000 during the same year, we simply add to the cost of pig iron, molding, mounting, electro-plating and trimmings of a specified stove 40 per cent. of the amount, thereby adding to it is pro rata of the general manufacturing expense. If, in the same way, the total cost of selling goods amounts, say, to $84,000 on a business represented by the first and second items above, $300,000 and $120,000, respectively, making a total of $420,000, we add to the corresponding cost of the single stove 20 per cent. of the amount to cover selling expenses. We do not know of any other just or safe method of computing costs, and we regard this system as simplicity in itself.

The manager of the accounting of a prominent manufacturing firm in Chicago, making a line of specialties in sheet metal, writes as follows:

MISCELLANEOUS TINWARE.

The selection of a proper unit in spreading fixed charges must obviously be governed by the nature of the business. The guiding principle in such a selection should be stability under the varying conditions which are likely to arise. If the product is uniform in kind, a quantity unit of product would seem most natural, as, for example, in blast furnace work, where the unit is the ton of pig iron. In lines where a varying product can all be referred to one principal type of machine, as in sheet mill work, the machine hour would be an excellent unit. In the greater majority of industries, however, variety of product or process makes such units impossible, and here the ordinary method is to apply fixed charges as a percentage on the sum of values of labor and material.

The principal objection to this method is that the amount of product which can be turned out in a given time by a given organization with a given plant, does not vary with the varying markets on labor and material. As the labor market, as a rule, is comparatively stable, it is, perhaps, better to accept the value unit than to endeavor to establish a quantity unit. The only practical quantity unit of labor is time, and the quality of labor is so various that this is not a fair measure. As regards material, however, a quantity unit is preferable, if attainable.

GALVANIZED SHEET IRON.

The manager of a very prominent concern engaged in rolling sheet iron and in the manufacture of galvanized iron writes that their preferred plan is to ascertain what percentage the general expenses and fixed charges are to the amount of production for a given period, say for one year, or where fluctuations are occurring with some degree of rapidity, less than one year. The percentage determined upon this plan is then added to the direct cost of materials and labor in any given lot of goods.

Political and Social Science

We are indebted to the American Academy of Political and Social Science, Philadelphia, for copies of several of the pamphlets which they have issued on political topics. Two of these are of particular interest at this time. One is "The Recognition of Cuban Belligerency," by Professor Amos S. Hershey, of the University of Indiana, and bears date June 16, 1896. The other is "The Intervention and Recognition of Cuban Independence," by the same author, and bears date in 1898. This latter paper was sent to press before the President's message on the Cuban situation was laid before Congress. Accordingly, it discusses the situation as it was before the war was commenced. Two other pamphlets are likewise of interest in this connection. One bearing date January, 1896, is entitled "McKinley and the Monroe Doctrine," and is by Lindley M. Keasbey, Ph. D., Bryn Mawr College. The other is entitled, "The Nicaraugua Canal and the Economical Development of the United States," and is by Emery Johnson, Ph. D., University of Pennsylvania. The object lesson which the people of the United States had a little while since in the matter of the journey of the Oregon from a harbor on the Pacific coast to join the Atlantic fleet in Cuban waters, a sail of some 18,000 miles, brings home the necessity of the Nicaragua Canal to every business man and to every voter. At present there is a demand for information concerning the Nicaragua Canal, and it will increase as the days go by, rather than diminish. Still another pamphlet before us, of the series referred to, is on "International Arbitration," by Eleanor L. Lord, of Smith College. Other pertinent publications on political topics, issued by the American Academy, include the following: "State Supervision for Cities," by Professor John R. Commons, of Syracuse University; "Problems of Municipal Government," by E. L. Godkin; "Home Rule for American Cities," by Ellis P. Oberholtzer, and "National and State Banks," by Horace White.

Press Clippings

Every business man sooner or later has thrust upon his attention the advantages that a press clipping bureau would be to him, either in his private capacity or in connection with his business. Periodicals are so numerous and time is so short that no one has the opportunity to read all that are put out, nor to watch the columns of a given class for paragraphs upon any stated subject. A press clipping bureau is an organized agency for doing for the individual what the individual is never able to do for himself. These remarks are suggested by a little pamphlet recently issued by the Press Clipping Bureau, managed by Robert and Linn Luce, with principal office at 68 Devonshire street, Boston. The bureau has been in existence ten years, and now employs sixty-three persons, occupies sixteen rooms and reads no less than 4,250 papers regularly. Among its customers are some who receive as many as 19,000 clippings a month. As many as 4,000,000 clippings a year are turned out. Every one who is interested in this subject will profit by writing for a copy of the book referred to, mentioning ACCOUNTICS.

Whatever you are from nature, keep to it; never desert your own line of talent. Be what Nature intended you for, and you will succeed; be anything else, and you will be ten thousand times worse than nothing.—Sydney Smith.

Have you not observed that there is a lower kind of discretion and regularity, which seldom fails of raising men to the highest station in the court, the church, and the law?—Swift.

Long and Short Leaf Ledgers

Several subscribers to ACCOUNTICS have requested information concerning the decision in the equity case of the Safeguard Account Company against Edward F. Wellington, in the Circuit Court of the United States, District of Massachusetts, the opinion in which was handed down by Judge Putnam some time since. The suit was argued largely upon Claim 1 of U. S. patent No. 393,506, which reads as follows:

"A blank book having full leaves of the same or substantially the same width, a part of which are provided near their outer edges with lines of perforation to form removeable margins, and the rest of which are unperforated, the perforated and unperforated leaves being introduced between each other throughout the book, with one or more of the perforated leaves between the unperforated ones, substantially as set forth."

Judge Putnam, in his opinion, first recites the nature and purposes of the invention, using language as follows:

"The advantage of a long and a short leaf ledger is that one column of names will answer for the pages on several narrow leaves of the book as well as for the wide page on which it stands and the opposing wide page. A book with a long and a short leaf is old. The book of the patent, however, is not made with a long and a short leaf, but with leaves of the same width, or substantially the same throughout, and so constructed by perforation, or its equivalent, that the user of the book can, without difficulty, make a long and a short leaf book, by removing so much of certain intervening leaves as is necessary, in order to so expose the name column of one page that it may be used with the other pages of the series.

"Before the invention in suit, to make a long and a short leaf ledger, it was generally best to make a book, in which all of the leaves were of full size, and then to cut from one or more leaves, following the leaf which contains the names column, a margin of proper width. Such a construction of a long and a short leaf book is difficult and expensive, from the book-binder's point of view, owing to the fact that the book, if it is to have the ordinary finish—namely, a flat, heavy, broad binding and colored, burnished edges—must be made and finished exactly like an ordinary book, and then have certain of its leaves shortened by cutting by hand. If the employee carelessly cuts the wrong leaf, the book is ruined. Moreover, the result is a book in which the outer edges of the leaves are flabby and liable to collect dust and become dog-eared, the covers themselves also being liable to become warped when not used. Looked at from the bookkeeper's point of view, such a book is difficult to use, for the reason that there is no firm, solid surface upon which to enter in the names column the various accounts. On the other hand, in the complainant's book, the leaves which are to be made short leaves are perforated before the book is bound up, and, in case of any error in the perforations, the leaf or sheet may be discarded when the sheets are gathered before stitching.

"The various processes which follow are those ordinarily practiced in making a long leaf book of equal thickness. The book may receive proper pressing and the edges of the leaves may be colored and burnished in the ordinary manner, and, in fact, be made without any increased expense in its manufacture over that of the ordinary long leaf book, except the cost of perforating. As the result, the accountant has a book in which the names may be easily written in the name column, for the reason that the book is solid throughout like an ordinary ledger, and yet, when it has been partially used, he may convert it into a long and a short leaf book, so that the same name column may apply to a number of pages."

Near the end of the opinion, Judge Putnam says:

"Sitting as triers of the facts, as well as of the law, we must take notice that the use of perforated lines in paper for the purpose of permitting easy separation, has for many years been common to all the arts where paper is used. Under these circumstances, its application to any particular art or any subdivision thereof cannot be regarded as involving invention, unless under special circumstances. We have great doubts whether the advantages claimed in this case exhibit utility of that striking character which stamps on the mind an impression of the actual presence of the spirit of invention. Nevertheless, in Thompson vs. Citizens' National Bank, the Court of Appeals for the Eighth District found invention in a patent in this same art, issued for a device of substantially the same nature as that at bar, though not the same. We feel constrained to follow the analogy of that decision, especially as the case at bar is one of doubt. Applying to the question of novelty the rule stated by Judge Lowell, we conclude that the patent has not been anticipated. No definite point has been made that the complainant may not prevail on the second claim of patent No. 393,506, if it does not on the first. Let there be a decree for the complainant under Rule 21, sustaining its suit on both claims of patent No. 393,506, with costs for complainant."

The above decision is apparently very broad and should be eminently satisfactory to the Safeguard Account Company, as no doubt it is. It places the wide and narrow leaf ledger in a proper light before the accounting public, and also clearly defines the status of improved methods of constructing books of the general class.

Correspondence

Percentage of Profits

From W. H. C., Boston:

I have a question that I would like to propose for such discussion as the readers of ACCOUNTICS may see fit to give it. It is as follows: In 1896 the operations of a certain factory showed a loss of $500; in 1897 the operations of the same factory made a profit of $1,500. What was the increase in 1897 over 1896, and what was the per cent. of increase in 1897 over 1896? It appears to me that 1897 shows an increase of $2,000 profit over 1896, but I am unable to name the per cent. of increase. Will some reader of ACCOUNTICS help me?

Accounting of Receiverships and Assignments

From J. B. G., Manitou, Colo.

I should be glad to see discussed in ACCOUNTICS methods of handling the accounts of receiverships—that is, a discussion of the general principles. The details, of course, I realize, must be adapted to the requirements of the business involved. I have tried different plans in the accounting of assignments and receiverships, but desire to keep pace with the general progress that is being made, hence my suggestion.

The plan that I adopted in the case of a receivership I now have in hand is as follows: I closed the books of the corporation and transferred the assets and liabilities to the receiver's ledger. Supplies and manufactured stock were, of course, carried over according to the fact. The difference in form as to the liabilities between those shown on the corporation ledger and those transferred to the receiver's ledger is that on the latter the accounts payable appear under the title of "Accounts Payable of the Jones Manufacturing Company." The notes are designated as "Bills payable prior to ——, 1898." The Profit and Loss Account I have placed on the receiver's ledger under the head "Profit and Loss Account of the Jones Manufacturing Company." This plan has its defects as well as other plans that I have used. In each case, of course, a report is made showing what the receiver does with his trust during the period covered by the report.

I had in view the plan of taking the inventory and charging it on the receiver's ledger under the different classifications and making the contra-entry "The Jones Manufacturing Company," whence the assets were derived, as a brief method of dealing with the assets on the receiver's main ledger. However, I saw objections to this plan.

In closing the books of the corporation I did not close to Profit and Loss such items as Unexpired Insurance Premiums and accounts of like nature on the one side, and accrued interest due on the various issues of bonds, and taxes accrued and due on the other, so that as far as the assets are concerned they followed into the receiver's ledger at the face value shown by the corporation ledger. While the unearned premiums from one point of view amount to, say, $5,000, yet the receiver could collect at short rates only.

I have before me statement of assets and liabilities of a receiver as follows:

ASSETS:	
Operating Assets, Materials and Supplies	$170,000
Current Assets, Cash and Accounts.	600,000
Other Debit Accounts, Additions to Plant and Equipment..............	550,000
	$1,320,000
LIABILITIES:	
Current Vouchers, Pay Rolls and Debts Due............................	$275,000
Other Credit Accounts:	
Receiver's Certificates................	200,000
Sundries	20,000
Balance Credit of Income Account.	825,000
	$1,320,000

The statement of the Income Account, of course, bears out the above balance. When the receiver assumed charge of the estate, he received a plant costing about $1,500,000, and there must have been $100,000 in materials and supplies on hand and a large amount of debts due, but how are the amounts accounted for?

In what I have presented I trust there will be found enough to call out expressions from accountants who have had experience in matters of this kind, and that a discussion may be started which will be of general advantage. I shall be very glad indeed to read the experience of those who have had to do with receiverships.

A Possible Balance

"My dear sir, your books are in frightful disorder. Don't you have to make up a deficit sometimes?" "O, yes, sometimes. But then, sometimes there's a surplus!"—Fliegende Blaetter.

Accountics

The Office Magazine.

A. O. KITTREDGE, F. I. A., C. P. A., EDITOR.
E. R. KITTREDGE, ASSOCIATE.

Accountics is devoted to the Science of Accounting, to the Art of Bookkeeping and to the advocacy of Improved Office Methods.

Subscription.—One dollar a year, payable in advance.

Postage is prepaid by the publishers in the United States, Canada and Mexico. For all other countries in the Postal Union, subscribers must add 50 cents a year.

Discontinuances.—In the absence of specific orders to discontinue at the end of the subscription term the magazine will be continued and a bill sent.

Remittances should be by Draft, P. O. Order or Express Order, payable to the order of the ACCOUNTICS ASSOCIATION. Money and postage stamps are at the risk of the sender, unless sent by express or in registered letters. Add 10 cents each to checks on local banks to defray collection charges.

Advertising Rates will be quoted on application.

Official Journal.—This publication, by resolutions duly passed, has been made the official publication of the following organizations :—
THE INSTITUTE OF ACCOUNTS.
THE NEW YORK CHAPTER of the Institute of Accounts.
THE WASHINGTON CHAPTER of the Institute of Accounts.
THE HARTFORD CHAPTER of the Institute of Accounts.

ACCOUNTICS is the accredited medium of intercommunication between members of the Institute of Accounts wherever located.

ACCOUNTICS ASSOCIATION,
Publishers,
Wool Exchange, New York.

Entered at the Post Office New York as Second Class Matter

The Tatum Automatic Order Holder

There exists in every office the need of a binder or holder adapted for retaining a single sheet or a small number of sheets. What is wanted is the equivalent of a book when in use, and yet something having such features of construction as will release the sheets instantly when required and readily permit a new supply to be inserted. Many merchants, especially in wholesale lines, follow the plan by which salesmen's orders are entered by the salesmen directly on an order sheet and sent into the house with all the original markings. This order sheet is used not only to ship from, but also to charge from. By this means an immense amount of copying is avoided, resulting not only in a saving of labor, but also diminishing the danger of error. For this purpose a holder adapted to retain a single order or a number of orders in a cover, the substantial equivalent of a book, is eminently desirable.

The illustration shows a form of holder recently put upon the market by the Sam'l C. Tatum Company, Cincinnati, Ohio. The peculiarity of the holder is that the jaws lock open automatically when the top cover is folded back and pressed down. By pressing the catch or spring button shown in the cut, the jaws automatically close so as to tightly grip the papers that have been inserted. The holder is without projecting springs or wires, and therefore a number can be stacked up in good shape wherever required. The parts of which the holder is composed are very simple, and are made to stand the hard usage to which such appliances are usually subjected. No tools or keys are required to open or close the holder.

THE TATUM ORDER HOLDER

To put in a new sheet the cover is bent back so that the front and back covers are about in line. To remove or sort the sheets already in, the top cover is pressed back still further, until the small catch underneath has set, and thus holds the boards apart at an angle. When in this position any desired sheet is easily removed, while by pushing the catch forward with the fingers, the jaws close again and nip the papers, as already described. A stock of these goods is carried at the New York office of Samuel C. Tatum Company, 102-104 Fulton Street, and the goods are also handled by the stationery trade.

We are indebted to the B. F. Goodrich Co., Akron, Ohio, for a mammoth colored lithograph, appropriate for framing, representing the company's plant. The group of buildings is impressive, and is so shown in the picture as to give the customers of the house an excellent idea of what they have got to depend upon for their supply of goods. The floor area is upwards of nine acres. The steam boiler capacity is given as 3,700 horse-power, and the engine as over 3,000 horse-power. The dynamo capacity of the establishment is 261 kilo Watts. In the way of fire protection there is an independent fire brigade, supplied with 2,650 feet of fire hose, and called into action from fifty-four fire-alarm boxes. Every box is also connected with the city fire department

Accountics

The Office Magazine

ONE DOLLAR A YEAR / TEN CENTS A COPY
AUGUST-SEPTEMBER 1898
VOLUME III / NUMBERS 5-6

CONTENTS.

Published by the ACCOUNTICS ASSOCIATION: Wool Exchange New York

Accountics

VOL. III AUGUST-SEPTEMBER 1898 NOS. 5 and 6

The Monthly Statement

This number of ACCOUNTICS is sent out in an enlarged form and with a double date in the head line. The preparation of its contents falls to that time of the year usually recognized among accountants and business men in general as the vacation period, and during the present year characterized by high temperature, excessive humidity and conditions generally that have made prolonged labor a matter of great difficulty and hardship. The editor has had no vacation, and to make up for the lack of a vacation as well as to be able to meet the many imperative demands upon his time, this plan is resorted to. It may enable him to obtain a little breathing space. It is always easier to produce in a single lot a stated quantity of goods of given quality, or perform at one time a stated amount of work of a given character, than to turn out two lots of goods or perform two amounts of work that in the aggregate amount to the same. We offer these remarks by way of explanation and not as apologies. The magazine by its contents in quantity and kind must speak for itself.

By way of further personal explanation, and as indicating the need of a vacation, or rest period, using the term in the sense of cessation from labor and freedom from stated duties, it may be mentioned that since the middle of June the editor has kept professional engagements in no less than seven different States, together with appointments in the District of Columbia and Province of Ontario. While covering many miles of travel, by rail and boat, much of it over so-called routes of summer tours, visiting many of the larger cities in the Union, meeting numerous business acquaintances and greeting hosts of friends, the whole experience being a complete change from usual office routine, there is withal in the final result a sense of weariness. Rest is sometimes defined as a change of labor, and before now we have secured very complete rest by even so small a change as removing from one desk to another, or transferring our work from one office to another. In the work of this summer, however, we seem to have had too much change to feel entirely refreshed. The old farmer encouraged his men all the morning in hoeing corn by the promise of a rest—that is, change of labor—in the afternoon. When the midday lunch had been dispatched he put them at the enticing work of building stone wall. We feel as though it were a stone-wall-building kind of rest that we have been having.

Business becomes so active at times that the bookkeepers, including ledger clerks and entry clerks, find it hard to keep abreast of the demands made upon them. They fall behind in the narrative save only as they are reinforced by extra help. So it is in the grand account of the nation's progress at this time, and not alone of the nation's progress but of the progress of the world, of which our nation is a most important part. It is more than the ordinary historian can do to keep abreast of the facts as they daily transpire. Scarcely four months have passed since the declaration of war against Spain, and yet how much history has been made in that time? In the East, in the language of Commodore Dewey, "we have taken an empire, without the loss of a man," and in the West we occupy Cuba and Porto Rico. Incidentally we are already administering the public schools of our new possessions, and in Santiago alone 4,000 pupils commence a course in English in September. Our veterans are now marching homeward, and the volunteers generally are being mustered out of service, for the war is over. That the returning troops are veterans is amply sustained by a glance at the bronzed faces of some as they march up Broadway, and the haggard features of others as they are tenderly transported in street cars and carriages.

Nor is history being rapidly made in and by our own country alone. On the contrary it would appear that the whole world is alert, and so used to surprises have we become that it seems as though there was no news in the morning papers whenever they fail to announce some great accomplishment or make public new schemes of diplomats and plans of governments in general.

The advanced and aggressive position of the Czar of Russia, in asking for a conference of the nations looking to disarmament and the settlement of questions in dispute by peaceful arbitration, is one of the most important events in the history of the century. No one can doubt that the success of Dewey in Manila Bay, of Sampson and Schley in the destruction of Cervera's fleet, and of our gallant army in the capture of Santiago, have made times propitious, for such a suggestion as the Czar alone, of all the potentates of the world, could offer in a way to command attention. So after all our own country remains the actuating cause. From present indications the balance sheet to be made up at the close of the nineteenth century is something very different from anything that could have been estimated at the beginning of the period, even as the close of a year's business in commercial affairs is often very different in profits and losses and in distribution of capital from what was expected when the year was begun.

On another page in this issue we present a very interesting paper on "Partnership Accounts," prepared by Wilton C. Eddis, Chartered Accountant, and read in May last before the Ontario Institute of Chartered Accountants. This paper, while read before a considerable body of expert accountants and experienced business men, was primarily intended for instruction of the accountant students, who were about to take the Institute examinations. It has the merit of being a very explicit and straightforward discussion of the principles of partnerships, arranged in a way to command the attention and respect of the expert, and also to be of special advantage in instructing beginners and learners. This paper, taken in series and compared and contrasted with that on "Corporations: Their Importance and Use," by Chas. Dutton, read a short time since before the New York Chapter of the Institute of Accounts, constitutes a very desirable addition to business literature. It is to be noticed that Mr. Eddis refers to the corporate form of doing business primarily, and contrasts therewith the partnership method of conducting business. Without saying so, it is very evident that he prefers the corporate form. Mr. Dutton's treatment of the subject made the contrast the other way, referring to the partnership form as the original type, and contrasting therewith the advantages gained by the corporate form. He also recommended the latter plan.

To one point particularly would we direct attention in passing, and that is to the remarks made by Mr. Eddis with respect to partners keeping a separate account, to which profits should be placed, thus leaving their capital accounts untouched, except at such intervals as are designated by mutual agreement. He asserts that this method of keeping capital accounts is occasionally adopted, and deplores the fact that it is not more generally brought into use. An accountant of wide experience and connected with prominent organizations in New York, discussing the same point some time since, advised in the matter of partnerships that capital account on the books be treated the same as capital account in the case of a corporation. The position that he took, in the light of special experience in matters of this kind, was that the articles of agreement should establish the investments, and, assuming that there were two, three, or even five or more partners, that their capitals should be pooled, so far as the general books were concerned, and therein their capital be represented by one amount. He advised, in turn, that each be allowed a salary or a drawing account, and that finally, when profits were declared, that they be divided according to the articles of agreement and carried to the respective accounts of the several partners, thus offsetting drafts, other than stipulated salary allowances. Although he did not touch upon the adjustment that would be necessary in the case of the partnership making a loss, undoubtedly his thought provided a means for it that would be equally appropriate and as readily applied. His intention in the matter was to save accountants and bookkeepers very much of the special labor there is in adjusting partnership accounts where disputes have arisen, or where something has gone wrong, by having all those matters attended to in the article of agreement, thus letting the partners adjust their differences between themselves outside of the books of the business. There are arguments on both sides of this proposition, both of a legal character and those affecting general expediency, and the matter is alluded to here only for the purpose of provoking thought on the part of those who are interested in the subject.

Every accountant who sets out to analyze a system of accounts or to write a paper upon some division of practical accounting, is almost sure to encounter early in the work the condition of uncertainty which prevails with respect to many terms that he finds necessary to use. The terminology of bookkeeping and accounting at best is in a deplorable state of uncertainty. It shows the lack of effort upon the part of some master mind to arrange its terms into something like scientific order, and to assign to each a definite meaning. Just what the remedy is to be we do not pretend to guess. In the general evolution through which accounting is passing a better order of things is likely to come about in the course of time, but just at present the same terms are being used with different meanings by various accountants and authors, and the same meaning is being indicated by different terms. When we turn abroad for precedent in matters of this kind and examine the works of British accountants, the confusion becomes greater. There are not only numerous dicrepancies in the use of terms among them, but they employ certain terms in very common use wherever the English language is spoken to mean very different things from what the same terms are understood to mean in this country. Not only do these difficulties exist with respect to the names of individual accounts, but they also prevail wherever the effort is made to designate operations. The accountant is obliged in many cases to borrow terms from the mechanical trades, particularly when his accounts deal with mechanical items, but even the mechanical trades fail to supply the proper quota of words, with meanings so thoroughly established as to leave no ground for misunderstanding or dispute.

Is the art of accountancy advancing and is accounting science making progress? To the first question the answer is undoubtedly in the affirmative. With regard to the second, some readers may be disposed to ponder for a moment before giving a reply. Assuming that the science of accounucs is advancing, a question that might well be raised is, At whose hands is the advancement being made? Is scientific accountancy being developed by those trained in the traditions of the art, or is it being advanced at the hands of those who have recently come into the ranks of the profession and who attack the problems which are presented without any knowledge of precedents?

This train of thought with respect to accounting is suggested by a paragraph which appears in one of the newspaper accounts of the life of Sir Henry Bessemer, who has recently died. Of all the generation of which he was a representative, Bessemer left a more indelible mark upon metallurgical science than any other. Bessemer steel, the discovery of which was his, introduced an era of industrial development, the boundaries of which are not yet fully understood. But Bessemer was not originally a metallurgist. His education and training in early life were in other directions, and he is a conspicuous example, out of many that might be cited, of those who have contributed in a remarkable manner to the advancement of applied science, who were not originally trained for their chosen work.

It is said of Bessemer that he always had a leaning toward mechanical pursuits. He was educated as an engineer, but while he was demonstrating to the French military authorities at Vincennes the results of a system which he had invented, of firing elongated projectiles from high, smooth-bore cast-iron guns, a military man said to him that such projectiles would be of little use unless stronger metal could be obtained for the guns. The invention was limited by the strength of cast-iron. There was the need in order to utilize the invention to have better metal for the guns. This was Bessemer's incentive to investigate the properties of iron and steel, and the methods in use of making iron and steel. At the outset he did not have the least idea of how he was to accomplish his purpose, which was to secure a metal strong enough for artillery purposes, simply because the science of metallurgy was not familiar to him. However he went at his work thoroughly in earnest and altogether untrammeled. The world knows the result. Concerning this he afterwards formulated a theory as follows: "I find that persons wholly unconnected with any particular business have their minds so free and untrammeled to view things as they are, and as they would present themselves to an independent observer, that they are the men who eventually produce the greatest changes." It is unnecessary to particularize further. Sir Henry Bessemer's life work is the best evidence of the correctness of his theory.

Returning to the art and practice of accounts: If progress is being made, by whom is it being made? Are the bookkeepers and accountants, trained from youth up in the conventional methods of bookkeeping, the ones who are the most aggressive in investigation and the most successful in adaptations and applications? Without particularizing in the least, we venture to say that those who consider themselves thorough accountants, because they have "been in the business all their lives" and know very little outside of the narrow lines of their profession, are very likely to lose sight of the opportunities which others, entering the profession later, and without their drill and discipline, will perceive and avail themselves of. Accounting science is progressive in its nature, and is destined to be developed to a point undreamed of by many who are in the ranks at the present time. If the usual rule holds good, a large share of that development will be made by those who have been primarily trained, not for bookkeeping and accounting, but, instead, in some other branch of applied science, and whose view-point, therefore, is so lofty and whose vision is so unobscured that they are able to perceive things as they really are and as they would present themselves to an independent observer.

Some men deem it an honor to be elected a director in a company; others regard is as a responsibility from which they would gladly free themselves; still others are perfectly willing to be directors for the glory and money there is in it. In a busy center like either one of the great cities of the land, and more especially like New York, it is hard to get men to attend board meetings without some special stimulation thereto. Accordingly a number of the financial institutions proceed upon the plan of compensating directors, not by salaries, but by an amount paid in hand at the directors' meetings. Those directors who assemble and direct get compensation and those who are absent from the meetings do not get anything. Some of the big companies in New York pay their directors $20 each for every meeting they attend, and for the smaller companies the fees are $10 and $5. It is astonishing how eagerly men of considerable wealth and of high standing and responsibility in the community look after the matter of their fees as directors. At least one very prominent financier makes it a point never to accept a director's place in any company that does not pay a fee of $25 per meeting. He looks upon his time as worth at least that much.. Very often the meetings are purely formal and last but a few minutes. Usually, regular meetings are held monthly or quarterly, or, in case of panics may be weekly or oftener.

Not only are companies obliged to give their directors good reason for attending the meetings of the board, but they are also under the necessity of securing their prompt attendance upon committee meetings; and, therefore, the compensation of directors is frequently increased by a scale of fees extending to committee work. They get extra pay when they attend committee meetings. When there is important work to be prepared for submission to the whole board, the committee meetings may be held two or three times a week, or even daily, and frequently extend over a considerable period. The committee attendance fee is usually about one-half of the director's fee. From this it will be seen that the occupation of a director in New York, in a certain class of companies at least, is remunerative.

The Farmer's Cost Accounts

By Rollin Jeffries

While discussing the general subject of Cost Accounts in Manufactures, it is pleasant to turn to the use of cost records in other branches and divisions of business activity. Farming would, perhaps, seem to be the last industry in which scientific cost records would be kept, and yet a moment's thought shows that there are as good reasons for the farmer knowing what it costs him to produce his different crops as for the manufacturer to know what his output costs. A recent issue of the Journal of the American Statistical Association contains a resumé of facts and conclusions reached by the Agricultural Experiment Station of Illinois, touching the production of corn and oats in that State in the year 1896. The account presented by our contemporary is of great interest to the thoughtful student, for much that is contained therein emphasizes the value and importance of cost records.

Various attempts have been made in the past to ascertain the cost of wheat growing in particular States, but the answers resulting therefrom have been unsatisfactory and widely divergent. We presume that similar inquiries addressed to the different factories throughout the land in any line of industry would have produced similarly unsatisfactory and divergent answers. There is no satisfactory basis of comparison. Therefore, in this regard agriculturists and manufacturers may be said to be upon a similar footing. The divergence of the answers with respect to the cost of wheat growing, it is pointed out, may have been due to the fact that the investigation was made in different years. As a fact, the harvests of no two years are exactly alike.

A farmer spends a certain sum in cultivating say fifty acres of ground. The cost per bushel of wheat raised depends upon the amount of the yield. He may reap ten bushels to the acre, or a considerably larger amount, the varying results being due to wetness, dryness, hailstorms, ravages of insects, or other contingencies. His cost for the fifty acres will be the same in every case, but the cost per bushel will vary with the quantity harvested. Therefore the result of one year is no sure criterion for another. In the light of these facts it would seem that various industries are somewhat alike in their uncertainties. Manufacturing and farming are not entirely dissimilar.

While the farmer may feel that his success depends largely upon causes beyond his control, the experienced manufacturer knows that there is also an element of chance in his business. The history of every factory in almost every line of industry will show that there are periods of business drought, as well as periods of drought affecting the farmer's growing crops. General expenses are the same, although the output may prove to be less than half what was expected. The result is a large loss where otherwise there would have been a generous profit. Continuing the parallel, there is a wide difference between different farms in the same year, and between different cultivators of the farms, even where the farms are of approximate equal fertility. Some farmers are skillful, methodical, industrious and economical. Others are lazy, shiftless and wasteful. On the other hand, some managers of factories are skillful and up-to-date, having the ability to avail themselves of every opportunity of saving cost that offers. Others are far behind the times, are terribly conceited in their self-sufficiency, and in general continue to do things as they used to be done, regardless of the demands of the present moment and the great advancement that has been made in processes.

It is not likely, in the near future at least, that there will be reached a statement of the general average of cost among the factories in any line of industry. We are not likely, for example, to have spread upon statistical records the average cost of a pair of shoes or of a ton of pig iron, or of a yard of cotton cloth, or of any other article. Nor is it to be supposed that the investigation of the various agricultural experiment stations will ever produce a satisfactory average as to the cost of any item of agricultural products. The agriculturist is interested in records of cost in comparison with selling prices as much as is the manufacturer in similar statistics of his business. If a certain crop in a given territory cannot be produced to sell profitably at the price fixed by those who enjoy the greatest advantages, then the farmer should change his crop, substituting something upon which he can make money. So the manufacturer, if he cannot produce goods to sell in competition with those factories which are most thoroughly equipped and most favorably located, should either change his location and equipment or get to manufacturing something better adapted to his location and the facilities he has. The law of the survival of the fittest can no more be disregarded in making goods than in tilling the soil.

Partnership Accounts*

By Wilton C. Eddis, C. A.

In dealing with the subject of Partnership Accounts and the numerous interesting problems frequently arising therein, I have thought it best to preface our inquiries by very briefly considering how partnerships may be formed. First there must be an agreement between the partners, and this agreement may be either in writing or verbal. In short, when any persons jointly work together with a view of making a profit, even though one takes no active part, there is a partnership, at any rate as far as the particular undertaking is concerned.

The principal difference between the partner in a firm and the shareholder in a Joint Stock Company is that the former is liable to the firm's creditors until they are paid; whereas the shareholder is only liable for the amount of shares he has subscribed for, and that have been duly allotted to him. There are certain exceptions as regards the liability of partners, but the principle involved is, that a partner who wishes to escape such liability must be so described in the articles of partnership and must take no part in the management of the business. Where the liability of any partner is thus limited the partnership is called a Limited Partnership, and to form such a partnership a certificate as provided by the act (this refers to Ontario) has to be signed, giving inter alia the following particulars:

(1) The name or firm under which the partnership is to be conducted.

(2) The general nature of the business to be transacted.

(3) The names of all the general and special partners interested therein and their usual places of residence.

(4) The amount of Capital Stock which each special partner has contributed.

(5) The period at which the partnership is to commence and the period at which it is to terminate.

No such partnership shall be deemed to have been formed until certificate referred to has been made as required by the act respecting Limited Partnerships in Ontario.

In such a Limited Partnership the partners are known as General Partners and Special Partners. "General Partners" are responsible as General Partners are by law, and they only are authorized to transact any business and sign for the partnership and bind the same. Special Partners are not liable for the debts of the partnership beyond the amount by them contributed to the Capital, but besides taking no part in the management their names must not be used in the name of the firm, if they are with their privity they will be deemed General Partners.

In Ontario, all persons associated in partnership for trading, manufacturing or mining purposes must deliver a declaration to the Registrar, duly signed by them in the proper form required. This declaration has to be filed within six months next after the formation of the partnership.

It can readily be conceived how difficult it becomes to settle accounts between partners when the agreement is merely verbal and the evidence has to be carefully weighed.

Common sense and experience clearly show that all partnership agreements or "Articles" should be in writing, and further, too much care cannot be given to this most important, and far too neglected matter. It is strange how careless otherwise shrewd and careful business men often are where agreements are concerned. The basis or structure of all partnerships is this agreement, right along, and many a poor widow or orphans would be better off to-day had proper provisions been included in the "Articles" of the deceased father to provide for the contingency of death.

T. M. Stevens, M. A., Barrister-at-Law, in a paper read before the Institute of Chartered Accountants in London, refers to the drawing up of Partnership Articles as follows:

"I desire to point out the necessity of carefully settling the Articles of Partnership so as to arrange for these questions (viz., 1. The method of valuation of a retiring partner's share. 2. His position relating to the good-will. 3. His rights to profits earned or interest accrued after the date of his retirement), whilst there is as yet no probability of a dispute. Let what is desired be stated in so many words: the Articles may be altered at any time by general consent, so that if the plan adopted at the beginning of the

*Paper read before the Institute of Chartered Accountants of Ontario, at Toronto, on the 19th of May, 1898.

partnership does not prove workable, there will be no difficulty in making any alteration. I think, whenever the firm is intended to carry on a large business or where the property is considerable, that the Articles should be submitted, after consideration by the solicitor, to counsel expert in these matters, and also to a Chartered Accountant, whose views might be embodied in the instruction to counsel; the initial expense will generally be saved over and over again before the lapse of many years."

The subject now before us is not merely one of bookkeeping as regards the conduct of any particular business, but bookkeeping as regards the accounts of the partners themselves.

There are two accounts which are treated differently in the books of a partnership as compared with those of a Joint Stock Company. These accounts are Capital Account and Profit and Loss Account, to use a well-known term.

In a Joint Stock Company the "Capital Account" should represent the amount of paid-up Capital, and this balance cannot be withdrawn during the existence of the company; and the Profits or Losses are carried to a separate account, and when a dividend is paid it can only be taken from the balance at credit thereto. On the other hand, in a Partnership Account the Capital Accounts of the partners show their respective Capital invested in the business; and any profit or loss resultant from said business is duly credited or charged to their Capital Accounts in proportion to their interests thus shown, or in the terms arranged in their Partnership Articles. Lindley defines "The Capital" of a partnership as "the aggregate of the sums contributed by its members for the purpose of commencing or carrying on the partnership business and intended to be risked by them in that business."

Partnership Articles often and wisely make provision to prevent the impairment of Capital by prohibiting the partners from withdrawing the Capital originally invested. Of course there would be nothing to prevent the partners from keeping a separate account to which profits could be placed and leaving their Capital Accounts untouched, except at stated intervals and by mutual agreement. This method of keeping Capital Accounts is occasionally adopted, but far too often the accountant finds that the business he is called in to report upon has been simply starved to death by the partners withdrawing too much cash for their own personal expenses, in anticipation of the big profits, which, unfortunately for their own interests and their creditors, never eventuated.

Let us now consider the subject from a practical and elementary standpoint; and in writing this paper I have borne in mind that while I have the privilege of addressing some of our leading accountants and business men, yet these papers are primarily intended for students, who contemplate going up for the Institute Examinations. Let us then take for our first illustration, "the formation of a new partnership and the opening of the books." Jones and Smith have gone into partnership and each places $1,000 in the business. In all cases of new partnerships or when a change of partners is made involving a fresh opening of the books, the best and invariable rule is to make out a balance sheet, as I shall endeavor more clearly to demonstrate later on. In this case it is very simple.

LIABILITIES.		ASSETS.	
Jones' capital ac't	$1,000	Cash	$2,000
Smith's " "	1,000		

Now, supposing Jones has an established business and has arranged to take Smith into partnership. Before opening the new books it will be necessary to have full particulars of the liabilities and assets of Jones, as well as the amount that Smith is investing. Let the following represent Jones's balance sheet, which Smith has duly examined and approved of.

LIABILITIES.		ASSETS.	
Sundry creditors	$1,000	Cash on hand and in bank	$ 390
Jones' capital ac't	6,000	Sundry debtors	2,670
		Merchandise	1,990
		Fittings, etc	450
		Goodwill	1,500
	$7,000		$7,000

The balance sheet then made for the new firm of Jones & Smith, supposing Smith introduced $3,000 capital into the business, would be as follows:

LIABILITIES.			ASSETS.	
Sundry creditors		$1,000	Cash on hand and in bank	$3,390
Jones' capital acc't	$6,000		Sundry debtors	2,670
Smith's capital acc't	$3,000	$9,000	Merchandise	1,990
			Fittings, etc	450
			Goodwill	1,500
		$10,000		$10,000

and from this balance sheet the new books would be opened.

I might here notice the item "goodwill"

account $1,500 in the assets. Jones, in preparing his statement for Smith increased his capital account by this amount so that it should represent his proportionate interest in the business, the Partnership Articles in this case stating that profits were to be declared on that basis.

It must be clearly understood that, where any arrangement is made for a division of profits, this also holds should losses have to be made good instead, even though this latter contingency has never been contemplated or mentioned.

In cases where the Capitals invested are of equal amount or bear the same ratio in which the profits are paid, no difficulty would occur in the adjustment of losses; but where the capitals invested are not equal or do not bear such a ratio, difficulties and apparent inequities may arise and this should be provided for in the Partnership Articles. Lindley refers to this point as follows:

"The only case which practically gives rise to difficulty is when partners have advanced, or agreed to advance, unequal capitals and to share profits and losses equally. If nothing more than this is agreed a deficiency of capital must be treated like any other loss, and the assets remaining after payment of all debts and advances must be distributed amongst the partners so as to make each partner's loss of capital equal; and if the assets are not sufficient there must be such a contribution amongst the partners, or some of them, so as to put all on an equality. But, if the true meaning of the partners is that all debts shall be paid out of the assets, and that any surplus assets remaining after payment of debts shall be divided between the partners in proportion to their interests therein or to their capitals, effect must be given to such an agreement, and those partners who agree to bring in most capital must lose most."

I will illustrate this by an example which will explain the matter clearly. A. B. and C. are three partners, investing respectively, $200, $500 and $1,000, and dividing profits equally. The business is wound up and results in a loss of $900 after paying all claims. Under the former method A. pays $300, B. $300 and C. $300, leaving their capital accounts as follows:

A. owing $100, or losing all his capital and 5-10ths besides.

B. owing $200, or losing 6-10ths of his capital.

C. owing $700, or losing 3-10ths of his capital.

Under the latter arrangement the loss would be divided in proportion to their interests, viz., A.s $200 would pay 2-17ths of $900; B.s $500 would pay 5-17ths of $900; C.s $1,000 would pay 10-17ths of $900.

It is quite possible that the preliminary balance sheets of Jones & Smith might be made up without Smith's name appearing. Suppose, for example, that Smith introduced no cash but brought valuable knowledge and a business connection with him—in this case, when profits were declared and divided as per agreement, Smith's share would be credited to his Capital Account, when making up the next balance sheet.

In the former balance sheet of Jones & Smith I have not considered the question of discounts upon the debtors' and creditors' balances. It is certainly right that some allowance should be made for these, but in opening the new books the actual amounts due and owing must be shown and the discounts debited and credited to Reserve Account as the case may be. You will notice that had this been done in the balance sheet referred to it would have reduced the amount of Jones's Capital Account. This is an important point for an incoming partner to consider. The amount owing to the creditors is known and will clearly have to be paid, less possibly some discounts; but the value of the debtor's balances can at best only be estimated. Let us suppose that Jones has agreed to value this item at $2,670, whereas the actual figures show $3,200; and has guaranteed Smith against any loss. Under these circumstances the books will have to be carefully kept with this object in view, and the balance sheet would then be as follows:

Liabilities.		Assets.		
Sundry creditors	$1,000	Cash on hand and in bank		$3,390
Jones' capital acc't	6,000	Sundry debtors	$3,200	
Smith's " "	3,000	Less reserve	530	2,670
		Merchandise		1,990
		Fittings, etc		450
		Goodwill acc't		1,500
	$10,000			$10,000

(1) Let these accounts realize only $2,500, then the difference, $170, will have to be charged to Jones's account.

(2) Suppose these accounts realized

$3,000, then there would be a profit of $300, which would belong to the firm and would ultimately be divided between the partners in the proportions agreed upon.

So far we have dealt with the opening of Partners' Accounts, as I stated before, the keeping of the business books involves no especial treatment. In the distribution of the profit between the partners, care is required, and especially where the Articles of Partnership make no provision for interest on capital.

As a general principle it must always be remembered that when interest is allowed to partners, the cost of it is borne by the firm; and as a general rule the best way of dealing with this item is to charge it to Profit and Loss Account after you have arrived at the profit made from the business.

Now, supposing the business shows no profits, is this interest to be charged and credited the partners' accounts? The answer is, yes.

There is a further point to be remembered in the division of profits when it is agreed to be in proportion to the partners' capital, and it is this: That the proportion is then calculated on the respective amounts of capital originally invested by each partner, and not by the balances at later dates. Of course, this could be altered by mutual agreement or by the terms of the Articles. If interest is agreed to be allowed on capital it does not necessarily follow that it is to be charged on drawings, though as a matter of practice this is usually agreed upon.

On the principle that practice is better than theory I will work out some of the questions set by the Institute bearing on the division of Profit and Loss.

"Brown, who owned a one-third interest in a business, gave Smith, who owned a two-thirds interest, $100 for his interest in a doubtful account of $300 against Jones. The bookkeeper made the following entry to arrange the transaction in the books:

Brown	Dr.	$200	
Profit and loss,	"	100	
	To Jones		$300

Was the entry correctly made? If not, how should it be made?

Answer: The entry was not correctly made.

1st. What was Smith's interest in the doubtful debt? It was $200 or two-thirds of debt. Now Brown is willing to give him $100 for this interest, so the entries should be as follows:

(1)	Brown	Dr.	$100	
	Smith	"	200	
		To Jones		$300
(2)	Brown	Dr.	$100	
		To Smith		100

which would show Jones's debt wiped off and leave Brown to be charged $200 and Smith, $100, or to complete the transaction at once

(3)	Brown	Dr.	$200	
	Smith	"	100	
		To Jones		$300

Frank Yeo and Walter Page are equal partners in a firm without any fixed salary for services rendered. Excess of capital is subject to a charge of 5 per cent. per annum, and excess of drawings to a like charge.

Their capital account shows as under:

Frank Yeo,
January 1, 1896, By balance $50,000
Walter Page,
January 1, 1896, By balance 30,000

On closing the books on December 31, 1896, their drawing accounts for the year were:

Frank Yeo $9,000
Walter Page 5,000

The net profits of the business for the year showed $10,000. Raise the Partners' Accounts.

The respective capital accounts of Frank Yeo and Walter Page after the various entries mentioned in the question will be as follows:

FRANK YEO.

Dr.					Cr.
1896.			1896.		
Dec. 31.	To drawings..	$9,000	Jan. 1.	By balance.	$50,000
	By balance..	46,150	Dec. 31.	By half profit	5,000
			"	By interest	150
		$55,150			$55,150
			Dec. 31.	By balance	$46,150

WALTER PAGE.

Dr.					Cr.
1896.			1896.		
Dec. 31.	To drawings..	$5,000	Jan. 1.	By balance	$30,000
"	" interest	450	"	By half profit...	5,000
"	" balance	29,550			
		$35,000			$35,000
			Dec. 31.	By balance.	$29,550

The amount of capital invested on the 1st of January, 1896, is $80,000. F. Yeo has, therefore, $10,000 in excess of half this amount, and is entitled to $500, being interest thereon at 5 per cent.; W. Page is $10,000 short on same date and must be, therefore, charged $500. These entries could be charged and credited to Profit and Loss Account, but the simplest way in this instance is to credit the one partner and charge the other. Now with reference to the drawings: We are furnished with no information as to the dates at which the amounts were drawn, but we are told they drew no salaries. I have concluded that each draw so much a month. The total drawings amount to $14,000, or say an average amount of $7,000, roughly estimating, during the year. F. Yeo draws $9,000, or an average of $4,500, and would have to pay interest on $1,000, being the excess of half the total average drawings, the interest to be charged being $50, which being taken off the $500 leaves $450 to go to his credit. W. Page has drawn $5,000 or an average of $2,500, being $1,000 below, and would be credited with $50 interest, which comes off the $500 charged him above, making it the $450 as shown in the account.

The principle involved in problems of this nature is that the firm is credited or charged with any interest paid by or credited to the partners' accounts. But the invariable guide must be the Articles of Partnership. An exception to this seems to be that interest is allowed on fresh capital introduced by a partner, when such fresh capital may be urgently required by the exigencies of the business, even though not specified in the Articles; but it is very clear that interest must not be allowed partners, however great may be the difference in their respective capitals unless so provided. It must also be remembered that where interest on capital is provided for, that unless specially mentioned, such interest stops at the date of dissolution of the partnership; and further, that profits which from some cause or other have not been divided, do not bear interest, even where the Articles provide for the interest on capital, unless, of course, this is specially mentioned.

So far we have touched upon the partnership accounts as regards the opening of them, and the division of profits, which I should think would present no difficulties to my hearers, but in the adjustment of partnership accounts great care and discretion are required. A partnership may be terminated by various causes, such as:

(1) Death of one of the parters.

(2) The termination of the period for which it was entered into.

(3) By one of the partners wishing to retire, or by mutual agreement.

(4) By the creditors thereof.

I feel I cannot do better than quote the rules to be observed as given by Lindley. "In adjusting the accounts of partners, losses ought to be paid, first out of assets, excluding capital, and lastly by having resource to the partners individually, and the assets of the partnership should be applied as follows:

(1) In paying the debts and liabilities of the firm to non-partners.

(2) In paying to each partner ratably what is due from the firm to him for advances as distinguished from capital.

(3) In paying to each partner ratably what is due to him from the firm in respect of capital.

(4) The ultimate residue, if any, will then be divisible as profit between the partners in equal shares, unless the contrary can be shown.

"If the assets are not sufficient to pay the debts and liabilities to non-partners, the partners must treat the difference as a loss and make it up by contributions 'inter se,' If the assets are more than sufficient to pay the debts and liabilities of the partnership to non-partners, but are not sufficient to repay the partners their respective advances, the amount of unpaid advances ought, it is conceived, to be treated as a loss, to be met like other losses. In such a case the advances ought to be treated as a debt of the firm, but payable to one of the partners instead of to a stranger. If after paying all the debts and liabilities of the firm and the advances of the partners, there is still a surplus, but not sufficient to pay each partner his capital, the balances of capitals remaining unpaid must be treated as so many losses to be met like other losses."

I will now endeavor to show you in a simple form how to adjust a partnership account. As I mentioned in the earlier part of this paper the first thing is to prepare a balance sheet from the books, and this appears as follows:

BALANCE SHEET.

Liabilities.			Assets.	
Creditors..........		$2,500	Sundry items......	$5,500
Partners' capital				
acct's ...A.	$1,500			
B.	1,500	3,000		
		$5,500		$5,500

For the sake of simplicity I have not

detailed these in this illustration. Let us assume that these assets have been realized and net, after paying all expenses, $3,500. The next thing to be done is to open a realization account, to which we have charged all the assets as follows:

REALIZATION ACCOUNT.

To assets..........	$5,500	By cash...........	$3,500
		" balance........	2,000
	$5,500		$5,500
To balance........	$2,000	By A. half loss....	1,000
		" B. "	1,000

It is very clear, then, that there is a loss of $2,000, and this loss will have to be borne by each partner equally, unless otherwise provided for. I have shown the Realization Account as closed, the balance being transferred to the partners' account as follows:

A. CAPITAL ACCOUNT.

To half loss.......	$1,000	By balance.......	$1,500
" balance........	500		

B. CAPITAL ACCOUNT.

To half loss.......	$1,000	By balance.......	$1,500
" balance........	500		

We now form a final balance which will show how the assets of the partnership will be distributed, as the assets are now in a distributable form.

FINAL BALANCE SHEET.

LIABILITIES.			ASSETS.	
Creditors..........		$2,500	Cash..............	$3,500
A. capital acc't	$500			
B. " "	500	1,000		
		$3,500		$3,500

I have here illustrated a simple case where the assets realized sufficient to pay all the creditors. Let us now look at a case where the assets are insufficient to pay the creditors, not forgetting that a partner, if he had lent the firm money, would rank next to the creditors. The balance sheet in the next instance stands as follows:

LIABILITIES.			ASSETS.	
Creditors..........		$3,500	Sundry items.....	$6,000
Partners' capital acc'ts..A.	$1,700			
B.	800	2,500		
		$6,000		$6,000

The assets have been duly realized and net $3,000, and from the realization account and partners' accounts which I show worked out, the process is clearly seen. The partners in this case also shared profits equally, and consequently, have to bear the loss in the same proportion. In this example the position of the partners is shown by examining their respective capital accounts. It will be observed that B. has to pay $700, and that A. is to receive $200.

REALIZATION ACCOUNT.

To assets..........	$6,000	By cash...........	$3,000
		" balance.......	3,000
	$6,000		$6,000
To balance.......	$3,000	By A. half loss....	$1,500
		" B. " "	1,500

A. CAPITAL ACCOUNT.

To half loss.......	$1,500	By balance.......	$1,700
" balance........	200		
		By balance.......	$200

B. CAPITAL ACCOUNT.

To half loss.......	$1,500	By balance.......	$800
		" "	700
	$1,500		$1,500
To balance.......	$700		

FINAL BALANCE SHEET.

LIABILITIES.		ASSETS.	
Creditors..........	$3,500	Cash..............	$3,000
A. capital acc't...	200	Cash paid by B...	700
	$3,700		$3,700

I have assumed that B. was in a position to pay this $700, if he could not, A. would have to stand the further loss, and if A. had no other means the creditors themselves would not be paid in full, but would have to share the $3,000 in proportion to, or as their claims ranked.

From the two illustrations here given almost any adjustment can be worked out, and I will again refer to some questions taken from the Institute Year Book.

On December 31, M.'s capital was $25,000; N.'s capital, $15,000, and O.'s capital, $10,000. They shared profits equally. Their creditors of $50,000 demanded payment of their debts and the assets realized $55,000.

(a) What were the assets stated at in the firm's books?

(b) What was the loss of each partner?

(c) What became of the $5,000 left?

(d) What was O. to pay M.?

Coming back to our rule we first prepare the balance sheet from the information given, which will give the answer to question (a) as the assets will equal the total liabilities in the firm's books.

LIABILITIES.			ASSETS.
Creditors..........		$50,000	$100,000
Capital accounts			
M.......	$25,000		
N........	15,000		
O........	10,000	50,000	
		$100,000	

REALIZATION ACCOUNT.

To assets	$100,000	By cash	$55,000
		By loss	45,000
	$100,000		$100,000
To loss	$45,000	By M	$15,000
		" N	15,000
		" O	15,000
	$45,000		$45,000

The loss of each partner would, therefore, be $15,000, and the Final Balance Sheet will give the answer to questions (c) and (d).

FINAL BALANCE SHEET.

LIABILITIES.			ASSETS.	
Creditors		$50,000	Cash	$55,000
Capital accounts			O. to pay	5,000
M	$10,000			
N	nil.	10,000		
		$60,000		$60,000

M. had, therefore, to receive $10,000 which he would receive as follows, the $5,000 mentioned in the question and the balance from O.

In making up the Realization Account the receipts would be entered in a special Cash Book. The best form is with columns with a separate heading to each important asset, thus practically showing all the details at a glance.

I would here like to compare two simple Partnership Balance Sheets.

First—

LIABILITIES.		ASSETS.	
Sundry creditors	$2,000	Sundries	$4,000
A. capital	1,000		
B. "	1,000		
	$4,000		$4,000

Second—

LIABILITIES.		ASSETS.	
Sundry creditors	$2,000	Sundries	$3,000
A capital	1,000	B. private acc't	1,000
B. "	1,000		
	$4,000		$4,000

In the latter balance sheet there is only $3,000 in assets to pay the creditors and carry on the business. B., by drawing on his private account has practically withdrawn his capital. In practical business this is a matter of far more common occurrence than might be supposed, and is a constant cause of trouble between partners. There should always be a definite understanding between partners as to the amount to be drawn by each partner. The best plan is probably for each partner only to draw a definite salary. I merely draw attention to this to show how simply a firm could be rendered practically insolvent.

As a final illustration I will direct your attention to a very interesting settlement which I have extracted from a business journal. Ballard, Haley, Moore and Butler were partners. Ballard and Haley being general partners and contributing experience; Moore and Butler were the special partners and contributed cash, the former $25,000, the latter $15,000. The profits were to be divided as follows:

Ballard	40
Haley	20
Moore	18
Butler	22

The general partners were permitted to draw for living expenses. At the general "round up" matters stood as follows:

All debts were paid and all assets exhausted excepting the debts owing by the partners. The special partner's capital had also been returned. The Balance Sheet was as follows:

LIABILITIES		ASSETS.	
Moore	$17,922 82	Ballard	$15,243 08
Butler	9,286 77	Haley	11,966 51
	$27,209 59		$27,209 59

They could not settle amongst themselves so referred the matter to a referee, Ballard and Haley being insolvent and unable to pay anything. The referee did not consider the balances owing by these insolvents in the matter, and taking only into consideration the amounts to be received by Moore and Butler from the firm, equalized them upon the basis of their respective interests in the profits and (of course) the losses, viz., 18 per cent. and 20 per cent., and decided that Butler should pay Moore $5,678.49. Moore thought he should receive more and appealed to the Court who awarded as follows, overruling the referee's decision:

Ballard had 40 and owed	$15,243 08
Haley " 20 " "	11,966 51
	$27,209 59
Moore had 18 and was owed	$17,922 82
Butler " 22 " " "	9,286 77
	$27,209 59

The decision as affecting Moore and Butler was as follows:

Butler owes Moore 22 of $17,922 82 on	$3,942 84
Moore owes Butler 18 of 9,286 77 on	1,671 62
Moore gets judgment against Butler for this amount	$2,271 22

Typewriter Batteries

One of the daily papers, a short time since discussing the possibility of war between the United States and Spain, somewhat facetiously alluded to the typewriter batteries that may be engaged in the struggle. Underneath the surface, however, there is so much truth that the suggestion merits at least a moment's consideration. That the typewriter is a useful instrument in the operations of war as well as in the pursuits of peace is very evident. Consider what it is to business and then remember that there is such a thing as the business of war. The typewriter, manipulated by an expert, is rapid and accurate, and in addition to producing a single copy can, by the manifold process, be made to produce a considerable number of copies. Therefore, every commander, every military post and every headquarters will have its proper equipment of typewriters. In many emergencies the typewriter will be as important as the largest gun that is available.

Every war sees new instrumentalities brought into operation. The War of the Rebellion revolutionized modern naval warfare and made various changes in other directions. A war waged in the year of grace, 1898, would develop, it is safe to say, many novelties and innovations, and last, but not least, would make extensive use of the writing machine, an instrument which did not exist at the time of the War of the Rebellion.

The old-style secretary or aide, it is safe to say, is as useless at the present time as the old smooth-bore guns which were employed during the Rebellion. Before the ordinary amanuensis could write one order for his commander, to be taken to one regiment or battalion, the nimble fingers of the expert typewriter operator would be able to take the words of the commander verbatim, and at the same time make a sufficient number of copies to supply every officer into whose hands the order should go. Accordingly, all the forts, all the officers of rank, and even the hospitals, surgeons and physicians, will find the use of a typewriter practically indispensable.

Especially will the typewriter be serviceable where telegraphic orders and advices are being sent and received. With a typewritten order in his hands, there would be no room for doubt or mistake on the part of an officer. His orders would be as plain as the text of his tactic books studied at West Point. For all the routine clerical work in the headquarters of the line officers, as well as in the commissary, the War Department has become so accustomed to the typewriter in times of peace, that its advantages could not be dispensed with in the field in case of war. Just as the telegraph brought the men at the front in close touch with the Department during the War of the Rebellion, so the typewriter will bring the American soldiery in the next war much closer to Washington than was possible as far back as in the sixties.

Bankruptcy Law

We are indebted to Bates & Holliday, attorneys and counsellors-at-law, 711 Tremont building, Boston, for a neat little pamphlet, entitled "Some Features of the New Bankruptcy Law, in effect July 1, 1898." The passage of the Bankruptcy Act brings into use new legal provisions affecting business, with which, of necessity, accountants, and bookkeepers as well, must be familiar in order to intelligently discharge their duties. Every accountant owes it to himself to have in convenient form a copy of the law as it was passed, and he will also be serving his own interests by accumulating pamphlets of the character of the one above referred to, as well also as the various legal blanks relating to bankruptcy matters which are already on sale in the stores of the law stationers.

Gross and vulgar minds will always pay a higher respect to wealth than to talent; for wealth, although it be a far less efficient source of power than talent, happens to be far more intelligible.—Colton.

We must despise no sort of talents; they all have their separate duties and uses, all the happiness of man for their object; they all improve, exalt and gladden life.—Sydney Smith.

It always seemed to me a sort of clever stupidity only to have one sort of talent—almost like a carrier-pigeon.—George Eliot.

He that would relish success to purpose should keep his passion cool and his expectation low.—Jeremy Collier.

Such a nature, tickled with good success, disdains the shadow which he treads on at noon.—Shakespeare.

Talent is that which is in a man's power; genius is that in whose power a man is.—Lowell.

It is not always the highest talent that thrives best. Mediocrity, with tact, will outweigh talent oftentimes.—Joseph Cook.

Talent is a cistern; genius, a fountain.—Whipple.

Accountants' Associations

Associated Accountants of New Orleans

This organization has maintained its regular meetings through the hot weather, which many people suppose to be more severe in the Southern cities than in the Northern cities. For the most part, accountants' associations in the Northern cities omit meetings through the heated term.

At the stated meeting of this association on the third Thursday in July, which was largely attended, the newly-elected president of the organization, A. L. Soule, read a paper on "The Proper Use and Treatment of the Merchandise Account." Incidentaly he gave numerous blackboard illustrations of different methods now in use among progressive bookkeepers. The paper served as the introduction to a very animated discussion, which was participated in by Messrs. Benedic, Kuehne, Fowler, Prentiss, Sherwood and others.

The first method explained was that originally brought to the attention of the accounting public in the "Manual of the Self-Proving Accounting System"—namely, dividing the Merchandise Account into two parts, one for purchases and the other for sales, in accordance with the two sets of values which are used in merchandise transactions. Purchase Account is credited and Sales Account is debited with the cost of the goods parted with. Then the balance in the Purchase Account shows the goods on hand at cost prices, while the balance in Sales Account shows the gross profit. It was argued by some of the speakers that this method is not adapted to all lines of business, and for this reason, it was explained, it is not in general use. This, however, was combatted by other speakers. On the other hand, it was very generally admitted that the plan is highly satisfactory in all those lines of business where such subdivisions of the Merchandise Account are easily maintained.

The second method outlined employed a Rebate and Return Merchandise Account. By subtracting the debit of this account from the credit of Merchandise Account, and the credit of this account from the debit of Merchandise Account, the true net cost and net sales of the merchandise for the year are shown. This method, it was asserted, is very simple, and, when used, saves the Merchandise Account from the charge of being "a trash box" account, as is often the case when all discounts, drayage, insurance, returned goods, expenses, etc., are dumped into it.

At the August meeting of this organization, after regular business had been disposed of, the members proceeded to a discussion of the subject which had been nominated for the occasion, namely, "Are sales journals necessary adjuncts to the sales sheet system of handling sales?" The debate was opened by President A. L. Soule, who spoke of the progress that has been achieved in accountancy methods in the last few years, and of the constant object of progressive accountants to record transactions clearly, concisely, and with no unnecessary details. The demand of thinking bookkeepers, he declared, is for something better than the old sales book, and this has given birth to what is known as the sales sheet system. At present there is a diversity of opinion and practice as to whether the sales sheet alone or the sales journal adjunct to the sheet should be employed. He asserted that, in conversation with bookkeepers practicing both methods, he had been unable to elicit a statement of any real advantages which follow upon using journals in connection with the sales sheet. On the other hand, from a personal examination of the books in many houses, he was inclined to think that the sales sheet could be so ruled and treated as to overcome the need of the journal as commonly used.

Among those expressing opinions who have had personal experience on the subject were Messrs. Sherwood, Cuny, Fowler, Rhea, Wadsworth and Ficken. It was the concensus of judgment of these speakers that as sales journals are generally used there is great loss of time entailed upon bookkeepers. The experience of Mr. Wadsworth, who uses a sales sheet system adapted to the cost system of keeping books, was especially interesting to the audience. He declared that his practice is in keeping with the method of treating Merchandise Account, which has been given prominent place in the proceedings of the previous meeting. His use of the sales journal is simply as a reverse posting test to prove the accuracy of posting. It causes, therefore, little if any, extra work. On the contrary, the speaker declared it to be a great help when trial balance period comes around.

At this meeting five new members were admitted, being gentlemen connected with some of the leading mercantile, insurance, railroad and manufacturing enterprises of the city. Additional applications for membership were also considered. At the September meeting Associate McNathan will discuss "Railroad Bookkeeping."

C. P. A. Examinations

At the stated examination of accountants for the degree of C. P. A., held June 14, seven applicants presented themselves, only two of whom passed. Two others passed in three of the four subjects, but failed in the fourth. They will be allowed the opportunity of re-examination in the fourth at some future date.

At the June convocation of the Regents of the University of the State of New York, a new Board of Examiners was appointed for one year, thereby putting into effect a resolution of the board, adopted some time since, which brings the accountants' examinations into strict agreement with all the other examinations conducted by the Regents. The Board of Examiners is constituted at present as follows: Chas. W. Haskins, of Haskins & Sells; Rodney S. Dennis, of Teele & Dennis, and John R. Loomis.

Previous to making the selection of examiners for the current year, the Board of Regents requested nominations from the New York State Society of Certified Public Accountants. From a list submitted by the Board of Directors of this organization, the three named above were selected.

Nothing is impossible to the man that can will. Is that necessary?—That shall be. This is the only law of success.—Mirabeau.

It is unfortunate that superior talent and superior men are so seldom united.—Marie Ebner-Eschenbach.

Public Accountants

The business community is beset at the present time by representatives of two classes of so-called public or expert accountants, for neither of which has it any use. One of these classes is composed of the frauds and confidence men who masquerade under the name of accountants, and the other of honest, but mistaken, men, who, having acquired a little skill as bookkeepers, imagine that thereby they have compassed the whole art of accountancy. The only class of public accountants for which the business community has any use whatever is composed of men of character and integrity, possessing high technical skill and backed in their work by extensive experience.

The rapid development of business in progress at the present time makes necessary a larger force of public accountants and auditors, as well as of other classes of skilled help, than has ever before been required. While to the superficial observer the accountants' ranks may seem full to overflowing, yet there are constantly being made places for all who present themselves with an equipment of skill and experience superior to that of those who are at present at work. In the profession of accountancy, as in all others, there is always room at the top.

Young men who aspire to accountancy as a profession, and bookkeepers who have the ambition to leave the office for a career in public work, are likely to be misled in their plans if they base them upon the results of a superficial examination of the situation. Business conditions have changed so radically in the last few years, and are still so rapidly changing from day to day, that nothing short of a critical analysis of requirements with the advice of men experienced in reading the signs of the times will save them from serious mistakes.

Accounting is much more than mere bookkeeping. A man may be an expert bookkeeper and yet fail signally as an accountant. As a rule, the bookkeeper gives very little attention to systematizing accounts, or to a consideration of the scientific plan upon which the accounting of a given establishment is based, and yet such matters as these are among the first that are demanded of the public accountant. There is far more in auditing than detecting minor errors of the bookkeeper, or ferreting out the methods of defaulters or embezzlers, and yet it is the latter which is most generally brought to public notice.

The equipment of the public accountant or auditor should, of course, include thorough training in bookkeeping, but, in addition, he particularly needs a training in commercial law, in business customs and in scientific accountancy. Withal, he should be thoroughly familiar with modern office appliances and the economical uses to which they may be put.

The first step in distinguishing between those public accountants who are entitled to the confidence of the public and those who are practicing with insufficient equipment and without proper credentials, has been taken in New York State by the passage of what is known as the Accountancy Law. The regents' certificate, which it provides, is likely for the future to be regarded as proof positive of the character and ability of the men who hold it. This first step is being ably sustained by the work of the New York State Society of Certified Public Accountants, which organization stands ready to support still other advances. Other States are emulating the example of New York, and at the next session of each of several legislatures, bills are likely to be introduced which, if passed, will put upon the statute books laws similar in their provisions to the New York Accountancy Law. In several States societies of public accountants have already been formed, which are intelligently working toward this end.

It is to the best interests of all those who are looking forward to a career in public accountancy to become familiar with the requirements of the regents' examination in New York State, whether they are allowed by reason of their places of residence to avail themselves of it or not. By this means there will be secured a standard by which to measure attainments. Further, it will be profitable for them to co-operate in their several States, so far as they have the opportunity to do so, in furthering the passage of laws similar to that at present in force in New York.

At the present time, in view of the exacting requirements of business interests, it is inexpedient for young men to commence upon the duties of a public accountant without first submitting to a sort of apprenticeship to a well-established firm, or at least working for a time in association with an accountant of extensive practise. In lieu of these, a careful course of coaching by some one who is competent to instruct, to suggest methods and answer questions, will be found of great advantage. Considered as an economical measure, it may be depended upon to save many times its cost.

A Poetical Dun

Bookkeepers and accountants, by reason of their intimate association with the financial department of business, are frequently called upon to make collections and to dun delinquent debtors, either in person or by mail. In dunning there is every opportunity in the world for displaying skill and special tact. On the one side there is the danger of offending the debtor, who may, in fact, be a valuable customer. On the other hand, there is the danger of failing to collect the money. A pleasant and agreeable dun, and one that is effective as well, is a great desideratum. A Cleveland hardware man is currently reported as being especially successful in this line. As a clerk in a store he put in his spare time writing letters to slow customers, and thus secured the practice that makes perfect. Up in Michigan there was a particularly bad case. A man by the name of William Rose owed twelve dollars, which had become outlawed, and was considered a dead duck. Nevertheless, it was the rule of the concern to write to William Rose occasionally. This was the situation when this clerk reached the position of dunning correspondent, and this is the letter that he wrote:

"Oh, William Rose, oh, fragrant rose,
Yourself it is who surely knows
Unsettled bills are bad.
They soil our books, they spoil our looks,
And make the heart grow sad.
So William Rose, feel in your clothes,
And find twelve dollars there.
The goods were sold in days of old
Before we had white hair."

Much to the surprise of the proprietor the debtor sent the money inside of a week. His letter declared that he had always intended to pay the account some time, and that he could not hold out longer against a demand couched in such pleasing language. It is not every one that is a born poet, and comparatively few are able to acquire the art of versification, but polite dunning is possible, even though each line of the letter does not commence with a capital letter and end with a jingle.

The Bookkeeping of Department Stores

By Charles F. Jones

(Concluded* from page 41 of the May number.)

In taking up the ledgers used in department store bookkeeping it may be well to say at the outset that no matter how many different ledgers are used, or how many differenet accounts a department store may have, the principle of the double entry ledger always remains the same. There is no difference in principles as compared with the double entry ledger of the smallest store. Circumstances, however, require an expansion of the system. Instead of having all the accounts in a single book, it is necessary for convenience sake to divide them between a number of books. It would be impossible to make a single ledger large enough to accommodate every thing; and if only one ledger were employed, then only one person could work upon it at a time. Accordingly, the ledger in a department store is arranged in several volumes, each volume being devoted to a given class of accounts, and the several volumes being arranged so that different clerks can work upon it.

In keeping more than one ledger—that is, having the ledger in several volumes, there are two ways of viewing the matter. Either the several ledgers may be considered simply as parts of the whole, which must be taken together in the trial balance in order to find the balance of the whole, or each volume may be so posted that each ledger will balance in itself, irrespective of any other ledger. The first plan requires fewer entries, but is not so generally used, nor yet is it so satisfactory as the second plan, because if all the ledgers must be taken together to make a balance and an error is discovered, then all the ledgers must be gone over in order to find the error. There is no possible means of localizing it. On the other hand, if the store, for example, has four ledgers and each is posted in such a way as to be in balance within itself, then any error which is discovered will require no further checking for its detection than the one book in which it becomes apparent. Three of the ledgers, for example, may be in balance, while

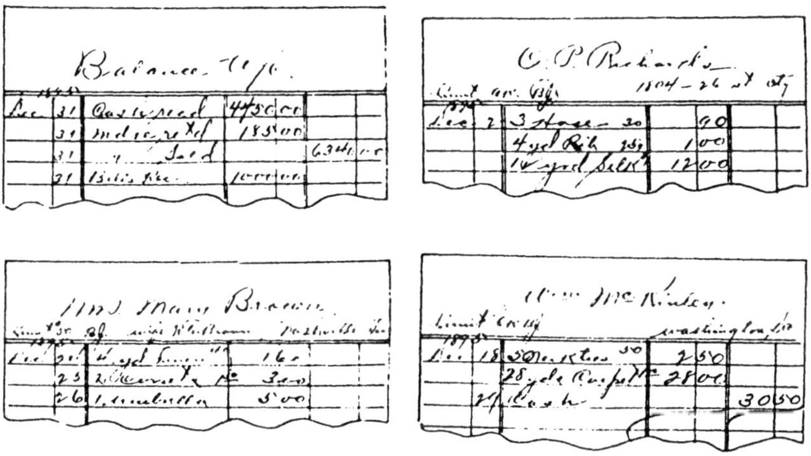

FIG. 52.—EXAMPLES OF ACCOUNTS OF CREDIT LEDGER.

*With this instalment we bring to a conclusion the very interesting treatise on department store bookkeeping which has been running in these columns for a number of months. The pressure upon our space is so great that we are obliged to omit several interesting diagrams with which Mr. Jones brought the original manuscript to a conclusion and to condense in certain other particulars. We omit, as being of comparatively small interest to the majority of our readers, the author's description of converting partnership books of a department store into joint stock company books, and also a portion of the routine of posting.—Editor of Accountics.

the fourth is out of balance. Only the one that is out of balance needs to be checked back.

In causing each ledger to balance itself, the main, or general, ledger is to be considered the principal book, and the other ledgers, such as the purchase ledger, the credit ledger and the department ledger, as supplementary books. The general ledger includes in detail those accounts which belong to the general business, and includes in lump also the balance footings of the supplementary ledgers. To make each of these ledgers balance individually, it becomes entries are to be made, so that each ledger shall balance itself, irrespective of the totals which may go into any other ledger.

Fig. 52 shows the ruling of the accounts of what is called the credit ledger—that is, the ledger in which are posted the amounts due the store. Fig. 53 shows the ruling of the accounts of what is called the purchase ledger—that is, the ledger in which are posted the sums that the firm owes to those from whom it has bought goods. Figs. 54 and 55 show the rulings of the accounts of the department ledger, in which is kept the record of the

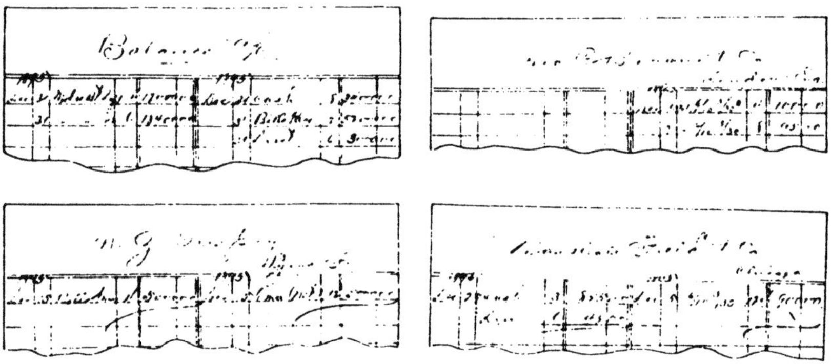

FIG. 53.—EXAMPLES OF ACCOUNTS OF PURCHASE LEDGER.

necessary that every entry should have a debit and a credit in each ledger in which any entry is posted. This is where the extra posting comes in in making the ledgers balance separately. However, this is not very much work, since the additional debit and credit (where the original debit and credit are not in the same ledger) can usually be carried in columns in the journal and cash book until the end of the month, and then posted as a total instead of posting each entry individually.

Where the ledgers are not supposed to balance themselves separately only one debit and one credit is made of any entry, the debit coming sometimes in one book and the credit in another. By this plan the totals of all four books will have to be joined together in order to get the balance. This is a very simple transaction, although sometimes a very laborious one. It does not need any further explanation. Brief attention, therefore, will be given to the plan by which the business of each department. These accounts show the purchases of each department, its expenditures and its sales, and, finally, the profit and loss. Fig. 56 shows the ruling of the accounts in the general ledger.

We have already shown that the entries to the credit ledger are made by the bookkeeper direct from part Y of the original sales check. Sometimes a department store has so many credit accounts that it becomes necessary to keep several credit ledgers in order to hold them [illegible] In cases of this kind, the alphabet is divided into a number of parts. The accounts with those persons whose names begin with the letters from A to F will fall to one ledger, while those that begin with G to M another; from M to R a third, and from S to the end of the alphabet to the fourth. In such cases the charge slips are divided up between the bookkeepers allotted to these several ledgers, each one posting a single book. Each bookkeeper takes his package of the sales checks, and, turning to the accounts with the several customers, makes entries therein from the sales checks direct.

In order to facilitate balancing, it is always well for the bookkeeper to have at hand a number of long, narrow blotters, to be used as book-marks. As the postings are made, he slips a blotter in between the leaves where the entries are being recorded and continues this until he has completed the posting of all the sales of the day. He then lays aside his sales checks, so putting them away that they can be referred to as may be necessary, either in the sense of correcting an error which he may have inadvertently made, or adjusting a dispute with a customer. He then takes a book of the kind shown in Fig. 56 and in it enters back from the ledger the items that he has posted. In the illustration it is assumed that we are tracing the work of the bookkeeper in charge of Ledger A. The first posting that he made was on page 34 of the ledger, and the amount was $4.82. He records this in the column Ledger A, and then turns to the next place indicated by the blotter, which is page 82, and records the item $4.50. He proceeds in this manner until he has recorded in Ledger A column all the entries that he has made in the ledger that day. Then by referring to his original sales checks, he can quickly run over them and check off the amounts. If they check correctly, he has proven by this work that his posting for the day is correct, and he is then ready to take up the next day's work. All the different credit

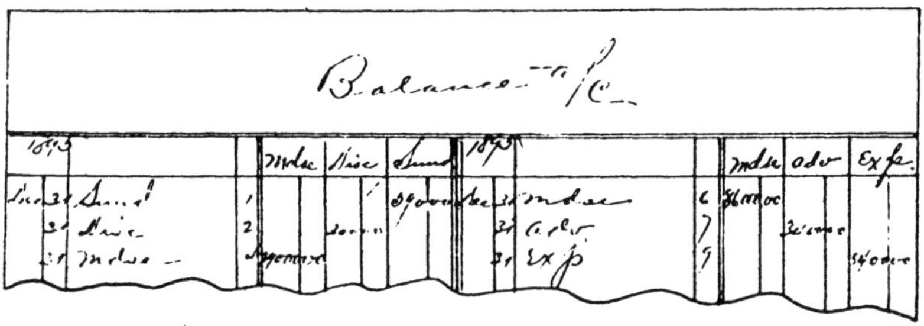

FIG. 54.—BALANCE ACCOUNT OF DEPARTMENT LEDGER.

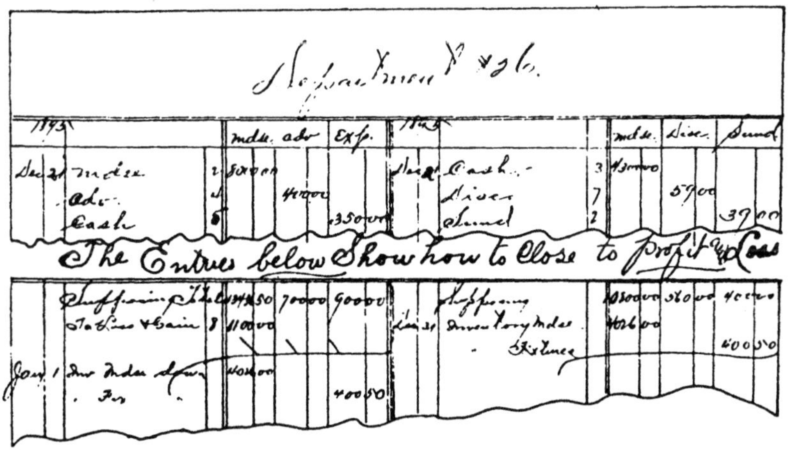

FIG. 55.—EXAMPLE OF ACCOUNT IN DEPARTMENT LEDGER.

ledgers having been thus checked up, the bookkeeper may take up the charge sales book, and enter in the column marked Ledger A the total footings of the corresponding column in the form shown in Fig. 56, and in the other columns of the charge sales book the total of the corresponding columns. Suppose that there are only two credit ledgers. The totals then recorded $600 in column A and

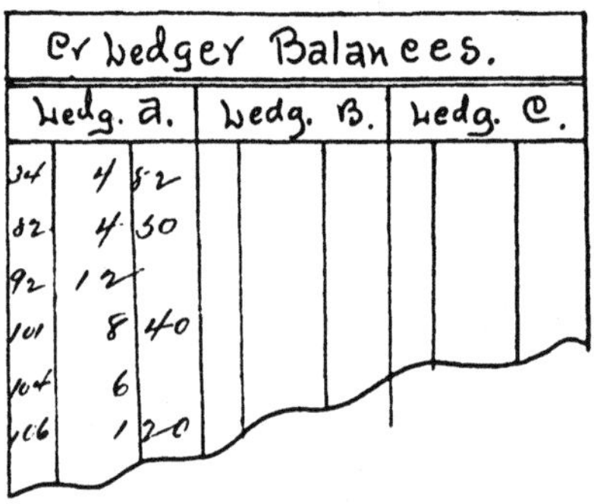

FIG. 56.—CREDIT LEDGER BALANCE SLIP OR BOOK.

$350 in column B, making a total of $950, should exactly balance with the sum total of the amounts of all the columns devoted to the various departments shown in Fig. 41.

Since the totals of the columns, Ledger A and Ledger B, have been arrived at through the entries made from part Y from the original sales check, as already explained, and as the total in columns Department 1, Department 2, etc., have been arrived at through entries made from part X of the original sales check, and since the totals on parts Y and X are the same, then by proving with the totals of the columns in the left of the form shown in Fig. 21, balance with those in the right of the same form, we are assured that all entries are correct.

Let us next give brief attention to the balance account shown in each of the several divisional ledgers. The duty of a balance account is not to show any part of the business. Its function is merely to carry such an amount as may be necessary to make the ledger balance within itself. The balance account supplies the missing debit for every credit, and the missing credit for every debit, thus keeping the total of debits and credits alike.

Returning now to a consideration of the posting mediums, and referring particularly to Fig. 41, already presented, the figures in column Ledger A are allowed to accumulate until the end of the month. Then the footing of this column is posted to the credit side of what may be called the balance account in the credit ledger. See Fig. 52. This figure, of course, equals all the charges for merchandise which have been made to the debit of the various people who have accounts in this credit ledger. Referring back to the pay-roll book, already illustrated, it will be recalled that in the extreme right hand column is placed the amount which is to be charged to each department for salaries for which it is responsible. The total will be posted direct from this pay-roll book to the debit of the account in the department ledger of the department to which each account belongs.

Referring to the department ledger, Fig. 55, it will be noticed that it has a number of columns ruled both on the debit and on the credit sides. These columns may be employed to any number, as may be desired. The more that are used the more explicit will be the information which the face of each department account in this ledger will show. This form of department ledger is preferred merely because of its simplicity, for looking at it and considering the footings for each column the bookkeeper can see at a glance, without the necessity of compiling information from other sources, the exact amount of merchandise which has been purchased, the advertising that has been done, the amount of general expenses to date, etc. On the other side of the ledger will be seen at once the amount of merchandise that has been sold, the amount of sundry accounts that are due the department on account of prior payment of bills by the firm, and any other sundries which may be accumulated to the credit of the department. Usually in this Sundry Account is posted merchandise which has been returned to the sellers—that is, if the form of deducting it from the invoice book has not been used. The latter plan, however, is strongly recommended. As has already been mentioned, as many more columns similar to these may be employed as is desired in order to make the information as minute, or present it in bulk, as the firm may desire. Having posted the total of each of these amounts shown on the pay-roll book form, which should go to the debit of each department in the department ledger at the end of the month, the total footing of the extreme right hand column is posted to the opposite side (credit) of the balance account in the department ledger so as to make a balancing credit for the debit which has been posted to each of the individual departments.

It may be well to remark here that in keeping four or five ledgers, each of which is to balance within itself, if all the balance accounts are wiped out or omitted, then all the ledgers become one —that is, one ledger becomes necessary to the other in order to make a balance, and when the footings of all are brought together, the whole becomes one symmetrically-balanced piece of work.

All the different books from which postings are to be made to any of the ledgers are handled in the same general manner as has been explained. For instance, we take up the invoice book. Here, as previously stated, each department has a separate book and the bills are posted in the order received, according to their dates. From this book the total of each bill is posted to the credit of the account of the firm in the purchase ledger from whom the bill has been received. The total of all the bills of the month is carried forward to a column provided for them until the end of the month, when, as a total, the sum is posted to the debit side of the Balance Account in the purchase ledger. This is the debit which offsets all the credits which have been made from the bills individually to the various accounts in the purchase ledger. These are two of the entries necessary to make the purchase ledger balance, and now the sum total at the end of the month, which, in this case, as shown in Fig. 44, amounts to $5,601.30, must also be posted to the debit side of the account in Department 3 (merchandise column) in the department ledger, and also to the credit side (Merchandise column) of the Balance Account in the department ledger. These four entries may be summed up as follows: Two are in the purchase ledger, making a credit and a debit; two are in the department ledger, making a credit and a debit. Again, looking at them from another point of view, we have two of them in the Balance Accounts (debit side in the purchase ledger and credit side in the department ledger), while two of them go to the main accounts of the system (credit side in the purchase ledger and debit side in the department ledger Thus it will be seen, as in the case of our former explanation, that if the two balance entries are wiped out, the books will cease to be in balance as distinct ledgers, but the two ledgers taken together would still balance as a whole.

Referring to Fig. 48, which is the general cash payment book, it will be seen that each entry is handled in the same way as has been explained for the other books. The individual items in the column of the purchase ledger, credit ledger and general ledger, are posted to the debit side of these ledgers. The totals of these columns, at the end of the month, are posted to the credit of the Balance Account of its respective ledger. This makes a debit and a credit. The totals in the columns, general expense, light, fuel, etc., are not posted individually, but are held until the end of the month as a whole. Then the footing of the column is posted to the debit of the account designated by the name of the column. The various amounts in the columns called Department 1, Department 2, etc., are not posted as individual items, but are held in the column until the end of the month, and then the totals are posted to the debit side of the accounts of a department indicated by the name of the column. The grand sum total of all these columns—Department 1, Department 2, etc.—must then be posted to the credit side of the Balance Account in the department ledger. At the end of the month the total of the column marked Purchase ledger must have its corresponding debit by the total being posted to the debit side of the Balance Account in the general ledger. The same remark applies to the total of the column called credit ledger A. The sum total of the column of the several departments forms practically a credit item on account of being held on the credit side of a portion of the cash book. There must, therefore, be a corresponding amount posted to the debit side of the Balance Account in the general ledger. It will thus be seen that practically four entries have been made of the columns—first, purchase ledger and credit ledger, and second, of the columns representing the several departments, but only two entries made of the columns entitled General Ledger, Expense, Light,

Supplies and Sundries. This is because the columns last mentioned do not need a Balance Account to balance them with the general ledger, since their credits and debits both appear in one ledger—namely, the general ledger. The credit in this case is the cash and the debit is the postings which have just been explained.

It may be well to explain here that the general ledger is really incomplete in itself, unless there be taken into consideration the balance of the various cash books would go to make up the Cash Account, provided a regular Cash Account is not kept in the general ledger. If this seems too complicated to the bookkeeper, he may keep a general Cash Account in his general ledger and post the balance of each of the cash books to this Cash Account at the end of the month. By this plan his ledger will be in balance without referring to the sums of the cash books, which have been closed into the ledger. It is, however, almost a universal custom at present among bookkeepers not to carry the general Cash Account in the ledger, but, instead, to figure the balance of the cash book in with the trial balance as the footing of the Cash Account.

The cash receipt book, Fig. 47, is handled in the same general manner. The individual items in the four columns shown in this form are posted direct to the credit of the accounts to which they belong. Thus, John Brown & Co. are credited with $100, the same as would be the case in posting from any other form of cash book. The four columns are used simply to keep the purchase, credit and department ledgers separate from the general ledger, so that the totals of each of the first three columns may be posted to their corresponding Balance Accounts in the ledgers in which they belong, thereby constituting the debit for the individual credits which have been posted from time to time. The sums of the three columns, purchase, credit and department ledger, are also finally posted in the general ledger to the credit of the Balance Account, thus balancing the debit represented already in the Cash Account.

The cash sales book is another part of the Cash Account, and the totals in each department in it are posted to the credit of the department's accounts in the department ledger, while the grand total of all the departments is posted to the debit of the Balance Account in the department ledger. Then, in order to make a credit for the debit, which this cash book is in itself, the total is, at the end of the month, posted to the credit of the Balance Account in the general ledger. If, as previously explained, a Cash Account is being carried in the ledger, instead of allowing the cash sales book total footing to represent the debit item, the total will be posted again to the debit side of the Cash Account in the general ledger.

The charge sales book has already been described, and the manner of securing the figures therein has been explained. The total of the columns at the end of the month is posted to the credit of the account of the departments whose number they bear. The grand total of all the columns is posted to the debit side of the Balance Account in the department ledger. The total of the column marked Ledger A is posted to the credit side of the Balance Account in Ledger A. The total of the column B is posted to the credit side of the Balance Account of Ledger B. These two amounts have already been posted to the debit side of these two ledgers, as previously explained, by the original entry which has been made direct from the sales check to the account of the person purchasing the goods.

Referring again to Fig. 43, which may be described as the general journal of the system, it will be seen that it is constructed with four columns on either side and that it is adapted for receiving journal entries which cannot be made by any of the other books. The one entry shown therein is where $120 worth of merchandise has been returned by the firm to R. R. Jones. As before explained, this entry is best made from the invoice book, being an opposite entry from what would be made for a purchase. In order to explain, we have made this entry solely for the purpose of illustration. The sum of $120 on the debit side of the journal is posted to the debit of Jones' account in the purchase ledger, and the $120 on the credit side of the journal is posted to the credit side of Department 6, the department which is returning the goods in the department ledger. This makes one debit in the purchase ledger, and, in order to get its corresponding credit, the total of the debit purchase ledger column is at the end of the month posted to the credit side of the Balance

Account in the purchase ledger. We also have one credit in the department ledger, and to get its corresponding debit, the total of the department ledger column is posted to the debit side of the Balance Account in the department ledger at the end of the month. When all the entries have been made for the month and properly posted, as instructed herein in connection with each of the several books, it will be found that the credit ledger is in balance. The figures given in the illustration are independent from the posting shown, and, of course, do not balance, since a number of accounts belonging to this ledger are missing in the illustrations, being represented merely by the "and so forth," which is to be understood as meaning that there may be any number of accounts in this ledger. The same remarks in this respect apply to all the other ledgers. Very few accounts have been shown—simply enough to give the ruling and explaining the postings without making a complete ledger. Supposing all the accounts to be present in the credit ledger, the difference between the debit side and the credit side of the Balance Account will be equal to the difference between the credit side and the debit side of all the accounts added together. These remarks also apply to the purchase ledger and the department ledger.

The general ledger, when all the accounts are together complete, will in reality include the sum total of the business. The Balance Account will represent the total balance of the purchase ledger, the credit ledger and the department ledger taken together. It will be found that the various accounts of Merchandise, Light, Expense, Rent, Advertising, Insurance, Help, etc., do not appear as main accounts in the general ledger, and that they will only contain the entries of such items as are not subdivided between the different departments at the time of the entry. It will also be seen that the Balance Account in the department ledger will show in its various columns the grand totals of the items of Merchandise, Expense, Advertising, etc., the amount of which have been divided among the various departments and are shown in the columns of Merchandise, etc., in each department account in the department ledger. From this it will be evident why the more columns there are in the accounts of the department ledger, the more explicit the statistics will be presented. The amounts that are carried into the general ledger under the heads Merchandise, Light, Expense, etc., are at the end of the season to be closed out by a journal entry, being divided among the various departments as is just and equitable.

The Pen vs. The Machine

The utility of the typewriter is so great in modern business offices for various kinds of literary work and for the preparation of documents in general, that it seems strange that it should be barred out from any place under any circumstances. Yet it is a fact that a rule of the House of Commons requires that all petitions must be laid before that body in written or lithographic form. It is also true that many in the legal profession in this country, as well as certain noted lights in the profession of accountancy, prefer hand-written documents and reports to the finest work that could be done upon a writing machine. A prominent member of the Institute of Accounts, who, perhaps, files more documents with the surrogate of New York County than any other one accountant, is an example in point of the latter class, while a leading firm of lawyers on Broadway, New York, whose office is exceptionally well equipped with typewriting machines and skilful operators, serves as an illustration of the former. They prefer that documents to be filed with the Secretary of State, for example, such as applications for incorporation, shall be hand-written rather than typewritten.

In view of the really magnificent work which is done from time to time on typewriting machines, it is hard to understand why penmanship should be so persistently preferred in the cases cited. Perhaps this clinging to hand-written documents is not unlike the course of certain prominent institutions, among which may be mentioned the Bank of England, that has only recently allowed the use of steel pens. It clung to the use of the quill pen for years after the world at large had found a substitute that is infinitely its superior. While a typewritten communication on official subjects will not at present be received in some of the British offices nor in the courts of Great Britain, we, in America, are almost as far behind, for it is only since the Harrison administration that typewriters have been used in the State Department at Washington. Even at present, all communications to the foreign legations of the United States and to the diplomatic representatives of other governments at Washington have to be written by hand. Our ministers abroad are still required to use the same method in preparing their despatches to the government. Secretary Blaine was the first official to introduce the typewriter, and it is to be supposed that if he had remained in office several years longer that convenient instrument would have been furnished to all the foreign representatives of the United States.

Correspondence

The Balance Column in Progressive Ledgers

From Frank J. Sager, White Oaks, N. M.

I was much interested in the forms of progressive ledgers shown in the pages of ACCOUNTICS some months since. I refer to the Private Ledger, or Balance Sheet Ledger, shown in the issue of December last, and the Mercantile Ledger, or Customers' Ledger, presented in the issue for October last. Shortly after examining the latter, I prepared the form which I now enclose, having intended to send it to you more promptly. For some reason, however, I failed to do so, and have only recently encountered it among my papers. You will recall that, in the form of Boston ledger sent to you some time since, and reproduced in the issue of ACCOUNTICS for February last, I dispensed with the balance column usually found in such ledgers. I believe that it will be found that both the Balance Sheet Ledger and the Customers' Ledger, as presented, would be improved by dispensing with the balance column and utilizing the space now occupied by it for an item and folio column.

A balance column, to my mind, serves no real purpose, except to make work. The Private Ledger, or Balance Sheet Ledger, would be considerably improved by doing away with the balance column, for the reason that, as illustrated, all balances are brought down into one horizontal line. Hence, nothing but balances appear upon this line. If those balances were brought down into the debit or credit columns of their accounts, there would be shown at a glance whether they were debit balances or credit balances. When extended into the balance column, this must be ascertained from the entries appearing in the account above the balance line.

In the form of Customers' Ledger enclosed herewith you will note changes made, other than dispensing with the balance column. So long as all accounts on a page, referring now to the form shown in ACCOUNTICS some time since, are debit balances, the form there shown will be self-proving, but when, as frequently occurs, there creeps in a credit balance, there is no provision for making the page self-proving. These ideas may seem, and perhaps are, crude and of little value. They are, however, offered simply as suggestions.

Note.—It affords us much pleasure to reproduce herewith the draft of Customers' Ledger, progressive form, submitted by Mr. Sager. It is to be compared, rulings and entries included, with what is shown in the October (1897) number of ACCOUNTICS, page 6. The point made by this correspondent with respect to varying balances—that is, an occasional credit balance creeping in among the debit balances, etc.—is well taken, but it is to be observed that with the close classification by which accounts of a kind are kept together, the variations in the nature of the balances are less frequent than might be supposed. Where a column is provided for balances, as in the case of the Self-Proving Mercantile Ledger above referred to, the bookkeeper finds ample space for writing above the irregular balance either Dr. or Cr., as the case may be, distinguishing it from the other balances, or he may insert the irregular balance in red ink. He, therefore, encounters no difficulty whatever in proving the pages of his ledger. Thousands of bookkeepers who are using progressive ledgers, ruled essentially the same as the Self-Proving Mercantile Ledger, will bear us out in the statement that these irregular balances make them no trouble when managed as above described.

There are several radical objections to the suggestion made by Mr. Sager, of omitting the balance column, when viewed from the standpoint of the commercial bookkeeper who is rendering monthly statements, and also from the standpoint of those who desire to prove the ledger by comparison with the auxiliary books.

First, with respect to statements of accounts. Where each account is balanced and the balance thrown into a column by itself, as is the case with the Self-Proving Mercantile Ledger, the pages are proven by taking the total of the old balances, adding the total of the debits, and subtracting the total of the credits, thus producing an amount which should agree with the total of the new balances. This work is done on the ledger page. Assuming that it proves, the statements are sent off without the necessity of refooting, and yet with the assurance that they are correct.

Next, with respect to proving the ledger

with the auxiliary books. By keeping the current items separate from the balances, the debits in the Self-Proving Mercantile Ledger may be proven with the footings of the auxiliary books from which the debits are posted—for example (principally), the sales books. In the same way, by keeping the credit items separate from the balances, this column of the ledger may be proven with the auxiliary books from which the credits are posted—for example (principally), the cash book. The very careful computations shown at the bottom of Mr. Sager's ledger page scarcely meet the requirements of the case, and will be regarded by many bookkeepers as more intricate, requiring more thought and greater labor than the balance column as commonly managed, and which Mr. Sager would have abolished.

With respect to the suggested improvement in the Balance Sheet Ledger, it is to be remarked that the balances are thrown out in this book—not every day, but rather once a week or once a month, according to the business. The bookkeeper's report goes in daily, forming solid columns of figures, and the balances are thrown out into the third column as often as they may be required for a complete or partial statement of the business. By dispensing with the balance column and bringing balances into debit and credit columns, as Mr. Sager proposes, some of the statistics of the business would be lost or there would arise the necessity of special computations for them. The total amount of sales, the total amount of goods put out, the total amount of credits to customers, etc., would be lost sight of if the balances were brought into columns, as he suggests.

While disposed to reject, for our own use at least, the suggested improvements of Mr. Sager, still we are not prepared to say that what he has offered is of no value. Other accountants may see their way clear to employ, in whole or in part, what Mr. Sager suggests. Mr. Sager's contribution is of great value, inasmuch as it is likely to provoke discussion and, therefore, will have the good effect of directing the attention of many bookkeepers to the whole subject, who otherwise might have neglected the matter entirely. And this leads us to say that we shall be glad to hear from any of the thousands who are using progressive ledgers on any of the points here raised, or those which have not yet been brought out, to the end that the very best may be discovered for use.

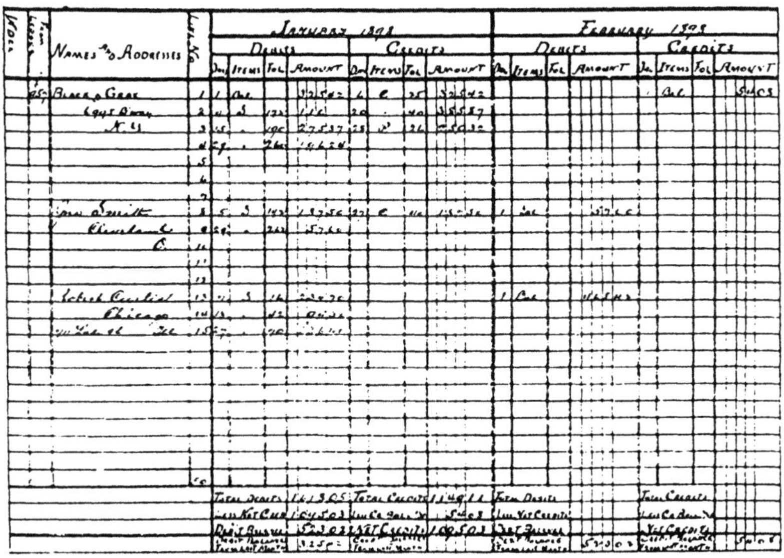

A PROGRESSIVE LEDGER IN WHICH THE BALANCE COLUMN IS OMITTED.

Managing the Bank Account

From J. B., Washington, D. C.

In the April number of ACCOUNTICS the following test question was printed: "Explain the various ways in which a banking account can be recorded in one's books, etc.?" What I now submit I do not claim is an answer to this question, but still it treats of one of the various ways in which a banking account can be recorded in one's books. The object in view is to point out some of the advantages to be maintained by keeping the bank account exclusively upon the check bock. By that I mean that the check book should cease to be used as a memorandum, as is usually the case, and that it be treated and kept as an integral part of the cash book. This is accomplished by entering the amount of the checks in the cash book, and refraining from entering the amount of the deposits in that book. The cash book then shows the total balance on hand, and the check book shows the amount of deposit in bank. The difference between these two balances should be the cash in the drawer. The daily deposits should be entered—itemized or in gross—upon the left hand stub of the check book, and the totals, including the last balance, should be carried forward from one bank settlement to the next. The check totals should be carried forward likewise and the book should be as carefully kept as any of the others in the office. When a settlement with the bank occurs the balance, as shown by the check book, should be brought down and the difference between it and the balance shown by the bank book should be explained. This explanation should be entered upon the deposit stub, somewhat after the following form:

Bank balance, as per check book......		$1,000
Checks out:		
No. 210......	$100	
No. 211....	50	
No. 212....	250	400
		1,400
Bank balance, as per bank book,		$1,400

Among the numerous advantages pertaining to this system of keeping the bank account, the following deserves specian mention: Since the cash account cannot be balanced without balancing the bank account at the same time, and since any error in the latter is bound to appear in balancing the former, certainty as to the correctness of the cash account insures certainty as to the correctness of the bank account. The managing man has only to glance at his check book in order to ascertain his bank balance. The bank account is always posted. By other systems the setting forth of differences between the check book and the bank book balance is a matte: of considerable difficulty. The plan here proposed saves valuable ledger space. The bank account far outranks all others in importance. To it certainty is an ever-present and indispensable necessity. Questions respecting its condition are among those most frequently asked in a business office. Since a bookkeeper is appreciated by his employer in exact proportion to his ability to return prompt and certain answers to the many questions which are asked him, the value of the advantages possessed by this system of keeping a bank account can be readily perceived.

Note.—We have pleasure in giving space to the argument presented above, supporting the practice which is followed by the majority of competent bookkeepers at the present time—namely, keeping a bank account upon the stubs of the check book. There are comparatively few bookkeepers at the present time who open an account with the bank in the ledger and post to it the deposits of the checks drawn. Such a plan would be considered inadequate in almost every office that could be mentioned. The common plan, and the one that gives the greatest satisfaction, is to regard the bank account as a division of the cash account, and to manage them very much as this correspondent sets forth.

In some concerns the very excellent practice prevails of passing all cash received through the bank, and of making no payments save by check. Incidental expenses, including those items ordinarily designated by the term "petty cash," are paid from a small amount represented by a check drawn for the purpose, which is advanced to the cashier as a fund out of which to pay them. Before this fund is exhausted he presents his vouchers for the payments that have been made, and a check is drawn covering them, recounting the vouchers by number or name. By this method his funds are replenished, and so the work proceeds. Three divisions of cash result from this method. First, the cash in hand not yet deposited in bank; second, the bank account, and third, the petty casn.

With respect to posting to the bank account and the argument that our correspondent advances—namely, that it occupies space, it is to be remarked that those bookkeepers who first have learned to keep the bank account upon the stubs of the check book, thus avoiding ledger work in connection therewith, learn a little later to keep the cash account entirely in the cash book and avoid ledger work in connection with it also. In other words, they omit the cash account from the ledger and take the balances from the cash book at the time of the monthly trial balance. This plan is found to work very well and undoubtedly results in a considerable saving of labor.

Filing Catalogues

From M. H. H., Philadelphia.

I would like to learn through ACCOUNTICS of some of the best systems of filing catalogues. I suggest that an article relating to a standard size of catalogues and pamphlets would be very interesting to the readers of the magazine.

Answer: The two suggestions of this correspondent can be treated together, for they are so closely related as to be virtually the same thing. If catalogues were all of one size and shape, the matter of filing them would be greatly simplified. Therefore, the second proposition, in a sense, includes the first. However, catalogues are not of a uniform size and shape, and, therefore, the system that is best to be employed for filing them becomes a matter of careful consideration in any office where the accumulation of printed matter is considerable in quantity.

With respect to an article relating to a standard size of catalogues and pamphlets, we would say that many such have been published, and the subject has even been exploited by some of the engineering societies.But catalogues continue to appear in all shapes and sizes, and bound in more colors than appeared in Joseph's coat, however much those who receive them may protest against odd shapes and urge that a few standard sizes would serve their convenience, while less variety in colors would also be appreciated.

The manufacturer or jobber who issues a catalogue is going to do exactly as he pleases in these particulars. In putting forth a catalogue he is governed in matters of this kind by several considerations. In the first place, he selects the size page that is best adapted to his illustrations already made, or to the illustrations to be made of the special goods he desires to show. This may or may not result in dimensions satisfactory to those who have given attention to standardization. After this point has been settled, he next takes up the question of what will make the most certain and lasting impression upon those to whom he sends the book. Then come in the questions of an odd shape, of wide margins, of fancy bindings, and, perhaps, of extreme colorings to the cover.

The favorite definition of advertising, whether expressed or implied, among many of those who send out catalogues, is "the colored bean among the white ones." That manufacturer, therefore, who succeeds in sending out a catalogue which is unlike all others with which it come in contact, or with which it may be filed in the office, is most sure to keep his goods, or at least the suggestion of his name, obtruded upon the customer all the time. On the other hand, the modest man, who shows his goods in a book of conventional size and shape, loses his identity, and his book ranks as only one among a hundred on the shelves of the office libraries of his customers. With all deference to those who are laboring for standard sizes of catalogues, and in full view of the utility of all that is claimed for such methods, we are compelled to say that we do not believe that standard sizes will ever be adopted, and that, instead, odd sizes and extreme shapes will be the rule for all time to come. This leads us to the first question which our correspondent asks—namely, systems for filing catalogues.

The subject divides itself into two parts—first, the convenient storage of the books and pamphlets, and second, the means of finding a book when it is wanted. With respect to storing the books, the work of librarians has practically exhausted the subject. Adjustable shelves for books, thereby adapting them to books of different sizes, and drawers or boxes and cases for pamphlets, seem to exhaust the list of facilities. With the book or pamphlet put away upon the shelf—that is, duly labeled by number or letter, or put in a case likewise properly designated, the best plan for reference is undoubtedly one or the other of the different forms of card indexes now before the public. The card index lends itself to almost any system of cataloguing or indexing that may be required, and several plans may be combined in single card system. The books and pamphlets may be catalogued by name of firm, and also by general line of goods. In turn, an index of contents may be distributed through the same set of cards, thus giving a reference to the shelf, book and page of any special article that is liable to be required; or the card index may be divided by guides so as to keep the references to books of a given kind all by themselves.

Speaking in the most general terms and advising in the interest of those whose requirements are the average rather than special, we suggest that the best plan is to divide the card index by guides with respect to lines of goods, the individual cards within the divisions being the names of firms or companies issuing the books. Each book or pamphlet filed will then be represented by a single card. As often as a book is taken out, in the sense of destroying the dead wood which is always accumulating, its card would likewise be withdrawn. Or, if a new book is substituted for an old book, no change need be made in the card, unless, indeed, to record on its face the date of the edition that has been put in place.

Most offices would benefit by keeping on file more catalogues than they do. Most offices also would benefit by having a better system for putting the books away and for finding any book required on call than is at present employed. Our advice above is expressed in general terms for average users, but it contains the essence of what is best for the most elaborate systems that may be adopted.

Reviews and Criticisms

Banquet Speeches

Model Banquet Speeches by Famous Banquet Speakers. Compiled by William C. Sprague. 207 pages, bound in cloth. Published by the Collector Publishing Company, 1897. Price $1.50.

This book should be invaluable to those who aspire to distinction in post-prandial oratory. It is up to date, in that it discriminates against old chestnuts and presents efforts of the recent past and addresses delivered on occasions with which the reader is familiar. The speeches included in the book cover a large variety of subjects and occasions, including banquets of members of the bar, political banquets, celebrations and various kinds and conditions of society gatherings.

Newspaper Directory

American Newspaper Annual, containing a catalogue of American newspapers, a description of every place in the United States and Canada in which a newspaper is published, including railroad, telegraph and banking facilities, and a list of the newspapers of the United States and Canada arranged by counties, with a description of each State, Territory, Province and County, giving location, character of surface and soil, chief products and manufactures; with separate lists of religious and agricultural publications, class publications, newspapers published in foreign languages, etc.; also the press and editorial associations of the United States and Canada, with their officers. 1,500 pages, bound in cloth, published by N. W. Ayer & Son, 1898. Price $5.

This book is so thoroughly described in the title-page, from which we have freely quoted above, that a very careful review of its contents would reveal little else than what is indicated. It is a volume that should have a place in every office, by reason of the information that it furnishes, which is not so readily obtainable from any other source. The table of population of those cities, towns and villages in the United States exceeding 5,000 people each, as shown by the last official census, or by later estimates, is exceedingly valuable, and can be put to many business uses. It covers four pages. From the introduction to the directory proper we learn that only 137 papers were added to the list in the preparation of this volume, as compared with its predecessor. The grand total of papers and periodicals enumerated is 22,092. Attention is directed to the fact that the net increase in newspapers and periodicals has shown a decline since 1894. A large number of new papers were started last year, amounting in the aggregate to something like 2,000. Some of these failed to survive, and many that were older likewise dropped out, making the net increase as above quoted. Following most of the papers listed are figures referring to circulation. These are of several different varieties, indicating statements supported by affidavits, statements supported by detail records, statements resting upon the publishers' unsupported claims, and circulations which are merely the estimates of the publishers of the directory.

Cuba

The Real Condition of Cuba To-day. By Stephen Bonsal, late Secretary of the United States Legation in Madrid, special correspondent of the New York Herald in Cuba, etc. With frontispiece and map. 160 pages, paper cover. 1897. Published by Harper & Brothers. Price, 60 cents.

Cuba At a Glance. By Emma Kaufman and Anne O'Hagan. With an introduction by T. Estrada Palma, President of the Cuban Junta. 107 pages, folding map, paper cover. 1898. Published by R. H. Russell. Price, 25 cents.

Cuba in Wartime. By Richard Harding Davis. With illustrations by Frederick Remington. 143 pages, with folding map, paper covers. 1898. Published by R. H. Russell. Price, 50 cents.

Cuba is no nearer to the United States geographically than it has been since the beginning. It is very much nearer to the hearts and consciences of the people, however, than it has ever been before. Accordingly, there is a demand for particulars concerning Cuba historically and geographically, and more particularly with respect to Spain's treatment of the inhabitants of that ill-fated island. Each of the three books presented above tells its story in an interesting and graphic style. Mr. Bonsal's work preceded the Spanish-American war by about a year. It is dedicated to the starving and plague-stricken thousands in Cuba who, he says, in piteous accents besought him while he was with them, to go and tell his people the story of their unimaginable woe. While interesting from beginning to end, the contents of the book are almost gruesome and are not the most pleasant reading by the very nature of the facts presented. But that this and various other volumes of its class have, in some degree, done their work, is evidenced by the hearty approval of the nation of the interference of our government in Cuban affairs.

The second volume in the above list is based largely upon historical works and documents, together with newspaper correspondents' work. It is not an argument but rather an unprejudiced statement. It shows the condition of Cuba and also recounts the historical facts leading up to that condition. This book made its appearance very shortly after the destruction of the Maine, and has proved its usefulness by a very large sale.

The third volume named takes still another view of the subject, but contributes in an important degree to the same general cause—namely, the amelioration of Cuba's condition. Mr. Davis visited Cuba last winter in the employ of one of the leading daily papers. He writes of what he saw. The illustrations, which are numerous, were made by the well-known artist, Frederick Remington, from personal observation while in Cuba, and from photographs. The chapter heads give a fair idea of the contents of this book. They include "The Fate of the Pacificos," "The Death of Rodriguez," "Along the Trocha," "The Question of Atrocities," etc.

Directory of Directors

Directory of Directors in the City of New York; 600 pages, octavo, bound in cloth. Published by the Audit Company, 1898. Price, $5.

Various directories have been compiled and issued in the past, ranging from the general city directory to those of classified trades, membership of clubs, elite society and other specialties. It is, we believe, altogether unique, so far as New York is concerned, to have a directory of directors, but that such a book is useful becomes apparent upon the most casual inspection of its contents. It may be assumed, therefore, that the Audit Company, in preparing and publishing such a work has done the business community a substantial service. The names of the directors are arranged in alphebetical order, and under each name is a list of the companies in which the individual is serving as a director. Under the names of many prominent men are lengthy lists, but the majority of names included show connection with but a single corporation. The names in the directory embrace those of directors who are residents of New York, even though they are connected with companies that are not domiciled here; and in turn they include directors who are not residents of New York, but who are connected with corporations having offices in this city.

With respect to the extent that prominent men are connected with companies, it may be stated that the greatest director of them all is Charles H. Coster, of J. P. Morgan & Co., who is a director in no less than fifty-nine corporations, nearly all of them railroad companies. Cháuncey M. Depew, however, approaches Mr. Coster closely, as he is a director in fifty-eight companies, his list including not only railroads, but a warehouse and storage company, a dock company, a coal company, a gas company, a telegraph company, and insurance and trust companies.

The members of the Vanderbilt family are well up in the list, Cornelius Vanderbilt being a director in fifty-four companies, William K. Vanderbilt in forty-two, and Frederick W. Vanderbilt in thirty-one. H. Walter Webb holds directorships in thirty-five companies. J. Pierpont Morgan is a director in twenty-three companies, being in this respect far outstripped by his partner, Mr. Coster.

It will doubtless surprise a good many to learn that Russell Sage is by no means near the top of the list. He belongs to the boards of only twenty-four corporations. George J. Gould is one behind him, belonging to twenty-three. Edwin Gould belongs to thirteen and Howard Gould to eleven.

Daniel S. Lamont, Cleveland's Secretary of War, who is now a power in the world of finance, is a director in forty-seven companies. Here is a list of other well-known men and the number of corporations in which they are directors: John Jacob Astor, 18 companies; William Waldorf Astor, 7; Samuel D. Babcock, 25; George F. Baker, 29; August Belmont, 19; John D. Crimmins, 12; Roswell P. Flower, 8; Henry O. Havemeyer, 4; Abram S. Hewitt, 10; Collis P. Huntington, 20; William J. Kelly, 24; Edward Lauterbach, 10; Darius O. Mills, 18; John G. Moore, 19; Levi P. Morton, 5; John D. Rockefeller, 2; William Rockefeller, 14; John E. Searles, 21; Samuel Sloan, 32; James Stillman, 17; William L. Strong, 6; Samuel Thomas, 24; William C. Whitney, 14.

Promissory Notes

Promissory Notes, Bills of Exchange and Checks, with General Remarks on Contracts. By J. W. Johnson, F. C. A. Published by the Ontario Business College. Seventh Edition, revised and enlarged. Nearly 100 pages, octavo, bound in cloth. Price $1.

Previous editions of this very valuable contribution to business literature have been noticed in these columns. The work had its origin in lectures delivered by the author to the students of the Ontario Business College, commencing the year 1877 and continuing up to the present date. It may be described as an accurate, safe and trusty guide for business men in dealing with bills and notes. It is based on wide practical experience, close observation and minute study of the subjects upon which it treats. While arranged in the light of Canadian law, it still is of interest and value to business men in the States, and presents many matters pertaining to checks and notes not to be found in any other volume. No one will peruse the pages of this book without having his knowledge increased in various important directions.

The Arithmachinist

A Practical Self-Instructor in Mechanical Arithmetic. By Henry Goldman. 4x6 inches. 126 pages. Published by the Office Men's Record Company. Price $1.

The fame of Henry Goldman has spread throughout the land. As the author of an advanced system for locating errors, of short methods for computing interest and discount, of methods for averaging accounts, and as the inventor of the Security System for Preventing Forgeries, the Instantaneous Index and Automatic Binder, etc., he is known among bookkeepers and office men from one end of the country to the other. More recently he has brought out a calculating device known as the "Arithmachine," which is described in his circulars as the simplest, strongest, smallest, lightest, cheapest and most reliable computing machine now before the business public. "The Arithmachinist" is, in a sense, a companion piece or introduction to the mechanical device above referred to. It is more than a manual of instruction in the use of the calculating machine mentioned, in that it discusses mechanical arithmetic broadly.

The work is divided into several leading chapters, following the one that is introductory and explanatory. These discuss in general terms elementary arithmetic and higher mathematics, with explanations of how mechanical devices are made to play an important part in calculations. The history of mechanical arithmetic is taken up, tracing its development from the earliest records down to date. This chapter concludes with a brief survey of present conditions. The next is technical and opens with a classification of computing machines. At this point the Arithmachine is formally introduced and the balance of the volume is largely devoted to a description of what the machine will do and how it performs. Numerous illustrations are presented, showing the Arithmachine in different positions, and by dotted lines in the several views indicating the motion of the hand in using. Numerous illustrations are also presented showing what may be readily accomplished with this device. The machine is also presented in a form adapted for English currency, thus illustrating its very wide applicability. Appended to the text are some thirty pages devoted to advertisements, wherein various articles are presented, ranging from false teeth to sewing machines, and including various articles useful in the office.

Osgoodby's Shorthand

Osgoodby's New Phonetic Shorthand Manual. A Complete Manual of Pitman Phonography, with all the modern improvements. By William W. Osgoodby. 124 pages, bound in cloth. Eighth edition. Published by Williams & Rogers. Price, $1.25.

The author of this work was for thirty-four years official stenographer of the New York State Supreme Court. He has held high positions in the stenographers' associations of the world, and is widely known as an author and teacher. The fact that his exposition of the Pitman method has passed through eight editions is evidence of its wide acceptability. The work is a treatise on Pitman Phonography with modern improvements. In system it holds to the original vowel scale, namely, long e in the first place, employs the horizontal inverted curved stroke for h, or, as the phonographer would call it, "hay," and employs those specials features of contractions and phrasing which have made Pitman phonography generally acceptable for amanuensis and reportorial work. The book is handsomely printed on excellent paper, and the shorthand characters have been most carefully engraved. It is attractive to the eye, and its arrangement is such as to take the student, whether in a class or acquiring the art by self-instruction, through easy stages from the beginning to the conclusion.

Some of the chapters which old phonographers will specially enjoy, particularly those who have been familiar with other text books, include the one on the Choice of Outlines, the Table of Contrasts and the one on Special Hooks. The chapters devoted to Contractions and Word Forms, and to Word Signs, are very comprehensive and very logically arranged. The Outlines for Important Words indicated by the longhand equivalents of shorthand characters is also a very important chapter. Another chapter entitled Illustrated Phrases Similarly Expressed is likewise valuable. The chapter entitled Optional Expedients will give various shorthand writers some new ideas.

From mere success nothing can be concluded in favor of any nation upon whom it is bestowed.—Atterbury.

The Excelsior Perpetual Ledger

Dennison & Sons, No. 2 Liberty street, New York City, are putting upon the market the form of perpetual or loose leaf ledger shown in the accompanying illustrations and which has been named by them the Excelsior Perpetual Ledger.

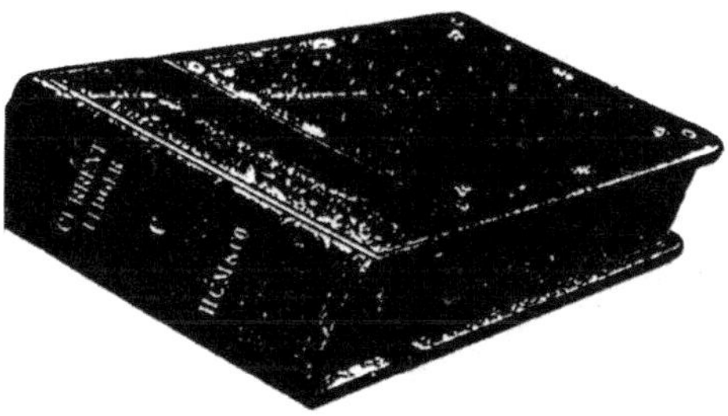

EXCELSIOR LOOSE LEAF LEDGER.

One of the engravings shows the ledger closed; another shows the binder unlocked and extended, with indication of the method of removing or inserting leaves, while the third shows the transfer binder, which, for economy, is extended beyond the capacity of the ordinary ledger.The binder is adapted for holding securely locked as many as a thousand leaves, whereas the ordinary ledger would be limited, for convenience in size, to perhaps half that number. The Excelsior Perpetual Ledger, as manufactured, has the feature of expansibility, which permits the insertion of leaves beyond the nominal capacity.

We assume that our readers are well acquainted with the advantages of perpetual or loose leaf ledgers,which include

TRANSFER BINDER.

self-indexing, the removal of filled pages, the substitution of blank pages and the ready weeding out from among the accounts everything that is finished or dead. This being the case, they are more particularly interested in such a matter as we bring to their attention at present in the mechanical features of the device. The ledger sheets, it will be seen, are punched with a slotted hole—that is to say, there is a cut from the edge of the sheet to the hole through which the posts of the binder pass. The binder post is flat and is adapted to be placed with its length in a longitudinal direction, for putting in or removing a leaf, as shown in oné of the cuts, and turned to a transverse position when the book is closed. By this means the sheets are securely held in position when the book is in use, and yet they are readily unlocked to be withdrawn whenever required. The cover or case slides upon itself in a way to expand when unlocked, as shown in the cut representing the book opened. By turning the posts, provision for which is made on the outside of the binder, as shown in the first view, the position of

BINDER UNLOCKED.—NEW LEAF BEING INSERTEI

parts is secured, which permits the removal of a sheet, as shown in the second cut. All this, perhaps, will be better understood by reference to the directions for operating the ledger, which the manufacturers are sending out. To remove a leaf, the user is directed to unlock the book and turn the posts with the key. He then opens to the leaf which he wishes to remove, spreads the leaves apart, and withdraws that which is to be taken out, as shown in the cut. The new leaf is then inserted, the book is closed, the cover is pressed down, and is thereby locked automatically. An attractively illustrated circular and price list has been prepared by the manufacturers for general distribution and will be sent to any one who applies for the same, mentioning ACCOUNTICS.

The world is always ready to receive talent with open arms.—O. W. Holmes.

Handy Document File

The A. C. Barler Mfg. Company, 104 Lake street, Chicago, Ill., are introducing a form of document file which possesses various new and attractive features. The file is in a sheet-steel case, provided with an excellent lock. The case is enamelled black and is ornamented with gold striping. Within the case are separate manila pockets, with metal eyelets, the system tending to complete classification.

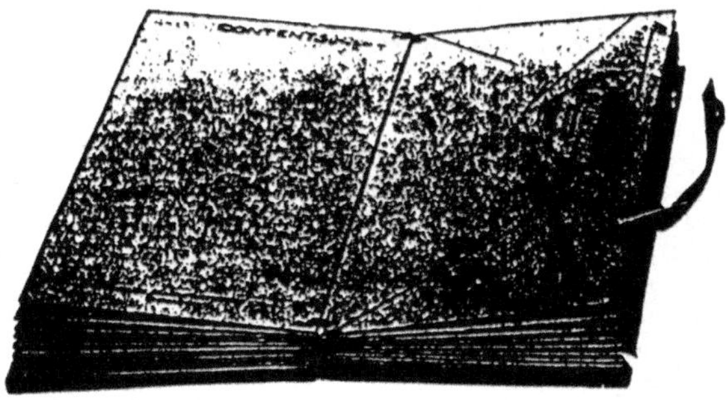

HANDY DOCUMENT FILE OPEN.

The acompanying illustrations show another device much on the same line, put upon the market by the same concern. It is known as the Handy Document File. The covers in this case are enamelled sheet-steel, provided with flanged edges to protet the pockets. An adjustable leather strap, shown in both views, provided with a snap fastener, serves to close the file. The files in this case, as in the other, are in envelope form and are held within the covers by cords which automatically bind the parts and, by a peculiar arrangement, adjust instantly to varying requirements. The envelopes, or pockets, are removable and may be exchanged, or additional ones may be added to suit requirements. The low price at which these goods are put upon the market insures a very large sale for them, while their intrinsic merits give them hosts of friends wherever introduced.

HANDY DOCUMENT FILE CASED.

Accountics

The Office Magazine.

A. O. KITTREDGE, F. I. A., C. P. A., EDITOR.
E. R. KITTREDGE, ASSOCIATE.

Accountics is devoted to the Science of Accounting, to the Art of Bookkeeping and to the advocacy of Improved Office Methods.

Subscription.—One dollar a year, payable in advance.

Postage is prepaid by the publishers in the United States, Canada and Mexico. For all other countries in the Postal Union, subscribers must add 50 cents a year.

Discontinuances.—In the absence of specific orders to discontinue at the end of the subscription term the magazine will be continued and a bill sent.

Remittances should be by Draft, P. O. Order or Express Order, payable to the order of the ACCOUNTICS ASSOCIATION. Money and postage stamps are at the risk of the sender, unless sent by express or in registered letters. Add 10 cents each to checks on local banks to defray collection charges.

Advertising Rates will be quoted on application.

Official Journal.—This publication, by resolutions duly passed, has been made the official publication of the following organizations :—
THE INSTITUTE OF ACCOUNTS.
THE NEW YORK CHAPTER of the Institute of Accounts.
THE WASHINGTON CHAPTER of the Institute of Accounts.
THE HARTFORD CHAPTER of the Institute of Accounts.

ACCOUNTICS is the accredited medium of intercommunication between members of the Institute of Accounts wherever located.

ACCOUNTICS ASSOCIATION,
Publishers,
Wool Exchange, New York.

The "Acx" System of

Filing Invoices

Pronounced by those who are employing it, simpler, more convenient and more serviceable than any other. A new and time-saving application of elements more or less used in every up-to-date office.

Copies of orders, records of arrivals of goods, and the invoices brought together in sets, adequately indexed and permanently bound in book form. Posting may be made direct to credit of Purchase Accounts, with daily, weekly or monthly summaries for charges.

No journalizing necessary. Some of the more prominent features of the system include the following:

1. A strongly-bound book, and one of even thickness, whether holding 10 invoices or 1,000 invoices. Books may be large or small at pleasure.

2. Each record contains a copy of the order, the report of receiving clerk and the seller's invoice.

3. Copies of orders are presented seriatim according to their numbers. Leaves of book are regularly numbered.

4. Knowing the name of the seller or the number of the order or the date of the invoice, the required place in the book is found instantly.

5. No special form of order is demanded.

6. Full provision is made for recording partial shipments, shipments of a single order distributed through a considerable period of time, or several orders combined in one shipment.

7. Always up-to-date. Less labor than by any other plan.

8. Book is built up progressively. No blank pages or dead stock to lift or carry around.

9. The "Acx" System is the bookkeeper's delight, because it saves labor, keeps everything ship-shape and enables him to answer questions about invoices and prices instantly from the actual figures.

10. The "Acx" System is greatly enjoyed by the buyer as well as by the proprietor and business manager, because it instantly furnishes all required information about purchases and orders out whether examined by order numbers, by names of sellers, by date of order or by date of invoice.

11. The "Acx" System employs cheaper equipment in view of the results accomplished than any other.

Samples, together with full and complete specification for construction and management, forwarded carriage paid for **One Dollar.**

ACCOUNTICS ASSOCIATION

Publishers and Booksellers

Wool Exchange Building - - - - New York

Local checks are not acceptable unless 15 cents be added for collection costs. Remit by banker's draft on New York, post-office or express money order, or send currency by registered letter at our risk.

Accountics

The Office Magazine

ONE DOLLAR A YEAR
TEN CENTS A COPY

OCTOBER 1898

VOLUME III
NUMBER 7

CONTENTS.

Published by the ACCOUNTICS ASSOCIATION: Wool Exchange New York

Accountics

VOL. III OCTOBER 1898 No. 7

The Monthly Statement

The lawyer and the accountant in the matter of incorporations would be a subject on which many men of both professions might write intelligently and instructively. We imagine, however, that if both spoke the truth neither would indicate an exalted opinion of the capacity of the other. It is a question which should lead in a case of this kind. The lawyer, in the interest of his clients, is careful with respect to every feature of law, while the accountant, not unmindful of the bearing of the law upon those matters in his charge, is equally anxious to pilot his clients through balance sheet details which to many are somewhat bewildering. The difficulty with the lawyer, from the standpoint of the accountant, is in many cases that he has no conception of accounts, and, therefore, is very apt, when confronted by a matter of a few thousand dollars on one side or the other of an account, to pass it by with the sweeping assertion, "Write it off," or "Fix it most any way you can," overlooking the fundamental principle which every accountant recognizes — namely, that for everything charged there must be a credit, and for everything credited there must be a charge.

Again, the accountant having an eye single to the orderly arrangement of the schedules fails to appreciate the tedious routine which the lawyer specifies and insists upon. Take it in the case of the incorporation of a business heretofore conducted by a firm. The accountant sees little else in the affair than a continuation of the old régime under a new name, and therefore would issue the stock for the visible assets and the business as a going concern. The lawyer, on the other hand, is anxious to draw a line between the new and the old, thus defining the liabilities of all parties, and insists upon the stock of the corporation being issued solely for cash. The fiction is transparent to the accountant, but the destruction is vital from the standpoint of the lawyer.

If lawyers were a little better accountants they would be able, perhaps, to manage an affair of this kind unaided; and in turn if accountants knew a little more of law they might be able to carry it through without assistance from the legal fraternity. In either case there would be a saving of expense. There are two classes of responsibilities, however, well defined, and, therefore, it is better for the two professions to work together than for either to try to get on alone. By thus working together they are likely in time to understand each other better and to develop a larger measure of mutual respect and confidence than would otherwise result.

"Brother" Beach, to paraphrase the style which our esteemed contemporary in Detroit effects when referring to the Editor of ACCOUNTICS, devotes a column of the last issue of his paper to a consideration of certain paragraphs in the last number of this magazine relating to summer conditions and the refreshment which change of occupation, when carried to an extreme, fails to afford. He concludes that not only does the editor of this publication need a rest of a different sort from that referred to, but that very possibly the readers of ACCOUNTICS also need such a rest as would follow the indefinite cessation from work of the said editor. At least that is to be read between the lines. All this serves to show the consideration that a fellow-editor has for the dear reader of the other publication, always forgetting, however, that the said dear reader is a man of discretion and abundantly able to select for himself what he is to read. If we were disposed to engage in a tilt with our contemporary—not, however, such a one as he informed us privately the other day, is like a spat between lawyers in the court room, merely professional, for the effect it may have on the jury—we could say several things about the rest "Brother" Beach might take. Selfish interest, however, prevents the pleasure of the fray. We might thereby down our adversary and accordingly be the loser of the large measure of free advertising we are now getting. So on second thought we vary the programme that is usual in such cases and say, "Brother" Beach, do not take a rest. Keep up the fusillade with which you have been honoring us for some time past. It evidently pleases you. Your readers should not object to being informed that there are those in the field who are really influencing accounting methods, even though your publication fails in its effort, and what you print about us from time to time is doing us a lot of good.

How not to do it is aptly illustrated by the conduct of many a bookkeeper who fails to rise above the mere routine of his daily duty and who sees no advantage in developing plans that shall meet business requirements. A bookkeeper does not post from his sales book because, as he claims, by rewriting the transactions in the journal he is likely to detect any errors that have occurred in the sales book entries. In this he shows that he does not rise to the thought that mistakes should not be made, and if made should be discovered where they are rather than detected as a result of extra or unnecessary labor. Many a bookkeeper uses two colors of ink on ledger and journal for no reason that he can explain, but simply because he has always done it. He sometimes forgets the order of the colors, and accordingly his books soon present a chromatic appearance of a peculiar character. In this and in other matters the bookkeeper is inconsistent with himself. He does a certain thing one way to-day, forgetting that he did it a very different way yesterday, and when confronted by his inconsistency, even though both methods are correct or allowable, he flounders about for an explanation. He fails to see the advantage of holding to a method and putting all his energy into driving his work forward upon a consistent plan. The lost motions in an average bookkeeper's work, the backing and filling, and the time serving, which, as a result of a tendency never combatted, becomes a part of his daily life, are still further illustrations in point. If bookkeepers could realize that employers are prone to see all these things and treasure them up against them, they would strive to substitute for all that could be cited as illustrative of how not to do it, that more interesting chapter of incidents, which embraces rules of how to do it. It is in this respect that the bright, active, enterprising and intelligent young man, with an eye to the main chance, has material advantage over the old fogy, who is set in his ways, and who is too conceited to attempt to learn his trade over again.

It is generally supposed that the amount of red tape, using a colloquial expression, that is encountered in every transaction with the Government makes official business far more difficult to transact than that which arises in everyday life, and yet whenever the subject is investigated it is found that the Government does everything possible to meet the business man half way. Particularly is this true in all matters connected with the post-office, not only in the delivery of mail, but also in the money-order division. An example in point will illustrate the latter: A clerk who was directed to get a money order gave the address of the payee wrong. The order should have been made out to John Smith, Providence, but by his mistake in directions it was made out to John Smith, Boston. Of course by post-office regulations it would have been useless to send the money order so made out to the Providence correspondent, and therefore it was necessary to have the matter corrected at the office of issue.

In the New York Post Office, in the money-order division, there is a window marked "Inquiries.—Money orders issued at this office." To this window application was made for information as to the method of correcting the mistake that had been made. In a very short time the situation was comprehended, and the order properly marked and cancelled. It was then given back to the messenger with directions to proceed to the cashier. Here the money was refunded to him, and then he proceeded to do again what had been done in the first place—make new application for such an order as was required. Of course he took good care this time to give the address correctly.

The net cost of the error was the loss of the fee paid for the first money order and which amount the Government got for the trouble to which it had been subjected by the mistake. The sender paid for one order and got the amount of the order back, though not the charge for the order. Then he had to pay for the second order. So much for the way in which a matter of this kind would be managed at the main post-office in New York. It no doubt would be somewhat simpler at each of the local branches, because less business is done and there are not so many departments organized in the money-order branch. In the country, particularly in small towns, it would be still further simplified. However managed in detail, it shows that the red tape of the Government is more a fiction than a fact when applied to the money-order division, and that the Government is in touch with business men in various details, facilitating their operations instead of hindering or retarding them.

"A chip to displace" is the significant phrase with which J. W. Warr, Editor of the Practical Age, opens the first article in the September number of that periodical. After referring to the address of the Editor of ACCOUNTICS before the Business Educators' Section of the National Educational Association at Washington and quoting remarks concerning that effort which were published in July issue of ACCOUNTICS, he says:

"Now, is it possible that the authors of bookkeeping treatises are going to allow judgment to go by default in favor of Mr. Kittredge? If his claim is correct and works on bookkeeping are teaching wrong doctrines, then business colleges come in for a large share of condemnation for promulgating what the books teach. Messrs. Packard, Williams, Soule, Bryant, Sadler and other great lights of the business college fraternity, will none of you step up and knock this chip off Brother Kittredge's shoulder? If Mr. Kittredge is right in his sweeping claims, there should be reform instituted at once; if he is wrong, the world ought to know it."

It is a matter of sincere regret to Mr. Kittredge that none of the representative commercial college men and authors of bookkeeping treatises was present at the Washington meeting. An open discussion on that occasion would no doubt have been profitable to all concerned. The next best thing perhaps is to exchange courtesies in print. In another part of this issue there is presented an extract from the address containing those paragraphs to which the editor of the Practical Age specially alludes. The entire address is too long for publication at this time.

Referring to the remarks of Mr. Warr, it should be stated in this connection that Mr. Kittredge's contention is not so much that works on bookkeeping are teaching wrong doctrines as it is that they do not go far enough or that what they do teach falls short of what modern business requires. That all treatises on bookkeeping would be improved by such revision as would recognize two or more accounts in place of the merchandise account as at present very commonly expounded, is a contention so manifestly correct that it does not need argument to support it. So long as the majority of the commercial schools are willing to teach bookkeeping on a plane so low as to make it comparable in importance with penmanship, stenography and typewriting, probably the present edition of text books will be entirely satisfactory. But whenever a considerable number of schools realize the opportunity that is at present presented to teach practical accounting as well as routine bookkeeping, a text book to be entirely satisfactory for the purpose will have to be prepared, for none of the present works is up to the requirements of the case. Mr. Kittredge does not claim discovery or originality in his plan of treating the merchandise account, for many eminent accountants have preceded him in it. He does claim a certain degree of originality in method of presentation and in the accounting facilities, which make the employment of the method easy and likewise readily understood by the average business man.

Uniform Bookkeeping

By A. O. KITTREDGE, F. I. A.

The only possible basis for uniform bookkeeping in a given industry or line of trade is to be found in the accounting principles which underlie that bookkeeping. Given a correct statement of principles as a foundation, then the only difference there will be in the arrangement of books of accounts for different establishments in the same business by different accountants will be in minor and unimportant details.

That uniformity in business methods is something greatly to be desired, so long as the methods are correct, is so manifestly true that it is universally conceded. Uniformity in the bookkeeping of each given line of trade is likewise desirable, for bookkeeping is a business method. Especially desirable is uniform bookkeeping in each division of trade and industry, if the bookkeeping is of the very highest type.

The most advanced interpretations of accounting and the most scientific forms of bookkeeping are far less complicated than are the ordinary unscientific plans in common use. As a fact the best and highest forms are the easiest for the business man to comprehend and work with. They cost less in original equipment and also in daily labor than do poorer methods. There is, therefore, business economy of the most pronounced character in using the very best that can be obtained. On the other hand, there is wilful waste and profligacy in adhering to the poor and the commonplace.

The immediate object of all bookkeeping is to produce a correct balance sheet or business statement, as it is frequently called. When we open the accounts representing our business venture we begin with a statement of our assets and liabilities. We then proceed to do business for a certain period, buying and selling goods, and exchanging values in various ways. Each of our transactions results in either a profit or a loss. Each transaction is also accompanied by an expense, more or less clearly defined. So long as our profits are larger than our combined losses and expenses, we make money. Whenever our losses and expenses, taken collectively, exceed the profits on our transactions, we lose money. To ascertain our standing at the end of the period we turn to our accounts for the data by which to make out a new balance sheet or business statement. A measure, therefore, of the adequacy of the bookkeeping we are employing is afforded by the ease and celerity with which the new balance sheet can be produced.

The highest type of bookkeeping provides a perpetual balance sheet: In other words, a going balance sheet and a going profit and loss statement are made integral parts of the bookkeeping system itself. They are always complete and up-to-date and are ever in shape to afford answers to all the questions that arise in the business man's mind as to his progress and as to his exact financial condition.

It is only through the introduction of uniform bookkeeping in the different trades and industries that the cost of instruction in the most advanced methods and the cost of equipment and supplies for the same can be kept down to the lowest possible figures. The wide employment of what are regarded as special books has the effect of reducing their cost to figures closely competing with the prices of regular stock books such as are usually carried by stationers. Again, the use of a common bookkeeping plan by a large number of business men in the same line of trade has the effect, in the course of time, of developing its various strong points and perfecting all of its details.

Army Bookkeeping

By Walton Day

Among the war matters which are being discussed of late is that of the bookkeeping routine of the army. In these modern times nothing can be done without a record. No property can be delivered without a requisition or a receipt, and every officer, according to his rank and the duties assigned him, is obliged to make a report and give account of his stewardship. The records extend down to the minutest detail. Each company must maintain its proper accounts. The company accounts contribute to the regiment records, and so on, to batallions and divisions, until finally the whole account of the entire army is made up.

The bookkeeping of a regiment of volunteers, for example, just entering the national service, is fairly characteristic of that which prevails in many other directions The detail work devolves upon the sergeants. A brief enumeration of the books may interest the reader. First there are the company books. Of these the most important is the "Descriptive and Clothing Book." This contains all the information about each man that has gone on the muster roll, such as age, nationality and home address, with such remarks as one usually finds in police records respecting eyes, hair and the like. There is also a column in which to chronicle such facts as death, desertion, discharge and promotion. The clothing account is kept in the same book. Every time a man gets a hat, a pair of shoes or other equipment from the quartermaster's stores, the articles are charged up against him, and against the amount he is entitled to draw upon for the current half year. The book is balanced at the end of June and December. For the first six months a man in the army is entitled to sixty dollars for his clothing, and the account is for the purpose of showing to what extent this appropriation has been exhausted by his drafts.

The next book is called the "Daily Report Book," and requires, as its name indicates, more constant looking after than the one previously referred to. The name of every man in the company, from the captain down, is entered in this book. Accordingly, it shows the complete status of the company. The entries in it are made early in the morning. By a glance at it one can tell the company's effective strength for the day. It records absences, sicknesses, stragglers—in short, how many men are ready for duty. As soon as the book is made up in the morning, it goes to regimental headquarters, where a draft is made from it for the consolidated report of the regiment. It is then returned to the company. The Daily Report Book is made the basis for the returns for rations, which are only to be drawn for the actual number of men in the company at the time requisition is made.

Another regular book kept by the sergeants of the companies is the "Sick Report." In it are recorded the names of all who report at sick call. When the book is made up it goes to the hospital tent, where the regimental surgeon on duty records in it the disposition of cases. If a man reports sick that needs only a simple remedy, the surgeon writes "for duty." If a man is ill enough to need relief from work, but not ill enough to go to the hospital, the surgeon writes "in quarters." If a man is very ill, he goes to the hospital and the record inscribed is "in hospital." The contents of the Sick Book then go into the Daily Report Book.

As a rule, no other regular books are maintained. Some sergeants keep a book for roll call, but a good sergeant usually calls the roll from memory, and in his memory, in turn, he stores away the names of the absentees. The sergeant major, the man who keeps the regimental books, must know all about the commissaries and quartermaster's department, about ordnance, about the hospital and about the adjutant-general's routine. He, in a measure, belongs to the adjutant-general's staff. He must keep a careful record of all orders received and issued, and he also keeps a voluminous letter-book of letters sent and received. His most important book is the "Consolidated Morning Report." This is only a compilation from the company books, but there is great need of accuracy in making it up. When completed, it shows the status of the regiment for the day. Another book kept by the sergeant-major is that in which is reported the field court-martials. This book goes directly to the Judge Advocate at Washington, and is extremely valuable. A man's liberty often depends on its accuracy, for the Judge Advocate can set aside trials in which there has been the least irregularity. A court-martial, as many have observed, is under great temptation to be a law unto itself.

The sergeant-major also keeps a descriptive book, which is identical with the company book, save only that it has fewer names in it. The book he keeps is only the record of the non-commissioned staff. Still another book that should be referred to in this connection is the guard-house or tent-book, which is kept by the sergeant of the guard, who enters in it the names of the guard for the day and their relief, whether first, second or third. He also records therein all prisoners found in the guard-house when his guard was mounted, and all prisoners brought in, with their alleged offences, and all liberations when made by the proper authorities. This goes to the sergeant-major at guard mount, and is returned immediately. In many respects it resembles a ship's log. The bulk of army bookkeeping and of bookkeeping that is purely military in its nature is covered in this general outline. The other books that are kept—those in the Subsistence and Quartermaster's Departments—are such books almost as might be kept by storekeepers anywhere, who deal in candles, bacon and other articles.

Silas Sadler Packard

In the death of S. S. Packard, which occurred at his residence in New York October 27, the community loses a good citizen, business education loses a man who for many years occupied a position in its foremost rank, and the Institute of Accounts a member and ex-officer, who, throughout his connection with the organization covering the entire period of its existence, did, up to the limit of his ability and opportunity, whatever would promote its interests.

The announcement of Mr. Packard's death reaches us just as this number of Accountics goes to press and, therefore, it is impossible to give a lengthy account of his life; suffice it to say that he was born in Massachusetts in 1826, emigrated to Kentucky in 1845, served in the Mexican war in 1848, and returning spent some little time in Ohio. In 1851 he went to Lockport, N. Y., as a commercial teacher. Later he lived in Tonawanda, where for several years he conducted a periodical known as the Niagara River Pilot. In 1856 he went to Buffalo and there became interested in the management of a business college. Later he spent a year in Chicago and shortly before the sixties founded in New York, in connection with Bryant & Stratton, a business school. Later he purchased the interests of his associates and the school became known as Packard's, which title continues to this day. Mr. Packard was the author of a number of commercial text books and was, for many years, foremost in the counsels of the commercial instructors of the country. He was a clear writer, a fluent talker and a master of debate and argument. He was a leader in almost every movement with which his name was associated and will be very generally missed in the business and social community of which he was a conspicuous part.

Accountants' Associations

Institute of Accounts

On Thursday evening, October 6, there was held at the Waldorf-Astoria the National Convention of the Institute of Accounts. Delegates were present from the various out-of-town chapters as well as those representing the New York chapter. The only business transacted was the election of general officers and members of the Executive Council, the choice being as follows: President, Charles E. Sprague, of the Union Dime Saving Institute New York; Secretary and Treasurer, Henry Harney, Certified Public Accountant, 88 Wall Street, New York. Members of the Executive Counsel for three years were chosen as follows: J. H. McNish, Boston; W. P. Plant, New York; A. O. Kittredge, New York, and R. H. Broderick, Bridgeport, Conn.

New York Chapter Institute of Accounts

Following the convention of the Institute of Accounts, the New York Chapter gave a dinner, to which were invited all of the out-of-town delegates and a number of guests residing in New York and vicinity. After a very attractive menu had been discussed in the usual way a number of brief addresses were made.

Charles Dutton, president of New York Chapter, acted as toastmaster, although there were no toasts. Among those who spoke were Messrs. Fitzgerald, who, in an effort to further advance the science of accounting and art of bookkeeping, suggested special courses of study; Jaudon, who deprecated uniformity of accounting methods because they might serve to lessen the volume of business usually flowing to public accountants; Gershon Smith, who gave a most interesting account of the formation and progress of the Hartford Chapter; Todd, who urged upon the Institute the necessity of a larger membership, thereby increasing its usefulness many fold; Richardson, who gave some account of conditions prevailing in Bridgeport and the chances of organizing a chapter of the Institute at that point; Broderick, who continued the same general line of thought, with assurances that results entirely satisfactory to the Institute would be reported from Bridgeport at an early day; D. C. Smith, auditor of the American Cotton Company, who dwelt briefly on the necessity of accurate accounting in the interest of capital; Rohne, who referred briefly to branches of specialized accounting, illustrating his remarks by allusions to the mathematics of building association work; Tipson, who referred to the work of a sister society; Ott, former Secretary of the New York Chapter, who alluded to the better opinion in which accounting is held in the community at large at present, as compared with what formerly prevailed, and Kittredge, who gave a résume of the work that is being done by the Association of Street Railway Accountants of America and other societies, which have been formed for developing special lines of accountancy. The addresses were delightfully informal and entirely void of the restraint of a pre-arranged programme. In all respects the dinner was one of the most successful and satisfactory that the New York Chapter has ever given.

Hartford Chapter of the Institute of Accounts

A brief synopsis of the work accomplished to date by the Hartford organization will no doubt interest many of our readers, while perhaps it will also specially encourage other branches of the Institute in different parts of the country. Meetings of the Hartford Chapter are held monthly in the rooms of the Hartford Board of Trade, which are centrally located and well adapted for the purpose. There is ample accommodation for from 50 to 75 persons.

The first regular meeting after the organization was established was held on the 26th of April. P. H. Woodward, Secretary of the Board of Trade, opened the meeting with an informal address welcoming the Institute of Accounts to Hartford and to the Board of Trade rooms. He gave a brief history of the Board of Trade from its formation to date and drew interesting parallels between its work in the community and what a society of accounts might do in the same community. At the conclusion of this address the question, "What is the proper basis of valuation of unsold goods to be credited to merchandise account when closing the ledger?" was introduced and discussed by nearly all of the members and visitors present. The consensus of opinion seemed to be that present cost value was the proper basis of valuation.

At the May meeting the question, "Is a journal indispensable in any kind of business?" was introduced by Charles W. Rohne in a very interesting paper. A general discussion followed. The conclusion reached seemed to be that a journal is not indispensable, but that it may be in any one of a number of different forms.

At the June meeting, although the weather was very, warm, there was a large attendance. Several subjects had been assigned to different members for special treatment. "What is the advantage of having a cash account in the ledger?" was discussed in a paper read by Frank W. Hawley. Mr. Hawley's conclusions were that a cash account is of no special advantage in the ledger. This position, however, was not concurred in by all of those who took part in the discussion that followed. "What is the difference between a trial balance and a balance sheet?" was treated in a paper by Horace S. Seymour. "What items should appear in expense accounts?" was discussed in a paper by Daniel P. Colton. "What points should be considered in a partnership contract, so that the division of gain or loss may be equitable?" was treated by George L. Vannais. "How can it be proper in a bank statement to put expense and other items of loss down to resources?" was ably handled by Gilbert W. Chapin. Each of the papers was profitably discussed at the conclusion of the reading and not a few original ideas were expressed. The plan was followed of inviting visitors to take part in the discussion as well as the members.

Meetings were suspended during July and August, but were resumed in September, and on the 27th of that month there was a meeting which had a very large attendance. Short papers were read as follows: "What is the distinction between bank discount and true discount?" by the President of the Chapter, George A. Reynolds; "Credits and Collections," by F. H. Boson; "Procedure in changing from single to double entry," by J. A. Butler, and "What is the significance of a sinking fund?" by Elmer M. White. The discussion of these papers by many of the members present proved conclusively that questions along the general lines indicated are well worthy of thought and consideration in every community.

The meetings of this organization to be held during the fall and winter months promise to be more interesting and valuable to the members than those which have preceded. Interest in the work seems to be constantly increasing and good reports as a regular thing are to be expected from the Hartford Chapter.

Educating Business Men

Business education, as the term is ordinarily employed, refers to the preliminary drill given young men in bookkeeping and allied arts before they enter upon office work. That the term from this time forward is to have a higher and broader significance is clearly indicated by the following extract from an address by F. R. Boocock, Secretary of the National Association of Credit Men, delivered a short time since before the Credit Mens Association of Rochester:

In seeking for one of the best means of improving credit conditions, it is impossible to overlook the necessity for educational work. It is very important to bring constantly to the attention of merchants the newest ideas and latest methods for the conduct of business. There is nothing of greater importance to the business world than the dissemination of sound business doctrines and the publication of the safest and truest systems. Our experience proves conclusively that a very large proportion of our commercial failures are caused by the ignorance of correct principles and the execution of incorrect ideas. By the adoption of the method we have selected of bringing to the attention of merchants the pitfalls into which so many honorable men have fallen, exposing the rocks upon which others have foundered, and exhibiting the methods that should be practiced, and the problems to which proper attention should be given, we can be reasonably sure that very much can be done to increase our business stability and to enhance the character of our commercial enterprise.

In success be moderate.—Franklin.

Systems of Accounting and Bookkeeping

It may be safely assumed that all the accounting in use may be grouped under three heads—double entry, single entry and X. The latter class we designate by the algebraic symbol commonly employed to designate an unknown quantity, for the reason that whatever there is outside of double entry and single entry involves so much of an unknown quantity that it becomes its main characteristic. We occasionally encounter those who claim to keep their books upon plans that are neither single entry nor double entry, nor yet arranged upon the asserted still more advanced plans included under the head of logismography. Hence the necessity of providing the third class in this survey.

It is the purpose of this series of articles, which will be continued until the field has been fairly covered, to present for the consideration of our readers a brief account of each of the considerable number of accounting systems now before the public, and which are candidates for favor. Our investigations, however, will be restricted, for the most part, to those systems which are essentially double entry in principle, and we shall not feel called upon to spend much effort in other directions—that is to say, upon investigations into the domain of X, as indicated above, nor yet into the realms of single entry.

We invite the reader's co-operation in these articles. If anything appears, descriptive of specified systems, with which the reader does not agree and with respect to which, by reason of his position of advantage, he is able to give further information, we shall be glad to have communications accordingly. If the reader sees anything described in these articles which is known to him by another name, he will confer a favor by communicating the fact to the editor. If the reader is acquainted with any system of accounting which is not mentioned in these articles, he will likewise confer a favor by sending forward such particulars as will enable us to prepare a paragraph concerning it. Our readers generally are invited to ask questions concerning systems. Those questions which we cannot answer off-hand, we will very carefully investigate, to the end that these columns may present the information sought.

I.—THE ROBINSON SYSTEM.

A system of bookkeeping which has attained considerable local prominence in the neighborhood of Boston, and notably in Lynn, was introduced some fourteen years ago by John L. Robinson, whose Boston office is No. 63 High Street, and Lynn office at 43 Sachem Street. The features of the system, we are informed, are the outcome of an examination of a set of books made many years since, wherein the work was largely duplicated. Mr. Robinson characterizes his system by the assertion that it is absolutely accurate and is maintained with the use of a minimum number of figures and words, and also a minimum amount of space. A number of special books are employed and these are carried in stock to meet the demand which has been created.

The leading feature of the books is the explanatory headings for the guidance of the bookkeeper and the ready information of the employer. The books embrace sales books, invoice files, cash books, note books for posting direct to the ledger, ledgers of various varieties, trial balance books, etc. The cash books include those made upon the columnar plan and also the variety known as double debit cash books for use by concerns whose receipt items are much more numerous than their disbursement items. The note books are arranged for posting direct to the ledger. The ledgers are provided with center money columns, also with right and left money columns. The sales books, invoice files, etc., are so arranged that all the debits made in a month to representative accounts can be offset by a single credit, and all credits by a single debit.

Referring to his experience, both prior to the introduction of the system which bears his name and since it has been employed, Mr. Robinson says: "I have found that a large percentage of firms desire medium-priced bookkeepers, inexpensive systems and relatively cheap books. They also demand correct work, upon simple, common-sense plans, that are easy to understand and analyze. It is to this field of business that I devote my energies. My books were originally designed for the shoe manufacturing business in its various branches, and without much advertising and no agents, they have found their way into about one thousand firms, engaged in about one hundred branches of the trade."

Reviews and Criticisms

Averaging Accounts

Martin's Equation Tables, designed to furnish merchants, manufacturers and other business men with an accurate set of calculations for averaging accounts and enabling the bookkeeper to perform with great facility and dispatch what has hitherto been a tedious process in the science of equations. By George W. Martin. Tenth edition. 1882. Published by Wilbur & Hasting. Price, $2.

The book above described is a standard work and one that is in extensive use in offices in various lines of business, and yet one that has been so little pushed as to be unknown to many who are needing just the assistance which it offers. The tables were calculated by a practical accountant many years since, when labor-saving devices were less in demand than at present, but when, nevertheless, any reasonable plan of shortening tedious processes of averaging accounts and of performing other problems in equations was of substantial value. The author prepared these tables at the outset for his own use. According to the preface he was laboring at the time with only six hundred accounts, whereas many a bookkeeper at the present time is required to oversee several times as many.

At the outset there is a chapter on equation of payments, wherein the principles are very clearly explained, and wherein the routine of the bookkeeper's work in this regard is clearly set forth. The problems which arise are divided into simple equations and compound equations. The first tables presented are tables of quotients and show the number of days from January 1 to any other date of the same year; also from January 1 of one year to any date of the next year, and from January 1 of a given year, counting backwards, to any date of the previous year. Following the tables of quotients are tables, seventy-two in number, arranged with reference to dates continuously from January 1 to December 31. There is a column of figures for each day of the year, and each page presents ten dates, the right-hand page being a continuation of the left, and having the same dates. Upon the margins of these tables are printed words and figures as follows: "January 10, 20, 31;" "February 10, 20, 29," and so on through the months of the year. These refer to the ten dates upon the pages and are employed in a cut index. There is also a column of figures at the extreme right of each page marked "Second year," to be used when the account embraces parts of two years. The amounts contained in these tables against the several dates corresponding to the dates in the account to be averaged are to be added together and divided by the total amount of the account. The quotient thus obtained is a key to the table of quotients giving the date that the account averages. In compound equations there are explained the processes by which is ascertained the date at which the balance of an account becomes due, where there are both debits and credits. From this description it will be seen that the tables are in very convenient form for use. Their utility is certified to by a large number of practical accountants who have employed them.

Printers' Style

Style-Book of the Chicago Society of Proof Readers. Pamphlet, sixteen pages. Published by the Ben Franklin Company. Price fifteen cents.

Every printing office has its style, by which is meant its own peculiar way of managing with respect to spelling, capitalization, abbreviation, citations, italics, hyphenating, punctuating, etc. We have never known of a printing office that was able, satisfactorily to itself, to accept any of the dictionaries for its style. There are exceptions to all rules among printers as well as others, and these exceptions to a large degree constitute the peculiarities of the style of any given office. The Style-Book of the Chicago Society of Proof Readers is not the style of any one printing office, but is the style upon which the Society has been able to agree. As stated in the preface, it is necessarily the result of compromises.

A book of this kind is of value in every business office, because every business office prepares copy for the printer, and whoever prepares that copy should have something at hand by which to determine the answers to various questions which arise. It is useful to stenographers, and a very casual examination of it by one who is fresh from school will show the vast difference between theory and practice. It is in convenient form for reference. It has been approved by many scholars of high standing and has been recommended for typewriters by such authorities as Mrs. Burnz, of New York, and the Phonographic Magazine, of Cincinnati. It is a work that will mark the path for many who are at present wandered in the wilderness of style.

Correspondence

Partnership Agreements

From John Vaughan, Pittsburg, Pa.:

The August-September issue of ACCOUNTICS is a most excellent one. It bristles with well-digested information, which will please thousands.

The point you call attention to on Page 100, to wit: That of keeping partners' capital and partners' personal accounts separate and distinct on the account books of the firm is a practice followed by the writer for years in the course of his professional experience. Professionally I invariably advocate, and introduce if possible, a capital account as well as a personal account for the books of a single proprietor even. When there are partners I insist upon it theoretically, and if not opposed by owners adjust those accounts in that way, or open the books in that manner.

Last December, in a partnership article of agreement (two partners), prepared and written by the writer, the following paragraph appears:

"3. The capital stock shall be $——, to be contributed equally by said parties; losses and gains to be equally distributed. The capital contribution shall be kept in a separate account on the account books to be called "Capital Stock." There shall be kept a personal account with each partner on which interest shall be allowed at six (6) per cent. per annum as per averages, the said interest to be a part of the current expenses of operation. The capital stock may be increased by mutual consent and record herewith."

From the above it can be seen that profits, if made, could be added to capital stock, as provided; otherwise they would be transferred by credit to the partners' personal accounts, which would be the partners' withdrawal accounts.

The same partnership agreement has an article, or paragraph, providing an allowance of wages to each partner, it having been prepared for a mechanical business.

"8. No verbal agreement shall contravene any of the terms of this 'Article of Agreement' without endorsement herein."

This is a good proviso and has saved trouble in several cases under my observation. Under it I have undone entries previously made by a bookkeeper and with the fullest sanction, approval and acceptance of the resultant by all directly interested.

"6. A balance sheet of all assets and of all liabilities of this partnership shall be made up for use and inspection of both partners at least once a year after proper appraisement and inventory. The books of account shall be kept by double entry method and be at all times open to the inspection of either member of the firm, or to his duly authorized representative."

This paragraph, you will note, calls for double entry bookkeeping; it also gives the professional accountant access to the books of account if either party desires to call him in.

The writer has been frequently debarred from access to books by the pigheadedness of one partner. In not a few cases I could have pointed out the way to the firm, by a simple analysis, how to avoid ruin, had I seen the accounts in due season.

The article above could be improved upon by calling for a trading account, setting forth expenditure and income, although to the professional accountant that must be done in order to develop the balance sheet after going to the trouble of appraising, etc. The trading account is, therefore, a latent factor in the paragraph like the heat in a piece of coal. It was omitted for brevity's sake, as people who don't understand bookkeeping prefer short agreement. They are suspicious of an article whose working out they do not quite understand. My experience suggests brevity; to say no more than vitally necessary in partnership articles; to drop redundancy, and yet enough to insure substantial equity, the true basis of confidence between partners. In case a professional accountant is called in for expert opinion, he can readily dispense equity if the provisions are made fair. Non-essentials are to be omitted preferably in so far as the writer's experience has gone.

I suggest your calling for a series of model "Articles of Agreement" for general partnerships, small, medium and large capital, and for mechanical, mercantile, manufacturing and professional businesses. By mechanical I mean a class not exactly manufacturers, or only in a small degree, but using manufactured goods. Say tinners, plumbers, painters and such. Such contributions to your columns would develop those points which each author may deem essential, and a "boiling down" of the whole series might develop one true model. Evolution is the law of progress. Lawyers frequently insert provisos, not capable of a practical carrying out in the bookkeeping, because contradictory in more than one direction.

Did the Court Err?

From J. B. Glasser, Manitou, Colorado:

Referring to the interesting paper of Mr. Eddis on partnership in the August-September issue, in the settlement of the Ballard-Haley et al. affair, the court allowed judgment in favor of Moore against Butler for $2,271.22. Should the amount not have been $2,957.55? Suppose the sum $27,209.59 had been due outside creditors and the solvent partners paid according to their respective interests in the profits and losses, the results would have been: Moore, 18 per cent., 18-40, or 45 per cent. of $27,209.59—$14,965.27; Butler, 22 per cent., 22-40, or 55 per cent. of $27,209.59—$12,244.32.

The creditors having been paid by Moore and Butler, they proceed to adjust as between themselves. Moore paid to the creditors $17,922.82, when he should have paid 45 per cent. of $27,209.59, or $12,965.27; hence he paid more than his share by $2,957.55. Butler paid to the creditors $9,286.77, when he should have paid 55 per cent. of $27,209.59, or $12,244.33; hence he paid less than his share by $2,957.55. Therefore, owes the latter amount to Moore.

What is the difference as far as the premises are concerned, whether the $27,209.59 was due members of the firm or outside creditors?

Business Requires Experience.

By G. W. Werlin.

During the last twenty-five years there has been a very material change in almost everything connected with our existence. War, for example, is at present conducted on very different lines from what formerly prevailed and the change in business is no less conspicuous. Any nation that engages in war or any man who enters upon business to-day, without such an experience and preparation as insures the use of the best up-to-date methods, is almost sure to meet disaster. Experience in war and experience in business are alike essential to success.

It may be possible occasionally to point out a business in which a man has succeeded without previous experience, but it is far easier to point out a very large number of cases wherein lack of experience has brought on disaster. That experience was lacking on the part of the one who failed may have escaped notice in some cases when the failure occurred, from the fact that some years had intervened between the time the business was begun and when the failure occurred. Nevertheless, it was inexperience that caused the disaster, and the disaster was delayed only during the period necessary to exhaust or consume the assets of the business.

Business cannot be learned from books nor acquired at school. A theoretical course in business is only an introduction to its practice. It requires thorough training to make a successful business man. Employment in a prosperous and progressive establishment, affording as it does the opportunity for watching causes and effects, and stimulating a desire to excel in the duties imposed, is the only practical training school.

To enumerate causes of business failures would be an almost endless task. The causes are extremely numerous, but for the most part they are mixed up with one kind or another of inexperience. Buying cheaply and selling at high prices are not the only conditions to insure success. Good buying is an art, the practice of which requires one to know many things and to understand many conditions. Speaking in general terms, goods can be bought cheapest when bought in a manner that causes the seller the least expense to make the sale. Therefore, the buyer's condition of solvency, his ability to pay promptly, his management of the details of his business and other conditions peculiar to himself all affect the prices that he pays for his goods. But all these are things which require forethought; that demand for their proper employment an intelligent study of conditions and a thorough acquaintance with surroundings, which are only other names for experience.

Talent is the capacity of doing anything that depends on application and industry; and it is a voluntary power, while genius is involuntary.—Hazlitt.

Talent is always queer-tempered.—Miss Braddon.

The Merchandise Account*

By A. O. Kittredge, F. I. A.

* * * I have already alluded to the inadequacy of a single merchandise or trading account for representing the complicated transactions of such a business as we are considering, but there is still more to be said about the Merchandise Account, as it is ordinarily conducted. Since the difficulties which this account presents are fundamental, making necessary, as they do, a radical departure from the ordinary interpretations of double entry bookkeeping, in order to meet the requirements of modern business, I shall ask you to bear with me long enough to show the reasons for certain features of the analysis which follow. What I have in mind to say amounts to an impeachment of the conventional Menchandise Account, namely, the Merchandise Account as set forth in various treatises upon double entry bookkeeping. But of that you must judge when I have finished.

It has long appeared to me as though there had been a mistake made by some one in the early days of the literature in English of double entry bookkeeping, and that those writers who have come after, while elaborating many features of the system, greatly to the advantage of modern business, have failed to detect the mistake made by their predecessors in the art, or to perceive the omission, if that is the preferred term, and, therefore, have gone along accepting the original pattern without a question.

Consider for a moment, if you please, the Merchandise Account as one of the several property accounts which double entry recognizes. It is peculiar among the ordinary property accounts, in that it is made up of two sets of values. There are cost prices on the one side and selling prices on the other. The balance is a mixed quantity. Compare it with Notes Receivable or with Cash, which accounts are of a similar nature. In each of them the same value appears on both sides of the account. Accordingly, the balance in each of these accounts shows the amount of the property on hand. Not so, however, with Merchandise. Its balance is an amount which represents goods on hand, minus the profit made on what has been sold; or an amount consisting of the sum of the goods on hand, plus the loss that has been made on what has been sold. This is very confusing, and it becomes still more so when expense items are taken into consideration.

Take another view of the case. Consider how we treat the Merchandise Account as we proceed with the record of transactions, and what the result is to the business. First, at the beginning of the fiscal period, we debit the account with the inventory—that is, with the amount of goods on hand. This inventory, of course, represents goods at real value or cost prices. Next we debit the Merchandise Account with the goods we buy, again using cost prices. The third step is to credit the account with the goods we part with, in this case taking them at selling prices. Some of the goods that we have bought from manufacturers or jobbers are unsatisfactory to us, and, therefore, we return them. Inasmuch as the items have been debited to Merchandise Account, that account must be credited with them when we charge them back to the seller. Here we bring in on the credit side of the account items expressed in cost values. Again, some of our customers return part of the goods which we have sold them. In crediting their accounts we necessarily debit Merchandise Account for the goods brought back. Here we bring in selling prices on the debit side. We now have selling prices and cost prices mixed in on both sides of the account.

All this is bad enough, but it does not yet represent the whole of the absurdities which are very commonly found by the public accountant in the Merchandise Account, as usually conducted. If there is a manufacturing department to the business the Merchandise Account is debited, in addition to what we have described, with the cost of the materials bought, with the amounts paid out for labor, with the salaries of the superintendent and general manager, with insurance, taxes and all the other expenses of manufacture. What bookkeeper, with such a hodge-podge of an account before him, is able to tell from the amount appearing as the balance in the Merchandise Account in the monthly trial balance what it really represents?

I have said that it has seemed to me that by some of the pioneers who wrote upon the subject of accounts, there was

---

*Extract from an address before the Business Educators' Section of the National Educational Association, Washington, July, 1898.

a link left out, or, at least, that there was a slipping of a cog in the wheels, and that those who have come after have been disposed to follow copy without question. For it is very evident that two or more accounts should have been placed where Merchandise stands alone at present.

The distinguishing difference between single entry and double entry, as often explained, is that in double entry there are property accounts which in single entry there are no property accounts (save Cash). In double entry we are supposed to be able to show the condition of the business with respect to its gain or loss by the books, but in single entry we determine the profitableness of the business only by comparing a complete statement of the proprietor's condition at the first of a fiscal period with a similar statement made up at the close. How much better does double entry do than this? By reason of that missing link or slipped cog among the property accounts, it is necessary to inventory or to count and value the goods on hand whenever a profit and loss statement is to be made out, not for the purpose of verifying a balance shown by an account, as in the counting of cash and in the listing of Notes Receivable, but for the primary purpose of determining what there is on hand.

As our books are usually opened and conducted, there is no account with stock and stores, but all is dumped into Merchandise Account, with the result of the confusion I have described. I am aware that there are some notable exceptions to what I have described, but the exceptions that are to be found in teaching and in the treatises upon bookkeeping which have general circulation are few and far between. Since it is necessary for me to bring to your attention in the analysis that we are about to consider a division of the Merchandise Account, first with respect to the departments of the business, and second with respect to the stock carried in those departments and to the sales made by the departments. I have felt that it was not in the least out of place to emphasize this feature by the criticism of the Merchandise Account to which I have directed your attention.

• • •

Two Views of Business

A recent writer, alluding to the work in which the National Association of Credit Men is engaged, says that it is of such a character as to command the sympathy of reputable and patriotic men everywhere. To save themselves from losses, says this writer, following from the practices of dishonest men, wholesalers and manufacturers have been obliged to take various precautionary measures, ranging from petitions for the enactment of new laws to arrangements for the co-operative investigation and prosecution of fraudulent failures. In protesting against crooked methods, false pretences and deception upon the part of their customers, jobbers and manufacturers have found it expedient to set a good example, showing in every reasonable way how business may be conducted honorably and free from deception and misrepresentation. Not only are they doing this, but they are demonstrating that business in general can be conducted fairly and honestly, and yet with satisfactory returns by way of profits.

The writer next alludes to an address delivered by ex-President Preston, of the National Association of Credit Men, in St. Paul a short time since. Mr. Preston dwelt upon the bad reputation attaching to business in the past, and contrasted therewith its better character, as demonstrated by business men of the present day. He asserted that the Roman philosophers despised commerce, regarding it as an unworthy calling. He quoted Cicero as saying that a merchant could never make any money unless he lied in the most atrocious manner. He quoted Saint Crysostom to the effect that it is scarcely possible for a man to be a Christian and a merchant at the same time. He showed that this sentiment has extended down almost to modern times. Benjamin Franklin said that commerce is badly tainted. Referring to the other side of the case, the speaker said: "We are teaching differently now and our credit organizations stand as sentinels pointing to honesty." The above fairly indicates the best sentiment of the community at the present time relating to business. Business is being made honorable, for honorable men are engaged in business. Contrast with this view of business the following taken from an exchange and which fairly illustrates an earlier conception of business:

At one of the annual fairs held at a small town in Russia, a gipsy and a Jew were haggling over the sale of a horse. Finally the bargain was struck and an observer called the gipsy to him and inquired how much he had got for the animal. The gipsy opened his hand and showed a ten-rouble note.

"But isn't that very cheap?"

"No," said the gipsy, "he is dead lame."

The gentleman then sought out the Jew and said:

"So you have given ten roubles for a lame horse?"

The Israelite laid his finger on his nose and said:

"Lame! He's as sound as you are; I saw he was badly shod, and only limped in consequence."

The inquirer returned to the gipsy and reported what the Jew said. The former gave a tremendous and most significant wink, and whispered:

"He's as lame as a two-legged stool. I had him badly shod on purpose, to make them believe that was the cause of his limping."

When this was communicated to the Jew he seemed for the moment taken aback, and hung his head; then, with a little sigh and a shrug of the shoulders, he said, quietly:

"Ah, well—it's all right—it was a bad ten-rouble note!"

Can Account Books be Standardized?

By Rollin Jeffries

It is the day of standardizing. Engineers meet in conventions to agree upon satisfactory forms and dimensions for important articles of use in their work. Conventions are also held to determine upon uniform and standard names in different departments of science, and in the several arts. Machines are built with interchangeable parts. Even accountants in certain lines of business get together for standardizing their systems and securing uniformity in methods throughout the industries which they represent. The savings every year, by reason of standardizing in the different fields in which standardizing has been accomplished, amount to fabulous sums of money. While much has been accomplished in the mechanical trades, the end is not yet. The ultimate result to flow from standardization is still in the distance.

The majority of account books, ledgers, journals, sales books, cash books, records and posting mediums in general, in the leading commercial and manufacturing concerns of the country, which are made to order, cost from 25 per cent. to 300 per cent. more than books of the same class of materials and involving the same amount of work would cost if manufactured in considerable quantities. The lack of standardization, assuming for the moment that standardization is possible, costs the difference between the price of stock books and the price of books made to order. The question then is, Can account books be standardized in a way to meet every requirement while conserving economy?

At first blush, every bookkeeper, every accountant and many business men will say that the idea of uniformity is preposterous; that the individual requirements of each office are so different from those of all other offices that anything like uniformity is out of the question, and, therefore, there is no use of argument. Let us consider, however, the elements that enter into these books.

In the first place, there is the paper to be considered, both with respect to quality and also as to thickness or weight. Paper manufacturers have reduced the question of paper to a very neat formula, and accountants and bookkeepers have been quick to perceive the advantage of the best grades which paper manufacturers produce. In texture, color and general quality there is so little difference at the present time in the ideas of those who order books that certainly there should be no difficulty in agreeing upon a standard in paper for each of the several books that are wanted.

Next with respect to size. There are fewer sizes of ledgers, for example, in use than might at first be supposed, and assuming that there are reasons why more than one size should be available, there does not seem to be any insuperable difficulty in arranging two or more standards in this regard.

Consider next the question of bindings. There is nothing, perhaps, in which the business man has been so frequently humbugged as in the bindings of the account books he uses, and there is nothing, perhaps, that goes into the office wherein there is as much waste, by which I mean needless expense, as in the bindings of account books. It is true that for every strong, well-bound books that is to be found in use some one can point to a book practically torn to pieces in use, thus demonstrating that the binding has been insufficient. This proves nothing, however, for in some cases it can be shown that the poor binding costs as much as the strong binding, and in many other instances it can be shown that in the strong binding, where special expense has been incurred, there is needless strength. Further than this, the strength of a binding does not represent its cost. There are many cheap bindings that are as strong as the most expensive ones.

From the foregoing, without further details, it may be concluded that a standard in bindings might be established which would be satisfactory from one end of the country to the other. There may be reason for having more than one style of binding, but in features of strength and of the material that enters into the binding, it would seem that certain standards might be agreed upon that would secure to the business man strength and durability with the smallest expenditure of money.

It is becoming the custom of late years to arrange ledgers on the time basis. Horizontal account ledgers or progressive ledgers, as they are more frequently called, are usually arranged to receive the transactions of a single year. A binding, therefore, on such books is a less important item than on ledgers that are intended to remain in use for several years, and finally to store away to be referred to as occasion demands. By the old plan, ledgers were made so large that the accidental dropping of a book was liable to injure it very materially. By the new plan, and with the sub-division of work among several ledger keepers, the volumes are made relatively very small, and, therefore, accidental dropping is not likely to do so much damage. All these facts have a material bearing upon the question of binding.

With quality of paper, thickness of paper, size of book and kind of binding established, which, we are disposed to think, many would assent to as being quite possible, there remains still the question of rulings, which, indeed, is the crucial question. Can rulings be standardized?

Rulings are of two kinds—horizontal and vertical. Of horizontal rulings there are certainly different spaces required for different purposes. A ledger to which postings of figures alone are made may be very much more closely ruled, and yet be satisfactory in use, than a record like a day book or journal, the pages of which are to be written full. Still, other variations will suggest themselves, which lead to the thought that if horizontal rulings are to be standardized there would have to be several well defined spaces and characters of lines.

Next let us consider the question of vertical rulings. While at first glance it would seem that of vertical rulings there is no end of variety, still, when an investigation is made it is found that vertical rulings can all be comprehended in a comparatively small number of groups. Within these groups the variations are almost nothing. Printing and heads may differ, different accountants may call the same account and the same group of accounts by different names, but details of that sort are scarcely sufficient to warrant the extreme expense of a new construction whenever a variation is required.

The present article is not intended to be an exhaustive discussion of the subject. Instead, it is only the embodiment of a suggestion sent forth with the hope that it will call out discussion from practical men. If horizontal rulings alone were standardized and blank book manufacturers were able to keep ruled paper in stock, which means that they would be able to rule paper in very large quantities, instead of ruling it in small lots; if bindings were standardized to such an extent that the supply houses catering to bookbinders' requirements could carry in stock book covers partially completed, made up in large quantities by special machinery; if the wants of bookkeepers in general could be standardized to such an extent that manufacturers of specialties could depend upon a demand for a reasonable quantity so as to make up their books in lots of 100 to 1,000 at a time, as other articles are manufactured, the cost of blank books to the average business concern would be reduced 25 per cent. to 75 per cent. of the present figures. Is the game worth the candle? Can it be done? Is it possible for accountants and bookkeepers to co-operate in a way to bring about such a condition of affairs as will enable blank books for special purposes to be manufactured at a cost closely approximating the stock books which are now found on the shelves of every stationer?

Terms of Sale

In a recent article entitled "The Tax on Wholesalers," wherein is discussed the expenses foisted upon wholesalers for collecting the checks of out-of-town customers, F. R. Boocock, Secretary of the National Association of Credit Men, presents the following sentences with regard to terms of sale:

I know there is a laxity on the part of some regarding their relations with the merchant, and that there are individuals who consider it clever to make some deduction for a puerile claim when making payment, or to exact an extra discount, or for some cause or other, to take advantage of the creditor and make a few cents or a few dollars in that way. All honor to the man that observes the strict terms of a sale and makes payment in accordance therewith, and all honor to the house that refuses to be defrauded by the petty devices that are frequently exhibited in the payment of bills for the purpose of gaining an additional percentage of profit or an increase of time on the account.

Nothing succeeds so well as success.—Talleyrand.

Talents constitute our very essence.—Charles Rollin.

The History of Bookkeeping*

By John Row-Fogo

No attempt has ever been made in this country (England) to study the history of bookkeeping in a scientific spirit, and to trace the gradual development in the art of recording the transactions of commerce from the early times when a worthy schoolmaster would annex to a treatise on arithmetic a few chapters dealing with the science of accounts, "after the manner of Debitour and Creditour," and by an "exquisite method," to the present day, when we have books by the hundred, doubtless no less exquisite in the eyes of their authors, since some of them take out a patent for their system—we suppose to prevent imitation. In the nation of shopkeepers this indifference causes surprise. But our neglect of this field has in reality its excuses. At the end of the fifteenth century, when complete systems of bookkeeping were first propounded, England occupied a very subordinate position among commercial nations, so that in our language no old treatises on bookkeeping exist; indeed, it may be doubted whether even up to a period considerably later than the period of the first book on the subject there was any English writer of originality. Some of our authors, it is true, deplore this absence of native talent, but they do nothing to remedy the grievance, and content themselves with translating, without acknowledgment, the most advanced foreign authors of the day; so that both in performing the deeds and in the more humble task of writing their chronicle we English have proved deficient. The performance we left to the Italians, the chronicle to the Germans, and all that remains to us at present is to give an appreciation of the work that has been done.

It has been impossible to discover the inventor of double entry bookkeeping. Probably, indeed, it grew up gradually, step by step, and its authorship will most likely remain, like that of the poems of Homer, all uncertain, except, as the schoolboy said, that it was not "made by one person." Certain, however, it is, as Dr. Jager has been at much pains to point out, that modern bookkeeping was not developed out of a system of single entry; and, further, that it dates back no farther than the time of the greatness of Venice and the cities of northern Italy. Many passages in old writers have been cited, of which Dr. Jager gives a list, from which it has been sought to prove that double entry was known at the time of Cicero and Pliny, and even to the Assyrians. These, however, prove nothing more than a familiarity with the custom of entering debits and credits on opposite sides of the page. Much more important are the extracts which have been published from the business books of the Barons von Fugger, the Rothschilds of medieval finance. These books were kept at Augsburg between 1413 and 1427, and show no signs or even rudiments of double entry.

The beginnings of the science are, therefore, unknown, and when we first meet with it in the "Summa de Arithmetica" of Luca Pacioli, printed in 1494, we find it full grown, almost as we know it to-day, and already bearing the evident traces of improvements suggested by years of experience. Fra Luca was a Franciscan monk, and known, even in an order rich in the names of men of learning, as one of the greatest scientists of the day. As the name of the book implies, it deals with the science of figures rather than with that of accounts, and, indeed, the chapters containing the masterly exposition of double entry were added as an appendix—almost as an afterthought. Coins, weights and measures in these days were in a state of dire confusion, and, after having given the rules and principles of arithmetical and algebraic calculation, Pacioli adds his chapter on bookkeeping, as he says himself, to give his readers in the same book all the instructions for bringing order into their commercial affairs. He lays no claim to be the author of double entry. "We shall follow the method of Venice (al modo di Venezia), which, without doubt, is much to be preferred before all others." How much the art of bookkeeping gained by passing through his clear brain it is impossible to say, but certainly

---

Originally published in the Accountant's Magazine, June, 1898.

Uber einige altere Bearbeitungen des Buchhaltungs-tractates von Luca Pacioli. Ein Beitag zur Geschichte der Buchhaltung. By Carl Peter Kheil. Prague, 1896.

Beitrage zur Geschichte der Doppelbuchhaltung. By Dr. Erhet Ludwig Jager. Stuttgart, 1874.

Luca Pacioli und Simon Stevin, nebst einigen jungeren Schriftstellern uber Buchhaltung. By the Same. Stuttgart, 1876.

Pacioli presents its principles with a lucidity which is hardly surpassed by the standard treatises of to-day, and, moreover, weaves into his narrative such quaint remarks and such wise advice that we cannot refrain from giving our readers some quotations from Dr. Jager's German translation. Should any one familiar with their language be interested in reading the first treatise on bookkeeping, they will find Dr. Jager's book well worthy of their attention. Not having access to the original, we cannot criticise its merits as a translation, but a German professor may be trusted in this respect, and, undoubtedly, Dr. Jager has caught the spirit of the book and provides us with most entertaining reading. The work of Pacioli, indeed, is a classic. The writers on bookkeeping—Italian, as well as foreign—for a century after the publication of the "Summa de Arithmetica," are nothing but more or less intelligent translators and adapters, most of them less rather than more; and even after the lapse of two hundred years, M. Kheil has found passages in the writings of eminent authors acknowledging their indebtedness to the work of the great Franciscan.

What we would nowadays call the chief defect in the bookkeeping of Venice, namely, to insist on passing each transaction through the journal before it finds its destination in the ledger, was in these days not an error of clumsiness, but a necessity called for by the circumstances of the time. The state of the coinage was chaotic. Transactions had to be carried on by means of a mass of coins which flowed in from every country, and from a host of petty states and cities; they were worn, clipped and often base—in fact, they were as varied as the pebbles on the beach. Sales and purchases were entered in the "day-book" as they occurred, and it was a work of considerable time for the head bookkeeper to convert them into the one standard medium in which his ledger accounts were kept. In this way every entry came to be journalized.

Let us now pass to a consideration of Pacioli's work and see what progress had been made in 1494 in the science of accounts. "The object of bookkeeping," says our author, "is to enable a merchant to conduct all his affairs in good order, so that he may quickly see how he stands in regard to each part of his business, as well as to his debts and to the moneys that may be owing to him." Does this not show a perfectly clear appreciation of the results to be obtained by double entry?—a record of the profit or loss of any department of a business, and a balance sheet at any date showing assets and liabilities.

"But before beginning to trade, the merchant must make a careful inventory in such a way that he writes on a sheet or into a special book all that in the world he possesses, movable and immovable, even if they were a thousand things. This whole inventory must be made on one day, otherwise it would disturb future trading." Here follows an example of an inventory, written out with great care and full particulars. "Everything must be mentioned—name, designation, mark, as much as possible. To a merchant nothing can be too clear. For this reason he has been compared to a cock, which, of all animals, is most watchful, and in winter and in summer never ceases its vigils." It is also said of the nightingale, quaintly remarks the author, that she sings all night, but this is only true during the summer and in warm weather—not in winter.

A note which pervades all these old treatises on bookkeeping, and which strikes us as strange nowadays, is the never-failing appeal to the religious feelings of the reader. The example of Pacioli of gently pressing his doctrines on his readers was hardly out of place in a member of an austere religious order, which was then at its height and full of the enthusiasm created by a cruel persecution; but by his immediate imitators it was done perfunctorily, and strikes us as nauseous. "These precepts," says Pacioli, "I have given you that you may not weary of the daily trouble of your business, especially not of your writings, when you enter up day by day all that occurs in the manner which I will show you. But, above all things, keep God before your eyes. By almsgiving riches are as little cut off as the road to heaven by holy mass." Again, in beginning a new book, the reader is reminded that among true Catholics it is the custom to mark the book with that glorious sign of the cross, before which every spiritual enemy flies and the angels of hell deservedly tremble.

"At once after the inventory," says Pacioli, "I declare that for orderliness and convenience a merchant requires three books—the one called Memorial (day-book), the second called Journal, the third called Great Book (Quaderno), although it sometimes happens that people who have few dealings use only the last two, namely, the journal and the ledger." Instructions are then given for writing up the day-book, and through the nature of the commerce of that day, it must have been a very rough, untidy kind of book. The merchant princes of Venice were retail dealers as well as traders on a large scale. The vaults and lofts of their dwelling houses were their chief emporium, but active business was also transacted in the wooden booths which were erected in the market places and streets of the town. "The day-book," says Pacioli, "is written up in the pressure (furia) of business, and the entries must be made by the principal, the clerks, the apprentices, or the women (if they can write), in the absence of the one or the other." Here again the author enjoins that a careful note be taken of the coins and measure in which each bargain is transacted. The day-book was evidently used to record every possible transaction, sales as well as purchases, bargains made for cash as well as on credit, and it is not till much later that a thorough separation takes place in the books of original entry.

We must now, however, leave the day-book and journal and examine Pacioli's treatment of the ledger, for, quaint and interesting as the former may be, it is the ledger which will show the extent of his proficiency in the science of double entry. We find that the old monk has no cause to shrink from such a scrutiny. Taking first the "inventory," he directs the reader to open accounts for each of its items, and to enter the creditor's on the left hand side of the page, the debtor's on the right; then to set apart a page for his own capital, which he credits with the assets and debits with the liabilities. "For in this book (the ledger) you must never put anything to the debit of an account which you do not credit to some other account, and conversely you must never credit an account without debiting another account with the same amount. In this way you can balance your ledger. In the debits there must be as much as in the credits. And when you add up all the entries, even if they are 10,000, then the one sum must amount to the same as the other; if it were otherwise, this would prove that an error is contained in some account, as I will show you more clearly when I instruct you how to take down the balance of your accounts."

Pacioli has no separate cash-book, and, indeed, so long as it was necessary to journalize each cash transaction to put in readiness for posting, it would have been a waste of labor to post a cash-book as well as a ledger account. Pacioli refers, for instance, to the custom among some merchants to keep separate books for such outlays as wages, cost of carriage, etc., but dismissed the subject with the remark that he finds no fault with such a practice, but considers it additional labor. But, granted that the form of recording dealings with cash was defective, in the account itself there was no error of principle: "The balance on cash account can never be a creditor, but must always be a debtor, or else the account must be square, and as soon as the balance appears as a creditor there will be a mistake in the account."

Putting aside, however, questions of mere form, which must be judged by the requirements of the circumstances, and turning our attention to matters of essential importance, we find that Pacioli has a clear grasp of what is necessary for recording a complicated transaction. Take, for instance, the instructions given for keeping the accounts of a branch shop. "You make the shop a debtor in your books for all goods which you may send into it day by day, making these goods creditors. You must imagine that the shop is a person who becomes your debtor for the things you give him, or for all expenses you defray on his account. On the other hand, you must credit the shop in your books with everything you take out of it, or which you receive from it, in the same way as if it were a debtor gradually paying off a debt. As often as you wish to make an accounting your books will show what the shop yields you, whether much or little, and you will then know what to do and how you should manage it." The same care to keep apart accounts relating to distinct transactions is shown in the treatment of partnership accounts, and the accounts of travellers sent with goods to fairs or foreign countries. In regard to bank accounts, a piece of advice is given which surely must contain a deep cardinal truth, for it stands to-day, unshaken and supreme, in spite of the changes wrought on every side by the five centuries which have passed since first it was uttered. "And because it sometimes happens that you deal with the banker on account of different businesses, both for yourself and for others, therefore you must keep different accounts with him in order to escape great confusion."

At the period for closing the books a trial balance was made by taking down the summations of all the ledger accounts, and, after securing an agreement, a profit and loss account was formed and the balance transferred to capital account. We say, if an agreement of the books was secured. Failing this happy result, a device was resorted to with which we are not wholly unfamiliar at the present day; and, as it may, perhaps, cheer some weary auditor to hear of the antiquity of the task at which he is engaged, and even inspire a placid sense of veneration in place of the impatient feelings which animate him to-day, we shall describe the process as it was practised five hundred years ago. "If the summa summarum of debits and credits in your trial balance are not equal to one another, you will conclude that there is an error in your ledger, and this error you must look for with diligence and patience, and with such talents as God has given you. You will proceed after the following manner: Take a companion, for you will hardly do this by yourself. Give him the journal into his hand, and hold you the ledger. Tell your companion that he is to begin with the first entry in the journal and call the page of your ledger, first the debit, then the credit. You must obey him and look up everything that he gives you. If your entry agrees with that in the journal, you will make a mark against it, a stroke (loncata) or any other sign (pontatura), and this mark your companion must also make in the journal, taking care that no entry is marked by you and not by him, or vice versa, because great errors may arise if you do so. When you are finished comparing the journal with the ledger, you must go over the ledger, and if you find any entry which is not marked, you will conclude that it is superfluous and delete it. In the same way you must examine the journal, and if you find an entry without a mark you will at once enter it in the ledger. In this way your error will be found, and the trial balance will agree."

It is curious that Pacioli, with his clear perception of the principles regulating double entry, and with the minute attention which he gives to matters of technical detail, should give no direct instructions in the method of passing "stock" through profit and loss account and the "inventory," which did rough service for a balance sheet. This silence and the confused ideas suggested by such indirect references to the subject as are found, have led Dr. Jager to the conclusion that the chief object of old bookkeeping was to obviate the necessity for a detailed stock-taking. Although much internal evidence can be brought to support this view—such, for instance, as the great weight laid on the necessity of recording a minute description of every bale of goods purchased or sold, which we have already referred to in the case of coins—we cannot help thinking that the learned writer has failed to establish his case, and has been too inclined to follow up a preconceived conclusion, which, no doubt, gave a plausible explanation of an invention which seems so cumbersome and gives such simple results. Nevertheless, Pacioli is certainly weak at this point, and the same defect is shown by a subsequent writer of considerable merit. Manzoni's treatise on bookkeeping was published in Venice in 1534, and although for the greater part it is nothing more than a literary robbery perpetrated on the work of Pacioli, the author has added detailed examples to the theoretical part of his book, and these show that he got over the difficulty in regard to stock by assuming that the balances of the various goods on hand were sold for cash.

The first instance of a goods account which can, without doubt, be said to be kept on correct principles, is found in the "Nieuwe Instructie" of Jan Ympyn, which is dealt with by M. Kheil at considerable length in his recent book mentioned above. M. Kheil's object in writing this "Beitrag" was to show how, without exception almost, the old writers on bookkeeping made the most extensive use of Pacioli's "Summa de Arithmetica," never, however, acknowledging their indebtedness. M. Kheil's treatise is a production of considerable interest. He has brought to its composition the results of many years of study and of close research, and if in this essay we take advantage of only a small portion of the material he offers, it is because we wish to use it only in as far as it supplements Dr. Jager's work in showing the complete stage in which bookkeeping had attained in the sixteenth century. In reality, the most valuable portions of M. Kheil's work are those in which he gives bibliographical notices of the completest list of old writers on bookkeeping which has yet been published; but this we leave untouched just now, for we understand that a further "Beitrag" is in contemplation, which will deal more exclusively and in greater detail with these matters.

Ympyn's book was published in 1543, and again its first part is borrowed directly from Pacioli, although in this case with due acknowledgment. Part second illustrates the first by examples, which are decidedly an advance on Manzoni, to whom we have briefly referred, for not only has the Dutch author considerably improved the wording of the entries by making them more clear and concise, and further introduced important subsidiary books—for instance, a separation of cash sales from sales on credit—but he has, for the first time as far as we can gather, dealt with stock in a satisfactory manner. The price which is placed on the balance of unsold goods is also the proper one, being cost price, not present value.

It is sad to have to note that this most deserving disciple of Pacioli, who not only showed such appreciation of the teaching of his master, but the far rarer quality of frankly disavowing all claims of originality himself, should have been the man who committed the blunder which has defrauded the great author of the "Summa de Arithmetica" in the very country which, from the size of its commercial interests, ought to have been most anxious to do honor to his name. Ympyn died when his work was still in manuscript, and the publication was undertaken by his widow, who brought out a Dutch edition in 1543, a French translation in the same year, and, four years later, an English version. Now, whether it was that Frau Anna Ympyn was no better and no worse than other sprightly widows and was a little careless, or whether the truth of it is that old Ympyn wrote a most undecipherable hand, in any case the much-prized acknowledgment to Pacioli pays its blind tribute to one Lucas de Bargo. The mistake was incorporated in the English translation, and, having found its way into the literature of a nation not much given to historical research, it remained there until a few months ago, when things were put right in the pages of this magazine.

Of the writers following Ympyn no notice need be made except, perhaps, of Paschier Goessens, a native of Brussels, who published a treatise on bookkeeping in Hamburg in 1594, in which he mentions the practice among some merchants to keep a special cash-book, although he does not consider it essential. Other writers go on copying the work of their predecessors, prescribing the general use of the journal as an integral part of their system long after the conditions had passed away which made its adoption a necessity, mentioning the mark of the cross as an essential formality, and in general showing the abhorrence for change which, even from Pacioli, earned them that taunt that each bookkeeper declares stubbornly that the old system is the best.

Bookkeepers' Extra Work

Every bookkeeper sooner or later is afforded the opportunity, if not actually requested, or specifically directed, to do what he fairly regards as extra work—that is, work over and beyond what he was engaged to do, and for which he is receiving a salary. The question at once arises: Can he draw extra pay for this extra work? The best answer to this is that it depends very largely upon the fairmindedness and liberality of the men for whom he is working. He may decline to do the extra work unless he is assured of extra pay, but this, in many cases, would only produce as an answer the statement that his services are no longer required. If he goes ahead and does the extra work, hoping to receive extra compensation for it, he is very likely to be refused when he makes demand for the money he thinks he has earned. If he persists in his claim and brings suit it would seem, in the light of several decisions of the courts, that he is doomed to disappointment in this direction also. In a case before the Supreme Court of the State of New York a little time since, it was held that no implied contract for extra compensation to a bookkeeper arises from the request by a member of the firm by which he is employed to go over his individual books. Certainly to go over a different set of books from the set he was employed to keep would appear to be extra work without the chance of successful dispute. The decision, however, went even further, for the court held that there was no implied contract for extra compensation in the case, even though the work involved was so considerable that it had to be done nights and Sundays in order to accomplish it without interfering with regular duties.

This case, possibly, is not so sweeping as would seem on the face of it. The decision was upon the question of an agreement for extra compensation. Did the order for the work and the performance of the work for which special compensation was sought imply a contract or not? The court held that it did not.

The difficulty at the root of the whole matter seems to be this. Bookkeepers as a rule are engaged for their time and services, not to do a certain amount of work. The bookkeeper sells his time; he agrees to work a year for so much money; he does not agree to do such and such work or accomplish such and such results for so much money. By the very nature of the bargain made at the outset he is obliged to give all his time to his employers, and it becomes their privilege to get out of him all the work they can in that time. Of course there remains to the bookkeeper the right to protest against being overworked. Any complaint he may make in this regard, however, is likely to be interpreted by a certain class of employers as something else than what it is represented to be. Some bookkeepers, as a fact, do nurse their jobs while putting up a bluff of extreme industry, and employers generally have been made aware of the fact.

Faithful and conscientious employees and fair-minded employers seldom have any trouble in matters of this kind. Where either party, however, is inclined to work the other for his own advantage, actual or apparent, there is very generally trouble in store. No employer can afford to employ a time-serving bookkeeper or clerk, and on the other hand no bright, honest and industrious bookkeeper can afford to work for a dishonest, overreaching, unscrupulous employer. Too much care, therefore, cannot be exercised in the matter of selection, not only of the office assistant by the business man, but also of the business man for whom to work by the bookkeeper.

Identifying Checks

A matter of perennial interest to business men, and one that is frequently discussed at considerable length in the trade papers, is the operations of forgers with checks and the methods that are employed to detect alterations and substitutions. The following incident, which is derived from a recent lecture by Professor C. A. Doremus, on chemical tests for detecting interpolations, bears upon it: Professor Doremus stated that the interests involved in the case which he was about to narrate were very large, and, accordingly, that it was not practicable that the original check should be tampered with or chemically treated. For purposes of testimony, therefore, a large photograph of the check was taken. The first trial resulted in no decision, and on the second trial what purported to be the original check was produced. It was handed to the cashier of the bank for identification, who examined it and said: "This is not the original check." "How do you know that?" demanded the amazed lawyer. "Because in the heading of the original check I pricked a hole in the center of each of the noughts with a pin. This check has not those holes." In all other respects the checks seemed to be identical. The court called for Dr. Doremus' photograph, which plainly showed the pinholes. Upon this the lawyer for the defence threw up his case, and the guilty substitutor of the false check fled the country. This incident suggests that while marks upon checks such as pinholes may be impossible in the majority of cases in the hurry of modern business, still it is a fact that in various other ways identifications are put in place by those who sign the checks. Peculiarities of signature, position of signature on the check, with respect to the amount, methods of dotting i's and crossing t's, and numerous others are resorted to more or less systematically by many business men. These serve the purpose of identification whenever occasion may arise.

With the talents of an angel a man may be a fool.—Young.

Talent rules without a sceptre.—Cælius.

Examination Questions

The following are sample questions selected from those which were set by the Scottish Chartered Accountants' General Examining Board, for the examinations in June, 1898:

Arithmetic:

After paying an income tax of 7d. in the £, a man's net income is £922, 5s. 10d. What was it before the tax was deducted?

A carpenter receiving a wage of 35s. per week of 54 hours can make an article 6 feet long by 2 inches wide by 3 inches deep in 3¼ hours. At what price per dozen must these articles be sold to realize a profit of 20 per cent., if the wood costs 1s. per cubic foot?

Algebra:

A person, after spending £10 more than a third of his yearly income, found that he had £15 more than a half of it left. What was his income?

The expenses of a given golf club, which is supported by an annual contribution from each member (no entry money being charged), have increased to £110 per annum, and it has been found necessary either to increase the annual subscription by 2s. or to obtain ten new members. What is the number of members and the annual subscription at present?

British History:

Enumerate the principal measures which were passed subsequent to 1868, and which are associated with the name of Mr. Gladstone?

Geography:

Why, in comparing the manufacture of sugar in Trinidad with that in Barbadoes, should Mill characterize the latter as "wasteful?"

Geometry:

Prove that if any side of a triangle be produced, the exterior angle so formed shall be greater than either of the interior and opposite angles.

Professional Knowledge:

A and B agree to be co-partners in carrying on a general merchant's business. Give a list of the books you would recommend them to keep and state the uses of the respective books.

Show the form of a statement of affairs where the assets consist of—

House property	£4,000
Stock in trade..	13,000
Works (including ground, buildings and fixtures)..	18,000
Book debts......	10,000

and the liabilities consist of—

Heritable bond, covering house, property and works	£10,000
Preferable claims for wages, salaries and taxes	1,000
Trade creditors	15,000
Loans from friends without security	10,000
Bills payable....	20,000

Laws of Scotland:

If a check is drawn upon a banker for a larger sum than stands at credit of the drawer, what right does the grantee or holder acquire on presentation of the check?

Actuarial Science:

If the present value of £10 be £200, what, at the same rate of interest, is the value of an annuity certain of £20 for 8 years deferred 8 years?

Political Economy:

Explain and criticize this definition: "Capital is that portion of wealth which is employed in the production of more wealth."—Walker.

Would capital include money, skill, land? Give reasons.

State and explain the Equation of International Demand and show the bearing on Protection.

Business of an Accountant:

A wholesale firm send out their goods in bottles, barrels and cases, all of which are charged in the invoice to the customers along with the goods; but full credit is allowed for all empties when returned. Many customers pay their accounts under deduction of "empties to be returned:" others pay for the bottles, etc., with the goods, and claim credit for them when returned. Explain briefly what details of bookkeeping you would advise should be adopted to enable the bookkeeper to ascertain at a glance how much of the sum due by any customer consists of unpaid goods, and how much consists of empties still to be returned. Illustrate your answer with a customer's ledger account, showing at least three transactions.

Auditing:

You are asked to examine the books of the cashier of a Tweed manufacturer who has embezzled over £300 of his employer's money. He had charge of all the principal books, which were kept by double entry. Name at least six methods by which he may have tried to conceal his theft.

In making a cash audit some paid checks are produced to you as the only vouchers for certain payments. Under what circumstances would you treat the same as vouchers? Are such checks evidence of the discharge of liabilities. Is there any danger in accepting checks as evidence?

Management of Trusts, Bankrupt Estates, Etc.:

O died on the 1st of January, 1897, leaving a widow and family by second marriage, and three children, X, Y and Z, by a former marriage. In terms of deceased's settlement the widow and her family were to receive £4,000 in full of their share of the estate on the 1st of June, 1897, and interest at 5 per cent. on that sum or any part of it unpaid, at that date, till paid, and the balance of the estate was to be divided equally among X, Y and Z. A sum of £2,000 was paid on June 1, 1897, to account of the widow and family's claim, and a further sum of £1,000 on December 1, 1897. X was paid £1,000 to account of his share on June 1, 1897, and Y was paid £500 on December 1, 1897. The estate was fully realized on June 1, 1898, and the sum in hand for division at that date was £4,012 10s. Make up a statement showing how this sum falls to be divided, interest to be charged on advances to X and Y at 5 per cent.

Letters and Answers Thereto

There is scarcely a business man from Maine to California who has not at one time or another raised the question of the necessity of preserving everything in the voluminous mail which reaches him. When business was small it was a comparatively simple matter to keep a copy of everything that was sent out and also to file away everything that was received, but with the increase of business conditions have materially changed, and at present to keep copies and files complete in many establishments would be a very large undertaking, indeed. Now and then is the great army of business men one is encountered who, with the courage of his convictions regarding utility and economy, does not pretend to keep all his letters, and who unhesitatingly consigns to the waste basket many of the communications that he receives. Men of this kind are increasing in number at the present time.

The difficulty of the matter is to determine what is worth saving and what may be unconditionally destroyed. If some things are to be preserved and other things are not to be kept, then a decision must be reached at the time each letter is received or written as the case may be, as to what shall be done with it. The necessity of so deciding has deterred many a man from resorting to this method of diminishing expenses and reducing the storage space required for his numerous and ever-accumulating store of documents.

Occasionally, an original suggestion is encountered still further looking to the reduction of labor in copying and filing. For example, a letter has recently come to our attention which had printed conspicuously upon it the following: "If this letter needs a reply it will greatly facilitate our office records if you will answer on the back of this sheet."

Various utilities are served upon this plan: First there is the saving of stationery, and next there is the saving of at least a part of what is ordinarily written in the date line. The dating is likely to be abbreviated to the utmost limit. Again there is the saving of the polite salutory with which letters are usually commenced, and perhaps also the closing salutation. A letter answered in this manner permits of various abbreviations, not only in the specific items above mentioned, but also in words and in style and character of composition. It more nearly corresponds to what would pass in conversation were the same message to be conveyed orally. The idea is certainly a good one and the suggestion or request will undoubtedly be acted upon by the recipient in a majority of cases. The old theory that every scrap of paper must be preserved and every letter answered is gradually becoming obsolete. This result has been hastened by the presence of typewritten and lithographed imitation letters, the genuineness of which it is assumed none but an expert can question. Whenever the business man feels sure he has an imitation letter he destroys it. The habit of destroying useless papers thus commenced soon extends to various other documents.

Accountics

The Office Magazine.

A. O. KITTREDGE, F. I. A., C. P. A., EDITOR.
E. R. KITTREDGE, ASSOCIATE.

Accountics is devoted to the Science of Accounting, to the Art of Bookkeeping and to the advocacy of Improved Office Methods.

Subscription.—One dollar a year, payable in advance.

Postage is prepaid by the publishers in the United States, Canada and Mexico. For all other countries in the Postal Union, subscribers must add 50 cents a year.

Discontinuances.—In the absence of specific orders to discontinue at the end of the subscription term the magazine will be continued and a bill sent.

Remittances should be by Draft, P. O. Order or Express Order, payable to the order of the ACCOUNTICS ASSOCIATION. Money and postage stamps are at the risk of the sender, unless sent by express or in registered letters. Add 10 cents each to checks on local banks to defray collection charges.

Advertising Rates will be quoted on application.

Official Journal.—This publication, by resolutions duly passed, has been made the official publication of the following organizations :—
THE INSTITUTE OF ACCOUNTS.
THE NEW YORK CHAPTER of the Institute of Accounts.
THE WASHINGTON CHAPTER of the Institute of Accounts.
THE HARTFORD CHAPTER of the Institute of Accounts.

ACCOUNTICS is the accredited medium of intercommunication between members of the Institute of Accounts wherever located.

ACCOUNTICS ASSOCIATION,
Publishers,
Wool Exchange, New York.

Entered at the Post Office New York as Second Class Matter.

Filing Cabinets and Business Furniture

We have received from the Globe Company, with factory in Cincinnati and salesrooms in Chicago, New York, and Boston, catalogue No. 26—a most interesting publication, and one that contains much which will be profitable for accountants, bookkeepers and office men in general to examine. The book is upwards of 150 pages in extent and is extremely attractive typographically.

At the outset there is presented what must be regarded by all as a most important notice. All discounts are abandoned and in their place the company has adopted the one-price system—that is, a net delivered price. Whoever gets the catalogue, therefore, and sees the representation of an article of furniture in it, in which he is interested, has before him the net price of the article delivered at his railway station. This saves delay in writing for discounts and removes all the uncertainties of freight charges. In addition to being fixed and definite, as here described, the prices have the special merit of being extremely low. The reputation of the goods made by the Globe Company is well established and its productions are everywhere the standard for high quality. The company announces that all the goods are guaranteed to be as represented.

The goods illustrated in the catalogue include the Globe Ideal and Columbia files, cabinet indexes, filing cabinets in a large variety of styles and sizes, together with illustrations of special suspending devices and other conveniences. There are also supplies for various filing cabinets which are in extensive use, document files, document cabinets in very large variety, pigeon-hole cabinets, revolving cabinets, check files and check file cabinets and mercantile report cabinets. The representations of goods included under the above heads occupy the first 76 pages of the book. Then follows a section devoted to the card index system, which embodies in the text pages and illustrations one of the best practical essays on the card index plan that has ever been issued. Different styles of record cards and guide cards are illustrated and different rods for holding the cards in place are likewise shown in extensive variety. Card index cabinets ranging from a single drawer and a card index case with cover, to cabinets to hold hundreds of thousands of cards are shown in great variety. Card index outfits for use in safes are also presented.

Legal blank cases occupy several pages. Pigeon-hole cases variously equipped are next presented, following which are miscellaneous goods, including book racks, revolving book cases, copy press stands and cabinets, office wardrobes, telephone closets and illustrations of bank fixtures and trimmings, etc.

A special section in the book is devoted to the Globe-Wernicke sectional cabinets. Our readers are already acquainted with this device, which is made up of various convenient units, in a way to enable the office man to build up his cabinet from time to time as his growing needs may demand. The standard units are illustrated in a large variety of styles and there would seem to be left little to be demanded by the business man that is not here supplied. The catalogue is supplemented by a very comprehensive index.

We have also received from the Globe Company the stationers' edition of their catalogue, which is equally complete in its details and profusely illustrated, with representations of the numerous lines of goods which this company manufactures for the stationery trade, and which are kept on sale at stationers' in every part of the country.

Buying and Overbuying

By F. C. Brunhouse

It has been truly said that ours is a nation of great producers and great consumers. We make no mistake when we declare that it is a nation of gigantic enterprise. Manufacturing merchandise of every description and in great abundance as we do, no one need suffer because of lack of supply. As buyers, we can get more than we need, with a little additional thrown in gratuitously. Big houses and little houses in competition with each other for trade, fling out almost innumerable inducements to the retail merchant in matters of price, style, quality and finish, and even tempt him with extra datings and discounts. Occasionally rebates are offered. Able and persistent salesmen are sent out, whose persuasive powers are so great that the retail merchant must possess unusual strength of mind to avoid falling a victim to their allurements.

The picture is not in the least overdrawn. It indicates the conditions with which every buyer must contend, whether he purchase for a wholesale house, for a department store, or for a store of any other description. The conditions apply with equal force to country merchants and to city merchants.

Everything is made extremely pleasant for the buyer. Accordingly, it is extremely easy to overbuy.

The successful buyer is one who is conversant with his business and who is likewise a man of resolute character. He is one who keeps close tab on his stock and who can tell you in a moment just what amount of stock he has on hand of every grade. He is one who studies his trade and the requirements of his customers. As a result, he knows what novelties he can sell and to what extent. He is always in position to regulate his purchase and thereby keep his stock in proper condition. He is always wide awake and well informed on what is being offered in the market. Does he read? Yes. He carefully scans every trade journal that is issued touching the line of goods that he buys, and thereby he attains new ideas and very frequently secures most valuable information. In a word, he is a thoroughly posted man.

Cash Discount Limit

By G. S. Mann

Now that we are entering upon a new era of prosperity, we should not forget the lessons of the depression through which we have recently passed. In perpetuating our enforced economies lie the possibilities of future success. To sell closely and quickly, to credit carefully, to discount purchases and to collect promptly, are going to be the rules from this time forward of the majority of those who have weathered the storm. In some lines of trade the discounts for cash will amount to enough to pay the expenses of the business. In such lines, therefore, one should never fail to take advantage of the discounts offered.

Some retail dealers appear to think that a few days later than the terms stated will make no difference. In such conclusions they are greatly mistaken. "Three per cent. 10 days" means just what it says, and the purchaser ratifies the contract of sale of which this is an important part whenever he accepts the goods. He should, therefore, be as scrupulous to observe that part of the agreement as any other.

The clause above quoted does not mean: "Send the money when you get ready and take off your discount," but instead, it is: "If your remittance reaches us within ten days from date of invoice, we will give you 3 per cent. discount."

Does the retail merchant ever realize that anything less than this is not a payment in full? The amount of the discount or the delay beyond the date may be trifling, but the times through which we have been passing have been of the kind to demonstrate that it is trifles which make or mar business. As a fact, the aggregate of such trifles is a considerable amount.

Certainly, no fair-minded and honorable business man would continue the practice of varying from the letter of the contract after once giving the matter careful thought.

The practice of exceeding the discount limit on invoices is an indication of a desire to get the best of the jobber in little things that often proves a forerunner of worse to come. Hence, in part, the attention that the jobber is likely to pay to such matters, and hence, in part also, the reason why the merchant should refrain from such things in the sense of avoiding the appearance of evil.

Dating Ahead

By Chas. Biggs

Every merchant and every manufacturer understands the meaning of dating ahead. Few, however, recall the adoption of the plan which of late years has become a fixed custom. Dating ahead within proper limits may be desirable, but, as it is commonly practiced, it has become a nuisance, and is a direct and certain cause of loss to the retailer.

During the past twenty years the population of the country has immensely increased. Immigration has also added its millions. As a result, the rivalry among the workers in manufacturing centers, where the wage has not been lessened, has been intensified. A larger output per hand employed than ever before has been forced. Again, the lowering of freights, due to the increase in facilities for transportation and the creation of improved machinery and better methods of manufacture, with the reduction of profits to the minimum, due to the intense competition for an outlet, have combined to cause a continuous reduction in the price of almost every product of skilled labor that is put upon the market. This has been true in spite of protective tariffs, which have only temporarily checked the fall. As a consequence of this condition, the manufacturer was long since obliged to abandon the old system of accumulating a stock of merchandise ahead of the season, for, as a rule, his stock declined in value upon his hands before it could be distributed to those who supplied the consumer. The remedy was to manufacture only upon definite orders and thus insure beforehand a market for the product of the mills at a known and agreed price.

As an inducement to the jobber or distributing buyer, the manufacturer said: "You want goods for the spring trade. If they were made and in stock now you would not buy them before spring. Therefore, if at present, say in September, you will give me an order for such merchandise as you will want next spring, I will manufacture it and deliver it to you from time to time from this date on, and date the whole of it as if you had purchased it February 1."

This proceeding was and is entirely legitimate, because it enables a manufacturer to run his factory during a series of months upon a certainty and because it lessens the cost of his product. For example, he has upon this plan no insurance to carry upon completed stock; it is all shipped as soon as finished.

The abuse of the scheme came later. The jobber or distributing buyer argued something as follows: "Well, here I have these goods on hand. The invoices do not date until February 1. Therefore, I may do with my customer, the retailer, what the manufacturer has done with me. I will give him the same date that I got, or even something better, as an inducement for him to buy. I will deliver as soon as he will accept the goods, thus getting ahead of some of my competitors and throwing upon my customer the burden of insurance."

Of course, at first only a few followed this plan and perhaps they reaped an advantage from it, but in this country there is no monopoly of ability to grasp a situation. Ere long the whole business community followed the practice. The bait to the retailer was an extension and enlargement of credit. It was a fancied but fictitious benefit. By this means there was established a custom which, carried to the extent of the original intention, was for the manufacturer a gain, but which, carried to the extent which now obtains, is an actual disadvantage, especially to the retailer.

The retailer is the one who should, above all others, buy on short time and carry the smallest stock necessary to the business that he does. He should open up at the proper season fresh lines of each class of goods that he carries and these new goods should be bright and seasonable. Too often tempted, however, by dating ahead, he makes his purchases out of season and thereby cumbers his shelves with goods that long before the proper time for consumption arrives have become shop-worn, undesirable and, in the eyes of employees and customers, old or past style. All these disadvantages follow upon the plan of dating ahead. In addition, the retailer under the offer is very generally tempted to overbuy in his early purchases, because the time of payment seems so far ahead.

Look back at the history of the past five years, which has been so disastrous to many business interests. Let us inquire who are the men who have succeeded during the period? They are those who have done business within the just limits of their capital and credit, whether large or small; who have bought frequently, who have managed to have seasonable and attractive merchandise to offer to their trade at the proper time, and who have not been burdened with old and undesirable stock.

Institute of Accounts

Incorporated
Under the Laws of New York
1882

A National Organization

Represented
Throughout the United States
By Chapters

The Objects of the Institute are

To secure a proper recognition of accounting as an element of business

To discover new principles of accounting, and to orderly arrange them for the enlargement of the science

To originate and circulate the literature of accountics

To maintain the dignity and uphold the importance of the profession of accountancy

To broaden the scope of the science of political economy

To establish harmonious relations of mutual dependence between itself and the business world, and to induce able and experienced men everywhere to devote their energies, in association with it, to the accomplishment of its purposes

Information and printed matter relative to the formation of new Chapters will be furnished upon application to

HENRY HARNEY, C. P. A., Secretary

88 Wall Street, New York

Accountics

The Office Magazine

ONE DOLLAR A YEAR
TEN CENTS A COPY

NOVEMBER 1898

VOLUME III
NUMBER 8

CONTENTS.

Published by the ACCOUNTICS ASSOCIATION: Wool Exchange, New York

Books on Accounting

and all other subjects sent carriage paid to any address in the United States, Canada or Mexico on receipt of publishers' price. All orders promptly executed.

Accountics Association, 260 W. Broadway, New York.

---

50 YEARS' EXPERIENCE

PATENTS

TRADE MARKS
DESIGNS
COPYRIGHTS &c.

Anyone sending a sketch and description may quickly ascertain our opinion free whether an invention is probably patentable. Communications strictly confidential. Handbook on Patents sent free. Oldest agency for securing patents.

Patents taken through Munn & Co. receive *special notice*, without charge, in the

Scientific American.

A handsomely illustrated weekly. Largest circulation of any scientific journal. Terms, $3 a year; four months, $1. Sold by all newsdealers

MUNN & Co. 361 Broadway, **New York**

Branch Office, 625 F St., Washington, D. C.

S. R. HOPKINS

PUBLIC EXPERT ACCOUNTANT

59 Wall Street, New York

25 years in the business

ACCOUNTANT
AUDITOR
ADJUSTER

HERBERT F. FRENCH

Successor to JUSTIN WHITTIER,

116 Bedford St., Room 302, Boston.

W. T. SIMPSON

Public Accountant and Auditor

Mills Building, NEW YORK

W. BAINBRIDGE JAUDON, C. P. A.

Expert
Accountant

40 Broadway, New York

CHARLES DUTTON & CO.

Counselors in Accountancy and Auditors

NEW YORK:—
29 PINE STREET

JERSEY CITY, N. J.:—
GREENE and GRAND STREETS

EAST ORANGE, N. J.:—
PEOPLE'S BANK BUILDING

Examiners of Municipalities, Corporations and Litigated Accounts

---

Henry Harney
Certified Public Accountant

Sylvester E. Strickland
Certified Public Accountant

HENRY HARNEY & CO.

88 Wall Street

New York

Telephone, 4281 Cortlandt

ITEMS	MDSE.	EXPENSE	TOTAL

James Arnold, 531 Chestnut Street, Philadelphia, Pa., Manufacturer of Columnar account books and special ruled forms for labor saving at manufacturers prices

Accountics

VOL. III NOVEMBER 1898 No. 8

The Monthly Statement

In the interesting and exceedingly valuable article on "Balance Sheets and Balance Accounts," by James B. Macdonald, which appears upon another page in this issue, there are several points made which should command the attention of all American accountants. Bookkeepers and business men as well, will also profit by giving it careful consideration. The object of all bookkeeping, as defined in the first sentence of the article, is something that we commend to the thought of all who have to do with business accounts. What is owing us and what we owe have in the past so filled the vision of those who have been responsible for the accounts of American firms and companies that there are few, comparatively speaking, who really appreciate that there are any other objects possible in bookkeeping or any other results that may be shown

The writer's distinction between a Balance Sheet and a Balance Account will appear new and novel to many—even including some prominent public accountants. The changed position of the debits and credits in the balance sheets submitted from what is current in this country will also command attention from all save those who have encountered this feature previously. The distinction that is made between what is appropriate or allowable with a private firm as contrasted with a public company will be followed with interest, while the reference to the lack of the advice of an accountant when the bill was drafted, resulting in one of the earlier Companies' Acts, will cause many of our readers to recall similar instances in our own governmental regulations. The discussion of "What is Profit?" and "What is Capital?" contains various suggestions that are valuable to students.

The conclusion to the article is specially noticeable: "It would * * * be better form to produce the ledger with its balance and subsiduary accounts as the sole repository of all facts relating to the financial situation." In other words, business statements are detached sheets, are apt to be lost. They may contain matter that the books do not show, and which, if not subsequently written into the books, leaves the real records of the business deficient. Further, the detached statement may be absolutely false and not show the business at all as the books disclose its condition to be. What better arguments than these could be presented for making the Profit and Loss Statement and the Balance Sheet going and integral parts of the bookkeeping system? Such management of accounts is now an accomplished fact in numerous mercantile and manufacturing concerns throughout this country, due to the employment of that unique and labor-saving device, the Balance Sheet Ledger.

In our October issue we presented a selection from the questions set by the Scottish Chartered Accountants' General Examining Board for the recent examinations, and in this issue on another page we present the official answers to a portion of these questions. It is to be remarked by way of showing the thoroughness with which the work of training young accountants is being done on the other side of the Atlantic, that not only are the questions proposed at the different examinations printed in full, but that subsequently the complete answers are given to the same questions, thus helping along those who are looking forward to submitting themselves to the ordeal at a later date. In addition the students are encouraged and instructed by the publication of general comments upon the examination of which we give the following as a typical example:

"The good results of late obtained at this examination have been maintained. Both of the Law papers, as usual, have been very well answered. The effect of a "poinding of the ground," and a "decree of mails and duties," in competition with the trustee in a sequestration, seemed unfamiliar to many candidates, though a common question in actual practice. The question on Cautionary Obligations appeared also strange to not a few. The paper in Actuarial Science was not a heavy one, and the questions were all well answered with the exception of No. ii., which does not present any special difficulty, and No. viii., which, though more technical, is well within the range of knowledge of this subject which is expected. The work in Political Economy was on the whole poor. The weakness of the papers appears most in the answers to the questions which require clear thinking and understanding rather than mere memory. The Board have again to emphasize the necessity of better preparation in this subject. The papers dealing with the General Business of an Accountant were well answered by most of the candidates. In Bookkeeping, where they showed to least advantage was in connection with consignments abroad, and in giving specimen rulings and explaining the parts played by certain books. The Auditing paper was rather searching, and revealed deficiencies in the candidates, notably in answering questions iii., vii. and ix. In Bankruptcies, Factories, &c., fair knowledge was shown, and the scheme of division was very well prepared. Some of the candidates were a little at sea in ranking claims under a trust deed, and dealing with the claims of creditors of a firm on the partners' estates. The paper relating to Company Work, References, &c., produced very good answers to most of the questions. The last three dealt with matters with which a number of the candidates did not seem to be acquainted, and unfamiliarity was also shown with the subject of question No. iii."

The growth of the accountants' profession of late years is something of which every one is aware, and yet actual figures are not on every one's tongue. A recent issue of our contemporary, The Accountants' Magazine, contains the following interesting statement of facts concerning Scottish accountants:

Ten years ago there were 398 Scottish Chartered Accountants: now there are 665—an increase of 267, or 67 per cent. The rate of increase from 1860 to 1870 was 23 per cent.; from 1870 to 1880, 45 per cent.; from 1880 to 1890, 63 per cent. When individual societies are looked at it is found that during the last ten years the Edinburgh Society has increased by 97 members, being at the rate of 41 per cent.; Glasgow Institute by 156 members, or at the rate of 111 per cent.; and Aberdeen Society by 14 members, or at the rate of 67 per cent. The addition to the Glasgow Institute is very striking. During the ten years from 1880 to 1890 the increase of membership of that Institute was only 46 per cent,, against 76 per cent in the Edinburgh Society. This was probably due to the Institute having in 1880 commenced the practice, which is still continued, of admitting "associates," who no doubt in consequence delayed making application for admission as members. But as soon as this temporary check to the increase of membership was past, the vitality of the profession in Glasgow again became apparent.

Similar investigations in other parts of the commercial and manufacturing world would no doubt show similar records of growth. In the article from which the above extract is taken the question is raised: Where do all these young accountants find employment? In reply, it is pointed out that the chief development of accountant work of late years has been in what may be called the commercial side—that is, audits and investigations. Consequently, the increase of accountants is greatest in commercial centres, where the demand for them is an increasing quantity depending upon the growth of business and the recognition upon the part of business men of the value of their services.

Export business is a benefit in two ways, first by opening up new fields, and, second, by relieving the pressure of competition at home.—The Furniture Worker.

The Relationship of Factory Books and Records to the Principal Books of Account

By Rollin Jeffries

From a careful study of cost-keeping methods, extending over a series of years and covering various lines of manufacture, I am impressed with the idea that very few manufacturers and comparatively few accountants as well, have a correct idea of the relationship that should be sustained between the cost accounts of a factory and the principal books of the establishment. Perhaps I would be stating the same idea in a way to be better understood, by asserting that in almost all cases what are called cost accounts are mere bookkeeping features and find no proper place in the accounting system of the establishment in which they are maintained.

By "accounting" I would indicate the fundamental plan or scheme or the records in their entirety. By "bookkeeping" I mean the mere method of record. Accounting may be compared to the plans and specifications of an architect, which epitomized are the theory of the building, while, from the same point of view, the bookkeeping would be the work executed by the builder, or the manner in which the theory is embodied in materials. A builder who proceeds with strict regard to the plans and specifications of a building produces a symmetrical structure adapted to the purposes for which it is erected, up to the limit of the technical ability of the designer. He shows the practical embodiment of the architect's idea. But builders frequently proceed in the erection of structures without any plans or specifications, trusting entirely to their own general conception of what is appropriate, and planning more or less as they go along, with respect to what is current in structures of the same class in the immediate neighborhood in which the building is being put up. Buildings so constructed seldom rank high in design or in matters of convenience of arrangement, or in completeness of detail. They are, rather, below the general average. And so it seems to me is the case in cost accounts.

To secure the best there must be a fundamental plan. There must be a scheme or a theory, put it as we may, underlying the entire accounting system, and so broad and so comprehensive in its nature that the cost records of the factory shall become an integral part of it.

Where cost accounts are managed as a part of the general accounting system of the establishment, there is likely to be method and purpose to them; but where cost records are maintained independent of the general accounting system, without any direct relationship thereto, or, to put it otherwise, without being a part of the general system and subject to the same rules of balance as are applicable to the general system, the work proceeds, as it were, by rule of thumb. The form and substance of the resulting work is very much like the building that is erected without the supervision of an architect.

The first conception of cost records or factory accounts, as they are frequently designated, is a plan by which the mere cost of the articles produced may be determined. Frequently, the manufacturer sees no reason for going further in this matter than putting upon any odd piece of paper the more prominent items which enter into the cost of an article or a given lot of goods, and guessing at the remainder. He walks into the factory some fine morning, and after consultation with the superintendent and foremen of different departments, makes out a list, wherein are noted the amount of material of each of several kinds, entering into the goods under investigation, and the amount of labor. These he prices. Then he makes extensions and adds up. He says by way of conclusion, without any effort being made to demonstrate the correctness of his calculation: "I will add so much for general factory expenses and so much for selling costs. I guess we can make the price list just about so and so." Thus he determines a policy without any proof of the correctness of the premises.

The fallacies in such a cost estimate are too apparent to need discussion, but the illustration serves to show the point I desire to make—namely, that nothing short of making the cost accounts a part of the general accounting system and subject to proof by balancing will demonstrate the correctness or incorrectness of the assumptions in such an estimate as I have cited. With a separate account covering factory expenses, and with another account covering selling costs or commercial expenses, it becomes comparatively easy to say that the allowance made for either is or is not sufficient for the purpose. Without the assurance that all manufacturing costs are included in the accounts and properly spread, the question of prime cost is still left wide open.

Every accountant is accustomed to rely upon the principle of balance for demonstrating the correctness of his records. Take the cash account by way of illustration. Cash is debited as it comes in and credited as payments are made. The balance between the two sides of the account shows the amount on hand. The cash is then counted to verify this balance. Consider for the moment the factory as a separate institution and apply the foregoing method of treatment for the purpose of showing its relationship to the general system of accounts. Debit the factory with all it costs; credit it with what it produces, at the actual cost of production. The balance remaining will be the inventory of materials on hand and work in progress in the factory. Verify the correctness of the account by taking stock or inventorying.

The above is a bald statement with everything in gross. Cost systems, properly considered, are analyses of the transactions in a factory, by which the various kinds of costs are properly distributed down to the minutest detail. The principle, however, is the same.

A single account in the general books of the establishment should stand for the factory, to be debited in gross with all that the factory costs and to be credited in gross with all that the factory produces, always taken at actual cost, as shown by the cost records of the factory. Sub-divisions should distribute down to the single article, and the correctness of the whole should be demonstrated by inventories taken as often as circumstances permit. It is by this plan only that the manager or proprietor can determine the profitableness of the factory. The detail accounts of the cost are comprised in such grand divisions as Material, Labor and General Factory Expenses. The method of the sub-division of these, according to the line of goods produced, should be such as will serve to distribute the expenses in a way to show what each lot of goods or each individual piece that is produced really costs.

Many managers of factories fail of a clear conception of the function of their manufacturing enterprise. Some are so confused, apparently at least, as to entertain the idea that a factory account should show a profit. This is an unreasonable assumption for several reasons. In the first place, no one is justified in operating a factory save only when the goods therein made are produced at a smaller cost than articles of like kind and quality can be bought in the open market. Nothing short of a showing of actual costs of production, making sure always that the recorded costs are equal to the actual outlay, is sufficient to demonstrate the expediency of continuing to operate the factory. Selling expenses have no part in the question at this stage. Second, no profit can be considered to be made on goods until they are actually sold. Supposing, for sake of illustration, that a given lot of goods has been produced in the factory at a cost of $5 per article. Assume further that these same goods sell in the market for $7.50 per article. It would be very poor business to go on piling up goods without selling them, on the assumption that $2.50 is being made on every article produced. The business man will at once say that the $2.50 is made only when the article has been sold and the money collected. Selling expenses, therefore, are always to be considered after actual cost of production has been determined.

Again, many manufacturers confuse factory expenses and selling expenses. In the illustration above, the five dollars is supposed to cover materials and labor (which, united, form prime cost), and also a proper pro rata of general factory expenses, such as superintendents, and the salaries or wages of other non-producers, insurance, cost of night watchman, heat, light, power, repairs of machinery and buildings, and depreciation of machinery and buildings. Selling expenses, on the other hand, include advertising, cost of show room, traveling salesmen, bad debts and all the other items that enter into the distribution of goods and must be paid out of the gross profit—namely, out of the difference between $5, the factory cost, and $7.50, the selling price. This demonstrates the necessity of showing in the main books of the establishment the cost of commercial expenses as well as factory costs. To blend the two in one account would be simply shutting one's eyes to very important business facts, and yet this mistake is often made as I know from experience.

Balance-Sheets and Balance-Accounts*

By James B. Macdonald

The ultimate end of all bookkeeping being the elaboration of a balance sheet, or balance account, either of which purports to contain in itself a complete resume of all past detail, we consider the best method of treating this subject is to take a few representative balance sheets and explain their component parts. This system is different to that adopted in existing treatises on bookkeeping and to the way it is taught in schools. Nevertheless it lends itself readily to the explanation of principles—a most essential point in any educational system. Another reason for adopting this course is that it immediately imparts the minimum knowledge of accountancy necessary to the conduct of a large business. In our day a high standard of excellence is attained in preparing these statements of accounts, but it should not be forgotten that this is the outcome of generations of experience and expediency.

WHAT IS A BALANCE SHEET?

A balance sheet is simply a memorandum containing the Capital and Liabilities of a business at a given date, together with the assets, or funds available to satisfy these. It is usually stated in the following form:

A. B. & Co.

Balance Sheet as at 31st December, 1897.

Liabilities	£15,000
Capital	20,000
	£35,000

Assets	£35,000
	£35,000

From this it will be seen that a balance sheet is nothing more or less than a statement of affairs at a given date, compiled from any data — not necessarily from book records. It is not a ledger account, or part of any bookkeeping system, but merely a memorandum containing figures based on the acounts — if such exist. Hence the term "balance sheet" (or statement) to distinguish it from a "balance account" as used on the Continent.

Before going further it may be as well to consider—

WHAT IS A BALANCE ACCOUNT?

A balance account is a general account in the ledger into which, at a given date, the balances of all other accounts are transferred. Thereafter one obtains at a glance a kind of panoramic view of the financial situation of the business. For convenience those items of receipt and expenditure which relate to Revenue are collected into an intermediary account called the Profit and Loss Account, and the balance of the latter only is transferred along with the others.

The following is the form of a balance account:

A. B. & Co.

Balance Account as at 31st December, 1897.

Dr.

To Assets	£35,000
	£35,000

Cr.

By Liabilities	£15,000
By Capital	20,000
	£35,000

WHEREIN DOES THE BALANCE ACCOUNT DIFFER FROM THE BALANCE SHEET?

First, the former is part of the bookkeeping system, while the latter is not.

Second, the same items are placed on opposite sides of each form.

Third, the "balance account" bears the symbols of an account proper with its "Dr. to" and "Cr. by," while the balance sheet should not.

Fourth, as regards the bookkeeping, where the balance sheet is adopted the books are "opened" for the new period by the balances brought down from the old, but where the balance account is in use the new accounts have to be "opened" by journal entry, because all ledger balances have already been cleared off to the balance account, and the latter itself balances.

These simple rules do not appear to be generally known.

A balance sheet is more frequently used in this country than a balance account.

*Originally published in the Accountants' Magazine.

owing mainly to this particular form being appended to one of the earlier Companies' Acts. Had practical accountants been consulted at the time the bill was drafted, they would have had this form reversed and converted into a balance account. The figures could then have been evolved from the financial records by natural transition. Private traders are not bound by the regulations affecting public companies, and there is nothing to prevent them recording the results of their business in the form of a balance account if they wish to do so. The commercial community, however, have become accustomed to the use of balance sheets, and they are likely, therefore, to remain with us.

The example we have given shows a balance sheet in its most rudimentary form. It is natural to assume that the parties interested in the business would require fuller information as to how their capital, liabilities and assets are made up. The sole art of framing a balance-sheet consists in subdividing these three main divisions — Capital, Liabilities and Assets—in such a manner as to show the salient features of the business. To what extent this should be carried is entirely a matter of judgment and experience. A few facts are readily grasped, while many tend to obscure the principal features.

Another important matter is to display the various items in an intelligent manner, so as to bring out their relationship to each other. A good method is to set down, first in order, those liabilities which have to be paid at an early date, and against this the funds which would then be available to meet them. Likewise with future liabilities, as far as possible. A statement so displayed offers useful information and looks symmetrical. It is perfect in substance if it contains all the liabilities, funds and capital of the business. Perfection in form is, on the other hand, only approximately attainable, because it is largely a matter of fancy, accuracy of principles, experience and practical knowledge of the business. The latter is, for all practical purposes, a minor matter compared with perfection in substance, which all may attain.

Two typical balance sheets are worth considering in detail—those of a private trading company and of a public limited company.

A. B. & Co.

Balance Sheet as at 31st December, 1897.

Liabilities—		
Bills payable	£10,000	
Current accounts	5,000	
		£15,000
Capital—		
A	£10,000	
B	10,000	
		20,000
		£35,000

Assets—		
Cash in bank		£3,000
Bills receivable		2,000
Current accounts		15,000
Stock		10,000
Freehold property	£15,000	
Less mortgage thereon.	10,000	
		5,000
		£35,000

It will be observed that the subdivisions are so arranged as to bring out conspicuously the amount of each principal heading; and that, in the nature of things, the total assets must equal the total capital and liabilities, if the business is solvent. If insolvent, the amount of loss, or deficiency, added to the assets must equal, or "balance," the capital and liabilities taken together.

In private firms any loss is deducted from the partners' capital, and any profit added on.

THE RAND EXPLOITATION COMPANY, LIMITED.

Balance Sheet as at 31st December, 1897.

Capital—			
Share Capital—			
Ordinary.	£350,000		
Preference	350,000		
Founders'	3,500		
		£703,500	
Reserve Fund		100,000	
Profit		425,000	
			£1,228,500
Liabilities—			
Bills payable		£100,000	
Ordinary creditors		140,000	
Dividends unclaimed.		1,500	
			241,500
			£1,470,000

Assets—		
Cash in bank	£110,000	
L'ns against securities	500,000	
Investments	840,000	
Ordinary debtors	14,000	
Office furniture	1,000	
Live and dead stock	5,000	
		£1,470,000

All balance sheets are reducible to the form of three principal divisions—capital, liabilities and assets; although in the case of public companies it is not usual to do so, the reason being that "Table A" of the Companies' Act, 1862, recommends a particular form which, in the case of companies not having their own Articles of Association, is obligatory. This form does not commend itself to us, as it discloses a want of knowledge respecting the theory and principles of accounts.

Any observations on the best manner of displaying the various items in a balance sheet are equally applicable to a balance account. In either case the statement is simplified and more clearly explained by adopting the three-division principle, hence our using it.

The various items composing the assets and liabilities in the above balance sheets are more or less self-explanatory. With the subdivision of capital, however, some debatable points are involved, which we will now consider.

WHAT IS CAPITAL?

In the case of a private individual or trading firm, capital practically means excess of assets over liabilities. With a joint stock company, however, a little more discrimination is necessary.

Theoretically and in the abstract the same rule is true, although it is seldom used in this sense even by accountants, owing to the peculiar constitution of these companies. The term capital in connection with public companies is more often employed as meaning share capital. This, of course, is a more restricted application than the wider meaning, to which we may apply the term actual capital.

Therefore, the actual capital of a corporation, as well as of a trading firm, is the excess of its assets over its liabilities. This admits of two subdivisions: (1) Share capital, and (2) Profit. The former may be split up into the different kinds of share capital, as preference, ordinary and founders', and the latter into—

(a) Reserve fund.
(b) Profit available for dividend, and
(c) Profit carried forward.

Share capital is regulated entirely by the Memorandum of Association of the Company and any subsequent modifications thereof.

It should be noted that debentures, being of the nature of mortgages, come under the heading of liabilities, and not of capital.

We shall now consider—

WHAT IS PROFIT.

Profit in the accounts of a private individual or trading firm means the increased difference between the capital in the business at a given date and the actual capital at a subsequent date — say the beginning and end of a year. If a decrease has taken place, the difference represents the loss incurred during the period under review.

Where joint stock companies are concerned, the matter is not so obvious. Their share capital being fixed, and irreducible except by legal process, any excess of funds after providing for liabilities and repayment of share capital is actual profit. In most cases it is inadvisable to make an unreserved distribution of this among the members. The law is very severe if more money is paid away by way of dividend than has actually been earned as income—a process commonly described as paying dividends out of capital. In practice, it is seldom possible to value the assets of a business precisely at a given date; and consequently any statement of profit and loss, under such circumstances, must be considered as only approximately correct. Prudence, therefore, suggests that a portion of the profits should be withheld for the time being. Other motives also may occur, such as the possibility of contingent, or unexpected, liabilities, arising.

Any fund so set apart out of profits is a reserve fund, and may be general or special according to the directions given by the proprietors for its application. The actual dividend fund would be described as profit available for dividend. If the profits of the business fluctuate considerably from year to year, part of the surplus in good years may be carried forward to help to equalize the dividend in less prosperous times. It is immaterial whether or not this is treated as a sum apart from the general reserve fund, because they are both undistributed profit.

With regard to the respective advantages of balance sheets and balance accounts, we are of opinion that the balance account is the only logical method.

If a balance sheet is written into the ledger, the items are seen to be on the opposite sides to the balances of the accounts which they represent, and by no possible means can they be worked into the present system of recording the double nature of each transaction. It is otherwise with a balance account, which is the pinnacle of double entry bookkeeping.

As to classifying the various trial balance entries, what is possible in the one case is equally so in the other, with this advantage in favor of the balance account, that the different steps by which all ultimate items are arrived at is recorded in the books and can be traced at any time.

This permits of the auditors inscribing their certificate in the ledger below the balance account which they have approved, and being held responsible for all that appears therein.

Likewise with the signatures of the directors or the managers.

On a question of fact, the production of the books would be conclusive evidence.

We suggest that this procedure should be made compulsory in every business.

It may be asked, "Does a balance sheet not also give this evidence?" and we answer, "Not always." Some companies which print their annual statements and do not write the balance sheet into the ledger, after a few years have not a single copy in their possession for certain years. In such circumstances how is one to know whether the balance sheet subsequently taken out from the books is identical with the one issued to the proprietors? These remarks apply more particularly to misrepresentations perpetrated in connection with personal accounts—say the listing of large loans to directors or officials among ordinary debts. The difficulty is mainly due to the slumping of items—a practice which, generally speaking, is not unseldom carried to the point of palliating facts which it is undesirable for the proprietors to know, or of burking discussion at the general meeting. Such bookkeeping prevarications, if we may so call them, would in all cases be ear-marked in the journal were a balance account in use, and the party responsible could afterwards be brought to book.

A balance sheet, as we have shown, would mask certain transactions of this nature.

Again, the books may be all right, but the balance sheet all wrong. Discovery is only possible by checking each item in detail. But we know from the evidence given in the Law Courts of late years that some non-professional auditors do not always do so. Here is a method of fraud peculiar to balance sheets.

How often at a general meeting of shareholders do we see one of the officials produce a working balance sheet, with several pages of appendix, from which to answer a question concerning the accounts. It would, in our opinion, be better form to produce the ledger, with its balance and subsidiary accounts, as the sole repository of all facts relating to the financial situation.

Sprague's Speeches

A Collection of After-Dinner Speeches and Miscellaneous Addresses. By Wm. C. Sprague. 188 pages, bound in cloth, top gold and deckel side edges. Price $1.50

Almost every one knows or has heard of Wm. C. Sprague, editor of the Collector and Commercial Lawyer, and of the Law Students' Helper, author of a number of works that have become exceptionally popular among lawyers, and president of the Sprague Correspondence Schools of Law and Journalism, Detroit. As an after-dinner orator and occasional speaker, he ranks high among the very best of the younger men now before the public. Accordingly, special interest attaches to his remarks on various occasions, particularly upon the part of those who, in a semi-business capacity, aspire to be able to acquit themselves creditably when upon their feet. The collection embraces speeches to lawyers, credit men, school teachers, churches, societies, college fraternities, editors, newsboys, Chautauqua assemblies, young men's clubs and various others. They are not merely such addresses as one is interested in reading, for they are much more, in that they are of a character to be helpful to the one who is preparing for any similar occasion. The addresses teem with sound sense, brilliant wit, humor that is catching and eloquence of a very high order.

The College Man

"I beg your pardon," said the passenger in the skull cap, leaning over and speaking to the young man on the seat immediately in front of him, "but are you not just returning from college?" "Yes, sir," replied the young man. "I am one of the graduates. In fact, I was the valedictorian." "I was sure of it," rejoined the other. "I would be greatly obliged if you would tell me in a few words who wrote 'Junius,' who the man in the iron mask was, what was the origin of protopsalm, explain the Schleswig-Holstein question, give me the reasons why republics are superior to limited monarchies, and tell me why evil is permitted on earth."—Chicago Tribune.

Accountants' Associations

Associated Accountants of New Orleans

We have the most favorable reports of the prosperity and good work of this organization. Meetings are well attended, membership is increasing and the attention of the business community is being drawn to the importance of good accounting and the value of the investigations and discussions which this association is promoting.

The subject before the October meeting was "Debentures," and the essayist was Aug. M. Benedic, secretary and treasurer of the Lambou & Noel Lumber Co. Among the guests on this occasion was Hon. M. J. Cunningham, Attorney-General of the State of Louisiana, who followed every demonstration with careful attention.

Mr. Benedic's paper proved to be an arraignment of certain debenture organizations now current in Louisiana, whose promises to the public he demonstrated to be beyond reasonable probabilities when analyzed in the light of mathematical facts. The paper, and the answers to questions which were asked of the speaker consumed the whole evening, so that discussion was carried over to the next meeting (November 17). It was expected that on this occasion some of the debenture companies, who had been invited to do so, would put in a reply to Mr. Benedic's impeachment of their foundation principles. Only one was heard from. The Louisiana Debenture Company, Limited, sent a letter which was read. This communication was to the effect that since the company was the defendant in a suit brought by the Attorney-General of the State, which suit was now pending in the courts, it would prefer not to be considered as seeking to influence or forestall the decision to be soon rendered by attempting to mould public opinion. Thereupon Mr Benedic continued his criticisms of the course of these companies, making his points clear by comparisons with other forms of investments, and by numerous pertinent illustrations.

Institute of Chartered Accountants of Ontario

We are in receipt of the programme of the meetings to be held at the Canadian Institute, Richmond Street, East, Toronto, during the present season, which is as follows:

October 19th, 1898, paper by Mr. A. C. Neff, C. A., subject, "Old and New Methods of Keeping Cash and Bank Accounts."

November 16th, paper by Mr. George Kappele, Barrister-at-Law, subject, "Points in Mercantile Law."

December 14th, paper by Mr. David Hoskins, C. A., subject, "Mercantile Arithmetic."

January 18th, 1899, paper by Mr. Wilton C. Eddis, C. A., subject, "Auditing."

February 15th, paper by Mr. George Edwards, F. C. A., subject, "Books of Account."

March 15th, paper by Mr. Harry Vigeon, F. C. A., subject, "Profits."

April 19th, paper by Mr. W. B. Tindall, C. A., subject, "Cost Accounts."

May 19th, paper by Mr. J. M. Scully, C. A., subject, "Fire Insurance Accounts."

The officers cordially invite members to bring these meetings before their commercial friends, so that the aims of the Institute may be forcibly brought before all business men. The programme announces that the intermediate and final examinations of the Institute will be held on the 17th, 18th and 19th of May, 1899.

OPENING ADDRESS.

At the opening of the session for 1898-1899 of the Institute of Chartered Accountants of Ontario, the president, Harry Vigeon, F. C. A., gave a brief resume of the history of the reorganization of the society and the steps which have brought it up to its present state of efficiency and usefulness. He spoke in part as follows:

As you are aware the Institute of 1893 was in a moribund condition consequent on the apathy of its members who, for the most part, were not public, practicing accountants. In that year a few earnest men, regretting the state of the body to which they belonged, determined to put life into the institution and place it upon its feet. They carefully studied the records of its history and set themselves out to profit by the mistakes of the past. The by-laws were thoroughly revised—brought up to date, and made more practical in their workings. The dead wood of the Institute was lopped off and the remaining membership were those who took some interest in its welfare. This small band of enthusiastic accountants struck at the core of the matter by making the examinations of the Institute not only worthy of the study of accountants generally, but also so practically thorough and comprehensive in their workings that the manufacturer, merchant, and other employers of accountants were seized with the fact that the "Bookkeepers' Certificate" of the Institute was a high recommendation to any person seeking employment with them in their office. At the same time the higher certificate, C. A., was only obtainable after years of careful study, practical experience, and public recognition. The course of study as outlined by the Institute was tested, and the number of candidates who presented themselves for the examination in the intermediate and final subjects is a conclusive proof of the success of the reorganization.

The active men then took hold of the other part of the Institute's work, namely, its contact with the public. For two years the monthly meetings were carried much similar to those of preceding years. Papers were read by gentlemen other than members of the Institute and on subjects that were in some cases only remotely connected with accounts. The attendance at these meetings was very discouraging, and at last a change in the method of conducting such meetings together with the subject for discussion was determined upon. Much anxious thought, and I might say, fear, was entertained when the new order of meetings was promulgated. It was thougnt that the subjects might appear too dry and heavy for a successful session, but the four or five gentlemen who took hold of the matter, spent a good part of the summer of 1896 in compiling a practical programme, and gathering together information from all quarters as to the best method of handling accountancy subjects, with the result that they approached the first meeting in 1896 with much doubt as to whether the new departure would meet with approval.

The programme thus arranged was successful and a better attendance of the members and those interested in accounts took place. The Executive were encouraged to make yet further efforts to bring those interested in accountants in Ontario in close touch with the Institute. The holding of the meetings in the Canadian Institute seemed to be appreciated. The facilities for gathering together in this room with the appliances by which illustrations and the general elucidation of the papers was far better than in the previous place of meetings. The meetings held during the session of 1897-98 were pre-eminently a success. The programme of meetings was calculated to draw together the best students of accounts and the papers read were not only of interest at the time of the reading, but were also the subject of thought and discussion after the meetings were held. The next branch of the reorganization to which these few gentlemen gave their attention was in the direction of the examinations.

It was felt improper and unfair to ask candidates to present themselves for a three days' examination without giving them any intimation of the scope of the subjects on which they were to be examined. The examinations of the Institute, or in other words the course of study necessary for a thorough knowledge of accounts, was deemed too narrow in the direction of practical accounts. Special work in branches such as Marine Insurance were considered as being outside of the ordinary range of accountants' work, and the subjects on which candidates were to be examined were set out as follows: Bookkeeping, Auditing, Bankruptcy, Mercantile Law, Joint Stock Companies, Partnership and Executorship work. Following the first examination after the reorganization the questions set were printed and distributed among those who applied for same. The examinations in the intermediate subjects were largely attended both at the November and May sessions. The questions were practical, comprehensive, and broad, so that no candidate was in any way inconvenienced by either technicalities or special subjects. The examinations showed that those who had embraced the opportunity of attending the monthly meetings obtained such an incentive to study that their proficiency was pronounced above those attending from outside points. After each examination the questions were printed and distributed, and in the present Year Book the questions set in the 1897 and 1898 examinations form a completion to the charter and by-laws and information regarding the reorganized Institute.

The programme about to be commenced embraces subjects of practical information and follows much on the lines of the past session. Subjects of practical utility are to be discussed, and we hope the results as shown by the next examination will fully bring out our expectations.

So much for the work as viewed from the outside. Much remains to be done. The standing of the members of the Institute has been acknowledged far and wide and the files of the Institute will bear me out in showing that our practicing members and their work are known from Halifax to Vancouver.

The Provincial Government has so far acknowledged the standing of the Institute by enacting in the Municipalities Act of 1897—that a Fellow of the Institute is recommended to the Municipalities as a fit and proper person to be an auditor of their accounts. A few more changes in the Statutory Enactments are required to place the profession of accounts and those who are possessed of the Institute's standing, in the professional ranks of which their skill and attainments qualify them. To this end the Council will direct their attention and it will be a source of pride if during my term of office as President of the Institute such Statutory enactments may be obtained, which will be giving to our members their just rights in the accountancy world.

Retail Bookkeeping

The following extract from an address delivered by F. R. Boocock, Secretary of the National Association of Credit Men, before some of the Western local associations affiliated with this body, indicates the appreciation of what the new accounting may be to retail merchants and the business public at large:

It is impossible for a merchant to give an accurate and comprehensive statement of his condition unless he keeps his books with intelligence and regularity. This is done to-day by the minority of merchants; in fact, it is the one irregularity against which credit men have most to contend. An imperfect knowledge of affairs is the ruination of most merchants. This is strictly true of those who keep practically no books, and largely so of those who know only periodically what is their true financial standing. It seems to me that this presents a condition that should be met by our association perfecting and encouraging a Uniform System of Accountancy for Retail Stores. I recognize that there is a great diversity in the character of businesses, and that no one set form of bookkeeping is practicable. While we concede this, however, we contend that there is a uniformity in accountancy which is possible, and which, while recognizing and observing certain cardinal facts, permits of such elasticity in bookkeeping as to cover every complication. If we can perfect such a system, and establish it in fifty or one hundred retail stores before the time of our next convention, I will feel that we have performed a labor of incalculable significance to business interests. Such a system would show at the conclusion of each day's or each week's business, as might be elected, the exact condition of the stock, profit or loss sustained, volume of trade, and every detailed knowledge so essential to prosperous management. The possibility of this field of activity is to me alluring, portentous and suggestive.

Question of an Annuity

From E. S. J., Tacoma, Wash.

On looking into the problem presented in the May number, page 46, I find myself perplexed with respect to the item "Annuity credit $2,500." I cannot as yet see how this account should show a credit of an annual payment and show no cost. It looks to me like getting something for nothing. I would like some information on this point, for I am interested in the general solution of the problem. It is, so to speak, a very pretty one.

Note.—In another part of this issue we present Mr. Benedic's solution to the general problem referred to. While it does not bear specifically upon the question here presented, it does give general information concerning Mr. Benedic's treatment of the question which he raised. Perhaps he will see fit to respond to the particular question which this correspondent raises.

Conversion of Partnership Books, Etc.

By Aug. M. Benedic

In the May number of Accountics, pages 45 and 46, we presented a question that had been arranged for discussion at the June meeting of the Associated Accountants of New Orleans. It was

TRADING AND MERCHANDISING ACCOUNT
At year ending Dec. 31, 189

Net Sales........	100%	$194,750	
Purchases...........$165,000			
Less stock on hand.. 10,000			
Amount of goods consumed.	79.6%	155,000	
Gross profit on goods.....	*20.4%*	*$39,750*	$39,750
General expenses...........		$1,000	
Salaries.....................		5,000	
Rolling-stock expenses.....		200	
Live-stock expenses........		500	
Stable expenses.............		800	
Feed consumed.............		2,300	
Taxes and License..........		380	
Insurance..................		125	
	5.3%	$10,305	$10,305
Gross profit on trading...	*15.1%*		*$29,445*
Rolling-stock depreciation.		500	
Live-stock depreciation....	.6%	600	1,100
Net profit on trading.....	*14.5%*		*$28,345*

entitled "The Conversion of Partnership Books Into Those of a Limited Company Under Certain Conditions." We have now before us the schedules which Mr. Benedic presented on that occasion, in

LOSS AND GAIN ACCOUNT.

	GAINS.		
Trading and Merchandising..		$28,345 00	
Commissions..................		7,110 00	
Real Estate Revenue...........		3,300 00	
Int. coupons, U. S. Bonds, 4's..		480 00	
Int. coupons. O.R.R. " 6's..		300 00	
Mdse. from Livingston........		313 33	
Fidelity } Annuity	$ 2,500 00		
Trust Co.. } P. worth	20,277 24	22,777 24	
Interest from A................		50 00	
Interest from B................		105 00	
Interest from Notes Rec........		400 00	
Total Gains.......(180.51%)		$63,180 57	$63,180 57
	LOSSES.		
Notes Receivable..............		500 00	
Accounts Receivable..........		1,200 00	
Shipment to Havana.........		165 00	
Interest on Notes Payable.....		75 00	
Int. coupons Bonds Payable..		1,750 00	
Total Losses.......(*10.54%*)		$3,690 00	$3,690 00
Net Gain..........(169.97%)			*$59,490 57*
A's pro-rata.....(3/7 or 72.84%).		$25,495 96	
B's pro-rata......(4/7 or 97.13%)		33,994 61	

exemplifying the methods which he recommended. In his letter to us, Mr. Benedic says:

"I enclose the solution of the problem mentioned. I have made no comment, nor have I furnished you anything but the plain solution. In presenting this

RESPECTIVE PARTNER'S ACCOUNTS.

A'S CAPITAL ACCOUNT.		
Capital invested...		$15,000 00
Loss and Gain.....		25,495 96
Withdrawals..................	$3,500 00	
Interest on Withdrawals......	105 00	
Net Capital.................	*36,890 96*	
	$40,495 96	$40,495 96
B'S CAPITAL ACCOUNT.		
Capital invested...		$20,000 00
Loss and Gain.....		33,994 61
Withdrawals..................	$2,500 00	
Interest on Withdrawals......	50 00	
Net Capital.................	*51,444 61*	
	$53,994 61	$53,994 61

problem last June, every entry and the results arrived at were illustrated and explained, particularly the Trading Account, the Merchandise Account, the Loss and Gain Account and the Balance Sheet. The classification of these ac-

BALANCE SHEET
Of the partnership A & B at year ending Dec. 31, '9...

	ASSETS.		
Cash.........................		$ 5,946 93	
U. S. 4% Bonds................		12,000 00	
O. R. R. 6% Bonds.............		5,000 00	
Collat. Notes Receivable.	$7,000		
Accrued Interest........	300	7,300 00	
Notes Receivable.. $5,000			
Less Rent N. not due 500	4,500		
Accrued Interest........	100	4,600 00	
			$34,846 93
Real Estate..................			52,000 00
Fidelity Trust Co.............			20,277 24
Book Accounts Receivable....			8,965 00
First M't'ge Bonds, Fund Acct.			3,053 07
Stock on hand, per inventory.		$10.000 00	
Stock on hand, 400 bbls. Flour.		2,400 00	
			12,400 00
Rolling-Stock.................		2,000 00	
Live-Stock		2,400 00	
Feed (on hand)...............		200 00	
			4,600 00
Office and Office Fixtures.....			750 00
Taxes and License (pre-paid).		120 00	
Insurance (pre-paid)..........		75 00	195 00
Total Assets...............			$137,087 24
	LIABILITIES.		
Collat. Notes Payable....	$2,500		
Interest due.............	35	$2,535 00	
Notes Payable...........	4,000		
Interest due.............	40	4,040 00	
Accounts Payable.............		4,926 67	
1st Mort. Bonds Payable.	$35,000		
Interest coupons due...	1,750	36,750 00	
Contingent Fund Acct. Notes Receivable................		500 00	$48,751 67
Total Net Capital..........			$88,335 57
A's Net Capital...............		$36,890 96	
B's Net Capital...............		51,444 61	

counts, the partners profit accounts and capital accounts, treasury stock and good will, received special treatment, and the different methods used in handling these accounts."

(We have reproduced the several

ENTRIES TO CLOSE PARTNERSHIP'S BOOKS.

The A & B Co., Ltd.	$137,587 24	
To Cash		$5,916 93
" Notes Receivable		5,000 00
" Notes Rec (collateral).		7,000 00
" Accounts Receivable		8,965 00
" Real Estate		52,000 00
" Office and Office Fixt		750 00
" Fidelity Trust Co		20,277 24
" U. S. 4% Bonds		12,000 00
" Orleans R. R Bonds, 6%		5,000 00
" First Mort Bonds, Fund Account		3,053 07
" Trading and M'disn'g		12,400 00
" Insurance		75 00
" Tax and License		120 00
" Rolling Stock		2,000 00
" Live Stock		2,400 00
" Feed		200 00
" Interest		400 00
Sunds. To "The A & B Co., Ltd."		$137,587 24
First Mortgage Bonds	$35,000 00	
Notes Payable (collateral)	2,500 00	
Notes Payable	4,000 00	
Accounts Payable	4,926 67	
First Mort. Bonds, Int. Coupons.	1,750 00	
Interest	75 00	
Real Estate Revenue	500 00	
Cont. Fund Acct. Notes Rec	500 00	
A's Capital	36,890 96	
B's Capital	51,444 61	

Write the full history, with necessary explanations for making the above entries (for future reference.)

schedules which Mr. Benedic has furnished us and present them herewith,

TRIAL BALANCE OF THE A & B CO., LTD.

The items for the trial balance are the same as set forth in h (9), with the following exceptions:—

Cash, increased	$27,500 00	
Collateral Notes Receivable, increased	12,500 00	
Subscription acct. in balance		
Total footings of trial-balance.		$249,251 67

over captions that clearly indicate their use and purpose.)

Easing the Mind

Who is there that has not been provoked in business to the verge of distraction; and, therefore, tempted to vent his wrath upon the offender in a letter? Who, again, is there who has written a business letter in anger that has not lived to regret it? To write what one is prompted to say while "hot around the collar," serves to ease the mind and clear the atmosphere, but the results of the letter mailed under these conditions frequently prove that the easing has been secured only at unreasonable cost. Not to write what one feels, is to keep the anger pent up in one's system, greatly to his physical discomfort. Is there no middle course? Here is the story of some good advice given to Secretary Stanton by President Abraham Lincoln:

Mr. Stanton, it seems, was greatly vexed because an army officer had refused to understand an order, or, at all events, had not obeyed.

"I believe I'll sit down," said Stanton, "and give that man a piece of my mind."

"Do so," said Mr. Lincoln, "write it

ENTRIES TO OPEN A NEW SET OF BOOKS FOR THE A & B CO., LTD.

Sundries To Sundries:—		
Cash	$ 5,946 93	
Notes Receivable	5,000 00	
Collateral Notes Receivable	7,000 00	
Accounts Receivable	8,965 00	
Real Estate	52,000 00	
Office and Office Fixtures	750 00	
Fidelity Trust Co	20,277 24	
U. S 4% Bonds	12,000 00	
Orleans R. R. 6% Bonds	5,000 00	
First Mort. Bonds, Fund Acct	3,053 07	
Trading and Merchandising	12,400 00	
Insurance	75 00	
Taxes and and License	120 00	
Rolling Stock	2,000 00	
Live Stock	2,400 00	
Feed	200 00	
Interest	400 00	
Subscription to Capital Stock	40,000 00	
Treasury Stock	60,000 00	
Good Will	11,664 43	
To Capital Stock (common)		$150,000 00
" Capital Stock (preferred)		50,000 00
" First Mortgage Bonds		35,000 00
" Notes Payable (collat).		2,500 00
" Notes Payable		4,000 00
" Accounts Payable		4,926 67
" 1st M't'g B'ds, Int. Coup.		1,750 00
" Interest		75 00
" Real Estate Revenue		500 00
" Contingent Fund Acct, Notes Receivable		500 00

Here insert a copy of the act of incorporation, and all other information pertinent to the act of incorporation.

In the stock-ledger, each shareholder will be credited for the amount of his holdings, giving the number of each share issued, date of issue kind held, etc. The total credits to correspond with the capital accounts in the check or key ledger.

Sundries. To Subscription to Capital Stock		$40,000 00
Cash from "C"	$20,000 00	
Cash from "D"	7,500 00	
Collateral Notes Rec. from "D" (With explanations)	12,500 00	

now while you have it on your mind. Make it sharp; cut him all up."

Stanton did not need another invitation. It was a bone-crusher that he read to the President.

"That's right," said Abe, "that's a good one."

"Whom can I get to send it by?" mused the Secretary.

"Send it!" replied Lincoln, "send it! Why, don't send it. Tear it up. You have freed your mind on the subject, and that is all that is necessary. Tear it up. You never want to send such letters; I never do!"

What Would Be Your Procedure in Changing from Single to Double Entry?*

By J. A. Butler

At our last meeting in June, when the chairman honored me by the request to speak on a subject to be assigned, and then announced the subject as, "What Would Be Your Procedure in Changing from Single to Double Entry?" I remarked that I had not the faintest idea. It occurred to me that my preferred method would be to get some one to do the work for me. One of my fellow accountants of the Institute came to my assistance with this suggestion: "Burn up the old books and start fresh." At the time this plan seemed feasible, and its advantages were apparent, but, upon reflection, I could see that the original entries would prove valuable by the saving of trouble and labor, and also time, which is money.

I do not understand that the subject requires a description of either single or double entry. If a paragraph in a recent paper is true, double entry has been in use since the fourteenth or fifteenth century. Therefore, its principles should be familiar to accountants and business men by this time. The article above referred to states that the earliest treatise on Double Entry was written by a monk, Lucas di Borgo, and published at Venice in 1495. The earliest book on the subject is entitled the "Keepying of the Famous Reconynge, Debitor and Creditor." It was published in London by John Gowghe, in 1543. Mr. D. A. Keister, in his book, "Expert and Stock Company Accounting and Auditing," states: "It is surprising to know to what extent Single Entry Bookkeeping is practiced, even in houses doing a large business, because business men themselves are ignorant of the superiority of Double Entry." In view of this statement, I trust you will pardon me for taking the liberty of imposing on your good nature to the extent of quoting this definition of bookkeeping taken from the Standard Dictionary:

"The art, method or practice of recording business transactions distinctly and systematically, in blank books provided for the purpose, so as to show the goods and moneys received, disposed of and on hand, the credits given, and the assets, liabilities and general status of the business, person or house."

"Bookkeeping is practiced by either Single Entry or Double Entry.

"In Single Entry the day book (a day book and journal kept as one) and the ledger are the essential books; in Double Entry, a day book, journal and ledger are the essentials, though a cash book, bill book, stock book, invoice book, etc., are usually added for accuracy and convenience of reference, but all are finally united in the ledger.

"By the Double Entry system, every transaction is made to appear on the record as both debtor and creditor by observance of the governing principle that in every instance the thing obtained is debtor to the thing given, and the thing given is creditor to the thing obtained, by means of which a correct ledger balance is always at command."

It is to be presumed that the great majority desire to be able to ascertain at any time the exact condition of their business, and whether they are making or losing money. Although there are exceptions, as in the case of two men, partners in a business not a great way from Hartford, who had their own ideas of the value of accurate account keeping. Having purchased a quantity of sweet potatoes, one partner remarked, "We must keep strict account of our sales of these potatoes to see if we make or lose," to which the other member of the firm replied, "Oh! if we make we will know it fast enough, and if we lose, we do not want to know it." It might be added as a moral that the first of these men was successful in business, while the other wound up in disgrace.

While not familiar with Single Entry Bookkeeping, my idea has always been that it consisted principally of memoranda, more or less in detail, according to the size of the business, of charges to individuals or firms for goods sold, the charges being offset by a cash or merchandize equivalent, and having no accounts to indicate whether a business was profitable or otherwise. Without going into the matter carefully, and in the absence of the advice of an experienced accountant familiar with the subject, the method I should naturally pursue in changing from Single to Double Entry would be as follows: First, to take as ac-

*Paper presented by J. A. Butler at the September meeting of the Hartford Chapter of the Institute of Accounts.

curate an inventory as possible and ascertain the amount of the resources and liabilities. The next thing in order would be to open the several Representative Accounts, charging Real Estate, if any to Real Estate Account, and the Merchandise Inventory to Merchandise. Charge Cash with the amount on hand. Open a Bills or Notes Receivable Account, debiting it with the amount of notes maturing, if any. The amounts of these accounts, with the sum of the Accounts Receivable already charged would comprise the Assets.

The Liabilities would be shown by crediting all accounts payable to the persons or firms to whom indebted. They would also include outstanding notes, if any, to be credited to Notes Payable Account. The difference between the Liabilities and the Assets, which latter we will assume are in excess, would show the capital or surplus, and when credited to an account representing the capital stock, the ledger correctly footed would be in balance.

To quote from the book: "Transforming the Single Entry Ledger into a Double Entry One," though simple as the process may appear after it is explained, it will be found that many accountants are not aware that there is any way of changing the principle of keeping the books, but by the laborious and tedious process of transforming all the accounts to a new ledger, an operation that is seldom necessary, unless the old ledger is filled. The process of changing a set of books from Single Entry to Double Entry is very simple. The characteristic difference between Single Entry and Double Entry consists in the use and application of the terms Dr. and Cr. This in Single Entry being applied only to persons or their representatives, it follows that the Single Entry Ledger can contain none other than personal accounts. Before proceeding to change a set of books from Single to Double Entry, it is necessary first to ascertain the loss or gain in business.

General Rule for Ascertaining the Gain or Loss in Single Entry: To the Liabilities, add the balance of the stock account when a credit, but when a debit add it to the assets. The difference between the Assets and Liabilities, when thus increased by the balance of the stock account, is the net gain or loss in business. Net gain, when the former exceeds the latter; net loss, when the latter exceeds the former.

Process of changing: From the Inventory you get the results and effects of the business in Single Entry. To change to Double Entry is only to debit the Assets to the Liabilities.

If the old ledger is to be used, the opening entry should not under any circumstances be any different than if a new one is to be opened. To use the old ledger, it would be necessary to post only the new accounts to be opened, while all the personal accounts are already in Double Entry condition, and are marked in the journal posted.

If a new ledger is to be opened, you would have to debit and credit the Personal Accounts separately instead of taking them collectively.

The subject is rather a barren one, and affords but little opportunity for elaboration, and, as Mr. Keister says, "The operation of the changing from Single Entry to Double Entry is so simple, and has been so thoroughly illustrated and explained, that further treatment would be useless."

The most fertile soil does not necessarily produce the most abundant harvest. It is the use we make of our faculties which renders them valuable. Talent, like other things, may lie fallow.—T. W. Higginson.

It always seemed to me a sort of clever stupidity only to have one sort of talent—almost like a carrier-pigeon.—George Eliot.

Such a nature, tickled with good success, disdains the shadow which he treads on at noon.—Shakespeare.

From mere success nothing can be concluded in favor of any nation upon whom it is bestowed.—Atterbury.

Wealth is the least trustworthy of anchors.—J. G Holland.

Nothing succeeds so well as success.
—Talleyrand.

Talents constitute our very essence.
—Charles Rollin.

In success be moderate.—Franklin.

Examination Questions

The following are the answers to some of the questions set by the Scottish Chartered Accountants' General Examining Board for the June, 1898, examinations, as published on pages 152 and 153 of our October issue:

Algebra: Golf club problem:—

Let x — original number of members,

then $\frac{110}{x+10}$ = original subscription,

and $\frac{110}{x+10} = \frac{110 - \cdot 1x}{x}$; ($\cdot 1 = \frac{1}{10}$th of a £1, or 2s.)

From which equation it will be found that $x = 100$, and present subscription is 20s.

WHAT IS A TRIAL BALANCE?

A "trial balance" of a ledger is a statement showing in detail the debit and credit balances appearing in the ledger on a certain date. Its main purpose is to prove that the ledger has been correctly posted.

POLITICAL ECONOMY: EQUATION OF INTERNATIONAL DEMAND.

As this existence of ratios of exchange is explained by the relation between supply and demand, anything which interferes with that relation must affect the ratio of exchange. Hence, if protection were introduced by import duties into one country, the supply of the "protected" productions of the other countries would decrease, and the equations of international demand would be disturbed, and new ratios of exchange would be set up.

Auditing: The Embezzling Cashier of a Tweed Manufacturing Concern—The cashier of a Tweed manufacturer whose books were kept by double entry might attempt to conceal the embezzlement of £300 by any of the following methods:—

1. Actual cash in hand may be short of the balance shown in the Cash Book.

2. Checques drawn from bank might be omitted from the debit side of the Cash Book, the payment being entered on the credit side.

3. Cash may be entered as paid in name of wages, and the Wages Book might be made to agree with the payments in the Cash Book by the entry of fictitious names of workmen.

4. Accounts amounting to £300 may have been collected by him and not entered in his books.

5. The balance on the Cash Book may purposely have been carried forward £300 short, and the trial balance of the books cooked to agree.

6. Fictitious credit accounts may have been entered in the Ledger, and the sums entered in the Cash Book as payments of these accounts might be appropriated by the cashier.

Management of Trusts, Bankrupt Estates, etc.—Statement showing division of £4,012 10s., being balance of estate of the late O, as at 1st June, 1898.

The sum in hand for division is				£4,012 10 0
And is divisible thus:—				
1. Widow and family's share of estate			£4,000 0 0	
Add: Interest at 5 per cent to 1st June, 1898			300 0 0	
Less: Payments to account		£3,000 0 0	£4,300 0 0	
Interest thereon at 5 per cent		125 0 0		
			3,125 0 0	
Due to widow and family			£1,175 0 0	
Note of Residue for division.				
Cash in hand at 1st June, 1898		£4,012 10 0		
Payments to X, with interest		1,050 0 0		
Payments to Y, with interest		512 10 0		
		£5,575 0 0		
Less: Due to widow and her family		1,175 0 0		
Divisible by 3		£4,400 0 0		
Yields to X, Y, and Z, each		£1,466 13 4		
2. X's share of residue		£1,466 13 4		
Less: Payment to account	£1,000 0 0			
Interest thereon	50 0 0			
		1,050 0 0		
Due to X			416 13 4	
3. Y's share of residue		£1,466 13 4		
Less: Payment to account	£500 0 0			
Interest thereon	12 10 0			
		512 10 0		
Due to Y			954 3 4	
4. Z's share of residue		£1,466 13 4		
Due to Z			1,466 13 4	
As above				£4,012 10 0

DIVISION OF ESTATE, JUNE 1, 1898.

Accountics

The Office Magazine.

A. O. KITTREDGE, F. I. A., C. P. A., EDITOR.
E. R. KITTREDGE, ASSOCIATE.

Accountics is devoted to the Science of Accounting, to the Art of Bookkeeping and to the advocacy of Improved Office Methods.

Subscription.—One dollar a year, payable in advance.

Postage is prepaid by the publishers in the United States, Canada and Mexico. For all other countries in the Postal Union, subscribers must add 50 cents a year.

Discontinuances.—In the absence of specific orders to discontinue at the end of the subscription term the magazine will be continued and a bill sent.

Remittances should be by Draft, P. O. Order or Express Order, payable to the order of the ACCOUNTICS ASSOCIATION. Money and postage stamps are at the risk of the sender, unless sent by express or in registered letters. Add 10 cents each to checks on local banks to defray collection charges.

Advertising Rates will be quoted on application.

Official Journal.—This publication, by resolutions duly passed, has been made the official publication of the following organizations :—

THE INSTITUTE OF ACCOUNTS.
THE NEW YORK CHAPTER of the Institute of Accounts.
THE WASHINGTON CHAPTER of the Institute of Accounts.
THE HARTFORD CHAPTER of the Institute of Accounts.

ACCOUNTICS is the accredited medium of intercommunication between members of the Institute of Accounts wherever located.

ACCOUNTICS ASSOCIATION,
Publishers,
Wool Exchange, New York.

John Vaughan, Public Accountant and Auditor, 413 Fourth Ave., Pittsburgh, Pa.

Publishers' Desk

The Weis Binder Company, 314 Jackson Street, Toledo, Ohio, is putting upon the market the most convenient form of mucilage or library paste for office use that it has been our opportunity to inspect up to this time. It is described as the Weis Handy Brush Mucilage Tube. It is a collapsible tube with a brush in the neck, the end of the tube being provided with a cap that slips into place. Any amount of mucilage that may be wanted for the work in hand is secured by the pressure that is applied to the tube. The mucilage exudes through the centre of the brush, and, therefore, is evenly distributed. From practical test, we are satisfied that the manufacturers' claim—namely, that the brush and tube will not gum, clog or dry up—is strictly true. The device is always ready, clean and convenient. It is something that seems destined to come into very general use in offices, wherever its merits become known.

We have received from George B. Forrest, 1002 Huron Street, Indianapolis, Ind., a copy of the National Mail Order Register and Business Record, a device which he is selling to those who are doing a mail order business. The book, which is in pamphlet form, bound at the side, has a page 6½ inches deep by 9½ inches long, on which is printed a form, the faint lines being indicated by printer's leaders in place of ruling. Columns in succession are provided for the following: Number of Order; Buyer's Name and Address; Article; Price Received; Cost; Gross Profit; Advertising Medium; Date the Order is Received; Date Filled, and How Sent. From an accountant's point of view the proximity of the three columns, Price Received, Cost and Gross Profit, is to be specially commended.

We have received from A. C. Bausman, Minneapolis, Minn., a sample sheet of his Check Register, a device which, in conjunction with loose checks or checks padded, takes the place of the conventional check book. The advantage of the check register is that the business man is thereby enabled to keep for a number of years in compact form a complete record of checks issued, also his bank account, showing the balance from day to day. The check register is arranged in a form to be a convenient posting medium. The manufacturer states that by having checks put up in pads instead of binding in the book, the price of the register can be saved on each thousand checks. The register provides the following features: A column for date, following which is space for name; then a column for recording the purpose for which the check was issued. Next there is a column for noting checks returned, another for the number of the checks, then the ledger folio. Following these are money columns entitled General Ledger, General Merchandise and Discount. Next is a pair of columns for the bank account, one entitled Deposits and another headed Withdrawals. Following these are two balance columns headed Debit and Credit. Evidently, Mr. Bausman approves of a liberal plan of banking, since overdrafts are regularly provided for. The registers are 14x17 inches in size, and are issued of different capacities, ranging from 5,000 to 15,000 checks. Circulars from the same manufacturer are at hand relating to the Quick Index and to Standard Trial Balance Books.

Very flattering reports from Pittsburg and vicinity reach us of the accounting and auditing work being performed in that neighborhood by John Vaughan. At the annual meeting of the Pittsburg Trust Company held in November, President C. B. McVay, who presided, and who also submitted the regular yearly report, directed special attention to the examination of the assets and accounts of the company which had been made by Mr. Vaughan. This report is said by disinterested financiers who were present at the meeting to be the most complete audit ever made of a Pittsburg corporation. It was highly satisfactory to the stockholders.

Subscribe Now.

Many persons delay forwarding their subscriptions to periodicals to which their attention is drawn, thinking that "some other time" more convenient will "do just as well." Back numbers of ACCOUNTICS are *not* kept in stock to accommodate tardy subscribers. Subscribe now, or you may miss a number worth many times the subscription price. Fill in the subjoined blank with your name and full address, enclose with it one dollar, and mail to us without delay.

ACCOUNTICS ASSOCIATION,

260 West Broadway, New York.

SUBSCRIPTION ORDER.

(20)

ACCOUNTICS ASSOCIATION,

260 West Broadway, New York. Date,________________189___

Gentlemen :—

Enclosed find one dollar, for which mail Accountics for one year, addressed as follows:

(Name)______________________________

(Full Address)______________________________

Remit by draft on New York, express or postal money order or currency in registered letter. Currency or stamps not registered at the risk of sender.

Institute of Accounts

Incorporated
Under the Laws of New York
1882

A National Organization

Represented
Throughout the United States
By Chapters

The Objects of the Institute are

To secure a proper recognition of accounting as an element of business

To discover new principles of accounting, and to orderly arrange them for the enlargement of the science

To originate and circulate the literature of accountics

To maintain the dignity and uphold the importance of the profession of accountancy

To broaden the scope of the science of political economy

To establish harmonious relations of mutual dependence between itself and the business world, and to induce able and experienced men everywhere to devote their energies, in association with it, to the accomplishment of its purposes

Information and printed matter relative to the formation of new Chapters will be furnished upon application to

HENRY HARNEY, C. P. A., Secretary

88 Wall Street, New York

Accountics

VOL. III DECEMBER 1898 No. 9

The Monthly Statement

The advantage that the country boy has in the life race over the boy born and bred in the city is forcible, if not elegantly, put in an article which appeared a short time since in one of the evening dailies of New York. We have not room to quote the article in full, and therefore epitomize it, using, so far as possible, the words of the original. It was addressed to young men, each of whom, it asserted, is ambitious in a vague sort of way. "You would all like," it says, addressing them, "to be recognized as great, and you would really do a good deal in the way of self-sacrifice to achieve fame, but do you know what the situation is? In twenty years from now, or in thirty years, some man will be the big boss of the country. He will be in the White House, after a hard fight, and all the country will be looking at him in admiration and envy. That individual is a young man now, about your age. Do you know where he is or what he is doing? He is out on a farm somewhere, feeding pigs or building fires at four o'clock in the morning; or he is selling trash on a train, or working in a machine shop, or trying to learn law in some little one-horse town. Wherever he is and whatever he is, he is living a life that prevents his wasting his vitality on nonsense. He is saving up his strength and growing all in one direction. He is not dividing his fine energies between clothes, cigarettes, neckties, photographs of girls and looking glasses. He is at the very bottom of the ladder. He has not one-half your chances or advantages. He has perhaps a very imperfect education, and you would be shocked at his clothes and his coarseness if you could see him in his present crude condition. But he will beat you all, and twenty or thirty years from now your boast will be that you slightly know the great So-and-So, and you will hang about telling how he used to feed pigs and is not too proud to admit it, and you will be asking the pig-feeder for favors."

These words are addressed to city young men. Their truth has been demonstrated thousands of times. The city boy is handicapped. The country boy, suffering the privations inseparable from poverty in the country and from country life in general, acquires a manliness, a sturdiness, a strength of character and will that carries him to the goal of his ambition. Dissipated energies, fittingly portrayed in a sentence above, are the rock upon which the ambition and comprehensive plans of the city boy are wrecked. There are exceptions to all rules. It is not all country boys that succeed in becoming leaders of men; nor do all city boys fail. It is true, however, that very few of those who have luxuries in their youth and who are not compelled to struggle for a mere existence succeed in reaching eminence. The same principles prevail so far as accountants are concerned. Those bookkeepers who fall into "soft snaps" of jobs when they first start out seldom advance. On the other hand, there is hardly an accountant of eminence at the present time who has not come up from small beginnings, and who has not advanced step by step as the result of hard study and heroic struggle. The moral of this is not necessarily to remove to the country, nor to desert a comfortable home in the city, nor yet to give up a comfortable office engagement, but rather to avoid those distractions which occupy time, consume energy and restrain the bright young man from the accomplishment of his purpose in life.

The tendency in business handwriting the last few years is in the direction of the plain and practical rather than toward the ornate or the copper-plate copy-book style. It has been clearly demonstrated that the legibility of a very commonplace, straightforward, clean handwriting is far greater than the legibility of matter written in conventional copy-book style. Many of the schools are teaching at the present time what is called the vertical system of handwriting, and a very business-like, utilitarian system it is. The change in penmanship which distinguishes the body of books of accounts and business correspondence is also gradually affecting business signatures. There are found to-day less involved and ornate business signatures than were current a short time ago. At first it might be supposed that a very plain and legible business signature would be one easy to imitate and, therefore, one which would really invite attempts at forgery. Quite the reverse is the case, as has been demonstrated by the expert testimony of many eminent penmen. A signature scarcely legible and composed of many flourishes and bold strokes is far easier to imitate than one that is straightforward, legible and which has an individuality of its own in every stroke. This individuality, by the way, is there, although the casual observer may not perceive it. When it comes to forgery trials it is clearly demonstrated that the plain signatures are those that are proof against successful imitation, while the involved signatures are those offering the greatest facility to those who would imitate them to their pecuniary advantage.

"Commercial Education" is the subject of a report of the Committee on Foreign Commerce and the Revenue Laws, of the Chamber of Commerce of the State of New York, unanimously adopted by that body November 3, 1898. By reason of its completeness, as well also on account of the recommendations embodied in the resolutions with which it concludes, it is of special interest to business men and accountants everywhere. The report is the result of an investigation that has been made by the committee in pursuance of the following resolution passed by the Chamber at its meeting, June 2, last, as follows:—

"Whereas, Much attention has been paid in Germany, England and other countries, to the subject of commercial education, and it is becoming generally recognized that such education has an important bearing upon the extension of commerce:

"Resolved, That the Committee on Foreign Commerce and the Revenue Laws of this Chamber be requested to investigate and report as soon as practicable the extent of such education in the principal commercial countries, its effect upon the development of commerce, and whether any of the methods pursued in such educational institutions abroad are desirable and practicable in this country."

The body of the report contains a brief yet very complete review of what is being done in this regard in England, France, Germany, Austria, Italy, Russia, Belgium and Switzerland. Schools are named and the courses of study in several are enumerated. There is also a review of the little that has been done in this country, specific mention being made of what is undertaken by the Wharton School of Finance and Economy, Philadelphia; the University of Chicago, the University of California, and by some of the leading institutions of general learning; notably, Yale, Harvard and Columbia Universities. Reference is also made to certain advances in the general direction indicated made in certain public schools, including those of Philadelphia and Brooklyn. A brief reference is likewise contained to what has been accomplished by Prof. Edmund J. James in this work, in the several fields of activity in which he has been employed.

The concluding paragraph of the report is as follows:—

"Your Committee are of the opinion that the importance of the development of both secondary and higher commercial education in this country cannot be overestimated. Not only do the interests of education demand the organization of such institutions, but commercial reasons alone imperatively require that immediate and decisive steps in the direction of improved commercial education be taken by the business men of this country. The increasing competition of the world, the successful efforts put forth by European nations, as shown by your Committee, to equip their merchants and bankers with every means of carrying on the intense competitive struggle for enlargement of markets and advancement of business demand that our commercial youth shall receive better training and sounder education in all that is essential to the carrying on of successful business enterprises. At the same time the higher commercial training that it is proposed to impart would secure a supply of properly equipped and trained experts, from whom our consular and lower diplomatic service, and even many branches of our administrative service could advantageously be recruited, as is now the case in European countries."

The resolutions, including preambles offered for the consideration of the Chambers, and which, as before stated, were unanimously adopted, are as follows:—

"Whereas, The modern conditions of commerce and industry require wider knowledge and higher education on the part of business men;

"Whereas, The present educational facilities offered to business men in business colleges and similar institutions are inadequate and fail to equip them for competition in the world's commerce;

"Resolved, That the Chamber of Commerce of the State of New York earnestly favors the establishment and development of sounder commercial education, both in secondary schools and in higher institutions of learning in this country.

"Resolved, That a Special Committee of five be appointed by the President, with power to add to their number, for the purpose of further inquiry into the subject of commercial education.

"Resolved, That the Special Committee so appointed be instructed to lay such plan or plans before the Chamber as may, in the opinion of the Committee, best lead to the accomplishment of the object had in view and favored by this Chamber."

The committee of five appointed under these resolutions is as follows: Seth Low, Gustave H. Schwab, James G. Cannon, W. Bayard Cutting and F. B. Thurber.

Bookkeeping Absurdities

By Walton Day

Is there a greater absurdity in all double entry bookkeeping, as taught by some of the schools and in many of the text-books, than the balance account? It may be described as an element brought in for the sake of consistency and maintained by reason of precedent, a useless affair, a meaningless account and in many cases amounting to a misleading statement of affairs. It would seem as though the writers on double entry bookkeeping, who first conceived of this absurdity, found it impossible to discriminate between a statement of resources and liabilities and a loss and gain statement. Else why did they attempt to bring everything into the balance account, and then from the balance account carry it back to the individual accounts? To close an account with a customer, for example, "By Balance," and to debit the balance account with this amount and then in turn to reopen the account by crediting the balance account and debiting the customer for the amount brought down may be consistency, but it is also absurdity.

With an inventory of merchandise to be entered as a balance on hand, no doubt the question arose with the original pioneer in bookkeeping science, where to put the debit at the time he was entering the credit. With the merchandise balance entered, and the profit or the loss, as the case may be, determined, he could see that the loss and gain account took the one side, while the merchandise account carried the other. However it may be, the balance account came into existence, and to this day it is honored and worshipped by many an old line bookkeeper to the exclusion of a proper idea of accounting from his mind, and to the disgust of the clear-headed business man who attempts to inquire into the matter and gets along only far enough to appreciate its absurdity.

Why should a personal account be balanced before it is settled? What reason is there in the conduct of an account with a debtor or a creditor for bringing down a balance that is analagous to the balance that is brought down in cash or merchandise? Why should a set of books ever be closed in the sense in which the term "closing" is used by the old line bookkeeper? A profit and loss statement should be made from time to time, as determined by inventories, but with the profits written off into the proper accounts, with the inventory balances brought down in the several accounts in which an inventory appears, what more is there that real business requires? Personal accounts, both debit and credit, may go on, and therefore the absurdity of writing in a balance with red ink and bringing it down in black ink, or vice versa, with conventional footing lines, may be avoided. It is to points of this order that the attention of the student of bookkeeping should be directed. Double entry bookkeeping should be only applied common sense, and so it will be if one has sense enough to see the application. Whatever there is of absurdity is something that is not essential to the system, but has been grafted on or allowed to come up by those who have paid more attention to form and ceremony than they have to the necessary elements.

Accountants' Associations

Hartford Chapter of the Institute of Accounts

The October meeting of the Hartford Chapter was held on the evening of the 25th of that month. About fifty members and guests were present. James W. Green read a paper entitled "At What Particular Time Does a Gain or Loss Occur in Business?" Mr. Green treated the question from a manufacturer's point of view. He was listened to throughout with marked interest. We shall have the opportunity of publishing this paper complete in an early number. Charles W. Rohne, Treasurer of the Co-Operative Savings Society, then presented an exhaustive treating on "Interest and Discount." He explained and illustrated the methods of operation and effect in the different lines of business to which his subject applied. The paper was an exceedingly interesting one.

At the November meeting of this organization, held on the evening of the 22d of November, about thirty persons were in attendance. Charles E. Gross, of the firm of Gross, Hyde & Shipman, one of the leading law firms of Connecticut, also President of the Hartford Board of Trade, gave an informal talk on "Some of the Legal Aspects of Accounting." He explained the difference between open and stated commercial accounts, and showed when an open account became a stated account in the eye of the law. He explained trust accounts in their various phases, pointing out some of the complications likely to arise in connection therewith, and showed the proper course to be pursued. At the close of his remarks a number of questions were proposed which Mr. Gross answered clearly and in a way to afford a large fund of information.

The December meeting of this organization, by regular order, would occur on the evening after Christmas. In view of the holiday season it was decided to omit the December meeting, and accordingly the next gathering of the Hartford Chapter will be on the third Tuesday in January.

New York Chapter of the Institute of Accounts

At the regular monthly meeting of the New York Chapter of the Institute of Accounts, held at the Waldorf-Astoria, Thursday evening, December 1, a paper was read by Charles W. Rohne, M. I. A., of Hartford, Conn., entitled "Interest and Discount." Mr. Rohne's address proved to be both historical and scientific. In the first place, he briefly traced the history of a charge for the use of money, including a glance at usury laws, both ancient and modern. In the second place, he presented what may be termed the mathematics of interest and discount, in a form to be extremely interesting to his audience. We expect to present the address in full, including illustrations, or, at least, copious extracts from it in future numbers.

At the conclusion of the paper there was an animated discussion of certain points which were contained in the speaker's remarks. Not a little of the debate turned upon sinking funds, and the different points of view from which sinking funds may be regarded.

Do you fear the force of the wind,
  The slash of the rain?
Go face them and fight them,
  Be savage again.
Go hungry and cold like the wolf,
  Go wade like the crane.
The palms of your hands will thicken,
  The skin of your cheek will tan;
You'll grow ragged and weary and swarthy,
  But you'll walk like a man!

—Hamlin Garland.

The Europeans are themselves blind whe describe Fortune without sight. No first-rate beauty ever had finer eyes, or saw more clearly. They who have no other trade but seeking their fortune need never hope to find her; coquette-like, she flies from her close pursuers, and at last fixes on the plodding mechanic who stays at home and minds his business.—Goldsmith.

The power of fortune is confessed only by the miserable; for the happy impute all their successes to prudence and merit.

—Swift.

Modern Accounting*

By A. O. Kittredge, F. I. A., C. P. A.

The subject assigned me on the program is as comprehensive as the conventional toast at a banquet. Almost anything may be said under it, so long as the title is once and a while mentioned, just to show that the speaker is not trespassing upon his neighbor's preserves. I am at a loss how best to interest you. My sympathy with the work of the business schools is such that I would be very glad to say something, if I could, to encourage to continued effort all those who are actively in the field, and in general to help along the cause.

The business world owes much to the commercial colleges,—far more than it usually acknowledges. The common course of the business man is to scoff at the instruction that the schools afford. He declares that he wants practical men in his office, not theorists. He affects to discriminate against the graduates of such institutions as you represent, and to favor those who pick up the theory of accounts while struggling for their bread as office boys and entry clerks. He is usually very free in his criticism of what you teach and how you teach it,—as he understands the matter,—but he seldom, if ever, visits your schools, to ascertain just what you are doing, or to discover how he might help you to approach nearer to the practical.

I, personally, am on record as a free-lance critic of the business schools, for, during my whole career as writer and editor, I have not hesitated, whenever the occasion has seemed to warrant it, to voice the criticisms of the business world and to contrast, so far as I was able, the actual instruction of the schools with practical requirements. Not once, nor twice, but very many times have I said those things which have caused a breeze in your camp, if I may use the expression, and which have put some one or more of your number upon the defensive.

The eminent teacher whose death we mourn to-day,‡ has repeatedly gone up to your conventions with an address more or less of which was in reply to something I had written or allowed to be printed, or which was a defense of what he assumed the business world would suppose had been attacked. Yet he, of all the extensive circle of commercial teachers knew best that I was no enemy of the business schools, and that I never criticised them for any other reason than to help them to higher attainments and to greater influence.

He also knew, as some of you know, that the foundation of my own work in the field of accounting was laid in a commercial college, and that within the four walls of a business school, at a time, too, when business schools were not what they have since come to be, I obtained an insight into those principles and methods which are fundamental to all that I have done in the past, or that I am undertaking at present.

I owe an apology for this long introduction and declaration of my position with respect to the schools, but from one point of view at least it is entirely justifiable. One of the journals, ostensibly published in the interests of practical business education, has recently characterized me, in the light of what transpired at the National Educational Convention at Washington last Summer, as strutting around in sight of the schools, with a chip on my shoulder. The editor, therefore, has called upon representatives of the business schools and authors of text-books in particular, to promptly knock it off. So far, however, I am notified of but a single strike in this direction. One of your number,—a teacher and author whom I have had the pleasure of knowing for a long term of years, and whose abilities and work I hold in high esteem, has come gallantly forward and made a desperate lunge,—but, unfortunately for him, has entirely missed the mark. He has most energetically replied to what I did not say at the Washington meeting, and has not touched in the least upon what I did say.

I went to the Washington meeting only because I had something to say that I thought would be profitable for the managers of the schools and the writers of works on bookkeeping to consider. I am here to-day for the same reason.

I did not say at Washington that "no up-to-date business man and no first-class enterprise, no matter in what line of business engaged, nor how small, nor how large, would dare to keep books at

*An address delivered before the Eastern Commercial Teachers' Association, at the Packard School, New York, November 26, 1898.

‡S. S. Packard.

the present time as bookkeeping is taught in the schools and as set forth in the ordinary text-books." Those who think I said this, or anything resembling it, are invited to read again.

Such sentiments, however, are frequently attributed to me by those who think they know just what I am thinking about, and one of this class did actually introduce me to several whom I met at Washington, with this as his explanation of my position.

What I really did say at Washington and what is pertinent to this occasion is in part as follows:—

Here the speaker read what was presented on pages 142 and 143 of Accountics for October, entitled "The Merchandise Account."

This is the essence of all that I have said in the impeachment of the teachings of the books and schools. In arguments upon these points, I shall welcome every one who sees fit to contest my position.

If I were to go still further in my criticism of bookkeeping "as she is wrote" and bookkeeping "as she is teached," I would say something about the apparent confusion there is between the trial balance and the balance sheet, and the mistaken effort that is frequently in evidence, of making the trial balance serve in the capacity of a balance sheet, or business statement. With your permission, bearing upon this point, I will read an extract from the preface to a new trial balance book that I have recently designed, and which a prominent company in the stationer's supply line is about to put upon the market. It defines my position in this regard, as well as anything I have ever put forth:—

"The only use to which a trial balance should be put is to determine the equilibrium of debits and credits in the accounts which are tested by it. The trial balance was never intended to be a business statement. Its use as an indicator of the progress of a business has grown out of the fact that no other statement has been available. Its use as a collection record has grown out of the fact that by the form of ledgers commonly used, it is a much handier exhibit of accounts collectable than the ledger itself.

"A correct balance sheet," in the words of one of the most practical and advanced British authors of accounting treatises, "is the supreme object of all bookkeeping." I am of the opinion that our American authors and commercial teachers have not been giving the balance sheet nearly enough attention in their work, nor bringing it out in proper relief. I am moved to say this in part, because some time since, one of the members of your organization, (a gentleman, who, unfortunately, is not here to-day,) asserted, in the presence of several accountants, that he knew no difference between a balance sheet and a trial balance. On being questioned, he strengthened his assertion by declaring that the trial balance was everything that was needed in any business. I have faith to believe he was expressing his real convictions, because I have encountered many bookkeepers,—some from the schools and some who have not had the advantages the schools afford,—who hold the same opinion.

Let me quote further from the preface to the trial balance book already referred to. In a paragraph following the one already read is this:—

"The balance sheet of a business may be described as the orderly presentation of the assets and liabilities of that business, with an indication of the capital invested. The standpoint with respect to capital commonly employed in making out balance sheets is that it is the amount which the business owes the proprietor. It is in no respect the function of a trial balance to present the facts which a balance sheet should show. Instead, the balance sheet is a form of an entirely different character. When a balance sheet of the conventional style is made out it employs the figures composing the trial balance, but, in addition, certain amounts which the trial balance ordinarily does not furnish,—namely, the inventory, or amount of goods on hand."

A profit and loss statement necessarily precedes the preparation of a balance sheet. It also is something that has not been explained in treatises and courses of instruction, (so far, at least, as I have been able to ascertain by very careful inquiry,) in the way a practicing accountant would consider appropriate and necessary. Let me quote again from the same source as before:—

"The profit or losses of a business are determined by a comparison of the expenses of the business with its revenues. If the expenses exceed the revenues or gross profit, a loss is incurred. If, on the other hand, the gross profits exceed the expenses and losses, a gain is being made. It is never the proper function of a trial balance to show profits and losses. This can only be satisfactorily and accurately done by another form of statement,—namely, that which is commonly designated as the Profit and Loss Statement."

Classification of accounts, it would also appear to the professional accountant has not received, at the hands of the authors of bookkeeping works, and the schools, the attention it deserves. The day has long since gone by when the artificial, or, shall I say academical classifications, that rely upon such general terms, as "Real" accounts, "Personal" accounts, "Impersonal" accounts, "Representative" accounts, and others of like character, for the purpose of designating classes and divisions, were sufficient. If an accurate and comprehensive balance sheet is the object of all bookkeeping, and for my part I firmly believe that it is, then the only proper guage of classification of accounts is the requirements of the balance sheet. In my practice I occasionally encounter bookkeepers who refer to their "debtor" accounts and to their "creditor" accounts as though these names designated the two leading classes into which all the accounts of a business can be divided. If any school or any text-book is responsible for this perversion,—and, mind you, I do not so charge,—I am indeed sorry. A moment's consideration must convince any one that such a scheme is woefully deficient. It is manifest that there can be both debit and credit balances in every class into which the requirements of the balance sheet and profit and loss statement would divide the accounts of a business.

I venture again to quote from the preface to the new trial balance book:—

"The balance sheet of a business, and the profit and loss statement as well, demand a correct and rigidly enforced classification of accounts. Customers' accounts are to be kept in a class by themselves, Property accounts are to be kept in a class by themselves, Accounts with Creditors are to be kept in a class by themselves, while Special forms of indebtedness, such, for example, as Notes Payable, are likewise to be separately indicated. Expense accounts are to be kept in detail for statistical purposes, but grouped or aggregated for purposes of statement. Revenue accounts,—that is, accounts of earnings and other sources of profit, are to be kept singly, for statistical purposes, but grouped or aggregated for purposes of statement."

"In the classification of expense accounts it is necessary to discriminate between those which enter into the cost of the product, as, for example, in a manufacturing enterprise, and those which belong to the sales or commercial department. Where accounts are properly classified and grouped in the ledger, the construction of a Profit and Loss Statement, as well also as the construction of a Balance Sheet, becomes easy of accomplishment."

There are still other points upon which I might offer suggestions to the writers of text-books and the managers of business schools, if time permitted, but quite enough has been said in that direction for this occasion. Let me now draw your attention to what some have been pleased to call "New Accounting." What I am about to read is an extract from an article that will shortly appear in print:—

"The tendency of the new accounting is to shorten the fiscal period,—in fact to practically abolish it, by doing pro rata, weekly, or monthly, as the case may be, those things which heretofore have been done only at the close of the period, say once a year, or, as in some cases, semi-annually."

"For example, a reserve for bad debts is made as often as there is a credit to sales account. The amount of the reserve is established by a percentage corresponding to the rate of loss shown by the records of past years. Then, when a loss is made, it is charged,—not to Loss and Gain Account, for that account has already been debited with the allowance made for the purpose, but to the reserve account. By this means the business man has before him always the means of knowing, not only what his actual losses are from bad debts, but also whether or not his losses of this class are running more or less than in previous years.

"In a similar manner, a reserve is provided, as the business proceeds, for taxes, and for each of all the other expenses and losses that cannot be paid or met until some future date.

"Suspense accounts, on the other hand, take the charges for all those items which, by their nature, are distributive,—that is, in whole or in part, falling to some future month or months. Then, as the months pass by, the proper expense accounts are debited and suspense is closed out.

"In short, the scheme is to make each month complete in itself,—standing its own costs or expenses, whether paid in that month or not, and having nothing charged to it except what properly belongs to it, even though the items are paid within its limits.

"Again, the omissions and errors of the old or common bookkeeping are corrected. A goods account and a trading account, to borrow names from our British accountant-cousins, are employed in the place of the conventional merchandise account. As goods are bought, they are charged to the goods account, and as they are parted with they are credited to the same account, both entries being at cost prices. This method leaves in goods account a balance corresponding to the amount of goods on hand, or to the inventory. Listing the goods or inventorying is resorted to from time to time, only to prove the correctness of the account.

"The goods parted with, which as before stated, are credited to the goods account at cost prices, are taken over to the trading account, also at cost prices. Trading account, in turn, is credited with the selling prices. The balance in Trading account then represents gross profit.

"The cost of doing business,—that is to say, rent, clerk hire, advertising and all incidentals, are cared for in a third account. Gross profit, diminished by costs of doing business, gives net profit.

"The facilities that have been devised to use with the new accounting make all these changes and innovations extremely easy. In practice it is found that with all the special adjustments referred to, no more labor, and in many cases even less labor is required than by the old plan.

"By dividing the Merchandise Account into Goods Account and Trading Account, as described, the balance in one showing the cost value of the goods on hand, and the balance in the other representing gross profit to date, and by keeping costs of doing business in a third account, two very important results are reached. The books are always in shape to permit the construction of a Profit and Loss Statement, instantly and on demand. With net profit (or loss) determined by such a computation, the books are in shape to permit a complete and accurate balance sheet to be made up. From this point of vantage, it is only a very short step to a perpetual Profit and Loss Statement and a perpetual Balance Sheet, both made integral parts of the bookkeeping system just as the Cash Account is an integral part of the system of accounts in common use.

"With the Balance Sheet and Profit and Loss Statement made going parts of the bookkeeping of the business, the books are always closed and are also always open. The degree of the profitableness of the business is ever in sight. There is no more waiting for the end of the fiscal year and the formal closing of the books at that date to learn whether a fair profit has been made or a considerable loss has been sustained. Just what the results of the business are is shown at all times by the Profit and Loss Statement, while the solvency of the concern is correspondingly shown at all times by the going balance sheet. Both are always complete and up to date."

The practical application of this method to the accounts of a business is very much simpler than it can be made to appear by mere verbal description. It depends solely upon an adequate quota of accounts properly classified and arranged. I can best explain what I mean in this regard by referring to some charts of classification and arrangement of accounts, which I have brought with me for the purpose. These have been selected from the files of the Account, Audit and Assurance Co., Limited, of this city, a corporation which I have the honor to represent, and indicate the current practice of that organization in this regard:—

CHARTS SHOWN:

1. Department Store.
2. Manufacturing Business.
3. Electric Street Railway.
4. Furniture Instalment Business.
5. Accounting and Auditing Business.

Each of these charts is in effect the key to the arrangement of the accounts of the business represented in what we term the Balance Sheet Ledger. This book consists of a series of adjacent vertical columns, so arranged as to receive at the outset the figures of the balance sheet of the business with which it is opened, and daily thereafter, the totals of all the transactions. It is divided into two principal parts—the Balance Sheet proper and the Loss and Gain Statement. As many accounts are provided in each part as the business requires—and as indicated by the chart. The book is also constructed in a way to permit the necessary cross entries between the accounts in the Loss and Gain Statement, and between the Loss and Gain Statement and Balance Sheet to be formulated or journalized in the ledger itself and posted as required.

By this means the advantages of a perpetual or going Profit and Loss Statement, and of a perpetual or going Balance Sheet are secured. The Balance Sheet Ledger is the summary ledger of the business. It presents the whole business and is always in balance. It is supplemented by the necessary auxiliary ledger, which contains the detail accounts of the several groups. The samples of Balance Sheet Ledgers that are presented for your inspection include the following:—

1. Instalment Furniture Business.
2. Department Store.
3. Manufacturing Business.
4. Standard Form.

Keeping Eternally At It.

One step won't take you very far,
You've got to keep on walking;
One word won't tell folks what you are,
You've got to keep on talking.
One inch won't make you very tall,
You've got to keep on growing;
One little "ad" won't do it all,
You've got to keep em going.

—Publicity.

When the desire of wealth is taking hold of the heart, let us look round and see how it operates upon those whose industry or fortune has obtained it. When we find them oppressed with their own abundance, luxurious without pleasure, idle without ease, impatient and querulous in themselves, and despised or hatred by the rest of mankind, we shall soon be convinced that if the real wants of our conditions are satisfied, there remains little to be sought with solicitude or desired with eagerness.—Dr. Johnson.

The greatest and most amiable privilege which the rich enjoy over the poor is that which they exercise the least,—the privilege of making them happy.

—Colton.

Riches seldom make their owners rich.

—Dr. Johnson.

The Work of an Accounting Engineer

The function of the designer of accounting systems that are adapted to special requirements, is strikingly set forth in a circular recently issued by the Account, Audit and Assurance Company, Limited, of New York. The circular bears the title, "The Utility of an Accounting Specification," and in part is as follows:

If you were going to put up a fine building, you would first of all engage an architect. You know what an architect does and therefore, you appreciate his value.

When, however, it comes to a consideration of the bookkeeping of your business and the fact begins to be apparent that the present plan ought to give way to something better, to be superseded by something that is scientific and up-to-date, you are not quite so clear as to your proper course.

There are competent architects in every city, any one of whom it would be safe for you to engage to look after your building, but, so far as you know at present, the best you can do to better your accounting methods is either to copy, fragment by fragment, from any and every source that seems to promise something useful, or an improvement over that which is at present in use, or to bring into your office a new man.

The new man would be either a professional accountant at a good round price per day, without the number of days necessary to the work fully determined, or a new bookkeeper commanding a higher salary than you have heretofore paid.

The professional accountant would come in to tell and show how your bookkeeping work could be better done. Very likely he would devise whatever new feature he recommended for your use while working in your office.

Such service would be very unsatisfactory at best, if for no other reason, because you would have no means of knowing in advance just what the complete system would be like, nor what special advantages it would afford in the way of exhibits of losses and gains, nor in keeping before you constantly your general financial condition.

The high-price bookkeeper is usually out of the question, either because the business cannot afford his salary or because there would really be no special need of him after he had improved the office system. Bookkeepers, irrespective of the amount of their salaries, are seldom successful in this regard, for, as a rule, they are routine men rather than planners. They are followers in method rather than originators.

With this brief introduction, we ask your attention to the following parallel between the architect, as you know him to be, and the Accounting Engineer, to whom these pages will introduce you.

Very few buildings nowadays are erected without the services of an architect. It is true, occasionally, that the assistance of the architect is dispensed with by copying the form and arrangement of some structure previously put up. The result of such an effort, however, is seldom satisfactory. Buildings so constructed lack perfect adaptation to the purpose in view, as well as individuality in appearance. They are deficient in conveniences, and very generally, for want of the technical skill of the architect, cost more to build than those which are specially designed. Besides all this, they do not have the advantage of the latest development in materials and finish. In various respects they are out of date before they are completed.

Very much the same conditions prevail in accounting and all other branches of office work. Those office systems which are copied, either in whole or in part, from others, are usually misfits. They not only fail to give results in the best form for business use, but they are also unnecessarily expensive in administration. The best methods, and those most economical of operation, are secured only when the services of an experienced Accounting Engineer are brought in to plan and specify to meet actual requirements.

Accounting Engineers and Architects are specialists whose functions include a careful and constant study of their respective arts, the keeping abreast of all improvements in methods and appliances, and a readiness to embody the best of their experience to date in the service of each client. The wider the experience of the specialist, and the more he has done, whether in erecting buildings, or in devising accounting systems to meet special requirements, the more able he is to perform new commissions, and the greater assurance his clients have of satisfactory results from whatever he recommends.

An architect who relied entirely upon verbal orders to get his work done would be wofully deficient in method. He would soon be the laughing stock of his town. No builder would be willing to estimate upon his work. No one would be safe to undertake a contract under his superintendence, for it would be impossible to ascertain in advance what would be required, nor could it be satisfactorily shown when the work was done that all requirements had been complied with. The human mind is so fallible that there are few persons having many details to look after who do not, sooner or later, contradict themselves in their verbal directions. Written instructions, therefore, which are specific, unchanging and always in evidence, are the only satisfactory dependence.

Every one who attempts to install an accounting system by personally explaining it to the manager and office employees, and who waits around to give the necessary instructions as they may be required, or for opportunities to exemplify its peculiar features, is in the same position as the architect who relies upon verbal directions to secure proper construction in a building. Even though the instructor in accounting does not make a complete muss of the matter, as is most frequently the case where he relies upon personal instruction, he fails of serving his employers in the best and most satisfactory manner. They usually get very tired of him before he thinks his work is done. Besides this, whenever his back is turned something is very likely to go wrong. On the other hand, comprehensive and adequate written instructions not only insure the proper progress of the work in the instructor's absence, but, in addition, secure in the final work a symmetrical system, with all its parts in accord and adapted to work together without friction.

The foundation of every architect's specification is the plans and elevations which represent the appearance and dimensions of the structure that is to be built. The specification explains the drawings, describes the materials to be used and the character of the workmanship. The drawings and specifications taken together indicate the features of the building in every part. Upon the care and accuracy with which the plans and elevations are prepared, depend the symmetry of the structure, the proper correspondence of parts, and the absence of annoying and expensive mistakes in construction.

It is just as necessary to construct in advance a correct chart of a proposed accounting system, as it is to draw correct plans of a projected building--in fact, more necessary. The Accounting Chart, like the plans of a building, shows the dimensions and proportions of the proposed system, its departments and subdivisions, and their relations one to the other. Taken with the Accounting Specification, it portrays correctly just what is necessary to be done to replace the unsatisfactory method at present in use by something that is strictly scientific and thoroughly adapted to requirements. All this is accomplished before any change or expense has been made in the work itself. The Accounting Chart and Specification taken together show the special advantages that will flow from the system and what will be required to operate it. This is so well set forth that the system can be intelligently criticized before it is installed.

It is the special work of one of the departments of the Account, Audit and Assurance Company, Limited, to prepare Charts and Specifications of accounting systems, and to give careful attention to the proper installation of the systems described. In this work the company has the services of the most experienced Accounting Engineers. It employs none but the best expert talent in any of its undertakings. It nas at its command eminent specialists in every division of accounting practice.

The circumstances, conditions and requirements of each case intrusted to the Account, Audit and Assurance Company, Limited, are first carefully ascertained and thoroughly studied. Then, in the light of the manifest needs of the client and the accumulated experience of the company's Accounting Engineers, an accounting system is formulated that exactly meets requirements.

The proposed system is first charted, and then all its features are carefully explained in the specification. So thoroughly is this work done, that with the aid of the Chart and Specification, the system can be readily and satisfactorily installed by the client's regular office employees.

The accounting system set forth in the Charts and Specifications sent out by the Account, Audit and Assurance Company, Limited, is known as the Balance Sheet System of Accounts. The leading features of this system are a perpetual balance sheet of the business and a going profit and loss statement. Both of these are always up to date, and each is made an integral part of the bookkeeping, just as the cash account is a part of the general system. Actual net profits are shown as often as once a month. In some lines of business the showing in this regard can be made weekly. Profits are determined and a correct Balance Sheet constructed without waiting to take stock or inventory, for there is always shown by the accounts the amount of goods on hand.

The Self-Proving Accounting System

In a recent issue of The Bookkeeper there appeared a review of the Self-Proving Accounting System, of which we make the following synopsis, omitting all irrelevant parts:

.. ..
.. .. Mr. Kittredge .. ..
.. ..
.. .. Keeley's Motor
.. ..
.. ..
Mr. Kittredge .. ..
.. .. Mr. Kittredge
.. ..
.. ..
.. .. Mr. Kittredge .. ..
.. ..
Free Silverites .. ..
.. .. Mr. Kittredge
.. ..
Mr. Kittredge .. ..
.. .. Mr. Kittredge
.. .. Mr. Kittredge .. ..
.. ..
.. .. Mr. Kittredge .. ..

In some 800 words the name of the author is used nearly twenty times. Concerning this matter Mr. Kittredge was heard to remark: "Still more good advertising, and it doesn't cost us a cent."

Of all paths a man could strike into, there is, at any given moment, a best path for every man,—a thing which, here and now, it were of all things wisest for him to do; which, could he but be led or driven to do, he were then doing like a man, as we phrase it. His success, in such a case, were complete, his felicity a maximum.—Carlyle.

Eastern Commercial Teachers' Association

The meeting of the Eastern Commercial Teachers Association, which was held in connection with the New York Teachers' Association, at the Packard College, New York City, November 25 and 26, was a most successful gathering. The attendance was large, the subjects discussed were pertinent to the work in hand, and the interest was sustained from beginning to end. The following is a copy of the official programme:

Friday, November 25, 1898.

Address of Welcome, Byron Horton, New York City.

Response, W. H. Sadler and W. J. Kinsley.

Semi-annual Address, William J. Amos, President, Stamford, Conn.

Secretary's Report and Reports of Committees.

Business Practice, F. T. Clute, New York City.

Discussion opened by M. J. Connor, Brooklyn.

Commercial Geography in the Short Course.

Commercial School and Methods of Presentation, J. P. Byrne, Boys' High School, Brooklyn.

Discussion opened by A. S. Heaney, Packard College, New York City.

Ideas in Advertising, E. H. Morse, Proprietor Hartford (Conn.) Business College.

Discussion opened by W. J. Kinsley and J. E. King.

Should We Aim to Maintain One or Two Year Courses in Our Commercial Schools? If so, Why?" N. P. Heffly, Brooklyn, N. Y.

Discussion opened by W. E. Drake, Jersey City.

Banquet (Evening, at St. Denis Hotel.)

Saturday, November 26, 1898.

What Effect Will the Teaching of Bookkeeping, Shorthand and Typewriting in the Public Schools Have on Our Business Colleges in the Future?" George P. Lord, Salem (Mass.) College.

Discussion opened by C. C. Gaines, Poughkeepsie, N. Y.

"How Can We Make Our Shorthand Department More Practical?" Charles M. Miller, Packard College.

Discussion opened by Charles T. Platt, Morse College, Hartford, Conn.

The Business College, Past, Present and Future, C. T. Cragin, Child's Business College, Worcester, Mass.

Discussion opened by J. D. Odell, New York City.

Business Schools vs. Commercial High Schools, Dr. H. M. Rowe, Baltimore, Md.

Discussion opened by E. M. Barber, New York City.

Best Method of Teaching Business Correspondence. A. S. Osborne, Rochester.

Discussion opened by A. H. Barbour, St. Johnsbury, Vt.

Development of Our Teachers, A. J. Scarborough, Boys' High School, Brooklyn.

Discussion opened by A. R. Kip, Morse College, Hartford, Conn.

*Modern Accounting, A. O. Kittredge, Editor of ACCOUNTICS, New York City.

Discussion opened by R. J. Shoemaker, Fall River, Mass.

Election of Officers for 1899.

On several occasions during the progress of the meeting, the resolution passed a short time since by the New York Chamber of Commerce, with respect to higher commercial education, came up for consideration. This resolution in its preamble points out that the commercial colleges are not affording the higher business education which the present needs of the business community demand. Evidently many of the speakers were considerably perturbed in mind concerning this matter.

Another question that was fundamental to much of the discussion that took place was the relationship of the commercial colleges and private business schools to the commercial departments in the high schools and other branches of the public school system. Still another subject which received consideration was the proper scope of the commercial course, either in a high school or a private business college. The drift of opinion seemed to be that the course should be broadened rather than narrowed, and that still more subjects should be attempted.

*Printed in full in another part of this issue.

Gaming is a kind of tacit confession that the company engaged therein do in general exceed the bounds of their respective fortunes, and therefore they cast lots to determine upon whom the ruin shall at present fall, that the rest may be saved a little longer.—Blackstone.

Old and New Methods of Keeping the Cash Account and the Bank Account*

By A. C. Neff, C. A.

These two accounts are so closely connected that neither can be fully dealt with without the other.

It is not my purpose to dwell at any length upon the elementary forms of the Cash Account, but I shall endeavor to trace the development from them into the more elaborate and complex forms, discussing the purpose and effect of the changes as we proceed.

The most elementary method of keeping the Cash Account is by journalizing the Cash transactions along with the other transactions, in their consecutive order, and posting them to a Ledger account.

It is well that the fledgling in accounts should get his first glimpse of the Cash Account through this medium, as it enables him later on to realize the journal character of the entries in the Cash Book. It fulfils its sphere of usefulness by forming part of the foundation of his knowledge of the theory of Bookkeeping.

But in even a small business, it is found inconvenient and laborious to depend upon journal entries and their posting to a Ledger Account for the record of Cash transactions, and especially for the balance of Cash which ought to be on hand; and a need is early felt for some more direct method of arriving at results.

This necessity is met by the first of many departures from the pure Italian methods, which have been introduced by the developments of modern bookkeeping.

The Cash Account is taken out of the Ledger and put by itself in a separate cover or book and called the Cash Book. The skeleton entries are filled in, with the full particulars of the transactions, the account takes on the day book character of a book of original entry, and the journal character of an important posting medium, in addition to its former ledger character, of a collection of all transactions affecting cash.

This improvement becomes the parent of a series of changes upon itself.

*A paper read before the Institute of Chartered Accountants of Ontario at the opening of the session for 1898-99.

It first appears in a journal form, the columns of Cash received and paid being side by side, and the transactions, whether receipts or payments follow each other in chronological order, the changing balance of Cash on Hand being readily apparent after each transaction, like a bank deposit ledger.

This form of Account is seldom used for the Cash Book, although the means of following the consecutive order of the transactions is an advantage to the investigating accountant which he sometimes regrets the loss of in the more advanced forms.

As it is usually desirable to entirely separate the receipts from the payments, the Cash Book commonly used follows the form of the ordinary ledger account, but extended so as to include the particulars, each side of the account occupying a page of the Cash Book, the left hand page being devoted to receipts, which are debited to Cash, the right hand page to the payments which are credited.

This is the standard form of Cash Book, upon which the later developments have been ingrafted.

With the use of the Cash Book, the totals of Cash received and paid may or may not be posted to a summary of the Cash Account in the Ledger. Formerly it was considered a serious breach of principles to omit it, but high authorities now sanction the omission.

The former idea of the relation of the Cash Book to the Ledger Account appears to have been akin to our present idea of the relation of a Sales Ledger, for instance, to the adjustment account representing it in the General Ledger. That is, the Ledger Account carried a summary of transactions of which the Cash Book furnished the details. But as the Cash Book furnishes its own balance, without extra effort, there seems to be no object gained by inserting the account in the ledger, other than furnishing a reminder of its existence, when taking a balance. And this existence even a junior is fully conscious of, after he has omitted it once or twice.

As the size of a business increases and the work of bookkeeping with it, there comes an increasing demand for labor-saving methods. This is met in the Cash Book, by setting apart into a separate column all the items requiring to be posted to a frequently recurring account, the items being thus condensed into a monthly total, which is posted to the ledger instead of the separate items.

The first applications of this principle are usually a column on the debit side of the Cash Book headed, "Mdse. Cr" for Receipts from Cash sales of Goods, and another on the credit side headed "Expenses Dr." for payments on that account.

I am quite in favor of the classification of the journal entries into parts which can be gathered into monthly totals, and in most businesses this can be largely done, but I have not yet found a business in which it can be made absolutely complete, and the journal entirely got rid of, and I think with Whatley and others that it is usually an undesirable

CASH

Date	Account to Credit	From Whom and For What Received	L.F.	Credit			Debit		Totals
				Mdse.	Bills Receivable	Acc't Paid	Discount	Cash	

FIG. 1—COMMON FORM OF

A need that is also soon felt is a column on each side for Cash Discount allowed off bills for early payment.

These allowances are not Cash Transactions, but properly belong to the journal; and the provision for them in the Cash Book is an example of a tendency to take advantage of the journal character of the Cash Book, and use it for recording what are not strictly cash trans-

abuse of the Cash Book to introduce into it entries which properly belong to the journal.

But I have no objection to make to an exception in case of the discount columns in the Cash Book, because of the convenience of posting both Cash and Discount to the Personal Account in the Ledger at the same time.

There are two methods of applying it,

CASH

Date	Account to Credit		Debit		L.F.	Credit			
			Cash	Disc't.		Sundries	Account Paid	Mdse.	Bills Receivable.

FIG. 2—PREFERRED FORM OF

actions. This is a tendency which I think is frequently carried too far.

The effort to get rid of the journal leads to recording journal entries in other books where they do not properly belong.

the one being the reverse of the other. In the first, the full amount of the account paid is credited to a customer, and on the credit side of the Cash Book an entry is made for a payment of discount, the amount being entered in a special column for the purpose.

In the second method a column on the debit or receipt side of the Cash Book is headed "Discount Dr." and a customer is credited with the amount of discount allowed him and the cash received from him in columns side by side. These methods are reversed for dealing with discount deducted from bills paid.

While the first of the two methods may balancing; or we may simply post the total from the foot of the column, being careful to post it to the same side in the ledger as that on which it appears in the Cash Book. If one keeps in mind the character of the entries when posting, the reversal of sides of which this is an example will give no trouble.

This principle of separating any class

CONTRA

Date	Account to Debit	To Whom and For What Paid	L.F.	Debit				Credit		Totals
				Expense	Mdse.	Freight	Bills Payable	Discount	Cash	

COLUMNAR CASH BOOK.

be nearer to the principles of bookkeeping, the second is much the more convenient and labor-saving method, and it appears to me keeps nearer to the facts, in that it includes in the Cash column only the Cash actually received.

It is also very convenient to be able to post to a customer's credit in the ledger, "Discount $5.00, Cash or Cheque $95.00, total, $100."

of recurring items into special column, may be applied to any desired extent, each particular business usually furnishing its own special requirements.

For many businesses it is found convenient to introduce on the debit or receipt side, columns for "Bills Receivable" which have been realized on, and for "Accounts Paid In," in addition to those above mentioned.

CONTRA

Date	Account to Debit		Credit		L.F.	Debit				
			Cash	Disc't.		Sundries	Expense	Mdse.	Freight	Bills Payable

COLUMNAR CASH BOOK.

In balancing the Cash Book different methods are employed of dealing with these columns. We may enter the totals either into the discount or Cash column on the opposite page, and post them from there, including the amount in the

On the credit or payment side, it is often convenient to provide for Bills Payable, Freight, Cash Purchases of Merchandise and sometimes Accounts Paid.

The object for the column for "Accounts Paid In" on the debit side is to enable one to keep an eye on the fluctuations on the open Accounts Receivable, by comparing the charged sales with the collections from customers.

While the columnar analysis is a very desirable improvement within reasonable limits, it often develops into another example of the present tendency to carry labor-saving too far, and just as I think it a mistake to try to do away with the journal entirely. I also think it a mistake to endeavor to analyze all the Cash transactions of a business into special columns.

It leaves some of the columns with such a few items, that it would have been easy to post them in detail, and the tendency of the columnar posting is to cover up and lose important information, which can then only be got at by dissection of the columns.

This labor-saving tendency sometimes takes the form of an effort to do entirely without a Ledger by columnar analysis of the Cash Book and summarizing the analysis.

In the case of Willson's Municipal Day Book and Ledger combined, the columnar arrangement undertakes to provide for all possible transactions, and to require no aid from a Ledger.

The new Ontario Municipal Cash Book follows the same idea. As the accounts must be reported in detail, these Cash Books must be dissected again for the items, so that the saving is doubtful.

There is no provision or requirement for a Ledger in the law regarding Municipal Bookkeeping, although a journal is required to be kept by all Municipalities except Townships, and they may do so if they so desire.

It appears to be the common custom in planning a Cash Book to set the special columns next to the particulars, leaving those items which are to be posted in detail to go into the sundries column, the farthest to the right.

As the number of columns increases, it

RECEIPTS

Date	Particulars	Resident Taxes	Non-Resident Taxes		Post Column	Total

FIG. 3—FORM OF MUNICIPAL CASH BOOK,

RECEIPTS

Date	Particulars	Debit Cash	L. F.	Credit Posting Columns		
				Sundries	Interest	

FIG. 4—SPECIAL FORM OF CASH BOOK

increases the distance that one has to travel across the page in tracing those amounts in the sundries column which are to be posted. It has seemed to me a better plan to put the sundries column, the one to be posted next to the particulars, where the items can be readily seen, thus doing away with the danger of erroneous posting through faulty tracing of to be posted in detail, and following that to the right are columns for the monthly postings, keeping these columns which are most used, nearest to the Cash Column.

This form being a complete posting analysis of the Cash, is also a self-balancing test of the accuracy of the Cash Book.

PAYMENTS

Date	Particulars	Bank Account					Salaries		Total	Balance on Hand
		Vouch. No.	Bank		Balance					
			Debtor	Credit	Debtor	Credit				

SHOWING MANNER OF DEALING WITH BANK ACCOUNT.

the line which the item is on.

The common method of using special columns is to enter the receipts in the column to which they belong, and only carry them into the Cash or Total Column when balancing at the end of the month.

This increases the difficulty of testing the Cash during the month.

These objections have gradually led me

In order to illustrate the difference between the two methods I now give examples of the ruling for each.

Thus far I have purposely avoided any mention of the Bank account, as I wished to deal with it by myself so far as that is possible.

The first method of keeping this account, as in the case of the Cash Account, is by journalizing the Bank trans-

PAYMENTS

Date	Voucher Number	Particulars	Credit Cash	Mercantile Bank Checks	Bank of Commerce Checks	L.F.	Debit Posting Column				
							Sundries	Mercantile Bank Deposits	Bank of Com'erce Deposits	Bank Charges	Trav'ling Expenses

SHOWING MANNER OF DEALING WITH BANK ACCOUNT.

to favor and in some cases to adopt what appears to me to be an improved form of Cash Book, in which the amount of Cash received or paid appears in a column next the particulars; beyond that the first column is devoted to the sundries which are

actions with the other transactions and posting them to a ledger account.

While this method has its advantages in that it shows to the junior in accounts the true character of the entries, in these

(To be continued.)

Accountics

The Office Magazine.

A. O. KITTREDGE, F. I. A., C. P. A., EDITOR.
E. R. KITTREDGE, ASSOCIATE.

Accountics is devoted to the Science of Accounting, to the Art of Bookkeeping and to the advocacy of Improved Office Methods.

Subscription.—One dollar a year, payable in advance.

Postage is prepaid by the publishers in the United States, Canada and Mexico. For all other countries in the Postal Union, subscribers must add 50 cents a year.

Discontinuances.—In the absence of specific orders to discontinue at the end of the subscription term the magazine will be continued and a bill sent.

Remittances should be by Draft, P. O. Order or Express Order, payable to the order of the ACCOUNTICS ASSOCIATION. Money and postage stamps are at the risk of the sender, unless sent by express or in registered letters. Add 10 cents each to checks on local banks to defray collection charges.

Advertising Rates will be quoted on application.

Official Journal.—This publication, by resolutions duly passed, has been made the official publication of the following organizations:—

THE INSTITUTE OF ACCOUNTS.
THE NEW YORK CHAPTER of the Institute of Accounts.
THE WASHINGTON CHAPTER of the Institute of Accounts.
THE HARTFORD CHAPTER of the Institute of Accounts.

ACCOUNTICS is the accredited medium of intercommunication between members of the Institute of Accounts wherever located.

ACCOUNTICS ASSOCIATION,
Publishers,
Wool Exchange, New York.

Entered at the Post Office New York as Second Class Matter.

PUBLISHER'S DESK

Treatment of the Merchandise Account

The Practical Age, for December, commenting upon Mr. Kittredge's address before the Eastern Commercial Teachers' Association, presented the following:—

A. O. Kittredge, the editor of ACCOUNTICS, certainly makes a point that is worthy of consideration when he states that the account (the merchandise account) as ordinarly treated shows absolutely no result. The difference between the sides of the cash account shows the amount on hand; in bills receivable account the difference shows the amount of notes on hand; the difference between the sides of the interest account shows the net gain or loss from that source. The difference between the sides of the merchandise account, however, gives no definite information, for it neither shows the amount of merchandise on hand nor loss or gain on it. To make it exhibit tangible results we must take an inventory of the merchandise itself, and add it to the credit of the merchandise account, when the difference will then show a loss or a gain. Now, if Mr. Kittredge has a practical plan of keeping the merchandise account so that at any time the proprietor of a business can ascertain his exact financial condition without the necessity of taking an inventory, the business world ought to know it and the business educators ought to teach it. The world isn't perfect yet, and it is not to be supposed that the science of accounting is unsusceptible of further improvement. Our columns are wide open to further light on this dark subject.

An Opinion Clearly Expressed

The following letter explains itself, and is commended to the attention of those who assume that anything said in criticism of the business schools, or of text books on bookkeeping, necessarily casts the speaker into outer darkness:

Hartford Business College,
Hartford, Conn., Dec. 10, 1898.

MR. A. O. KITTREDGE, C. P. A.
260 to 266 West Broadway,
New York City.

My Dear Sir:

It gives me pleasure to acknowledge receipt of a copy of your paper on "Modern Accounting," as read before the Eastern Commercial Teachers' Association, in its New York meet November 26. I note that you did not include copies of the charts, and surely could not expect you to do so.

Allow me to say, however, that your paper, including the remarks you made and the books you showed, contained more meat for my teachers and myself than any other paper I have ever heard read before any teachers' commercial association.

You may rest assured that the best of business college men are with you in your views, and we only envy you the opportunity you have to derive benefits from your continual contact with up-to-date accounting, as it is to be found in the best concerns of the practical business world.

Should you ever have occasion to come to Hartford and will put up with our hospitality, we shall be glad to treat you as best we know how.

Yours for business,
(Signed) E. M. MORSE,
Principal.

We have received from the L. L. Brown Paper Company, Adams, Mass., several sample books of linen ledger and typewriter papers. The books are strongly bound with handsome cover papers, and each bears an attractive cover design.

Volume IV, Nos. 1 to 6
January 1899 to June 1899

ting is the Vital Element of Business

Accountics

The Office Magazine

JANUARY 1899

CONTENTS

ACCOUNTICS ASSOCIATION
Publishers
260-266 West Broadway NEW YORK

Card Index Competition

Applications of the Card System to Business Uses

Prizes: $150.00 Cash

For the purpose of exciting a lively interest in card index methods, and also by way of paying something for the work which may be done by contestants, we have arranged a cash prize competition in

Lists of Uses with Illustrations

No one has yet compiled an exhaustive list of the uses to which card systems may be applied, with illustrative examples. Perhaps a complete list is impossible, for new applications are continually arising. No two persons who may undertake the preparation of such lists will agree in all details. Hence the advantage of interesting a large number in compiling lists.

Each contestant will necessarily reflect his own experience and observation, and indicate his own peculiar preferences. For example, if Card Ledgers were under consideration, A would present one form of ruling, while B would present another. Each would have his reason for so doing. As a fact, cards for ledger accounts may be ruled in a great many different forms, each specially useful for one particular class of accounts. We desire to secure the largest possible variety at the hands of practical users. Again, take it in Cards for Subscription Lists in periodical publishing; various rulings are current. We would like a showing of all of them,—and so on to the end of all the uses that can be suggested.

For the best list of practical applications and set of illustrations that is sent us, on or before the date named below, we offer a First Prize of $100.00, and for the next best a Second Prize of $50.00.

General Particulars

1. Under each title in the list the contestant is required to give a brief outline of the application of the method that he has in mind, together with various general conditions. The dimensions of the cards to be employed are to be stated or indicated. Whatever variety in colors would be necessary to employ for the purpose in view is to be mentioned. How tab and guide cards would be used is also to be described.

2. Sample rulings are particularly desirable. In all cases illustrations are to be on separate sheets and are to indicate the exact size of the card that [illegible] contestant would advise [illegible] reference from text to illustrations should be made numerically, calling the first ruling Fig. 1, the next Fig. 2, and so on.

3. The quality and variety of the exhibit of rulings and illustrative examples will have special weight with the committee of award in deciding the contest. A mere list of uses, without showing the manner of application, would be comparatively valueless. Hence the advice to contestants to give special attention to those details. The object in view is to secure the largest possible variety of rulings in connection with the largest list of uses.

Accountics

VOL. IV JANUARY 1899 NO. 1

The Monthly Statement

It has been the policy of ACCOUNTICS to devote itself to the science of accounting, the art of bookkeeping and the advocacy of improved office methods. While there is no desire upon the part of the publishers to alter this fundamental principle, it will be their aim during 1899 to improve upon all past efforts; to broaden the publication upon these lines, and make it at once more valuable to present readers and interesting and instructive to an ever widening circle of new acquaintances.

From a very small beginning, the magazine has grown to the dignity of five thousand regular readers. That it is deserving of this success is evident from the fact that, up to the present time, no great effort has been made to place it before the public. It has sprung from a wind-sown seed, as it were, in untilled soil and has grown into a strong young tree solely because of its own hardiness. Beginning with this number, an effort will be made to place it before the public in an attractive and effective manner. The addition of a handsome cover is the first step in this direction, and this will be varied in color and design with each successive number.

The best business writers already are numbered among the contributors, and the subjects dealt with will be more widely diversified than ever before. Business problems of many kinds will be intelligently and thoroughly discussed by men of practical experience and unquestionable ability. ACCOUNTICS aims to advance steadily and surely and the publishers desire it to deserve every inch that it gains.

The funny men of the newspaper press know a good thing when they see it, but very frequently when they get the good thing in hand they work it so hard as to wear it out, if not actually to spoil it. A while ago it was the mother-in-law joke, upon which the changes were rung until there seemed to be no possible variation left. A little later it was the plumber, and this worthy individual came in for an undue share of obloquy and shame. More recently the Klondike, that vast region of severe cold and plentiful gold, has had a large measure of attention, while the war, of course, contributed ideas to both joke writer and cartoonist. Just now the woman in business seems to be the joker's special theme. The papers abound with suppositious stories of what the woman does when confronted by a demand for identification on presenting a check in bank; what she does when she is informed by the bank that her account is overdrawn, and how, in general, she keeps her accounts. Some of the stories are worked up with much ingenuity, if not technical skill.

For example, the young husband presented his wife with an expense book and explained to her how to keep it. She faithfully scrawled her accounts in the book every evening, like the thrifty housewife she aspired to be. Finally the husband asked to see the book. His wife beamed with pride as she glanced at the red lines under the amounts and the neat array of figures while handing over the book. It was certainly a pleasing thing to look at, but every few days this cabulistic entry appeared: "G. K. W., 25 cents," or "G. K. W." some other amount. The sums varied, but the initials were always the same, and they appeared with astonishing regularity. Naturally the inquiry was made: "Who is this 'G. K. W.?' and why do you give him or her so much money?" The good wife laughed. Why, that isn't any one," she said. "You see, every now and then there is a certain sum for which I cannot account and so I put down 'G. K. W.'—goodness knows what. Don't you see?"

Another story of the same kind represents the wife receiving a certain amount of money and entering it thus: "January 2. Received from Bertie, $85." The contra-entry was explicit and sufficient, even though not satisfactory in detail: "January 3. Spent it all." We have not space to refer to many other stories of a similar character which are current at the present time. The attempted identification of the woman at bank by the production of a handkerchief with the initials worked in it, only to find that she was carrying the handkerchief of a friend, is one of them, and another is the suggestion that a strawberry mark or a mole, or some similar physical mark should meet the requirements of bank identification. Some of the stories are good and some are very silly. Just at present the woman who essays to do business is in the same position in the mind of the joke writer that the mother-in-law and the plumber have been in the past.

Cost Marks

There are numerous words in the English language that may be used as cost marks or cyphers for marking goods. There are also many short phrases that are adapted to the same end. The requirements of a word for cost mark purposes are that it shall consist of exactly ten letters, all different, each of which shall be used to represent one of the digits. For example, "blacksmith," which has ten letters and no duplication, is something that is entirely appropriate for the purpose, and is found in use in different directions. The phrase "Why not save?" is an illustration of the second class and is something that is employed by various merchants. Whether a cost mark shall be based on a word or a phrase, or shall be a set of arbitrary signs, depends largely upon taste and inclination. A writer in one of our exchanges, discussing cost marks in general, gives several examples arranged in a somewhat attractive form. We quote as follows:

Once upon a time I compiled a list of cost marks, and I had quite a collection of them. There were "Republican" and "Democratik" for politics. "Snug Profit" and "Cash Profit," both of which are pleasing. "Now be Sharp" suggests a horse trader, while "Black Horse" is in the same direction. A sporting man might prefer to use such phrases as "Cigar Smoke," "Bad Whiskey," "Big Jack Pot," "Bucket Shop," "Prison Gate." These might be the chapters from which to write a romance, but they are simply cost marks of various firms I have known. A hardware man uses "Fish Tackle." A plumber might like "Gainful Job." "Profitable" has a good sound. "Big Factory" is used in a manufacturing town. Shoe dealers have chosen such words as "Tan Blucher" and "Kip Brogans." Several geographical names answer the purpose, such as "Charleston," "Perth Amboy," "Blackstone," "Cumberland." Other suggestive phrases are: "You are Sick," "Corn Basket," "Don't Be Lazy," "My Wife Joan," "Big Scholar," "Elucidator." One man who reads his Bible every Sunday uses the sentence, "He is my Rock."

Reviews

SPENCER'S COMMERCIAL LAW.

A manual of commercial law, containing a clear, concise and logical exposition of the rules relating to business transactions and the management of affairs. By Edward W. Spencer, of the Milwaukee Bar. Published by the Bowen-Merrill Company. Size 5½ by 8½. 654 pages. Price $2.00.

The object of this work is to give instruction in American law to business men, general readers, and members of schools and colleges where business branches are taught. It has been made as practical as possible. Technical details have been left out, and this space is devoted to rules regarding the formation, interpretation and discharge of contracts in general, to bills and notes, to the rights and liabilities of shareholders in business corporations, to sales of chattels, etc. Subjects having no direct bearing upon commercial law are condensed, while those of direct interest are expanded and carefully treated. Lists of leading text books are given at the end of chapters and topics to aid those who may desire to go more deeply into the study of the various subjects.

The work ought to be of value to every business man, as well as useful to the student and the teacher.

Evolution in Accounting and Cost Keeping*

By A. O. Kittredge, C. P. A.

In whatever direction the manufacturer or business man gazes at the present time, he finds changes, as compared with what was current practice a short time since. New machinery has supplanted the old; scientific processes have taken the place of empirical methods; steam power has superseded horse power and water power; factories are lighted by electricity instead of gas; power is distributed electrically in place of belts and wire ropes; and by thousands of steps, some very small and few very large, the production of goods in factories has advanced to its present position of scientific vantage as compared with the puny efforts of individual artisans of a few generations back.

Nor is the end yet reached. Development is still in progress, and so rapid are the strides in certain lines that far-sighted men are deterred from buying for their establishments the equipment of machinery that is offered to-day, knowing full well that almost before they could get it set up and put in motion, something very much better would be available.

If we read the story of industrial development, we find special emphasis put by the historian upon the invention of the steam engine by Watt; of the power loom by Cartwright; of steam propelled boats by Fulton; of printing by Gutenberg, and upon various other leading incidents. For the moment we have the feeling that the ancients have done everything and that, therefore, there is little or nothing left for those of the present day. And yet within our own experience has come the electric light, the telephone, the typewriter, the X-ray, liquefied air, and a hundred other inventions, discoveries and improvements the use of which distinguished the daily life of the people of the present from that of other generations. Progress is being made in all directions, and the one difference between the development in evidence at the end of the nineteenth century, and that which has characterized preceding periods, is the difference between an ox team or a canal boat for the transportation of passengers, as compared with an express train on one of the trunk lines; or the difference between a courier bearing dispatches through a trackless wilderness, and the telephone or telegraph wire, which gives us instant communication without regard to distance. It is the difference of rate of speed. The evolution of the day is something unprecedented in the history of the world. It is proceeding at the rate of a lightning express train.

With all the development that is in progress, it would be strange indeed if some of it were not to be found in the realm of accounts. Accounting, perhaps, is the last division in which men are likely to seek for evidence of progress. As a fact, it would seem that business men have been content to let accounting severely alone, while promoting advancement in every other department of their business. Certain it is that for one reason or another accounting has been kept in the background, and only lately, with the rising tide of actual necessity, have the accountants of America taken such a stand as enables them to meet the real wants of business enterprises. Societies of mechanical engineers, mining engineers, electrical engineers and various others have been in existence for many years, but not until recently have societies of accountants been organized for the promotion of the mutual interests of their members and the advancement of the science to which they are devoted. It is somewhat singular that accounting has been so much neglected, for upon it depends almost everything there is in business.

The importance of accounting was so

*An address by A. O. Kittredge, C. P. A., before the Manufacturers' Club, Cincinnati, December 12, 1898.

ably presented some time since, in an address by Charles Dutton, before the Institute of Accounts, New York, that I cannot do better in this connection than to refer briefly to what he said. I quote:

"Accounting is a component of all business of every kind and nature, not here and there not now and then, but everywhere and always. It cannot be eliminated from business. Close your halls of legislation, adjourn your courts of law, and business in the main would go on with but little interruption; but remove the element of accounting and business would be paralyzed. It would be impossible until that element was restored. What would be the result in this city, if those who are entrusted with the practical application of this element should for a single day desert their posts, leaving business to get along without their assistance? I ask, what would happen to business under these circumstances?"

The speaker's conclusion, in the light of a somewhat extended argument was one in which we all must concur—namely, that "Accounting is the vital element of business."

There is an evolution in progress in accounting. It is being more and more adapted to the real needs of business. It is constantly giving results in better form for the business man's use. It is being regularly reduced in expense, increased in efficiency, and adapted to the growing needs of the manufacturing and mercantile world.

I invite your attention this evening to a brief survey of certain analytical methods of applied accounting, through which certain adaptations to needs are secured, as well as results in special form. If time permitted, what I shall proceed to explain might be contrasted with other methods, for the domain of accounting is so vast and what its science covers is so broad, that there are methods and methods, each with special merits of its own, but all, when handled by competent accounting engineers, adapted to work to the one end—namely, the advancement and development of business interests.

The leading features of the system that I shall present for your consideration, are a perpetual or going balance sheet and a perpetual or going profit and loss statement. The system outlined proceeds upon the theory that the fiscal period may as well as not be obliterated and that the books of account can be made to show actual conditions at all times, instead of occasionally, as, for example, at the end of a year. Or to put it otherwise, the fiscal period, instead of being a year, may be reduced to a month. In many cases it is reduced to a week, and in some lines of trade it is brought down to a single day.

One of the greatest difficulties to be met in considering cost accounts, and for that matter in considering any other special division of the accounts of a business, is to comprehend the relative position of the group in the collective accounts of the business. So great is this difficulty that in many cases business men appear to entertain the idea that cost accounts are something separate and distinct from the regular accounts of the business, that cost accounts are something which cannot be made a part of the regular accounting system, but instead are a separate and distinct effort, something necessary to be done by reason of the information afforded, but something in which those who have charge of the general accounts of the enterprise have no particular concern.

I am disposed to take a different view of the case. I am disposed to believe that the general system of the accounts of any business should include everything that had to be recorded concerning that business, whether it occurs in the factory, in the salesroom, in a branch house, or in the main office. I will admit that details in many cases can best be conducted away from the main office, but boiled down results, the thing in the aggregate, should always be known in the main office and always represented in the general books. From several points of view this is a very broad proposition, and not a few, perhaps, may be disposed to ask how this can be. It is partly with a view to answering that question that I have thought well to bring to your attention the charts of an accounting system, to which your attention will be directed.

There are just two grand divisions in which all the accounts of any business may be arranged. There are just two leading questions which every business man asks from time to time concerning his business as represented by the accounts. The two grand divisions referred to are the balance sheet and the profit and loss statement. The two questions referred to are his degree of solvency and the rate of his profit or loss.

The confusion that exists in the minds of many people, with reference to these two classes of accounts and the nature of the statements that are made from time to time under these heads, was strikingly illustrated in a number of the daily papers a few days since. Secretary Gage's annual report contained a statement of the income of the national government and its disbursements, with a balance struck, showing the deficit. This statement was manifestly a revenue and expense statement, the equivalent of the profit and loss statement of a private corporation, and yet it was referred to in the head lines of some of the papers, and also in certain paragraphs in accompanying articles, as being the nation's "balance sheet."

For the moment I do not remember ever having seen a national balance sheet. To say the least, it would be a remarkable document. A balance sheet is a statement of assets and liabilities. What are the assets of the nation? Cash in the treasury is one item; real estate, including the public buildings thereon, would also figure conspicuously in the statement; fortifications, river and harbor improvements, the navy and army equipment, materials of war, and hundreds of other items of less magnitude representing property the nation owns, would go to complete the accounts. On the other hand, the liabilities of the nation would consist of its bonded debt and its floating indebtedness, by which is meant accounts in process of adjustment, etc. The difference between assets and liabilities from the standpoint of the individual business man represents present worth or invested capital. The nation, however, is not a firm nor yet a stock company trading for a profit, and therefore right here the parallel breaks down.

The operations of the nation are so gigantic, and the purpose for which it exists is so different from that of a mere money-making enterprise, that individual citizens, and other nations as well, in passing upon the question of the nation's solvency, content themselves with comparing expenses with revenue. If the revenue is equal to or greater than the expenses the nation is solvent beyond question. When the revenue is considerably less than the expenses there is trouble ahead, as witness the conditions which immediately preceded and extended into the panicky period through which we have recently passed.

After all, is it not very much the same with private corporations and business firms? As long as the profits of the business are greater than the expenses very few care particularly about the relative standing of assets and liabilities. Conditions very evidently are steadily improving. But when it is known that the expenses of a business are greater than its revenues, no matter how solvent it may be by the balance sheet statement doubt is cast upon the financial standing of the concern and ultimate disaster is looked for.

Comparatively few establishments make money every month of the year. Some of the most profitable enterprises show considerable losses through certain months in the year, and then very large profits through the remaining portion of the year. The fact that they are making a loss day by day during the dull season does not necessarily impair their credit, for it is known to be the nature of the business that things are so. Our nation falling behind for a short period, in the sense of having greater expenses than revenue, does not necessarily lose credit among the nations of the world, nor in the minds of its citizens. Even at present, thanks to the Spanish war, the expenses of the government are greater than its revenue, and for several years to come it looks as though there would continue to be a deficit, save only as legislation securing larger revenues may remedy the condition; and yet, in view of other well-known facts, we have unlimited confidence in the nation's solvency.

In order to make proper application of what there is to be said concerning the accounts of a manufacturing business let it be assumed that we have a going enterprise with which to deal. It makes comparatively little difference from what line of trade we choose an enterprise for illustration. Since we shall be dealing with an imaginary institution instead of some special enterprise there will be afforded the opportunity of carrying the system of analysis and classification up to ideal limits. In other words, there will be no reason why we should stop short at any point in pursuing our theory and illustrating its application, simply because the actual conditions of a business make unnecessary certain requirements. Accordingly, the diagrams will contain some things that would not necessarily appear in the accounts of any particular organization. Or, to make this point clearer, given a number of factories in the same line of business, the accounts of all of which are arranged upon the plan here shown, no one of them, perhaps, would have everything that is illustrated, and no two of them, perhaps, would make the same variations from the chart.

A chart to illustrate such a paper as the present must of necessity be ideal in its completeness. When a business is organized upon the plan that the chart indicates certain omissions are of course made, according to the special requirements of the case, and very likely certain changes in names of accounts will occur, but the principle of analysis will be the same.

With the two grand divisions before us —namely, the balance sheet and profit and loss statement—let us first consider what the balance sheet shows. Before entering upon this let me direct your attention to the point of view from which this analysis is made. It is that the business is an institution that owes the proprietors or the stockholders the money that they invest in it. The definition of a corporation which appears in the statutes of some of the States at the present time is that it is "a person created by law." We will suppose that our factory is a corporation. Then it is a person in the eye of the law. From the stockholders' point of view it is a person that owes him and his associates the money that he and his associates have advanced to it. The corporation also owes for its other indebtedness, whether it be funded, in the shape of bonds, or floating, in the shape of notes, purchase accounts, etc. From this point of view, which is by no means an exceptional one, we have an equilibrium in the accounts. The assets will exactly balance the liabilities.

The assets of a business, as we ordinarily find them, may be divided for purposes of analysis in the sense of indicating their relative importance, into four classes. Right here let me remark that the terms of classification inside of the brace entitled "Assets" amount to very little from the accountant's point of view. These terms are introduced solely for the benefit of the business man, in the sense of indicating the character of the assets with which he has to deal.

The active assets of a business consist of Cash, sometimes subdivided into the amount that is in the office and the deposit that is in a single bank or in each of several banks. The next item is Notes Receivable; following which is Accounts Receivable, divided into Customers' Accounts and Sundry Debtors. Next we have Materials on Hand, subdivided as may be required.

In a foundry business, for example, the principal material account would be pig iron; in a furniture manufacturing business one of the leading material accounts would be lumber, and where lumber is bought considerably in advance of consumption, for the purpose of keeping on

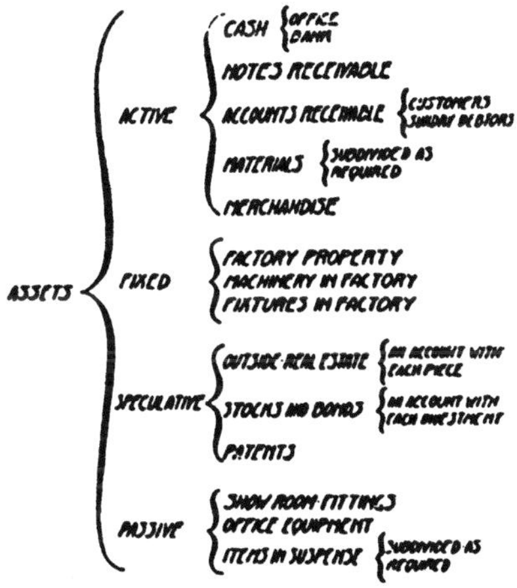

FIG. 1—ASSETS.

hand a good assortment and also for securing proper seasoning, the lumber account becomes a very important asset.

Finally, among the active assets is what I have called Merchandise. Let me define this Merchandise Account. It is not the Merchandise Account which usually appears in a set of books, but instead is a subdivision of the account commonly indicated by that name. In this case it records the goods on hand ready for sale, whether these goods were made by the concern itself or bought in the open market to sell again. It is the "stock" on hand.

The merchandise account is debited with the goods as they are turned over by the factory, taken at actual cost. It is also debited with goods as they are bought in the market. In turn, it is credited with the same goods as they are parted with, likewise taken at cost. This process leaves a balance in the account equal to the inventory or the cost value of the goods remaining on hand. Inventorying or "stock taking," then, is resorted to only for the purpose of verifying this account.

When we get down to the accounts of the Profit and Loss Statement I shall have something to say about a Selling Account, or, as our English contemporaries sometimes call it, a "Trading Account," which takes the goods over from the Merchandise Account at cost and sells them for what it is possible to get for them. The balance in the Selling Account, therefore, represents gross profit or loss, as the case may be.

The next division in assets is designated as Fixed, the items being Factory Property, Machinery in Factory, and Fixtures in Factory. These assets are always worth more to the business than they would fetch in the market if disposed of at forced sale. They are necessary to the business, and yet they are not immediately available for paying debts; hence the distinction between active assets and fixed assets.

The third division I have called Speculative Assets. Many concerns, for business reasons, in the sense of forming alliances or for investing surplus profits and for other reasons, carry on their books accounts of real estate outside of the needs of the business, and occasionally they own stock in other companies, or have capital invested in bonds. Speculative in this sense means investments outside of the nominal requirements of the business.

I have also included under the head of Speculative Assets, Patents. Almost every business owns patents. Some enterprises buy patents, paying exemplary prices for the same. Others acquire them at much smaller expense in the development of the business itself. Whatever the Patent Account is charged with, the real value of the patents is an undetermined amount until a sale has been made. A sale, however, is seldom made when the patents are really valuable to the business and are being used therein. Whatever figure, therefore, stands opposite Patents is a speculative asset, but in a different sense of the word, however, from that in which speculative has previously been used.

Finally, we come to Passive Assets. The fittings of a show-room are important to the business, and are of a kind to require frequent replacement; they are easily destroyed, but they differ in kind altogether from the fixtures and machinery in the factory. The office equipment is of a similar character. Hence the head under which they appear. Some preferences in classification might throw these two items back into Fixed Assets. With such a change I would have no quarrel, for, as before stated, all these terms are matters of choice and their only value is in keeping before the business man the real nature of the figures which his balance sheet displays.

Finally, under the head of Passive Assets we have Items in Suspense. An item in suspense means something that is paid in the present month or present fiscal period, the charge for which belongs to some other month. Take a familiar example: If we pay three months' telephone services in advance at the beginning of the present month it is unfair to charge all that bill to the present month. One-third of it belongs to the present month, one-third to the next month and one-third to the month thereafter. Therefore we carry the whole amount into Suspense, and then from time to time take out of Suspense whatever applies to the month in progress.

Let us next consider the Liabilities of the business. These also, as shown on the chart, divide into four classes. Every business has Active Liabilities, which may be subdivided into Accounts Payable, including both Purchase Accounts and Accounts with Sundry Creditors, and Notes Payable. Many enterprises have Funded Liabilities, in the form of mortgage bonds or debentures, or both. Every business should also have Reserve Liabilities.

Here let me define a reserve or reserve liability. A reserve is an amount set aside from current income to provide for a future expense. The theory upon which our analysis proceeds, as I have already explained, is that a perpetual balance sheet and perpetual profit and loss statement are to be maintained. Reserves, therefore, are very important elements. If the business incurs an expense as it proceeds, which cannot be paid at once but which will have to be paid at some future time, then the expense should be charged into the business at it proceeds, and at the date to which it belongs. The

Credit Account then will be a fund or reserve to be employed in discharging the amount whenever the bill is rendered.

For example, take it in the second item shown under this head on the chart, namely, Taxes. Taxes, as a rule, are paid once a year; but taxes, considered as an expense, are in progress all the time. If each month is to stand upon its own footing and this is entirely feasible in manufacturing lines as well as in mercantile lines, then the monthly expense of taxes should be charged up each month. But we cannot walk up to the county treasurer's office and pay our taxes each month. Therefore we are obliged to create a reserve for taxes, debiting the business month by month with the monthly pro rata of taxes, and crediting Tax Reserve Account. The business

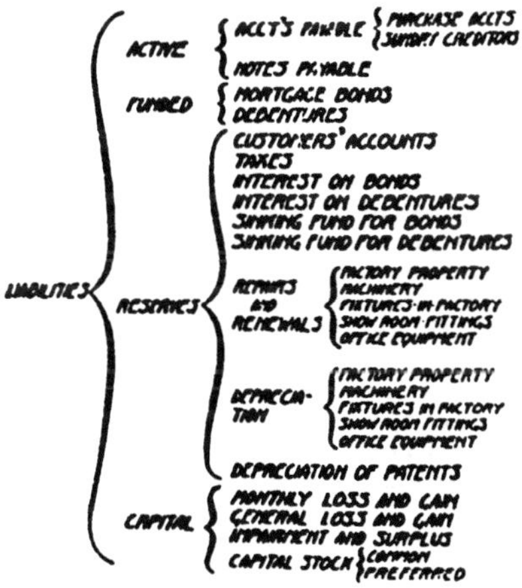

FIG. 2—LIABILITIES.

thereby is charged with its real expense at the proper time. Tax Reserve Account, on the other hand, accumulates a fund out of which to pay taxes. When tax paying time arrives the reserve fund is used for paying taxes. Tax Reserve Account is debited with the cash paid out and thus the liability is discharged.

Take for another example the first item in this division of the chart, namely, Debtors' Accounts. We are morally certain that we shall never collect the exact amount from customers that we have charged them. If, for example, we put out $10,000 worth of goods this week we can say for a certainty that we will not be able to collect the full $10,000 for them. There will be a deduction, or a rebate, or an allowance, or a bad debt, or the expense of a trip somewhere to straighten out some difficulty, real or imagined, that will reduce this $10,000 by its amount, whatever it is. Since we want each month's business to stand by itself, and since there is always a shrinkage in debtors' accounts, it is only right to set aside at the outset a reserve to meet this shrinkage. If, in the light of past years' business, we discover that our bad debts, our costs of collection, rebates, allowances and all other items of the same class, are amounting to one-quarter of one per cent upon the face of the accounts, or one-half of one per cent., or some other amount, then it is only good business management to charge into expenses and credit to a reserve account such an amount each month as will meet this cost whenever it comes to be paid.

Interest on bonds and debentures is an expense month by month, to be paid quarterly or annually. Hence the necessity of a reserve fund in these cases.

The next item under the head of Reserves is Sinking Fund for Bonds, and following it is Sinking Fund for Debentures. A sinking fund may be regarded from various points of view, and therefore when the term is used in a chart of this kind it is necessary to define exactly what is meant. I take it that the average business concern as a rule borrows money only because it needs additional capital. If it had all the capital the business required it would not borrow. It borrows money and pledges as security a part or all of its property upon the theory that sooner or later it can pay out. Accordingly, the ambition of the management is to discharge the indebtedness as soon as possible. Its only chance of discharging that indebtedness, however, is to make money during the time the indebtedness runs, to meet it at maturity. In order to be in shape to pay the bonds when they fall due the plan is followed of setting aside a certain amount of money each year out of the profits, thereby accumulating the fund out of which to pay the bonds at the agreed date. A sinking fund, considered from this point of view, absorbs a certain amount of profits, or, what is the same thing, and, as the chart before you is arranged to show, the credit to the sinking fund is made a charge against the business by way of expense.

The thought underlying this is that we

always want to know just what is left for dividends after provision has been made for every possible claim and emergency.

So much for the sinking fund as it appears in this chart. Now for a thought with respect to sinking funds from an altogether different point of view. A sinking fund may be established simply by the conversion of assets. A concern may be property rich and cash poor. It borrows money, pledges as security certain property, not with the expectation of repaying that money out of profits but out of conversion of the property into cash. In a speculative way, perhaps, it has bought a large tract of mining property, or it has invested largely in unproductive real estate. Its funds are tied up, and for operating purposes it needs ready cash. The financial institution that lends the cash stipulates that a sinking fund shall be created and maintained, with a reserve carried to it each year. As fast as the property which is unproductive opens up or comes into the market for sale a certain amount, therefore, is set aside from receipts from sales, according to the contract, to form the stipulated sinking fund. This, as will at once be perceived, is a different theory altogether from the one first explained, and yet the same terms are used.

There is left in the classification of reserves certain items that are of more importance to manufacturers, perhaps, than any of those that have been previously considered. These are Reserves for Repairs and Renewals of Factory Property, Machinery, and Fixtures in Factory. Then there are reserves against depreciation of these same assets, and likewise to provide for depreciation of patents.

It is an admitted fact that factory property, machinery, fixtures, etc., will get out of repair, and therefore that there is a standing expense of the nature of maintenance. This expense is a charge that ought to be spread over the product. If, for illustration, it costs $10,000 a year to repair the factory and keep the machinery in good order, then in the stated cost of the product, over and above all other items, there should be included this $10,000.

It is not the best management that deducts the actual cost of repairs from the profit showing at the end of the year. It is much better to estimate in advance the charge that repairs will really be for the year, making the estimate in the light of the records of previous periods and then charge one-twelfth of this amount into the cost of the monthly product. Credit that amount to the corresponding reserve account. When it comes time to make the repairs make them as they should be made, debiting the reserve account with the expense. At the end of a year, or of any other long period, an inspection of the accounts will show whether or not the reserve has been made too large or too small. If too large then there is an amount to be carried to the profit side of Loss and Gain; if too small, there is an amount to be carried to the debit side of Loss and Gain, and a corresponding adjustment of charge rate for the future.

No matter how thoroughly machinery and buildings are kept in repair there is still a constant depreciation in value. A factory building that is twenty, thirty or forty years old, as the case may be, although it has been kept in what may be described as "perfect" repair, is to-day condemned by the average manufacturer as being too old and therefore undesirable for use. All around us we see such buildings being torn down and new ones put up in their places. This is a broad illustration of the fact of depreciation, independent of repairs.

Again, take it in the case of machinery. Machinery is being constantly superseded by new inventions and new designs. No matter how thoroughly a given machine is kept in repair sooner or later it is discarded and a new device is put in its place. The prime cost of machinery, therefore, and the prime cost of buildings as well, are parts of the product.

It would be manifestly unfair to charge the cost of machinery and buildings into the first month's product, but into a certain number of months' product their cost must inevitably go. Is the life of a building fifty years? Then one-fiftieth of its cost, independent of the expense of repairs, should be charged into the expenses of each year. Or, what is the same, one-twelfth of one-fiftieth of the cost of the building should be charged into each month's product. Is the life of a machine ten years? Then one-tenth of the cost of that machine should be charged into the product each year, or one-twelfth of one-tenth should be charged into the cost of product each month.

(To be continued.)

Revenue Accounts*

By W. T. Kernahan, C. A.

In the days before the electrical engines and iron horses ran all through the country there was not the necessity there is now of watching closely all the details of and influences connected with one's business. In these, the closing years of the nineteenth century, we find the laborer and mechanic being pushed aside by the introduction of labor-saving machinery and devices, and, as improvements increase in this line, and competition becomes keener every day, the business man who desires to be successful and keep abreast of the times must needs be fully alive to every move in the direction of progress. While it is an essential feature in a man's business that he should take advantage of rapidly increasing improved methods for the carrying on of his undertakings, it is equally, if not more important, that he should fully realize to what extent his success and progress depend upon a thorough and efficient system of keeping his accounts. Day after day we find private concerns, partnerships and companies launching out upon the business world, invariably with the one object of gain in view. The question, which we have come to consider this evening, is not what is the manner in which this end should be reached, for that in each case will depend upon the nature of the undertaking, but rather what are the best methods for arriving at a knowledge of the true state of the business at any time, and at the actual results of it for the period under consideration.

Such is the purpose of this paper, which has been termed Revenue Accounts. In turning to Webster, I find that he defines Revenue in this way:

(1) In a general sense, the annual rents, profits, interest or issues, of any species of property real or personal, belonging to an individual or to the public, when used of individuals it is equivalent to income. In modern usages "income" is applied more generally to the rents and profits of individuals and Revenue to those of State. In this latter application Revenue is:

(2) The annual produce of taxes, excise customs, duties, rents, etc., which a nation or State collects and receives into the treasury for public use.

(3) Return, reward, as a rich Revenue of praise.

A great landed proprietor whose whole income is derived from rents, or a millionaire, who derives his entirely from interest on bonds, or dividends on stocks, might state with a certain degree of correctness that Revenue was his total receipts without any deduction on account of expenditure; but considerable qualification would have to be made in this definition before a firm or company trading in cash and goods could do so. Revenue, as applied to the latter, represents the amount earned during any period under consideration, and this amount is shown by the excess of the profits and income over the expenses and losses. If, however, as it sometimes occurs, the expenses and losses are greater than the profits and income, then there is no Revenue, but rather a loss and a reduction of capital.

Here let me call attention to the fact that, in many instances, there will be found parties who confuse cash receipts with Revenue and who think they are identical. Such, however, as you are aware, is not the case; the debit side of the former represents only the actual cash received, while in the latter the credit side includes the earnings of the business whether they have been received or not. The credit side of cash gives a list of the actual amount of cash paid out, and on the debit side of Revenue account is found the expenditure whether the amounts therein set forth have been paid or not at the time such statement is made out. The difference between the two sides of the cash account will be the cash on hand. In the Revenue account the difference will show the profit or loss. If the credit side of the Revenue is the greater the result will be a profit. If, unfortunately, the debit side is the larger, the excess will be a loss. Now that we fairly understand what the Revenue account is we will next consider the form of Revenue account that will best show the results of the undertaking and also the various ledger accounts which affect the result of it.

*Paper read at a meeting of the Institute of Chartered Accountants of Ontario, Thursday, 14th April, 1898, by W. T. Kernahan, C. A., Second Vice-President.

To raise a correct Profit and Loss Account is not such an easy matter as inexperienced people would suppose. To know how a man is doing it is not enough that he be asked how his bank account is and how much he owes now as compared with the same time last year, although there will be found not unfrequently persons who think this sufficient; but rather his books should be kept in such a manner that he may be able to know from them not only what the Profit and Loss has been for any term, but they should also contain the particulars of income and expenditure from which comparative statements can be made, so that in the event of the results of the business not being satisfactory, the proprietor could tell which department was drawing too heavily on the concern.

In his admirable paper read here two meetings ago, Mr. Tindall pointed out the necessity of keeping the accounts so that the manufacturer could tell the exact cost of the articles which were being turned out, and as he spoke of the wisdom of having such records as to the cost of articles, so I state that it is equally essential that the various departments of a concern should have separate accounts kept for them, each of which should be charged with all the amounts pertaining directly to it, so that when the Revenue Account is drawn up it will show the actual results of each department.

In an ordinary manufacturing concern the Revenue Account is generally separated into three parts, or, as some prefer to call them, divisions, viz.: 1st, The Trading Account, showing the gross profit; 2d, The Profit and Loss Account, showing the net profit or loss, and 3d, the distribution of such profit.

Taking the first division called Trading Account, we find it debited first with the stock on hand at the date of last stock taking, which in a manufacturing concern would include raw materials, materials manufactured, and in process of manufacture. To this is added the purchases during the period, and care must be taken to see that all the goods which have been receiv?d and taken into stock have been correctly charged and proper credit given for them. The amounts representing stock and purchases would include freight and duty charges and fuel used in production.

REVENUE ACCOUNT FOR THE YEAR ENDING MARCH 31, 1898. TRADING ACCOUNT.

To Stock on Hand, 31 Mar., 1897.		
Raw Materials	$3,000	
Stock Unfinished	1,000	
Stock Manufactured	8,000	$12,000
Purchases	54,500	
Less Returns	500	58,000
Freight and Duty		1,000
Fuse for Power		1,000
Wages		8,000
Balance carried down, being Gross Profit		23,860
		$103,860
By Sales	$90,862	
Less Trade Dis.. $1,000		
Less Returns 562	1,562	$89,300
Stock on Hand, 31 Mar., 1898.		
Raw Materials	2,000	
Stock Unfinished	3,000	
Stock Manufactured	9,560	14,560
		$103,860

PROFIT AND LOSS.

To Rent	$2,000	
Less paid by Sub-Tenants	600	$1,400
Taxes		200
General Expenses		1,380
Traveling Expenses		2,200
Salaries		2,820
Salaries of Management		3,000
Insurance		250
Advertising		400
Interest		150
Cash Discount		300
Law Costs and Collection Charges		100
Stable Expenses		800
Fuel Heating		350
Repairs		800
Depreciation on Building, 2½% of $20,000		500
Depreciation on Machinery, 7% of $12,000		840
Commissions		125
Bad and Doubtful Debts		660
Preliminary Expenses being 4th, last division		125
Balance being Net Profit for year, carried down		7,480
		$23,880
By Gross Profit from Trading Account		$23,860
Transfer Fees		20
		$23,880

PROFIT AND LOSS, No. 2.

To Special Reserve, being 5% on Capital Stock of $40,000 in conformity with By-Law No. 10	$2,000
Dividend being 10% on $40,000	4,000
Balance carried down to next year	3,000
	$9,000
By Balance at credit, 31 March, 1897	$1,520
Net Profit for year ending 31 March, 1898	7,480
	$9,000

The item of wages should include the amounts paid and due to all those who are directly engaged in the manufacture of the goods, including, where practicable, those of the foreman. I say where practicable, for the reason that in some instances the foreman's time is spent in several departments and, therefore, it may not be easily ascertained how much of it should be charged to each department. If, however, such a division can be made, the result will be more satisfactory. The amount charged for wages should correspond with the entries in the wage-book, which should be kept by one of the office staff, the amounts paid out by another of the office staff. In this way there would be no payments to others than those actually employed.

These three items constitute the total debits against which on the credit side are entered the sales during the period (less returns and trade discounts) and the stock on hand at the end of the term.

In checking over the sales, attention should be paid to see that credit was not taken for sales which were not filled until after stock had been taken and were not deducted from stock at the time the account was being made up.

The item representing stock on hand, is one which can be made the temporary escape of the results of a bad year, and a person desirous of selling out to advantage, not unfrequently uses the stock item as the means of fraudulent misrepresentations.

The stock should be taken by the heads of the various departments, each of whom should certify to the correctness of his returns, and hand them in to one of the proprietors who should see that the proper prices are entered and that the extensions and additions are correct. Of course, proper allowance would have to be made in the stock-taking for depreciation on shop worn and out-of-date goods.

The balance of the Trading Account will be the gross profit which is carried down to the second division to the credit of Profit and Loss. I say the balance so carried down will be the gross profit, for the reason that the first division should always show a gross profit, unless the goods were sacrificed below cost, or were destroyed.

In making up the Trading Account some prefer to enter in a subsiduary column the last stock-taking and add thereto the purchases during the period, and from the total deduct the stock on hand at closing, carrying the difference into the outer column—thus showing the goods actually used. The result in either case, however, is the same. Some there are who contend that rent and taxes should be a charge in the Trading rather than in the Profit and Loss Account, but to me it appears that the trader, who adopts the plan that I have above set out, will have a better idea of what his gross profit is, and as it is upon this that he bases his estimates of net profits, I think that only the items which I have just named should be considered under the first heading.

There is, however, another very strong reason why rent and taxes should not be included in the first division or Trading Account, which can, perhaps, best be explained by way of example.

There are three men, friendly to each other, in the same line of manufacturing business, but operating at different points, the factories being in Montreal, Toronto and Peterboro. The Montreal man pays a heavy rental and a good sized tax bill. The Toronto man owns his own factory, free of incumbrances and, therefore, has only taxes to pay. Peterboro being a bonusing town, the factory man there is free from taxes and pays a low rental. Now assuming that these three men came together for the purpose of comparing their gross profit percentages, in the first instance the difference, if any, would probably be very slight, but if each had included in his Trading Account the items of rent and taxes, you will readily see that, so far as comparisons are concerned, the results would be useless, for the Peterboro man, whose gross profit percentage under the first proposition was the lowest, shows up differently under the second method.

Referring to gross profits Mr. L. R. Dicksee, F. C. A., says: "It would be difficult to find an exact definition to the term gross profit, inasmuch as the items from which it is calculated will be found to vary in different undertakings, but seeing that the whole business of a trader is based upon calculations of a fixed percentage of gross profit upon each different class of goods dealt with, I think it necessarily follows that any form of accounts which does not recognize the existence of such a thing as gross profits fails to afford the trader that assistance which he is entitled to look for from his accounts, and consequently to a very great extent fails to justify its existence.

"I have heard it argued by many experienced accountants that gross profit cannot be considered to arise until such things as rent of warehouse, salaries of warehousemen, etc., have been debited to the Trading Account, but as it is the almost universal custom of traders to reckon their percentage of gross profit entirely from the cost price of their goods (although as a matter of convenience they actually make the calculation backwards from the selling price) it seems to me that, however correct it may be in theory, it is in practice nothing more than pedantic to include in this first section of the Profit and Loss Account anything more than sales and the closing stock upon the credit side, and purchases and the opening stock upon the debit. It is, of course, quite possible to argue that the resultant credit balance means absolutely nothing at all, but, even if this is so, the fact remains that, unless we so prepare an account, it is impossible for us to see, or for the trader himself to see, whether the aggregate transactions of a period actually result in the percentage of gross profit which he had been calculating upon throughout the period, and therefore, I think, that whether we choose to call the balance of this first section "Gross Profit," or whether we merely employ the indefinite term "Balance," the overwhelming weight of advantage lies in our bringing our account, in this respect at least, into accord with the custom of every trader, and so enabling him to ascertain whether during any period he has actually achieved the results which he anticipated."

Before leaving the Trading Account let me say this to those who are just starting out, if there be any such here, that on assuming the position of bookkeeper or accountant an endeavor should be made as early as possible to ascertain upon what basis the proprietor has been making his calculations of Gross Profit, and having become conversant with it this system should be followed, so long as no principle is involved, even though it may not be on the same lines as those advanced by experienced accountants. For a man who has been for years following the same method of computations cannot be expected to switch off from the old way to accept the new ones unless there are very strong reasons for doing so, for this would necessitate the adjustment of a new basis of figuring which to him might be confusing. If, however, the system under which he is working does not meet your views, it would be no difficult task after preparing the statements for him to make out another set in a different manner showing the results by the other methods. The proprietor would in this way thoroughly grasp the results of his business.

In the second division against the balance of gross profit brought down we will find such charges as these, rent, taxes, general expenses, traveling expenses, salaries, insurance, advertising, interest and discount, law costs and collection charges, commissions, stable expenses, repairs, fuel, bad debts, depreciation, etc. The balance will then show the net profit or loss of the business for the past term.

Some of these charges require particular study and we shall consider them in the order in which they appear in the account.

Rent. As I pointed out before, amounts due regardless of the fact as to whether they are paid or not at the time at which the statement is being made up, must be taken into consideration and the proper accounts charged therewith. This applies to Rent Account, which therefore must be charged with the amount paid and due at the date of closing. If, as in many instances, the premises are too large for the requirements of the undertaking, and parts are rented to sub-tenants, the rents so derived from the sub-tenants are credited to Rent Account, and the balance only of this account is charged to Revenue Account, instead of charging that account with the total rent paid and crediting it with the amount received from the sub-tenants. In making the charge, however, in the Revenue Account, the total rent can be entered in the subsidiary column, from which will be deducted the amounts paid by the sub-tenants and the balance carried to the other column.

Taxes. If the taxes have been paid to the end of the calendar year and the financial year ends at a different period, the Revenue Account must be charged only with a proportionate amount up to the time of closing, and the balance carried down will appear in the balance sheet as an asset. Insurance premiums will be treated in the same manner. If, however, the taxes have not been paid then Revenue should be charged with the pro rata amount due, and this will be shown in the balance sheet as a liability. The taxes for the current year can generally be figured out from the Assessment sheets, but, if the rate has not yet been made, it is usually fair to make the charge on the basis of the past year unless it is known that a considerable difference will be made for the year under discussion. In this event an estimate based upon the peculiar circumstances will suffice.

General Expenses. This is an item which can be made to cover a multitude of sins, and, therefore, is one which should be gone into minutely in order to see that there is a voucher for every item as well as authority for every payment, and that nothing has been charged to it which is not proper, for frequently items which should have gone to personal accounts have found their way into this account.

Traveling Expenses. The same remarks apply to this, but in addition the Travelers should make out a detailed list of their expenses for each trip on forms furnished them, giving the railway fares from place to place, livery if any, hotel bills at each point, and any incidental extra expenses that there may be, which should be signed and sent in weekly or handed in with the Traveler's collection account at the end of the trip. These are then examined to see that the charges are not too high, and in case a limit is placed on his expenses, to see that such limit has not been exceeded. As the day and date are on each statement, double charges cannot be very well made. Where a stipulated sum per day is allowed, out of which the Traveler must pay all his expenses, there is no necessity for such forms being sent in, but, in lieu thereof, some form of report should be adopted which would show the actual time the Traveler was out on the road and entitled to expense money. Most Travelers spend periods of the year in the warehouse, and during that time should not, as a rule, draw the full expense money.

Salaries. These are treated in the same manner as wages, although there is not the same opportunity for carrying dummies on the salary list as there is in connection with wages.

Advertising. This is an expenditure upon which there is considerable difference of opinion, and the amounts charged against Revenue will in a great measure depend upon the nature of the business and the advertising done. If it were confined to newspaper and magazine lines, the account could be dealt with much in the same manner as taxes and insurance, but where the concern has sent out "Specials" in the shape of fancy and expensive show cards, souvenirs, etc., then the question arises, should the total expenditure be charged against the period in which the advertising is done, or should credit be taken for part of it, and be treated in the balance sheet as an asset? My opinion is that where the business is such that this class of advertising is done year in and year out the total expenditure for such should be charged against its own year, save of course any advertising matter that may be on hand; but if it is something extra, then it might be divided over as many years as the estimated life of it. It is contended by some that, as the benefits of the advertising do not accrue some times until long after the expenditure, that part of it only should be charged against Revenue in the year in which the advertising was done, but if this procedure were followed year after year, it would, I think, be the means of raising a will-o'-the-wisp asset that might eventually prove to be a source of trouble.

Interest and Discount. Interest received on investments, and accrued interest to date of closing, should go to the credit of Profit and Loss, but in the event of interest having been paid in advance credit only should be taken for the amount earned. If the company has borrowed money on debentures or mortgages, the interest on them should be charged in a separate sum in the Revenue Account. The principal charges of interest and discount are familiar to every one, but, at closing, an examination should be made to see that, in cases where large sums have been paid in advance for the use of money, allowances have been made for the balance of the time the money had been borrowed beyond the date of closing. In ordinary trading concerns this would not be of much consideration, but in a bank doing a large discount business this would be an important item. Provision must be made in a manufacturing or trading concern for discounts that will be allowed for cash payments, the volume of which will depend upon the amounts outstanding subject to discount, and the time in which payments may be made subject to such cash discounts. As it frequently requires thousands of dollars of a reserve for those discounts it will, therefore, be seen that the question of how much should be charged to Revenue is a most important one, particularly where the year has not been as prosperous as had been expected, for the tendency with the directors of a company desirous of paying a dividend might be to reduce such reserve below the proper figure.

LAW COSTS AND COLLECTION CHARGES. "Keep out of law" is a common expression, and though we are all disposed to follow this advice, yet, in spite of all our carefulness, occasions do arise where, even though we keep out of a lawsuit, we have run up a fair-sized bill of costs and under this heading we must charge such expenditure regardless as to whether the bill has been paid or not.

STABLE EXPENSES AND FUEL. These require no special comment apart from the observation that attention should be paid to the items making up these accounts to see that they do not contain any charges that should have been made to personal accounts, for it is an every-day occurrence to find the employees of large concerns purchasing through their firm fuel at reduced rates, and, unless a strict supervision is kept over these accounts, some of the items which should have been paid for by the employees could be charged to Fuel Account.

DEPRECIATION. Of all the questions that are open for consideration there are none I think which provoke so much discussion as the subject of Depreciation. It is not in the fact of the necessity of charging for it that the difference of opinion arises, but rather in the methods of arriving at what should be written off as well as the volume. In writing on this question, Mr. E. Guthrie puts it in this way: "What is a manufacturer? and what is involved in the performance of the acts necessary to his business? A manufacturer is one who produces goods for sale. Production implies consumption. The value and volume of consumption represent the cost of the produce. The difference between the volume or value of that which is consumed and the volume or value of that which is produced is the profit or loss of the manufacturer. How important then that the volume or value of that which is consumed should be accurately ascertained. To ascertain that volume or value of cost every constituent element must be ascertained, weighed and measured. What are they in this case? What does the manufacturer consume? Raw materials, stores, labor direct, outside services, machinery and buildings. There is, however, an essential difference between the first four named and the last two named elements of cost. The difference is (and in this relation it is the only difference) that the first enumerated are consumed absolutely within the period concerned, excepting a measurable residue for immediate consumption in the succeeding period, while the last enumerated are consumed over a number of years. From year to year neither the precise value consumed nor the residue of value carried on from year to year is exactly measurable. We have, therefore, to base the charges for depreciation upon the assumption of a certain term of useful existence of the machinery or building; this term is called 'the life' of the machine or building."

From this, then, it follows that the total value of the building or machine must be written off during its estimated life or a reserve fund of sufficient size should be set aside year by year to provide for its replacement. That which has no residual value should be divided by the number of years and an equal amount be written off annually, while depreciation on property having a residual value should be charged on the diminishing value.

There is one serious and important consideration in connection with writing the depreciation off the several accounts which it is, perhaps, wise to mention, for this method may in some instances lead to litigation. Take a company, the directors of which thoroughly appreciate the importance of depreciation, and who in their desire of placing the business on a sound financial basis, rather than paying large dividends, write off each year large sums for depreciation on machinery, etc. In a few years they have practically written off the total value of the machines which to all intents and purposes are quite good and will do the work for some time to come equally as satisfactory as new machines. Now just at this juncture a fire occurs, the property is entirely destroyed and is fully covered by insurance. In the adjustment of the loss the books are produced and it would indeed be a most difficult matter to convince the adjusters that the amounts set out in the different accounts did not represent the full value of the machines, etc., and consequently if a loss were paid on the basis of the balances set out in the books, the trading company might sustain a considerable loss. On the other hand, if, instead of writing off the depreciation on the various accounts, a special account were opened for depreciation and adequate amounts credited to it the results of the Profit and Loss Account would be the same, while the difficulty above cited would be overcome. In the event of a loss an independent adjustment of the various items covered under the policy could be made each on its own merits.

Let me not be understood as suggesting that the insurance companies in the adjustment of losses are desirous of taking advantage of every or any point in their favor. From my experience in the insurance business, I can bear witness that they are always anxious to ascertain and pay for the actual loss sustained; but it is a difficult thing to convince any man that the actual value of that which he is buying is more than the value placed upon it in the owner's books. If the latter case were followed in the Balance Sheet, Capital Account of Buildings, Machinery, etc., would show in a subsidiary colume the total amount at the debit of each, from which would be deducted the sum standing at the credit of depreciation, and the balance carried to the outer column would be the same as though depreciation had been deducted from each of the accounts.

REPAIRS. This is an account which can very easily be misused, and the results of a business can be materially affected if expenditure properly chargeable to it is posted to Capital Account. Repairs is the term used to designate what has been expended to keep the property of the business in good working condition, and no item which only represents a replacement of a worn or broken part should find its way into Capital Account. But in extraordinary cases where the value of the property has been materially increased in a permanent manner, then it is in order to charge Capital with the bare amount of such increase. In a factory that is well looked after and where every weakness in the buildings and plant is immediately strengthened, and where a properly kept Repairs Account is opened, very little trouble will arise in arriving at the proper sum to be written off for depreciation, and the better the condition in which the property is kept the less will have to be deducted for depreciation.

BAD AND DOUBTFUL DEBITS. Every concern doing a credit trade is bound to make losses on some of its accounts, and, at the time the books are being closed, it become necessary to go through the list of outstanding balances to ascertain what are the probabilities of collecting them. Such balances as are known to be irretrievably bad must be written off without any hesitation, but the trouble arises in estimating what will be the probable loss on the remaining accounts. Every item outstanding is subject to some degree of uncertainty, but many of them can be passed under ordinary circumstances as being good. Some there are who write off a fixed percentage each year for bad accounts, but I think the surest and most effectual method is, when at all possible, for one of the proprietors to go through with the credit clerk the list of the ledger balances and consider each on its own merits. This will undoubtedly take more time than figuring by a guess rate per cent., but the results should certainly make up for the extra labor, although in some instances the estimates in each case might be similar. By doing this the proprietor is brought in closer touch with the true condition of the accounts outstanding, and he will then be in a better position to know whether any immediate action should be taken in connection with the collection of any of them.

COMMISSIONS. Where the nature of the business is such that Commission is a factor in arriving at the amount which should be charged to Revenue, a similar method should be adopted as was followed in Interest and Discount.

PRELIMINARY EXPENSES. In new companies, where the expenses of organization have been large, it is customary and allowable to open an account under the heading of Preliminary Expenses, in order to distribute the charges over a period of say three and not more than five years.

The balance, therefore, will represent the net profit or net loss for the period and is brought down to the third division where the distribution of the profits (if such there be) is made. In the case of a partnership in which any of the partners are entitled to interest on capital it is charged there, and the balance is divided according to the terms of the partnership. With a company, this division will show the balance, if any, carried forward from the previous year's profits, and it is in this division that the proposed dividends are charged, as well as any special reserve fund that is being raised, the balance being carried forward to the next account. If, however, there had been a deficiency in former Revenue Accounts, it would be necessary to cover such deficiency before any profits would be available for dividend, and if the past year has also proved disastrous, of course no dividend can be paid at all. It has been held that the holders of preference shares were entitled to their percentage of the profits of the year's business, regardless of any deficiency shown in previous years, so long as the Capital was restored to the position it was in at the commencement of the year.

In a small partnership concern it might not be necessary to have a second division of Profit and Loss Account, but if such were omitted it would, however, be best to show in the Profit and Loss Account the amount, if any, of interest paid each of the partners on Capital. In closing I may say there are many other items which would appear in a Revenue Account that I have not touched upon here, for each particular business has its own accounts, but I think the ones to which I have called attention will properly serve the purposes for which this paper was intended.

How Fortune plies her sports when she begins to practice them!—Ben Johnson.

Blest are those whose blood and judgment are so well commingled that they are not a pipe for Fortune's finger to sound what stop she pleases.—Shakespeare.

Credits and Collections*

By F. H. Bosson, C. A.

It is an indication of breadth in the Institute of Accounts to include in its subjects for discussion business topics that are not technically connected with the details of accounting. While credits and collections are very closely allied with the accounts of all concerns, yet many accountants have nothing whatever to do with them, the responsibility being assumed by the financial partner, treasurer of the corporation, or, in large concerns, by the so-called "Credit man," who has charge of this department.

The bookkeeper, however, should consider himself a possible candidate for promotion to this grade of service. His familiarity with the accounts renders him one of the most available persons for the position, and not a few accountants have developed into credit men. Some principles and methods suggested by long experience and producing satisfactory results may, therefore, be of interest and some profit to the members of this chapter.

First and foremost, the same man should bear the responsibility of deciding credits and making collections. The reason is obvious. No matter how good his judgment in extending credit, an element of wholesome caution is introduced when he realizes that he is to be held responsible for the collection of the account on which he has authorized credit.

Beginning at the credit end, the first question suggested is, What constitutes a basis for credit and how should the various credit limits be regulated? Information (facts in preference to opinions) relative to the prospective customer must, of course, be the guide for establishing his credit; and this may be obtained in various ways. Commercial agency reports, trade experience, bankers' opinions, and, better than all else, a personal financial statement from the party himself, are some of the common methods of acquiring the desired information. The facts in the case should be carefully studied and a credit limit placed on the account. Now, in an ideal

*A paper read before the Hartford Chapter of the Institute of Accounts September 27, 1897.

basis for credit, three essential elements always exist—character, capital and capacity; three C's, and, therefore, easily remembered. Unfortunately, they are not always present, and the absence of any one should have an important bearing on a man's credit limit.

The first element mentioned—character—should always be considered absolutely necessary. No person who is known to be dishonest, that is, lacking in integrity, should be considered worthy of a line of credit. No matter what his capital, he can easily evade his debts and cause greater expenditure in the collection of his account that the profit on his patronage amounts to. Besides there is no comfort or satisfaction in dealing with people of that class.

The customer, then, must be honest to begin with. But some say, "Is not that sufficient?" It may be for a very limited line in the necessaries of life, where the party is not in business on his own account and has a permanent position, but in considering commercial credits, honesty alone is not a sufficient basis, for the reason that any one of several conditions often make it impossible for an honest man to pay his debts. He may have character, but no capacity; incapable and a poor manager; his losses through poor judgment become his creditors' losses; or he may be unfortunate; and, in case of accident, sickness, etc., somehow the living expenses are usually taken care of before the outside creditors are provided for.

Next comes the element of capital or net resources, the man's financial worth. The character question having been settled, the line of credit that should be extended is determined largely by the amount of capital involved, although a very important item is the relative amount of liabilities to net worth. For instance, two customers show the same amount of capital, say $10,000; one has assets amounting to $22,000, liabilities $12,000; the other assets $12,000 liabilities $2,000. The first would be entitled to very limited credit, if any; in fact, this condition usually reveals a candidate for failure. The latter is in a healthy condition and the account could be accepted with reasonable safety on a credit limit of $1,000. "Isn't that pretty small?" some one may say, "for a $10,000 capital and a healthy condition?" Well, there are various other questions involved, and this suggests our third element, capacity or ability.

If the debtor has just inherited his resources and is known as a man of inferior capacity and little business experience, give him a moderate limit and watch the account carefully. On the other hand, if he is known as an energetic, capable man who has accumulated his capital by his own efforts, and, therefore, knows the value of it, the risk is correspondingly reduced and the credit limit can safely be increased. It will thus be seen that no two cases are exactly alike; hence the difficulty in establishing a definite rule to regulate credit limits.

In a general way, and as a foundation to be built upon, 10 per cent. of the customer's capital is a reasonably safe limit with which to open an account, other conditions being favorable. Once on the books, the behavior of the customer has a vital bearing on limit already fixed. If he discounts his bills or pays promptly at maturity and causes little or no trouble with unjust claims and disputes, his limit may safely be increased to 20 per cent. or even 30 per cent. If, however, he is slow and unsatisfactory, credit should be restricted and the limit reduced accordingly, and in some cases entirely revoked.

A large volume of business is transacted without any credit basis or limit whatever, that is, for cash with order, C. O. D., draft against bill lading, and under a guarantee or bond. Is this class of trade desirable? Some think not; but a little thought will reveal the fact that it is perfectly safe, a fundamental requirement, and, in some cases, more goods are sold than could be disposed of to another party on credit and time.

The writer has in mind a case where $10,000 worth of goods were purchased in a year on a strictly cash basis (draft against express receipt). It is doubtful if another customer could have been found in the town to have done one-quarter the amount on credit, because the first man had the trade and understood remarkably well the sale of the goods handled. So circumstances alter cases, and the credit man cannot afford to be too technical and watch only his personal record, represented by percentage of losses, to aggregate sales at the end of the season. He must have in mind that unseen line representing the largest amount of business for his concern at a conservative and reasonable risk; for risk there is bound to be and losses from bad accounts. These, however, reach their minimum when correct principles are applied and a proper system of collections is established and rigidly adhered to.

This brings us to the second division of our subject—Collections.

Twice each month, the 1st and the 15th, has been demonstrated to be the most effective plan for sending dunning letters. Greater frequency is apt to cause indifference and bad feeling on the part of the debtor. Less frequency is decidedly unsafe and should never be allowed. Efficiency in collections is due very large to absolute regularity. On the dates mentioned above, every account on the books should be examined and treated in accordance with its age and condition.

The first letter sent is one of the most important. It is a simple request for settlement of account overdue and contains nothing that can offend the most sensitive, and yet it educates the customer to feel that payments are expected promptly at maturity. This may be sent if account is from three to fifteen days overdue. Failing to bring remittance, No. 2, a little stronger, is sent at the next dunning period. If this fails in its purpose, the next time for dunning finds the account a month overdue and a draft at three days' sight should now be sent, in connection with letter No. 3. If draft is returned unpaid, No. 4 is the letter, expressing surprise at such an occurrence and insisting on immediate attention with settlement. The next number on the programme, 5, hints at legal measures. No. 6 threatens to hand the claim to attorney for decisive action, unless settled within one week from date. No. 7 is the last resort, in the shape of a telegram, "Must have settlement immediately. Will positively wait no longer." If the telegram is ignored for two days, nothing remains excepting to place the claim with attorney for collection. These claims should be kept in a separate attorney's file, containing particulars of the account and all correspondence bearing upon it. When paid or returned as uncollectible, transfer them to a "defunct" file, alphabetically arranged.

Watch the attorney and obtain reports on the claim in his hands at reasonable intervals.

In cases secured by guarantee, letter No. 5 on the programme is to be replaced by No. 8, which threatens to call on surety for payment. This, in cases of guarantee, to be followed by No. 9, calling on surety for payment under the bond. Failing of result, No. 6 is to be sent both customer and surety.

Care should be exercised at point of letter No. 5, to ascertain if account is secured by guarantee, in order to modify subsequent letters accordingly.

Courtesy, dignity and firmness should characterize all correspondence bearing on credits and collections. One should never lower himself to the plane of the man who tries to be smart by using cheap, impertinent language. There may be temptations to "answer back." Always resist them and pursue the "even tenor of your way" to the end of the "programme."

Old and New Methods of Keeping the Cash Account and the Bank Account*

By A. C. Neff, C. A.

(Continued from page V, December issue)

While this method has its advantages in that it show the junior in accounts the true character of the entries, in these progressive days, it can scarcely be considered a satisfactory method for use, in any business, but one having a very limited Bank account.

Still, one sometimes meets with the use of a Ledger Account, the deposits being posted for the Cash Book, and the cheques being journalized and posted from the Journal in total or detail.

As it is often desirable to know the full amount of receipts and payments, and of the Cash on hand, including both Cash in office and Cash in Bank, it is a common practice to treat the Cash in Bank as though it were part of the Cash in the office, the Ledger Account for the Bank is therefore dropped, and the record of the transactions with the Bank is kept on the stubs of the cheque book.

This method is largely taught and used, but I have never found it satisfactory. It takes no account in the books of the relations of the Bank, as a corporation, with the business.

*A paper read before the Institute of Chartered Accountants of Ontario at the opening of the session for 1898-99.

The record depends upon the paid cheques and drafts, the cheque stubs and the Bank pass book. The pass book shows amounts only, and does not include unpresented cheques. The record on cheques and stubs is liable to be very meagre as to particulars, and the entries on the stubs are often entirely neglected, and are not as likely to be safely kept as records in regular books. If they are lost all record is gone.

I recently met with a case where the only record of the expenditure of over $50,000 had been the pass book, cheques and stubs, the only book record was a printed report of a part of the expenditure. Part of the stubs and part of the cheques were lost, and we were obliged to get copies of the pass book from the Bank.

A common result of this method is that there is not sufficient record in detail of the bank transactions to enable one to use it to the best advantage as a check upon the cash book.

Where any doubt rests upon the Cash account, important light upon the case is usually got by comparison of the Bank account with the Cash, item by item. If there is a proper record of the account in the books, it is much more readily compared, and more likely to be correct, than by the method now under discussion.

Another objection to this method is that a cheque book has but a few items on a page, and the totals must be constantly forwarded, and but a small portion of the account can be seen at a time, and when the balance in the bank is required after the issue of a score or so of cheques, some figuring is necessary to arrive at it.

In order to meet this difficulty, there is sometimes provision made in the front or back of the cheque book for a list of the deposits and cheques, in the usual deposit Ledger form.

An improvement upon this method is the one in which the Bank transactions are incorporated into the Cash book by means of special columns. For this purpose there are two distinct methods taught and in use.

The first is that in which the deposits are entered in a special column, among the payments on the credit side, the cheques being entered in a special column, among the receipts on the debit side of the Cash Book, the payments made by these cheques being included among the payments made in Cash.

In the other method the deposits are entered in a special column for the Bank on the debit side of the Cash book, and Cash receipts which are deposited are entered there direct, as far as possible.

When the deposits do include Cash which had appeared in the Cash column of receipts, it is necessary to charge the amount thus included in the Cash column of payments. The payments by cheque are entered on the payment side in a special column for the Bank.

In the first method all the transactions with the Bank are incorporated into the Cash.

The monthly totals of deposits and cheques are posted to a Bank account in the Ledger, the balance in the bank being shown there, though the adjustment is frequently worked out as a memorandum in the Cash Book.

The Cash Balance covers only Cash in the office.

The second method is a combination of the Cash account and the Bank account in the same book in columns side by side, but entirely separate, each account having its own balance.

Both these methods present the advantage of bringing together all the receipts and payments whether in Cash or through the Bank.

In the first method each cheque calls for an entry on both sides of the Cash Book. In the second method only a part of the deposits call for two entries.

For ordinary use, the first is probably the better of the two, but the second is convenient where all or nearly all cash received goes on deposit, and all payments are made by cheque, as in the case of a Municipality or an Association.

Where there are considerable transactions with the Cash in the office as well as with the Bank, and where it is not necessary to report the receipts and disbursements, I have for many years used a method which I have not until recently seen described by any author.

Just as the Cash Account is taken out of the Ledger and put in a separate cover, and developed into a book of original entry and a posting medium, so I have separated and developed the Bank account.

Discarding the cheque stubs, I have first entered in the book the full particulars of a payment to be made by cheque, then filled in the blank cheque in accordance with the entry. The particulars of a deposit are entered here at the time the deposit is made.

The deposits and cheques with full particulars are thus always entered right up to date, and the balance in the bank undrawn against is apparent at any time. Thirty or forty transactions are in full view on a page. By checking off the checques presented at the bank, whenever the pass book has been written up, it is at once apparent what cheques are outstanding. At the end of the month it is balanced and adjusted with the Pass Book, by allowing for cheques outstanding.

It can be kept posted up from day to day, and all desirable provision can be made for posting in monthly totals, by the use of special columns, just as in the Cash Book. In fact, it is but a sub-division of the Cash, but with the added feature of keeping up the personal account with the Bank.

Where several Bank accounts are current, I open a separate place for each in the book, devoting to each as much space as seems necessary.

This method has proved so convenient and satisfactory wherever I have used it, that I have never known it to be discarded where once established.

It gives the completest kind of control over the Bank account, and is an exceedingly satisfactory kind of record for an auditor to have placed before him, for he can test it with the bank pass book with such comfortable certainty, and there is no intervention of cash or any other transactions to interfere with the clearness of the record.

It is equally useful for either a small or large account. It is just the thing for a pocket book record of a private bank account, and it has proved to be almost indispensable in a business where more than five hundred cheques a month were being issued, for it gives the financial manager full control of his Bank Account.

Where it is necessary to report the Receipts and Disbursements of a business, as in the case of financial companies, this method scarcely answers the purpose.

Some record is required which combines the Cash and Bank Accounts, but which also provides for all the desirable features which we have been discussing, and avoids as far as possible the undesirable ones.

The recently authorized Municipal Cash Book introduces a novel effort in this direction. It consists of four columns for the Bank Account, on the payment side of the Cash Book, immediately following the particulars and voucher number. The columns are Dr. Bank, Cr. Bank, Dr. Balance, and Cr. Balance.

The ruling distinctly separates these columns from those which follow, which are for salaries and other expenses of the Municipality. This form seems to present a peculiarity in balancing owing to the situation of the columns for deposits, but as I have had no experience of it in operation, I am not in a position to criticise it.

I submit as much of the form as is necessary to illustrate the point which I refer to.

I had occasion early last year to draw the form for a Cash Book, and with the object of combining the Cash and two Bank accounts under one set of voucher numbers, and into one columnar analysis, I introduced the Bank accounts on the payment side, but in quite a different manner from that just mentioned. I submit as much of the form as is necessary to bring out the method of dealing with the Bank account.

Besides the advantage of having the vouchers all together and in consecutive order, no matter from what source paid, it provides or those cases where payments are made partly in Cash and partly by cheque, or partly by cheque from one bank and partly from the other.

The form has proved a success in all but one respect.

It does not furnish any better means of balancing the Bank accounts, and adjusting them by the cheques outstanding, than that furnished by the usual combined Cash and Bank Account, and it becomes desirable to keep a summary of the Bank Account in the Ledger.

It will be noticed that it retains the previously mentioned features of complete posting analysis, and self-balancing test of the accuracy of the Cash Book and posting totals.

I should, perhaps, have dealt with the Cash Journal earlier in the paper. This is an example of an effort at labor-saving by putting the entire transactions of a business including the Cash into one book, and analyzing them into monthly total columns, only the sundries column.

which includes personal accounts, being posted in detail.

I am not familiar with the use of this book, but while I recognize some advantage in the gathering into one monthly posting total of all the expenditure for any purpose, whether cash or credit, it appears to me it must interfere with the division of labor, as soon as a business reaches those proportions which require it.

It appears to me I should prefer the columnar analysis of the Journal distinct and separate from the Cash Book.

I cannot claim to have exhausted the subject with which I have dealt, though I have endeavored to present all the features of main importance, so as to provide that which I think all our paper should claim to furnish, namely, the basis for discussion.

I leave the paper to your friendly criticism with the hope that I may reap a benefit from it, in new or clearer ideas on the subject. For I expect to class myself with our student associates as a seeker after new light right through to the end of my humble career as an accountant.

In the course of my study, I have frequently felt the meagreness and elementary character of material dealing with the subject I have discussed. The result of the thought and development of which we see constant examples in the Cash Books in the better conducted offices around us seems not to reach publication.

Theory of Accounts

From various sources the information reaches us that on test occasions competent bookkeepers and accountants,—that is to say, those who appear to be competent, wofully fail in the theory of accounts. It has been intimated by those who know, that the lowest percentages of the candidates who submit themselves for the C. P. A. examinations in this State are found in the division entitled "Theory of Accounts." Those who pass well on practical accounting, auditing and commercial law, sometimes fall down completely in the theory of accounts. The reason for this is hard to explain.

We present below the questions on the theory of accounts used in the Regents' examination for the C. P. A. degree, June 14, 1898. They are well worth the consideration of all who aspire to proficiency in accounting according to the conditions established by the Regents. According to regulations, the first five questions are to be answered and five of the others, but no more. Each complete answer receives ten credits. Accordingly, there would be a total of one hundred credits. Seventy-five credits are necessary to pass:—

1. Describe fully each of the following accounts, showing what entries may be made on each side and what disposition should be made of the balance: (a) cash account, (b) interest account, (c) merchandise account, (d) suspense account, (e) real estate account.

2. Describe the following securities and show the essential features of each: (a) common stock, (b) preferred stock, (c) income bonds, (d) debenture bonds, (e) mortgage bonds.

3. Describe the process of taking a trial balance. State the purposes of the trial balance and show its relations to the balance sheet.

4. Give a rule for averaging the maturity of the balance of an account containing items of various dates on each side.

5. State in the form of journal entries the following transactions: (a) a note of a customer returned with protest charges from the bank where it had been left for collection, (b) the setting aside for wear and tear of a portion of the value of machinery, (c) the adjustment of interest accrued but not yet payable on a mortgage, (d) accommodation paper indorsed by the firm when coupon bonds are received as security.

6. In case of bonds purchased at a premium or at a discount, to be held till maturity, state how the price should be disposed of on the books at purchase, at maturity and at any intervening time.

7. Formulate, in an imaginary case, the journal entry or entries for the conversion of a partnership into a joint stock company with the same resources and liabilities.

8. Describe a voucher record for the expenditures of a corporation.

9. What is meant by good-will? What kind of property is good-will? May the good-will of a partnership be sold?

10. What names are given to accounts that represent the excess of assets over liabilities? Differentiate these names in their application to various kinds of business.

11. What is the proper course of procedure in taking charge of the bookkeeping of a firm that has either no books of account or very imperfect ones?

12. Describe fully a system by which occasional small sales made on credit to persons not regular customers may be recorded without opening a separate account with each purchaser.

13. Describe the most complicated form of cash book with which you are acquainted, showing its functions, the sources from which its materials are derived and where its results are carried.

14. Describe fully the method of keeping a bills receivable account, and state the connection of the account with the bill-book.

15. As the bookkeeper of a firm that had no articles of co-partnership, what would be your duty on learning of the death of a partner?

The Leaven in the Meal

It requires but a casual glance at current copies of the trade and commercial papers to perceive that the broad question of accounts is being brought more and more into prominence. That "accounting is the vital element of business," is being demonstrated by hundreds of pens to-day, where only one or two were in evidence a little while ago. It is well for business interests that this is so.

In a recent issue of the Outfitter, under the title, "The Books Were Wrong," we find the story that is reprinted below, and which has an obvious moral. It was preceded by a quotation from Charles Lamb, as follows:

"To a genuine accountant the difference in proceeds is as nothing. The fractional farthing is as dear to his heart as the thousands behind it."

The story thus introduced has its frequent counterpart in business life and was as follows:

One of the saddest scenes in the rough and tumble of life is a business failure—a failure that has come after honest and industrious effort, a sincere and apparently well-deserving struggle.

It is impossible in such a case not to feel the throb of sympathy, and it is equally impossible not to seek for the causes of such a failure. Not infrequently the trouble is with the books. Let us tell you a story.

Tall and handsome and good-natured was young Harry Effleham. He was a partner in the firm of Oaks & Effleham, outfitters in Tarbury, one of the smartest towns in the State. Oaks managed the business and Harry's father supplied the capital, at least half of it. They did a business of $70,000, nearly all credit, and had broad ideas. They failed and then, of course, they learned all about their affairs, when it was too late to do any good. The bookkeeping had been so blundering and slovenly that it would have been impossible for them to know where they stood at any time for three years back without an expert investigation.

Effleham senior lost heavily by the failure, but he had money left, the savings of a lifetime, and he started Harry again, this time in partnership with a hustling, brass-bound fellow, who had made a few thousands by a stroke of genuine luck, rare as such things are. Call him Jackson, if you like. He at once took the helm of the new concern and inside of a year had appropriated every cent of value he could carry away from under the noses of the Efflehams, and the result was another wreck. For lack of a proper record of the business the victims did not know what was happening to them until the wrecker had his booty and had fooled it away.

Still again Harry was started in business, this time with an honest and industrious partner. Harry kept the books, but his partner found that Harry's ideas of a business record were extremely hazy and unique. He kept no cash book at all. He kept no ledger account with the creditors, only with debtors. Though buying largely on four months and paying "on account," the payments were merely minuted on the bills, and to find out how much was due to pay at any time required a considerable search and mathematical calculation. A fair business was done, but it was impossible to predict a safe future, and after two or three years of hard work and growing anxiety the partner told Harry they must separate. Harry had not the means to buy—his father's were exhausted—and he sold out and went to clerking. And there he is now.

To be a shrewd planner or an energetic worker is scarcely more important to a business than to maintain an accurate account of the transactions, affording at all times a quick and intelligible view of the firm's standing and responsibilities.

Correspondence

ANALYSIS OF A BUSINESS.

From F. H. K., Toledo, Ohio.

I enclose, for the benefit of the readers of ACCOUNTICS, a copy of an analysis of a business which I submitted to a client a few days since. The information has been compiled from cash and credit sales slips covering the dates indicated. The form in which the matter is condensed, having met with the approval of my client, suggests the idea that there are probably many other business men who would be pleased if their bookkeepers would compile information of their respective enterprises in a similar form. The figures are "pro forma" for the purpose of demonstrating the utility of the formal statement.

Information of this character could be readily gathered from day to day by a single clerk, and entered in a production book kept for the purpose. It would be necessary to exercise care to group articles of a kindred nature together, and where possible also to group together those which bear a relatively average profit, thus making the information more valuable to those whose business it may be to peruse it.

Golden roofs break men's rest.—Seneca.

The difference between talent and genius is this: while the former usually develops some special branch of our faculties, the latter commands them all. When the former is combined with tact, it is often more than a match for the latter.

—Beaconsfield.

Analysis—Paint Department Sales—1897

Goods	Jan.	Feb	Mar	Apr	May	June	July	Aug	Sept	Oct	Nov	Dec	Total
D. Mixed Paint	40.30	695.45	1010.22	674.95	994.67	717.52	224.49	250.42	175.82	205.58	75.92	74.76	5938.05
F. Mixed Paint	5.45	11.26	6.90	14.15	5.76	5.65	9.65	.65	29.45	477.28	115.56		681.76
H. Floor Paint			5.48	2.25	7.88	5.66	.25	3.20	2.10	2.50	.25	1.25	31.12
Brushes	38.09	92.93	92.98	182.29	146.52	120.43	73.20	134.05	64.45	85.74	77.02	22.64	1130.84
Turpentine	44.50	45.13	34.21	48.01	121.93	38.20	73.58	29.21	27.71	49.92	38.45	65.52	568.81
Linseed Oil	238.33	1008.99	620.37	354.57	458.60	265.32	227.95	322.77	218.33	366.64	105.44	55.06	4265.57
Gold Leaf, Bronzes, etc.	29.62	18.37	59.43	59.97	55.71	82.83	33.81	66.25	70.64	55.30	56.80	10.23	598.96
Liquid Filler	51.15	86.05	44.65	62.55	102.30	40.90	24.40	32.90	50.25	24.90	32.20	21.75	572.
Paste Filler	1.72	6.39	18.81	.57	12.51	.75	1.80		3.37	3.74	4.85	.63	56.14
Dry Colors	104.29	80.30	141.25	184.79	257.07	179.58	125.70	112.74	163.11	99.63	80.62	62.98	1706.06
Oil Colors	32.78	45.06	74.45	57.96	99.98	84.99	56.16	88.48	62.19	67.60	37.42	15.67	719.76
Varnishes, Shellacs, Dryers	131.54	151.39	204.44	94.13	149.45	172.60	91.42	120.78	144.56	106.08	82.19	49.55	1499.54
Japan Colors	4.75	8.96	7.08	21.18	15.49	35.47	16.29	28.42	30.24	28.06	17.67	6.60	213.58
Pure Leads / Graded Leads	85.89	306.94	604.09	374.64	545.72	544.90	466.23	633.91	498.59	427.87	204.39	132.55	4798.64
Oil & Varnish Stains	7.14	2.30	29.52	7.59	22.04	14.42	.20	5.57	10.33	10.37	7.49	8.10	125.07
Special & Paste Paints			73.98	521.33	241.03	26.14	27.65	7.75	17.74	5.87			931.48
Putty	6.–	21.24	14.37	23.88	25.64	11.41	9.30	30.53	57.38	22.77	24.21	21.73	272.46
Carriage Gloss Paint	6.75	5.30	15.33	21.55	11.90	74.01	24.76	41.40	54.23	6.12	10.18	9.32	281.75
Wood Alcohol	34.88	1.01	.20	6.70	26.40		8.50	3.25	7.–	26.68	9.80	25.78	170.30
Artists Materials	4.21	5.96	6.55	17.61	16.53	3.45	3.67	6.94	26.49	18.51	20.55	11.85	142.32
Fresco Colors												14.40	14.40
Sundries	38.55	37.93	49.17	61.04	151.54	18.07	45.43	42.13	38.47	21.06	34.61	13.67	622.57
Totals	925.98	2113.58	2908.05	4366.98	3870.56	2442.44	1574.54	1964.98	1728.75	2122.98	1037.42	642.54	25,362.16

DIAGRAM ILLUSTRATING LETTER FROM F. H. K.

Men pursue riches under the idea that their possesion will set them at ease, and above the world. But the law of association often makes those who begin by loving gold as a servant finish by becoming themselves its slaves; and independence without wealth is at least as common as wealth without independence.

—Colton.

Accountics

VOL. IV FEBRUARY 1899 NO. 2

The Monthly Statement

A very carefully considered paper on auditing, by Wilton C. Eddis, C. A., the first section of which is published in another portion of this issue, is a very valuable addition to the literature of accountics. It is something that will bear study, both upon the part of professional accountants and the men in active business. The advantages of audits, and the qualifications of auditors, and what is to be done and what is to be expected, are all so clearly indicated, that whoever reads it will be better qualified than before for the duties of his position, whatsoever it may be. Auditing, in this country at least, is yet in its infancy. By this we do not mean that the process of auditing is not understood, but that the business public does not appreciate auditing as it should, and, therefore, does not have nearly the amount of auditing done that would be advantageous. There is no concern, from the smallest to the largest, that would not be benefitted in a very large degree by having its books periodically examined by a competent, disinterested and independent auditor. Few concerns there are whose books are so well kept that they could not be improved, and, as a rule, an examination precedes the suggestion of improvement in the system. For these reasons, and many others, we commend to the attention of our readers the paper referred to.

When this magazine brought to the attention of the business world the somewhat peculiar and altogether new word "accountics," there was the attempt in certain directions to characterize the term as pedantic and unnecessary. Others pretended to frown upon it as though it were an unwelcome addition to the language and an unnecessary term as well. All this, however, has passed away, and to-day the word "accountics" is recognized on its merits and finds its proper place in the dictionaries, wherein it is defined as expressing the science of accounts.

No doubt stimulated by the success of this magazine in popularizing a much needed new word, various attempts have been made by others to bring into use new and strange terms, that defined, as their inventors intended them to be, would indicate the business or industry upon which they are engaged, or, more properly speaking, the science of that industry. For example, Mr. Donaldson, of The Billboard, brings forward "advertics," which he describes as standing for the science of advertising. Here is a quotation from an editorial in the December issue of the journal referred to: "Advertics is such knowledge as we possess of advertising, severely tested, coordinated and arranged in order. Great care must be taken to avoid confusing advertics with advertising. They are and always must be kept separate and distinct. The one is the science, the other is the art. They are related only in that a principle of science is a rule of art. Science is knowledge; art is the application of knowledge to practice."

We are not called upon to pass upon the character of the word "advertics," its roots, elements, etc. Its etymology is something to be described and defended by others than ourselves. Suffice it to say, it sounds odd and looks queer, but, for that matter, others could have said just as much about accountics a short time since. A thought or two, however, with respect to the science of advertising, whether it be indicated by the term "advertics" or something else. In the January number of The Billboard we find an account of an interview with some one who, it is asserted, has written much on advertising that is valuable. We are assured that this person is interested in advertics. He is, in fact, not adverse to engaging in the work of defining, outlining and illustrating the science which advertics represents. We are told that he has already accomplished very much in another field which is comparable to the one referred to. This gentleman, it is said, has argued somewhat against the feasibility of outlining the science of advertising in a way to lay down rules to which practical advertisers should comply. He has stated, it is asserted, that in these days the artisan inventor is the one who leads. The scientist, he has asserted, follows after, co-ordinating and arranging the facts which the inventor has brought to light. All this, and more which transpired at an interview, seems to have troubled the editor of The Billboard, for, under these conditions, he inquires, of what real practical value and utility could advertics ever be? Our contemporary continues: "If a rule of art becomes a principle of science instead of the reverse, then surely science has but a poor place in our workaday world." Finally, he quotes from an unnamed authority the following: "While art utilizes all rules, it also transcends them all. A really grat painting, a masterpiece, cannot be made by rule."

If we were involved in this discussion, as we are not, we would be disposed, as at present advised, to agree with both sides. Art, it seems to us, unquestionably precedes science—that is, recorded science. At least, it was so in accounting. The score, the notched stick and various other primitive methods of recording obligations, long preceded any formulated rules or principles. Double entry, which was a manifestation of the science of account-keeping, followed long after definite methods of accounts had been in extensive use. At the present time, the practice of the most able accountants is far ahead of the recorded science. A little later some writer will take from accountants in the field somewhat of their practice and combine it with somewhat of theory and produce the scientific basis for the development of another set of men or another generation of accountants. The art is always in the van.

We are glad to know that some one is determined to formulate the principles or science of advertising. Wnile we doubt the ability of any one to lay down in fine detail all the rules to which advertisers must conform in order to be successful, we firmly believe that principles can be generalized sufficiently to cover all practice, and that, as time goes on, this generalization will gradually be brought down to specific rules. There are less variations from certain basic principles to-day in the practice of the most successful advertisers than would at first be supposed. While a "master stroke" in advertising—to paraphrase a quotation above—cannot be made by rule, yet the rule can be pointed out as soon as the master stroke has been manifested. Who knows but what the advertiser would have been able to make the master stroke much sooner than he did, if only he had had an inkling of the rule beforehand? And who will say that others might not also have been successful if only they had some general rules for their guidance. So here is success to advertics, if that is to be the name.

We think we shall only be serving our readers acceptably by using a small space on this page for the purpose of directing their attention to one of the advertisements which appears in this number, and which also appeared in our last issue. We refer to the card index competition conducted by The Globe Company, Cincinnati, and which by its terms brings us indirectly, if not directly, into the work. Card indexes are used for a multitude of purposes. They are in growing demand in every department of business. They would be used a thousand times more extensively at the present time, if only the business community fully understood the utility of the system and its wonderful adaptibility to all requirements.

The genius of modern business is to record a fact, whatever it may be, upon a loose sheet of paper, and then to combine several sheets of a kind into a holder, a filing case, or into some special form for convenient access and reference. A letter-filing system fairly exemplifies the principle. The so-called card index is a very common form of loose sheets arranged in drawers for convenient reference. Because for the most part the sheets are small, they are called cards; and because in the infancy of the use of cards in this general way, mere indexing, as, for example, in library work, was pre-eminent, the name became "card index." In some cases it was called "library index." Modern uses, however, have outstripped the name and business adaptations have gone far beyond what is fairly designated by the term "card index." In the advertisement referred to, The Globe Company points out some of the various uses for which it has constructed cards in the past, and indicates a range of dimensions for cards that, to the uninitiated, will be surprising.

The competition, which is stimulated by liberal cash prizes, ought to develop a practical literature on card indexes and their application, which will be of the greatest advantage to the business community. We commend the matter to the attention of our readers, not only by suggesting to those who are in position to compete for the prizes to take active part, but also to others who are not so situated, to give the matter attention and thereby discover what can be done in directions that will specially serve their business ends. Even though you do not send in your list with examples for consideration in the award of prizes, the mere making up of such a list as far as you can go will be of advantage to you in broadening your knowledge and in enabling you to make new applications of a universally convenient method. In any event, take the first step and send for the catalogues of the company. They contain information of the greatest value in every office.

There are excellent business reasons for having attractive, well arranged and comfortable offices. In the first place a very large fraction of the business man's time is spent in his office, and, therefore, there should be comforts as well as conveniences. The more convenient the office is and the better supplied it is with labor-saving devices, the less it costs to transact the business to which the office is devoted. In the next place, the more handsome and elegant the office is, the more of an advertisement it proves to be. The saying is that clothes make the man. To a certain extent, in the same sense the office indicates the business.

There is always a utilitarian side to the office question. With what conveniences is the office supplied? Is it up to date in all particulars? Again, given the elements that enter into the office equipment, are they arranged in the best manner? Can improvements be suggested?

A long article could be written on office facilities and office arrangements, but that is not our object at the present time. Every man likes to know how the other man is doing the same thing. Whenever Jones calls upon Brown he glances at his office arrangements, and if he is an observing man, he takes advantage of the suggestions and hints that this sly glance gives him. Many men are proud of their offices and like to show them. Many men change their offices frequently, for the sake of keeping them up to date and making the office the best advertisement possible.

We would like to establish for editorial purposes an office exchange, so to speak. In other words, we solicit photographs of office interiors for reproduction in these columns. Connected with almost every office is some one who works the camera. If there be no amateur photographer, there is some one near by whose services can be secured at a moderate price. Therefore, send us along photographs of your office arrangements. Let us see the private office, the bookkeeper's office, the shipper's office, and as many other divisions of the office as you see fit. Give us good, clear pictures that are suitable for reproduction and see what we will do with them. We imagine that something will follow from this that will be of interest to the readers of the magazine and to business men in general.

The name of a weekly paper which is at present achieving a large measure of popularity is such that a phrase concerning it that properly tells all its achievements can hardly be formed without mentioning the name of the paper itself. Its name is Success and it is a success. We commend especially the magnificent engravings (half-tone work) which have characterized the pages of this exchange for some time past. It is a desirable addition to the reading of every family. The articles in its columns are wholesome, and in many cases eminently practical. The office of Success is in the Cooper Union building, New York.

Interest and Discount—I

By Charles F. Rohne

History of Interest

The history of interest goes back to the time of the Mosaic law. For upward of thirty centuries the mind of man has been engrossed with this subject, and yet no unanimity of opinion has been reached as regards the individual rights of men who loan and borrow money to affix the rate of compensation to be paid the owner and lender thereof. In the early ages the charging and receiving of compensation for the use of money was called usury and was denounced as unjust. This mistaken and prejudicial use undoubtedly arose from a misunderstanding, or misinterpretation, of some of the enactments of the Mosaic laws, which read as follows:

"Thou shalt not lend upon usury to thy brother; usury of money, usury of victuals, usury of anything that is lent upon usury; unto a stranger thou mayst loan upon usury, but unto thy brother thou shalt not lend upon usury." (Deuteronomy xxiii, 19-20.) "And if thou lend money to any of my people that is poor by thee, thou shalt not be to him as an usurer, neither shalt thou lay upon him an usury." (Exodus xxii, 25.) And again, in speaking of a poor brother, "Thou shalt not give him thy money upon usury, nor lend him thy victuals for increase." (Leviticus xxv, 37.)

These laws are specific and direct in their application, and do not forbid the charging of usury except to poor brothers. For ages, the followers of Moses and the disciples of his teachings were the money lenders of Europe for usury; and, by reason of this, and the fact that they were as a class shrewd, trafficking, and a money dealing people, is to be attributed the unjust prejudice that, in a measure, to this day exists against them and others who follow the profession of money lending.

Aristotle, the Grecian philosopher, gravely contended that, as money could not beget money, it was barren, and that usury should not be charged for its use.

In this regard, as in many others, the old philosopher did not philosophize aright. He did not see that with money the borrower could add to his flocks, his fields, and his merchandise, and thus profit by the increase of all.

The Greeks were not, however, governed by the opinion of Aristotle, for in his age they paid an average rate of about 30 per cent on the capital employed in the shipping trade, and about 12 per cent for capital employed in business on land.

The Roman law allowed interest of usury, and during the days of the republic, the rate of interest or usury was very high. This resulted mainly from the fact that the debtors, the plebians repeatedly threatened and sometimes made efforts to deprive their creditors, generally the patricians, not only of the interest on their capital, but also of the capital or principal itself.

But from the time of the fourth century the writings of the Romish church Fathers and the Canon Law prohibit interest. This prohibition was based upon the Mosaic law as above quoted and upon the sophistry of Aristotle.

The council of Vienna, Austria, in 1311 declared any defence of interest to be heresy.

[The chapters comprising this serial are from a paper bearing this title, read a short time since by Chas. F. Rohne, of Hartford, before the Hartford and New York Chapters of the Institute of Accounts. The paper in its entirety exceeds the space that could be devoted to it in a single number, or even in two numbers, and therefore we have decided to spread the essay before our readers in the form of a serial.

Mr. Rohne requests that we give prominence to the statement that the matter in the first chapter is borrowed from Soule's Philosophic Practical Mathematics, a copyrighted work. He also makes acknowledgment to various other works for different portions of what is here presented, including Harper's Advanced Arithmetic, Geo. King's Theory of Finance, Bond Tables of the Mutual Life Insurance Company, New York; Wentworth's Complete Algebra; J. Watts Robinson's Tables; Lieutenant-Colonel W. H. Oakes' Compound Interest Tables; Cohen's Present Worth Tables; Croad's Car-Trust Building-Loan Association and Instalment-Plan Monthly Tables, and The History of Banking of All Nations, published by the New York Journal of Commerce.—Editor, Accountics.]

In England, from the earliest period of history to the reign of Henry VIII, interest was forbidden to all persons except to Jews and foreigners, and they were often plundered to enrich the crown, on the miserable pretext of punishment for what the government called their "hellish extortions."

But the opposition of the people to this ruinous interdiction against interest, by the government, resulted in a statute, passed in 1546, allowing interest to the extent of 10 per cent per annum. Yet, in the reign of Edward VI, in 1552, the government again prohibited the taking or charging of any interest, and passed an act declaring that taking interest was "a vice most odious and detestable" and "contrary to the Word of God."

On the passage of this act, interest arose to 14 per cent, and continued at this rate until 1571, when an act was passed repealing the act of Edward VI, and re-enacting that of Henry VIII, allowing 10 per cent interest.

The word interest was now substituted for the word usury, and the meaning of usury was changed to mean the rate per cent charged in excess of the legal rate.

By the middle of the 17th century, nearly all the governments of Europe followed England in abolishing the Usury Laws, and established fixed rates. But as the fixed rates were evaded, just as the prohibition had been evaded before, and as the legally fixed rates resulted in making the rate of interest higher than it would have been without such laws, all European States have since abolished Usury Laws.

In 1829, England abolished Usury Laws on commercial paper running less than twelve months, in 1850 on all capital except loans on real estate, and in 1854, they were abolished altogether.

The United States stands almost alone in retaining Usury Laws. The legal rate of interest in the National Banking Law is 7 per cent in States where no rate is fixed. In States where the State Laws fix the rate per cent.. the National Banks are to be governed accordingly.

The highest excellence is seldom attained in more than one vocation.
—Bovée.

Wealth is nothing in itself; it is not useful but when it departs from us.—Dr. Johnson.

Scottish Chartered Accountants

We are indebted to Richard Brown, Secretary and Treasurer of the Chartered Accountants of Scotland, with office at No. 23 St. Andrew's Square, Edinburgh, for a copy of the official directory of the Chartered Accountants of Scotland for 1898-1899. The directory is upwards of one hundred pages in extent, and is printed on excellent paper and bound in limp covers. It presents first the personnel of the general examining board, composed of representatives of the Edinburgh Society, the Glasgow Institute, and the Aberdeen Society. Following are the officers of each of the three organizations named.

Thirty pages of the book are devoted to an alphabetical list of the members of the several organizations, following which is a topographical list of about the same extent. Referring to the latter, it is interesting to know that members of these organizations are to be found in Australia, British Columbia, Canada, Central Africa, Central America, China, India, Japan, New Zealand, Philippine Islands, South Africa, South America, and the United States. Eleven members are classed under the head last designated. Of these, seven are in New York, one in Seattle, two in Chicago, and one in Waco, Texas.

The next section of the book is devoted to the agreement between the Society of Accountants of Edinburgh, the Institute of Accountants and Actuaries in Glasgow, and the Society of Accountants in Aberdeen, by which are secured uniform rates for qualification for and admission to membership. Succeeding this is the syllabus of examinations by the general examining board. The whole is supplemented by a very comprehensive index.

Incorporated Accountants' Journal

We are indebted to James Martin, Secretary of the Society of Accountants and Auditors, 4 King Street, Cheapside, London, E. C., for a bound volume of the Incorporated Accountants' Journal for the year ending September, 1898. This periodical is well sustained and is one of the most useful published in the interest of accountants at the present time. As our readers will bear us out, we have had occasion in the past to make extracts somewhat frequently from the current numbers as they have appeared. The book is sent out neatly bound in cloth, with gilt side and back title.

A Business Barometer

If business upon the New York Stock Exchange can be trusted at the present time, as in the past, to foretell faithfully the general business conditions that will prevail, then the current year will be a most prosperous one. Even thus early in the new year, some records of long standing regarding the volume of business transacted have been broken, and the exchange has experienced several days which have surpassed any others in its history.

The scene here reproduced was taken upon Broad Street, which, during business hours, is one of the most interesting sections of New York. The crowds of men in the foreground belongs to a class known as "curb" brokers. Among many people there seems to be an idea prevalent that curb-stone brokers are of not much consequence, but, nevertheless, a great amount of business is transacted by them. They constitute a sort of informal stock exchange, being unorganized and without officers. The same action and excitement that takes place upon the floors of the various organized exchanges may be witnessed here, day after day, regardless of passing vehicles or the condition of the weather.

In the background, situated upon the corner of Wall and Nassau Streets, stands the United States Treasury building. In old Federal Hall, upon this site, George Washington took the oath of office as President of the United States in 1789. The statue directly in front of the entrance is that of the "Father of his Country." In front of the Treasury building, upon the corner of Broad and Wall Street, is the handsome Drexel Building, upon the first floor of which are situated the offices of the well-known banking firm of J. Pierpont Morgan &

LOOKING UP BROAD STREET, (NEW YORK). THE SUB-TREASURY BUILDING AND THE FOOT OF NASSAU STREET IN THE BACKGROUND.

Co. The Mills Building is next on the right, in which is the office of Henry Clews & Co.

On the left, in the foreground, are seen the lamps at the entrance of the Commercial Cable Building, which is one of the newest "tall" buildings in the lower part of the city. Further toward Wall Street, though not shown in the illustration, is the building of the New York Stock Exchange. Here is the heart of a financial district, which, perhaps, has become the most important in the world, and which is regarded by many persons as the business barometer of the nation.

National Association of Manufacturers

The fourth annual convention of the National Association of Manufacturers was held at Cincinnati, January 24-26, 1899. The local committees had made elaborate preparation for the entertainment of their guests. Governor Bushnell welcomed the delegates in behalf of the State of Ohio, and Mayor Gustave Tafel, of Cincinnati, made the welcoming address in behalf of the city. President Search, of the Association, responded.

The president's annual address was a feature of the convention. It referred to the rapidity with which our nation made historical events during the past year, how it had come into possession of colonies in several parts of the world, and how some 12,500,000 people had been brought under our charge. These rapid developments have as rapidly enhanced the commercial welfare of our country, for the newly-acquired territory is all tributary to the United States, and will grow in commercial importance.

Reference was made to the efforts of American manufacturers toward the extension of our foreign trade. The efforts of this Association to obtain legislation calculated to expand our merchant marine have resulted in the bill introduced into the Senate by Senator Hanna, aims to encourage the building and operation of ships under the American flag.

The president spoke of the bearing upon the United States of the Nicaragua Canal agitation. Two problems pertaining to the coming Paris exposition were mentioned, and the necessity for action in these directions was urged. In closing, some suggested changes in the basis of association membership were discussed, and the effective work of the Asociation for the past year was tersely described.

The treasurer's report showed a balance on hand of $2,637.57. The reports of the various committees were interesting, and told of much that had been accomplished. The city of Boston was selected as the meeting place for next year's convention.

The election for officers resulted as follows: President, Theodore C. Search, Philadelphia; Secretary, E. P. Wilson, Cincinnati; Treasurer, Charles A. Schieren, New York.

The following is a list of the State Vice-Presidents: Alabama, A. F. Bend; California, J. G. Hamilton; Connecticut, Pliny Jewell; Delaware, Charles W. Pusey; Georgia, J. F. Hanson; Illinois, C. F. Quincy; Indiana, D. M. Parry; Kentucky, R. F. Balkey; Louisiana, F. M. Young; Maine, Chas. R. Mulliken; Maryland, David L. Bartlett; Massachusetts, George T. Coppins; Michigan, O. H. L. Werneke; Mississippi, W. T. Adams; Missouri, L. D. Kingsland; New Hampshire, F. B. Pike; New Jersey, Benjamin Atha; New York, Charles A. Moore; North Carolina, D. M. Tompkins; Ohio, H. C. Yeiser; Oregon, L. D. Cole; Pennsylvania, John H. Converse; Rhode Island, Samuel M. Nicholson; South Carolina, Ellison A. Smythe; Tennessee, C. D. Mitchell; Vermont, Henry Fairbanks; Wisconsin, Frederick W. Sivyer.

The question of handling the wires and gas, water and drainage pipes in great cities, and even in towns, is becoming with each year one of the greatest importance. A prize was offered to the engineers of the United States by The Cosmopolitan magazine for the ablest article suggesting a scientific, economical solution of this problem. The paper of Henry F. Bryant has been selected by the committee as the one most ably meeting the conditions. It appears in the February number.

Fortune turns everything to the advantage of her favorites.—Rochefoucauld.

Many dream not to find, neither deserve, and yet are steeped in favors.
—Shakespeare.

Of all pure things, purity in the acquisition of riches is the best. He who preserves purity in becoming rich is really pure, not he who is purified by water.—Manu.

Practical Auditing*

By Wilton C. Eddis, C. A.

In undertaking to write a paper on Auditing, I have found that I had undertaken, when I came to do it, a far more difficult task than I thought when the President was arranging the subjects for the present course, and suggested the subject to me. To define a subject, which is, after all, a matter of individual experience, would be too presumptous for me to attempt, and further, to laden an auditor with the responsibilities which he could not reasonably undertake would clearly be unfair to the auditor and misleading to the public, so I have contented myself with giving you, to the best of my ability and the time at my disposal, a chatty paper on auditing, which I trust, however, will give my hearers some idea of an auditor's responsibilities and also be of service to such of my hearers who are students coming up for examination.

That the terms auditing and auditors are well known amongst business men is a recognized fact, and that there is a recognized meaning to these terms is also true, and further they are referred to in Acts of Parliament, but their meaning is not defined.

Under the Municipal Acts of Ontario, besides laying down that audits of the accounts must be made, the qualifications of certain auditors are defined as being "a Chartered accountant," or some other expert accountant. But there is no legal definition as to what an audit entails, beyond what custom has established, and even that is of a vague nature. Consequently, where an audit is called for, the auditor has virtually to decide, from his own experience, what is necessary to be done.

With the phenomenal growth of joint stock companies in recent years, so has the demand for audits increased, and not only with incorporated, but in private companies and firms, are audits made, where a few years ago such a procedure was not known.

When the head of the firm personally superintended the whole of his business, even in details, he required no one to vouch for the accurateness of his books or statements, his transactions were also limited, but his profits were large. Now, however, he finds, with more numerous transactions and closer profits, that it was more profitable to have his books audited, also that it keeps his office more up to the mark and leaves him more time to extend and conduct his business.

Shareholders in companies who have put money into them and cannot personally superintend their business, naturally look for some guarantee that the periodical statement presented to them is correct. Unfortunately, the average investor is perfectly satisfied if he gets a good dividend, forgetting the fact that a few dividends possibly may be all the return that he will get for his investment, if the company is badly managed, or was not justified in paying such dividends.

It is only a matter of time when investors will demand that their interests are properly protected, and that they shall have a guarantee that is worth something, that they are informed periodically as to the true state of their investments. Certainly, nearly all companies now have these annual statements vouched for as audited and found correct. The whole question then arises, what is the value of these audits?

The successful man, or the successful company, is often looked up to with feelings of envy, and supposed not infrequently to have had a run of luck, or opportunities not available to others. Not so; with few exceptions, success can be commanded by all those who are prepared to seek for it in the only way in which it can be found, by work and thoroughness, by doing something of selling goods just a little better than others, or by looking after all the details. Look at our successful companies, and trace their career—that the best companies look that their books are carefully audited, though with these companies, where everything is a matter of perfect system, there is far less risk for the shareholder in this respect than with companies not so well managed. That good auditors are essential may, however, be demonstrated by

*Paper read before the Members of the Institute of Chartered Accountants of Ontario, Jan. 18, 1899, by Wilton C. Eddis, C. A.

the statement that often a company is supposed to be well managed until it fails; an effective audit would have exposed the weakness possibly early enough to have saved the shareholders from heavy loss.

Investors, like the public, are as a class long-suffering, and joint stock companies, and large institutions, too, are often managed by a few. These few, as a rule, doubtless intend for the best, but in the case of companies, they know that the average shareholder wants dividends, and as long as they get them will be easily satisfied that all is well. Now, I want it clearly understood that in the remarks I am about to make, I do not in any way intend or wish to refer to our numerous well-managed financial or trading companies. The auditor who would injure any company, even if it may be struggling along against adverse circumstances, is not worthy of his calling.

Well, then, if losses are made, there is always the hope that times will mend, that possibly the depression in business is only temporary; very likely this is perfectly true. Perhaps the manager lacks the moral courage to lay the true state of affairs before the directors, not realizing that if they and the shareholders were working in harmony with the management, that all could pull together and wait for better times. He, the auditor, with that moral courage that is an essential characteristic, would come in and decline to sign the balance sheet which purported to show that there was so much profit available for dividend, whereas, in reality, proper provisions had not been made for liabilities not shown therein.

The company may have elected an auditor, who, not knowing his duties, thought all was right because the manager told him it was so, and further that it was approved in the minutes of the directors. The manager may also have feared that the shareholders would take some unpleasant action.

One false step always leads to another, too big a dividend paid this year must cut into next year's profits, and if the deception is kept up there can be only one result, viz., failure.

In making such a statement as the above, one would think that with auditors appointed the shareholders would be at any rate comparatively safe, but then, there are auditors and auditors, and many poor shareholders to-day are ruined through the failure of a company under such circumstances.

Men learn by making mistakes, commonly at someone else's expense. It is a fact that the cleverest men in the professions and in mercantile life have first to gain experience, and by making mistakes then arrive at the highest eminence. But to do this, they must be men of ability and education. By education I do not necessarily mean college education; some of our best men have educated themselves. If the auditor, who has been elected to audit the company's books, is a man of ability, if he does not know his work, he will undoubtedly in time learn it, probably at the company's expense. But if the auditor has no ability for that line of work, what then? The answer is self-evident.

When companies are ably managed and all is going well, and there is a good system of internal check, the incapabilities of the incompetent auditor are not brought to light.

When a gale overtakes a vessel at sea and the vessel is strained to the utmost, is hardly the time to be looking after the repairs which were neglected when the ship was in port.

Occasionally a storm breaks in on the financial world and wrecks a big company, and Toronto has been no exception to this rule. In good times the incompetent auditor is found to be sufficient, but when troublous times come it simply means ruin, when the management is also found wanting. There is a well-known axiom, "experience docet," or experience teaches. So it does, but it often takes a long time.

While admitting the fact that well-managed companies exercise the same care in the appointment of their auditors as is shown in all the departments of their business, yet it cannot be denied that, commonly speaking, the auditors who are appointed are chosen because they happen to have the most influence with the directors, not because they understand their duties or are best qualified for their position.

It is feared, though, that some companies, as far as the management is concerned, don't want a proper audit, and here, perhaps, I may say that I have no company that I am even thinking of, in mind. They are quite willing that the accounts should be signed as audited, but the auditor must do as he is told. It is to prevent cases like this from being possible that the Government should legislate to protect the interests of the shareholders.

Let us assume two companies, the one audited by a man who will certify anything so long as he gets a good fee; the other is also audited, but the work is thoroughly done, and also found correct. The former company pays a large dividend, and the latter a small one; and yet this latter may be the far stronger company of the two. Of what value under such circumstances is auditing unless the shareholders insist that competent men are appointed to look after their interests.

We hardly, I suppose, realize that not so many years ago, any man could style himself a doctor, or practice as a lawyer, without proving that he held any special qualifications which entitled him to so designate himself, but as civilization advanced, so the necessity arose that the community should be protected. Where life was at stake the necessity for this would soon become apparent. At a later stage, when men required advocates to plead for them, only those who had studied the law, and had proved their knowledge, were allowed to act.

It is very clear, then, that unless auditing means something, it is only worse than useless. Let us glance at a common method of appointing auditors, and then I propose to touch on their qualifications and responsibilities, finishing my paper with a few points in the audit itself, and in conclusion, briefly reviewing some of the questions on auditing set by the Institute of Chartered Accountants last year. It may not be out of place here, perhaps, to refer to and bear tribute to the excellent work done by the men who have guided the destinies of the Institute for years past. It is easy enough to criticise, but far more difficult to construct. One object of the Institute has been to raise the standard of auditing. Bookkeeping may be defined as an exact science, and can be studied and applied by reading; but auditing is a distinct branch of the accountant's profession and requires not only the thorough knowledge of bookkeeping, which a good accountant must possess, but also numerous other qualifications, which I can only refer to briefly.

Business men are slowly but surely realizing that the position of auditor is one of great responsibility, and entails something more than merely ticking off and checking additions. A capital question in one of the Institute examinations was "What is the nature and scope of an audit?" and, partially answering this, it may be stated that the usual object of an audit is that the periodical balance sheet may be vouched for as correct; and in the same way the scope of an audit may be defined as an investigation or checking, which the auditor considers necessary to enable him to so vouch that the balance sheet shows the true position of the company or firm. In the case of a joint stock company, the responsibility of the auditor is more defined than when acting for a firm where his duties may be specifically detailed and his responsibilities limited.

Unfortunately, a number of auditors consider that their duty begins and ends if they satisfy themselves that the balance sheet is correct if it agrees with the books, and do not trouble themselves to ascertain that the books represent the true state of affairs.

Again, a percentage of auditors will certify anything that is laid before them. Personally, I have felt a good deal of sympathy with the auditors of the late Farmers' Loan Co., and have little doubt that they intended, and thought they were doing, everything all right. But when an auditor is expected to protect the interests of the shareholders, it stands to reason that he must be a man of some experience and position. Further, it stands to reason that a man in a subordinate position in one firm is scarcely the man who could be expected to oppose what he feels to be wrong possibly, but when he is assured by the manager, sitting in his handsome office, that he need not be afraid, that he (the manager) will vouch for it. Further, perhaps the manager is a personal friend of the so-called auditor's employer.

It is clear, then, that the auditor must be an independent man, a man with moral courage.

At this point it might be well to clearly say that the auditor has nothing to do with the conduct or management of the business; that is the responsibility of those who are chosen for that purpose, or who own it. His duty is to certify to the correctness of the statements periodically made, to the best of his belief, having audited the accounts.

It goes without saying that the auditor, further, must be a man of honor, who will be a party to no deception. Let us examine this for a few minutes by an illustration. The bank manager has been applied to for an advance, and has called for a statement of the affairs of the firm. An auditor is asked to certify to the same. In this case he is equally bound to satisfy himself as far as is reasonable that it is correct.

A few weeks ago I was discussing these statements of affairs with a bank manager, and he told me he always divided the assets in half and then decided how much to advance. But does not the merchant, on the other hand, feel justified in writing up these assets, if he feels assured that his figures are to be subjected to such a heavy discount?

The bank system of internal auditing and checking is one of the finest pieces of mercantile machinery we have, and yet the banks could easily procure reliable balance sheets from customers worth dealing with, by insisting that they are certified to by first-class and reliable auditors.

There has been a good deal of stir of late years as to municipal audits. What should be the qualifications of a municipal auditor? He must be a first-class accountant, one thoroughly acquainted with the principles of bookkeeping, both practically and theoretically. He must be conversant with the Municipal and Assessment Acts, and further must understand his duties as auditor. He must be able to trace the receipts back to their original source, and see that the total cash received and accounted for by the treasurer is correct, and tallies with the collector's rolls, and that the list of taxes in arrears is also correct. Further, he examines all vouchers for payments, sees that they have been paid to the proper parties, and that such payments have been duly and properly authorised. He will have to see that all investments are in proper order and duly accounted for, etc. Also that all the items are properly summarized and presented to the proprietors of the institution, viz., the ratepayers. Thus, briefly sketched out, it can readily be appreciated what a responsible position this must be, that only a man who devotes his time to auditing and accounting work could possibly carry out these duties, so that the certificate attached to the summary referred to could be relied upon as correct and true.

Times are different now from what they were a few years ago; it is an age of experts; unless a man is a specialist he cannot expect to rise above his fellows. In all classes of undertakings, the public demands that only experts be employed in works that involve heavy responsibility, experience and skill. Why should this be so? The answer is simply that it is a matter of economy. Men in these days of competition cannot afford to experimentalise; they must know for certain what they are doing. The contractor, if he is to be successful, must know exactly what the work he is tendering for is to cost him before he gives a price.

(To be continued.)

Two Kinds of Gambling

The writer of the following lines seems to have a wrong idea of legitimate business. He plainly depicts two kinds of gambling, giving to one sort the dignity of a business transaction:

You go upon the Board of Trade
  Where margin merchants meet
And take some little options
  On January wheat;
You watch the little ticker
  Till the hands swing round the ring—
Then you find your little boodle
  Has gone a-glimmering.
          That's business.

You go into a faro bank
  And buy a stack of chips,
And watch the cards come from the box
  Which the dealer deftly flips;
When your head is dull and aching,
  At the breaking of the day,
You see that fickle fortune
  Has gone the other way,
          That's gambling.

It requires as much talent to spend as to make.—Whipple.

Gaming has been resorted to by the affluent as a refuge from ennui. It is a mental dram, and may succeed for a moment; but, like all other stimuli, it produces indirect debility.—Colton.

Institute of Accounts

Hartford Chapter

The meetings of this organization continue to be well attended and interest is fully sustained. The only exception to the general rule of attendance was the meeting for January, which, unfortunately, fell upon an evening that was peculiarly inclement. For this reason alone a comparatively small number attended the meeting. The evening was spent in a general informal talk, which some of the members had the enthusiasm to say was worth more to them than some of the stated addresses by which other meetings have been characterized. This only shows what an advantage there is in a free interchange of opinion upon the most informal basis. The February meeting of the organization is appointed for the last day of the month, and particulars of it are necessarily deferred until our next issue.

New York Chapter

At the January meeting of this organization, a paper by Powhatan Wyndham Robertson, of Washington, D. C., was read, in the absence of the author, by the Secretary of the Chapter. It was entitled "The Advantages of Bookkeeping in Schools, and How It Should be Taught to Best Fit the Student for the Practical Requirements of Life."

This paper was longer than we have space to spare, and, accordingly, it is impossible to reproduce it in full. Further, its treatment of the subject was of a kind to more particularly interest teachers and the managers of schools than business men and accountants. In the course of the paper the point was made that in the present age of business activity the student must prepare to enter into active service at once upon leaving school. Bookkeeping, it was argued, is an important part of a thorough business training. The author asserted that the mental discipline to be derived from the study of bookkeeping is quite as good, if not better, than that derived from the more ornamental but less practical studies often pursued. On the other hand, the prospects of pecuniary reward are much better. After presenting a general definition of the term bookkeeping and a short statement of its objects, Mr. Robertson went on to describe how it should be taught, presenting in substance the following: In order to understand the science of accounts, it first becomes necessary to understand the accounts themselves. Therefore, in teaching, one must deal with the individual account, recognizing in this the most essential part of the science.

With this general foundation laid, the following method of procedure was recommended: First, teach students an account in its entirety, then its component parts and then its object; following the latter with the peculiar characteristics applicable to the account most commonly used. Second, make them understand when and why the accounts are to be debited and credited. Third, illustrate the use of the day book, instructing them when and how to enter transactions naturally and accurately. Fourth, make plain the use of the journal. Illustrate what is meant by journalizing, and instruct in journalizing transactions. Arrange the transactions used for illustration, so that they may be well graded, making every step one in advance, so that each successive entry may give a broader knowledge of the science. By this plan the students are never permitted to lose sight of the fact that every debit must have a credit of equal amount and vice versa, and also that in every journal the total debits must equal the total credits.

The fifth point made by the writer was instruction in posting and how to post correctly. There should be inculcated in the minds of the students, he declared, the habit of executing their work accurately, naturally and in a businesslike manner. The sixth item of instruction would be with respect to the trial balance, how to make it out and the objects to be served. The seventh was when and how to close the several accounts in the ledger, how to open the Loss and Gain Account, and how to transfer the differences from the several speculative accounts to the Loss and Gain Account, and from there to the final account. The last point made was with respect to the balance sheet or balance statement, how to make it out and its object.

In the course of his remarks the speaker asserted that the names and distinctive characteristics of the books and business papers most commonly employed should be made clear. The record of a series of transactions should be carried on from the first day, and should advance by degrees from the simple to the higher and most complex account. In this manner, the speaker asserted, the science will unfold itself naturally. The student will know why certain things exist and how to apply them. Accordingly, he will work by reason rather than by rule.

At the same meeting a paper by Lewis Cornelius Muzzy, F. I. A., of Worcester, Mass., was read. Mr. Muzzy likewise was unable to be present at the meeting and, accordingly, his paper was presented by proxy. The title to the paper was lacking, but leading phrases in the introduction will give an idea of the subject. One of these was as follows, "Figures do lie." Another, in close proximity, was the following, "Liars do figure."

The author aimed to show the cause for the apparent truth of the somewhat common saying that figures do lie. One reason very tersely expressed was that liars do figure. It was in this sense that the phrases above quoted were brought to the attention of his audience. Mr. Muzzy believes that lying figures are caused either by ignorance, carelessness, or downright dishonesty. To this latter cause he lays the blame of many very serious losses that usually occur through the dishonesty of trusted employes. He believes that the greater percentage of losses from this source will be found among ordinary business houses, because in those cases where the accounts are often closely and intelligently watched, as occurs in large corporations and private firms, it is more difficult for the dishonest man to avoid detection. Several examples were presented of the manner in which figures are made to lie, in order to cover the tracks of dishonesty.

Mr. Muzzy looks upon ignorance and carelessness as sources of great loss throughout the business world. He believes that an ignorant or careless bookkeeper will incur losses as the direct result of his ignorance or carelessness. He believes also that such a one will drive trade away indirectly, if not directly, because of the offense to customers by these bad qualities. The author claimed that the grand and prolific cause of business failures will be found in insufficient or careless bookkeeping. He cited examples where business men, who were models of uprightness and integrity, have failed from these causes alone. The author was disposed to attribute this ignorance and carelessness to the superficial training afforded by schools and colleges. He declared that these institutions practically ignore important branches of instruction, and accordingly many enter the field of office work who are in reality very incompetent.

As a remedy, the author strongly endorsed periodical auditing. This he defined as an excellent safeguard against losses caused by dishonesty, ignorance and carelessness. He declared that independent and disinterested audits should be welcomed by accountants and bookkeepers, as well as by business men. Such effort results in mutual protection and affords bookkeepers the proof of their efficiency and honesty.

"An Ideal System of Street Railway Accounts" is the title of a lengthy article in the January number of the Street Railway Journal, New York, by A. O. Kittredge, C. P. A., Editor of ACCOUNTICS. The article is illustrated by a chart showing the general classification of accounts and with the subdivisions carried to the same degree of minutiae that has been recommended by the Street Railway Accountants' Association.

The Youth's Companion Calendar for 1899 is one of the most attractive of those which have come to the publisher's desk. It bears out the reputation of this popular juvenile journal for doing everything well.

Fortunes made in no time are like shirts made in no time; it's ten to one if they hang long together.—Douglas Jerrold.

They make their fortunes who are stout and wise.—Tasso.

It is a law of the gods which is never broken, to sell somewhat dearly the great benefits which they confer on us.—Corneille.

Men may second Fortune, but they cannot thwart her.—Macchiavelli.

Evolution in Accounting and Cost Keeping

By A. O. Kittredge, C. P. A.

(*Continued from page 9, January issue*)

It is very frequently argued that what value, is quite enough in the case of real estate to offset the depreciation of buildings, and that therefore it is safe to carry the property on the books at the original figure. Every one here knows the fallacy of that argument. Every one here can cite instances of factory property in this city, which to-day is worth very considerably less than it sold for twenty or thirty years ago. Other instances are in evidence where the property has quadrupled in that time—not the value of the buildings but the value of the land.

The accountant then says: Let each tub stand upon its own bottom. There is a depreciation in buildings no matter how rapidly the land value is advancing. Charge the depreciation into product and you will be on the safe side. If your land is advancing in value so much the better. But rising values in land ought never to be used to offset the wear and tear of the buildings on that land.

Before now land has become so valuable that the manufacturer could not afford longer to use it for factory purposes. Thereupon he has moved his factory to the suburbs and sold the old factory site for building lots. This move lost the building to him. It should have been paid for by the product made in the factory prior to the removal. Certainly the rise in the value of the land did not cheapen his product. Making money as a manufacturer is one thing. Making it out of a rise in land values is another thing entirely.

The last item shown in Reserves is Depreciation of Patents. Every American patent has a natural life of seventeen years from date of issue. Extensions, under the present law, are out of the question. Assuming that a patent is valid and valuable, and, further, merely for the sake of convenient illustration, that it has cost the concern by purchase $17,000, then the use of that patent costs $1,000 a year. Therefore costs of product should stand this $1,000 a year. It is not safe, however, in all cases to assume that the life of the patent is the full seventeen years. Frequently there is such radical change in the art that a patent that is extremely valuable for three, five or ten years becomes of little or no value at the end of the period. New discoveries or improvements supersede it. The point to be made is that the life of a patent is to be estimated according to the best judgment of the management, and that its cost, whatever the amount, must be distributed over the product during the term of its assumed life.

Before dismissing Reserve Accounts let me call your attention to the form in which this writing off of values appears upon the books. A reserve account is treated in a sense the same as an insurance account, not, however, in the sense of the premium paid on an insurance policy, but instead in the sense of a sum set aside to meet the loss when the loss occurs. It accumulates little by little very much as the insurance companies accumulate funds out of comparatively insignificant premium amounts.

Ordinary practice in certain directions is to write down the assets themselves. For example, suppose the machinery in a given manufacturing establishment originally cost $100,000. Suppose, for sake of convenience in illustration, that the management decides that the depreciation in that machinery is $10,000 a year. If the $10,000 depreciation per year should be carried directly to the credit of Machinery Account, then Machinery as an asset on the balance sheet would stand at the beginning of the second year $90,000, at the beginning of the third year $80,000, and so on until at the beginning of the eleventh year it would be represented by a zero or naught. Now this plan is nonsensical and is very rightly objected to by business managers generally. They will very readily accept the theory that $10,000 or some other sum ought to be charged into expenses every year, but they do object to continually writing down an asset of the kind that machinery is, particularly in view of their relationship to the insurance companies. The machinery cost, as we assume, $100,000. It is worth a large sum to the business as a going institution, but whether at this date its value is $75,000 or $50,000 or less nobody can tell to a certainty. It would cost approximately $100,000 to replace it with new machinery strictly up to date, and yet to sell it now at forced sale would produce perhaps little more than the value of so much scrap iron. It will ultimately wear out and have to be replaced entirely. Therefore its cost, in some ratio or other, ought to be spread over product during the months of its use.

These are conflicting conditions. The machinery ought to be insured in view of its value to the business, irrespective of what has been written off. Suppose, for the sake of argument, that what we have been considering is kept insured for $50,000, and that in the eleventh year, by the plan of crediting depreciation directly to the machinery account, it appears on the balance sheet represented by a row of naughts. This surely is a queer predicament to be in, that of insuring property for $50,000 which is represented on the books by no amount at all.

By the reserve account brought into play as described the product is charged as the years go by with a percentage of the cost of the machinery, just as it ought to be charged on the basis of prudent management. The machinery account at the beginning of the eleventh year still stands at $100,000, but Reserve Account against Machinery having been credited $10,000 each year, now stands ready to replace the machinery whenever it is necessary to replace it without any loss or drain upon the business. Upon this showing there is nothing wrong in insuring the machinery for $50,000, or any other sum that the insurance companies may agree to. Further, the company owning the machinery is solvent beyond question, for it has reserved out of profits the sum of $100,000 against machinery that cost $100,000. It is able to discard all its old machinery and to replace it with new to the same value without calling upon its stockholders to put up any new capital.

The practical working out of the plan differs slightly from the letter of the illustration. Instead of replacing the entire equipment of the factory at one time, after a term of years, the replacement proceeds continually, item by item, year by year; now one machine, now another; now a new engine, again a new set of boilers, all the costs being provided out of this reserve fund, created by charging to cost of product what the wear and tear of the machinery has been estimated to be.

One thought more with respect to Reserves before we proceed. It is often urged against trusts, which are the largest corporations at the present time, that they have less strength within themselves to carry them through seasons of depression and panic than private firms, and that therefore they often fail when private firms remain solvent. Let us see what the reason is.

Trusts are capitalized, as a rule, not in view of the actual value of their assets but strictly in view of their earning ability, or, as it is sometimes expressed, upon their dividend capacity. The promotor of the organization does everything he can to keep the capitalization up to the highest limit. There is where his profit comes in. When the organization is effected and the management comes to survey the field it is discovered that every cent that can be earned, even under favorable conditions, must be paid out for interest on bonds and in the form of dividends in order to live up to promises. To pay stipulated interest and as much dividends as is expected makes it impossible to set aside anything by way of reserves against wasting assets, or for any emergency whatsoever. The trust, therefore, is kept poor, even in good seasons, by paying out all that it earns.

The private partnership, on the other hand, is seldom put in that position. The individual members of the firm, desiring to accumulate, spend less than their profits in good seasons, or, even if they spend it, they invest the money in residences, in rental real estate, in interest-paying bonds, in dividend-paying stocks in other companies, and in various ways put it where it is satisfactory to them but nevertheless where it can be reached in case of need. Inasmuch as the members of a private firm are individually liable for all the debts of the concern, the property that has thus been bought out of the profits of the business is still virtually in the business and forms an important part of the strength of the firm for tiding over periods of hard times.

In Ohio your corporation law is very different from that in many of the States of the Union. Here, if I understand the case, a stockholder is liable to the creditors of the corporation in an amount equal to the par value of his stock. An Ohio corporation, therefore, has a certain amount of reserve in this direction, which does not apply to corporations formed under the laws of many of the States, and I assume, therefore, that your manufacturing corporations escape some of the trials that others are subjected to.

The reserve funds to which I have directed your attention are the safety props of corporations of the ordinary class, and tend to keep within its treasury so much of the profits earned as may be necessary to insure the integrity of the enterprise and its solvency under all conditions.

The fourth division in Liabilities is Capital. I have already directed your attention to the theory upon which this chart is constructed, namely, that the business owes its stockholders the amount they have invested. Therefore the re-

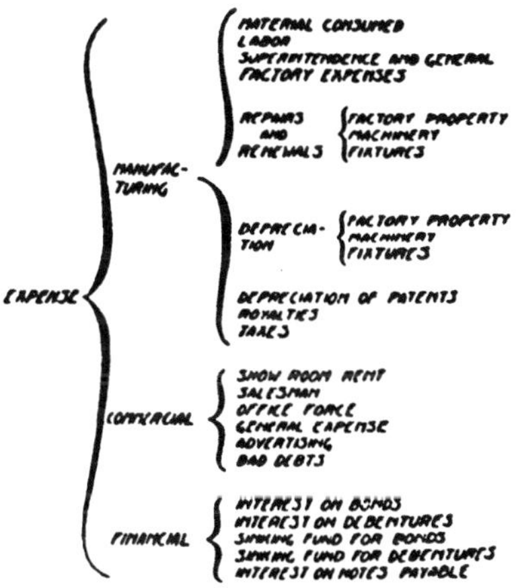

FIG. 3—ANALYSIS OF EXPENSES.

sultant from comparing the outside liabilities with the total of the assets produces the Capital Account.

Capital in a manufacturing or mercantile concern appears in two or three different forms. There is capital in process of development, if I may use the term, represented by the Loss and Gain accounts of the business. These are shown her as a monthly Loss and Gain Account, and what is termed the general Loss and Gain Account. The latter may be described as the summary for a quarter, for six months, or for a year. Next appear Impairment and Surplus. Surplus means the net earnings left in the business and not paid out in dividends. The opposite to this is Impairment, which has the relationship to it of a minus to a plus. It is the provision for recording the impairment of capital where the business is running at a loss. Finally, there is the Capital Stock Account, divided, as circumstances require, into Common Shares and Preference Shares.

Now let us consider the Profit and Loss Statement of the business. Expenses precede revenues. We must put up some money for store rent, clerk hire and advertising before we can do business even upon the smallest scale. A factory has a multitude of expenses which must be paid before it has any product for sale. After its product has been made and its goods are ready for the market there are still another series of expenses to be met before any money comes back to the treasury. Let us consider these somewhat analytically.

Our chart divides the expenses of a manufacturing company into three classes—Manufacturing, Commercial and Financial. Let us glance at the Financial first, because the expenses under this head are the exceptional expenses de-

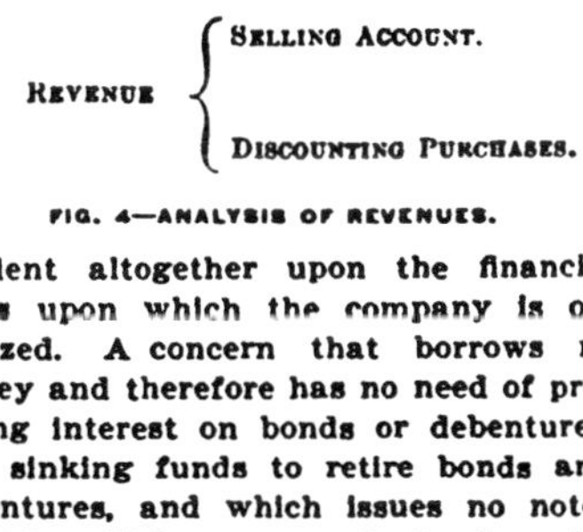

FIG. 4—ANALYSIS OF REVENUES.

pendent altogether upon the financial basis upon which the company is organized. A concern that borrows no money and therefore has no need of providing interest on bonds or debentures, and sinking funds to retire bonds and debentures, and which issues no notes payable, will have no need of a financial division in its expenses. With this explanation we will dismiss the third class.

There then remains Manufacturing Expenses and Commercial Expenses. By Manufacturing Expenses I mean those expenses which are a part of or go into the cost of product. By Commercial Expenses I mean those expenses which are necessary to the sale of product and to the conduct of the enterprise in all particulars outside of the mere running of the factory.

It is possible to conceive of a factory that has no selling or commercial expenses. For example, it has bargained with some one to take its entire product at an agreed price. Upon this basis it has no need of salesmen; it maintains no showroom; it has saved the expense of samples; it has no need of an extensive bookkeeping system to look after customers' accounts; it has no collections to care for, and no credit departments to maintain; it has no losses from bad debts; it does no advertising, and in general it escapes all of those items which are here classified as Commercial Expenses. The expenses are limited strictly to those items which we have called Manufacturing.

The factory consumes material and it employs labor. A necessary expense beyond these items is the salary of superintendent. Then there are certain general factory expenses, such as insurance, wages of cost clerk, foreman and other non-producers, and those small supplies like oil and waste that cannot be charged to any particular order, and also those larger items like power, heat and light, cleaning, night watchmen, etc., which are of such a character that they must be spread over the product by some such plan as a percentage, because it is an impossibility to charge them specifically to the orders as they pass through. Then there are repairs and renewals, divided under such heads as Factory Property, Machinery and Fixtures, the reserves for which I have already described. There are also depreciation of Factory Property, Machinery and Fixtures, depreciation of Patents, and the cost of royalties —in case royalties are paid for the use of patents owned outside of the establishment—and, of course, there are state, county and city taxes.

This division of Expenses into Manufacturing and Commercial is vital to any proper consideration of costs, and yet is one on which business men are perhaps more frequently confused than upon any other. They are prone in many cases to group the two classes together. Instances are on record where an excessive amount of advertising or the increase of the president's salary, his time being devoted exclusively to selling, has been assumed to affect the cost of product. The idea is of course absurd.

Now let us glance at the Commercial Expenses. The goods that are produced in the factory, whether under the best possible management or otherwise, cost a certain additional sum to sell. Certain commercial expenses are involved. What are those expenses? They classify under such heads as the following, varying, of course, according to the commercial conditions of the business: Show Room Rent, Salaries of Salesmen, Salaries of Office Employes, and General Expenses. The latter would include Repairs and Renewals of Show Room Fittings and Office Equipment, and also the depreciation of each of these items, together with incidental expenses generally. In addition, there are the costs of advertising and the loss from bad debts. All of these must be paid out of the gross profits made on sales before anything is available for dividends, and here let me again remark that no profit is ever made until the goods are actually sold, and the money collected.

If Financial Expenses exist, then Interest on Bonds and Debentures, Sinking Funds for Bonds and Debentures, and Interest on Notes Payable must also be paid out of gross profit on sales before anything is available for dividends.

Next let us consider the Revenues of the business. Under ordinary conditions a manufacturing establishment has only two sources of revenue. One of these would be represented by what in the chart before us is called the Selling Account, and the other would be the profit made on discounting bills for supplies and goods purchased. In some instances the revenue from the latter source amounts to a considerable sum. In other instances it is of less importance.

With respect to the Selling Account, you will recall that I have already alluded to it when discussing the Merchandize Account under the head of Assets. It is one of the two grand divisions of what is ordinarily called Merchandise Account. Selling Account is the second of these divisions. The first you will recall shows the goods on hand.

Before further describing Selling Account, let me point out, by referring to the complete chart, the course which a given transaction would take.

Suppose that the factory is called upon to make a thousand articles of a given kind, say wheelbarrows, wagons or bicycles. Materials are bought, and as they come into the stock room Material Account is debited. This account as pointed out under the head of Active Assets, is to be subdivided as may be required for statistical purposes. The order to make the articles is given to the superintendent of the factory. He draws on stores or materials on hand—that is Material Account—for such supplies as he requires. He hires labor as necessary and proceeds with the order. As fast as the goods are completed, we will say in lots of one hundred or any other quantity, they are credited to the factory, that is, to Manufacturing Account at what they cost, including materials consumed, labor, pro rata of superintendence and general factory expense, pro rata of repairs and renewals, pro rata of depreciation, pro rata of royalties, and pro rata of taxes. Their cost value is then carried to the Merchandise Account. Factory Account having been debited with materials, labor and general expenses, and now being credited with the exact cost of the goods finished, there is shown by the balance in the account the cost value of work in progress, etc.

Merchandise Account as stated is debited with the cost of the goods brought over from the factory. As sales are made, the goods are taken out of the Merchandise Account, still at cost prices, and are debited to Selling Account. The balance in Merchandise Account will then show the cost value of the completed goods remaining on hand. The Selling Account in turn is credited with price obtained for the goods. The balance in it, therefore, assuming that business is conducted on a profitable basis, will be gross profit.

Gross Profit, as we have already pointed out, must stand Commercial and Financial Expenses. Gross Profit, therefore, is carried to the credit of the Monthly Loss and Gain Account. If discounting purchases has made a profit, its amount is similarly carried to the credit of the Monthly Loss and Gain Account. Commercial Expenses are carried to the debit of Monthly Loss and Gain Account, and likewise Financial Expenses, if they exist.

The balance then in Monthly Loss and Gain Account will show the profit or the loss of the month's transactions. Then it, in turn, is closed into General Loss and Gain. General Loss and Gain continues to receive monthly results for a period of say three months, six months or a year, according to preference. Then, in the light of demonstrated results, the question of a dividend comes up. If there is a large credit balance, a dividend is very likely to be declared, but perhaps not for the whole amount. Whatever is left after the dividend has been charged is carried to the credit of Impairment and Surplus Account. On the other hand, if a loss is the result of the business for the term, it is carried to the debit of Impairment and Surplus Account.

The only possible ends that can be reached in conducting a business are either a profit or a loss. If a profit over and above the amount that is paid out in dividends is made, then capital is being added to and we call it Surplus. If the expenses are greater than the revenues, then the capital is being impaired and we face the music by charging the amount to Impairment Account.

(To be continued.)

Limitations of Auditing.

"The position of an auditor with regard to a company should be absolutely independent," says the London "Accountant," "and, to a large extent, of course, this is impossible while there is nothing to prevent the auditor being either directly or indirectly interested in the promotion. It is upon this point that some new rule of practice (or, if necessary, fresh legislation) should be sought; but the occurrence is, in itself, so unusual that we very much doubt whether, up to the present, it has produced any evil results that are worth considering. Still, the mere fact that an abuse has been kept within bounds is in itself no argument against its being suppressed, and, accordingly, we are only voicing the opinion of many, when we say that they would welcome any reform in the existing law which would have the effect of entirely dissociating auditors of companies from the promotion, the promoter, or any profits in connection with either."

It is madness to make Fortune mistress of events, because in herself she is nothing, but is ruled by prudence.
—Dryden.

The fortunate man is he who, born poor or nobody, works gradually up to wealth and consideration, and, having got them, dies before he finds they were not worth so much trouble.—Charles Reade.

The whole world is put in motion by the desire of wealth, which is chiefly to be valued as it secures us from poverty; for it is more useful for defence than acquisition, and is not so much able to secure good as to exclude evil.—Dr. Johnson.

The Unit System of Office Furniture

By Walton Day.

Who is there among accountants and business men that has ever bought an office cabinet of any kind and has not sooner or later wished that it was of different dimensions or of somewhat different arrangement? Who is there, in fitting up an office to-day, that can say just what the growth of the business will be in one, two or five years, and therefore knows exactly how to provide in the matter of equipment? I venture to say there is not one among those who read these lines that has not, first or last, bought something in the office cabinet line which was not either too large or

The Unit System of Office Furniture.
Fig. 1—A Globe-Wernicke Cabinet, one unit wide and four units high with cupboard base and cornice top.

too small for his purpose, as the circumstances of the case turned out to be, or that was not subdivided differently from what was really required? To every one, therefore, the unit system in office furniture, which overcomes all these difficulties, appeals with special force.

To those not initiated, so to speak, a definition of the unit system is necessary. By unit system is meant a series of component parts, or sections, each adapted to a special purpose, but all of the same

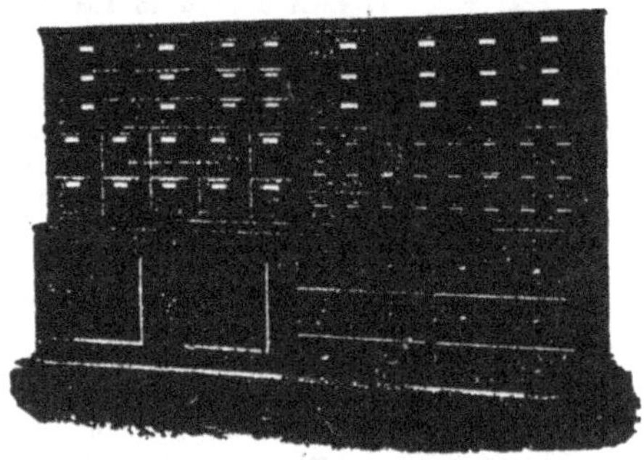

Fig. 2—A Globe-Wernicke Cabinet, two units wide with cupboard base on the left and high drawer base on the right and flat top.

dimensions, and so constructed as to be readily combined, according to requirements. The parts or units may be superimposed, or they may be joined together side by side, and they admit of as many

Fig. 3—A Globe-Wernicke Cabinet two units wide and five units high with low drawer base and cornice top.

variations in position as the permutation of their number. Suitable bases and cornices for finish are provided. If the way in which the cabinet is arranged in the office at the outset does not please, it can be quickly taken down and put up in

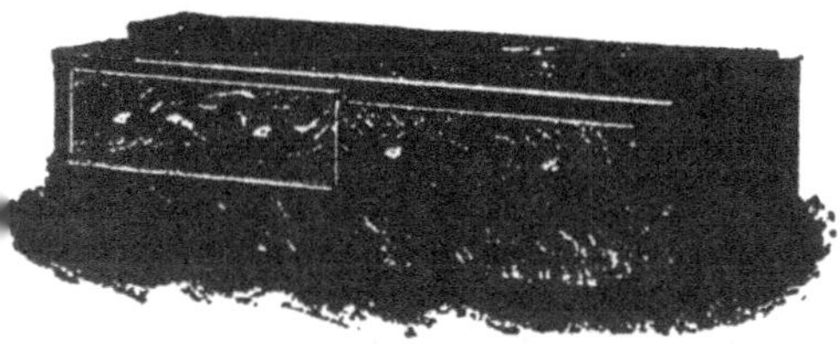

Fig. 4—Low Drawer Base.

some other form. If there is a lack of capacity in some certain division of the

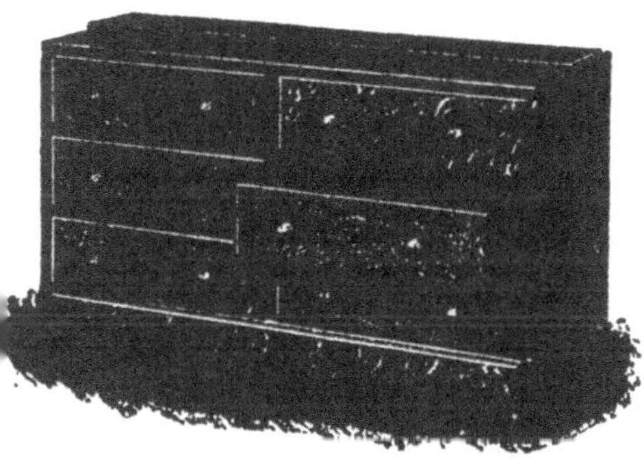

Fig. 5—High Drawer Base.

cabinet, an additional unit can be obtained and added thereto, thus supplying

Fig. 6—Cupboard Base.

the deficiency. All this will be made plainer by glancing at the illustrations.

Fig. 1 shows a Globe-Wernicke cabinet, which is the embodiment of the unit system, consisting of four units above a cupboard base and below a cornice finish.

Fig. 7—Flat Base.

Scrutinize the illustration closely for the purpose of discovering what it contains. The unit immediately above the cupboard base is devoted to card indexes.

Fig. 8—Flat Top.

The next unit is a combination, being part card index and part letter file, while above it, in turn, are two catalogue drawer units.

Fig. 2 shows a Globe-Wernicke cabinet

Fig. 9—Cornice Top.

of the same number of units, but set up in double width instead of single width. This necessitates an extra base and also an extra finish unit at the top. The cupboard base is used under one section and a drawer base under the other. In place of the cornice top, like the one in the first cut, a flat top is employed.

The bases in both Figs. 1 and 2 are

Fig. 10—Shelf Unit.

shown wider than the sections above, thus forming a narrow ledge for shelf, which not only adds greatly to the appearance of the cabinet in the office, but also contributes an element of convenience that is greatly appreciated.

Fig. 3 shows a Globe-Wernicke cabinet arranged two units wide and five units high. In this case a low drawer base is employed, under both sections of the same general width as the cabinet units. The same kind of a cornice top is used as in Fig. 1. Notice the variety of accommodations afforded by this cabinet. Commencing with the section at the right and at the bottom, there is first a legal blank unit. Above this is a pigeonhole unit. Above this in turn are two document file units, while at the top is

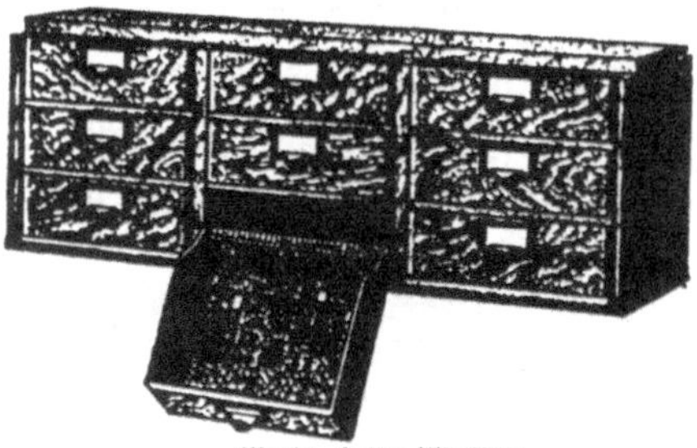

Fig. 11—Letter File Unit.

a unit devoted to transfer cases for the correspondence. The second section, commencing at the bottom, has first a unit of catalogue drawers, above which is a card index unit, and above it in turn a daily report unit. The two sections completing this part are letter file units.

Fig. 12—Card Index File Unit.

This description of what is certainly of great interest and importance to every man having to do with office work, will be better understood by a specific reference to the units from which choice is

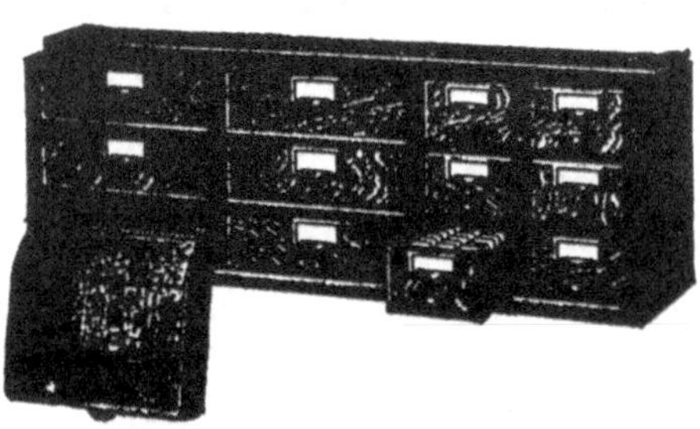

Fig. 13—Combined Letter File and Card Index File.

to be made in selecting a cabinet for a given purpose. First let us examine the bases that are available. Several of these are illustrated in Figs. 4 to 7 inclusive. In the first is a low drawer base. The dimensions of the drawers inside are 18⅜ inches long, 10⅞ inches wide, and 5¼ inches deep. There is next shown a high drawer base, containing six drawers, the inside dimensions of which are 18⅜ inches long, 15¼ inches wide, and 4¾ inches deep. It is said that no housewife ever yet found a dwelling with enough closets to meet her requirements, and we venture to say there never yet was an office in which one or two more drawers would not be acceptable. Hence the utility of these bases.

Fig. 14—Arch File Unit.

Drawers, however, do not meet every office requirement. There are articles to put away which are better accommodated by cupboards; hence the convenience of what is shown in Fig. 6. In some cases, however, there is no room in the office for either a drawer base or a cupboard base; and the height available is required for the regular units. For such

Fig. 15—Transfer Case Unit.

purposes the flat base shown in Fig. 7 comes in. The units composing the cabinet, whether letter files, catalogue drawers, document files, card indexes, or what not, are placed directly upon it.

Next with respect to the top finish. The choice between a flat top (F'g. 8) or a cornice top (Fig. 9) are offered. The first finishes the cabinet in a form to allow piling on top of it various articles like books out of use, transfer cases, stationery in bundles and boxes, etc., while the second affords a finish, at least to a high cabinet, that is in better keeping with the general appearance of the office. But Globe-Wernicke files are not always used of high dimensions. Some of the best illustrations of the utility of the system that we have ever seen have been restricted to two units height over a low base. They were surmounted by the flat top shown in Fig. 8, thus virtually adding a table or counter to the general outfit of the office.

Under a letter file, below a document

Fig. 16—Document File Unit.

file, and also in connection with the card index unit, a shelf is frequently a very desirable adjunct. A shelf unit, therefore, has been provided in this system, and is illustrated in Fig. 10. It can be located in combining the units wherever desired, and those who have already equipped their offices with this system of furniture, and who would find shelves a convenience in certain places, have only to buy the necessary shelf units and rearrange their cabinets with them in place, in order to be up to the front with

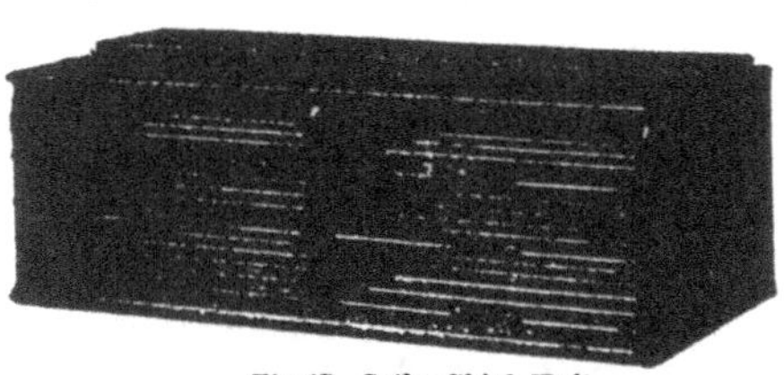

Fig. 17—Roller Shelf Unit.

the best accommodations the market affords. The shelves slide in and out.

Great care has been taken by the manufacturers of this system of office furniture in the finish as well as the details of the different units. It is up to the highest standard of quality, and many small conveniences have been thoughtfully worked out. For example, the letter file unit (Fig. 11) shows a suspending device. This is also repeated by way of further illustration in Fig. 13. To

Fig. 18—Pigeon Hole Unit.

have a file hung in the way shown is a great convenience whenever its contents are to be examined.

Fig. 12 shows the card index unit, which is as carefully constructed and equipped as the most complete card index cabinet that could be purchased. Those who use many arch files will appreciate the arch file unit shown in Fig. 14. The files are readily put away, the papers they contain are kept out of the dust, and all the while they are instantly available.

Fig. 15 shows the transfer case unit. It is as simple in construction as can be imagined, and yet it takes its place in the combination, whether at top or bottom, like any other unit. When the space that it occupies in the cabinet is wanted for an extension of the letter file, for example, it can be replaced by a letter file

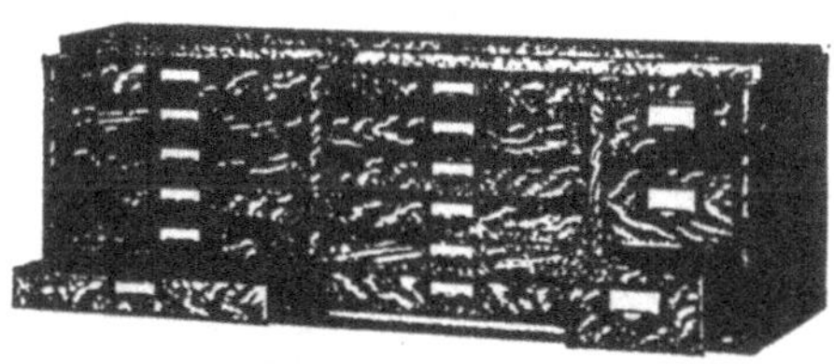

Fig 19—Legal Blank Unit.

unit, and then with its contents it may be relegated to some less valuable space. Furnished with a base and top another finished, yet always incomplete, cabinet is established, to be added to as required.

Document files are indispensable in the offices of lawyers, attorneys, insurance men, county officers and many others. In every business office a few documents at least are to be taken care of. What can be handier for the purpose than the unit clearly shown in Fig. 16? The entire cabinet may be composed of document file units, or one or two document file units may be used in combination with others, as illustrated in Fig. 3.

In almost every office there are large books to be kept and handled, like commercial reports, atlases, dictionaries, etc. How they can be put away compactly, and yet without special damage to their bindings, is clearly illustrated in the rolling shelf unit shown in Fig. 17.

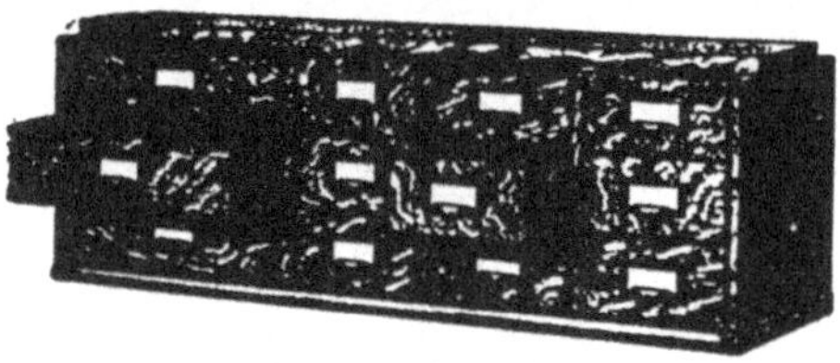

Fig. 20—Catalogue Drawer Unit.

Pigeon-holes are indispensable in every office. How papers can be properly assorted, kept clean and free from dust, and suitably labelled, and how the entire lot can be made a part of the general cabinet system of the office is clearly shown in Fig. 18. Again, every office has more or less blanks that should be kept flat and ready for instant use. The legal blank unit, shown in Fig. 19, providing twelve broad but shallow drawers, and three narrower drawers of greater depth, is adequate for ordinary purposes. Still another unit, not illustrated here, con-

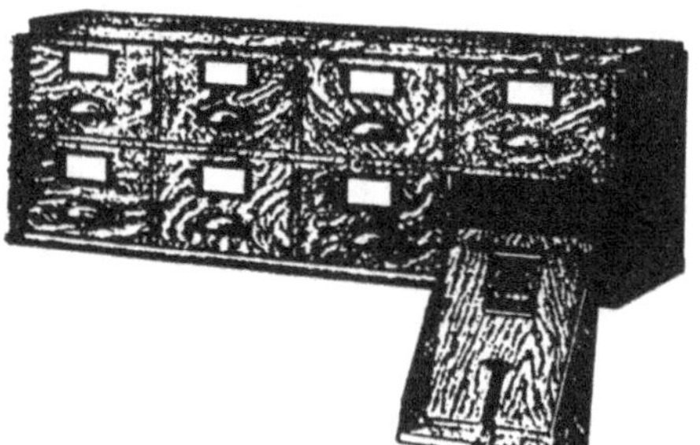

Fig. 21—Daily Report Unit.

tains a different arrangement of drawers for this purpose, something which is referred to simply as indicating the wide assortment from which selections may be made.

How shall we take care of the catalogues that come flowing into our office day after day, of various sizes, bound and unbound, and of a variety which makes it impossible to handle them as ordinary books in a library? Drawers seem to suggest themselves as being the best for the purpose. Note how a catalogue drawer scheme has been incorporated in one of the units of this system, shown in Fig. 20. There is just as little cabinet work about the drawer as may be, thus giving it the greatest possible capacity. There are several sizes of drawers contained, thus adapting the unit to the largest possible assortment. Holders for labels are provided in a way to clearly indicate the contents of the several drawers.

Fig. 22—Moving has no terrors now—waiting for the wagon.

Daily reports from salesmen, travellers, agents, managers of branch houses, and of various other persons, are regular features of the business routine of many concerns. How shall they be taken care of in a way to permit instant reference, while also securing adequate classification? The daily report unit, shown in Fig. 21, answers the question almost without words. A clamping board holds the reports in the files or trays in the most desirable manner, while the trays themselves are provided with a suspending device which makes instant reference a matter of pleasure and convenience. The clamp, or follower, in this case is similar to that which is used in tne document file unit, Fig. 16, and serves to compress and hold the papers flat.

And now let us suppose that the reader

has made his selection of units, and has put in place in his office a Globe-Wernicke file, and that, in course of time, it has become filled just as files are intended to be filled. It has been added to from time to time, unit by unit, as occasion has demanded, increased in width and increased in height as well, until finally, the capacity of the office for transacting the business that is to be done, as well as keeping the necessary papers, has been exceeded. It is now a question of moving. Note how the cabinet is made ready for the truckman (Fig. 22). The terrors of moving, where, as a rule, everything has to be emptied and separately packed, and wherein there is big furniture to carry downstairs, furniture, perhaps, which has been practically built into the office, are all overcome by the use of the unit system of furniture. There is not a unit in the Globe-Wernicke cabinets that cannot be taken through a space 17x24 inches. Further, the cabinets are combined and taken apart without a tool and in so simple a manner that even a layman, though not a handy man mechanically, will have no trouble.

The Globe-Wernicke cabinets, which, it should be stated, are manufactured by the Globe Company, with factory at Cincinnati, and salesrooms in Chicago, New York and Boston, are made in two sizes, known respectively as the 13 inch and the 17 inch. The 13 inch, meaning the width from back to front, accommodates papers flat or ordinary letter size, while the 17 inch accommodates full legal cap lying flat.

Notwithstanding the number of illustrations presented in this article, the entire assortment of units has not been presented, and, therefore, the reader is urged to send to the Globe Company, to either of the addresses above, for a complete catalogue. Among the interesting features which will be found in the book are prices on each article delivered to the buyer's address. The manufacturers pay the freight.

You have a disagreeable duty to perform at twelve o'clock. Do not blacken nine and ten and all between with the color of twelve. Do the work of each and reap your reward in peace. So, when the dreaded moment in the future becomes the present, you shall meet it walking in the light, and that light shall overcome its darkness.—George MacDonald.

Fortune smiled deceitful on her birth.
—Thomson.

Wanted—A Pencil Sharpener

The sharpening of a pencil, at its worst, is, with the aid of a good pen-knife, a simple operation. Many machines have been invented and placed upon the market, each one claiming many points of superiority over its sharp little competitor, the pocket knife. No less than three hundred American patents have been granted upon such devices, and there is yet to be found one of these machines which has not been rejected by one or another pencil-user after a fair trial.

Judging from all indications, however, it would seem that there is a good opening in this field for the right article, and sooner or later it will be brought out. To be a permanent success, a pencil sharpener must do better work than can be done by hand with a knife. The sharpening must be accomplished in less time, and that, too, without soiling the fingers or the desk. Further, the machine must be simple and durable. If it is complicated and liable to get out of order, it is doomed to failure, irrespective of its merits in other directions.

Steadfastness and Success

Brightness of intellect frequently exists without steadfastness of purpose. Mere ability to work has been declared by many men to be the sole reason of their success, but work cannot be continually pursued without steadfastness of purpose. Success, therefore, depends upon steadfastness. A writer in the Mechanic Arts Magazine discusses this subject as follows:

"It cannot be too often repeated that it is not men of genius who move the world and take the lead in it, so much as men of steadfastness, purpose, and indefatigable industry. Notwithstanding the many undeniable instances of the precocity of men of genius, it is nevertheless true that early cleverness gives no indication of the height to which the grown man will reach. Precocity is sometimes a symptom of disease rather than of intellectual vigor. What becomes of all the "remarkably clever children"? Where are the prize boys? Trace them through life and it will frequently be found that the dull boys, who were beaten at school, have shot ahead of them. The clever boys are rewarded, but the prizes which they gain by their greater quickness and facility do not always prove of use to them. What ought rather to be rewarded is the endeavor, the struggle, and the obedience; for it is the man who does his best, though endowed with an inferiority of natural powers, that ought above all others to be encouraged.

Accountics

VOL. IV MARCH 1899 No. 3

The Monthly Statement

The question of an international association of public accountants and auditors has been broached by the secretary of one of the largest and most influential organizations in continental Europe. He is at present seeking information as to the existing associations among accountants, the plans upon which they are organized and the objects which they have in view. He does not desire publicity just now, preferring first to decide for himself the apparent feasibility of the scheme that he has in mind. Accordingly we cannot make known his identity. His letter to us, however, opens up a question which may be profitably discussed either as a preliminary to what is to follow from his efforts, or merely as an inquiry as to the interests which accountants have in common in different sections of the world.

Business is universal. It extends from the torrid zone to the Arctic regions, and from the east to the west, until the globe is completely encircled. The Volapük of commerce is the account. Values may be expressed in whatever currency is lawful in the country where the accounts are made out, and therefore they often vary from each other in this regard. The descriptive terms and names of accounts may be in one language or in another, but the correct relationship of debits to credits, of assets to liabilities, and of revenues to expenses is always of the same kind and nature, and always of a character to correctly tell the story of profitable or unprofitable transactions. Whether the accounts are phrased in terms derived from the English, Dutch, French, German, Russian, Italian, Spanish, Japanese or Chinese languages, or whether the accounts are expressed in dollars, pounds sterling, francs, marks, or in some other units of value, the integrity of the records, the correctness of the statements and the adequacy of the reports are to be determined by the same general rules of auditing and investigating. It would seem, therefore, without extended argument, that accountants, wherever working, in whatever part of the world they may be situated, or whether of one tongue or another, have many interests in common and many interests that might be served by an international organization.

Less has been done in the way of organization among accountants in America than in various other parts of the world. We have almost nothing in this country in the way of societies among accountants, compared with what is current in Great Britain, or even what is in progress in the Netherlands, in France, in Germany, in Italy, and in Australia. If an international association were to be formed at the present time, America, it would seem, would have little to say relatively, because America is so little organized at the present time, and because professional accounting has at present so small a place in our affairs.

Organizations among accountants just now are most numerous and the societies in existence are largest in membership in Great Britain. It would seem probable, therefore, if an international organization is to be effected at any time in the near future that the accountants of Great Britain would exert the larger measure of influence, simply by reason of their preponderance in number. But because English accountants might exert the larger influence in an international organization is no valid reason why the accountants of America should withhold their effort in a measure which is calculated to bring accountants into closer and more advantageous relationship throughout the world. Our correspondent, whose letter has suggested these general remarks, has not intimated to us in the least what his ideas are concerning the basis of an organization, nor the means of communication between members, nor the plan of officering, nor even a list of the general objects to be served. All this is speculation at present. It will be time enough to give attention to these points when specific measures have been offered for discussion or approval. Meanwhile what do our readers think of the general proposition?

In view of a decision recently affirmed by the Court of Appeals of New York, it becomes an interesting question whether an accountant, auditor, or bookkeeper, employed by a corporation that fails, is a professional man or one living by manual labor. The stock corporation law of New York makes the stockholders of every corporation, jointly and severally, personally liable for all debts due and owing to any of its laborers, servants or employes, other than contractors, for services performed by them for such corporation. Is an attorney-at-law, for example, who is regularly employed by a stock corporation at a fixed salary, an employe within the meaning and protection of this provision? This question was raised some time ago by George R. Bristor, formerly a clergyman in Rockland County, and now a practising lawyer. He acted as the attorney for the Merchants and Manufacturers' Protective Company under a written contract, at a salary of fifty dollars a week. He sued one of the stockholders for a balance due him under this contract. The case was tried before Mr. Justice Hirschberg, of Orange County, who wrote so good an opinion that it was adopted by the Appellate division, and is pronounced elaborate and satisfactory by Judge Gray in the Court of Appeals, where the decision has since been affirmed. That decision is adverse to the claim of the attorney.

The preference which the stock corporation law gives to debts due to employes is held to be solely for the benefit of persons who earn their living by manual labor and not by professional services. Hence the question proposed at the outset of this paragraph: Is a bookkeeper, for example, one who earns his living professionally or by manual labor? The answer to this will indicate in some measure his chances of collecting back salary (or wages) when the corporation by which he is employed fails. Apropos of this question may be presented the old conundrum: "Why is the bookkeeper like an old hen?" the answer to which was: "Because he scratches for a living." But does he scratch manually as with a pen, or mentally by agitating the grey matter that is supposed to be within his skull?

The New York Clearing House has recently taken a definite stand in the matter of fees on country checks. Its action is such as to make it obligatory upon the part of the members of the Association, or concerns that clear through members, to charge fees for the collection of out-of-town checks. Under the rules, the fees will be discretionary with the collecting bank on dealings with the United States, the State or the city of New York, and for items collected in Boston, Providence, Albany, Troy, Jersey City, Newark, Philadelphia and Baltimore. For items not on the discretionary list and payable in Connecticut, Delaware, Indiana, Illinois, Kentucky, Maine, Maryland, Massachusetts, Michigan, Missouri, New Hampshire, New Jersey, New York, Ohio, Pennsylvania, District of Columbia, Vermont, Rhode Island, Virginia, West Virginia and Wisconsin the collecting banks are to charge not less than one-tenth of one per cent. For Alabama, Arizona, Arkansas, California, Colorado, Florida, Georgia, Idaho, Indian Territory, Iowa Kansas, Louisiana, Minnesota, Mississippi, Montana, Nebraska, Nevada, New Mexico, North Carolina, North Dakota, Oklahoma, Oregon, South Carolina, South Dakota, Tennessee, Texas, Utah, Washington, Wyoming and Canada, not less than one-quarter of one per cent. In no case is less than ten cents on any item to be charged. A group of items received from any one person at the same time and payable within one district may be added together and treated as one item. No rebates are to be allowed. For a violation of the rules, the collecting bank will be fined $5,000, and in the case of a second violation may be expelled or excluded from clearance privileges.

Bearing upon this subject, Matthew Marshall, the well-known financial writer, whose articles regularly appear in the New York Sun, asserts that the collection of checks and drafts upon distant points by the clearing house banks has been costing upwards of $2,000,000 a year. He attributes this loss or expense for which the banks have not been reimbursed to the fact that there is over-competition among the banks for business, and that by reason of this competition they are being drawn into practices detrimental to their real interests. Dwelling upon the number of banks engaged in business at the present time, the writer asserts that of national banks there are 3,700, and of State banks as many more. Contrasted with this, he points out that Scotland has but 10 banks and England but 91. Canada, with a population of 5,000,000, has only 40 banks, or one to every 125,000 inhabitants. In the United States, with a population of 75,000,000, we have a bank for every 10,000 people. How easily, among this multiplicity of institutions, all eager for custom, can practices detrimental to the bank creep in?

While accountants in America are struggling with the schedules of gigantic corporations, and wrestling with the problem of reconciling accounting systems with the requirements of trusts, consolidations, mergings and other enterprises both new and original in character, the accountants of some of the older parts of the world, notably Great Britain, are laboring with problems of an entirely different character, but no less important in their final results. It is accepted the world over that dividends may not be paid out of capital. On the face of it, it would seem that there was little chance for argument or dispute upon this proposition, but the courts of Great Britain, as accountants of that realm are beginning to understand, have learned of late to discriminate so finely between what is and what is not capital in the paying of dividends, that there is being revealed a large area of debatable ground.

For example: If a company invests a million dollars in five steamships costing $200,000 each, and there ensues a profitable business for a period of say three or five years, so profitable indeed that interest on debentures is promptly discharged, repairs and renewals fully sustained, and dividends regularly paid, and if at the end of the period the company by disaster loses one of its steamships, the loss, we will say, being nominally $200,000, or one-fifth of its capital, does this fact deprive the shareholders of their rights to dividends from the earnings of the remainder of the company's fleet or the remaining four-fifths of its capital? It is assumed that the other four steamships continue to do a profitable business. Must the profits which these steamships earn be turned in to restore the capital of the company to its original amount, or should dividends be continued to the shareholders to the limit of the earning capacity of the crippled fleet, leaving the loss to stand unreplaced, or, if replaced at all, to be replaced by contributions of new capital from the stockholders for that specific purpose? This illustration is a simple one, comparatively speaking, of the broad question that is being discussed both in and out of the courts and only serves to open up to a very limited extent the nature of contentions which are agitating the accountants of Great Britain, and which are being considered by court justices at the present time.

It would seem from certain decisions that have been handed down that the bench is disposed to hold that because a part of an investment has been lost, there is no reason why the other part should not go on earning profits and paying dividends as best it is able. It would seem that there is a disposition to hold that a loss of capital is a loss of capital, and not a loss of profits on capital that has not been lost, and that, save only by the unanimous consent of the stockholders, the management of a company has no right to withhold dividends in order to make up a loss of capital. Going a step further, the decision seems to point, in some cases at least, to the path that the management should pursue in the matter of reserves for contingencies. It would appear that reserves may not be laid aside out of profits in all cases and as matters of course to meet future losses, but that instead the stockholders are entitled to dividends up to the measure of the real earnings. From their receipts in turn they should establish their own reserves, out of which to replace the depreciation of their shares, caused by disaster, or occurring because they are founded upon wasting assets. In a single paragraph we are unable to present to our readers all the ins and outs of this very interesting problem with which, as before stated, the accountants and courts in Great Britain are at present laboring. On a future occasion we may go further into this matter. Our object at present is merely to draw attention to something, which, sooner or later, must come up for similar consideration in this country. Just now, as marked at the outset, the profession in America is too busy with other matters to give this attention and investors are too closely engaged in forming companies and trusts to give much consideration to the principles of their future management.

A pamphlet recently issued by the National Association of Credit Men, entitled "Business Hints as to Business Success," and which is being given wide circulation at the present time, deserves more than passing notice. It has been compiled by the Business Literature Committee of the organization and has been issued by the Secretary, F. R. Boocock, 20 Nassau Street, pursuant to a resolution passed at the last annual convention.

The pamphlet is less than fifty pages in extent but contains more real business meat than is ordinarily packed into such a space. The articles for the most part are selections from the best matter that has appeared in the monthly clipping sheet which has been published by the Association for some time past. The latter, known as "Business Topics," has been sent to a selected list of editors of trade and class papers, with the request that they make such use of its contents as to them seems best, coupled with the statement that no credit whatsoever is desired or expected. The result has been that a series of articles on pertinent business topics, written for the most part by practical credit men, has been given an extremely wide circulation.

This circulation, however, has not brought the matter directly to the attention of the class that may be supposed to be most interested—namely, the small merchants throughout the land. The present book, therefore, has been compiled for the purpose of bringing to the attention of the business men of all the towns and villages throughout the country such articles of advice and counsel on commercial and financial topics as cannot fail to be of advantage to them in their regular work.

The subjects discussed in the little book before us include the following: "The Cash Principle in Retail Business," "The Value of Getting Credit," "The "Merchant's Rating," "The Merchant's Bank Profits," "Fresh Stocks," "Early Buying and Systematic Buying," "Dating Ahead," etc. The selections from Business Topics are supplemented by a special chapter devoted to a method of recording the merchant's purchases and payments, of recording his notes payable, and of filing his invoices. Methods for these three important parts of the bookkeeping routine of every merchant are laid out in considerable detail upon a plan that will readily work in with the most complete accounting system. At the same time the methods are presented to the retailer entirely divested of bookkeeping technicalities.

The book will be circulated through the co-operation of a large number of wholesale merchants and manufacturers who are persuaded that the distribution of good literature among the merchants of the smaller towns will have an important effect in improving credits, that is in diminishing the risks of selling. It is, therefore, of the nature of a missionary effort—a distribution of tracts, as it were, with a very special and commendable business object in view.

An Accounting Term: "In Suspense."

(In many cases a charge to suspense only puts off the day of reckoning. Witness the haste of the man in the foreground to get away from a disagreeable fact.)

At What Time Does a Gain or Loss Occur?*

By James W. Green

In saying what little I have to say on this subject, I shall confine myself to its consideration from the point of view of a manufacturing business, as all my experience has been in that and kindred lines. Of course, it is natural to think that no other business is quite as difficult to look after as the one we ourselves are engaged in, and so it has always seemed to me that the account keeping in a manufactory excelled all others in the number and diversity of the petty little things to be classified and accounted for. It does not seem as if any other line could furnish as many chances to keep track of and investigate so many little things which, when finally disposed of, are like the Dutchman's horse—hard to catch and of very little value when caught. And in considering the main question I shall speak more of the losses than of the gains, as the latter are far less likely to provoke discussion or demand investigation. Not that I would underestimate or discourage the value and necessity of a continual comparison of costs and charges in profitable transactions.

Most successful houses owe their success to a careful and systematic examination of their most profitable trades, as these transactions indicate, for the most part, in what line the house is giving the public the most for its money. If the public contiuue to buy a certain line or class of goods which yields the manufacturer a generous profit, he may feel pretty sure that in that line he excells his competitors, and, therefore, that is the line for him to push to the utmost—lowering the price as fast as reduction in the cost of production permits, and thereby increasing the sales as well as discouraging competition. But the gains of a business are like children in a large family—they take care of themselves, and, further, they are always agreeable to investigate, to be responsible for, or to talk over. Consequently, every one connected with the management of a business is ever ready to discuss the gains and especially his share in them. He likes to tell you how smart he was in making the trade, and how much of the profit on this or that transaction was due to his fine business judgment and sagacity.

With the losses, however, it is quite different. Nobody wants anything to do with them. Nobody wants to talk about them, and and, above all, nobody wants to be held responsible for them. Consequently, the analysis of losses and the display of their whys and wherefores is always a disagreeable, though highly important, duty.

At what particular time does a loss occur? Losses in business may be roughly divided into three classes: First, those in which the price agreed upon is less than the cost at which contract is finally completed; second, those caused by a reduction in a bill after it has once been rendered, and third, those caused by the failure of the debtor to meet his obligations. This last class of losses belongs to what is usually termed the "commercial end" of the business and may be said to occur, so far as the books of the business are concerned, as soon as the loss is credited to the debtors' account. The other two classes of losses belong to the manufacturing end of the business. The losses here may be said to occur in the first class as soon as the bill is entered on the sales book, and in the second class as soon as the reduction is credited to the debtor. Both the second and third classes of losses are plain to see. They stand out by themselves on the books. Anybody at all familiar with business transactions understands them—or understands their effect—as soon as he sees the entries, and, if he considers himself anything of an expert, they are among the first things he looks at. Such losses, therefore, cannot escape the notice of those responsible for the safe conduct of the business and are sure to occasion discussion, investigation, and proposals for preventing their repetition in the future.

The discussion then narrows itself down to losses of the first class, viz.

*Read before a meeting of the Hartford Chapter of the Institute of Accounts, October 25, 1898, by James W. Green.

those caused by the contract price of a piece of work being less than the cost of its production. At what particular time does such a loss occur? Manifestly, at the time the bill is rendered and the amount placed on the sales book, for, up to that time, any statement of the assets and liabilities of the business would class this particular piece of work as a part of the unfinished orders or work in process. At such times it would naturally be included in the assets at its actual cost and would, therefore, have no effect whatever on the profit and loss account, although even at that time its cost might already be far in excess of the agreed price. As soon as it is billed, however, it ceases to be a part of the work in process and becomes an asset among the accounts receivable. And it is just at this moment that its value changes and it occasions a loss to the business—just here that it fails to return a new dollar for an old one. The trouble is, however, that the entry looks as innocent as the rest of its fellows and there is nothing in its appearance to indicate its shortcomings. Here, then, is where the accountant must get in his work. I hold it of extreme importance that the cost of all work done for a price should be ascertained as near to the time the bill is rendered as possible—before it is rendered is best, of course, but, when this is not possible, as soon after as it can be managed. By thus getting the facts together, when they are all fresh in everybody's mind, the occurrence of similar leaks is prevented in the future. I have myself seen a case where the same piece of work was done three times in succession at a loss because the cost was not ascertained in the first place, and when the job came along again it was accepted twice afterwards at the old figure because nobody thought of such a thing as its not having paid in the first place.

The Filipino Accountant

By Vannant

We are always ready to welcome an addition to the ranks of skilled labor, no matter from what source it proceeds. Mechanics and artisans, becoming citizens of this country, add to its wealth-producing power. Accountants who leave their homes and take up their residence among us also contribute in no unimportant degree to the prosperity of the country. What we have acquired as the results of the Spanish war, in population as well as territory, adds to the wealth of the nation. But it would seem, by at least one authority, that in taking over the Philippines we have acquired what we least expected. For the most part, we have been disposed to consider the Filipinos as a barbarous or semi-civilized race, but great is our astonishment when we learn that the Filipinos, first and last, excel as accountants. No less an authority than General Charles W. Whittier, U. S. V., makes this assertion. The occasion of it was the dinner of the Merchants' Association in Boston about the turn of the year. General Whittier was not present, but sent a letter of regrets, in which he expressed his opinions with respect to various matters in Manila, from which point he had recently returned. Incidentally, he gave some account of the natives, whom he had carefully studied. Of these General Whittier said: "The native is clever, excels as a mariner, musician, cigar and cigarette maker, railroad workman and station master; he is an excellent accountant, and weaver of pina (pineapple fibre) and tusi (pineapple and hemp); in fact, he seems adaptable to any skilled labor. He is not yet equal to governing."

Now all this is interesting in the extreme. Just what kind of a man an "excellent accountant" is, who is grouped in the same class as mariners, musicians, cigarette makers, railroad workmen and station masters, to say nothing of weavers, is a question. But, evidently, General Whittier knows what he is talking about, for he goes on to say that this clever native (accountant) is incapable of self-government. This statement begins to cast a ray of light where before all was dark. We supppose that before General Whittier sailed for the Philippine Islands he must have looked in upon some bookkeepers or accountants' association in this country, thereby discovering the fact that bookkeepers and accountants are notorious for their inability to govern themselves in an associated capacity or manage their own affairs in that business-like way in which they conduct the offices over which they are called upon to preside during business hours. The question now arises: Is the accountant's profession about to be overrun by Philippine cheap labor? For example, is the registration bureau conducted by the New York State Society of Certified Public Accountants soon to have the name of Filipino after Filipino recorded as an applicant for a position as an accountant's assistant? These are, indeed, grave questions, and they are of special importance to the rank and file of those who in various parts of this glorious land are now passing as expert accountants.

Novel Application of the Card Index Method

By Fielding West

I have noticed the advertisement of the competition in card index data published in recent numbers of Accountics. I am very much interested in this enterprise and hope that nothing will intervene to prevent its successful culmination. The business information that will thus be piled up will be of the utmost importance to the business world, and I hope in due time will be presented in the form of a handsome volume.

However, the object of this letter is to call attention to a novel application of the card index principle which came to my knowledge a short time since. Believing that it is one that is not likely to be included in the list of any of the competitors, I submit it for editorial consideration. It is Uncle Sam's ingenius method of detecting a professional enlister. It seems that various men have a passion for periodically enlisting in the army. After serving a while they desert and then turn up at some other recruiting post. The card index plan has been resorted to for the purpose of detecting the offenders. There are men also who have been dishonorably discharged from the service who have a hankering to get back. The card index plan works in their case also. The following is a quotation from a description of the way the government manages in this regard:

The papers for every recruit are made out in this way: One, the physical form, on which his physical fitness is determined; next, the oath of enlistment. Then what is known as the "picture card" is made out. It shows every mark on his body, like a photograph. It gives his size, color of hair, eyes and all peculiar characteristics, such, for instance, as scars, moles and so on. The eyes are graded, as blue, shades 1 to 10. This card is sent immediately after the enlistment to the Surgeon-General's office. Surgeon-General Sternberg designed the system. As soon as this card reached his office it is taken to a frame of pigeon-holes. The pigeon-holes are classified for height first, so that a "5-foot-7" card enters that department and comes along the sub-divisions until it reaches "eyes, blue, 10." In this frame it moves to "scars characteristic." By this process it reaches the only pigeon-hole that can contain picture cards of this character. By a still further and finer process of elimination it is brought face to face with the card of the man if he has ever enlisted before. Right in the office of the Adjutant-General is the record of every soldier to the minutest detail. Let us suppose that two cards face each other to-morrow which seem confusingly alike. One is marked "Thomas Jones, deserter from the Fifth Cavalry December 26, 1897; not apprehended. The other is marked, "James Smith, recruit, enlisted at Fort Porter, N. Y., February 9, 1899." In less than one hour after the receipt of this card word will come from the office of the Adjutant-General: "Arrest recruit James Smith, alias Thomas Jones. He is a deserter from the Fifth Cavalry. Evidence of same will be furnished at Fort Porter, N. Y., by mail." This man will be tried by court-martial for desertion under the 47th article of war and his apprehension will have been due to the card index system.

Change of Address

The attention of all our readers and advertisers is called to our change of address. Accountics is now very comfortably and eligibly located in the Lancashire Building, Pine Street, less than a half block from the corner of Nassau Street, and directly east of the Sub-Treasury Building. We shall be pleased to have all our friends and patrons visit us in our new quarters as often as it may be convenient for them to do so.

"I should like to know when you are going to pay that bill. I can't come here every day in the week?"

"What day would suit you best?"

"Saturday."

"Very well, then, you can ca'l every Saturday."—Tit-Bits.

Gentleman (entering)—Do you work here, boy? Office Boy—Only when the boss is looking.—Boston Transcript.

Practical Auditing

BY WILTON C. EDDIS, C. A.

(*Concluded from page 25, February issue*)

Let us now consider the audit of joint stock companies.

There are general principles in auditing receipts and payments, seeing that statements and balance sheets are correct as compared with the books, and then that the books are a true record of the transactions, and other information professed to be therein recorded. These general principles are applicable to all audits. In the case of the municipal accounts, the auditor, as I have shown, requires to understand the rules governing them, so with the audit of companies, the auditor must be familiar with the Act under which the company is incorporated; it will be his duty to study the by-laws and minutes to ascertain that the transactions, as affecting the accounts, are in accordance with the regulations laid down by the directors and shareholders.

The auditor, further, is appointed by the shareholders, though in the first instance he may be appointed by the directors, and he is bound to see that they have a true statement periodically presented to them. The subject of hidden reserves is, however, one that is often met with which means that the company is in reality better off than appears on the balance sheet. This is a subject which the experienced auditor will know how to deal with, but as a totally different matter to a balance sheet which attempts to show more than there are.

The auditor, then, besides having a good general knowledge of the various companies acts themselves, will require to understand the nature of the business, and the exteht to which he will have to examine into details.

Let us glance at another class of audits, viz., the accounts of executors and trustees.

Here, again, the auditor will require to have a sufficient knowledge of the law relating to this subject, so that he may be in a position to do his duty effectively. A good illustration of this may be given by again referring to another examination question of the Institute:

A trustee under a will being short of funds, paid a legatee to whom $1,000 was bequeathed, $50 per year as interest for two years from the death, and then paid the legacy in full. How would you debit the two payments of interest, and why?

Now, as a general rule, pecuniary legacies bear interest from the expiration of twelve months from the death of the testator, and are not entitled to any interest prior to then. So answering this question in a broad way, the two payments would be debited as follows, viz., one payment to the estate and the other payment to the trustee. But the professional auditor must not be content with a mere superficial knowledge of his work. He must post himself on all the matters that require his attention. His profession is one of endless work and study, and the first-class auditor is a student to the end of his days. The man who informs you that he is a first-class accountant and thoroughly understands bookkeeping probably does not realize how little he does know. It requires knowledge to know one's own ignorance, and the more learned a man is, the more humble he is, and consequently the more valuable.

So, after this preamble, let us reconsider this question. Perhaps the trustee was quite right to have paid this legatee the two years' interest. He may have been informed by his lawyer that as the legatee was a child of the testator, he was entitled to receive interest from the date of his father's death; or the legacy may have been in payment of a debt, possibly a debt of honor; so you see, there are in reality two answers to this question.

Further, in audits generally, it is often seen that the young auditor, very anxious no doubt to do his duty and distinguish himself, raises little trivial points and magnifies them, because he fancies that unless he finds something wrong, people will think he has not done his work properly.

The "true auditor" is a man who has a high standard, and who does his work so that he can satisfy himself that his standard has been maintained. Such a man does not seek to advertise his work. If he finds mistakes he gets them corrected, so that the correct results may be obtained. Some of the best auditing work is done in this way.

"Prevention is better than cure"—the auditor who, by his steady and conscientious work, prevents things going wrong, does far more useful work than when he is called in to ascertain the amount which has been stolen by a dishonest cashier.

The policemen who maintain order are better friends to the community than are the militia when called in to suppress a riot. Both necessary at different times, but how many a riot could have been averted if a proper police force had been maintained. And, indeed, how many poor, weak prisoners might now be respected citizens, and thousands of dollars saved to the merchants, had a proper system of auditing been maintained.

It does not pay to wait to insure until burnt out, but one thing is requisite, and that is to insure in a strong and respectable company. Equally so, is it a perfect farce to employ auditors who don't know their work, and only work for dollars and cents. The auditor who is worth anything, works for honor as well as a living, and, moreover, must be a responsible man. The man who has nothing to lose, either in reputation or livelihood, is not the man to do any professional work.

A professional man must devote his whole energies to his profession. So the professional accountant must not follow any other calling, and our Institute has wisely laid down the rule that only men devoting their whole time to the profession of accounts can obtain its highest honors. I have laid considerable stress on the importance to the community generally that only first-class accountants should be appointed auditors, and this is a matter of such grave importance that it is engaging the attention of the best men everywhere.

It is more and more being admitted that men should not be allowed to practise in the profession of accounts, until they have proved their fitness. For my part, I believe that all practising accountants should be licensed by the government, and that such license should not be granted unless the accountant has proved himself qualified by passing a sufficiently searching examination. It is very encouraging to the Council of the Institute to see the real and live interest taken in the work which they are striving to do in this direction. There is little doubt but that, in the near future, there will be as marked a difference between the bookkeeper who holds his diploma and the one who does not, as there is between the M. D. and the quack doctor, and also that when a man is known as "an accountant," people will understand that such a man is a fit and proper person to audit accounts, or advise generally in the multitudinous questions which arise daily. So much for auditors and their qualifications. On such a subject one could write for hours, but I wish now to give a short space to the subject of the accounts themselves.

We will choose a manufacturer's accounts. The auditor has audited the books, examined all the vouchers and found everything in order. The authority for all transactions, where such authority required looking into, has been found to be satisfactory. He now has to examine the profit and loss accounts and the balance sheet. As I before explained, the auditor must be a good accountant, so equally when discussing auditing, it is not the place to examine or explain the principles of bookkeeping.

Theoretically speaking, the auditor has the balance sheet handed him all complete, etc., but in actual practice the auditor often makes out the balance sheet himself, and passes the closing and final entries.

Accounts that have been badly kept have to be straightened out and audited, as well as books that are well kept. So often the auditor is practically engaged in a dual capacity both as auditor and accountant. The auditor, strictly speaking, should only audit, but in experience this cannot always be carried out, as the bookkeepers employed sometimes do not know how to prepare a proper balance sheet or straighten out accounts which have got mixed up.

First, let us look at the profit and loss accounts.

A manufacturer makes his profit by manufacturing goods and then selling them. So to ascertain his profits the auditor has to find out what it has cost to make them, then what he has sold them for. What is the cost of making goods? Goods are the product of labor and raw material, valued at what it has cost to land it at the factory. So the cost of goods consists of this labor and material, plus the expense of the machinery and other aids required to complete the process.

Let us divide them into three classes, then:

First, labor;

Second, material;

Third, other expenses.

To audit the labor, or, as it is called, the "wages," what vouchers should the auditor require to examine? The voucher for wages paid is primarily the wages sheet, which is confirmed by the check drawn on the bank, and strengthened by the evidence at the disposal of the auditor that the employes, whose names appeared thereon, actually received the cash. Where a proper system of cost accounts is kept, the check on wages is far more complete; because the wages and materials are shown as factors in providing the manufactured article, and the actual amount expended on these items is recorded on all goods manufactured, and can be compared with the corresponding accounts in the general ledger.

As regards the other items of expenditure, they are audited in the usual way. One very important point in an audit is seeing that items that belong to revenue are not charged to capital account and shown as assets. This often requires great care to look into. The manager of a company who is over-anxious to show a good dividend will try to keep his expenses down by charging items such as repairs, to a capital account, instead of an expense account.

We now come to the question of stock-taking, and the auditor's duty is to see, as far as is in his power, that the values of the raw material, stores and merchandise are shown in the balance sheet as correct.

There are several methods of doing this. In extreme cases the auditor might be required to be present when stock was being taken, and check each item. But as a general rule, he carefully examines the stock sheets, checks the figures therein, and ascertains that these have been prepared by responsible men. In valuing stock on hand allowance must always be made for depreciation through change in fashion, fall in market values, etc. He may occasionally, too, with advantage, refer to invoices for values, etc., but as a matter of fact, the reliability of stock taking depends upon the reliability of the men who have done the work. There is, again, a further valuable check, and that is by comparing the percentage of gross profits with those of former years, and if there is a marked discrepancy or increase it would require looking into. The question of auditing these items, and, in fact, all an auditor's work, is so guided by experience, that no hard and fast rules can be laid down by which the beginner can be guided. Quite a different procedure might be adopted in one audit as compared with another, and yet the main principles would be observed in each.

By comparing the percentages of profit and expenditure with former years, a most useful guide is afforded, not only to the auditor, but to the manufacturer himself. The auditor now having audited these accounts and found them correct, ascertains that all the liabilities have been included in the balance sheet, and to do this he must depend on the assurance of the responsible officer or member of the firm that this has been done. He can see for himself, though, that proper provision has been made for outstanding liabilities, such as rent, accrued interest, wages, etc. Theoretically, no balance sheet is complete unless all outstanding accrued items, whether as assets or liabilities, are included, but in actual practice many large firms find that it is more advantageous, and as it takes too much extra time to include such accrued items, so they omit them, on the ground that one year averages up with another.

I am not prepared to discuss this question here, but one point is very clear, that such items as depreciation on machinery or leaseholds, and provisions for bad and doubtful debts, must never be left out if the balance sheet is to show a fair and true statement of the firm's position.

The assets also in the balance sheet will require very careful examination. The cash on hand must be in existence, as on the date of closing the books, and must be carefully counted. If the auditor cannot do this on that date, he should count the cash on his first visit afterwards, checking the cash book up to that date. But the better and more modern system is to have little or no cash to count. The auditor should urge that all cash received should be banked daily. The best rule is that all cash taken on the one day should be banked the next to the exact amount. Auditing the bank account is a very important part of an auditor's work. The bank vouchers should be carefully compared with the payments made. Copies and full particulars of all the deposits made and bills discounted should be always kept and checked by the auditor. Because the bank balance agrees with the balance in the firm's books is no reason why the account should not be checked, and the following gives a good illustration of this:

A firm accepted a draft at sight, which was duly charged to their account by the bank on the 31st of the month, but which was omitted to be charged by the firm to their customer, not being entered in the Bills Payable book. On the 30th of the month, a check for a similar amount was drawn and sent to another customer. The bank account was balanced in due course. The auditor, however, in checking the items in the cash book with the bank vouchers found that the bill referred to was not entered. The mistake as above was discovered, and the bank balance had to be altered to its correct amount by a correcting entry. The check given on the 30th was outstanding, and had not been paid by the bank, as the bookkeeper supposed, on the 31st.

The merchandise has already been dealt with. The book debts and bills receivable will require careful examination. The auditor should go through these with the principal, and see that all doubtful debts are provided for and the bad debts written off. It is not the auditor's duty or province, however, as before mentioned, to manage the business; the management may choose to give long credit, but, as a general rule, the account itself will afford a good idea as to whether it is a safe one or not. Where a business is run on practically a cash basis, if an account was unpaid for twelve months it would invoke enquiry; on the other hand, some firms allow accounts to stand with good marks in the hope of getting further business. Experience can soon fix the rate for a particular business. Probably the simplest plan is to set aside a fixed percentage of the accounts as a provision for doubtful debts.

The valuation of machinery is always a difficult matter. It is often impossible to fix a true value on machinery, and the percentage to be written off is largely a matter of experience. From 7 per cent. to 10 per cent. would be about the rate. With new inventions always being made, it is evident that in some firms there must be available capital to purchase new machinery to keep abreast of the time. A good illustration of this is in printing machines. Machines that a few years ago were very valuable, are now only worth what the material they are made of will fetch. It is astonishing how changes in invention and fashion can affect values in assets, such as machinery and merchandise, and even in raw material. So, in auditing these accounts, no certain rule can be laid down. As far as possible the manufacturer should value these in his own interests, as near their real value as possible. Merchandise is, of course, not valued at its selling value, but at what it costs, the rule in all cases being that profits on sales belongs to the period in which the sales are made.

Such assets as goodwill and patent rights, also preliminary expenses, in the case of a joint stock company, can remain at their original cost to the business, though it is always satisfactory to see fictitious assets, so called, gradually written off.

Investments usually are not altered, but remain at their original cost, unless, of course, there should be a loss on realization. In the case, however, of a company formed to deal in stocks and shares, these would then require to be valued periodically at their market value and provisions made as required, but then they would cease to be investments, but would be bought and sold at a profit; whereas the term investment implies a permanent disposal of capital for the sake of the revenue to be derived therefrom.

Leasehold investments are valued at their original cost, less the amount set aside each year, so that their value shall always be correct, as it is very clear that they must, as a general rule, be steadily decreasing in value.

Finally we come to the available dividend. Human nature is much the same everywhere and in all classes. Even if we have an unusually heavy snow storm, there is a feeling of satisfaction at learning that it is the biggest on record. In this age of statistics we are always hearing of records being broken, and, unfortunately, many a company, through trying to establish or maintain a record for paying dividends, has failed and perhaps helped to swell the record for the year of insolvent businesses. So we see the tendency is to try and show the best year in business. Naturally the shareholder likes to see a big dividend and the business man likes to feel that his business is improving.

It is not the auditor's business to declare a dividend. A profit is, however, available for dividend in proportion to the extent in which profits are locked up in the business. Where a large profit is worked on a small capital, it might not be prudent or possible to declare more than a nominal dividend, though the figures show that a good profit has been made. In private firms too often the capital is too small owing to withdrawals, and in companies often the cash capital is too small, though the figures sound most imposing. The amount of the dividend declared or the profit withdrawn is the business of the shareholders or firm, and with the certification of the balance sheet the auditor's work is ended.

Hartford Chapter

At the meeting of the Hartford Chapter of the Institute of Accounts, February 28, addresses were delivered by Meigs H. Whaples, president of the Connecticut Trust and Safe Deposit Company, of Hartford, and by Henry S. Robinson, secretary of the same organization. The subject of Mr. Whaples' address was "Banking and Bank Accounting." He dwelt particularly on the latter part of his topic. He compared the methods that were in vogue when he entered the banking business some thirty or more years ago, at which time balances were drawn off monthly, with the system now in practice, wherein daily balances are the regular rule. He described in detail the various books now used in banks doing business in cities of moderate size, and also the methods of the Hartford Clearing House.

The subject of Mr. Robinson's address was "The Duties of Trustees, Executors and Administrators." He dwelt upon the requirements of the State of Connecticut in the matter of settling estates of deceased persons, and gave much valuable information regarding the procedure in administering an estate and the method of making up the accounts to be rendered the probate court. He also explained the duties of trustees under wills, and made some suggestions regarding the investment of the funds of the trust, calling attention to many points which are liable to be overlooked by any one not accustomed to the settlement of estates and the administering of a trust, and the neglect of which might be a source of embarrassment, if not actual loss.

Both addresses were very interesting and instructive, and were greatly enjoyed by the members and guests present. The meeting was well attended. The March meeting of this organization will be the annual meeting for election of officers, etc.

Fortune comes well to all, that comes not late.—Longfellow.

Can wealth give happiness? Look round and see, what gay distress! what splendid misery!—Young.

Without a rich heart wealth is an ugly beggar.—Emerson.

Poverty treads close upon the heels of great and unexpected wealth.—Rivarol.

Sovereign money procures a wife with a large fortune, gets a man credit, creates friends, stands in place of pedigree, and even of beauty.—Horace.

"Which of your studies do you like best, my little man?"

"Oh! Accounts."

"Accounts? What kind of accounts do you mean?"

"Personal accounts, mostly. I've got to get square with Jem Slattery for kicking my dog, I've got an old grudge to settle with Johnny Davis, and if I only can catch Mike Dugan alone I'll punch him 'till his capital is done for and his reserve's clean used up. I'll bet cash against book accounts he won't never make another statement after I've audited his ledger.'

Interest and Discount—II

BY CHARLES F. ROHNE

Evil Effects of Usury Laws

Usury laws, like other laws fixing prices, are not only ineffectual, but they prevent all persons, whose credit is not first class, from obtaining loans from capitalists of the highest character, and force borrowers to secure loans from those who are less scrupulous and who are also compelled to charge above the current rate a premium sufficient to compensate the lender for the extra risk.

Usury laws undertake to prevent what is not an evil, and hence what should not be interfered with; consequently they are productive of injury instead of benefit. Who would pretend that it is just for the Legislature to compel underwriters to insure extra hazardous or specially hazardous properties, on the same terms or rate per cent. as they write ordinarily hazardous risks? And yet such a law would be no more absurd and unjust than the law of usury which requires that the rate per cent. of all interest shall be the same on capital loaned to those whose security or character are widely different.

Again, it is impossible to make the legal rate a fair rate; for the market is continually changing, and independent of the hazard of the risk, a rate that would have been fair at one time would be too low at another time, and perhaps extortionate at another time. A loan for a short period commands a higher rate than for a long period; and a rate that is fair for a short period would be unfair for a long period. The only way a fair rate can be determined is by competition in the money market, when all the elements of supply and demand, of risk, of time and of profit, are duly considered by the borrower and the lender."

Borrowers and Lenders

When the Usury Laws were passed the poorer classes were the borrowers and the rich the lenders, and hence the Usury Laws were enacted mainly with a view to protect the poor against high rates of interest.

But, at the present time, the borrowers are largely the rich men and the rich corporations, and a large part of the lenders are the poorer or medium classes. Hence, considering the reason for the passage of the Usury Laws, it follows logically that they should be now abolished.

One evidence of this change of borrowers and lenders is the fact that in 1894 three million depositors, mostly poor people, had nearly $1,300,000,000 on deposit in the savings banks. Another evidence is the fact that hundreds of millions of dollars of bonds of various kinds of corporations, or States, and of nations, are held by the poorer classes.

Considering the Usury Laws in all their bearings, the conclusions are as follows: 1. They are unwise and unjust. 2. They are practically inoperative. 3. They are evidence of financial inexperience on the part of the law makers. 4. They are violative of the rights of borrowers and lenders, and of the ethical principles of business. 5. They should be repealed.

That a law regulating interest in cases of judgments, successions, and transactions in which no contracts of interest are made, is necessary, there is no question of doubt. But further than this, the question of interest should be left to the judgment of the contracting parties.

Definitions

Interest is the sum paid for the productiveness of capital.

Interest is calculated on a scale of a certain number of units on every 100 for one year, and hence it combines per cent. and per annum, from the Latin per centum, on a hundred, and per annum, for a year.

The principal is the sum of money or capital on which interest is charged or paid.

The rate of interest is the per cent. paid on the principal, for its use, for a specified time.

Time is the period for which the principal is loaned or bears interest.

The amount is the sum of the principal and the interest.

The proceeds is the difference between the principal and the interest.

The subject of interest is classified into several divisions, viz.: simple interest, annual, semi-annual, and quarterly interest, and compound interest, which we will present in the order here given.

Simple interest is the interest on the principal unincreased by interest, however long overdue.

Annual, semi-annual and quarterly interest is simple interest, and the interest on the simple interest from the time it becomes due until paid.

Annual, semi-annual, and quarterly interest is allowed by some States on notes and contracts where the interest is payable annually, semi-annually or quarterly.

Compound interest is interest on both the principal and the interest, i. e. it is interest where the principal is increased at the expiration of each period of interest payment by the interest on the principal for such period, whether for twelve, six, three, or one month or for one day.

Compound interest is allowed in some States, under certain conditions.

Legal interest is the rate per cent. fixed by the law of each State, to apply when no agreement is made. In many of the States the penalty for usury is the forfeiture of all interest. In Connecticut there is no penalty, but in New York the penalty is a forfeiture of principal and interest, and fine not exceeding $1,000, or imprisonment not exceeding six months, or both. However, in New York on demand loans of $5,000 and upward, which are secured by collateral, any rate of interest may be agreed upon in writing. In California and Idaho compound interest is allowed by written contract.

Usury is a higher rate per cent. than the law allows. The law of different States prescribes the different penalties for usury. In Louisiana the penalty is the forfeiture of all interest.

The principal, the interest, the rate, the time, and the amount of proceeds, constitute the five quantities involved in interest questions; and when any three of these are given the others may be found. Hence, there are five classes of interest questions.

Interest is defined by many political economists to be the sum the borrower pays for the use of money. But this definition is opposed by the more acute and critical political economists, who define interest to be the share of the product obtained by the owner of capital.

The rate of interest is the per cent. paid for the capital or money borrowed, for a specified time.

It was formerly believed that the rate depended upon the abundance or scarcity of capital in the money market at any given time. But this opinion has been proven to be erroneous. The rate is now shown by our best economists to be governed by the productiveness or profits of capital employed in the various lines of business.

Mill says, after thoroughly arguing the case, "It is an error to imagine that the rate of interest bears any necessary relation to the quantity or value of money in circulation."

Ricardo says that "The rate of interest is not regulated by the rate at which the bank will lend, but by the rate of profit which can be made by the employment of capital, and which is totally independent of the quantity and of the value of money."

The value of money is its purchasing power.

But independent of this general law based upon profits, the rate is sometimes affected by the greater hazard that is incurred by loaning to less responsible parties, or on less certain security, and also by reason of the difficulties that sometimes attend the transactions of loan, because of the legal limit placed upon the rate, called Usury Laws.

Again, the rate is influenced by the duration of the loan. Money loaned for a short period commands a higher rate than money loaned for a long period, and call loans bear a lower rate than loans made for a definite period of time.

Annual Interest

By the terms of contracts for the use of money for more than one year, the interest is commonly made due and payable annually or semi-annually. In some States interest not paid at the time specified in the contract draws interest from that time, on the legal principle that any debt should draw interest from the time it is due.

Annual interest is simply interest on the principal plus simple interest on each installment of interest on principal not paid when due. Annual interest is legalized in Michigan at the same rate as described by the contract, in Ohio, Wis-Iowa at 6 per cent., and in Pennsylvania, consin, Vermont, New Hampshire and Georgia, Illinois and Indiana by special contract only.

Evolution in Accounting and Cost Keeping

By A. O. Kittredge, C. P. A.

(Concluded from page 43, February issue)

And now before I close, although I fear the length of my remarks has already taxed your patince, let me say a word or two upon certain principles underlying cost accounts, the application of which is to be made in every factory, according to the nature of the product. What shall be done with general factory expenses? How shall they be spread over product? General factory expenses include the salaries of superintendents, foremen, cost clerks and other non-producers. They also include the reserves for repairs and depreciation, the use of patents, taxes, insurance, and the like. The aggregate sum is usually a very considerable amount.

For reasons already mentioned, it is not the best plan to deduct these at the end of a long period like a year from gross profits, because that method affords no insight as to the results of the business between times. These expenses, therefore, should be spread over product, first for the purpose of showing the real results of the business as it proceeds, considered as a single unit, and second for the purpose of determining the profitableness of different parts of the business and of different articles that are made.

It is comparatively easy to charge into any lot of goods the material consumed and the labor that is directly applied. Supposing that the lot of goods so produced is one hundred wagons, and that the cost of labor and materials has been $1,500, or $15 per wagon. What amount shall be added to the $15 per wagon to determine its actual cost, for the purpose of showing the price at which it must be sold to make a satisfactory product? The records of factories in some lines of business show that the general factory expenses are 15 per cent., 25 per cent., 40 per cent., or 50 per cent. of the specific shop costs. Various other ratios are also in evidence. One hundred and fifty per cent. is occasionally encountered. If the general expenses of the shop have amounted to 100 per cent. of the specific charges, then the cost of the wagon in this case would figure $30. So much for the result. Now as to method.

Many manufacturers, in attempting to solve the problem of cost accounts, proceed literally upon the lines just indicated by way of illustration. They say, "Our general expenses are of such and such a ratio to our product," and then make the application. Frequently they take the product at selling prices, which, of course, must include prime factory cost, general expenses of factory and commercial expenses, together with profit. General expenses of factory are variable, commercial expenses are also variable, for they are frequently influence by such things as changes in the salaries of officers. Therefore, it is at once evident that this plan is inadequate.

Again, if the profits commercial expenses are thrown out and prime cost is taken as the basis, certain other difficulties are encountered. Materials vary in price from time to time, not only as the market advances and declines, but also as a whim of the trade demands a substitution of one kind of material in place of another previously used, with corresponding variation in cost. What basis, then, can be found that is entirely reliable upon which to base the distribution of factory expenses?

It is the generally accepted opinion of accountants everywhere that labor being the least variable of all the elements entering into the cost of product, is the best foundation on which to spread general expenses. The labor may be taken in the dollars and cents of cost, the high-priced labor and the low-priced labor going in together at just what is paid for it, or, as certain accountants prefer, the labor hours may be taken as the unit, irrespective of the price paid per hour.

With respect to the choice between these two methods, I shall not attempt to speak to-night, but I do wish to leave this thought with you, that upon labor, as shown in the factory to be as an element of prime cost, should the general expenses be distributed.

In conducting the accounts of a manufacturing establishment, mechanical facilities should not be overlooked. If "accounting is the vital element of business," the only thing without which business cannot manage to get along, then in comparison it is like a priceless gem and deserves a setting in proportion to its value. The day has long since gone by when any dark corner was good enough for the bookkeeper; when any cheap

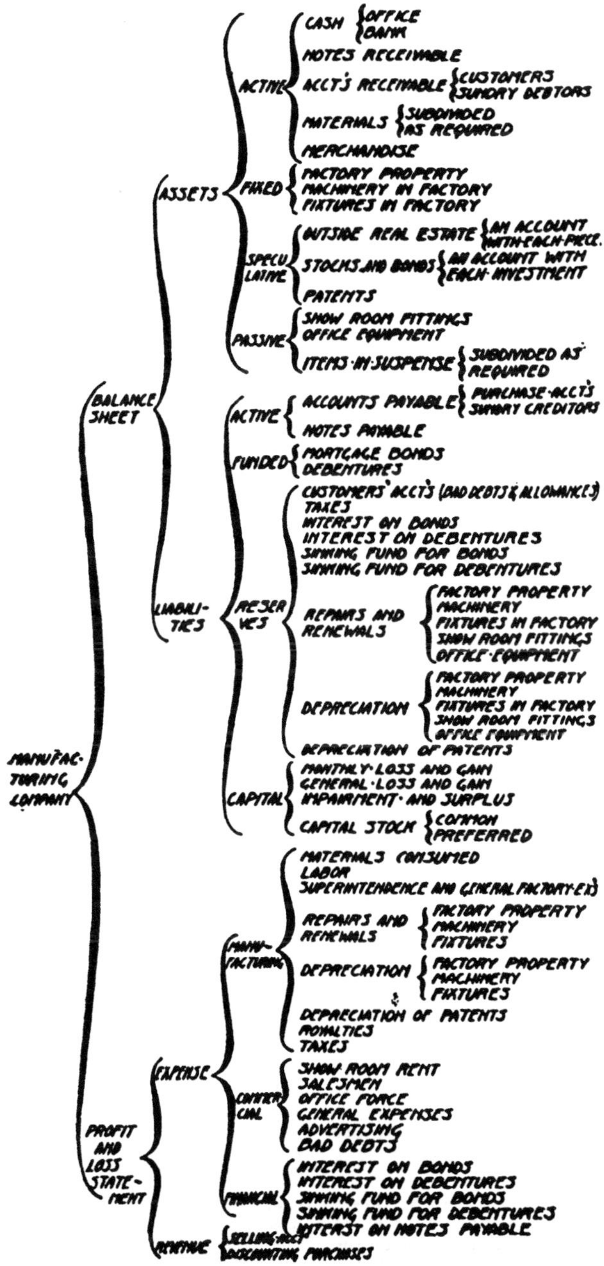

FIG. 5—FAC SIMILE OF COMPLETE CHART EXHIBITED DURING THE ADDRESS.

book that could be picked up at the corner stationer's was good enough for the accounts; when the ledgers of one business were exactly like the ledgers of every other business, and when bookkeeping was bookkeeping, irrespective of the line of industry.

Manufacturers have learned the value of first-class machines and do not hesitate to discard an old machine in favor of a new one, even though the latter costs an exemplary price, simply because the product will be 10 per cent. better, or 5 per cent. cheaper. They have learned the advantage of employing scientific and skilled superintendents and of keeping free from managing men who proceed by rules of thumb and whose methods are entirely empirical. The day is at hand when manufacturers are making the same changes in their offices that they have heretofore made in their factories. Good accounting systems are as valuable and as money-making as good manufacturing systems. Scientifically trained accountants in the office are worth as much relatively as scientifically trained superintendents in the factory. A well-lighted, well-furnished, well-equipped office is worth just as much relatively as a well-lighted, well-equipped factory room. Account books are specially adapted to needs. Ledgers are ruled according to the requirements of the special business that is to be done. Books in the conventional sense are superseded by card systems, by loose leaf ledgers and by various other modifications, each adapting the article to the special requirements of the case. The office engineer and the accounting engineer are as much in demand at the present time as the architect for the factory building, and the mechanical engineer for the construction and supervision of the machinery which it contains.

All leading and successful manufacturing concerns, it is safe to say, have good cost accounting systems in operation. They are not willing to forego the advantage which an adequate cost accounting system affords them merely on account of the small saving in expense that there would be in adhering to a guess-work plan.

I frequently assert that the best plans of modern scientific accounting cost no more for their administration than the slipshod methods of the past. This is literally true in hundreds of cases. But assume for the sake of argument that the very best accounting system in a factory does cost more than the poor plan, the advantages following from the use of a well-devised, well-organized and thoroughly administered system are a hundred fold greater than the small additional expense.

It is not a formidable undertaking to put in place in factory or in office the very best system that can be devised. It is not nearly so great an undertaking as those to which manufacturers are accustomed in making changes in their motive power and in the machinery for the production of goods. It is simply because they are not acquainted with such things and because their attention has not been specifically directed to the advantages following upon such a change, that so few changes and improvements in this line are made.

The one special thought or suggestion that I would like to leave with you tonight is this: Examine the grade of your accounting methods, both in factory and office, by comparing them with your mechanical methods. Are they both upon the same high plane of excellence? If so, you are to be congratulated. But if your factory is ahead of your office—as I venture in some instances will be found to be the case, then consider seriously the proposition that your next large profit in a business way will follow upon bringing your office up to a plane alongside of that of your factory, or even advancing beyond it. "Accounting is the vital element of business," and in its train follow numerous advantages in way of profits which fail of observation by those who have not carefully developed their office systems.

Mechanic Arts Magazine

When the magazine called Home Study was launched, we carefully scrutinized its name, with the wonder in mind if in time it would not outgrow that which it purported to be. "Home Study" was an excellent name in its way, but, after all, it had its limitations, and the magazine soon showed by the energy of its management and the aggressiveness of the policy upon which it was conducted, that it meant more than mere supervision of home lessons or lessons by mail. It was from the start an important addition to the literature of the practical arts. It was not a surprise to us, therefore, on receiving the first number of the new volume, to find that the name had been changed, and that it had become "The Mechanic Arts Magazine." This title is somewhat awkward to pronounce, and perhaps many will find it somewhat difficult to recall at will, but, nevertheless, the words clearly define the object and purpose of the magazine.

Correspondence

A Collection Method

From F. K. H., Toledo, Ohio.

What is here illustrated was born of necessity. In handling collections covering two or three States, I have found that better results are obtained by sending drafts direct to a local bank for attention, than by trusting to the tender mercies of our home institutions, who appear to find clipping coupons more profitable than chasing delinquent debtors. Hence the letter of instruction above the perforated line shown in the specimen.

The form of statement and letter to the customer were added in order to lay before the drawee a memorandum of the invoice for which the appended draft is made. I have found that seldom, if ever, is this form of draft returned for further information. On the other hand, in the past, 15 per cent. would hardly cover the number of ordinary drafts coming back, with some such notation as " no statement," or "invoice misplaced."

The draft itself was appended to the statement so that a merchant paying the same without question could afterwards, at his convenience, ascertain what bills were covered thereby. This plan of collections has proved, so far as I have used it, to be of real utility, which is the object we are seeking to attain in all business matters.

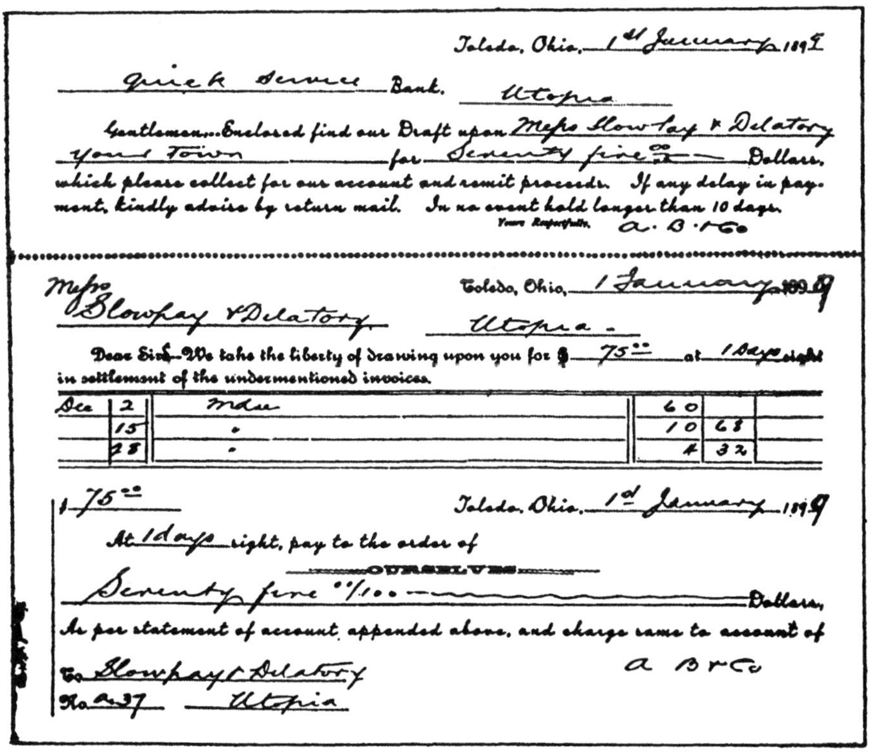

Toledo, Ohio, 1st January 1899

Quick Service Bank. Utopia

Gentlemen... Enclosed find our Draft upon Messrs Slowpay & Delatory Your Town for Seventy five 00/xx Dollars, which please collect for our account and remit proceeds. If any delay in payment, kindly advise by return mail. In no event hold longer than 10 days.

Yours Respectfully, A. B. & Co.

Messrs Slowpay & Delatory, Utopia.

Toledo, Ohio, 1 January 1899

Dear Sirs—We take the liberty of drawing upon you for $ 75.00 at 1 Days sight in settlement of the undermentioned invoices.

Dec	2	Mdse	60	
	15	"	10	68
	28	"	4	32

$ 75.00 Toledo, Ohio, 1st January 1899

At 1 days sight, pay to the order of

OURSELVES

Seventy five 00/100 Dollars,

As per statement of account appended above, and charge same to account of

To Slowpay & Delatory A B & Co

No. 37 Utopia

REPRODUCTION OF FORM ACCOMPANYING LETTER FROM F. K. H., TOLEDO, OHIO.

Builders' Accounts

From C. B., New York.

I have read in the Bulletin, published by the National Association of Builders, the series of articles upon Builders' Accounts, recently contributed to that journal by the Editor of ACCOUNTICS. In view of this fact I beg leave to submit some questions with respect to my system of keeping builders' accounts, upon which I would be glad to have an expression of opinion. To begin with, I adopted about three years ago a system very similar to that outlined in the articles referred to, with certain slight deviations. For instance, if we enter into a contract with Mr. Jones, I at once charge Mr. Jones with the amount of the contract, say, $10,000, the entry being as follows:

Jones. Dr.
To Contract Account........... $10,000

By this means the contract account is credited $10,000. Then I open an account with the job itself, charging it with all materials and labor expended on that job, until the job is completed. Then I credit the job with the amount of contract, debiting the contract account as follows:

Contract Account. Dr.
To the Jones job................

I then close the job account by carrying tha difference to Profit and Loss Account. By this plan I show how much we make on each job.

Inasmuch, as we have a good many subcontracts to deal with, I open a subcontract account with each job, and debit the same with all accepted proposals for, say, stone, carpenter work, etc. I credit the respective subcontractors with the amount bargained for, thus showing what we have sub-let and at what prices. If payments on account should be made to any of these subcontractors, I charge them with the amounts paid and credit the subcontract account of that job with the amount paid and debit the job with the same. For example, the entry is as follows:

Jones Job. Dr.
To subcontract Jones job...... $500
(Part payment to Miller for stone furnished for above job.)

This is continued until all the subcontract accounts are charged to the job. The purpose of this latter is to show just how the job is progressing.

ANSWER: Our correspondent's plan is unique in various features and is one which we do not recall to have encountered previously among builders' accounts. We have seen something very similar to it, however, in the advertising accounts of publishers. The purpose in the latter case, however, has been to show the total amount of advertising under contract.

Our correspondent has displayed considerable ingenuity in the method of arrangement which he has described, and if it works satisfactorily in the office in which he is engaged, we can see no reason why it should not be commended. It will, however, appear somewhat complex to those who have not become familiar with its workings, and other names for accounts and a less involved plan will suggest themselves to various accountants, some of which they will possibly prefer to what is here presented. We should be very glad to have our readers discuss this problem as to them seems best, giving this correspondent the benefit of such criticisms as they may offer.

Dutch Institute of Accountants.

We are indebted to J. G. Ch. Volmer, Secretary of the Nederlandsch Instituut van Accountants, for several pamphlets relating to that organization, and which is familiarly known as the Dutch Institute of Accountants. One of the pamphlets contains an address to accountants, pointing out the features of the organization and the use that it can be to the profession and to the business community. Another contains the constitution and by-laws of the organization. Without having a literal translation of the latter before us, we feel safe in saying that the fundamental principles upon which this organization is based do not differ materially from those of certain organizations in this country. One of the pamphlets is supplemented by a list of the questions which are presented to applicants for membership. The organization was formed the first of January, 1896, and is reported to be in a very prosperous condition.

Whatever's lost, it first was won.—Mrs. Browning.

All wealth is the product of labor.
—Locke.

Questions and Answers

Concerning the

BALANCE-SHEET SYSTEM OF ACCOUNTS

Conducted by the

Account Audit and Assurance Co., Ltd.

25 Pine Street, New York

What is an Accounting Specification?

From C. W. T., Grand Rapids, Mich.

I am interested in the general announcement of the Balance Sheet System of Accounts, but I do not quite understand what is meant by an accounting specification.

ANSWER.—No important work in the engineering line is undertaken at the present time without the supervision of an expert in that line. If a building is to be erected, an architect is employed. If waterworks are to be constructed, an engineer in that particular field is engaged, and if a machine to accomplish special results is required, the work is turned over to a competent mechanical engineer. An accounting engineer is an equally important person when an accounting system is to be devised and installed.

Almost every one understands what is meant by an architect's specification, or, as the phrase is commonly used, the plans and specifications for a building. If we are about to put up a factory building, a city block, or a residence, we first select the architect and proceed to give to him our general ideas of the structure to be erected. He then examines the site, considers the general question of materials to be used in the building, and the design that would harmonize with the purposes of the structure and look well in the surroundings which the building will have. These preliminaries settled, the plans of the building are drawn, the elevations are put upon paper, and the specification of construction is written. The latter is an explanation of the drawings and is a carefully prepared statement of just what the builder is to do, what materials he is to use, and how he is to combine them in putting up and finishing the building. Without an architect we scarcely attempt the meanest structure nowadays.

Now for the contrast in the office. For an accounting system an accounting engineer, or a person who has had special experience in accounting work and in designing accounting systems by whatever term designated, is called in. He first ascertains the conditions of the business, and the showings that are desired; he takes cognizance of the nature of the transactions, the force that is employed, and various other conditions, and then, after charting the accounts in a way to secure the results that are desired, proceeds to outline the plans and methods of the office in very much the same way that the architect gives directions in his specification to the builder.

A specification of an accounting system is just as reasonable a proposition for the office as a specification of a building is among builders. We are not yet, however, quite so familiar with the former as the latter. Both secure the results of skill and experience. A building built without plans and specifications, wherein each mechanic would be allowed to do exactly as he saw fit, would be a very peculiar structure; but the average office system and accounting system are very much of this order. Without a preliminary plan and without carefully prepared directions, it is a go-as-you-please effort from entry clerk to bookkeeper-in-chief, with the result that there is much lost motion, a great deal of useless labor and an important shortage in the way of useful results. For the lack of a scientific system, which the specification would afford, the business man fails of that information from his books which he ought to have.

The Balance Sheet System of Accounts is a definite method of accounting, worked out by accountants of wide experience, and carefully adapted from time to time to different lines of business. The system is conveyed from those who are entirely familiar with it to those who would employ it in their business by means of an accounting specification. The office man by this means has in written form directions just what to do and when to do it, and is never in doubt about his work.

Workings of the Balance Sheet System

From P. W. S., Harrisburg, Pa.

Will you give me some conception of the workings of the Balance Sheet System of Accounts, and the results secured by it, pointing out incidentally wherein it differs from other accounting systems? Is it expensive to operate?

ANSWER.—The Balance Sheet System of Accounts differs from ordinary bookkeeping, and also from other accounting systems. so-called, in various important particulars. First, by it the defects of ordinary double-entry bookkeeping are remedied and the omissions supplied. Second, there is nothing of mystery about the Balance Sheet System of Accounts, either as to method, nor yet in the nature of the results which it is guaranteed to produce. In this it differs from all other proprietary systems. The Balance Sheet System may be summed up in the assertion that it is good accounting science, intelligently applied and supplemented by the best possible bookkeeping methods.

The results secured by the Balance Sheet System may be briefly outlined as follows: It gives a going statement of profits and losses. This statement is made an integral part of the bookkeeping. It also gives a going statement of assets and liabilities—that is, it presents a perpetual balance sheet which likewise is made an integral part of the bookkeeping.

If the business man wants to know how much cash he has on hand, he glances at the cash book. With the Balance Sheet System of Accounts, if the business man wants to know how much money he has made, he glances in the same way at the profit and loss statement. He gets this information without any special calculation or figuring for the purpose. The profit and loss statement is a part of the regular books, and is kept up to date, just the same as the Cash Account is a part of ordinary double-entry bookkeeping and kept up to date.

Again, if the business man who has the Balance Sheet System in use wants to know just how much he is owing—that is, his liabilities—and just how much he has got to pay with—that is, his assets—a glance at the balance sheet, which, as already stated, is a regular and going part of the bookkeeping system, and which also is constantly kept up to date, at once shows these facts. The Balance Sheet System of Accounts includes a little more in various details than the ordinary double-entry system. It is labor saving in that it does not duplicate work. It is susceptible of proof by trial balance methods at every point and in operation never costs more than the ordinary plan. In many cases it costs to operate from 10 to 50 per cent. less.

Chart of Accounts

From P. A. A., Boston.

I have seen repeated references to charts of accounts, but I have a very indistinct idea of what is meant by the same. Will you kindly explain?

ANSWER.—Our correspondent undoubtedly understands the meaning of the word "chart" in its broad sense. He certainly would comprehend the idea conveyed by the expression "chart and compass," as applied to sailing a vessel. He would also understand what was meant if we should say that a certain course or route was charted, or even if we should say that a chart of the proposed plan was outlined. Chart and map, under certain conditions, mean the same.

Few enterprises, of either large or small dimensions, are entirely successful at the present time that are not thoroughly planned in advance. Haphazard work seldom avails much. To build a house without a plan previously drawn would be an unusual undertaking. Hence by analogy the desirability of a plan or chart of an accounting system before anything is done in the way of opening the books, or even deciding what particular books shall go to make up the set.

An accounting chart is an orderly arrangement of the accounts necessary to the proper statement of any business in a way to show their relationship one to the other, and to clearly indicate the function that is performed by each account.

Every one recognizes, to a greater or less extent, the necessity of classifying accounts. A chart only shows the classification completed. A chart of the accounts of a business indicates not only the classes into which the accounts are divided, but also the relationship of those classes, each to the other, and the ends to be served by each.

If the accounts in a ledger are properly classified and the classification carried to its logical conclusion, then the necessity of analysis and arrangement of facts at the end of a fiscal period is entirely overcome. Much that is usually done at the end of the year in closing the books is simply to make up for the defects in the bookkeeping as the business of the year has proceeded. Hence the need of classification, and hence the need at the outset of a chart that shall show the method of classification and indicate at a glance just what is to be done at all times, to maintain the order and to keep the business records up to date, complete and correct in all particulars.

The Accounts of a Trust

From O. C., Buffalo.

I desire to inquire if the Balance Sheet Accounting System is or is not specially adapted to the accounts of a trust? By trust, in this case, I mean a corporation that is organized to control and operate several minor organizations, each owning its own plant and heretofore carrying on its own business. The trust that I am concerned in owns a majority of the stock in several companies heretofore carrying on business independently, and has contracts with each, by which for the future it becomes sole operator of the plant, sole factor of the product, etc.

ANSWER.—The Balance Sheet System of Accounts is better adapted to the requirements of such a corporation as our correspondent describes than any other plan that has ever been devised. The Balance Sheet System is based upon such a classification of the going accounts as presents to the management, by the accounts themselves, a balance sheet statement from beginning to end as well also as a perpetual loss and gain statement. The latter can be subdivided as required and made to show not only the results of each plant but of each division of each plant. That which the management of a trust especially requires to know is, therefore, most clearly and satisfactorily set forth by the Balance Sheet System.

There is first the arrangement of the going accounts in balance sheet order of the assets and liabilities, and in turn, in profit and loss statement form, the accounts showing expenses and revenues. These general exhibits become integral parts of the bookkeeping system, instead of being separate statements drawn up outside of and apart from the books, as is usually the rule. Accordingly the books are always closed and likewise are always open. Everything, of necessity, is kept up to date. It is impossible for the bookkeeping to get behind. The showings of profits, according to the nature of the business, are either weekly or monthly. Monthly showings are found by experience to be quite long enough apart, and where shorter intervals are possible weekly exhibits are preferred. By the judicious use of suspense accounts and reserve accounts, profits are as correctly shown at weekly and monthly intervals as they are ordinarily shown at the end of a year or other lengthy fiscal period.

Several consolidations, although not commonly known as trusts, have lately adopted the Balance Sheet System of Accounts, after thorough investigation of its features, and it is now working in the offices of these companies to the entire satisfaction of the management.

The Balance Sheet Ledger

From W. W., Washington.

I would like to have a Balance Sheet Ledger sent on approval. If it suits me I will keep it; otherwise I will return it promptly.

ANSWER.—The Balance Sheet Ledger, which is the one special book employed in the Balance Sheet System of Accounts, is not a stock book, but instead is something that is always made to order. No two Balance Sheet Ledgers as yet have been sent out exactly alike, but instead each one has been especially designed for the business for which it has been intended.

The impression seems to prevail in certain directions at least that the Balance Sheet Ledger is comparable to other and common forms of ledgers, and that it is something which may be used as an adjunct to any bookkeeping plan. This assumption is in error as we will try to show. Preliminary to the designing of a Balance Sheet Ledger is a classification of the accounts of the business by which they are arranged in the order, and in the necessary classes or sections to give the results which are guaranteed to those who employ the system. With the scheme thus outlined the next step is recording it, which results in the chart of the accounts. Finally the chart is explained and described in what is called the specification. A Balance Sheet Ledger would be useless without the specification describing its use, for otherwise, differing from ordinary forms of ledgers, it would not be understood. Accordingly, the proprietors of this device decline to send out a Balance Sheet Ledger, save only when it is accompanied by a specification of use, showing its adaptation to the special line of business for which it is ordered.

The Acx System of Filing Invoices

BY WALTON DAY

Many of the readers of ACCOUNTICS are already practically familiar with what is known as the Acx System. Many others are acquainted with it on account of the advertising which our columns have contained for some months past and the circulars which have been widely distributed. We now have pleasure in illustrating the system in some detail.

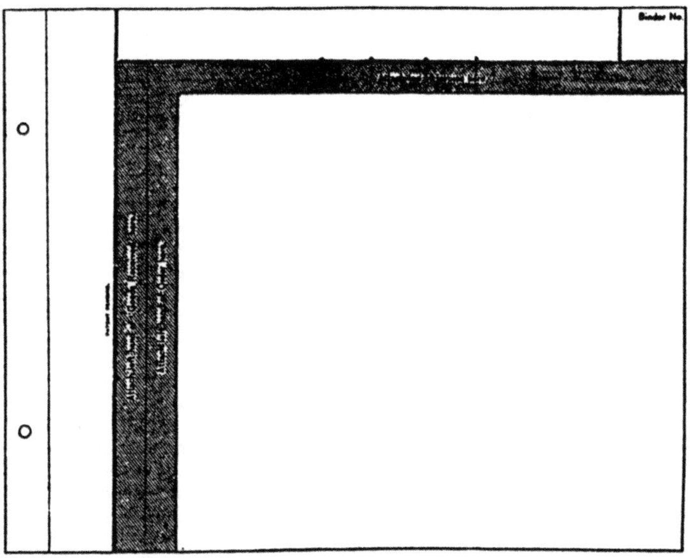

ACX SYSTEM OF FILING INVOICES. FIG. 1.—THE PRIMARY UNIT—THE ACX SHEET.

At the outset let it be said that the system is capable of various modifications and adaptations. It is essentially a unit system, with the possibility of a large number of variations in the arrangement of the units, as well as in the number of the units in themselves.

Whoever has filed invoices upon any of the plans now in common use, ranging from the old method of pasting in a book to what many have considered the acme of perfection—namely, placing the invoices loose in alphabetical order in a letter file after they have been journalized or otherwise entered—has experienced the need of something better. What is demanded is something that will take the place of journalizing or the laborious work of entering in a purchase register. What is wanted also is something that will admit direct posting from the invoice to the credit of the seller's account, and what is wanted still further is something that will permit direct reference from the goods or materials which the invoices cover back to the invoices. Incidentally, there is likewise demanded facilities for recording the receipt of goods apart from the invoice and also for keeping in convenient position the copy of the order which was sent for the goods. Checking invoices demands the comparison of the bill with the order, and also comparison of the bill with a list of the goods actually received.

The plan of checking receipts of goods with the invoice itself in obsolete at the present time in many establishments. It is urged against the plan, which was formerly in very general use, that it is very easy to make a mistake in checking goods when there is before the receiving clerk a list of what should be found. It is an exceedingly simple matter to put a check mark in front of any quantity noted. The temptation is to put the mark there without actually counting the goods, taking it for granted that the real quantity is that which the bill calls for. Opposed to this plan is that which has been in force for a long time past in many leading establishments, namely that of having the goods actually counted and listed on appropriate blanks, without the invoice in sight. This causes a report to be made to the office of what the shipper has sent, or at least of what has been found in his packages and cases, independent of the invoice. The checking of the "goods-received slip" with the invoice is another matter entirely, and one that is attended to in the privacy of the office.

Right here it should be remarked that there are very important objections to allowing tne invoice to go out of the office. It is inexpedient to make known to the receiving clerk the prices and terms upon which goods are being bought. Matters of this kind should be restricted to the office and therefore the plan of having the receipt of the goods checked, independent of the invoice, is greatly to be preferred.

The three prime elements to be dealt with, therefore, in any system of filing invoices are first the duplicate or copy of the order sent for the goods; second, the statement of goods received, made out by the receiving clerk, and third the invoice itself. There are various good business reasons, patent to every one upon reflection, for desiring a filing system that shall bring these three elements together in the final putting away of the papers, and also that shall keep them together at all times for inspection and reference.

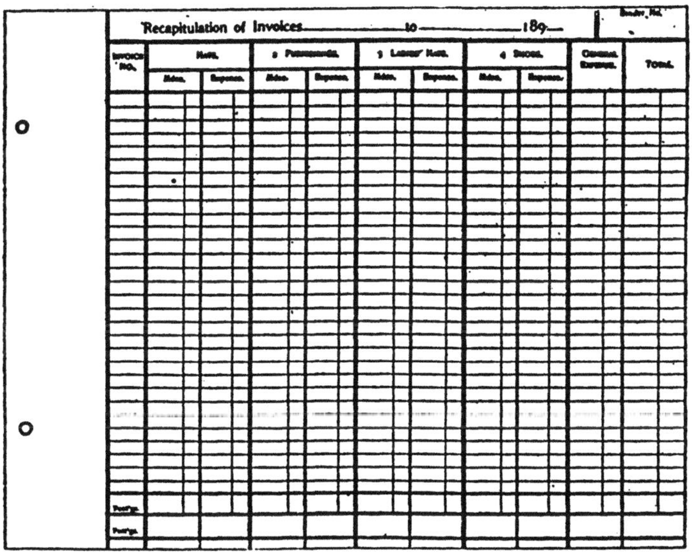

FIG. 2.—RECAPITULATION SHEET.

The leading unit of the Acx Filing System is what is known as the Acx Sheet and is illustrated in Fig. 1. This is a manilla sheet, ordinarily made 8½ inches deep by 11 inches long, and punched to fit a standard post binder. It is so reinforced or thickened at the left-hand end on the line of punchings that the extra thickness that is given it, or the presence of the false shank, builds up the sheets in the binding as rapidly as the free portions are built up by the addition of the parts attached. The Acx sheet is provided with three spaces of mucilage, clearly indicated in the engraving. The use of these is suggested by the lettering appearing in each. The vertical space at the left hand is entitled "Attach left hand of Goods-Received here." Second, and parallel to it, is that which is printed, "Attach left hand of Order here," while the strip across the top reads, "Attach top of Invoice here."

The copies of orders for goods may be kept in any shape desired. They may be letter press copies or carbon copies, as preferred. If special blanks for this purpose were being prepared they would be

FIG. 3.—THE GLOBE POST BINDER, PARTLY FILLED WITH ACX SHEETS, CARRYING ORDERS, RECORDS OF GOODS RECEIVED AND INVOICES, TOGETHER WITH COMPLEMENT OF RECAPITULATION SHEETS

restricted to dimensions less than the unoccupied space of the Acx Sheet, bounded by the lines of gum on the left and at the top, and by the margins of the sheet at the bottom and the right. Whatever may be the nature of the copy of the order that is kept, whether in one piece or on several sheets, and whether a small sheet or a large sheet folded, the first step after the order has been sent out is to attach it to one of these Acx sheets by simply moistening its edge and laying on to the gummed portions indicated. The Acx Sheets receiving the order in this way are thereafter in a sense in a condition of suspense, being kept loose in a drawer or held in a suitable loose sheet binder until such time as the invoices shall come in and the Goods-Received slips reach the office. Whenever an invoice has been checked with the Goods-Received slip and comparison has also been made with the copy of the order for the goods, these two additional elements are attached to the Acx sheet in like manner—that is, by moistening their edges and laying against the gummed surface as already mentioned. The Acx Sheet at this stage is ready to go into the post binder. It takes its place, forming with others which have preceded it such a construction as is shown in Fig. 2.

A rubber stamp of proper form, containing such items as "Checked with order," "Checked with goods received," "Prices checked," "Extensions checked," "Freights and allowances," Entered on recapitulation sheet," etc., is provided and is impressed upon each invoice. This forms a blank for all the uses indicated by the titles. As the Acx Sheets go into the binder they are serially numbered, the first one being No. 1, the next No. 2, and so on. For this purpose space is provided in the upper right-hand corner for the numerals, as shown in Fig. 1. In posting to the purchaser's account this number is carried to the ledger, the same as would a notation of the page of an invoice book or of the journal, in case the posting was from either of them.

For the debit postings—that is, the charges to Merchandise Account, or to the different departments of the business, recapitulation sheets of the kind shown in Fig. 3 are employed. These are necessarily made to order to suit the business that is being conducted. The illustration shows that which would be correct for a business run in four departments, and indicates the provision made for charging to the Merchandise Account of each department, to the Expense Account of each department, and to the General Expense Account of the business. The invoices for a week or month, according to the time schedule upon which the books are being conducted, are recapitulated on these sheets, the numbers being entered down the first left-hand column, and the amounts being distributed through the several distributing columns, according to requirements. The total amount is extended in to the extreme right-hand column. Proof of correctness is secured by footing in both directions. Recapitulation sheets are provided with a line for footings at the bottom, and also a second line for indicating postings. The proper distribution of the purchases, therefore, is posted from these sheets to the several accounts in a way to complete the bookkeeper's work with a minimum of exertion and trouble.

The result is that the invoices are put away serially numbered and arranged in book form, with references from the ledger accounts directly to the invoice, and in the case of retail stores, where price tags are employed, with references from the goods directly to the invoice. Thus the source of supply, the age of the goods, and various other important facts are revealed on call with the smallest possible amount of labor.

When the most is said about office work it is all summed up in the assertion that all that is done is only indexing. That index plan is best which requires the least work and which gives the most ready reference to any item that is required. Given the check on goods in the store, the Acx system presents at once the invoice of those goods, the record of the receiving clerk and the copy of the order. Given the date of an invoice, by turning to the division of the book corresponding to that date, the invoice is at once found. Given the name of the seller, a reference to his ledger account gives the pages in the Acx system covering the invoices that he has supplied. Other advantages following upon the use of this system are so apparent that enumeration seems unnecessary.

These goods are being manufactured by The Globe Company, Cincinnati, New York, Boston, Chicago. Sample sheets and other particulars will be sent on application.

Metallic Coin Case

Every one who has to do with considerable quantities of fractional currency, whether pennies, nickels, dimes, quarters, or larger coins, knows the necessity of some available plan for putting the coins in packages of uniform size for storage purposes and for convenient conveyance to and from depositories. The usual plan in use in such cases employs a

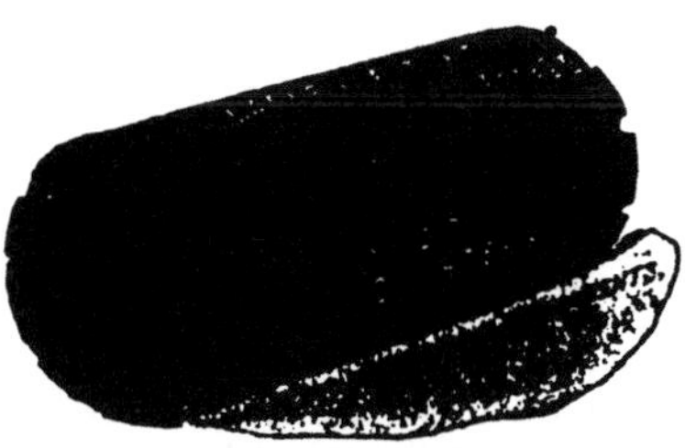

METALLIC COIN CASE

piece of paper rolled around the coins and fastened with mucilage or sealing wax. The paper, however, does not prove satisfactory in all cases, and with various qualities of paper in use with different numbers of thicknesses in rolling, the resulting packages vary in size. To be the most satisfactory, a standard size should be employed and the case should be of such material as not only to indicate the contents but also to admit of using repeatedly.

What is known as the Cable Metallic Coin Case, illustrated in the accompanying engraving, has been devised to meet the requirements of business men in this regard. The style of the device and its operation are so clearly indicated in the engraving that further particulars are scarcely necessary. Among the advantages referred to by the sole agents, William G. Johnston & Co., Ninth and Penn Streets, Pittsburg, Pa., are the following: The case can be filled and securely closed in one-fourth the time required to roll the money in an ordinary piece of paper. When filled, the case still reveals the coin enclosed in a way to indicate its denomination. It also presents the coins in a form to allow them to be counted without opening. At the same time the coins may be removed and returned to the case as many times as may be required. The device is of such a shape that it can be stacked on the counter. All rolling is avoided. It is sufficiently strong to resist breaking when dropped. This coin case is made in sizes to meet all requirements.

Clip Binder

In every office there is the need of some device for holding in position papers, circulars, pamphlets, etc. It should be of the nature of a binder readily adjusted in position and just as readily thrown out of use. A device of this kind which has come into extensive demand is known as the "Clip" and is illustrated in

THE CLIP BINDER

the accompanying cut. It is manufactured by H. H. Ballard, 99 Pittsfield, Mass. The device consists of the clip, which is made in a variety of sizes, and a pair of keys or handles. The latter serve to hold the clip open while the pamphlets or other papers are being inserted. When the clip is in position the keys are withdrawn. The utility of the device becomes evident upon inspection.

Accountics

VOL. IV | APRIL 1899 | NO. 4

The Monthly Statement

The Street Railway Accountants' Association of America is fortunate in having very efficient executives, who are always forehanded in plans and arrangements. Under date of March 20, a circular to the membership was issued, calling attention to the third annual convention of this organization, which is to be held in Chicago, October 17 to 20, inclusive. Notwithstanding that the date of the convention is yet several months ahead, still the secretary was able to announce that an exceptionally strong program has been provided, and that among other features papers on the following important subjects will be read: "Car Mileage," "Blanks and Forms," "Materials and Supplies Accounts," "What Does the General Manager Want to Know From the Accounting Department?" Following this announcement is the very significant statement as follows: "These papers will be the results of studies rather than the experience of the authors."

This sentence very aptly epitomizes the nature of the work of this organization for it is essentially a class of study, in which all are pupils and every one a teacher. The Association is organized upon the plan of free interchange of ideas and opinions, and no organization was ever established upon such a basis that did not prove of great value to its members at large. The headquarters of the Association during the convention will be at the Auditorium Hotel, Chicago. The meeting will be held simultaneously with that of the American Street Railway Association at Tattersall's, corner State and Sixteenth Streets. Railroad rates are promised the same as heretofore,—namely, at one and one-third fare, for the round trip, on the certificate plan. In concluding his circular, the secretary urges the members to commence now to make their arrangements to attend and to look forward to the pleasures of Chicago hospitality.

This organization is officered the current year as follows: President, J. F. Calderwood, auditor of the Twin City Rapid Transit Co., Minneapolis; first vice-president, E. R. L. Tighe, accountant of the Brooklyn Rapid Transit Co., Brooklyn; second vice-president, R. Lancaster Williams, treasurer of the Richmond Traction Company, Richmond, Va., and third vice-president, F. E. Smith, auditor of the Lynn & Boston Railway Co., Lynn, Mass., and secretary and treasurer, W. B. Brockway, ass't sec'y of the Toledo, Bowling Green & Fremont Railway Co., Toledo. The executive committee is constituted as follows: H. L. Wilson, auditor of the Boston Elevated Railway Company, Boston; H. G. Mackay, comptroller of the Milwaukee Electric Railway and Light Co., Milwaukee; H. E. Babcock, auditor of the Elmira and Horseheads Railway Co., Elmira, and J. D. Fraser, secretary and treasurer of the Ottawa Electric Railway Co., Ottawa, Canada. We know of no accountants' organization that has done more good to its members and to the interests which they represent than has this association in the time that it has been in existence.

The National Association of Credit Men is to hold its convention this year in Buffalo. The date in June 6, 7 and 8. Very extensive and careful preparations are being made not only by the National officers, but by the committees of the local association. From whatever point of view it is regarded the occasion promises to be one of great interest. A prominent feature, outside of the regular sessions of the Association, will be what is termed trade congresses, each presided over by a leading member of the trade represented. At the convention held at Detroit last year, the trade congresses proved to be of great value and brought men of like interests together in a way to benefit all concerned. The lines of trade to be represented, by congresses at Buffalo, with the chairmen so far selected, include the following: Boot and shoe trade, George G. Ford, of L. P. Ross, Rochester; dry goods, F. S. Evans, with Strawbridge & Clothier, Philadelphia; grocery trade, F. W. Standart, of the C. S. Morey Mercantile Company, Denver; hardware, F. J. Hopkins, of Jenney-Semple Company, of Minneapolis, and clothing, Thos. Davies, of L. C. Wachsmuth & Co., Chicago.

During the sessions of the convention of the Credit Men a number of addresses are to be delivered by prominent credit men and others, specially qualified to speak upon the movement for which the organization stands. W. A. Prendergast, who occupies a prominent position in the New York Credit Men's Association, will address the convention on "The Relation of Law to Commerce." H. E. Hutchings, of Burnham, Hannover, Munger & Co., Kansas City, will deliver an address entitled, "Relations of Salesmen and Credit Men." Still other speakers, the National officers say, will be announced later.

Another feature of the convention, in which business men generally will be interested, will be the exhibition of the equipment and method of conducting a model credit department. At the last convention Secretary Boocock was instructed to collect from the members generally, forms, blanks and special articles of equipment, together with accounts of any original methods employed, and therefrom to select what would constitute the general outfit of a model credit department, with the object of arranging the same for exhibition purposes. This work of necessity has been delayed to the latter part of the year, but now it is well in hand, and from indications everything will be in readiness to make the proposed exhibit at the convention. Considerable enthusiasm is being manifested by different members of the National organization co-operating with the secretary in this undertaking.

In connection with the model credit department, arrangements have been made by which more or less of a complete accounting department shall also be shown. The contemplated exhibit in this line will include a scientific accounting system, arranged in a form to apply to small mercantile establishments, and also shown in its interpretation for the largest mercantile and manufacturing concerns. The points to be emphasized are perpetual showings of financial conditions, and constant exhibits of profit and loss, together with the use of modern labor-saving methods. Still other and minor features of the convention will likewise be of interest and value to the business community at large, and those who can make it convenient to spend the week named in Buffalo, are sure of a good as well as a profitable time. Transportation rates on the certificate plan (a fare and one-third) are being arranged. Hotel accommodations, the secretary announces, will be abundant and reasonable in cost. The date of the convention falls in what is coming to be known as the vacation season. The natural attractions in and around Buffalo, together with the desire to encourage the general movement for which the credit men's organization stands, are quite enough to insure a very large attendance. The Iroquois Hotel has been selected as general headquarters.

In another part of this issue we present a paper by the eminent London accountant, Jas. B. Macdonald, on the "Treatment of Fixed and Circulating Capital in the Accounts of Joint Stock Companies." Our readers will recall a previous paper by the same author, printed in these columns (1898), entitled "Balance Sheets and Balance Accounts." In that article what is capital and what is profit were clearly defined, from the author's point of view. In the present article he discusses what is commonly designated among our English brethren as the single account system and the double account system in the treatment of phases of the capital in the accounts of joint stock companies. What is now presented bears in no unimportant degree upon various questions which are before English accountants' organizations and the courts dealing with business questions in Great Britain. The considerations presented also bear upon questions which, if not already up for debate in this country, will soon demand attention here. It is to be noted that near the end of the article Mr. Macdonald says that the terms "single account system" and "double account system" are by no means apt. He prefers the phrases, "the fixed capital system of accounts" and "the circulating capital system." The phrases "fixed capital" and "circulating capital" may appear novel to the minds of many of our readers, and to the majority will undoubtedly open up new fields of investigation. We commend the article to the attention of our readers as one worthy of careful attention.

We have referred in these columns in the past to the custom prevailing in various government offices, in diplomatic circles and in certain leading banking institutions of the world, which discriminates against the typewriter. Certain courts do not look with approval upon typewritten documents of any kind, and various legal firms affect to discriminate against machine work. The march of progress, however, is only delayed, not stopped, by such conservatism. Every now and again we learn of important steps forward. For example, a short time since the Emperor of Germany issued an order permitting the official so-called "immediate reports" submitted to him by the various German officers to be prepared on the typewriter. This is justly regarded by the manufacturers of typewriting machines as being a very marked concession, because that which becomes admissible at court will of course be approved by society in general. Accordingly, there will be for the immediate future in Germany at least more typewriting and less penmanship. The cable despatch which contained this important bit of information moralized to this extent: "Hitherto it has not been thought polite to use a typewriter for other than business letters," and concludes with the statement: "The Emperor has made a restriction directing the sort of machine that must be used in preparing the report." The blue pencil of the ever vigilant telegraph editor cut out the name of the machine, even though it was included in the despatch as it left Berlin. It is enough, however, to know that a typewriter is to be used, even though we do not know which typewriter. The situation in this respect reminds us of the old toper who heard some one condemn whiskey as being bad, to which he replied: "Do not call it bad. Some kinds are better than others, but they are all good." Some typewritten manuscripts are more pleasing to the eye than others, but all typewriter work decently executed, irrespective of the special machine on which it is done, is preferable to hand written documents for almost every conceivable purpose. The day will come, we think, when hand written matter, even for personal communication and social correspondence, will be practically obsolete.

Who shall decide when the school teachers and the college professors fail to agree? Professor James Bryce asserts that "advertising has now become so extremely important a part of commercial life that it would be very desirable if something could be done to reduce it to a science." To this Printer's Ink, which prides itself on being called "the little schoolmaster," says: "Advertising will never be reduced to a science because it is an art. It would be as easy to reduce literature, music or painting to a science as to do so with advertising. Certain principles underlie all the arts named. Yet a knowledge of these principles by no means insures to the possessor the slightest degree of proficiency in the art. After all, the ideal advertiser is born, not made. Unless he possesses an intuitive knowledge of how people are influenced most of the effort expended will be abortive. This knowledge may need cultivation and direction, but the germ of it must have been implanted by Nature before development can act. If it were possible, as Professor Bryce suggests, to reduce advertising to a science, all its uncertainties would disappear, and everybody could succeed in it without the aid of the advertising agent or ad writer."

This latter, in the estimation of the "Little Schoolmaster," is apparently so terrible a condition that it must be avoided at all hazards. The very thought of the ad writer and advertising agent being rendered unnecessary is shocking to many who are engaged in the lines of business named, and yet the leading ad writers of the day are beginning to line up on the broad proposition that the principles of advertisement writing can be better applied by those who are in immediate contact with the business that is to be advertised than by those who are at a distance and make a specialty of ad writing. In effect they say that advertising has been so nearly reduced to a science, and its rules so well formulated that any reasonably bright man familiar with the articles to be announced can better write the advertising than the born expert who has not this advantage.

Many business men are beginning to comprehend that the advertising agent in a very large number of cases is an unnecessary as well as expensive adjunct to his advertising enterprise, and that the buying of space in periodicals is no different in principle from buying commodities in general, and that therefore his general purchasing agent should be in request. It is even possible that the advertising agent as we now know him to be and the ad writer may, in the course of time, disappear from the face of the earth. Advertising, however, will not thereby be stopped. Instead it will probably grow by leaps and bounds as compared with its development in the past, when it has been hampered and restrained by these so-called specialists. Particularly will its development be rapid in the future if so much of science as even the "Little Schoolmaster" admits by the phrase, "certain principles," is formulated and communicated to the business public.

Broader education among business men and the advent of men of real education and culture in business circles are fast reducing the chances of the shysters and humbugs who in the past have fattened upon the ignorance and credulity of their victims. Not all advertisement writers are humbugs, nor are all advertising agents entirely useless, but there are those of both classes who have paraded before the public in the past that have been deserving of the severest terms of censure that could be devised. Above all things such men deplore light and the diffusion of intelligence. Darkness and ignorance are essential to their success. They would restrain the development of a science useful to the business world and the promulgation of its principles in order that their so-called art may be practiced without interruption and to their own personal advantage.

While referring to advertising, we are reminded again of what our friends of The Billboard are doing in the direction of developing the science of advertising designated by their new-coined word, advertics, previously mentioned in these columns. Friend Donaldson, in the course of his effort, is developing some most unusual, if not particularly effective phrases. For example, in the March issue of the journal named we encounter this: "Advertics is the science of disseminative incentive." We venture to say that many of our readers did not know this before, and that therefore they are very much pleased to have this information spread before them. We read further: "The matter about which it is engaged is intelligence. Intelligence, as here used, does not always signify acquired information nor inculcated knowledge. It may be and quite frequently is a priori; as, for instance, in the first cry of a babe. In this sense it may be said to be innate, that is, prior to experience." We were under the impression that experience in the matter of the babe, so far as pain is concerned, preceded the cry. That, however, is only common sense, and is not science. Our Solon continues: "It is intelligence none the less, for it is intelligible to the mother, nurse and attendants. Furthermore, it possesses incentive. If you doubt it, note the alacrity with which the mother responds to it." All of which seems plausible. We also find the following: "It is important that this definition of intelligence be firmly fixed in the mind, for it is used thus specifically throughout this treatise. It is ever to be distinguished from gathered experience in the shape of pure knowledge which may affect the cognative faculties alone. Intelligence is to be understood as going further and affecting the motive powers. That is to say, it stirs up feeling, excites evolution, prods the will, prompts determination and stirs up action." From the preceding it is evident that our author is floundering around in what we may venture to describe as the slough of metaphysics. In fact he says in another place: "Advertics is grounded in metaphysics." Recognizing this as a bold statement he explains as follows: "This assertion in the minds of some scientists will be tantamount to a damaging admission. The painstaking naturalist and the exact physicist speak with impatience of a science which deals with matters which cannot be seen, touched, tasted, smelled or heard." We wait further developments of advertics with great interest, not forgetting that certain authorities of late declare that there are more than the five senses enumerated.

Some of the Accounting Literature of the Netherlands

By A. O. Kittredge, C. P. A.

Books Received

It is popularly supposed that various experts in the higher sciences have in effect a common language which makes it possible for them to understand each other no matter in what particular tongue a given treatise may be written. Thus, chemical formulae is the same, whether used by a professor in one of the universities of this country, or in any one of the great continental schools. The rule, unfortunately, however, does not seem to have got down, or up—which shall we say?—to the accountant's realm. Accordingly, when an accountant, who is not also an accomplished linguist, gets a book on accounting from Italy, or France, or Germany, or the Netherlands, or Russia, he is obliged to do a great deal of guessing, which is only another name for free translating, or else put in an immense amount of study before he really knows what it is all about. There are so many points of view from which an account in itself, or a broad principle in accounting science may be viewed, that without getting into pretty close contact with the writer, who undertakes an exposition, whatever his nationality may be, it is practically impossible to tell just what he is driving at.

The foregoing, we think, should be regarded as a very satisfactory introduction to and an apology for the following review of three very important and no doubt equally interesting works, which we have recently received from the hands of J. G. Ch. Volmer, Professor de Comptabilite, and Secretary of the Nederlandsch Instituut van Accountants, Amsterdam. Two of the works are in Dutch and the third is in French. Of the former the first is entitled "De Rekening-Courant." In the authorship of this work Mr. Volmer shares the honors with P. Kats, a prominent accountant and mathematical expert of Utrecht. Fifty-six pages of the work are devoted to definitions, statements of principles, and methods and rules, while the thirty-three pages following are devoted to illustrative examples in tabular form.

The second book is entitled "Inventaris en Balans," and works out with much care the principles underlying these most important business documents, presenting incidentally an original scheme of analysis with various illustrations. Some of the latter are extended to the dimensions of folding plates.

The third volume, which, as before mentioned, is in French, is a translation of the work by Valentine D. Kempten, entitled "Practique Brifue Pour Tenir Livres de Compte," from the edition (Italian) of 1550. The translation is preceded by a preface by the translator, together with a brief history of the literature of bookkeeping. The type on the pages of the translation is turned the opposite way from that in which a book is ordinarily printed, a plan which gives a continuous column for the money amounts, and which also provides space in the opposite margins for post marks, etc.

Periodicals

Current files of De Accountant, and of Manndblad Voorhet Boekhouden, show that the accountants of the Netherlands are alive to the advantages of a periodical literature in their special field. The first of the periodicals above named is the official organ of the Nederlandsch Instituut van Accountants. It is under the management of J. G. Ch. Volmer, who is also the secretary of the organization. Referring now to the issue for January last, this journal opens with an article nearly three pages in extent, discussing the fundamental law of the institute and its interpretation in view of certain specified conditions. Following this is an official report referring to some of the undertakings of the organization: Other articles relate to meetings and transactions of the organization, including a special address from one of the executive officers. There is also a report of the

Committee on Examinations. Several pages are devoted to the questions set for an examination of students in accountancy. The range of subjects includes the languages—French, Dutch and English; arithmetic, theory of accounts, accounting practice, etc. Two pages of this journal are devoted to advertisements. The Yost typewriter is something that appears in this department that can be read without a translation. Various works on accounting and various accounting conveniences are also described.

The second paper above mentioned deals with accounting from a standpoint somewhat less official, and contains articles illustrating special applications of accounting principles. It also contains a reprint of the questions used in an examination of accountant students, with solutions of the problems. There is an article by J. G. Ch. Volmer, devoted to questions and problems for practice. This journal has a department of correspondence, also one of questions and answers, and still another of book reviews. The advertising in this paper is quite as limited as in the first journal above mentioned, and is devoted to about the same subjects, the American typewriter being replaced by illustrations of a photographic camera and a fire-proof safe.

When Shall Men Stop Studying?

The daily papers, a few days ago, contained the information that Francis B. Thurber, the well-known business man, formerly one of the leading wholesale merchants of the city, and more recently prominently connected with both the New York Chamber of Commerce and the American Export Association, had been admitted to the bar at the ripe age of fifty-seven years. Mr. Thurber to accomplish this result had to pass the Regents' examination. To qualify for this he had to attend lectures at the University Law Shcool, take examinations, flunk and try again, just like any other law student, but finally he has his diploma, and it now hangs over his desk in his office in Chambers Street. Mr. Thurber's own explanation of these circumstances is that he undertook the study of law partly as mental discipline, partly to set an example of studious industry to his son, who is preparing for college, and partly to make money out of it. An incident of this kind is notable, and is worthy of attention because of its rarity. It goes to show that there are some young old men, as well as some old young men in business.

Confidence in Oneself

The successful business man realizes more than any other, perhaps, the necessity of believing in himself. He knows wherein he would have failed had he doubted himself in the least, or allowed any one else to have a question concerning his confidence. Believing in oneself always goes far toward making others believe in him. Discussing this subject our contemporary Success offers the following:

The young man who would succeed in life must have great confidence in his own ability to achieve success. This is a foundation-stone, and without it his building will either never go up, or will topple. The men who have achieved results in life have been men who believed in themselves; men of large hope and of optimistic views. Despair never yet won a victory. Confidence must always precede action. A young man can never accomplish anything in the world until he is thoroughly convinced that he can.

Pessimists have never done anything, except to put stumbling-blocks in others' way. It is the cheerful, hopeful man, the man who believes that the world is growing brighter and better, that is of value to the world. The man who fears failure, talks failure, thinks his work will be a failure. As Job said, "The thing I feared has come upon me." The very attitude or habitual condition of one's mind has a great deal to do with his success. A stream cannot rise higher than its fountain, and to achieve great success a man must continually dwell in the atmosphere of high ideals. He must think upward, work upward, or he can never reach a high goal.

There is nothing which will take the place of downright confidence in your own ability. Years and years before German unity was an accomplished fact, or even likely, Bismarck said: "It will come; and it will come through me." The Iron Chancellor's confidence in his own ability and his unflinching determination to carry out to the letter whatever he undertook, made the German nation possible. His imperious will and gigantic confidence in his own ability won half the battle before he began. No man with a wavering policy, or with self-distrust, could ever have accomplished this marvel.

The Treatment of Fixed and Circulating Capital in the Accounts of Joint-Stock Companies*

By James B. Macdonald

For many years the well-known company lawyers, Mr. Palmer and Mr. Buckley, Q. C., have advocated rival systems of account for ascertaining "what are the profits of a company." These have been described as the single and double account systems. Neither of the writers originated the method he upholds, although great credit is due to both for having contributed to the issue being finally settled in point of law by the decisions in Lee v. Neuchatel Asphalte Co., and Verner v. General and Commercial Investment Trust, referred to hereafter.

The debatable matter really resolves itself into a consideration of the best method of treating fixed and circulating capital in the accounts of joint-stock companies.

Mr. Palmer, in his "Company Precedents," 6th edition, says:

"According to this system (the single-account system) the profits for any particular period are to be ascertained by a profit and loss account and a balance-sheet showing the true financial position of the company and the result, whether in the shape of profit or loss, of its transactions during such period. The balance, whether to the debit or the credit of profit and loss account, appears as an item in the balance-sheet; and the balance-sheet is not a capital account showing, as a matter of history, how the capital contributed has been applied in the past, but a living account showing the true financial position of the company at the date, and the difference in amount between the assets on the one hand and the debts and paid-up capital on the other hand.

"Everything depends, as in an ordinary partnership, on how the balance-sheet works out. The mere fact that the profit and loss account (disregarding losses and depreciation) shows a credit balance is not treated as establishing the fact that the company has made a profit during the period, since that balance may, in the balance-sheet, be counterbalanced by an equivalent or greater loss of capital sustained during the year (or previously, unless, indeed, the previous loss shall have been written off.)"

The single account system, then, is but another term for that which has been, for a long time, in general use among the commercial community.

We gave an outline of the system in our previous paper on "Balance-Sheets and Balance-Accounts," and need not further enlarge on it here except to observe that a new name became necessary as a distinguishing mark when the double-account system came to be recognized as a distinct method.

The theory of the double-account principle is that the proprietors adventure the greater part of their capital in a "fixed undertaking,"[1] such as a railway, mine or patent, which they have no intention of dealing in as a commodity with a view to making a profit on the sale thereof; that they look for their income from the produce or use of the said "fixed capital," and not from any appreciation in its value,[2] therefore, it is argued, any diminution of capital may likewise be disregarded in ascertaining the annual profits.[3] The double-account system is only the translation of these views into accountancy form. It consists in showing capital receipts and expenditure as a separate account from the general balance-sheet, and in maintaining capital expenditure in the books at cost price irrespective of any fluctuation in value which may take place.

By way of illustration we give the double-account forms prescribed in the Gas-Works Clauses Act, 1871, 34 and 35

---

*Originally published in the Accountants' Magazine.

[1]Mr. Justice Chitty in re Midland Land and Investment Corporation (8th November, 1886).

[2]Salisbury v. Metropolitan Railway Company (22 L. T., 839).

[3]Lord Justice Lindley in Verner v. General and Commercial Investment Trust, Ltd. (L. R., 1894, 2 Ch. p. 239.

Vict., c. 41, together with another set of forms which we suggest would be an improvement on them.

The feature we most object to in the statutory form is the entry of debenture proceeds and expenditure therefrom in capital account. "Debenture capital," says Mr. Buckley, "is not in fact capital at all in the proper sense of the word. It is available money raised by borrowing." We prefer, for this reason, to show such the principles involved in Mr. Dicksee's model capital account are more open to criticism. Diminution of "fixed capital," as we shall show hereafter, is not required by the Companies Acts to be made good out of revenue; but permanent assets acquired through the issue, or from the proceeds, of terminable loans or debentures are not in our opinion "fixed capital." On no other ground can their inclusion in capital account be justified.

SCHEDULE B.

FORM OF ANNUAL ACCOUNTS.

THE ____________________ GAS COMPANY.

Year ending 31st December 18—.

C.—CAPITAL ACCOUNT, for the year ending 31st December 18—.

	Expenditure to 31st Dec. 18—	Expended this year.	Total to 31st Dec. 18—		Certified receipts, 31st Dec. 18—	Received during year.	Total receipts to 31st Dec. 18—
1. To Expenditure to 31st Dec. 18—				1. By Ordinary shares of £— each			
Since that date—				2. " Ordinary shares of £— each			
2. " Lands acquired, including law charges . . .				3. " Preference shares of £— each			
3. " New buildings, manufacturing plant, machines, storage works, and other structures connected with manufacture . . .				4. " Debenture stock . .			
4. " New mains and service pipes (not being in place of old ones), including laying same, paving, and other works connected with distribution . . .				5. " Mortgages and bonds .			
5. " New meters (not in place of old ones), including fixtures				6. " Amounts received in anticipation of calls . .			
6. " Cost of promoting special Act							
7. " Special items (if any) .							
Total Expenditure .							
To balance of Capital Account . . .							
£				£			

FIG. 1—FORM OF ANNUAL ACCOUNTS AS PRESCRIBED BY ENGLISH LAW.

items in the general balance sheet or balance account, as the case may be.

On the other hand Mr. L. R. Dicksee, F.C.A., appears to adopt the statutory form in its entirety when illustrating the double-account system, as applied to colliery accounts, in his "Book-keeping for Accountant Students," Part iii., p. 249.

The statutory form, whether right or wrong, has at least the force of law. It does not, however, extend to colliery accounts, and, therefore, the correctness of

Economists are unfortunate in their choice of the terms "fixed capital" and "circulating capital." These names are apt to convey the impression of permanent assets and liquid assets. This misinterpretation has constantly to be guarded against. We give the precise definitions at a later stage.

The double-account system seems to have grown upon us unconsciously. It probably took its inception in the manner in which the national exchequer accounts are kept. The next steps in its evolution appear to have been the passing of the Companies Clauses Act, 1845, governing parliamentary companies, the Railway Companies Securities Act, 1866, the Regulation of Railways Act, 1868, and the Gas Works Clauses Act, 1871, the last two of which prescribe a set form of accounts for such undertakings. Its further development has been the outcome of private bill legislation, and of a series of legal decisions under the Companies Acts, which we will notice hereafter.

Meanwhile we quote a few economic definitions of "individual's capital" and of "fixed" and "circulating capital," which relate to the subject.

"Economists are agreed that whatever gives a profit is properly termed capital." —Senior, Political Economy (1850), p. 67.

Sidgwick asks—

"What is exactly meant from the point of view of the individual capitalist by wealth yielding a profit? . . . It merely means that the individual is using his wealth—either personally, or by lending it to others—in such a way that he continually finds himself possessed of the equivalent of what was originally devoted to such use, together with some additional wealth; this something more being what is called profit. Or, more precisely, we should say that the hope of finding himself possessed of this profit is his motive for thus using his wealth, since we should agree that capital does not lose its essential characteristics by in the special form of money; and this becoming actually profitless."—Principles of Political Economy, bk. i chap. v. p. 122.

Marshall, again, defines a person's capital as—

"That portion of his wealth by which he wins what he needs. Its most conspicuous elements are such things as the factory and the business plant of a manufacturer; that is, his machinery, his raw material, any food, clothing, and house-room that he may hold for the use of his employees, and the goodwill of his business. These are things from which their owner expects to derive an income may be called his Trade Capital."—Economics of Industry, chap. iv. pp. 62, 63.

I.—General Balance-sheet on 31st December 18—.

Dr.				*Cr.*
1. To Capital account . . . . Balance at credit thereof (acc. C).	£	1. By Cash at bankers		£
2. " Profit and loss account . . . Balance at credit thereof (acc. E).		2. " Cash on deposit or at interest .		
3. " Reserved fund . . . . Balance at credit thereof (acc. F).		3. " Coals for stock on hand, 31st Dec. 18— .	£	
4. " Depreciation fund (for works on leasehold lands) . . . Balance at credit thereof (acc. .)		4. " Coke and breeze, 31st Dec. 18— .		
5. " Unpaid dividends		5. " Tar and other products		
6. " Interest accrued and unpaid on mortgages, bonds, and debenture stock, and other loans, to 31st Dec. 18—		6. " Sundry stores .		
7. " Sundry tradesmen and others for amount due for coals, stores, &c., to 31st Dec. 18— . . .		7. " Gas and meter rental: balance of this acc. due to the Coy. on 31st Dec. 18—, less deposits and prepayments . . .	£	
8. " Wages and contingencies . . Amount due to 31st Dec. 18—		8. " Coke and other residuals, 31st Dec. 18—		
9. " Other items (if any) . . .		9. " Sundry accounts, 31st Dec. 18— . . .		
		10. " Special items (if any), including investments		
	£			£

FIG. 2—FORM OF GENERAL BALANCE-SHEET ACCOMPANYING THE ANNUAL STATEMENT SHOWN IN THE PRECEDING ILLUSTRATION.

These definitions show that the prime test in determining what wealth is capital is its profit-earning capacity, and that the use to which it is put is considered rather than its nature.

Mill's view is—

"The distinction between capital and non-capital lies in the mind of the capitalist—in his will to employ them for one purpose rather than another."

Two sub-divisions of "Individual's Capital" have been adopted, by economists, and are stated by Adam Smith as follows:

"'Fixed capital' is that which affords a revenue or profit without circulating or changing masters; and 'circulating capital' is that which affords a revenue only by circulating or changing masters."—Wealth of Nations.

An admirable explanation of the latter

is given in Maclaren's "Elements of Economics":

"Houses, lands, etc., are by no means invariably 'fixed capital.' It is quite common for speculators to buy up land capital.' . . . So a shipbuilder buys ships and sells them to a company. In the hands of a builder they are floating capital; in the hands of a company they become fixed capital."—Vol. 1., p. 212.

SCHEDULE B.

THE ________________ GAS COMPANY.

C.—CAPITAL ACCOUNT as at (say) 31st December 1897.

Dr. | *Cr.*

"Fixed Capital" Assets.	Expended during year 1897.	Expenditure to 31st Dec. 1896.	Total to 31st Dec. 1897.	Share Capital.	Received during year 1897.	Certified receipts, 31st Dec. 1896.	Total receipts to 31st Dec. 1897.
To Expenditure to 31st Dec. 1896		£0 0 0		By Ordinary shares, amounts paid thereon *N.B.*—Outstanding £ : :	£0 0 0	£0 0 0	
Since that date—				Preference shares, amounts paid thereon *N.B.*—Outstanding £ : :	0 0 0	0 0 0	£0 0 0
" Lands acquired, &c. .	£0 0 0						
" New buildings, &c. .	0 0 0						
" New mains and service pipes, &c. . . .	0 0 0						
" New meters, &c. . .	0 0 0						
" Cost of promoting special Act	0 0 0						
" Special items, if any .	0 0 0						
		0 0 0					
			£0 0 0				
" Balance, being working capital carried to General Balance Account . . .			0 0 0				
			£0 0 0				£0 0 0

FIG. 3—FORM OF ANNUAL ACCOUNTS PREFERRED BY MR. MACDONALD.

and build houses for the express purpose of selling them again. In the hands of these speculators lands and houses so traded in are floating capital; because the entire property in them is parted with in one operation. But if a person buys lands for the purpose of farming it himself at a profit, or of letting it out to farmers, or buys or builds the houses for the purpose of letting them to tenants, then such lands and houses are 'fixed

Further on he adds:

"If a person buys funds or shares as an investment to produce an income, they are 'fixed capital.' But there is a class of persons called stock-jobbers who buy this kind of property with the intention of selling it again at a profit, and they keep a stock of it as traders do goods; in the hands of such persons such property is floating capital."—Vol. 1. p 213.

SUMMARY.

I.—GENERAL BALANCE ACCOUNT as at (say) 31st December 1897.

Dr.		*Cr.*		
To Cash in bank or in hand . .	£0 0 0	By Capital account for working capital, brought forward		£0 0 0
" Permanent assets provided out of terminable loans or debentures	0 0 0	" Debenture stock, &c. . . .		0 0 0
" Sundry debtors	0 0 0	" Sundry creditors		0 0 0
" Stock, &c.	0 0 0	" Depreciation fund . .	£0 0 0	
" Investments	0 0 0	" Reserve fund	0 0 0	
		" Profit and loss account	0 0 0	
				0 0 0
	£0 0 0			£0 0 0

FIG. 4—PREFERRED FORM OF GENERAL OR BALANCE ACCOUNT.

These extracts illustrate very clearly the economic and legal conception of "fixed" and "circulating capital."

The terms are not the best which could have been chosen; but so long as one grasps the idea intended to be conveyed, it does not matter very much what names are given to them.

We shall now show that the legal view of "fixed" and "circulating capital" coincides with the economic doctrine. The following is found in Verner v General and Commercial Investment Trust (L.R. 1894, 2 ch. p. 239).

"A limited company was formed, the objects of which were to invest its capital in stocks, funds, shares and securities of various descriptions, and the receipts of the company from the income of these investments were made applicable to paying a dividend. The market price of some of the investments of the company fell and others of them proved worthless, so that the value of the company's assets was materially diminished; but the income received from the investments for the year considerably exceeded the expenses of the year. One of the trustees brought an action on behalf of himself and all the other stockholders in the company, except the defendants, against the company and the other trustees to restrain the company from declaring a dividend, on the ground that until the loss of capital was made up a payment of dividend would be a payment out of capital.

"Held (by Justice Stirling and by the Court of Appeal) that it was within the power of the company to declare a dividend, for that there is no law to prevent a company from sinking its capital in the purchase of a property producing income and dividing that income without making provision for keeping up the value of the capital; and that fixed capital may be sunk and lost, and yet the excess of current receipts over current expenses may be applied in payment of a dividend, though where the income of a company arises from the turning over of circulating capital no dividend can be paid unless the circulating capital is kept up to its original value, as otherwise there would be a payment out of capital."

Justice Stirling said:

"I think it is not made out that the payment of a dividend is beyond the power of the company. Whether it is prudent that a dividend should be paid is not for me to decide, but for the men of business of whom the company is constituted. I base my opinion on the peculiar nature of the constitution of this particular company; and it is not to be assumed that I should have arrived at the same conclusion if I had been dealing with an ordinary trading company—if, for example, the object of the company had been to carry on the business of a stock-broker, and the investments had been the ordinary stock-in-trade of that business. It follows, from my view of the nature of the company, that the shareholders would not be entitled to divide for the purpose of dividend any increase in the value of the investments, however great."

Lord Justice Lindley, in delivering the joint judgment of Lord Justice A. L. Smith and himself, in the same case, said:

"The capital of a company is intended for use in some trade or business, and is necessarily exposed to risk of loss. As explained in Lee v. Neuchatel Asphalte Co., the capital even of a limited company is not a debt owing to its shareholders, and if the capital is lost the company is under no legal obligation either to make it good or, on that ground only, to wind up its affairs. If, therefore, the company has any assets which are not its capital within the meaning of the Companies Acts, there is no law which prohibits the division of such assets among the shareholders. Further, it was decided in that case, and, in my opinion, rightly decided, that a limited company formed to purchase and work a wasting property, such as a leasehold quarry, might lawfully declare and pay dividends out of the money produced by working such wasting property, without setting aside part of that money to keep the capital up to its original amount.

"There is no law which prevents a company from sinking its capital in the purchase or production of a money-making property or undertaking, and in dividing the money annually yielded by it, without preserving the capital sunk so as to be able to reproduce it intact either before or after the winding up of the company.

"A company may be formed upon the principle that no dividends shall be declared unless the capital is kept undiminished, or a company may contract with its creditors to keep its capital or assets up to a given value. But in the absence of some special article or contract there is no law to this effect. . . .

"When it is said, and said truly, that dividends are not to be paid out of capital; the word 'capital' means the money subscribed pursuant to the memorandum of association, or what is represented by that money. . . .

"A dividend presupposes a profit in some shape, and to divide as dividend the receipts, say for a year, without deducting the expenses incurred in that year in producing the receipts would be as unjustifiable in point of law as it would be reckless and blameworthy in the eyes of business men. The same observation applies to payment of dividends out of borrowed money. Further, if the income of any year arises from a consumption in that year of what may be called circulating capital, the division of such income as dividend without replacing the capital consumed in producing it will be a payment of a dividend out of the capital within the meaning of the prohibition which I have endeavored to explain. . .

"The word 'profits' is by no means free from ambiguity. The law is much more accurately expressed by saying that dividends cannot be paid out of capital than by saying that they can only be paid out of profits. The last expression leads to the inference that the capital must always be kept up and be represented by assets which, if sold, would produce it; and this is more than is required by law.

"Perhaps the shortest way of expressing the distinction which I am endeavoring to explain is to say that fixed capital may be sunk and lost, and yet that the excess of current receipts over current payments may be divided; but that floating or circulating capital must be kept up, as otherwise it will enter into or form part of such excess, in which case to divide such excess without deducting the capital which forms part of it will be contrary to law."

It will be seen that while Mr. Justice Stirling was disposed to treat this as an exceptional case, the Court of Appeal, on the other hand, laid down general principles which in effect grouped all companies into those which had their capital represented by (1) "fixed capital, " or (2) "circulating capital," or (3) partly "fixed" and partly "circulating capital."

This legal distinction between fixed and circulating capital is further brought out in the following cases: Lee v. Neuchatel Asphalte Co. (L.R. 41, Ch. Div. 14); Bolton v. Natal Land and Colonization Co. (1892), 2 Ch. 124; Salisbury v. Metropolitan Railway Co. (22 L.T. 839); Midland Land and Investment Corp., Ltd. (8th November, 1886); Wilmer v. McNamara & Co., Ltd. (L. R. 21, Ch. Div. 1895, p. 245); and Lubbock v. British Bank of South America (1892), 2 Ch. Div. 198.

A consideration of these cases, and more particularly the first, leads to the conclusion that share capital may be represented by circulating assets which must be maintained at a corresponding minimum value, or by fixed assets, the value of which may be either known or uncertain, but stand in the books at a constant figure until realization or liquidation takes place. In the legal view share capital is more a measure of the respective interests of the proprietors in the profits and in the actual capital when realized and avalable for distribution than the determined amount of capital due to them at a given date. It is not even conclusive evidence as to the precise value of the capital originally put in by them if the shares were acquired under a registered contract.

So far as accountants are concerned, the net result is that they should apply these facts to the accounts of any particular company which they may be engaged on, and distinguish between the two kinds of capital assets in their balance-sheets. If the share capital is represented by circulating assets, the usual form of balance-sheet or balance-account will suffice, but if represented by fixed capital then the double-account system should be used. The use of the double-account system should imply that a portion of the share capital is represented by "fixed capital" assets. If this practice were consistently followed by accountants it would tend to educate the commercial community to a better understanding of the law on the subject. The fact of a company using a special form would help to indicate that it was open to such a company to claim the benefit of the law in respect of having a substantial portion of its assets represented by "fixed capital," and not to write off out of revenue any diminution in the value thereof; while if it should do so, from prudential motives the "depreciation fund" in the general balance-sheet would show the total amount set aside for that purpose ab initio as against the cost price of the assets set out in capital account.

Although adverse fluctuations in the value of "fixed capital" may legally be disregarded in accounts, ordinary wear and tear must be provided out of revenue. The leading cases on the point are Davison v. Gillies (L.R 16, Ch. Div. 347) and Dent v. London Tramways Co. (16, Ch. Div. 344).

The terms single-account system and double-account system are by no means apt. We should prefer to say "the Fixed Capital system of accounts" and the "Circulating Capital system," as the case may be.

Briefly, the difference between the two methods is that in the one system capital expenditure is ear-marked at cost price, apart from the other assets, and remains so up to the moment when it is decided to sell or liquidate the undertaking; while in the other case the assets are treated as a common fund out of which liabilities to third parties have first to be met, and the remainder constitutes the actual capital available for the proprietors.

Is Double-Entry Bookkeeping of Spanish Origin?

Of late the popular sentiment is such as to at once condemn everything that is Spanish, without stopping to inquire into the merits of the matter. Some are so patriotic that very possibly they would stop keeping books by double entry if convinced that the double entry system was invented by Spaniards. As a nation we are disposed to regard double-entry bookkeeping as Italian in origin. Almost every English work that has been published, wherein any attempt has been made to trace the history of modern bookkeeping, gives the credit to certain Italians, and yet it would seem that the Italians are not to bear the laurels without dispute.

In a recent issue of the Accountants' Magazine we find a discussion of the antiquity of double-entry bookkeeping, in which certain facts are presented that cannot fail to interest all who are working as bookkeepers or engaged in any branch of accounting work. The discussion is based upon certain statements in the recent work of Carl Peter Kheil, entitled "Valentin Mennher und Antich Rocha." Our contemporary remarks that it has been claimed that double-entry is of Spanish origin, and then proceeds to the following statement of facts in support of the theory:

Tabulative bookkeeping was impossible until the invention of our present system of counting and figuring, and this was introduced into Spain by the Moors in the tenth century, long before it was known in Italy. Further, bookkeeping by double-entry was prescribed in mercantile transactions by statute in the fourteenth century, so that it must have been well known in the country by that time, and lastly, paper mills were used in Spain about two centuries earlier than in Italy. Our contemporary then quotes the author under review, wherein he points out that the words of the old statutes hardly bear out the interpretation which has been put upon them, and that the other two arguments are purely hypothetical. Still, continues our contemporary, the point is of some interest. Pacioli was most certainly not the inventor of double-entry. He merely wrote the first systematic treatise in which he embodied the existing practices, "al modo di Venetia." It is quite possible, therefore, concludes the Accountants' Magazine, that Spain is the birthplace of double-entry. Account books dating from 1339 to 1345 and kept on double-entry have been found in Montauban, France, and it is improbable the system should have been known there and not on the other side of the Pyrenees. In the meantime, however, research has failed to bring out anything certain, and above all, Spanish treatises on bookkeeping, as far as is known, all date subsequent to the great "Summa de Arithmetica" of Pacioli.

Men have made of Fortune an all-powerful goddess, in order that she may be made responsible for all their blunders.—Mme. de Staël.

In this age of specialties in almost every line of business, it is little wonder that there should spring up such a valuable monthly paper as ACCOUNTICS, devoted to the science of accounting, to the art of bookkeeping and to the advocacy of improved office methods.—Hide and Leather, Chicago, Ill.

Interest and Discount—III

By Charles W. Rohne

Compound Interest

Compound interest is the interest on a principal formed by adding interest to a former principal. Compound interest is illegal in most of the States. In transactions involving compound interest the interest is commonly called compounded, i.e., added to the principal to form a new principal, annually, semi-annually or quarterly. The amount of the principal for the first interest term is the principal for the second interest term; the amount of the second interest term is the principal of the third interest term, and so on.

The number of years necessary to double any sum of money at annual compound can be ascertained usually correct to two places of decimals at all ordinary rates, say from 3 to 15 per cent., by dividing .693 by the rate expressed decimally and adding the decimal of .35 with result to be considered as years and decimals of years. To illustrate, .693 divided by .06 produces 11.55, add decimal .35 and we have a total of 11.90.

Turning to any compound interest table we will find that at 6 per cent. $1,000 will amount in twelve years to $2,012.19+, and in eleven years to $1,898.30. Deducting the amount at the eleventh year from the twelfth year and the remainder is $113.89. Ninety per cent. of this difference is $102.50, which added to $1,898.30 gives a result of $2,000.80. Thus the rule given only varies 80 cents on an amount of $1,000, which would mean a variation of .0008 of a cent on $1.00.

George King, Fellow of the Institute of Actuaries in England, in his work entitled "Theory of Finance," on the subject of interest states: "Capital is wealth appropriated to reproductive employment," and in the words of the late J. S. Mill, "The gross profit on capital may be distinguished into three parts, which are respectively, the remuneration for risk, for trouble and for the capital itself, and which may be called insurance, wages of superintendence and interest." It is with the last of these, INTEREST, that we have at present to do.

In civilized communities wealth is measured in money, and therefore in the following investigations it is of money that we shall speak; but evidently it is immaterial, in laying down general propositions, whether the standard units are of one value or of another, so long as we remain consistent with ourselves, and use the same standard throughout. We shall, therefore, as the most convenient course to suit all currencies, treat of units of value, without specifying to what currency these units belong.

The rate of interest is, in scientific investigations, the ratio between the interest earned in one unit of time—generally a year—and the original sum invested, and it may be represented by the amount of interest earned on one unit of money in one unit of time. In ordinary commercial transactions interest is calculated at the rate per cent., instead of at the rate per unit; and therefore, to convert the commercial rate into the corresponding rate employed in mathematical researches we must divide by 100. Thus, if 5 per cent. be the rate of interest charged by a banker for an advance the corresponding mathematical rate is .05.

The capital invested is called the principal.

It is usual to say that there are two kinds of interest, simple and compound. If the interest be calculated on the original capital only, for whatever length of time the loan may have been allowed to remain outside with interest unpaid, then it is called simple interest; but if the interest on each occasion of its becoming due be added to the original debt, and if the interest for each succeeding period be calculated on the original debt so increased by all the previous accumulations of interest, then interest is said to be compound.

It will, however, be found that the assumption of simple interest leads continually to reductio ad absurdum, which is sufficient evidence that a fallacy somewhere lurks in the supposition. Money, whether received under the name of principal or interest, can always be invested to bear interest, and therefore, from the very nature of the case, simple interest is impossible. It is true that borrower and lender may between themselves agree for only simple interest, but such agreement does not prevent the borrower from investing the interest which is thereby allowed to remain in his hands, and securing interest thereon; and it is because this interest on interest is ignored in the doctrine of simple interest that the mathematical formulas fail.

EFFECTIVE AND NOMINAL RATES.

If the nominal rate of interest is 6 per cent. per annum, and the same is compounded semi-annually, the effective rate is .0609. If it is compounded quarterly the effective rate is .061364.

The nominal rate to be charged semi-annually in order to produce 6 per cent. per annum is .059126. If, however, it is compounded quarterly the rate is reduced to .058695. An illustration of nominal and effective rates is as follows:

Commonly, one-twelfth of an annual rate is considered a monthly rate. Therefore, when the nominal rate is 6 per cent. per annum, one-half of 1 per cent. per annum would be considered the monthly rate, but compounding at the rate of one-half of 1 per cent. per annum for twelve months, or expressed decimally compounding 1.005 for twelve months will produce 1.06167776, or nearly 17/100 in excess of 6 per cent.; whereas, if we use the expression (1+r), one-twelfth, we find that the monthly rate is .004867551, assuming that (r) is 6 per cent., or .06. Now, using 1.004867551 as the rate and compounding the same for twelve intervals we have 1.06 within an infinitesimal quantity.

A comparison of the difference between the nominal rate due monthly and the effective or equivalent actual rate due once a year, is as follows:

Nominal rate due monthly.	Effective or Equivalent actual rate due once a year.
3 %	3.042 %
4 %	4.074 %
5 %	5.116 %
6 %	6.168 %
7 %	7.229 %
8 %	8.300 %
9 %	9.381 %
10 %	10.471 %

I am amazed how men can call her (fortune) blind, when, by the company she keeps, she seems so very discriminating.—Goldsmith.

Hartford Chapter

The annual meeting of the Hartford Chapter of the Institute of Accounts was held March 28, with the usual large attendance. The secretary presented the first annual report, reviewing the history of the organization to date and clearly indicating that the chapter's first year has been a satisfactory one in every particular.

The principal business transacted was the election of officers, which resulted as follows: President, Gershom Smith, auditor of Pope Manufacturing Company, and secretary, Edwin Brower, 41 Kenyon street. Clarkson N. Fowler was chosen a member of the board of governors for three years. The members of the board holding over are Frederick Plimpton and J. Henry Turner.

Several applications for membership were reported as pending. A new plan was adopted for the registration of those who apply for membership, but who do not care at the outset to submit themselves to examination. It amounts to what might be described as probationary period, admitting the applicants to the general privileges of the meetings, but of course with no right to vote. Prospective members thus recorded must apply for full membership within three years from date, and take the usual examination. Rules have been adopted for carrying this plan into operation, which we hope to have the opportunity to lay before our readers in full at an early date. They have not yet been promulgated.

Of High or Low Degree

"Did you sever your connection with the firm or were you discharged?" asked the friend.

The man out of a job gave a few minutes to thought before answering.

"I'm a little uncertain about that," he said at last.

"Uncertain?"

"Yes. Of course, I know that office boys are discharged and general managers sever their connections, but I can't be sure that I was high enough up to sever my connection, and I don't think I was low enough down to be discharged. Perhaps you'd better make it that the firm and I disagreed."

Reviews and Criticisms

Commercial Law*

It is, perhaps, unfair to judge of a book intended for school use by the paper upon which it is printed or the binding in which it is sent out, but the value of the volume above described is discredited by its publishers, in that an exceedingly cheap paper has been used and the poor binding given it. Its technical merits are far beyond what would be expected from the setting in which they are presented. The book is one of a series issued by the publishers above named, and has had a large circulation in schools. It has come into demand among practical men more recently on account of the special attention that is, of late, being given to matters of commercial law by accountants and all those who have the management of business affairs. There is at present a well-defined demand for good works on commercial law, and all that are in the market are getting an amount of scrutiny which has not heretofore been accorded them.

The theory upon which this book is arranged corresponds to many others which have preceded it, some of which have been previously reviewed in these columns. After a general introductory chapter, in which law, sources of law, property, etc., are discussed, there are taken up in succession contracts, sales of personal property, guarantee in suretyship, negotiable paper, agency, partnership, corporations, common carriers, bailment, insurance, interest and usury, real estate sales, patents, copyrights, and trade marks, and rights of married women. There are also included a glossary and an alphabetical index. The work is illustrated in various points by the introduction of fac similes of different business documents. The several chapters are followed by a series of questions for review, arranged under heads corresponding to the chapters. The book is of convenient size, and a careful study of its contents cannot fail to be of advantage to accountants, accounting students and office men in general.

*Commercial Law. A practical text-book for schools and a valuable book for reference. By H. T. Hilles, Esq., of the Cleveland Bar. 200 pages, 5¼x8 inches, bound in cloth, red edges. Published by the Practical Text-Book Co. Price $1.25.

Private Ledger*

The dimensions of the New Idea Private Ledger are 4 inches wide by 6 inches deep. The first few pages are devoted to what is called a Personal Account, and are ruled in conventional ledger fashion, the debit occupying the left of the page and the credit the right, each with spaces for date, items and amount. Following this is the Bank Account, having space first for date, then for number (presumably check number), then for check paid to, following which is amount and then balance. We are informed in italics that "the rule is to add deposits and subtract checks." After several pages devoted to Bank Account, the user is introduced to promissory notes receivable. Three-quarters of an inch of space is devoted to the maker's name, a half-inch to where due, following which are twelve very narrow monthly columns, and finally the amount.

Next comes what we are informed is the Ledger, which, in some respects, is the queerest bit of account ruling that we have ever seen. Where the name of the account would be written, is printed the word "Ledger," so that the name must be written over the printing. The page assumes to be divided into four spaces in depth, but there has been a mistake in the ruling between spaces one and two, so that no provision is made for the names of the accounts. At the conclusion of the ledger, promissory notes payable are taken up in the same liberal style as notes receivable, already referred to, following which are personal accounts payable, which, in the way of ruling, is also a curiosity and a law unto itself. The first column, a little over a half-inch in width, is entitled "Bills Re-

*The New Idea Private Ledger. Pocket Size. Arranged by Seymour Eaton. Published by P. W. Ziegler & Co. Price $1.

ceived," the next "To Whom Due," the third "Amount," and following which is "When and How Paid."

Life insurance next comes up for attention. The page is ruled in columns, the first devoted to the name of the company, the second to the amount, next premium, while the next four columns relate to dates of premiums falling due. The next section is really the most valuable of all that the book contains, for it is left entirely to the user's discretion how to employ it. It is entitled "Memorandum," and is without vertical ruling. The last two pages of the book are devoted to what is called "Five Years' Business." The months are printed in the first column, with five lines to each. The second column is devoted to year, following which, with unit ruling, is a column entitled "Gross Business." Two other columns without unit rulings follow, and are without heads. It does not appear how the author would have the business man use them. The book is sufficiently attractive in its general appearance to ensure it a large sale. It utterly fails of utility, however, when it comes to an examination of its contents, while, in addition, almost every section has the blemish of crooked rulings or absolute mistakes in lines.

Shorthand Errors

Whoever dictates and reviews business correspondence or documents of any kind is impressed with the limitation of shorthand as practiced by the average amanuensis. The enigmas and conundrums which from time to time are presented to him for solution are far more intricate than those which usually adorn the puzzle corner of a family paper. The plausibility of the errors which creep into the work is their most dangerous feature. Sentences which convey the most arrant nonsense are yet so complete, so smooth and so plausible as frequently to pass casual inspection. Many a business man receives from a valued correspondent a letter manufactured in this way, which he vainly strives to understand. The amanuensis has got one or more words wrong, which the business man in hastily reading before signing has entirely overlooked, just enough to destroy the sense and defeat the purpose of the person whose name is signed to the letter, thereby constructing a conundrum for which his correspondent finds no ready answer.

The business man, for example, dictates, "We send a box to-day," the amanuensis writes, "We sent the books to-day.' To confuse the articles "a" and "the," definite and indefinite, seems to be something that the average amanuensis is prone to do. The shorthand characters for these useful particles so nearly coincide that much is left to context, but few are among amanuenses, apparently, who can correctly apply the rule. In such a case as "box" and "books" the outlines in the Pitman shorthand, for example, are identical. The vowels are usually omitted. In "sent" and "send" the outlines and vowels are identical, the only difference being the thickening of the stroke in the word "send." This distinction is difficult with a pencil and, therefore, the context must be depended upon for proper reading of the notes. The average amanuensis, becoming a machine, fails to exercise enough brain to know whether it was "a box," or "the books." The difficulties which the average business man of the period encounters in this regard are duplicated in various other directions. Various authors and public men have complained of the shortcomings of their amanuenses and of the deficiencies of the shorthand systems which they write. Books have been published containing sentences, ridiculous in themselves, and yet deviating no more from the author's real intention than "box" from "books" in the specimen error quoted above.

When Fortune means to men most good, she looks upon them with a threatening eye.—Shakespeare.

The good things of life are not to be had singly, but come to us with a mixture,—like a schoolboy's holiday, with a task affixed to the tail of it.—Lamb.

A good man's fortune may grow out at heels.—Shakespeare.

Fortune, to show us her power in all things, and to abate our presumption, seeing she could not make fools wise, has made them fortunate.—Montaigne.

It is not always the highest talent that thrives best. Mediocrity, with tact, will outweigh talent oftentimes.—Joseph Cook.

Combined Purchase and Payment Record

By Walton Day

In the last number of Accountics we referred to the work of the National Association of Credit Men and mentioned among other interesting facts that this organization, for the purpose of making of small merchants better credit risks, is doing an important work in the direction of what we may call standardizing bookkeeping. In the article mentioned we alluded particularly to a method of recording the merchant's purchases of and payments for merchandise. We also stated that the plans which are being presented to the retailer for adoption are entirely divested of bookkeeping technicalities. We now have the opportunity of laying before our readers a general view of the book in which invoices received and payments made are recorded, and also reduced fac-similes of pages with entries.

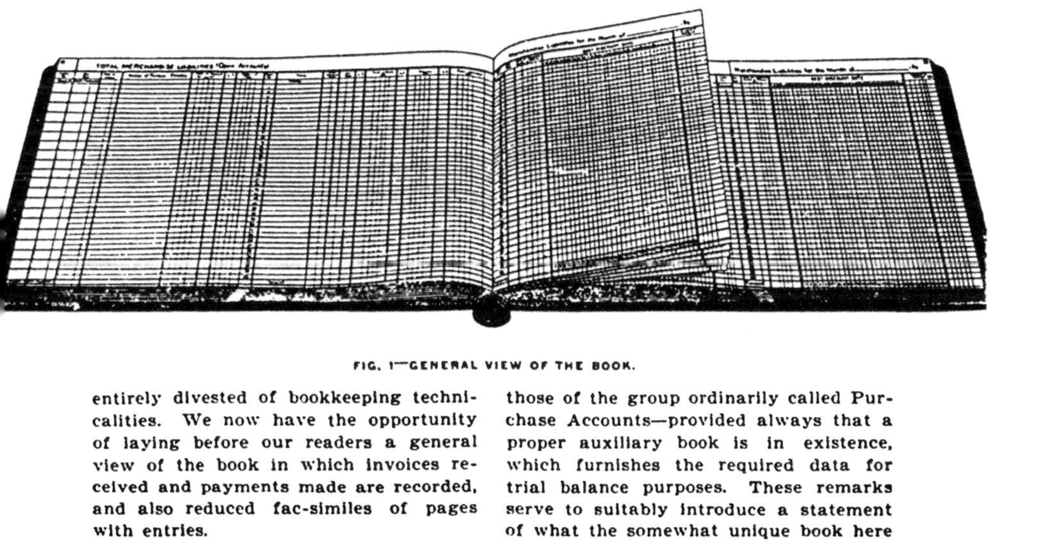

FIG. 1—GENERAL VIEW OF THE BOOK.

One of the first thing that the progressive bookkeeper does in getting away from the thraldom of routine, as commonly practised, is to omit the cash account in his ledger, and when taking off a trial balance to obtain figures for the cash direct from the cash book. One of the matters which the hard-headed business man of limited technical knowledge and slight office experience declares he cannot understand is the necessity of maintaining a ledger account with Cash, when the footings, and very frequently the items themselves as well correspond with the cash book. Why, he asks, should the same thing be done twice, producing exactly the same result? The progressive bookkeeper, after he has learned to dispense with the Cash Account in his ledger, finds out in the course of time that he may also dispense with his Notes Receivable Account and Notes Payable Account, depending in each case upon the note books for the required figures for the trial balance. It is only a step further along the same path to be able to dispense with other accounts that are usually kept in the ledger—for example, those of the group ordinarily called Purchase Accounts—provided always that a proper auxiliary book is in existence, which furnishes the required data for trial balance purposes. These remarks serve to suitably introduce a statement of what the somewhat unique book here illustrated performs, and the theory underlying its design.

In brief it shows at all times the merchandise liability (open accounts) of the merchant in gross and in detail, so far as individuals are concerned, without any posting to another book, and incidental thereto also shows in detail the same liabilities with respect to the dates of their maturities. In a single book, therefore, there is accomplished what in ordinary bookkeeping practice is secured only by several books, being the result of somewhat tedious posting from one book to another, and the subsequent drawing off of a statement.

When the book here illustrated is presented to the country merchant for use, none of the reasons for its existence above set forth is obtruded upon his mind. Instead, he is merely told, in the simplest possible language how to use it. The results that follow upon correctly conducting it at once become evident to his mind. The book is presented as a complete unit in itself, without any connection with anything else, and yet the accountant, as he reads this description, will immediately perceive that it is also capable of use as an element in an accounting system of the completest type.

Referring to the general view of the book it will be seen that it is of the long and short leaf variety. As made up it is demy size, opening at the end instead of at the side. The first long page is devoted to the general particulars of the purchases and payments. The several short pages and the second long page are devoted to monthly records, wherein are noted the amounts of invoices to be paid at certain dates, and the payments that are made thereof.

The second of the illustrations presented herewith is a reduced fac-simile of the long page with entries, while the third cut is a fac-simile of a short page with entries corresponding to those on the long page. While the fac-similes here presented are so much reduced as to make it a matter of some little difficulty, to some eyes at least, to trace all the details, still enough can be derived from them to make the following description intelligible:

All the pages of the book are divided horizontally by red lines into panels. Each panel is sub-divided by a blue faint line into two spaces. Referring to the second cut it will be seen that the red lines run to the extreme left hand margin of the wide page, whereas the intermediate blue lines stop short against the date column. Each panel is devoted to a single invoice. The first line in the panel is for recording the purchase in such items as the date of the bill, the name of the seller, the amount, terms, the best discount date and due date.

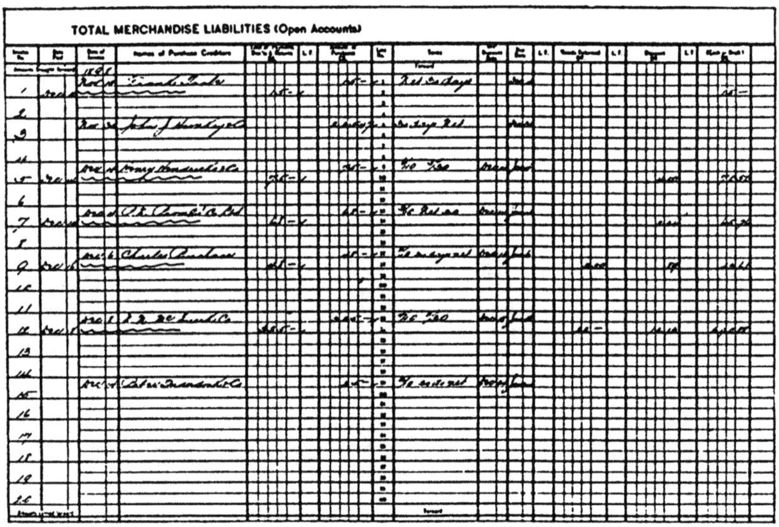

FIG. 2—REDUCED FAC-SIMILE OF LONG PAGE, WITH ENTRIES.

Of the two money columns in the left hand portion of the wide page, the right hand one, or the credit column, records the amounts of the purchases, while the left hand one, or debit column, the amounts of payments. The two money columns on each of the narrow leaves likewise record the amounts of purchases falling due in that month, and the payments made thereof.

As invoices come to hand, as already

described, they are entered in the various items above mentioned, and, in addition, according to their best discount date, are extended on one or the other of the narrow pages.

When invoices are paid, the second line in the panel is used, and then is brought into play the three money columns in the right hand portion of the wide page, devoted respectively to goods returned, discount, and amount of cash or draft. When the settlement that is made of a given invoice has been recorded in these items the total amount is entered in

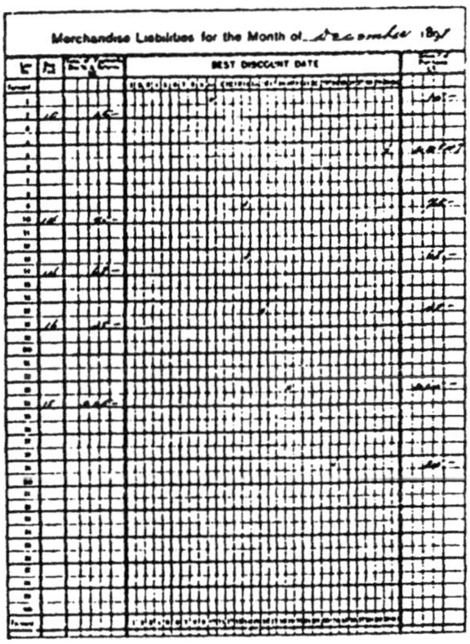

FIG. 3—REDUCED FAC-SIMILE OF SHORT PAGE, CONTAINING MONTHLY SECTION.

payment column on the first wide page and also in the payment column on the monthly page, in which the payment is made. The monthly pages, in the space between the money columns, are ruled into thirty-one narrow spaces, numbered for the days of the month. They are introduced for mere convenience in indicating the date of payment to be made. A check mark proves all sufficient for the purpose.

From this description will be perceived that the balance between the two money columns in the left hand portion of the first wide page always shows the total amount of the merchant's liability for merchandise on open accounts, whereas the balance between the money columns in each narrow page shows the amount to be paid in that month. There is, then, before him always a statement of his total liability (on open accounts) and also a detailed showing of when the amounts fall due.

For the purpose of increasing the usefulness of the book, ledger folio columns are provided, so that where it is desired to do so it may be used as one of original entry, from which to post to a ledger. This latter use, however, is likely to be far less in amount than the usual plan, as above described.

The equipment which the National Association of Credit Men is tendering country merchants includes, in addition to the book here specifically described, a notes payable book, arranged upon a similar plan, and an adaptation of the "Acx" Invoice Filing System, which was described in the March issue of ACCOUNTICS. These articles are being furnished to merchants at an extremely low price. The general movement for bringing the advantages of correct business methods to the attention of merchants throughout the land is being supported by contributions from prominent wholesalers and manufacturers, who believe that every step in the direction of better accounting for the small merchant, whereby he shall be lead always to know his exact condition, will render business safer and reduce the risk incident to credit sales. Several circulars, including price list and illustrated descriptive matter, have been prepared by the National Association of Credit Men, and can be obtained by addressing F. R Boocock, Secretary, 20 Nassau street, New York.

Good Bookkeeping and Poor Bookkeeping

BY WALTON DAY

The bookkeeping of a business is its historical record. The record to be of real value must not only be correct in details but must also be scientific in arrangement. The foundation upon which bookkeeping rests is the science of accounts. Scientific bookkeeping, therefore, is the only kind of bookkeeping which the progressive business man can tolerate. Bookkeeping as an art may be defined as the practical application of the principles of accounts to the records of business. Whatever methods embody the correct application of these principles constitute good bookkeeping. On the other hand, those methods which neglect or violate the principles of accounts serve to illustrate poor or inadequate bookkeeping.

Questions and Answers

Concerning the

BALANCE-SHEET SYSTEM OF ACCOUNTS

Conducted by the

Account Audit and Assurance Co., Ltd.

25 Pine Street, New York

What the Balance Sheet System does

From L. H. O., St. Louis.

Will you kindly explain briefly wherein the Balance Sheet System of Accounts differs from ordinary double entry bookkeeping? Perhaps a statement of what the system accomplishes will meet my requirements.

ANSWER—Our correspondent s question is perhaps a larger one than he supposed it to be when writing us. We may not be able in the space available at this time to answer him in full. We will attempt, however, to present one or two facts for his consideration.

By the Balance Sheet System of Accounts the ordinary fiscal period is abolished—that is, the business man no longer waits for the end of a year to ascertain the real results of his business, or to make those adjustment in his accounts which at that date for the first time conditions reveal to be necessary. The ordinary fiscal year, therefore, we may say, is abolished. It is reduced to a month in ordinary cases; in many cases to a week and in extreme instances to a single day.

Everything in the accounts is kept up to date and the showing is such that the actual condition is always revealed by the going accounts, thus eliminating the necessity of steering by dead reckoning or proceeding on general estimates between periods. Summed up, the Balance Sheet Accounting System gives a perpetual loss and gain statement and a perpetual balance sheet.

That business manager is most successful in directing affairs who has the least need for guessing at conditions. The Balance Sheet System therefore becomes an important aid in business management, because it eliminates from all the problems to be considered the fact of uncertainty. It gives the manager actual results, as the business proceeds, upon which to predicate his policy and base his directions to subordinates. This contrasted with the usual plan of issuing directions based upon assumed conditions, and of knowing the actual results of business only at the completion of the year, when in all probability current conditions have materially changed, puts into proper relationship the Balance Sheet System and ordinary double-entry bookkeeping. The Balance Sheet System is a modernized, up-to-date, scientific plan, while the usual interpretation of double entry is an antiquated, out-of-date plan that is so rusty in its bearings that it requires extra power (office expense) to operate it. At the same time the resulting product is far behind the times when measured by present business requirements.

For the Banking Business

From a Banker, Harrisburg, Pa.

Will you kindly inform me of the advantages of the Balance-Sheet Accounting System to the banking business, and the general adaptability to that line of business?

ANSWER.—The Balance-Sheet System of Accounts, particularly in view of the fact that its results are shown by contrasting earnings with expenses, is specially applicable to the banking business. When applied to the banking business it is made to show, by daily balances, the resources and liabilities of the institution and also the earnings to date, either in one amount or in several classified amounts, according to the nature of the business that is being done. The predominant feature of the System, and one that is very generally appreciated by bankers, is that it places before the managing officer daily such a statement as above described, in the most condensed form, and at the same time based upon the most scientific accounting principles.

The showing made by the Balance-Sheet System differs from the usual bank trial-balance in various respects, chiefly in the classification and grouping of accounts and the distribution of earnings and expenses. Earnings and expenses are so arranged in the Balance-Sheet Ledger as to be readily closed into the loss and gain account at a moment's notice. Unaccrued profits and items of expense, paid in advance, which are properly distributable over a future period, are carried in suspense accounts in a way to bring the proper proportions into the current accounts from time to time. Interest receipts, which are usually credited direct to profit, are by this system first carried into suspense, and thereafter properly distributed over the period to which they properly belong. Accordingly, the bank's profits per day or per week, according to the time-schedule upon which the system is arranged, are always clearly and correctly shown.

Another feature of the Balance-Sheet System, applied to banking, which will be generally appreciated, is that it is not necessary that the detail accounts be posted into the subordinate ledgers before making up the daily showing, as under the old system. Instead, the daily statement may be completed within a very few minutes after the closing of the banking day, even though details are not posted for some hours afterwards. Another feature of the Balance-Sheet System is that it permits of indefinite subdivisions upon a logical and scientific plan, in a way to accommodate any amount of busniess that is being done, or any amount of clerical force that it is desired to employ. The ordinary ledgers used with this system become auxiliary books for statistical purposes. The accounts which it contains are condensed under general heads in the Balance-Sheet Ledger, which alone shows the business in its entirety. The latter may be preserved as privately as may be desired. The Balance-Sheet Ledger in itself is self-proving, and in order to demonstrate its correctness it is not necessary to take off a general trial balance of all accounts in detail. Each group or class of accounts may be proved from time to time, by comparing its totals with the corresponding general account in the Balance-Sheet Ledger. In this respect the routine is similar to the usual method of proving the deposit account with the individual balances in all the ledgers of which it is composed. The principle, however, is carried to a much greater length to the manifest advantage of all concerned.

Abuses of the Merchandise Account

From T. C. D., Baltimore.

In a recent letter concerning the Balance Sheet System of Accounts, I note the statement that the "deficiencies of the usual double-entry method are supplied, and the abuses of the Merchandise Account corrected." I do not understand what you mean by abuses of the Merchandise Account. Will you kindly explain?

ANSWER—As bookkeeping is ordinarily taught by the schools, and as set forth in the text-books, the Merchandise Account is a greatly overworked element. It is made to perform various functions which do not belong to it, and there are put upon it duties which, by their nature, belong to accounts of an entirely different character. Whether or not the inventors of the double-entry system intended the Merchandise Account to be used as it is at present being used, it still is true that the Merchandise Account, of all the property accounts that are recognized in double-entry, is being employed for more than a single purpose, and that by the multitude of uses to which it is put it keeps out of the bookkeeping system certain other accounts which by rights should be present, and only by the use of which can the results of a business be correctly and satisfactorily shown.

As the ordinary student of bookkeeping sees the situation after he has taken a course at school, or investigated in ordinary treatises on bookkeeping, the Merchandise Account is a condition precedent to every set of books. The professional man, with nothing to sell but services; the financial institutions, dealing only in interest, discount, exchange, etc., and the transportation company, with no stock of goods on hand whatsoever but supplying a service; all these and still others that might be cited, must all have their respective Merchandise Accounts, because, as the student sees it, the Merchandise Account is the only account through which a profit can be shown.

Compare with the ordinary use that is made of the Merchandise Account a set of books arranged in a form to contrast earnings with expenses, and which restricts the Merchandise Account to a record of goods on hand. At once the absurdity of the usual method becomes apparent. Earnings contrasted with expenses affords a foundation upon which the accounting for every conceivable business enterprise may be established, and it is the only foundation that is common to all. The ordinary merchandising business is better provided for upon this basis than by the use of the Merchandise Account in the conventional way. Earnings in this case would be the gross profit on goods sold. Gross profits, diminished by the expenses of doing business, show net profits.

The overworked Merchandise Account, as it is usually conducted, is charged at the outset with the inventory, and thereafter with the new goods bought; also with rent, salaries, advertising and expenses generally, and likewise with those goods which are returned by the customers of the house. It is, in addition, frequently charged with bad debts, costs of collection and with all rebates and allowances. In turn it is credited with goods sold, and also with the goods returned to those from whom they were purchased, and very usually with the odd items of gain and income which may pertain to the business, including rentals of real estate, special services, etc. It requires no explanation to show that the functions of several accounts are here being loaded upon the one account, and it requires no analysis to demonstrate that such a mix-up is a positive disadvantage to the business and a great bewilderment to the management.

The very meaning of the word "merchandise" should suggest the exclusive use to which the account of that name is to be devoted. It should be an account of goods on hand—nothing more and nothing less. It should record the goods that are brought into the establishment, and likewise the goods that are sent out of the establishment, and its balance should show the goods remaining on hand. It should be no part of its work to record profits or show expenses. Such things belong to other accounts.

The professional man, the transportation company, the financial institution, the insurance corporation, and all other enterprises, of whatsoever name and character, which do not buy goods to sell again have no use for a Merchandise Account. Their transactions include other items, but not the selling of merchandise. A system, universally applicable, must therefore relegate Merchandise Account to those lines of trade to which by nature it belongs, and must have in its place such accounts as are appropriate to the business conducted. And this leads us to say again that the only system that can be regarded with any toleration whatever is one which has for its foundation the proper contrast of earnings with expenses.

Department Stores

From M. T., Troy, N. Y.

What advantages does the Balance Sheet System of Accounts offer for a department store, and can this system be operated in a store of moderate size—say of four to ten departments—as economically as the ordinary double-entry system?

ANSWER—Referring to our correspondent's last question first we would say that the results of the adoption of the Balance Sheet System in numerous department stores show a saving of from ten to fifty per cent. in clerical labor and other expenses of administration in favor of the Balance Sheet System as compared with what preceded it. Broadly, it is guaranteed that in no case will the expenses of the Balance Sheet System exceed those of the usual double-entry system in the same business. In a majority of cases the expenses will fall considerably under those of the double-entry plan, with all the special advantages secured by the system thrown in. While the Balance Sheet System makes necessary the doing of certain things which the old plans do not require, and while in some of its details it requires more work than is demanded by corresponding details of the usual plan, the savings in still other directions, and the fact that duplicate work is avoided, and further, that back work is entirely escaped, leaves the grand result in the position above described. The Balance Sheet System as a whole is the cheapest to operate.

Now, with respect to the first question proposed, namely, that relating to the special advantages which the Balance Sheet System offers in department store work. Without extra expense and without extra labor the following special results are secured, either daily or weekly, according to the time schedule upon which the system is based: 1. A profit and loss showing of each department; 2, the amount of goods on hand in each department, taken at cost prices; 3, the sales of each department; 4, the expenses of each department, and 5, the general expenses of the establishment to be prorated over the departments. These facts summed up—that is, taken collectively and properly arranged—mean a daily or weekly balance sheet of the business, showing correctly, under appropriate heads, the total assets of the business and under other appropriate heads the liabilities of the business. It means, also, at the same intervals, and in proper detail, a complete showing of the expenses of the business and its actual earnings—or in other words, a complete profit and loss statement.

The secret of the economy of the Balance Sheet System is that everything is correctly and properly done at the time that it is done, and that nothing is allowed to be done in duplicate. The majority of business men will bear us out in the assertion that a very considerable amount of the clerical labor in every office is devoted to what may be called back work, either in searching for some neglected or overlooked fact, or in the compilation of certain statistical showings to be derived from the books and demanded by the management for particular use. All this is avoided in the Balance Sheet System, by having the work correctly planned at the outset in a way to show perpetually just what the management desires to see, and therafter kept up to date on that plan, without variation therefrom.

Again, a part of the economy in the Balance Sheet System grows out of the fact that the very considerable labor and interruption to business incident to what is called closing the books or inventorying, or making out the annual or semiannual balance sheet, is entirely avoided. The work of each of the weeks and months of the year under the Balance Sheet System is exactly the same, for the books are always open and they are also always closed. The inventory as a unit and also subdivided into departments, is always known and the profits from transactions are likewise always in sight. It is fair to assert that the major part of the work that is involved in the annual closing, as it is frequently called, is devoted to making up that which was neglected as the business proceeded. If the books had been adequately and correctly kept all the twelve months of the year the work involved in closing would be avoided. The Balance Sheet System is based upon a plan of thorough work, scientifically planned and intelligently conducted. It entirely avoids the accumulation at the end of the year.

His Honor—The Mayor

It would seem that in Belleville, Ontario, the business man, the accountant and the teacher of young business men, is not without appreciation. J. W. Johnson, F. C. A., for upwards of twenty years one of the principals of the Ontario Business College, was some time since elected mayor of the town. More recently he has been returned a second and now a third time to the mayor's chair, all of which, we think, goes to prove, in addition to what is aserted at the beginning of this paragraph, that a prophet, in Belleville at least, is not without honor among his own friends and countrymen. We are sure that Belleville is to be congratulated in having at its head an eminently practical business man and one who, in a special manner, recognizes the fact that accounting is the vital element of business.

Ill-fortune never crushed that man whom good-fortune deceived not.—Ben Jonson.

A great fortune is a great servitude.
—Seneca.

Fickle Fortune reigns, and, undiscerning, scatters crowns and chains.—Pope.

"THE PEN IS MIGHTIER THAN THE SWORD"—BUT WHERE DOES THE INK COME IN?

The 3-A Line of Account Books

By Fielding West

The Globe Company, with factory at Cincinnati, and sales rooms in Cincinnati, Chicago, New York and Boston, and represented throughout the United States by prominent stationers in almost every business center, has recently become the sole manufacturers and sales agents of a line of improved account-books, which are being marketed under the trade name of 3-A Books. An announcement of some of these specialties was contained in the advertisement of the company named in the issue of this magazine for January. Among the articles then noted were the following: 3-A Progressive Mercantile Ledger, 3-A Progressive Bank Ledger, 3-A Trial Balance Book, 3-A Notes Payable Record, 3-A Notes Receivable Record, and 3-A Invoice Purchase and Payment Record. All of these books employ the long and short leaf principle, and embody a recently patented improvement, whereby the projecting edges of the long leaves are reinforced to compensate for the extra thickness of the short leaves, thereby presenting an even writing surface throughout.

There are presented herewith two illustrations of a book of this class, one being a back view showing the arrangement of the leaves above described, and the other a front or open view, likewise illustrating the special features described. These views are to be taken as typical only, for the construction named is capable of many variations and adaptations. For example, in the illustrations, five interleaves or narrow leaves are shown. The number of interleaves is subject to variation, and as a fact books are being constructed with anywhere from one interleaf to forty interleaves, according to the nature of requirements. In turn, the books may be of various proportions, with relatively very wide pages, or very narrow pages.

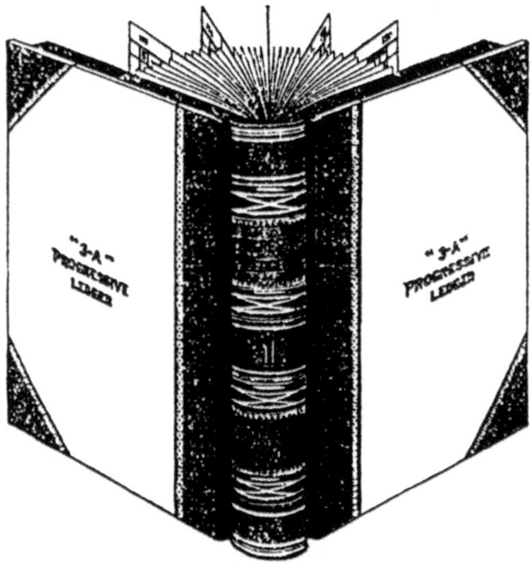

3-A ACCOUNT BOOKS—BACK VIEW OF A 3-A PROGRESSIVE LEDGER, SHOWING CONSTRUCTION AND THE THICKENED EDGES OF WIDE LEAVES.

Referring more specifically to some of the special account-books constructed upon this plan, it may be stated that "progressive ledger," as used by The Globe Company, signifies, for mercantile and banking uses, a design and construction, irrespective of the special patented improvement referred to above, that is the equivalent of what is widely known as the Boston ledger, or Safeguard ledger. The names of the accounts are written on the first wide page down the left hand margin, with as many lines allotted to each account as the activity of the account may require. The monthly divisions which are provided on the remaining space of the first wide leaf, and the several narrow leaves, record the transactions for the months in detail, with a balance carried forward from each month to the succeeding month. Unlike the usual design of Boston or Safeguard ledgers, as they are frequently called, wherein a single interleaf is all that can be used, the monthly spaces in a 3-A Progressive Ledger may be distributed over a number of interleaves, thus giving, for example, two years to a single writing of the account names instead of one year. Or the ledgers, restricted to one year, or twelve monthly spaces, may be of comparatively small dimensions simply by increasing the number of interleaves.

The 3-A Trial Balance, mentioned in the list above, is perhaps as good an example of the economy of this construction and the compactness of the resulting books as anything that could be referred to. It is only cap size in dimensions, yet provides for fifty accounts to the page, and by the quota of interleaves which is provided offers twenty-four sets of monthly columns, with an extra pair of columns for the end of each year for recording the balances after closing. Bookkeepers generally are pleased with a trial balance book of moderate dimensions and compact form on account of the convenience in handling, and they are also pleased with the requirement of writing the names of the accounts only once in two years. Instead of footings being carried forward in this book page by page, a novel arrangement of recapitulation sheets at the close of the volume takes care of this part of the work with a minimum of labor.

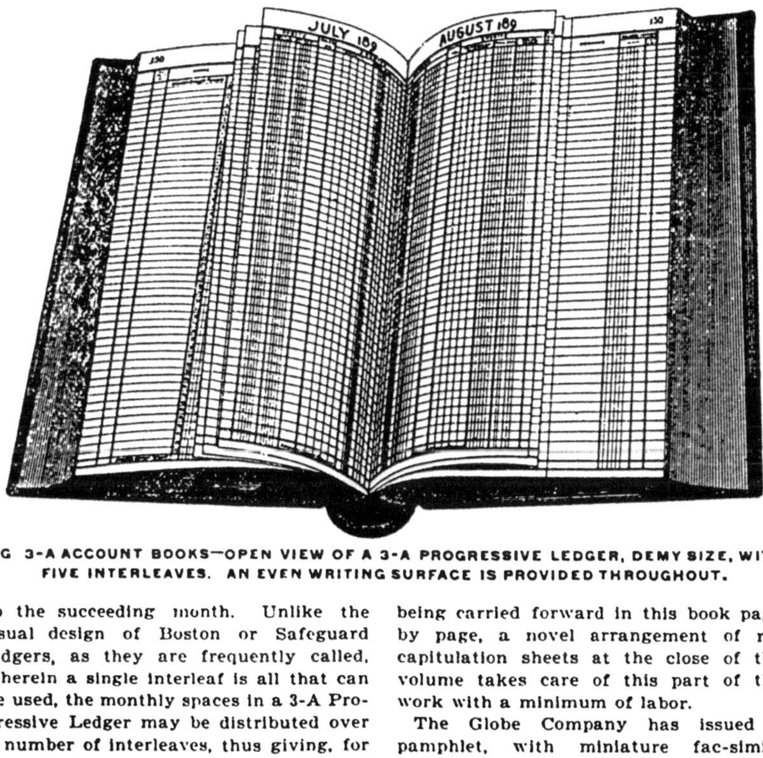

FIG 3-A ACCOUNT BOOKS—OPEN VIEW OF A 3-A PROGRESSIVE LEDGER, DEMY SIZE, WITH FIVE INTERLEAVES. AN EVEN WRITING SURFACE IS PROVIDED THROUGHOUT.

The Globe Company has issued a pamphlet, with miniature fac-simile pages with entries, of the 3-A Progressive Ledger, demy size, adapted for Sales and Purchase Accounts, copies of which they are ready to send to all applicants who mention this article. The pamphlet, in addition to general descriptive matter, contains full instructions for use, and is a desirable addition to the accounting literature of the period. It is much more than an advertising pamphlet, because it contains an exposition of certain advanced principles of bookkeeping, in which office men at large are interested. It is something that every progressive bookkeeper, accountant and business man will profit by examining.

Accountics

VOL. IV MAY 1899 No. 5

The Monthly Statement

It affords us pleasure to announce that the last of the several engagements of Mr. A. O. Kittredge as editorial writer for and correspondent of various trade and class papers terminates the present month, and that none of them will be renewed. For the future Mr. Kittredge's pen will be used exclusively for ACCOUNTICS. Commencing with the June number, there will be continued in the columns of this magazine much of the special work which he has in the past been doing for other periodicals along the lines of accounting and improved business methods. There will be found in ACCOUNTICS, hereafter a monthly survey and review of the work of the National Association of Credit Men, with appropriate references to what is being done by the local organizations affiliated with this movement, thus continuing in these pages what has been presented for many months past in a monthly letter, addressed to the Collector and Commercial Lawyer, Detroit. There will also be presented in these columns from time to time stated articles and short paragraphs relating to street railway accounting, thus carrying forward what has for two years or more been appearing in the pages of the Street Railway Journal, New York. A series of articles will also be presented, relating to bank accounting, bank auditing and banking routine in general, continuing in these pages what was commenced some time since in the American Bankers' Magazine, New York. Other articles from Mr. Kittredge's pen will be published relating to builders' accounts, thereby continuing what has been done in the columns of the Builders' Bulletin, Boston; and still other articles will appear relating to the routine and accounting of dry goods stores, department stores, etc., thereby carrying forward what started nearly two years since in the columns of the Dry Goods Economist, New York. A very considerable part of the special work which Mr. Kittredge has been conducting in some of the journals above mentioned, and in others not specified, has been that of answering questions on accounting matters and solving stated office problems. He will be glad to continue this service in the same manner, to all who may desire his help through these columns.

The recent action of the New York Clearing House in the matter of collection charges on country checks has brought up afresh the general question of what a bank should do for the accommodation of the public, or what it can afford to do in any direction without direct compensation therefor. The contention of many merchants is that their accounts are worth so much to the bank, that the bank can afford to make collections of country checks for them gratuitously, in addition to keeping their accounts. This contention should be easy of proof if correct. It is very easy to determine the interest value of a given amount on deposit. It is more difficult, however, to determine what it costs to keep a given account, since the accounts with the bank vary one with another in activity and in various details. Still banks know how to pro rate their expenses equitably over the entire number of depositors accounts. With the interest value of an account determined and the cost of keeping the account ascertained, it is very easy to strike a balance, thereby showing exactly what a given account is worth to a bank. Many banks undertake to make calculations of this kind, but the results, for manifest reasons, are held for their own use and are seldom made public.

It is evident that a bank is a public institution and therefore cannot stand so strictly on its rights as a private proprietor. It cannot escape doing a certain amount of business as a matter of accommodation to the public, and yet, if the business done as a mere accommodation should become excessive, the bank's profits would be seriously curtailed. Without profit, the bank could not exist. A given depositor's account may be worth but little at the present time, and yet it may grow into one of considerable value later. A depositor's balance may be really a source of expense, but the influence of the depositor in other directions may more than compensate for loss involved in his personal account. These are only a few of the considerations which the practical bank manager must take into account in determining the value of a given account to his bank. As said above, certain banks have very carefully devised systems for eestimating the value of accounts. Having determined the clerical cost of keeping the account, and having contrasted it with the interest value of the average deposit, they are then in shape to contrast the resulting balance with the general advantages of the account just alluded to.

In another page of this issue we commence as a serial the republication of a pamphlet, issued some time since, by Bernard Dale, of London, entitled, "How are Profits for the Year to be Ascertained?" The sub-title, as the essay was originally published, was as follows: "What is Capital of a Company Within the Meaning of the Prohibition that Dividends May Not be Paid Out of Capital?" In view of the interest which attaches to the general subject covered by this pamphlet and which sometimes finds expression in some such phrases as the "laws of capital" and the "laws of profit," a matter which has been referred to in recent issues of this magazine, we feel certain that our readers generally will find what is now begun of special value and importance. While treating entirely of the English law on the subject, the essay still develops principles which, sooner or later, will come before the American courts for a consideration.

It is not to be forgotten that in many details our American laws are based on English precedents, and that the intimate relationship, commercially, existing between Great Britain and the United States, tends toward uniformity in business laws, as well as in business methods. Our British cousins, by reason of having commenced earlier than ourselves, have made greater progress than we have made in laws regulating business operations. One of the results of the numerous gigantic schemes of capitalization, now commanding attention in this country will be to bring under review of the courts, sooner or later, various matters which, to a certain extent at least, have escaped attention in the past. Among these we may safely guess will be the principles which Mr. Dale so intelligently discusses in the essay referred to.

In the preface to his pamphlet, Mr. Dale asserts that one of his objects has been to show that the law (English) is not in the state of confusion in which it is so frequently represented to be, and that when the decisions of the courts are carefully examined and compared, they are found to be in harmony not only with each other, but with the principles upon which economists have based their division of capital into "fixed" and "circulating." He says further, that the recent adoption by the courts of this division as a ground of judicial decision has made it a necessary part of his task to investigate the principle underlying such division, and, as preliminary thereto, to examine the motion of capital. He carefully discriminates between what is capital in general and what is an individual's capital, and, as will be seen by a perusal of the article, closely adheres to the definition of an individual's capital as given by Adam Smith in his "Wealth of Nations."

As the weeks pass by, the action of the New York Clearing House in the matter of collection charges on country checks, full particulars of which were given in a recent issue of this magazine, seems to meet with the general approval of banks and bankers in various sections of the country, and also to be regarded by the majority of business men as entirely reasonable. The country merchant, for his own advantage, has been drawing checks upon his local bank and mailing them to New York and other business centers in settlement of bills there due. In this in some cases he has been encouraged by the local bank, apparently, however, upon a mistaken policy. The local bank, according to the argument, would have the use of the money represented by the depositor's balance during the time that the check was in course of transmission and in process of collection. However correct this may have been theoretically, the country merchant soon learned to take all the advantage to himself, and not infrequently his remittances of local checks to his creditors in business centers have been equivalent to acts of kiting. With a bill just due and yet no cash in hand to pay it, he has ventured to remit his check at a date to secure the discount on the bill, trusting to collections in the succeeding few days to make his account good before the check would get back. The local bank, therefore, gained nothing, for it had no balance on deposit during the time the check was out. The local bank actually lost by the operation, for upon another basis the merchant would have bought exchange and would have paid a proper fee for the same. The effect of the new order of things is likely to be beneficial to all concerned. The local merchant will gradually become accustomed to buying exchange, the habit of misusing local checks by mailing them away to a distance will disappear, the prices charged by the country merchant for goods bought at a distance will be fixed with reference to the fact that he pays exchange in remitting for the same, and the much neglected bill of exchange drawn by the local bank upon its city correspondent will once more come into vogue. The whole business of buying, selling and paying for goods conducted between buyers and sellers in distant points will finally reach a proper and equitable footing.

In another part of this issue we present selections from a very considerable number of letters which have reached us since our April number went to press, discussing the pros and cons of an international association of public accountants. The letters which we print are a fair selection with respect to the sentiments expressed. Some favor such a movement unconditionally. Others think that so far at least as this country is concerned, such an effort at the present time would be premature. Some assert that before anything can be done that would be creditable to the accountants of the United States, and particularly to the accountants of the Empire State, the rivalries and jealousies which are asserted to exist between different accountants' associations must be overcome. It is necessary, they argue, that the profession be shown to stand upon a common footing. As might be expected, the strongest endorsement of the scheme comes from some of our correspondents in Canada—the members of the Ontario Institute of Chartered Accountants. This association, which, as we have pointed out in the past, is by far the best organized and the most ably conducted of all of the organizations among accountants in America, is, therefore, in a better position to occupy advanced ground than any other. It is apparently ready to co-operate in whatever offers that promises to be beneficial to the profession. Our readers generally will profit by a perusal of these letters. While there is no probability of immediate steps being taken by any one —as we were careful to explain in the first instance—to consummate an international organization, yet, sooner or later, this question is bound to be presented in tangible and definite shape to be answered either negatively or affirmatively. The preliminary survey of the situation through our columns at this time is not without advantage, therefore, for it shows not only the differences of opinion which exist upon this question, but also indicates what different accountants believe must be accomplished as necessary preliminaries to the undertaking.

In another column of this issue, a full account is given of the law relating to accountancy, recently passed by the Legislature of Pennsylvania, and since signed by the Governor of that commonwealth. The law, which puts the Keystone State directly in line with New York, provides for the examination of public accountants for the degree C. P. A., the examinations to be held semi-annually in May and November. There is every reason to believe that the results of the law will prove beneficial to the profession at large. Other States are stirring in the same direction. Quite a little effort is at present being made in New Jersey, and in March last a bill was introduced in the Legislature of Minnesota. This latter bill is modelled upon the same general lines as that proposed in Illinois. The bill, we learn, has been referred to the committee in the Senate, by which committee it has been approved for passage, and at recent advices, was on "general orders." The expectation is that the bill will become a law. Naturally, the accountants of Minnesota are enthusiastic over the prospect, and business men at large have given the proposed law enthusiastic support. From present indications, it is reasonable to expect that ere long, the profession of accountancy will be recognized in all the States.

One by one the several States of the Union are falling in line in the matter of abolishing days of grace. The Legislature of West Virginia recently passed a bill, which takes effect the present month, defining the legal holidays in that commonwealth, and another bill which abolishes days of grace and sets forth the rule to be followed when negotiable paper falls due on Sunday and other holidays. This act also goes into effect the present month. A law has been passed by the Legislature of Massachusetts abolishing days of grace, the provision having gone into effect March 6. In this case the act was vetoed by Governor Wolcott, but subsequently the House of Representatives passed it over the veto, and a little later the Senate concurred with the House in the same.

National Association of Credit Men

The fourth annual convention of the National Association of Credit Men organization is to be held at Buffalo, June 6, 7, and 8. Elaborate preparations have been made for making the occasion one of great interest and benefit to the delegates and members who can attend. Hotel Iroquois is to be the headquarters. A number of important addresses are to be delivered, and the reports of the various committees and the discussions thereon, are likely to develop many matters of vital interest to business men in general. Trade congresses, which were an important feature of the convention held at Detroit a year since, will also be a feature of this convention, and not a little interest attaches to what will transpire in these informal gatherings of men of allied interests. The proposed congresses and the credit men who are to preside over the same are as follows: Boot and shoe interests, Geo. G. Ford, of L. P. Ross, Rochester, N. Y.; clothing, Thos. Davies, of L. C. Wachsmuth & Co., Chicago, Ill.; dry goods, F. S. Evans, of Strawbridge & Clothier, Philadelphia, Pa.; grocery, F. W. Standart, of C. S. Morey Mercantile Co., Denver, Col.; and hardware, F. J. Hopkins, of Janney, Semple & Co., Minneapolis, Minn.

F. R. Boocock, the secretary of the national organization, has arranged to display in one of the parlors of the Hotel Iroquois a model credit department in working order. This will be arranged as an object lesson for all those who seek the best mechanical means for managing the matters in their charge. Under the auspices of the Account, Audit & Assurance Co., Limited, of New York, an exhibit will be made of modern book-keeping methods, likewise in a parlor of the Hotel Iroquois. The Globe Company, with factory at Cincinnati, Ohio, and sales departments in Chicago, New York and Boston, has complimented the National Association of Credit Men by supplying the furniture required for the model credit department exhibition, and also for the display of bookkeeping methods mentioned above. The Globe Company on its own account will also display a very complete line of improved and labor saving account books, known as the "3-A" series.

The local Association of Credit Men in Buffalo, through appropriate committees, is making very careful and elaborate preparations for the entertainment of guests. A number of excursions and other features are planned. The business meetings of the convention will be restricted to one short session each day, leaving delegates and visitors abundant time for trade congresses, excursions, examination of the different exhibits and other features of interest.

Blest are those whose blood and judgment are so well commingled that they are not a pipe for Fortune's finger to sound what stop she pleases.—Shakespeare.

Well-gotten wealth may lose itself, but the ill-gotten loses its master also.
—Cervantes.

How are the Profits for the Year to be Ascertained?

BY BERNARD DALE

The term capital is used sometimes with reference to the capital of a community, and sometimes with reference to the capital of the individual. In the former case the notion presented is that of "social" capital; in the latter that of "individual's" capital. Adam Smith was careful to show that these two notions did not coincide, and, although almost ignored by his two great disciples, Ricardo and John Stuart Mill, the distinction is now well recognized by leading economists, and its importance insisted on in the solution of all questions bearing on the import of the term capital. In these pages we have nothing to do with "social" capital, and the definitions of capital given below are, therefore, only of "individual's" capital.

Adam Smith, who uses the term "stock" in the same sense that modern economists use the term "wealth," defines an "individual's" capital as follows:

> "His whole stock, therefore, is divided into two parts. That part which he expects is to afford him this revenue is called his capital. The other part is that which supplies his immediate consumption." (Wealth of Nations, Book 1, Chapter I.)

John Stuart Mill's definition is:

> "Precisely that part of a man's possessions, whatever it be, which is to constitute his fund for carrying on fresh production."

Again, speaking of those who live on the income of their property without being engaged in production, he says:

> "Let us, therefore, consider whether, and in what cases, the property of those who live on the interest of what they possess, without being personally engaged in production, can be regarded as capital. It is so called in common language, and, with reference to the individual, not improperly." (Principles of Political Economy, Book 1, Chapter IV.)

In his "Political Economy," page 60, Senior says:

> "But economists are agreed that whatever gives a profit is properly termed capital."

Macleod, who uses the term "economic quality" as denoting anything of which the value may be measured in money, says:

> "Now any economic quantity whatever may be used in two distinct ways. 1. The proprietor may use it himself for his own personal enjoyment. 2. He may trade with it, i. e., use it so as to produce a profit. When any economic quantity is traded with or, as it is termed in economics, used productively: it is termed capital." (Elements of Economics, Vol. 1, p. 204.)

Professor Marshall's definition is:

> "Capital is that part of an individual's wealth which is destined to be used as a source of income." (Economics of Industry, Chapter III.)

Professor Sidgwick says:

> "The man of business means by capital wealth employed so as to bring its possessor a surplus which we may call, in a wide sense, profit: or, more precisely, we should say that the hope of finding himself possessed of this profit is his motive for thus using his wealth, since we should agree that capital does not lose its essential characteristics by becoming actually profitless." (The Principles of Political Economy, Book 1, Chapter V.)

In his "Positive Theory of Capital," Chapter IV., Professor Boem-Bawerk defines capital in general as "acquisitive wealth," and adopts the idea of wealth used as a source of income as the distinctive feature of individual's capital

It will be seen from the above definitions that, according to economists, what marks out a man's capital from the rest of his wealth, is not the nature of the thing itself, but the use its owner is making of it. The very same thing may be capital or non-capital, according as its proprietor has or has not devoted it to productive purposes. There is no such thing as Absolute Capital, that is, that which at all times and in all places is capital. As Mill observes, the distinction between capital and non-capital does not lie so much in the kind of commodities as in the will of the capitalist to employ it one way rather than another; and although Professor Sidgwick has excepted to this view on the ground that wealth becomes capital not when it is destined for profitable employment, but when it is actually used for this purpose, he ultimately agrees "that we should take the intention of the owner of wealth rather than the consequences of his acts to determine whether that wealth is or is not capital."

Professor Marshall instances the case of a peasant's cart, which, when employed in the field, is capital, but which, when carrying him and his family for a jaunt on a holiday, is not capital. Again, he says, it is not always clear to what extent a doctor's house and his horse and carriage should be regarded as capital required for his business. A bare enumeration, therefore, of the articles composing a man's wealth, would not enable us to predicate of this or that thing that it was capital; in order to do this we should require to be informed whether its owner was using it productively or, varying our phraseology, using it as to yield to him an income or revenue. It is the possession of this characteristic of income or revenue yielding that, in the eyes of an economist, distinguishes an individual's capital from the rest of his wealth.

If now we were to take up the balance-sheet of any company, say a manufacturing company, we should find, among the assets, properties of widely different natures, namely, lands, buildings, machinery, dead and live stock, debts, patents, cash, etc. Any one of these assets, however, if destined to be used by the company as a source of income or revenue would, according to the above definition, be a capital to them.

An individual's wealth may perform this function of yielding an income or revenue to him in either of three ways:

1. The owner may retain the ownership of the thing himself and use it in his own trade—e. g., the boat of a fisherman used by him for fishing.

2. Or while retaining the property in the thing the owner may let the use of it to another on hire—e. g., a pleasure boat let on hire.

3. Or the owner instead of retaining the property in the thing and obtaining an income or revenue by its use by the letting out the use on hire, may part with it altogether, e. g., sell the boat.

In the first two of the three cases above given the boat would be termed a "fixed" capital; in the last a "circulating" capital.

Adam Smith is generally supposed to be the first economist to divide capital into fixed and circulating, and to stamp on those terms the meanings with which they now pass current in the commercial world.

He defined "fixed" and "circulating" capital as follows:

> " 'Fixed' Capital; that, of which the characteristic is, that it affords a revenue or profit without circulating or changing masters.
>
> " 'Circulating' Capital; that of which the characteristic is that it affords a revenue only by circulating or changing masters." (Wealth of Nations, Book 2, Chapter I.)

And in another passage he says:

> "In all countries where there is a tolerable security every man of common understanding will endeavor to employ whatever stock he can command, in procuring either present enjoyment or future profit. If it is employed in procuring present enjoyment, it is stock reserved for immediate consumption. If it is employed in procuring future profit it must procure this profit either by staying with him, or by going from him. In the one case it is a fixed and in the other a circulating capital."

Adam Smith gives several instances to show that one and the same thing may be either a "fixed" or "circulating" capital, according to the method in which its owner employs it. The cattle of a farmer employed in labor are his "fixed" capital, but the cattle which are bought, not to labor, but for sale, are his circulating capital, because, as Adam Smith says, the farmer makes his profit by parting with them. A flock of sheep bought by a farmer, not for sale, but in order to make a profit by their wool and by their increase is a "fixed" capital; because the profit is made by keeping them. Then again, although Adam Smith classifies agricultural implements as "fixed" capital to the farmer who retains them for their use, he points out that in the hands of the manufacturer who made them, they would be his "circulating" capital because he made them to be sold absolutely and so to change masters.

John Stuart Mill, speaking of "circulating capital," says, "The term, which is not very appropriate, " is derived from the circumstance that this portion of capital requires to be constantly renewed by the sale of the finished product, and when renewed is perpetually parted with in buying materials and paying wages; so that it does its work, not by being kept, but by changing hands." And speaking of "fixed" capital he says, "Another large portion of capital, however, consists in instruments of production, of a more or less permanent character; which produce their effect not by being parted with, but by being kept." (Principles of Political Economy, p. 57.)

In his "Elements of Economics," vol. 1, p. 206, Macleod devotes several pages to the distinction between "fixed" and "circulating" capital. He gives several illustrations to show that what singles out an individual's "fixed" from his "circulating" capital is not the nature of the thing, but the mode in which it is used as capital. Thus he says:

> "Houses and lands are by no means invariably 'fixed capital.' It is quite common for speculators to buy up land and build houses for the express purpose of selling them again. In the hands of these speculators, land and houses so traded in are floating capital; because the entire property in them is parted with in one operation. But if a person buys land for the purpose of farming it himself at a profit, or of letting it out to farmers, or buys or builds the houses for the purpose of letting them to tenants; then such lands and houses are fixed capital.
>
> "So a shipbuilder buys ships, and sells them to a company. In the hands of the builder they are floating capital; in the hands of the company they become fixed capital."

Macleod then points out that articles which are usually classed as "floating" capital may become "fixed" capital, and he instances furniture, clothes and plate, which are usually "floating" capital, because they are made for the purpose of being sold. They are, however, sometimes made for the purpose of being let out for hire, and then they are "fixed" capital. Then, anticipating, as it were, the recent discussion as to the distinction to be drawn between securities held as a permanent investment, and those held for sale by a jobber, he says:

> "If a person buys funds or shares as an investment to produce an income, they are fixed capital. But there is a class of persons, called stock jobbers, who buy this kind of property with the intention of selling it again at a profit; and they keep a stock of it as traders do goods; in the hands of such persons such property is floating capital." (Elements of Economics, vol. 1, p. 213.)

There are, however, some objects, which, from their nature, lend themselves more readily to their user as fixed capital than others. A railway might almost be said to be incapable, from its nature, of being used save as "fixed" capital; but even a railway may become "circulating" capital, as the history of the Potteries, Shrewsbury, and North Wales Railway Company shows. This company, having failed to work its line as a profit, ceased to use it as a road, and obtained authority from Parliament to sell it for what it would fetch. It then became their "circulating" capital, since they could only make it produce an income to them by parting with it.

The terms "fixed" and "circulating" capital are not, perhaps, the best that could have been selected, having regard to the requirements of scientific classification. But the danger of departing from an established nomenclature would probably be found to outweigh any advantage to be attained by a nearer approach to precision. The terms are certainly calculated to call attention to the physical properties of the subject rather than to its change of legal ownership, while performing the function of a capital. It is certainly difficult for a casual reader to understand that the steam horses let out for hire at a fair are not a "circulating" capital to their owner, or that the seed of Adam Smith's farmer, which, as he puts it, "went backwards and forwards between the ground and the granary," was a "fixed" capital. The distinction itself, however, is a real one, and one which, as we shall see hereatter, is of great importance in the solution of the question, "What are the Annual Profits of a Company?"

The Question of an International Accountants' Association

The Advantage of a Common Standard of Efficiency

From George Edwards, F. C. A., Toronto.

I am not prepared to say whether an International Association would be practicable. The difficulties of coming together upon common ground for the discussion of practical questions seem mainly to lie in the diversity of language, of monetary systems, and also in the distance separating the members of the profession in different parts of the world. I do not think that an International Association, having for its only apparent object, the meeting together of a number of delegates for three or four days' convention, at a pleasant watering-place, at which papers are read and officers elected, can accomplish much real good. There must be something more than this.

The benefits arising from an International Association would be, as I view it, in the formation of a committee composed of representatives from the principal Institutes, this committee having for its object the close personal investigation of the standards of efficiency required by different Institutes as a precedent to membership, and a further object of levelling up these standards so far as may be possible. The adoption of a common standard of efficiency is bound to create confidence in the minds of the investing public in the work of accountants of other countries. It should be of distinct advantage to practicing accountants in countries utilizing foreign capital to any extent in business undertakings.

The Work Should Commence at Home

From W. G. Mowat, C. P. A., Buffalo.

I am in sympathy with organization and believe that in unity there is strength. I also believe that the existence of at least three Accountants' Societies in this State has been the cause of the non-success of all efforts to accomplish any practical benefit. I did belong to the National Society of Certified Public Accountants in the United States, but have resigned. I took this step because there did not seem to be any effort made at organization nor any particular results. I do not know of any class of professional people that is so thoroughly disorganized as accountants. I think the cause of all the trouble is in New York City. Until the men at the top of the profession in New York decide to bury their differences, amalgamate the various societies and endeavor to accomplish some practical benefit, the best course for country accountants to pursue is to wait in patience and do nothing.

Likely to be of Great Benefit

From J. F. Calderwood, Auditor Twin City Rapid Transit Company, Minneapolis.

I can readily see a great benefit accruing to both the members of an International Association of Accountants and also to those who employ the service of such accountants, provided the International Association is organized upon the same basis as are the English Accountants' Associations.

A Word from Scotland

From the Editor of the Accountants' Magazine, Edinburgh:

I quite agree as to the great advantage to be derived from correspondence and interchange of professional views between accountants in different countries, having myself had experience thereof, but with regard to the question as to the advisability of endeavoring to establish an international association of public accountants there appear to be many practical difficulties. It is, however, highly desirable to fully discuss the project with the view of ascertaining whether these difficulties could be overcome.

There are great differences in the position of the profession in European countries, which is highly organized in some and almost non-existent in others. The different languages spoken would also be an obstacle. The scheme so far as English speaking countries are concerned, would be easier of accomplishment, yet it would lose much of its value if, for instance, Italian accountants were not embraced. The whole matter is worthy of careful consideration, and I hope it will everywhere receive this.

There are Others

From Maurice S. Kuhns, C. P. A., Chicago:

I would suggest that you place the matter of an international organization among accountants, before the American Association of Public Accountants, or the National Association of Certified Public Accountants, in order that any attempt toward such an organization may receive the official endorsement of the leading and representative associations of the United States, without which such an attempt would probably prove weak and abortive.

Accountancy Benefited by Organization

From J. W. Johnson, C. A., Belleville, Ontario:

I regard the proposition of an international association of public accountants favorably and think it is feasible. Organization among accountants in the United States and Canada has been progressing for a dozen years past. Speaking for the Province of Ontario, I voice the universal opinion of the public in the cities and throughout the country, when I say that through the thorough work accomplished by the Institute of Chartered Accountants of this Province, accountancy has been raised in the Dominion to the status of a profession. The services of its members are in demand from the Pacific to the Atlantic, and for such services they are receiving professional remuneration such as was neither asked for nor offered prior to the establishment and development of the profession.

The Institute of Chartered Accountants of Ontario has created a new class of students—namely, students of accounting, who are pursuing the Institute's curriculum in regular course, and for whom a future career, well assured and thoroughly recognized in the community, is provided. Locally, then, the public accountants of Canada have made a place for themselves and are making a name. The place and the name have come to them in such a way that they can respect themselves. They know that in other countries men engaged in the practice of accountancy have been equally successful—in fact, in the mother country even more successful—in creating and maintaining similar organizations, the methods of which command the confidence of the public, and secure for their members a wide and profitable field for employment.

The proposal to establish and maintain an International Association, that will bring these organizations and their units together to the extent that is possible, I regard most favorably.

Is the proposal feasible? I think it is. International organizations that are not ephemeral exist among doctors, engineers, teachers, scientists and various other classes, professional and non-professional. Permanent good must result from these associations, or they would not be maintained. Through them their members derive knowledge from each other. Their profession or business commands the attention of the public through the press reports of their proceedings. As accountants can and need to learn from their professional brethren in other countries, and would be benefited and stimulated by professional intercourse and printed communication with each other, and as they are as intelligent as any of the classes who find such organizations profitable, I think the scheme a feasible one.

Premature at Present

From J. E. Sterrett, C. P. A., Philadelphia.

With respect to my views upon the subject of an International Association of Public Accountants, I would say that in my judgment, such a move at the present time would be premature. Until Public Accountants are better organized, through associations more local in character, I do not see how it would be feasible to maintain a larger association, built upon uncertain foundations.

Wealth is a weak anchor, and glory cannot support a man: this is the law of God, that virtue only is firm and cannot be shaken by a tempest.—Pythagoras

---

Conscience and wealth are not always neighbors.—Massinger.

Much learning shows how little mortals know; much wealth, how little worldlings can enjoy.—Young.

Fortune brings in some boats that are not steered.—Shakespeare

Interest and Discount—IV

By Charles W. Rohne

Illustration Showing the Difference Between Interest and Discount

Profits made by trading in debts are made in two ways: 1. When the person who buys the debt agrees to defer receiving the profit until the end of the time agreed upon. In this case the profit is termed interest. Thus, when a person buys a debt of $100, payable one year hence, at 5 per cent. interest, he pays down the $100, and receives in exchange for it the right to demand $105 at the end of the year. The debt is the price of the money, and the money is the price of the debt. When the debtor pays the debt he brings the $105 in money to his creditor, and buys up the right of action against himself. Thus, every "loan" of money, as it is called, is a sale or an exchange; the lender transfers the property in the money to the "borrower," and in exchange for it receives the right of action to demand the principal and interest at the end of the year. The right of action is a new creation of property, and is the credit, or the debt. All "loans" of money are sales or exchanges; they are acts of commerce, and, therefore, enter into the science of economics.

2. Where the difference, or profit, is retained at the time of the purchase of the debt.

In this case the profit is termed discount. But discount of itself is of two kinds: (a) In the ordinary books of algebra it is said that discount is where the profit is retained at the time of the purchase; and the sum paid for the debt is such a sum as, improved at the given rate of interest, should be equal to the full amount of the debt at the end of the period of advance. It is, however, the present value of the sum agreed upon at the agreed-upon rate of profit. This may be called algebraical discount. It is used by insurance companies in determining the present value of future payments and in some other cases. (b) But this kind of discount is never used by bankers and dealers in money. In banking it is invariably the custom to retain the full amount of the profit agreed upon at the time of purchasing the debt. Thus, if a banker discounts a bill of $100 for a year at 5 per cent. he deducts and retains the full $5.00 at the time of the purchase, and gives his customer a credit for $95.00. That is, he creates a right of action of $95.00 to purchase the right to $100 at the end of the year. As this method of discount is invariably used in banking and money lending, it may be termed banking discount.

The rate of interest or discount is the ratio of the profit to the amount of the debt, made in some given time, as the year. The profits made by interest and algebraical discount are exactly equal, but banking discount is more profitable. In the example given in the former case a profit of $5.00 is made on the advance of $100; in the latter case a profit of $5.00 is made on the advance of $95.00.

So long as the rate of discount is low, there is not much difference in the profits by way of interest or banking discount. But as the rate increases the profit increases at a very rapid ratio, as may easily be seen. If a person lends $100 at 20 per cent. interest he advances $100, and at the end of the year receives $120, which is a profit of 20 per cent. If he discounts a bill for $100 at 20 per cent. he advances only $80.00, and at the end of the year receives $100, which is a profit of 25 per cent. If he lends $100 at 50 per cent. interest he advances $100, and at the end of the year he receives $150, which is a profit of 50 per cent. If he discounts a bill of $100 at 50 per cent. he advances only $50, and at the end of the year receives $100, which is a profit of 100 per cent. Discounting a bill of $100 at 60 per cent. is a profit of 150 per cent. If a person lends $100 at 100 per cent. interest, at the end of the year he receives $200, which is a profit of 100 per cent. If he discounted a bill of $100 at 100 per cent. he would advance nothing, and at the end of the year he would receive $100, or his profit would be infinite.

Usury dulls and damps all industries, improvements, and new inventions, wherein money would be stirring if it were not for this slug.—Bacon.

Accountants' Associations

Hartford Chapter, Institute of Accounts

The April meeting of the Hartford Chapter of the Institute of Accounts, which was held on the evening of April 25, was devoted to a discussion of the plans for the ensuing year. The attendance was confined to members, and a very considerable percentage of the entire membership was in attendance. After careful canvassing, it was decided that the meetings of this organization for the ensuing year should be of two classes. One of these is to be restricted to members only, in which discussions are to be of an informal character, and in which timid members and untrained speakers or rather those who have not gained the confidence which is to be secured only by practice, shall have an opportunity to express themselves as they would not be willing to undertake to do if strangers were present. Open meetings, as the other class is designated, are proposed, to which invitations are to be extended to the public, as it may be interested. A speaker from outside the immediate membership of the Chapter is to be obtained for each, if possible, and in addition, formal papers, prepared by the members, are to be read. These two kinds of meetings are to be alternated so far as possible, but the Chapter recognizing the fact that circumstances may often interfere with such plans, the President of the Chapter, in co-operation with the Chairman of the Topic Committee, is authorized to arrange for the one or the other class, as conditions may allow.

The Topic Committee is constituted as follows: Henry R. Hovey, Chairman; George L. Vannais, and Frank W. Hawley.

In the absence of the President, Gershom Smith, who was out of the city at the date of this meeting, the chair was occupied by Clarkson N. Fowler, of the Board of Governors. After the routine business of the evening had been disposed of, Mr. Fowler addressed the members on "The Accounting of Fire Insurance." He introduced the subject with a brief review of the early history of fire insurance, and then described the methods of keeping the accounts, of the cash transactions as well as the records which are necessary to the preparation of the annual reports to the several State insurance departments and for other purposes.

New York Chapter of the Institute of Accounts

A meeting of the Board of Governors of the New York Chapter of the Institute of Accounts was held Wednesday evening, May 3. There were present Messrs. Dutton, Plant, Althers, Dillon and Kittredge. The special matters of business brought before the meeting included arrangements for the annual meeting of the Chapter, which occurs on the evening of May 18; consideration of the annual reports of officers to be made at that time; nomination of officers and members of the Board of Examiners for the ensuing year, and nominations of the delegates to the annual convention of the Institute, which will occur a few weeks hence.

Chas. Dutton, president of the Chapter, occupied the chair. W. P. Plant, secretary and treasurer, presented an informal outline of the report which he is prepared to make to the Chapter at the annual meeting, which was approved. The financial condition of the Chapter was shown to be satisfactory, there being a tidy sum in bank, with all liabilities satisfied.

The following ticket, it was agreed, should be recommended for consideration of the Chapter at the annual meeting: For President, John T. Murphy, secretary of the American Type Founders' Company; for secretary and treasurer, W. P. Plant, with Driggs-Seabury Gun & Ammunition Company, and for members of the Board of Governors to fill vacancies, Frederick W. Child and William Dillon. The following, it was agreed, should be recommended to the Chapter as delegates to the convention of the Institute: F. W. Child, Chas. E. Cheney, Thos. S. Whitbeck, John T. Murphy, J. R. Loomis, H. H. Todd, A. O. Kittredge, Wm. Dillon, W. J. Althers, W. P. Plant and Chas. Dillon. The resignation of A. O. Kittredge as a member of the Board of Governors, which was tendered just before the meeting adjourned, was accepted, but action in the matter of filling the vacancy just made was deferred until the next meeting.

Pennsylvania Certified Public Accountants

By the law which went into effect in Pennsylvania on the 29th of March, the accountants of that State have secured legal recognition, with which they may be well pleased. They have struggled through a period of many months for what was manifestly to the advantage of the business community, and, finally, have acomplished their object. This work has been due largely to the efforts of the Pennsylvania Association of Public Accountants, of which John Heins is President; John Vaughan, Vice-President; Wm. M. Lybrand, treasurer, and J. E. Sterrett, Secretary. As likely to interest our readers, we present below the act in full, only remarking in passing that as yet the Board of Examiners has not been announced.

An Act to establish a board for the examination of accountants, to provide for the granting of certificates to accountants, and to provide a punishment for the violation of this act.

Section 1—Be it enacted by the Senate and House of Representatives of the Commonwealth of Pennsylvania in General Assembly met, and it is hereby enacted by the authority of the same, that any citizen of the United States, residing or having an office for the regular transaction of business in the State of Pennsylvania, being over the age of twenty-one years and of good moral character, and who shall have received from the Governor of the State of Pennsylvania a certificate of his qualifications to practice as a public expert accountant as hereinafter provided, shall be designated and known as a "Certified Public Accountant," and no other person shall assume such title, or use the abbreviation "C P. A.," or any other words, letters, or figures, to indicate that the person using the same is such certified public accountant. Every person holding such certificate, and every co-partnership of accountants, every member of which shall hold such certificate, may assume and use the title of Certified Public Accountants, or the abbreviation thereof (C. P. A.), provided that no other person or co-partnership shall use such title or abbreviation, or other words, letters, or figures to indicate that the person or co-partnership using the same is such certified public accountant.

Section 2—The Governor of the State of Pennsylvania shall appoint a board of five examiners for the examination of persons applying for certification under this act. Three of said examiners shall be public accountants, who shall have been in practice as such for at least five years, one of whom shall be appointed for the term of one year, one for two years, and one for three years, and upon the expiration of each of said terms an examiner shall be appointed for the term of three years, and after one thousand eight hundred and ninety-nine these three examiners shall be certified public accountants. The other two examiners shall be practicing attorneys in good standing, in any of the courts in the State of Pennsylvania. One of them shall be appointed for the term of one year, and the other for two years, and upon the expiration of each of said terms a successor shall be appointed for the term of two years. The examination for certificates shall be based upon an examination in commercial law and general accounting, said examination shall take place in Philadelphia, Harrisburg and Pittsburg twice a year during the months of May and November of each year, under these rules and regulations, as may be adopted by the Board. The fees provided by this act shall be twenty-five dollars for each applicant, from which shall be paid for the expenses incident to such examination for stationery and clerk hire a sum not exceeding two hundred dollars, and if any surplus above said expenses shall remain at the end of any year it shall be paid after the traveling expenses of the board shall be deducted therefrom into the Treasury of the Commonwealth. The results of such examinations shall be certified to the Governor and filed in the office of the Secretary of International Affairs and kept for reference and inspection for a period not less than five years, the Governor to issue the certificates.

Section 3—The Governor of the State of Pennsylvania may revoke any such certificate for sufficient cause upon the recommendation of the Board of Examiners, who shall have given written notice to the holders thereof and after he has had a hearing thereon.

Section 4—The Board of Examiners may in its discretion waive the examination of any person who shall have been for three years before the passage of this act practicing in the State of Pennsylvania as a public accountant and who shall apply in writing for such certificate within one year after the passage of this act.

Section 5—If any person shall hold himself out as having received the certificate provided for in this act, or shall assume to practice thereunder as a Certified Public Accountant, or use the initials C. P. A. without having received such certificate, or after the same shall have been revoked, he shall be deemed guilty of misdemeanor and on conviction thereof shall be sentenced to pay a fine not exceeding five hundred dollars.

Associated Accountants of New Orleans

The regular monthly meeting of this organization was held April 20th. Several applications for membership were favorably acted upon and several others referred to proper committees. The financial condition of the association, by the report of the Treasurer, was shown to be most excellent. The principal business of the evening was the election of officers for the ensuing year, resulting as follows: President, A. L. Soule; First Vice-President, Wm. Palfrey; Second Vice-President, P. W. Sherwood; Secretary, N. Cuny; Treasurer, A. A. Hart, and Librarian, E. E. Soule. The following members of the Executive Committee were also elected: Messrs. Jacquet and Benedic.

The annual meeting of this Association, which marks the seventh year of its existence, is to be held May 13th, at West End, Lake Pontchartrain. Messrs. Sherwood, Fowler and Benedic have been appointed as a committee of arrangements with full power to act.

The topic of the evening was "Co-Operative Societies," on which subject, a very able paper was read by Associate J. W. Prentiss. The aims and purposes of the organization as well as the history of its development, together with a statement of the volume of business done, were thoroughly and interestingly set forth.

It is significant that the daily papers of New Orleans give liberal space from time to time to the reports of this organization. The work of the association is beginning to attract favorable attention throughout the city, and as recently remarked by the New Orleans Picayune, its future discussions promise to be attended by many visitors.

Pennsylvania Association of Public Accountants

At the meeting of this organization, held in Philadelphia, April 17th, the following officers were chosen for the year: President, Charles N. Vollum, of Philadelphia; Vice-President, John Vaughan, of Pittsburg; Secretary, J. E. Sterrett, of Philadelphia; Treasurer, William M. Lybrand, of Philadelphia. Members of the Executive Committee were selected as follows: John Heins, John W. Francis and H. B. Hayes.

New York State Society of Certified Public Accountants

The regular monthly meeting of this organization, and the annual meeting as well, was held at the Waldorf-Astoria, Monday evening, May 8th. There was a larger attendance of members than has been present at any other meeting of the organization for some time past. Preliminary to those numbers on the programme which related particularly to the annual meeting, regular routine business was transacted. Francis Gottsberger, in behalf of the Legislative Committee, presented for consideration a memorial addressed to the regents of the University of the State of New York, requesting the modification of one of the rules at present governing the examinations for the degree of "C. P. A." The modification consisted in substituting in the rule defining those who are eligible to examination, a term of satisfactory experience as a public accountant, in place of a term of study. The presentation of this memorial opened up a discussion of the general subject of examinations, and the rules relating to the same, during the course of which it transpired that the Board of Examiners had been requested by the regents to report upon the rules, in whole or in part, governing the examinations. It was finally concluded that it was expedient for the Society to confer with the Board of Examiners before adopting the memorial, in order that the recommendations going from the Society to the regents, and also proceeding from the Board of Examiners, should, so far as possible, be in accord.

President Haskins, in his annual report, epitomized the history of the Society and briefly surveyed the work of the past year along the general lines for which the Society at present stands. He also referred to what was done during the year which preceded the organization. He congratulated the Society upon what has been accomplished, and the good influence which the organization is exerting in the general business field; and last but not least, upon the advantages to the members themselves, growing out of mutual acquaintanceship and frequent contact with each other. He said that the organization had made important progress during the year just closed, and that it would enter upon the third year of its existence under most favorable conditions.

The report of Treasurer Kelly showed a balance in bank, a relatively small amount due from members, and a liability to certain members of the Society for cash advances. Deducting the latter amount from sum of the cash on hand and the amount owing by members, showed the Society to be in a satisfactory condition of solvency. The heaviest expenses of the year were incurred by the Legislative Committee, which had faced special emergencies, in view of certain obnoxious and destructive legislation which had been introduced at Albany by those unconditionally opposed to the objects for which the Society stand.

The report of Secretary Teele in a sense traversed the same ground as that of the President and Treasurer who had preceded him, but giving, however, in definite figures and in considerable detail the progress of the organization, which had been generalized by the President. It was shown that the Registration Bureau conducted by the Society during the past year had produced an income greater than its expenses, and the significant statement was made that all those who had registered, who by their character and experience were competent to assist in the work of public accounting, had found more or less employment through this agency. It was also stated that if the registration had been larger, it was probable all would have found work.

The election of officers for the new year resulted as follows:

President, C. W. Haskins; Vice-Presidents, L. H. Conant and F. J. MacRae; Secretary, Leon Brummer, and Treasurer, J. N. Kelly. Directors: J. T. Anyon, H. R. M. Cook, D. J. Edmonds, J. R. Loomis, Edward Adams, R. L. Cuthbert, F. W. Lafrentz, F. I. Stott, A. W. Teele, H. S. Corwin, S. Roger Mitchell, D. C. Tate.

Illinois Association of Public Accountants

The annual meeting of this organization was held April 12th. The election of officers for the current year resulted in the choice of the following: President, John A. Cooper, of Holbrook & Cooper; Secretary and Treasurer, Laurence A. Jones, of Hawley, Jones & Co.

The Bank Auditor

In a recent issue of the Banking Law Journal we find the following discussion of the bank auditor, which presents certain thoughts that may be of interest to our readers:

The auditor is fast being recognized as an important and necessary officer in every bank that professes to keep abreast with the times in its methods of handling the clerical work. Generally speaking, the duty of the auditor is to check over the work and see that it is done promptly and correctly. From this point of view he might more properly be styled the assistant cashier in order that his office may carry the weight of official title and authority. If, however, the auditor is to be one of the clerical force, his duties may be limited to balancing the pass books on the individual ledgers and to making out and adjusting the accounts current on the foreign ledger. If time permits, he should also assort the checks and deposit tickets. In balancing the pass books, the auditor should do all the work, down to an including the striking the balance on the individual ledger. He should carefully compare the footings of the pass book with the footings of the ledger and, where a discrepancy occurs, he should be entirely satisfied as to the reason for it. If the ledgers are kept on the daily balance or "Boston" system the comparison of balances must be made with double care. A printed form embodying an acknowledgment of the correctness of the balance should be delivered to the depositor with the book and the auditor should see to it that this acknowledgment is returned promptly. The making out and reconciling the accounts current with corresponding blanks is a most important part of the auditor's duty. When properly and thoroughly done it constitutes a complete check on the general ledger. When the work of the auditor is carefully considered it will be seen that it is a mistake to assign the position to one of the younger men. On the contrary, it requires the skill of the most competent accountant in the institution and the office should rank next after the tellers and the discount clerk.

The Incapacity for Independent Action*

By Elbert Hubbard

"The point I wish to make is this: McKinley gave Rowan a letter to be delivered to Garcia; Rowan took the letter and did not ask, 'Where is he at?' By the Eternal! there is a man whose form should be cast in deathless bronze and the statue placed in every college of the land. It is not book-learning young men need, nor instruction about this and that, but a stiffening of the vertebræ which will cause them to be loyal to a trust, so act promptly, concentrate their energies; do the thing—'Carry a message to Garcia!'

"General Garcia is dead now, but there are other Garcias.

"No man, who has endeavored to carry out an enterprise where many hands were needed, but has been well-nigh appalled at times by the imbecility of the average man—the inability or unwillingness to concentrate on a thing and do it.

"Slip-shod assistance, foolish inattention, dowdy indifference, and half-hearted work seem the rule; and no man succeeds, unless by hook or crook, or threat, he forces or bribes other men to assist him: or mayhap, God in His goodness performs a miracle, and sends him an angel of light for an assistant. You, reader, put this matter to a test: You are sitting now in your office—six clerks are within call. Summon any one and make this request: 'Please look in the encyclopedia and make a brief memorandum for me concerning the life of Correggio.'

"Will the clerk quietly say, 'Yes, sir,' and go do the task?

"On your life he will not. He will look at you out of a fishy eye and ask you one or more of the following questions:

" 'Who was he?'

" 'Which encyclopedia?'

" 'Where is the encyclopedia?'

" 'Was I hired for that?'

" 'Don't you mean Bismarck?'

" 'What's the matter with Charlie doing it?'

" 'Is he dead?'

" 'Is there any hurry?'

" 'Shan't I bring you the book and let you look it up yourself?'

" 'What do you want to know for?'

"And I will lay you ten to one that after you have answered the questions, and explained how to find the information, and why you want it, the clerk will go off and get one of the other clerks to help him to find Garcia—and then come back and tell you there is no such man. Of course I may lose my bet, but, according to the law of average, I will not.

"Now if you are wise you will not bother to explain to your 'assistant' that Correggio is indexed under the C's, not in the K's, but you will smile sweetly and say, 'Never mind,' and go look it up yourself.

"And this incapacity for independent action, this moral stupidity, this infirmity of the will, this unwillingness to cheerfully catch hold and lift, are the things that put pure Socialism so far into the future. If men will not act for themselves, what will they do when the benefit of their effort is for all?

"My heart goes out to the man who does his work when the 'boss' is away, as well as when he is at home. And the man who, when given a letter for Garcia, quietly takes the missive, without asking any idiotic questions, and with no lurking intention of chucking it into the nearest sewer, or of doing aught else but deliver it, never gets 'laid off,' nor has to go on a strike for higher wages. Civilization is one long anxious search for just such individuals. Anything such a man asks shall be granted; his kind is so rare that no employer can afford to let him go. He is wanted in every city, town and village—in every office, shop, store and factory. The world cries out for such; he is needed, and needed badly—the man who can carry a message to Garcia."

*From an article originally published in the March number of The Philistine, of which Mr. Hubbard is the editor. The article had the effect of selling out the entire edition in a very few days, and further of inspiring Mr. George Daniels, general passenger agent of the New York Central Railway, to order a new edition of five hundred thousand copies for free distribution. The article is based upon a well-known war incident. President McKinley desired to send a message to General Garcia, who was somewhere in the mountain fastnesses of Cuba. Rowan was selected to be the bearer.

The Impending Trust Panic

By Walton Day

It seems to be the settled conviction of many business men that panics in this country are inevitable, and that, as the result of the American disposition to overdo things, there must be, at recurring intervals, a period of liquidation and general business reform. All this certainly seems to be borne out by the financial history of the nation up to date. Panics and financial crises have occurred from time to time in the past, at comparatively short intervals, and wise acres shake their heads and say it is only a question of a short time before another will be upon us.

Looking back over the panics which are best known to the present generation of business men, we find that one of them was of a nature to be called a railroad panic, brought about by too much energy in building railroads, and a too large expansion of credits, based upon bonds covering properties, the earning capacity of which had not yet been determined. Another and more recent panic is described as a financial panic, brought about by uncertainty concerning the financial system and the policy of the government with reference to silver.

Those who talk the most about panics of the past are the most ready to point out impending panics, and the consensus of opinion of the croakers of the period would seem to be that the next panic, the precise date of which, however, has not yet been established, is to be a trust panic.

The arguments which lead to the conclusion that we are to have another panic and that the impending panic is to be a trust panic, are based, to a certain extent, upon historical parallels. The amount of money that is being put into so-called trusts at the present time, the amount of bonds and stocks which the public is buying, the uncertain foundation upon which many of the so-called trusts are based, the evident overdoing of the thing, which, if not really in progress at the present time, it is believed will soon be manifest, leads these prophets of disastrous days to predict a sudden change in public sentiment, a period of disaster and lack of confidence, and a general shrinking of values. A little something of this kind has already occurred in Wall Street, due to the conservative action of the banks in declining to accept as collateral for loans, stocks of corporations, the standing of which had not yet been fully established. That it did not extend further and overwhelm many budding and promising enterprises was astonishing to many people.

With a steadily advancing market in various stocks and bonds Wall Street has also manifested, the last few months, a number of startling fluctuations. No principle underlying these fluctuations has been discovered, and the most careful students have failed to formulate the law that governs their occurrence. The only thing that is certain in the matter is that sudden changes in value take place at intervals, and always exhibit substantially the same characteristics. This being the case, a brief study of some of the periods of speculation of the past is not without interest.

Matthew Marshall, in a recent issue of the Sun, reviews the speculative eras and panics of the past as follows:

The speculations attending the South Sea bubble in England about 1720 and its contemporary, Law's Mississippi scheme in France, are classic examples of the way in which popular enthusiasm carries the prices of stocks up to a dizzy height and then, by a sudden revulsion, lets them fall again. The lesson thus taught did not, however, prevent a similar era of wild speculation in England, a century later, when the cessation of the wars with Napoleon Bonaparte and the refunding of the British national debt let loose in 1825 a flood of capital seeking investment. This was followed, in 1837, by a crisis resulting from participation in the land speculations of this country; in 1844 by the railroad building mania, in which the celebrated promoter Hudson made himself so conspicuous; in 1857 and 1866 by excessive mercantile trading on credit; in 1878 by the failure of the City of Glasgow Bank; and even so late as 1890, by the Argentine operations of the Barings. In France, except so far as the country was affected by its relations with England, the only recent great catastrophes of the kind have been those of the Panama Canal and the Secretan Copper Syndicate, the effects of neither of which were very widespread and disastrous. In England there have recently been several flurries in gold mining and in industrial investments, but they, too, have been confined to a comparatively limited circle, and the "Krach" in Vienna and in Berlin in 1873, with the numerous subsequent convulsions of a similar kind have been purely local.

Not until about sixty years ago did speculation in stocks reach large proportions in this country. The financial crises from which we suffered, previous to that time, were mainly commercial, that of 1837 being the result of wild speculations in real estate. The popular hostility to corporations, which found expression in the political war against the United States Bank, made Legislatures until about 1838 chary of granting charters, especially for banks, and the Manhattan Bank and the Chemical Bank are, to this day, monuments of the ingenuity by which their founders, under pretence of establishing waterworks and the manufacture of chemicals, secured banking privileges. In New England, charters for cotton factories were more freeley obtained, but they were hampered with personal liability provisions, which, when they began to be enforced, made the privileges to which they were attached less desirable. A little later general laws, permitting the free incorporation not only of banks, but of railroad companies, manufacturing companies, and, finally, every sort of enterprise, began to be enacted. Within recent years, also, the State of New Jersey, especially, has made the incorporation of companies for every imaginable purpose as easy as it possibly could be, and the result has been the creation of corporations with a total of capitals amounting to hundreds of millions of dollars.

These enlarged facilities for the multiplication of stock companies, aided by the stimulus given to enterprise by the gold discoveries of 1849 in California and Australia, so swelled the volume of stocks available for speculation as to lead to the revulsion of 1857. In the autumn of that year the failure of the Ohio Life and Trust Company precipitated a panic, during which stocks of the best kind fell in price one-third and one-half. New York Central sold at 50, which is equal to 25 at present, its capital having since been doubled. Harlem at 7, the old Michigan Southern, now Lake Shore, at about 15, Michigan Central at 35, Pennsylvania Coal at 46, Cleveland and Pittsburg at 8, New York State 6s at 91, Ohio State 6s at 80, and other stocks at proportionately low figures. The suspension of specie payments by the banks on October 13 and 14 put an end to this slaughter, a recovery in prices set in, the banks resumed payment December 12, and in three months everything was as cheerful as ever. In February, 1858, New York Central rose to 87, Harlem to 13½, Michigan Southern to 25, Michigan Central to 72, Pennsylvania Coal to 77, Cleveland and Pittsburg to 17, New York State 6s to 115, and Ohio State 6s to 101.

The election of Lincoln on November 6, 1860, followed by the secession of South Carolina and the prospect of a civil war, again produced a panic on the Stock Exchange. On November 21 New York Central, which had recently been as high as 84, fell to 71; Harlem, which had beeen 18, to 13. Michigan Southern suffered a decline from 18 to 13, Michigan Central one from 64 to 45; Tennessee 6s one from 87 to 75; Missouri 6s one from 77 to 70, and Virginia 6s one from 92 to 80. As civil war became more imminent there was a further reduction of even these low figures, which the firing on Fort Sumter in April, 1861, accelerated, and not until December, 1861, when the banks suspended specie payments, was there any marked recovery. The issue of legal tender notes in February, 1862, started an upward movement, which, with wild fluctuations, lasted until 1873, when another panic occurred, the details of which, as well as those of the panics of 1884, 1893 and 1895, are too recent to need to be recapitulated.

Every one who has glanced at the daily papers of the last few months, has been aware of the immense figures following the names of corporations forming and about to form. We are not alarmists and do not propose to string out figures here in a sensational manner, but only to show the limits to which the trust mania is carrying the nation at the present moment, we quote from one of our contemporaries. A list is given of the trusts formed and forming, occupying a solid page and producing the astonishing aggregate of capital of $6,000,613,000,000. One hundred and fifty-three so-called trusts are enumerated, and since the date of the list a considerable number of very large organizations have been formed. Our contemporary compares these figures with the cash in the treasury on January 1 last, and with the money in actual circulation on February 1 last. The circulation and cash on hand are added, with the result that the trusts are shown to be capitalized at a sum greater than two and one-third times all the money the country possesses.

We have no sympathy with the conclusions which our contemporary draws, but we do believe that trusts are being overworked and overdeveloped just at the present time, and that, accordingly, the panic which business prophets are foretelling is altogether reasonable to expect, unless, indeed, some sudden change in plans and methods should intervene After the storm is over, many large enterprises will be found that have entirely escaped, while many others, inadequately organized with an over-issue of stock in proportion to assets, with too little capital for the requirements of the case, or, broadly, based upon false assumptions of earning capacity and poorly managed, will be found to have been swept away.

Protecting Checks

Many are the devices which clever inventors have produced for foiling the operations of check raisers. The plan commonest in use among the business men of this country at the present time is perforated figures in the check, the figures cut out corresponding to the amount written in the body of the check. This plan is presented in various modifications, but all depending essentially upon cutting the paper into figures. In a few instances it has failed to prevent fraud, for the cuttings have been successfully changed through the medium of filling. Another plan in somewhat general use employs a chemically prepared paper, which, it is claimed, is of such a character that any attempt to erase the writing for purposes of alterations results in such a change in the appearance of the paper as to cause instant detection of the fraud. Experts, however, have succeeded in changing the writing on prepared paper, notwithstanding these precautions, until the opinion prevails today in various directions that none of the so-called chemical papers can be implicitly relied upon.

According to the London Post, Mr. Frank Nowlan has proved to the satisfaction of himself and many to whom he has exhibited his work that none of the existing methods of protecting checks is of any use whatever, if the forger only knows his business. Growing out of his experiments in this direction, he has produced what he considers the absolutely safe check, which is described as follows:

When held to the light it will be seen that in the parts intended to be written on there are colored lines, very much like the lines on which musicians write their manuscripts. The Nowlan check consists of two pieces of paper. On one of these the lines are ruled with an ink of India red, or any other prominent color, mixed with an easily soluble mucilage. The second piece is laid on over these lines. In other words, the check consists of two pieces of paper superimposed, united by mucilage, with lines on the inner surface of one of the two pieces. As soon as any liquid reagent is applied, in order to remove the writing on the surface, the mucilage between the two sheets becomes moist. The color then no longer keeps to the lines but wanders and forms blots and blurs, which are visible on both sides of the check and can in nowise be removed. Mr. Nowlan's invention was a short time since submitted to the London Bankers' Association, all the members of which, we are informed, being greatly pleased with the simplicity and certainty of the method exhibited for preventing check alterations.

"Jest Do Yer Best"

By James Whitcomb Riley.

The signs are bad when folks commence
A-findin' fault with Providence,
And balkin' 'cause the earth don't shake
At every prancin' step they take.
No man is great till he can see
How less than little he would be
Ef stripped to self, and stark and bare
He hung his sign out anywhere.
My doctrine is to lay aside
Contentions, and be satisfied;
Jest do yer best, and praise er blame
That follers that counts jest the same.
I've allus noticed great success
Is mixed with troubles, more or less,
And it's the man who does the best,
That gits more kicks than all the rest

Some Office Novelties

An Improved Trial Balance Book

The Globe Company, with factory at Cincinnati, and sales rooms in Chicago, New York and Boston, are putting upon the market at the present time a new Trial Balance Book, which possesses unique features. It is one of the series of account books which the company is introducing under the general trade name of "3-A." The book is composed of sections, each section having two wide pages with a complement of narrow pages between. Each narrow page carries two pairs of monthly columns. The space of the first wide page, that is covered by the narrow pages when turned, also carries two monthly columns. The same remark is true of the second wide page. The remaining space of the second wide page is devoted to two pairs of columns each entitled "After Closing." The book is only cap size (9x14 inches), and yet presents twenty-four pairs of columns for the months, that is, it is good for two years with a single writing of names, and also furnishes a pair of "After Closing" columns for each year. Each page is fifty lines deep. The compactness of the book is perhaps unparalleled in the annals of book construction.

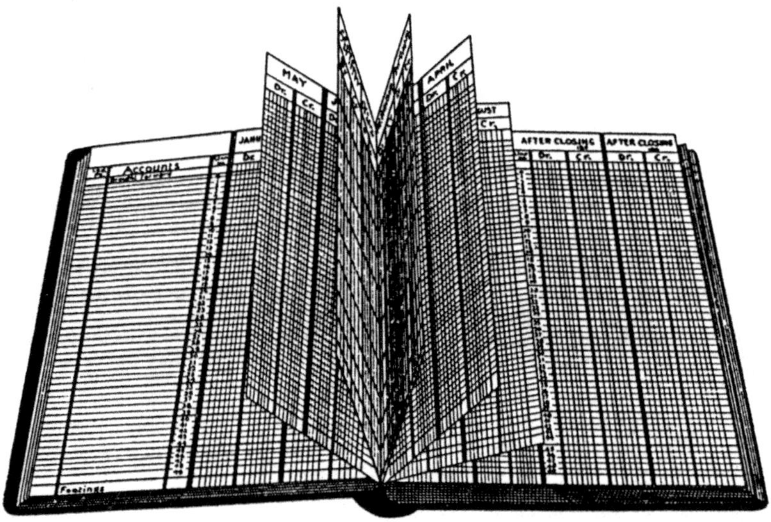

"3-A" TRIAL BALANCE BOOK

The several pages are provided with "Carrying Forward" columns, and yet it is recommended that the monthly footing be summarized on what are called recapitulation sheets, a supply of which is added to the book in the form of a folding plate at the back. Twenty-four footing spaces are provided, the lines in each of which are numbered to correspond with the signatures or sections from which the amounts are transferred.

The significant legend at the top of the title page of the book is "Every Debit Has Its Credit." The explanatory text which is bound in with the book is an essay on accounting that will be read with interest by many bookkeepers and business men as well. In addition to the stated directions for use there are short articles bearing such titles as: "Function of the Trial Balance," "The Profit and Loss Statement," "The Balance Sheet," "Classification of Accounts," and others.

Three-Ply Card Case

E. L. Prickett & Co., Mount Holly, N. J., are putting upon the market a line of up-to-date leather novelties which cannot fail to be of interest to business men everywhere. What is known as the Three-Ply Card Case is illustrated in the accompanying engraving. This device

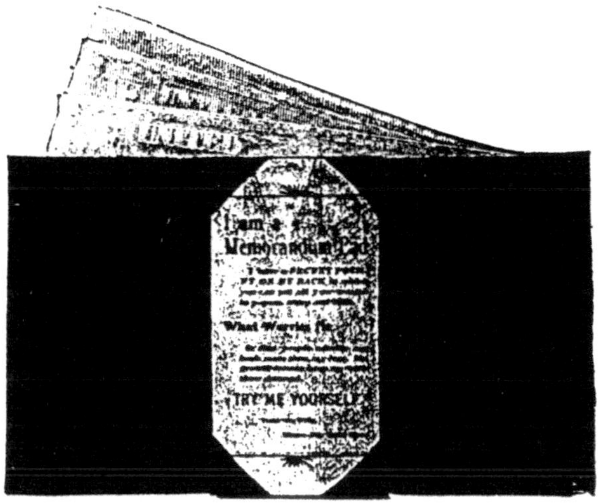

THREE-PLY CARD CASE

has the usual spaces for holding business cards, personal cards, etc., and, in addition, is so constructed as to furnish a space at the back for bills or currency. The latter are so ingeniously put away when the card case is in use as to be entirely out of sight, and at the same time the card case is not rendered the less desirable for use because the bills are in it.

Collection System

We are indebted to C. A. Sweetland, 110 No Eighth Street, St. Louis, Mo., president of the St. Louis Society of Accountants, for circulars and other particulars relating to Carl's Quick Collection System, which he is now putting upon the market. What is offered is not a collection agency, but an improved system of account arrangements for use in the business in which the purchaser is engaged. It facilitates the collection of bills, drafts and notes, etc., and is so organized that no items can be overlooked or allowed to run overtime, without the knowledge of the bookkeeper in charge.

In offering the system, Mr. Sweetland does not assert that it will collect bad accounts. He directs attention, however, to the large class of delinquents who occupy middle ground between the positively good account on the one hand and the irredeemably bad account on the other. He also directs attention to the loss of many accounts because the debtor's attention is not drawn to them. The fundamental plan is persistent work along lines that are calculated to avoid offense to the debtor. Rubber stamps are freely used, and they are so carefully devised as to the wording as to give no offense. In view of the fact that the system does not consist of mechanical contrivances, it is impossible to present a detailed description of it in this connection. Mr. Sweetland's circulars are accompanied by numerous testimonials of purchasers, all of whom seem to be well pleased with it.

The Scattergood Mucilage Pot

The illustrations presented herewith clearly indicate the features of an improved mucilage pot which is being put upon the market by the Scattergood Company, 491A Philadelphia Bourse, Philadelphia, Pa.

The pot consists of three glass parts—the mucilage receptacle, the inner well and the cover. The cover is larger in diameter than the mouth of the receptacle and so lifts off readily without sticking to the mouth. The contact is at the bottom only. The cover is formed with a ground joint where it rests on the re-

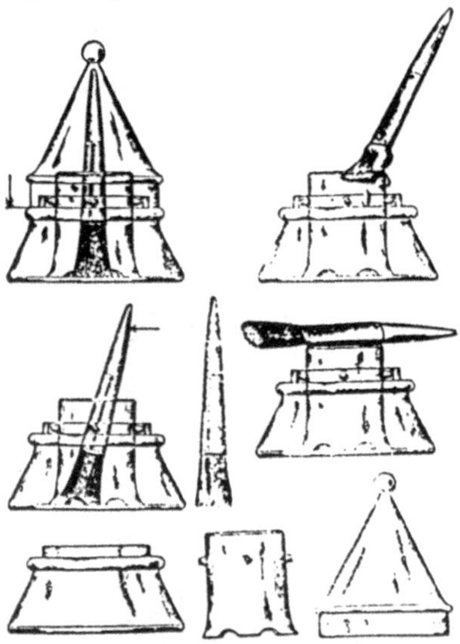

SCATTERGOOD MUCILAGE POT

ceptacle. The brush, which is clearly shown in the engraving, is of special quality, compared with mucilage brushes in general, and is of such dimensions and features of construction as to be kept within the mucilage and under the cover, thus preventing the drying up which so frequently injures a brush. The function of the inner well is to provide an edge against which to wipe the brush, for the purpose of dispensing with surplus mucilage and also to afford a resting place for the brush between times of use. The base of the pot is so wide that it is not easily upset. The construction of the brush handle is such that it is never fouled, and the presence of the cover is an assurance against evaporation. The makers call attention to the fact that this device is free from the objections of the roller, the sponge, and the automatic brush wiper, all of which are sure to clog.

Office Scale

The accompanying illustration shows the general appearance of what is described as the Commercial Office Scale, manufactured and sold by the Pelouze Scale & Manufacturing Co., S133 Clinton Street, Chicago, Ill. The scale shown is one of a considerable series put out by this company, all operating upon essentially the same principle. The present article is intended particularly for mail and express packages and has been designed to meet the recognized requirements of business offices. It is described as absolutely automatic and accurate. To lay a package, whether it be a letter or a bundle of printed matter, in the pan of this scale and notice by the pointer the exact postage required, is a vast improvement over the tedious manoeuvering of a poise on a beam, which was characteristic of the plan commonly current in the past. This scale gives instantly in cents the exact amount of postage re-

PELOUZE OFFICE SCALE

quired for letters, packages, circulars and newspapers in the United States and Canada. Its capacity is twelve pounds, which is quite enough for ordinary office requirements. The scale is handsomely finished with heavy nickel mountings. The dial is white enamelled, with figures distinctly printed thereon. Double upright steel supports distribute the weight and insure accuracy.

Many have made witty invectives against usury. They say that it is a pity the devil should have God's part, which is the tithe; that the usurer is the greatest Sabbath-breaker, because his plough goeth every Sunday.—Bacon.

Questions and Answers

Concerning the

BALANCE-SHEET SYSTEM OF ACCOUNTS

Conducted by the

Account Audit and Assurance Co., Ltd.

25 Pine Street, New York

Treatise on the Balance Sheet System of Accounts

From H. E. W., Emporia, Kan.

Please send me a treatise on the Balance Sheet System of Accounts. In the April issue of ACCOUNTICS I find this statement in the article entitled "Abuses of the Merchandise Account:" "It should record goods brought into," etc., "and likewise goods sent out," etc. "The balance should show the amount of goods on hand," etc. Now of what does the credit to merchandise consist? If it is sales and these sales represent cost and profit on goods solely, then how will the balance show goods on hand? * * * Please state the cost of the Balance Sheet System. I desire to examine into it with a view to adopting it in our store.

ANSWER. — If you had more carefully read the advertisement in ACCOUNTICS, you would have seen that the suggested treatise on the Balance Sheet System of Accounts is a carefully prepared specification of the system for the special purpose for which it may be ordered. In other words, we describe our specifications as practical treatises on accounting. We have nothing more by way of free literature than such pamphlets and circulars as are enclosed herewith. From these we believe you will be able to gain a very clear notion of what we have. We unhesitatingly guarantee all the results which our advertising matter sets forth.

In the dry goods business, departmentized as we presume your business must be, there will be constantly before the management when the Balance Sheet System is in operation, first the cost value of the stock on hand in such department, second the gross profits made in each department to date, and by gross profits we mean the difference between selling price and cost price; third, the expenses of each department, as distinguished from all other departments, and including its fair pro rata of general expenses, and fourth, net profits of each department to date; and further by way of total, net profits of the entire business, being the sum of the profits in each of the several departments. Additional to this showing and incidental thereto, will be all the usual details, such as amount of sales, amount of collections, amount due from customers (in one lump sum), amount of purchases, amount of payments to purchase creditors, and amount owing to purchase creditors (in one lump sum), cash receipts, cash disbursements, and amount of cash on hand. All these items appear in the Balance Sheet Ledger, which is a construction making these showings as the result of ordinary posting. There is no drawing off of statements, no special calculations, no extra work of any kind, but the system is gauged to produce these results as a regular thing, exactly as ordinary bookkeeping produces a balance in the Cash Account day by day, thereby indicating the amount of cash on hand.

We scarcely know how best to answer the special difficulties which you encounter in reading what has appeared in ACCOUNTICS with regard to our system. You are troubled with respect to our statements because you apparently have no other conception of the Merchandise Account than as that account is explained in the text-books on bookkeeping and taught in the commercial schools. If we were to say in so many words that the usual conception of the Merchandise Account is wrong, opposed to accounting principles, erroneous in results, etc., we should only be declaring what is a fact. How to explain all this to you through the medium of correspondence is something else.

Our usual course is to name a lump price for a specification and Balance Sheet Ledger, as described in our circulars. We are unable to make a figure, however, until we know something of the magnitude of the business, its division into departments, number of clerks, present system of conducting the books, etc.

Consider us not sellers of a proprietary system, but instead, accounting engineers who design systems for special purposes. You will then understand what we do. We have never yet installed two systems exactly alike, although we have sent out specifications for a very large number of installations in the same general line of business. Minor particulars always come up for consideration.

Cost of the Balance Sheet System of Accounts

From M. A. H., Buffalo.

This is in answer to your advertisement in ACCOUNTICS. Please advise me as to the cost of a Specification of the Balance Sheet System of Accounts:

ANSWER.—Every specification that we prepare is special to the business for which it is ordered. Our relationship to an accounting system, and to office work in general, is the same as that of an architect to a building that is about to be erected. Our work is done in the light of actual conditions and the requirements of our clients. Prices, therefore, of necessity, have to be adjusted according to the character of the work, its extent, etc.

Our circulars will give you a conception of what we supply and also of our general business methods. We put everything in writing, and our specifications are of a kind to be comprehended by every business man, and to be put into effect by any good double entry bookkeeper. In order to estimate upon your work, we ought to know some general facts, and we beg you to reply, so far as to you may seem appropriate to the following general questions:

Is your business entirely cash, or part cash and part credit?

If you are selling on credit, about how many accounts are there to take care of?

Is your business departmentized, and if so, into how many departmems is it organized?

Are your salesmen restricted to departments, or may the same salesmen sell through various departments?

Have you a good sales or counter system in operation?

Are you keeping track at present of the sales of each department, independent of all others?

Is there an indication on your goods of the cost price, as well as the selling price, or is there a lot number designation on each label, by which the cost of a given article can be ascertained in the office?

How many sales people altogether do you employ?

Do you do any manufacturing whatsoever, and by "manufacturing" in this question we would include dressmaking, if you conduct a dressmaking department; the trimming of hats, etc., if you conduct a millinery department; alterations and fitting of garments, in case something of that kind is done.

We find dry goods stores and department stores, while similar in general features, frequently with specialties attached which have to be provided for in the accounting system; hence some of the questions above presented. We trust to hear from you further.

Post-Dating and Long Credit

BY H. C. HARVEY

The retail dealer is very frequently injured by post-dating and long credit. A salesman representing a long-time jobbing house succeeds by the inducements of post-dating and four months' time to sell the retailer about twice as much as he ought to buy. Too frequently the retailer does not recognize this fact until he has received the invoice and opened up the goods. Then he becomes alarmed. He is seized with the fear that he will not be able to dispose of enough of the goods to be able to pay the bill by the time it falls due. In his anxiety of mind he takes risks. He sells to his customers on time, even making credit sales that he would not have thought of making had he bought his goods as he needed them from a short-time jobbing house, or for cash. The usual result is that when the post-dated bill falls due, the merchant has neither the money to pay it, nor yet the goods on hand. Accordingly, he is either compelled to ask for an extension or to borrow the money with which to pay the bill.

From experience I have found that the long-time, post-dating wholesale houses are an actual injury to the trade, and the real enemy of the average retail merchant, while on the other hand the cash houses are his true friends. The retailer that buys for cash and sells for cash never fails. He usually accumulates a handsome fortune. He is a benefactor to mankind, for he can and he does sell to the customer cheaper than would be possible under other conditions of buying. The honest consumer who wants to pay for what he gets is greatly benefited by the cash system. I hope to live to see the time when there will be no four and six months' jobbing houses, but that instead all retail dealers thoughout the length and breadth of this fair land will be buying for cash and selling for cash.

Accountics

The Office Magazine.

A. O. KITTREDGE, F. I. A., C. P. A., Editor.
E. R. KITTREDGE, Associate.

Accountics is devoted to the Science of Accounting, to the Art of Bookkeeping and to the advocacy of Improved Office Methods.

Subscription.—One dollar a year, payable in advance.

Postage is prepaid by the publishers in the United States, Canada and Mexico. For all other countries in the Postal Union, subscribers must add 50 cents a year.

Discontinuances.—In the absence of specific orders to discontinue at the end of the subscription term the magazine will be continued and a bill sent.

Remittances should be by Draft, P. O. Order or Express Order, payable to the order of the ACCOUNTICS ASSOCIATION. Money and postage stamps are at the risk of the sender, unless sent by express or in registered letters. Add 10 cents each to checks on local banks to defray collection charges.

Advertising Rates will be quoted on application.

Official Journal.—This publication, by resolutions duly passed, has been made the official publication of the following organizations:—
THE INSTITUTE OF ACCOUNTS.
THE NEW YORK CHAPTER of the Institute of Accounts.
THE WASHINGTON CHAPTER of the Institute of Accounts.
THE HARTFORD CHAPTER of the Institute of Accounts.

ACCOUNTICS is the accredited medium of intercommunication between members of the Institute of Accounts wherever located.

ACCOUNTICS ASSOCIATION,
Publishers,
Lancashire Bldg., Pine St., near Nassau,
New York.

Entered at the Post Office New York as Second Class Matter.

Publishers' Desk

In rsponse to the request of numerous readers, we have provided ACCOUNTICS with a very neat and serviceable form of binder, into which may be placed the serial numbers of the magazine as they are issued, without cutting, punching, or other mutilation. The binder is one of the neatest and best constructions of its class that we have been able to find, and is a desirable addition to the articles on any office desk or library table. There is less of the appearance of a binder about it and more resemblance to a finished book than anything we have ever been able to secure when investigating the binder market. Each binder is arranged to hold twelve numbers. Since the numbers can be put in and taken out individually, without disturbing the others, and readjustments in arrangement made at any time, the binders can be put into instant use. It is not necessary to wait for the beginning of a new volume. Further, if desired, a binder can be used over and over again. We offer these binders at 75 cents each, postage paid, and shall be glad to have the orders of those of our readers who desire a permanent filing case for their copies.

Mr. Clarence F. Chatfield, who was for a short time connected with ACCOUNTICS, announces that he is again giving his entire attention to general advertising. On his business card Mr. Chatfield describes himself as "Advertiser, with Gillam & Shaughnessy, Temple Court, New York." Those requiring the special service in advertising matters which Mr. Chatfield is able to render, will no doubt serve their own interests by corresponding with him.

Stamping tinware is comparatively an old industry, but extremely deep stamping is something quite new. The Seamless Metal Ware Company, with general office at 34 Nassau Street, New York City, and factory at Sing Sing, New York, operating under special patents and processes which it owns and controls, is producing single piece tinware in depths heretofore unattained by any one. For example, the body of a quart fruit can is made of a single piece of metal. The establishment has a model equipment of machinery, specially designed for it by the Ferracute Machine Company, of Bridgeton, N. J., under the immediate supervision of Oberlin Smith, President and Engineer of the company. It is also equipped with a model set of factory books—being the Proof-by-Balance System of Cost Accounts, while the general summary of the business is upon the basis of the Balance Sheet System of Accounts, all supplied by the Account, Audit and Assurance Company, Limited, of New York. Various new and ingenious expedients have been resorted to for producing and tabulating results, with the smallest amount of clerical labor. It is quite safe to say that there is no other manufacturing establishment in its line, the general manager of which is afforded so correct and complete a showing of operations week by week as this one.

J. L. Pvorman, a well-known public accountant of San Francisco, has recently visited Honolulu, H. I., on professional business.

A consolidation of important street railway interests occurred on the 1st of April, in New Orleans. The New Orleans and Carrollton Railroad Company absorbing the Canal and Claiborne Railroad Company. The policy of the management of the consolidated systems will be a continuation of that of late maintained by the New Orleans and Carrollton Railroad Company—namely, to have the best of everything. There is in progress at the present time extensive rebuilding of tracks, wherein unusually heavy rails are being employed; a considerable number of new cars of large size and excellent appointments are being put into service, and important extensions of lines are in progress. At a meeting of the Board of Directors of this Company, held early in April, Mr. A. O. Kittredge, of the Account, Audit and Assurance Company, Limited, of New York, was appointed consulting accountant of the company, with term of service dating from April 1st. Mr. Kittredge's first work will be the arrangement of the books of the company upon the most approved lines, and upon the Going Profit and Loss and Perpetual Balance Sheet Method.

No trouble or expense will be spared to give this company a model accounting system, for nothing short of that would be in keeping with its equipment in other directions. Mr. J. K. Newman, President of the company, spent some time in New York in March, and the report of his investigations, made to the Board of Directors on his return to New Orleans, resulted in the action above mentioned.

John R. Sparrow, C. P. A., announces that after May 1, 1899, his office will be located in the Astor Building, No. 10 Wall Street, New York City. Mr. Sparrow's telephone number is 3965 Cortlandt.

George Gonthier, Public Accountant, Montreal, Canada, makes a specialty of improved accounting systems, and working in conjunction with the Account, Audit and Assurance Company, Limited, of New York, has recently completed some very important and altogether satisfactory installations of the Balance Sheet System of Accounts. Mr. Gonthier visited New York early in May, and spent considerable time in investigating accounting methods in the metropolis and inquiring into other matters pertaining to his profession.

Wm. H. Hoskins, Stationer, 904 - 906 Chestnut Street, Philadelphia, conducts his business upon department store methods. His establishment occupies all the four floors of the large building in which it is located, extending through from street to street, and is a veritable bee-hive of industry. In the sales rooms goods are displayed on what are to be regarded as new and original plans so far as concerns the stationery trade, all prices are marked in plain figures, several new and unusual lines of goods are carried, and in various respects the methods of the store are revolutionary compared with what the public is accustomed to meet in the stores supplying office requisites. The first or street floor is the sales room for stationers' sundries; the second floor is devoted to office furniture, of which a very large variety is carried in stock; the third floor is devoted to storage of surplus stock, and the fourth floor to the manufacturing departments including commercial printing, plate printing, engraving, ruling and bookbinding. Commodious elevators connect the several floors. In the basement are located boilers, engine and dynamos, the light and heat for the entire building is produced on the premises, and the distribution of power to elevators and machines in the manufacturing departments is by electric motors. Mr. Hoskin's avowed ambition is to have the best of everything, and proceeding along these lines he is at present installing the Balance Sheet System of Accounts, supplied by the Account, Audit and Assurance Company, Limited, New York. The plan upon which the system is laid out will show him the net results of each of the several sales and manufacturing departments weekly, independent of all the other departments.

W. M. Williams, of Chicago, a member of the Illinois Institute of Accountants, has recently removed to New York, and is established as assistant credit man of the American Steel and Wire Company, with office in the Empire Building.

The McGraw Publishing Company, which, by agreement with the several companies owing the Street Railway Journal, the American Electrician, and the Electrical World and Electrical Engineer, has become the publisher of these several periodicals, has recently occupied new and commodious offices at No. 120 Liberty Street, New York. A new accounting system has been installed, under the auspices of the Account, Audit and Assurance Company, Limited, arranged upon the Going Balance Sheet and Profit and Loss Statement plan. It is safe to say, as the result of this installation that there is not another publishing concern in the country to-day that enjoys as thorough and complete an analysis of its monthly operations as does the McGraw Publishing Company. Each periodical is shown in all details, independent of all the others, and there is likewise a careful discrimination between expenses of administration and the expenses of publishing the several journals. The entire results are presented in the most compact form in the Balance Sheet Ledger, which in this case has been so arranged as to present first the profit and loss statement of each periodical, and subsequently the general exhibit of assets and liabilities.

We are indebted to P. S. Eustis, general passenger agent C. B. & Q. R. R., Chicago, Ill., for a copy of the new map which the Burlington Route has recently issued. While giving prominence to the Burlington Line, it is also a truthful map of railroads in general, and geographically goes down to such fine distinctions as counties and county seats. The map is a useful adjunct to any office, and is accordingly in wide demand. To the same source we are indebted for two handsome books, entitled "Colorado Outings" and "California," respectively. Both of these books are exceedingly interesting and beautifully illustrated. The idea of the Passenger Department of the Burlington Route in issuing these books, is to interest the readers in the countries they describe, trusting that in the future, some of those who examine them will be influenced to pass over the Burlington Route to view the district indicated.

Our enterprising contemporary, Profitable Advertising, Boston, has recently taken over by purchase the periodical long active in the same field, known as Art in Advertising, published in New York. We are informed that commencing with the May issue the two magazines will be consolidated under the suggestive title of "Profitable Advertising and Art in Advertising." Miss Kate E. Griswold, editor and publisher of Profitable Advertising, and whose effort in her chosen field has brought the magazine to its present enviable position at the head of the list, is to be congratulated upon her continued success. With the enlargement of title and enlargement of field which the combined magazines suggest, her work, which is at present greatly appreciated by advertisers everywhere, should be still more acceptable to the business public.

A leading stationery concern in Montreal is that of Granger Freres, doing a large business, both in the city proper and in the towns naturally tributary to Montreal. This establishment has been recently equipped with the Balance Sheet System of Accounts, supplied by the Account, Audit and Assurance Company, Limited, of New York, and installed under the personal supervision of George Gonthier, Public Accountant, Montreal.

The two establishments of the Edward Frohlich Paint and Glass Company, the main concern in Detroit and the branch house in Toledo, have recently been equipped with the Balance Sheet System of Accounts, supplied by the Account, Audit and Assurance Company, Limited, of New York. The adjustment of the system in the branch house has been made with special reference to the reports which the proprietor and manager at the general office desire to see. A duplicate of the Toledo Balance Sheet Ledger is maintained in the general office, and duplicate daily summaries, prepared at the Toledo office for posting to its own Balance Sheet Ledger, are forwarded to Detroit, thereby maintaining as complete a showing of the operations of the Toledo store in the Detroit office as in the Toledo office. The business of this concern is thoroughly departmentized, resulting in six distinct divisions, three of which are manufacturing, and three of which are purely merchandizing in character. The showing of each is made independent of all the others, and in every respect the profit and loss showing from week to week gives the manager just what it is necessary to know concerning expenses and earnings for the purpose of directing the business in a way to keep expenses down to the minimum, and in all other respects conserve profits.

C. A. Honecker, formerly cashier of the Illinois Steel Company, Chicago, is at present auditor of The American Steel and Wire Company, with offices in "The Rookery," Chicago. Mr. Honecker brings to bear upon his new position qualities of a very high grade, together with a long and successful experience as an accountant and office manager.

Accountics

VOL. IV JUNE 1899 No. 6

The Monthly Statement

The annual convention of the Institute of Accounts, which occurred the first of June, is reported in another page of this issue. No member of the Institute can read the account of what occurred on this occasion without feeling that the organization is now placed in a position to be specially useful to the business community and to go forward energetically with the work which there is for it to do. It enters upon a new year under most favorable auspices. The unanimous vote for James G. Cannon for President was indicative of the deep-seated determination upon the part of the delegates composing the convention to secure for leadership a man of broad experience, and one whose connection with other national movements has demonstrated his conspicuous ability for useful work along the lines of business reform and modernized business methods. Charles Dutton, who was elected secretary and treasurer, needs no special introduction to our readers, for, as President of the New York Chapter for two years past, and as a speaker before the New York and Hartford Chapters on various occasions, and, in addition, as a public accountant of national reputation, he is instantly recognized by every one. The resolutions which were passed by the convention declaring the policy of the Institute with respect to local chapters and the action that should be taken by the Executive Council in certain directions are exeremely significant. We dare predict that as soon as active work is commenced, which is to be undertaken by the general officers and the Executive Council as soon as the hot weather is passed, there will be a quickening of the pulse in all directions, and that for the future of the Institute will easily hold that position among national organizations to which by its usefulness it is justly entitled.

We noted in these columns a short time since the fact that the typewriter had been accorded a semi-official recognition in Germany, and at that time called attention to the steady onward progress of a mechanical device, the utility of which in business had long been apparent to every one. Our own government has been almost as backward as those of foreign countries with reference to the typewriter, officials seeming to believe that there was some hidden danger in its employment. From recent dispatches from Washington, however, it would appear that this prejudice has at last been broken down, and that for the future the typewriter in Washington is destined to be considered upon its merits.

It is only within the last year that typewriters have been used generally in all of the government buildings at the Capitol. The reluctance to adopt the machine in some of the departments appears to have been due to one or the other of three principal causes: First, the substitution of typewriter operators for penmen would necessitate the employment of many new clerks not acquainted with the routine of the departments; second, much of the writing had to be done in books of record in which the ordinary typewriter could not be employed; third, it was of the greatest importance that the records made by the respective departments should be permanent in character, and the opinion prevailed in many instances that typewriting was other than durable. These several objections have at last been overcome. The general utility of the typewriter in business overcame the first named above. The second objection was met by the appearance in the market of certain writing machines which could be employed as conveniently for copying in books as upon separate and detached sheets, and the third objection was set aside by investigations instituted especially for the government.

The strongest opposition to the typewriter's adoption was shown in the Department of State, where, only after numerous and scrutinizing tests and comparisons had been made by authorized agents, was the keyboard device permitted to supplant the pen. One of the tests referred to involved the question as to whether or not the impressions made with the machine were likely to resist the action of light, air and strong chemical solutions as satisfactorily as would writing done with fluid ink. To determine this it was ordered that expert chemical analyses be made of the ink used upon ribbons sent to the department and recommended as leaving an absolutely indelible copy. The Division of Chemistry of the Department of Agriculture was entrusted with the investigation. The result was that ink containing certain pigments in certain established proportions was found to be altogether satisfactory. Specimens of writing done with one of the ribbons, saturated with the ink referred to, were exposed over a week to a very powerful chemical, with the result that when removed, the writing was still distinct.

At the Columbian University the chemists sought to ascertain which was the more permanent the imprint made from the ribbons or the writing done with the ordinary fluid ink of the State Department. In each case samples of penmanship and typewriting were tested side by side. The typewriting, it was shown, offered much stronger resistance to the acid. When the penwriting was almost entirely effaced the typewriting showed scarcely any signs of impaired legibility. Exposure to the sunlight for eighty-four hours did not appear to affect the clearness of the ribbon's impression. A striking advantage claimed for the machine is that the stroke of the type forces the ink below the surface of the paper and places it beyond the reach of chemical agents, so that acids or alkalies, which will not destroy the paper itself, can have no appreciable effect upon the typewritten characters. These experiments, further, have proved that there is a marked difference between the permanency of writing done with copying ribbons, such as are used to a large extent in business offices and that done with non-copying or record ribbons, which, it is concluded, alone should be used whenever an unchangeable and absolutely ineffaceable copy is desired.

The tendency of the present day is to capitalize and incorporate enterprises of almost every conceivable kind and character. The corporate form of management, or perhaps it were better to say partnership, is that which has almost general approval at the present time. Accordingly, we have little corporations and big corporations, close corporations and general corporations, and in many cases corporations which are essentially family affairs. In the sense of study and comparison, the suggestion of incorporating private estates in this country has been made, although we do not recall an instance of an actual trial of the plan. Given, for example, a family, consisting of father and mother, with sons and daughters, living together in what may be described as the homestead, and being in what is commonly termed good circumstances, how would the idea apply? The children are the natural heirs of the estate and also its prospective managers. Naturally, there occurs to the father and head of the family the question of the ultimate division of the estate. A will, of course, comes up for consideration. But divisions of estates, to be made after the death of the head of the family, are not always satisfactory, and it frequently happens that the wishes of the deceased are not carried out. Then comes the question why not incorporate the estate, and through the medium of the capital shares divide it at once? Why not put upon the management of private property the restrictions usual in the case of manufacturing and mercantile corporations?

Suppose the idea is carried into effect. The father and mother would be majority stockholders, thereby controlling the policy of the estate or the corporation, as long as they live. The father would be president, the oldest son would be vice-president, and another child would be secretary. Regular meetings of the board of directors, which we may assume would include the whole family, would be held and would decide general questions of policy and management. This means the young people of the family would be brought into immediate contact with the responsibilities of the estate and have a share in its management long before it would be thrown upon their unaccustomed shoulders. Assume that the estate has certain investments outside of the homestead, and that there is a profitable income therefrom. Upon this plan the capital shares would be able to pay a dividend. The president we may suppose should have a salary, and in place of pocket money and allowances, upon the usual plan, each of the heirs would be put upon a footing of participating in the income of the estate. Vice-president, treasurer and secretary would have salaries and the stockholders in general would get dividends. This would be taking up in a practical way some of the features of actual business, and inculcating an object lesson, while also organizing a school of practical business.

Schemes of this kind, however, as remarked at the outset, have, as a rule, gone nc further than the stage of theoretical discussion, and yet something very like what is here pictured has been recently accomplished in England. The Earl and Countess of Warwick, as we learn from a correspondent, whose letter was recently published in one of the leading dailies, have converted their life interests in their Warwickshire, Essex, Leicestershire and Northamptonshire estates, the lease of the Clutton collieries and the insurance policies on their lives, into a limited liability concern, and the public, in answer to advertisements in the press, have rushed to subscribe for £210,000 four per cent. debentures. The correspondent gives certain particulars concerning the basis of the organization. Of the debentures £126,000 are repayable upon the death of the Earl at the latest, and £84,000 at the death of the Countess. These provisions indicate the uses to which the life insurance policies are to be devoted. Why not try in a practical way the experiment in this country? The question is one to be answered by business men who are spending their lives in building up estates that they must leave behind them.

Pensions for Accountants and Bank' Employes

In a pamphlet recently received from an incorporated organization of accountants in South Africa, we note provisions in the charter and by-laws for paying pensions and sick benefits to members, and, in specified cases, assisting their widows and orphans.

We also hear that the First National Bank of Chicago is operating a fund and plan for pensioning its officers and employes under certain conditions. It is to be hoped that plans of this character may become popular and universal.

The First National Bank experiment is in every way business-like, and provides that all employes shall furnish a yearly certificate of health from a physician, to be approved by the bank. All employes are required to contribute to the pension fund. The old employes have all become subscribers, though decision was optional as to them. The pension fund is created by each officer and employe contributing to it 3 per cent. per year of his salary, that amount being deducted in equal monthly instalments. No pension is paid until the pensioner has completed fifteen years or more of service and reached the age of 60 years. At 60, any one may retire if he wishes, or the bank may require him to do so. At 65, officers and employes must retire unless the bank especially requests them to continue their services.

New Form for Transferring Stock Certificates

"Look on the back of stock certificates of recent date and compare the new form of transfer which you will find printed there, with old form," said a prominent banker the other day. "The old form, which contained a blank power of attorney intended to be filled in by the transfer clerks, has been succeeded by a form which omits the power of attorney and merely 'authorizes' the transfer of the stock on the company's books. This modification renders unnecessary the 25 cent stamp which has heretofore been affixed to stock transfers. I wonder how much this diminishes Uncle Sam's revenue from this source!"

Many fortunes, like rivers, have a pure source, but grow muddy as they grow large.—J. Petit-Senn.

Accountancy in Great Britain

The present legal status of accountants in Great Britain is far from satisfactory to many members of the profession residing therein. For lack of information as to the exact situation, it is customary in this country to assume that the position of accountants in Great Britain, with respect to the law, is entirely satisfactory. Not a few articles have been published in the United States from this point of view, and in some of them American accountants have been urged to base all their efforts for legal recognition upon English precedents.

That things were not entirely satisfactory to British accountants in this regard, however, began to be evident about the time that the accountancy law in the State of New York was enacted. English periodicals devoted to accountancy, devoted considerable space to the letter of the law, directly after its passage with comments thereon, and plainly indicated by what they presented the thought that evidently was in the minds of the writers—namely, that the New York law in many respects was better for the profession than anything then existing in Great Britain. One article in particular that we recall suggested to British accountants that they would be doing well to base efforts for changes in the law under which they are working, upon the American precedent.

For some time past the broader-minded and more liberal men in several of the organizations in the United Kingdom have been working toward the adoption of a common standard of proficiency and the enactment of a law before which the members of all the different societies would stand upon a common footing. Several drafts of bills, with this object in view, have been prepared and have been more or less advanced toward their passage, without, however, any of them securing the necessary majority. Recent files of our exchanges contain what is described as the Accountants' Bill of 1899, which is still another attempt to accomplish the result so urgently desired by the best element in several of the leading organizations.

The object of the present bill, as declared by one authority, is registration and not amalgamation. The bill sets forth a registration scheme, by which it is proposed to recognize only qualified accountants, and to debar unqualified accountants from practicing. Clause 2 of the bill provides for the restriction of the use of the title of public or professional accountant to all save those who are registered in pursuance of the act. Every person is entitled to be registered as a public accountant under the proposed law who proves to the satisfaction of the provisional council within twelve months after the passing of the act, that at the date of the passing of the act he was a bona fide practicing accountant or was a member of the Institute of Chartered Accountants in England and Wales, or a member of the Society of Accountants and Auditors (Incorporated), or a member of the Society of Accountants in Edinburgh, or a member of the Institute of Accountants and Actuaries in Glasgow, or a member of the Society of Accountants in Aberdeen, or a member of the Scottish Institute of Accountants, or a member of the Institute of Chartered Accountants in Ireland. After the passing of the act, no person, save as excepted above, shall be entitled to be registered as a public accountant until he shall have passed the examination to be from time to time prescribed by the council, and shall have been admitted as a member of one or the other of the corporations, institutions or societies enumerated above.

The provisional council is to be made up as follows: Upon the passing of the act there shall be formed a provisional council, consisting of five members of the Institute of Chartered Accountants in England and Wales, four members of the Society of Accountants and Auditors, one member of the Society of Accountants in Edinburgh, one member of the Institute of Accountants and Actuaries in Glasgow, one member of the Society of Accountants in Aberdeen, one member of the Scottish Institute of Accountants, and two members of the Institute of Chartered Accountants in Ireland, all elected by the councils of the respective societies within two months after the passing of this act, along with not less than three accountants in public practice in the United Kingdom, who may be appointed by the President of the Board of Trade.

The permanent council is to be made up in the month of January, 1901, and is to be composed as follows: In the first instance, of the provisional council with nine members added, to be elected as follows: Two members of the Institute of Chartered Accountants in England and Wales, one member of the Society of Accountants and Auditors, one member of the Society of Accountants in Edinburgh, one member of the Institute of Accountants and Actuaries in Glasgow, one member of the Society of Accountants in Aberdeen, and one member of the Scottish Institute of Accountants, one member of the Institute of Chartered Accountants in Ireland, and one accountant in public practice in the United Kingdom, to be appointed by the President of the Board of Trade. At the end of the first year after the establishment of the permanent council, one-half of the members representing the provisional council shall retire, and their places shall be filled by nine persons elected in the same manner and from the same bodies as in the case of the election last above described. At the end of the second year, the second half of the members of the council shall retire, to be succeeded by another nine persons to be elected as mentioned. Thereafter, in each year, one-third of the members of the permanent council shall retire according to seniority, and their places shall be filled in the same manner as in the above mentioned elections.

From the above it will be seen that in effect this bill will bring the leading accountants' societies of Great Britain into practical co-operation and will give all of them the open door through which in the future accountants may qualify for public practice. We shall watch the progress of this measure, and the other efforts which are being made in Great Britain to advance the interests of the accounting profession, with lively interest.

Uniform Accounting

One of our exchanges, The Practical Age, specially devoted to the gas interests, recently published an article on accounting, wherein the benefits that would flow from uniformity in system and methods were ably set forth. From this article we make the following brief extract:

"The field of technical literature is noticeably lacking in the attention that is given to the subject of bookkeeping. This is not because of its insufficient importance, but rather by reason of the indefinite ideas which prevail among works officials as to what constitutes good practice in the classification of their accounts. As we have said repeatedly, there is a great deal of difficulty found when it is desired to compare the records of one company or works with those of another engaged in the same line of business, and this is not because the same items do not enter into the accounting classification, but is more often due to local conditions which have made it seem advisable to juggle the accounts, either for the purpose of deceiving or avoiding the mental effort and complexity in system required to provide for the proper placing of all items. In general, we may say that there is no such thing as uniformity in accounting, just as there is no such thing as uniformity in the results of operations. If the records of various organizations of the same character were readily available, and all made according to a uniform system, it would be possible for works managers to ascertain whether the results which they are obtaining are equal to or better than those obtained by others under the same conditions. It is a very inefficient manager indeed who will not endeavor to bring the standard of his work at least up to that obtained by fellow managers. * * *

The importance of a perfectly rational and uniform system cannot be overestimated. Any industrial enterprise, made possible by the means of capital received from investors, is under moral obligations at least to render its stockholders an honest and accurate report of its business. This cannot be done when the bookkeeper is at liberty to bolster up or detract from any particular account by being allowed to place some important item in favor of or against any one of several headings. "A place for everything and everything in its place" should hold here as elsewhere. While we are readjusting our business methods it would be well to look to our bookkeeping as well. If investors are asked to put their money into circulation they should at least be permitted the privilege of knowing what is being done with it. Fair dealing is the best way to establish confidence.

Worldly wealth is the devil's bait.
—Robert Burton.

The National Association of Credit Men

By A. O. Kittredge, F. I. A.

Every one who had the privilege of attending the convention of the National Association of Credit Men, held in Buffalo, June 6, 7 and 8, went away from that city with the conviction that the Credit Men's movement is steadily progressing and constantly increasing in strength. The general verdict was that there was never a more successful meeting among business men than this convention. The discussion, while animated, was always within bounds. The various committees in their reports presented for adoption resolutions embodying the legislation which they thought appropriate under the circumstances. To the outsider it may have looked like an attempt to gag the convention, or at least to lead it along prearranged lines. Nothing of the kind occurred, however. The convention approved of these resolutions that struck its fancy, and quietly laid on the table others which to the majority of the delegates seemed inappropriate or inexpedient at this time.

* * *

A little breeze occurred in the discussion of the country check matter. From the outset the National Association of Credit Men has been on record on this subject. The wrong of using local checks in remitting for city bills was discussed long before the National movement took formal shape, and at the Toledo convention several addresses which were made contained allusions to this matter. The question of the country check has been constantly before the National Association ever since the date of its organization, and several of the local associations have been conspicuous in their efforts to induce country merchants to remit by banker's draft, money order or in some other form than by checks on local banks. Notwithstanding these historical facts, one of the speakers on this occasion seemed disposed to charge the National Association with truckling to a movement fostered by the New York Clearing House. It is needless to say that he was not supported by the convention, and that his attempt to put the organization on the wrong side of this question was promptly defeated. The truth could be stated in this form: The National Association of Credit Men was the first to agitate the question of reform in local check matters, and up to a recent date had secured so much of business sentiment in favor of the reforms that it has advocated, that the New York Clearing House saw its way to enforce a charge for collecting these checks, thereby greatly helping the Credit Men in their effort at a reform.

* * *

The election of officers for the new year resulted in what was a surprise to many. Up to the date of the convention few were prepared to believe that Mr. Boocock, who has been secretary of the national organization from the outset, really intended to decline another term. When, however, his determination to engage in other lines became evident, many were at a loss to find a proper successor. The selection of W. H. Prendergast, however, as secretary was a happy solution of the difficulties which many delegates seemed to believe faced the organization at this juncture. Mr. Prendergast was one of the speakers before the convention and in that effort, as in others in the past, demonstrated his ability to handle business topics in a way to be a credit to himself and an honor to any cause that he may espouse. He brings to bear upon his new office talents of a high order and an experience that will be greatly to the advantage of the organization.

* *

James G. Cannon, the retiring President, who has held office for two years, was probably the unanimous candidate for re-election, but his declination of the honor was positive, as well as courteous. And then came the most important question of all: Who shall be the next President? A committee on nominations had been appointed, but every man in the whole convention felt that a share of the responsibility of selecting the right man rested upon himself, and therefore the committee had abundant help. There was no unseemly struggle for the position. There was no one, in fact, working for it. It was a very pretty illustration of the office seeking the man, and the gentleman, John Field, of Philadelphia, upon whom choice finally centred had to be urged a long time before he would consent to undertake the responsibilities which the convention was disposed to thrust upon him.

* * *

There was another peculiar circumstance in the case. The National Association of Credit Men is on record first as advocating, and more recently as supporting, the bankruptcy law. John Field is opposed to the bankruptcy law upon principle. The National Association of Credit Men, prior to the passage of the act, did much to influence business sentiment and legislation in support of the so-called Torrey bill. John Field, at the convention in Kansas City two years since, made a most eloquent address, opposing the Torrey bill and every other form of bankruptcy law. He only uttered his own honest convictions, but so earnest was his address that he had the convention with him to a man applauding his courage in facing an audience almost unanimously opposed to his sentiments. To be called to the office of the chief executive of the association with such a record was somewhat of a surprise to Mr. Field, and equally a surprise to many of those who nominated him, and yet Mr. Field seemed to be the right man for the place. Accordingly he was unanimously elected President. This does not mean that Mr. Field is likely to use his position in the National Association of Credit Men to forward his own views with reference to bankruptcy, but it does mean that a strong, honest, outspoken business man, who has the confidence of all who know him, will do his best to carry forward the work of the National Association along the lines in which it is working. Mr. Field's inaugural address, which was entirely extemporaneous, for he had no opportunity for preparing a stated speech, more than ever endeared him to the men whose votes had put him at the head of the organization. He has the satisfaction of knowing that, notwithstanding the differences that have existed between him and the rank and file of the association in the past, he will have the hearty and enthusiastic support of the members in his administration.

* * *

F. W. Standart, of Denver, was elected Vice-President. In his inaugural address (if inaugural address it could be called, being in fact only a few extemporary remarks in response to the calls of the delegates after his election had been announced), he very happily alluded to this incident in Mr. Field's career as a member of the association, saying that no other man in the organization could have commanded support under such circumstances. He also voiced the sentiment of all the delegates when he said that the unswerving honesty and outspoken courage of the president-elect carried the convention in his favor.

* * *

The National Association of Credit Men indicated its high appreciation of the services of the retiring officers in a characteristic and very appropriate way. Mr. Cannon was made the recipient of a loving cup, and the occasion of its delivery was made extremely enjoyable by the facetious remarks of Mr. Hanlon, of St. Louis, who, in his presentation speech, to the delight of his hearers, toyed with the ex-President's well known temperance habits. For a total abstainer to be referred to in terms similar to those which are usually applied to the hopeless drunkard, warning him of the evil of his ways and of the only end that is possible for such a career, was indeed unique. Nothing short of the exact words of the speaker, a view of his gestures and various other peculiarities of the address could convey an idea of the fun of the occasion. Suffice it to say, the audience was convulsed from the beginning of the address to the end thereof. Mr. Boocock was remembered with a very handsome and expensive scarf pin, something that he will ever treasure as an evidence of the appreciation of the men in whose interests he has worked so arduously for the three years just ended.

* * *

The discussion along the lines of an improved commercial agency service, together with the communications received from the different mercantile agencies, indicated that these organizations are beginning to have more respect for the work of their customers, the Credit Men, and the reasonable demands that they are making upon them, than they entertained a short time ago. Resolutions outlining the work to be done for the coming year indicate a campaign aggressively active and up to the limit of the funds that can be secured for the purpose. The exchequer of the National Association will have a little larger income in the future than in the past by reason of an increase of the per capita tax to be paid by the local organizations. The proposition for increasing it still further by advancing the annual dues of the members at large was defeated. The education of the country merchant along the lines of better accounting, better office system and better business habits in general, is to be continued, and special attention is to be given to improving the operations of the bankruptcy law by securing much needed amendments at the hands of the next Congress. The office of the National Secretary remains in New York, and the place for holding the next convention is left to the discretion of the Board of Directors.

The Question of an International Accountants' Association

Should be Deferred

From W. H. Vollum, Editor The Public Accountant, Philadelphia.

I notice that ACCOUNTICS is exploiting the idea of an International Society of Accountants. I have had some little correspondence with English Accountants on this subject, and the consensus of opinion seems to be that it would not be feasible at this time, for the reason that the profession in England is far more advanced than it is in America. The Englishman considers the belonging to professional societies and the contributing of papers on professional subjects as a part of his religion. Such, however, is not the case in America. If the idea of organization on an international basis can be postponed for a few years, until a number of the States have passed C. P. A. laws, I think the idea could then be taken up and pushed with success.

A Great Benefit to the Profession

From Charles A. Honecker, Chicago.

An international organization of Accountants would result in great benefit to the profession. We cannot dispute the fact that our first-class accountants, whose reputations have made them distinguished either in the public service or at the head of large interests, are as thorough in their knowledge of the profession as can be found. We grant that English accountants of the higher class are much older in experience and cover many more experts, besides furnishing the world with more first-class literature on this subject, than have those of other countries. We also know that the untiring efforts of the American profession to bring together the accountants of the highest standard, in an organization for the benefit of the entire profession, has met with failure in many instances. Yet, notwithstanding this, we have been brought in contact with that class of accountants whose thirst for knowledge and desire for association with the best brains of the profession demand that such organization be made permanent, and thus we have a few such institutions that are well-supported and accomplishing their purpose. The successful societies are composed mostly of first-class accountants, and they demonstrate that the great and broad interest in organization and the purposes to be accomplished thereby, exists at the top of the profession, while organizations composed in the majority of bookkeepers, with a light sprinkling of good accountants, have failed of their purpose. In a general sense we ascribe such failure to the fact that it is wisdom and knowledge and experience that a good accountant seeks, and the polishing of his own perceptions by association with those of equal and better knowledge than himself; and it unfortunately happens that these things are not obtained in association with bookkeepers whose ambition does not lead beyond their present status and who prefer to remain on the even plane of an excellent though non-advancing craft.

A proposition to effect an international organization of accountants would doubtless result in a hearty response from both sides of the water, and find all both willing and eager for the opportunity to associate with each other and the ensuing benefits.

The commercial aspect of the country is changing rapidly. Instead of many small concerns engaged separately and in competition for the business of each branch of trade, they are combining their capital into a comparatively few huge corporations. Varied interests and conditions are therefore brought together, which demand the highest standard of accounting in all departments. A number of years ago these corporations were few, but with the increasing number and the opening up of the wider field, we realize the sad fact that first-class accountants equal to the emergency are scarce, necessitating the plodding along with inferior help. The conditions impress upon us the importance of the special study of this broader field of "greater accounting." We need the education of broadening association, comparison of methods and interchange of ideas that an international society would bring to us, and we hope for the speedy consummation of such an organization.

It Needs a United Profession

From Alfred H. Thomas, A.S.A.A., Honorable Secretary of the South Wales and Monmouthshire Society of Incorporated Accountants and Auditors, Cardiff, Wales.

I think an international association among public accountants would be an excellent institution from many points of view, but having in mind the fact that the profession, even in this country, is anything but united, it seems to me to be impracticable, in its present condition, to bring about an international consolidation of the same.

Doubtful of Results

From R. H. Moore, Chicago.

I do not feel that I have much to say with regard to an International Association of Public Accountants and Auditors, since I am neither a public accountant nor yet an auditor. I may say, however, that I am heartily in favor of organization, and much deplore the fact that so little interest is taken in this matter in the United States, not only by public accountants and auditors, but by the accounting fraternity generally.

The fortunate circumstances of our lives are generally found at last to be of our own producing.—Goldsmith.

Avoid both courts and camps, where dilatory Fortune plays the jilt with the brave, noble, honest, gallant man, to throw herself away on fools.—Otway.

Liability Insurance

Rates for liability insurance, says our contemporary, Rough Notes, are high; they may be too high, but we don't believe it. Whether rates are too high or too low, the public must have liability insurance. There is no getting around that proposition. At the rate legislators, courts and jurors are going on, enacting statutes, construing the law and assessing damages, only by means of liability insurance can manufacturers and business men get along with any degree of safety. They dare not be their liability underwriters, for they never know when they may be compelled to face a damage suit even after their business affairs may have been closed for years. We are told that it is no uncommon occurrence for liability companies to settle under suits instituted five to ten years after the date of policies under which these claims are brought. There is no determinate period that a liability policy can be made to cover after which all liability ceases. Any time, from one year until the statute of limitation bars further action, may suits be brought and claims enforced by the insured. Conditions grow harder every year. The labor vote is a most important factor in carrying elections, and all political parties bid with all their might for this vote. Whatever this vote demands, sometimes in justice and sometimes against public policy, as a rule goes, and the tendency of legislatures and the courts is to limit the defenses of employers, and to strengthen the hands of employes in their demands for extortionate claims for damages. It is the universal experience that the ratio of claims to number of risks written is steadily increasing. Rates have increased, and still further advances must be made so long as public sentiment forces the issue as against the companies, compelling them to meet a steadily increasing loss ratio.

It is claimed, and fairly claimed, that the liability companies have made no money from liability underwriting. It is true that for the first three to five years a company is engaged in this business it seems to make money, but profits steadily diminish, and, after a few years, managers lose their tendency to boast over net results. In liability underwriting, as in other branches, "Pride goeth before destruction, and a haughty spirit before a fall."

Reviews and Criticisms

How to do Business *

Seymour Eaton, who is at present director of the Department of Industry and Finance in the Drexel Institute of Philadelphia, is well known to buyers of business books as the author of various attractive and more or less useful volumes. His "One Hundred Lessons in Business," brought out several years ago, had a large sale, and the present book may be described as a continuation of the same idea, as was fundamental to it. The volume is exceedingly attractive in appearance, whether examined outside or by carefully turning the pages. It appears to be full of those things which the student of business, the general reader, and even the expert, might utilize with advantage.

In the circulars accompanying the book there is an attempt at telling how the book was written. The statement is made that the author visited a large number of business concerns for the purpose of ascertaining how they did business, and that in his calls he collected material enough to have made a considerable number of books. He has, however, it is asserted, made judicious selection from what he collected, and has put into this book, only those things which are interesting, attractive and valuable.

Close inspection soon reveals that there is a degree of superficial gloss about the book which, while making it attractive to the general reader, causes a measure of disappointment to the one who really seeks practical information. More value perhaps attaches to the illustrations than to the text, and yet there are comparatively few matters in the text portion of the book to which exception can be taken, save only that which has already been intimated—the lack of going to the bottom, in the sense of giving the business man that information about the subjects treated which he really wants. The book has been arranged as a text-book, and the different chapters are followed by questions for recitation and examination. The fact that the illustrations throughout the book are in fac simile, and in many cases are in colors, the colors being for the most part the same as those in which the original papers are printed, gives the book an attractiveness which it would not otherwise present.

The work is divided into several leading chapters, a list of which, with running comments, will afford the reader a conception of the nature of the volume. The first chapter is entitled "Banking, Collections and Negotiable Paper." It is illustrated first by a plan of the Bank of England, followed by a fac simile of the deposit ticket of the Union Trust Company of Philadelphia, and then by reproductions of bank checks and bankers' drafts from Woodstown, N. J., and Knoxville, Tenn., and a money order issued by the Wells Fargo Express Company. We are particular in calling attention to these illustrations only to indicate the wide range which the author has given them. The second chapter is "Stocks, Bonds and Other Securities," in which is discussed the Stock Exchange, with illustrations of bonds, certificates of stock, etc. The succeeding chapter is entitled "Transportation of Mail, Money and Merchandise," and opens out very bravely with a history of transportation, which is boiled down to less than a page in extent. "Economic Results of Improved Means of Transportation" follows. "Transportation Rates and Freight Companies" are disposed of in less than a page. Fac similes of bills of lading of different prominent transportation lines are presented. "Transportation Accounts," in the form of an analysis that would be hard to apply in practical bookkeeping, are polished off in less than two pages. "Railway Management" is also analyzed and tabulated in about equal space. The transportation of mail enables the author to introduce a number of popular illustrations—namely, fac similes of envelopes with peculiar addresses, odd postmarks, forwarding records, etc. In like manner, but more briefly, "Life, Fire, Marine and Indemnity Insurance" are discussed, after which

*How To Do Business, as Business is Done in Great Commercial Centers, containing also Eaton's New Short Cuts in Figures. By Seymour Eaton. 324 pages, 6x8½ inches, with illustrations in colors. Bound in cloth. Published by P. W. Ziegler & Co. 1898. Price $2.

"Import and Export, Shipping and Warehousing" are taken up.

When the author reaches the end of two-thirds of the book, he gets down to his hobby, which is "How To Do Business." It is introduced by a chapter entitled "Hints and Helps for Young Business Men." "Business Experience" is disposed of in thirteen lines, after which a page tells "How to Succeed as a Salesman." "Failures in Early Life" take nearly two pages, while "A Poor Man's Chances" occupy one. The glittering generalities that are introduced in chapters bearing such titles as "The Talent of Success," "Favoring Circumstances in Life," "Use Money Carefully," "Character," "A Strong Will," etc., are entirely characteristic of the author.

He next takes up "Correspondence," in which he gives advice with respect to letters, pointing out those which bring success, and telling how to write them. Here, also, come in other popular illustrations, such as postal cards of foreign countries, with a superabundance of postmarks and extra stamps. "What Constitutes a Good Letter" is then defined. A good social letter, we are informed, is one which has an abundance of news, whether the news be sad or glad. Spelling and grammar, we learn, do not make the letter, any more than clothes make the man. All this is interesting, and may produce a condition of doubt in the reader's mind as to the author's real intention, for some believe that clothes have very much to do in making the man. "Hints for Corresponding Clerks," "Slips in Grammar Corrected," "How to Earn and Get a Good Situation," "Communication by Telegraph," "New Short Cuts in Figures," "Mechanics' Arithmetic," "Postscript Notes" and "Modern Bookkeeping Ideas" complete the scrap-book compendium, which really this book amounts to.

Under the head of "Modern Bookkeeping Ideas," we find several points which should have more than passing attention. For example, we are told that "it is much more important to learn the principles that govern correct systems of bookkeeping than it is to learn any particular form, according to which books should be laid out." Again, "An intelligent business man may learn bookkeeping by acquiring the fundamental principles of scientific accounting, and draw up his own forms in accordance with those principles." From this we are allowed to infer that there is a conflict in progress in the author's mind between bookkeeping and accounting, with the result not yet settled. We quote again: "When a note is renewed, the best way to record it is simply to make a memorandum in the bill book, marking out the old and entering the new. If something is paid on the note, a journal memorandum may be made, or if the note has been discounted by us, and we are obliged to take it up, the complete entries had best be made." We recognize the directions as aptly portraying "business as she is done"—in some cases at least. What we have quoted above is the total information under the head of "Modern Bookkeeping Ideas" relating to notes.

Space, however, will not permit to make further extracts. The bookkeeping ideas are accompanied by a number of pages devoted to rulings in colors. The first of these is declared to be a law ledger, and shows a docket combined with spaces for charges and credits. The next is a "Credit Ledger," whatever that may mean, wherein two columns are devoted to debits and one to credits. A Daily Cash Balance Book, a Mail Order Register, an Instalment Ledger, a Price Book, a Horizontal Sales Ledger, a Merchandise Stock Register, a Purchase Journal, a Pay Roll, and the Best Form of Balance Sheet (?), all of the blanks and forms being of an ancient, if not antediluvian character, complete the book.

Not only is Fortune herself blind, but she generally causes those persons to be blind whose interests she has more particularly taken in hand.—Cicero.

The possession of wealth is, as it were, prepayment, and involves an obligation of honor to the doing of correspondent work.—George Macdonald.

There is nothing which continues longer than a moderate fortune; nothing of which one sees sooner the end than a large fortune.—Bruyere.

The proverb is true, that light gains make heavy purses; for light gains come often, great gains now and then.—Bacon.

When wealthy, show thy wisdom not to be to wealth a servant, but make wealth serve thee.—Sir J. Denham.

Get place and wealth,—if possible with grace; if not, by any means get wealth and place.—Pope.

Accountants' Associations

New York Chapter of the Institute Accounts

The regular annual meeting of this organization was held in parlor 26, at the Hotel Marlborough, on Thursday evening, May 18. The business meeting was preceeded by a dinner.

Among those present were Charles Dutton, H. H. Todd, J. T. Murphy, W. J. Althers, William Dillon, Emil Opitz, W. P. Plant, D. C. Smith, F. J. MacRae, Thomas S. Whitbeck, John Moull, S. E. Sargent, L. C. J. Barthelémy, Owen Shepherd, F. W. Child and A. O. Kittredge.

The first business transacted was the election of delegates to the convention of the Institute. The Board of Governors recommended the following gentlemen: F. W. Child, Chas. E. Cheney, Thos. S. Whitbeck, John T. Murphy, J. R. Loomis, H. H. Todd, A. O. Kittredge, Wm. Dillon, W. J. Althers, W. P. Plant and Chas. Dutton, who were duly and unanimously chosen.

Mr. Plant, the Chapter's Secretary and Treasurer, then reported that during the past term seven new members had been added to the roll, and that the cash receipts were in excess of the previous year.

These new members were C. W. Haskins, Owen Shepherd, Charles MacLean, all of New York; Henry N. Jenkins, of Wilberforce, Ohio; G. P. Heidenrich, of Hazleton, Pa.; W. P. Godson, of Toronto, Canada, and Daniel Cranford Smith, of New York. Mr. Smith, last named, was accepted and elected as a member of the Chapter at this meeting.

The resignation of A. O. Kittredge as a member of the Board of Governors was then presented and accepted, and Mr. Charles Dutton was elected to fill the vacancy caused by Mr. Kittredge's resignation. Mr. John R. Loomis was also elected a member of the Board of Governors to fill the vacancy caused by expiration of term. The Chapter then proceeded to elect its officers for the ensuing year. Mr. Frederick W. Child was unanimously elected President, and Mr. W. P. Plant Secretary and Treasurer.

The delegates elected to represent the Chapter at the annual convention of the Institute of Accounts were then instructed to cast their vote at the annual meeting, for James G. Cannon as President, and Charles Dutton as Secretary and Treasurer of the Institute.

The holding of three meetings on the same evening left no time for the customary general discussion. It was therefore dispensed with, and the meeting adjourned about 11 p. m.

Hartford Chapter

The regular monthly meeting of this organization was held May 23, with a fair attendance. One new member was elected. Delegates to represent the Chapter at the annual convention of the Institute were selected. The Library Committee reported progress and displayed a number of works on accounting that had been purchased, as well as others presented to the Chapter. An additional appropriation for the purpose of books was voted. The Library Committee for the current year is composed of Gershon Smith, Chas. W. Rohne and Frank W. Hawley.

The subject of "How Should Accounts Payable be Treated?" was then discussed at length in two formal papers, read by Frank W. Hawley and Gershon Smith, respectively. We hope to be able to present these papers in subsequent issues. Edwin Brower, secretary of the Chapter, read a paper on "The Lawful Money Reserve of National Banks."

Third Annual Convention of the Institute of Accounts

The Third Annual Convention of the Institute of Accounts was held in the State apartments at the Waldorf-Astoria on Thursday evening, June 1, 1899, at 8 o'clock, with seventeen delegates present in person or by proxy.

The delegates of the New York chapter were all present in person, except one who was unavoidably detained.

Mr. Gershon Smith, President of the Hartford Chapter, held proxy for George A. Reynolds, Edwin Brower and Chas. W. Rohne, the delegates from that organization. Mr. Powhatan Wyndham Robertson, of the Washington Chapter, was represented by a proxy in the hands of A. O. Kittredge.

Col. Charles E. Sprague, President of the Institute, was in the chair. Mr. Henry Harney, the Secretary, being absent, on motion of Mr. Dutton, W. P. Plant was elected secretary of the meeting, pro tem. After the President had reported that the several chapters were maintaining their activity and interest, and that the affairs of the Institute were prosperous, he appointed the Secretary a committee of one to pass on the credentials of the delegates. The report of this committee having been received and accepted, the convention, on motion of Mr. Whitbeck, proceeded to the election of officers. Thereupon Mr. A. O. Kittredge, in a few well-chosen words, placed in nomination for President of the Institute the name of Mr. James G. Cannon, Vice-President of the Fourth National Bank, New York, and retiring President of the National Association of Credit Men. Ballots were then made out and delivered to tellers duly appointed, who announced that Mr. Cannon had been unanimously elected.

Mr. Child, in a timely and carefully worded speech, then nominated Mr. Charles Dutton for the office of Secretary and Treasurer. Mr. Dutton was also unanimously elected.

A committee consisting of F. W. Child and Wm. Dillon was appointed by the chairman to wait upon Mr. Cannon and inform him of his election.

The following resolution, offered by A. O. Kittredge, was unanimously adopted:

"Resolved, That it is the policy of the Institute of Accounts to encourage the formation of Chapters in all the business centres of the land."

After routine business had been concluded, on motion of Mr. Dillion, the Executive Council was instructed to take action under Section 6, Article XVIII. of the By-laws, which provides that "the Publication Committee may offer premiums to the members of the Institute, who, in competition, submit the best papers on proposed subjects, such premium not to exceed $50 in any one case, or more than $150 in any one year." The motion was unanimously approved.

On further motion of Mr. Dillon, the Executive Council was requested to instruct the Publication Committee to carry out the provisions of the by-laws relative to the distribution of literature to the Chapter members, containing the reports and proceedings of the various chapters and conventions of the Institute.

Mr. Plant, while not opposing the motion, suggested that a condition and not a theory confronted the Institute, and that the literal carrying out of the provisions in this regard would be impractical, because so very expensive. He intimated that ACCOUNTICS contained very full, fair and complete reports of the Chapter and Institute doings and discussions, and that an annual file of ACCOUNTICS contained in handy and compact form all the information that any member could desire.

Mr. Dillon's motion was carried.

Gershon Smith, of Hartford, Conn.; Henry Harney, F. W. Child and J. R. Loomis, of New York, were then elected to fill vacancies in the Executive Council caused by the expiration of terms.

After a vote of thanks to the retiring President, and also to the retiring Secretary and Treasurer, for their activity and efficient administration of their various offices, the convention adjourned.

Maryland Association

The latest organization of public accountants and auditors is the "Maryland Association of Public Accountants." As the name implies, the society is intended to include all the leading professional accountants in the State. A bill, similar to the New York bill, will be presented to the next meeting of the Legislature, and the Association will spare no pains to elevate the profession and to keep it upon the high plane that it deservedly occupies. The President of the Maryland Association is Max Teichmann, the Secretary Frank Blacklock, and the Treasurer Wm. F. Rogers.

We ourselves make our fortunes, good or bad; and when God lets loose a tyrant upon us, or a sickness, if we fear to die, or know not to be patient, the calamity sits heavy upon us.—Jeremy Taylor.

If Fortune has fairly sat on a man, he takes it for granted that life consists in being sat upon; but to be coddled on Fortune's knee, and then have his ears boxed,—that is aggravating.—Charles Buxton.

There is some help for all the defects of fortune; for if a man cannot attain to the length of his wishes, he may have his remedy by cutting of them shorter.

—Cowley.

Correspondence

Builders' Accounts

From A. W. T., Erie, Pa.

I have read the letter from C. B., on "Builders' Accounts," published in the March issue of ACCOUNTICS, and have found it very interesting. I have kept this class of accounts for several years past, and believe I have a system for the same which is superior to his both in the matter of simplicity and of accuracy. To begin with, your correspondent makes too many entries and opens too many accounts. A brief outline of my system, submitted merely to bring out further discussion, which will probably be beneficial to both C. B. and myself, is as follows:

If I secure a contract from Mr. Jones at $1,000, my entry would be as follows:

Jones, Dr.
To Jones Contract....$1,000.00

When I commence to execute the work, I do not make an entry against the work in the ledger until the end of the first month. Thereafter an entry is made at the end of each succeeding month. Every item of cost is kept in a cost book, which is divided into columns running lengthwise of the book, and extending across two pages, giving me about fifteen columns in all. In these I keep the cost of each class of work, viz., mill work, excavation, foundation, glazing, plastering, sundries, sub-contracts, etc. By keeping the record in this form, I can tell at a glance what a certain class of work is costing. We do not care so much about the work that we sub-let, for all our contracts are made within our estimate.

Every item that is charged to a contract goes through Merchandise. For example, if we let the stone work for Mr. Jones's house to John Doe for $500, the entry in the journal would be as follows:

Mdse., Jones's Contract, Dr.
To John Doe.........$500.00

I then charge the job in the cost book as follows: "John Doe's proposal for stone work, $500." Then, in regular form, I give him credit in the ledger. At the end of each month I foot up the total column of the cost book and charge in the ledger as follows:

Jones's Contract, Dr.
To Mdse.,

being the cost of contracts, per cost book, for the month of ——.

If Mr. John Doe draws on account, the entry would be simply:

John Doe, Dr.
To Cash.

When the page is completed, the balance in the account, whatever it may be and on whichever side it occurs, is transferred to profit and loss.

The above routine is the result of several years' experience in the building business, and I find by it that I can keep the exact cost of each class of work, with the smallest number of entries and the least labor of any plan I have investigated. I would like to have the opinion of your correspondent, C. B., concerning this and also the opinion of other readers of the magazine.

Management of Drafts

From E. S., Louisville, Ky.:

Here is a question over which a number of bookkeepers in this city are at present disputing: Made 60 days' sight draft on John Smith, Henderson, Ky., and discounted it at German Insurance Bank. One party to the dispute says that Bills Receivable should be debited and John Smith credited, and then, in turn, that Cash and Discount should be debited and Bills Receivable credited. The other side says debit Cash and Discount, and credit John Smith. Please give in reply an indication of which is the best practice.

ANSWER.—From the ear-marks on the question we are disposed to regard it as a school problem, rather than one that has arisen in actual business. It is not common in most lines of business to draw drafts at 60 days' sight. It would be much more natural to make the draft at 60 days after date. Further, it is not usual in business to secure the discount of a draft until after it has been accepted. Of course, there are exceptions to this rule. For example, where the draft is accompanied by a bill of lading, but such transactions are a law unto themselves and do not ordinarily come into what might be called common practice.

We are in all cases inclined to the rule that the record in the books of accounts should correspond to the facts of the transaction. Assuming that the draft is accepted before being discounted, we should certainly pass it through Notes Receivable Account. Even though it were not accepted before being offered for discount, the acceptance is implied, and, therefore, we should be disposed in that case, as well, to pass it through Notes Receivable Account. Then when the discount is accomplished, Notes Receivable Account would, of course, be credited, with Cash and Discount standing the debit.

We have no better means of knowing, perhaps, than the correspondent who sends us this question, what is the usual practice in this regard. There is a tendency in various directions to go across lots and thereby, apparently at least, save entries. It might be that an investigation of a considerable number of cases analagous to this, would show an opinion strongly in favor of the direct entry as cited in the question proposed. Usage, however, would scarcely determine our opinion in the premises of what it is expedient to do. Experience has taught us that a smart Aleck way of saving time in the original entry by cutting across lots usually results in a loss of several times as much time in discovering how the entry was made and why it was made, when it comes to checking up or auditing. The straightforward plan, with the whole history of the transaction recorded, is in our estimation always the best.

The Imprest System of Handling Petty Cash

To one who has not been to the trouble of looking up the definitions of the word "impress" and the derivatives therefrom, the term "imprest cash" will seem peculiar. In the sense ordinarily employed, imprest conveys the idea of pressure or confinement. We impress a stamp; an idea is impressed upon the mind. Again, seamen are sometimes impressed into service. If the one who undertakes the investigation of this word carries his inquiry a little further, he will find under the form "imprest," something as follows: "That which is impressed;" and still further, "A prepayment of money especially to carry forward some public service." The definition of the compound word "imprest-money" is, "Money advanced from the exchequer, or money paid to recruits on enlistment." The imprest office in the English government is a department of the admiralty, which has charge of loans or advances to paymasters. It is in the latter definitions that reason is found for the term "imprest cash," as now used in many business concerns.

Under the imprest system, the person charged with petty disbursements is provided with a sufficient sum as a working capital, which is debited to him in the general cash book. At the end of each month, or other period agreed upon, he presents to the head cashier an abstract of his petty cash outlays, which, after being verified from his cash book, are repaid to him and entered in the general cash book, from which they are posted to the proper expenditure accounts. The petty cashier thus starts each month or other period with the exact amount of the original working capital on hand. Receipts are obtained for as many of the payments as possible, and they are filed in the usual way. The above is the definition of the term and description of the imprest system which appears in the columns of one of our English exchanges.

The preferred system in this country differs from that set forth above, in details rather than in principle. The amount of imprest cash is determined in the light of the general requirements of the case, and once agreed upon, whether the amount be $50, $200, $500, or some other sum, is deposited in the imprest cash box. It is thereafter considered in the balancing of the general cash book as an amount on hand. It is the unvarying quantity with which the imprest cash box stands charged. As disbursements are made by the cashier in charge, receipts are taken and are dropped in the box, no effort being made to enter them upon what is frequently termed the petty cash book. From time to time the receipts and vouchers are withdrawn from the imprest cash box, are duly certified and audited, and then the amount is repaid to the cash box, thus restoring imprest cash to its original sum. The repayment may be from cash out of the general fund, entries for the vouchers in that case being made on the cash book, or, preferably, it may be by check on the bank. The latter plan prevails in all cases where the total cash received each day is deposited and every expenditure is evidenced by check. In such a case, a check would be drawn for vouchers number so-and-so to so-and-so, inclusive, and the proceeds of the check would be deposited in the imprest cash box in place of the vouchers taken up.

Interest and Discount—V

By Charles W. Rohne

Arithmetical and Geometrical Progression

In computing simple interest there are many problems in which the theory of arithmetical progression can be applied to advantage. An arithmetical progression is a series whose successive terms increase or decrease by constant difference. Five elements enter into computations in arithmetical progressions, as follows:

First terms for which the symbol (a) is used, common difference denoted by the symbol (d), number of terms denoted by the symbol (n), last term by (1), and sum of the terms by (S). If any three of these five elements are known, the other two can be found by computation.

A geometrical series, or progression, is obtained by multiplying the preceding term by a constant multiplier. Five elements enter into computations in geometrical progressions, as follows:

First term, symbol (a), ratio denoted by the symbol (r), number of terms by (n), last term by (1), and the sum of the terms by (S). As in arithmetical progression, if any three of these five elements are known, the other two can be found by computation.

Accounts in which Interest is an Element

Savings banks pay compound interest to their depositors; they add the interest to the principal either monthly, quarterly or semi-annually. An interest term is the regular interval, at the end of which interest on deposits is compounded. Monthly interest terms begin on the first day of each month; quarterly terms usually on the first days of January, April, July and October; and the semi-annual terms usually on the first days of January and July.

The interest term of most savings banks is three months. No interest is allowed on fractional parts of a dollar. Most savings banks allow interest only on those sums which have been on deposit a full interest term. Hence interest is computed at the end of the interest term on the smallest balance on deposit at any one time during the term.

Equation of Payments

Simple interest is used in the majority of formulas given for the average or equation of payments. Equation of payments is the process of finding the equitable time for paying in one sum several debts due at different times. The term of credit is the time that must elapse before a debt becomes due. The average term of credit is the time that must elapse before several debts due at different times may be equitably paid in one sum. The equated time is the equitable date of payment. A focal date is a date from which the terms of credit are computed. Any date may be assumed as a focal date, but the focal date usually assumed is the earliest date at which any of the debts become due.

Equation of payments is based on the following obvious principles:

1. Any debt is equitably subject to legal interest from the time it is due.

2. The interest of any sum for a given time equals the interest of two times that sum for one-half of that time, or of one-half of that sum for two times that time, and so on.

3. The use of any sum paid at any time before it is due equals the use of an equal sum not paid till the same length of time after it is due.

The present worth of a debt due at a future time is the sum of money that, loaned at interest to-day, will amount to the debt at maturity. True discount is the interest on the present worth of the debt from to-day to maturity; it is the debt minus its present worth. Bank discount exceeds true discount by the interest on the true discount. Commercial discount and bank discount have largely taken the place of true discount; the latter is but little used. In computations in true discount,

Present worth=principal.
Rate of discount=rate of interest.
True discount=interest.
Sum to be discounted=amount.
Amount—present worth=true discount.

The Wrong of Tardy Paying

By James G. Cannon

In talking with a representative merchant of New York some time since, he stated that he could not understand why it was that so many rich people were negligent about paying personal accounts, and, to use his expression, "allowed their bills to run so eternally slow." When their attention is directed to the status of the account, they will often affect to feel very much insulted. They cannot apparently bring themselves to realize that a debt contracted in this way is a just one, and as worthy of prompt payment as any other business obligation. Let me relate two or three instances that came under my observation, of the wrongs inflicted by the rich upon those in more humble circumstances, who could ill afford to be deprived of the use of money justly their due.

X is a poor dressmaker living in New York, who worked for Z, a wealthy woman. Z paid X $50 on account leaving a balance of $100 due her, and shortly afterwards sailed for Europe, where she remained for six months. In the meantime X, deprived of the $100, was unable to meet her rent and other obligations, and suffered much humiliation and inconvenience. When Z returned from Europe she paid X without even an apology for the delay.

A, a poor seamstress, working for $1.50 a day, was employed by one of the leaders of New York society, whose name is associated with most of the season's great social functions and charities. In many ways she was kind to this seamstress, sometimes giving her cast-off garments; but she was thoughtlessly unkind about paying her for her services. The rich woman could not understand why this servant should demand her wages, and consequently discharged her.

M is a well-known physician in Brooklyn. He has treated a wealthy family residing on one of the most fashionable avenues in the city; but for a year his bills remained unpaid—not even noticed. Finally he made an appeal to the lady of the house on one of his calls. "Doctor, please be patient with me," she said; "my husband has given me money for that bill three different times, but I used it for shopping, and I am afraid to tell him. I will try to pay the bill little by little out of my allowance." Meantime the physician is worried about his own bills because of the selfishness of this woman.

In illustration of the way credit is sometimes extended I will give you an example: D is a retail butcher doing a large business. E represents a family well-to-do, who dress in the latest mode, attend the theatre, drive on the boulevard and entertain lavishly. Their orders to the butcher are liberal and they are particular about getting the best cuts and tenderest birds. Although they occasionally pay a little on account, the end of each month finds the unpaid balance increased. The butcher does not refuse to serve the family, because he fears he might lose both the money and the customer. The account continues to grow. When D's patience is finally exhausted, and he intimates that he would like to have the bill liquidated in full, E goes to another butcher, repudiates his indebtedness to D; the other butcher welcomes him as a customer, and E still keeps up style and no doubt continues rolling up bills with other dealers.

Very often an account that has run for some time becomes difficult of collection merely because the debtor, whose moral sensibilities may be none too acute, feels he is asked to give something for nothing, especially when the goods bought on credit are worn out or consumed, and there is nothing in sight for the money he is expected to pay. One should insist upon the payment of all bills in strict accordance with the terms of sale, and no necessary expense should be spared in forcing the wealthy delinquent to a settlement. He may take umbrage and withhold his patronage, but, in my judgment, accounts that require extra effort to collect are not desirable.—From an address entitled "Individual Credits," delivered by James G. Cannon, Vice-President of the Fourth National Bank, New York City, before the National Association of Credit Men, at their annual convention, held at Kansas City.

Let Fortune do her worst, whatever she makes us lose, so long as she never makes us lose our honesty and our independence.—Pope.

It is only when the rich are sick that they feel the impotence of wealth.

—Colton.

The Higher Education of the Business Man

By Edmund J. James

Edmund J. James, Professor of Public Administration in the University of Chicago, has been for many years past a most careful student of business conditions and business requirements. His inquiry has ever been directed to what is best for business men and what will conserve business interests. For many years Professor James was associated with the Wharton School of Finance, Philadelphia, a department of the University of Pennsylvania, and for a long time he has been before the public as a representative of what may be called the higher business education. At the meeting of the Missouri Bankers' Association, held in St. Louis a short time since, Professor James read a paper on the "Higher Education of the Future Business Man," wherein he indicated what the college course for the future business man should be. He gave the history of the establishment and success of the Wharton School of Finance, and illustrated his paper by very interesting particulars of the work. The following extract will give our readers an idea of the position occupied by this eminent teacher:—

The reasons for the establishment of that school involved three points; the inadequacy of existing facilities for the higher education of the business classes; the desirability of having such facilities, and suggestions as to what can and should be done. The American youth who is looking forward to a business career and has completed the ordinary grammar school course stands face to face with an interesting and important problem. Shall I seek a situation in some business house, closing my school education with what I have now, and trusting to the friction of active life for a further education, or shall I go to some other school a while longer and trust to the benefits of the training there to make up for the greater practical knowledge which I might get in the same number of years in a counting house, bank or factory?

The average boy in American life decides in favor of going into business at once. Perhaps a reason may be found in the fact that the so-called higher education to be had in the colleges appears to bear but little relation to their future work. It may all be very nice. It may belong to the accomplishments of life. It makes doubtless a fine dessert; but it is in all probability an article of luxury which no energetic and vigorous person who is determined to succeed in the fierce conflict of competitive business can afford to acquire at the cost of years of effort.

Now what courses are open to the youth who determines to get something more before going into business? He might take a medical or theological course; the former would increase his knowledge of facts enormously, the latter would sharpen his logical acumen. Such a proposition, however, would seem absurd and very few students would think of adopting this plan. A law course, a course in civil, mechanical or electrical engineering would be of no more practical benefit. What then remains? Only the so-called business or commercial and the literary college.

The business college cannot be said to furnish a higher business education at all. It has to do with "facilities"—indeed chiefly with manual facilities—writing, reckoning and the things that go to make up a good clerk, things which may be of great value in themselves, things which every business man would be better off for the having, and yet things which, after all, are only facilities. As for the literary college, I think no one who has ever taught in one, but will admit that the traditional college curriculum has turned aside many a boy from a business career in which he might have succeeded to a professional one in which he failed.

Our college courses hold a boy during two very important periods of life—the preparatory from 12 to 16, and the college proper from 17 to 21. That a course of study pursued during these years, no matter how good it may be in itself, may work harm to a boy who comes under its influence cannot be denied. Fortunately for the world people who believe that a curriculum can be devised that will be suitable for all boys, no matter what may be their tastes or inclinations, are becoming fewer and are losing their influence. I do not think the fact can be denied that our colleges are not educating our business men as a matter of fact. The case may not be as bad by any means as it was represented some time ago by Andrew Carnegie, who declared that he did not know any successful business men who are college graduates.

The ratio of college men in business to the non-college men is declining. Even the proportion of college graduates in the professional schools is not increasing, even the number of physicians, lawyers and clergymen who are college graduates are not relatively increasing, and indeed may be decreasing, and yet the college is considered especially adapted to these classes. In other words, the old-fashioned curriculum may be just the thing for the business man, but if so he cannot be led to see it and has not been persuaded of it.

It was these facts that led to the establishment of the first school of finance. The primary reasons were: First, that the business class of the country needs a higher education as much or more than any other class; second, the view that the commercial college, however valuable its curriculum, is by its very nature unable to give this higher training; third, the fact that the American college, however real and valuable its higher training, does not in its present form furnish a kind of higher education which appeals to the business community, as is shown by the fact of the small number of youths who are looking to business careers who enter them.

Negotiable Paper for Patent Rights

In the very complete discussion of the negotiable instruments law recently presented in the columns of this magazine, being a report of the paper by Mr. Bartholemy, before the New York Chapter of the Institute of Accounts, it was made quite apparent that notes given for patent rights are required by the law of New York to contain upon their face the phrase "given for a patent right." The Scientific American, in a recent issue, discussing negotiable paper for patent rights, says that this requirement of the law seems unnecessary at the present time and inharmonious with the progressive spirit of the day. It serves, however, as a forcible reminder of the notorious patent right swindles which first called legislation of this character into existence.

The evil reached its height, says our contemporary, and indeed had its life in the Middle and Western States during the period of prosperity and wild speculation which followed the Civil War. The most glaring frauds were enacted. Large sums were paid for rights under void and worthless patents. Patent rights for the same territory were sold over and over again. Notes were taken to facilitate the sales, and were immediately discounted. By the time the purchaser discovered the deception, they were in the hands of bona fide holders, enforcible against the maker.

The courts were powerless to protect the victims of these and other similar impositions, and the State Legislatures were finally appealed to for relief, with the result that in 1868 Ohio passed an act which required any person, before offering for sale a patent right for any county, to submit the patent to the probate judge of that county, and make affidavit before him that the patent was in force and that the applicant had the right to sell. It also required that any written obligation taken on the sale of such right should bear on its face the words: "Given for a patent right." Failure to comply with this law was made an offense.

Continuing the discussion, our contemporary says that this statute in its entirety was of doubtful propriety, and this seems to have been realized, for within a year the provision requiring the making and filing of proofs was repealed. From this beginning legislation was enacted in several States, including Indiana and Illinois, in 1869; Minnesota in 1871, Nebraska in 1873 and Kansas in 1889. The law as amended in Ohio, requiring only that written obligations given for a patent right should bear such statement on their face, was passed by the Legislatures of Vermont in 1870, of Michigan in 1871, of Pennsylvania and Wisconsin in 1872, of New York and Connecticut in 1877 and of Arkansas in 1891. In the litigation which promptly followed the enactment of these statutes, their constitutionality was assailed vigorously and at first with uniform success.

Concerning this litigation, our contemporary gives a very long and interesting account, showing how different State Courts are arraigned on opposite sides of the question, and concludes that until the validity of these statutes is brought before the United States Supreme Court—if that should ever be—their validity must be regarded as finally established, as far as the State Courts of New York, Pennsylvania, Ohio, Indiana and Kansas are concerned That they will be declared unconstitutional and void if ever brought before the Supreme court is hardly to be doubted, for that has been the attitude of every Federal judge who has passed upon the question.

Long and Short Leaf Books

The Globe Company, of Cincinnati, New York, Chicago and Boston, are rapidly adding to the considerable line of long and short leaf books, all being marketed under the trade designation of "3-A Account Books." Included in the assortment

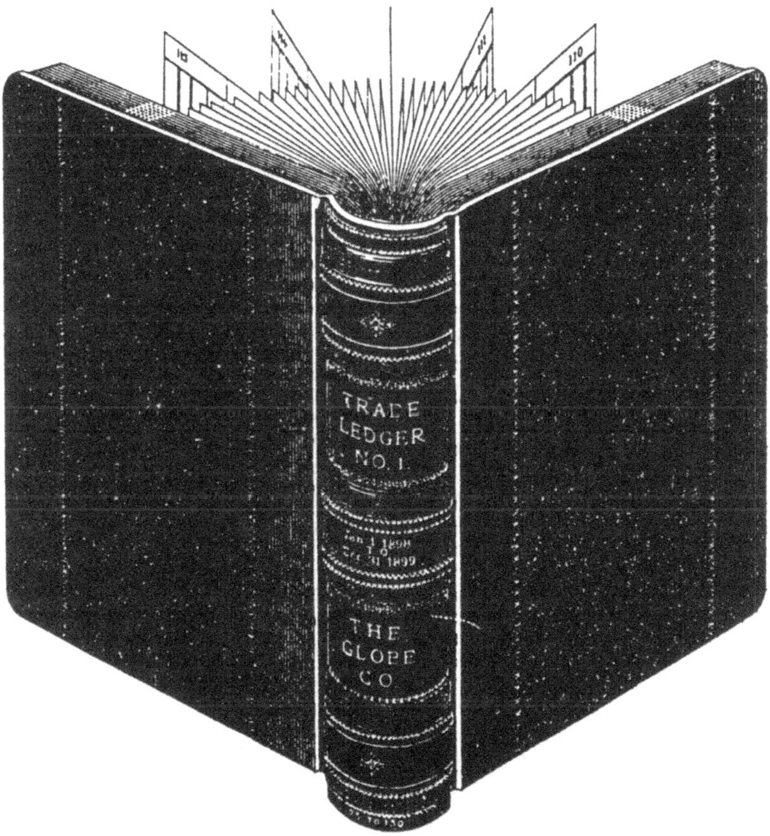

BACK VIEW OF A LONG AND SHORT LEAF LEDGER

are Sales Ledgers, Purchase Ledgers, Bank Ledgers, Trial Balance Books, Pay Rolls, Invoice Registers, Voucher Distribution Registers, Notes Payable and Notes Receivable, Records, Advertising Registers, etc.

The accompanying cut shows a general view of one of these books, and very satisfactorily indicates the peculiarities of construction. The margins of the wide leaves projecting beyond the narrow leaves are thickened or reinforced so as to produce an even writing surface, no matter where the book is opened. Compared with other long and short leaf books in common use, the reader will notice that there are no margins to cut off and no portions of leaves to remove along prearranged lines of perforations. Instead the book is a finished article from start to finish. The construction further admits of any required number of short leaves to each pair of long leaves. Accordingly, there is any desired amount of space for columnarizing opposite each writing of names or other data. Some samples recently produced show as high as eighty pairs of columns opposite a single writing of names, in a book that in general dimensions is of demy size. The columns might have been increased to double this quantity, if required, without changing the dimensions of the wide pages.

Rulings, printed heads, weight of paper and other conditions are adjusted to suit requirements. Those who are using long and short leaf books in any form will find it to their advantage to inquire into the 3-A productions of the Globe Company before placing additional orders, and those who have never used long and short leaf books will find it greatly to their advantage to examine these books on account of the immense saving of labor which their use insures.

Should Accountants Advertise

The apparent intolerance with which certain members of the accounting profession regard even the most modest efforts upon the part of their fellow-practitioners to secure publicity and draw to themselves a share of patronage or indicate to the business public their ability to serve it advantageously, and also the scepticism of certain official periodicals in the accounting field concerning similar matters, constitutes some of the interesting features of the period. One of our English exchanges maintains a carping mood over all matters of this kind. It asserts comparatively little. Its actual comments are few and far between, but yet, by insinuation, it holds up to scorn from time to time specimens of the announcements which advertising accountants are sending out.

This journal, in a single issue a short time since, presented two characteristic samples of its derision, and yet, unintentionally, perhaps, afforded those whom apparently it would chastise a real service in giving them a still larger sphere of publicity. We reproduce below the two examples, without change, allowing our readers to draw their own inferences. The first example was found near at home, as will be seen from an examination of the following:

CHARTERED ACCOUNTANT TOUTING.

The following circular has been issued broadcast in the City of London:

Bagster's Balance Sheet Forms.

These Forms contain a list of the various particulars which must be abstracted from the books for the purposes of preparing a balance-sheet and a profit and loss account for any past period.

They are intended to be filled up with the necessary figures by the applicant himself, and when so filled up to be returned to the author, who will from these figures prepare a balance-sheet and a profit and loss account for the period concerned.

The Forms are published at two guineas, and this sum will include the preparation of the balance-sheet and profit and loss account from the figures supplied by the applicant.

The Forms are suited to all businesses.

The accuracy of the balance-sheet and profit and loss account will, of course, depend upon the accuracy of the figures supplied, but should there be errors in these figures, except such as are of equal amount on both sides of the account, the balance of them will be revealed, and thus give a warning of the inaccuracy.

To all who desire to test the accuracy of accounts prepared by themselves or for them, these Forms will be of value, for they will only need to abstract from such accounts the figures required by the Forms, to have the test applied.

The author does not suggest that the accounts thus prepared are as reliable as those prepared by a Chartered Accountant after an investigation by him of the books themselves, but he claims that with care and attention, under the direction of the Forms, accurate figures can be abstracted by the applicant, which, of course, would result in accurate accounts.

The difficulty of obtaining accurate figures from the books consists principally in the fact that the books themselves may be inaccurate, and few laymen have the time and training which will enable them to set them right. The author will, however, advise as to the best way of extracting the figures, and by attention to the principles necessary to be followed in the future, there ought to be little difficulty in periodically obtaining reliable results.

JOHN BAGSTER,
Fellow of Chartered Accountants.

The other example was found in the accounting literature of far-off America, and was presented in the following form:

"WHAT WE DO."

The following advertisement is extracted from "Accountics," of New York:

"We design and instal scientific accounting methods and improved business systems.

We conduct audits and make examinations in all parts of the country. The correctness of our reports is guaranteed by suitable bonds of indemnity.

Further particulars on application.

ACCOUNT, AUDIT AND ASSURANCE CO., LTD.
260-266 W. Broadway, New York."

If we command our wealth, we shall be rich and free; if our wealth commands us, we are poor indeed. We are bought by the enemy with the treasure in our own coffers.—Burke.

Questions and Answers

Concerning the

BALANCE-SHEET SYSTEM OF ACCOUNTS

Conducted by the

Account Audit and Assurance Co., Ltd.

25 Pine Street, New York

Samples by Mail

From D. A. J., Hastings. Neb.

I have noticed advertisements of the Balance Sheet System of Accounts, with its Perpetual Balance Sheet, and Profit and Loss statement. Please send by mail samples for my inspection.

ANSWER: In asking for samples you are for the moment confusing an accounting system with mere bookkeeping details. We do not supply account books for ordinary use, nor are we specially interested in the kind of ledgers or the character of posting mediums that may be employed in any direction. We are furnishing an accounting system, however, which, in connection with ordinary bookeeping details, accomplishes results which have heretofore been impossible in the way books have been kept.

The Balance Sheet System of Accounts is essentially, first, a plan of classification of accounts, and, second, a method of supplying the deficiencies in the ordinary double entry in a way to round out and complete the plan upon which double entry is based. We produce in any business a profit and loss statement and a balance sheet that are integral parts of the books, just the same as the cash account is an integral part of the ordinary bookkeeping plan. By the Balance Sheet System of Accounts a reference to the profit and loss statement, which is always kept up to date, the same as the Cash Account is, shows the rate of profit or loss and the results to date. Again, reference to the Balance Sheet, which is likewise always kept up to date, shows the degree of solvency of the establishment; that is, the amount in gross and detail of resources, the amount in gross and detail of liabilities, the total profits to date, or the total losses to date, as the case may be. These are results that have never before been accomplished in bookkeeping. Without further particulars you must be able to perceive that what we are supplying is something that of necessity is always made to order and arranged to meet stated conditions. It is nothing that is kept in stock nor of which samples could be sent by mail.

Some Objections Answered

From T. A., London.

The following are some of my reasons for declining, for the present at least, to accept your offer on the Balance Sheet System of Accounts:

1. I consider that you want too much for your specifications.
2. You want more than I can afford to give.
3. I know enough about bookkeeping to make up a system of my own.
4. The system is not particularly well adapted to the tea business (my line of trade), carried on in a small way, where there is a large stock of printed matter, circulars and labels for different kinds and for different sizes of packages.
5. My experience is that any one who is thoroughly familiar with the business can tell whether it is making money or not, and about how much money it is making, without a going profit and loss account.
6. There is too much detail about the tea agency business in any case, and by any extra work it would be rendered more difficult.
7. I consider that the best man to draw out the forms is the party who is thoroughly familiar with the stock.
8. Any man who understands the principles upon which your going profit and loss account is kept and has seen the scheme you have for keeping account of stock, should be able to make out a system to suit his business better than you.

Answer—1. With regard to your assertion that we demand too much for our specification, we have only this to say, that we have priced them in the light of their cost to us to produce, and their value to the purchaser. If our prices were too high, we would not have any business. The fact that we do have a very large business is conclusive proof that our prices are reasonable.

2. With respect to your assertion that we demand more than you can afford to give, we have nothing to say, beyond the

general admission you alone must be the judge of that fact.

3. With respect to the statement that you know encugh about bookkeeping to make up a system of your own, we would say that not being personally acquainted with your attainments, we are in no position to admit or deny the assertion, but assuming, for the sake of argument, that you are able to make up a system of your own, still it would seem evident from what has transpired in this correspondence that you have not yet constructed a system. You may be able, for all we know, to make up a suit of clothes, or to construct a pair of shoes, and yet we venture to say that notwithstanding this fact you are wearing tailor-made clothes, and shoes made by shoemakers of experience and skill. We venture further to say that this is so, for one or the other, or both of two reasons—first, that the general quality of what you can buy is far better than what you could make in an amateurish way; and, second, that the cost at which the regular manufacturer can afford to sell is less than would be your expense in making up for so small a demand as your personal requirements.

4. Whether or not the Balance Sheet System is particularly well adapted for the tea business, carried on in a small way, where there is a large stock of printed matter in use, etc., is something, we submit, that you are not in position to assert, for as yet you know nothing of the details of the system, nor have you any practical experience in its operations. Four our part, with the advantage of this knowledge, we unhesitatingly assert that the Balance Sheet System of Accounts will do better for the particular line of business described, notwithstanding its details, than any other system than can be applied to it.

5. We do not dispute that any one who is thoroughly familiar with a business can tell whether or not it is making money, and about how much money it is making, without a going profit and loss statement. You are very judicious in using the word "about" in this declaration. It reminds us of the way in which school boys sometimes phrase their inquiries, addressed to their mates who are carrying new watches: "About what time is it by your new watch?" What the business man wants is not a notion of "about" how much he is making or losing, but the actual facts of his business which lead up to the result of either a profit or a loss. No one could afford to keep books upon any system at all for the mere satisfaction or the small usefulness of knowing nearly the amount of his profits or losses. The profit or the loss, as the case may be,. is the result of certain antecedent facts. These facts must be brought to the view of the manager, in order to enable him to so direct the operations of the business that losses may be diminished and profits increased. The Going Profit and Loss Statement, therefore, is of great advantage to a business for other and more important reasons than those which you name.

6. You say there is too much detail about the tea agency business in any case, and any extra work would render it more difficult. This is a gratuitous statement and our reply is that the Balance Sheet System is nothing if it does not reduce detail, and if it does not diminish work. Our testimonials from users in all cases are that clerical work is reduced rather than increased by the operation of the plans which we advocate.

7. We quite agree with you that one of the best men to draw out the forms for use in any business is one who is thoroughly familiar with the stock, but we submit that supplemental to his work should be that of another, who is thoroughly familiar with the requirements of accounting. The man who is familiar with the stock is seldom acquainted with accounting details. The best result can only be accomplished by combining the skill and experience of the two. For our part we never think of brushing aside the valuable assistance of the man who knows the business, but, on the other hand, we always insist that there is more involved in drawing up a blank than the mere knowledge of the business details. There must be correspondence and agreement of the blanks with the different parts of the accounting system, or else unnecessary work is done and details increased rather than diminished.

8. You say in conclusion that any man who understands the principle upon which our Going Profit and Loss Account is kept, and who has see the scheme we have for keeping account of stock, should be able to make out a system to suit his own business better than we can. If we should admit the correctness of this proposition, it would still prove

nothing, so far as relates to the present case. The man you describe is a purely imaginary person and in no event can he be yourself, for nothing has transpired in this correspondence which warrants you in the assumption that you do understand the principle upon which our accounting system is based. You have not seen, in whole, or even in part, the plan which we employ for keeping account of stock in your line of business, and, therefore, are in no position to form an opinion concerning it.

Inventorying

Inventorying, with the Balance Sheet System, instead of being a huge piece of work, to be undertaken once, or at most twice a year, wherein the whole establishment has to be regarded as a unit, becomes a series of smaller jobs, any one of which is to be undertaken whenever circumstances favor. Each department may be inventoried independent of all other departments. No two departments, of necessity, require to be inventoried at the same date. The accuracy of the showing of course is conserved by inventorying at irregular periods, and inventorying some departments more frequently than other departments, depending in this regard upon the nature of the goods and the volume of the transactions, and other special circumstances. To better illustrate this last statement, it may be asserted that in some department stores, where the system is in use, inventorying has been assigned to a special corps of employees, qualified for this work and rendered proficient by long and continual practice. These men commence the work of inventorying at the beginning of the year and continue it throughout all the months of the year. They take up in succession one department after another, doing the maximum of work themselves, and leaving only a minimum to be performed by the sales people in co-operation with them. Some departments are examined between Saturday night and knowledge of the sales people employed Monday morning, almost without the in those departments.

Each inventory thus taken is compared with the book account, which shows the goods that should be on hand. The advantages to the management, growing out of such exhibits, are too apparent to need lengthy explanation. If the goods on hand correspond with the book account, it is evident that the system is being correctly administered and that no pilfering is in progress. Any discrepancies, on the other hand, would at once suggest careful investigation or even the services of detectives to discover the nature of the leak that is draining the profits.

Finally the Balance Sheet System for departmental stores as well as for other enterprises may be described as a well devised, thoroughly constructed machine, scientific in all its parts, economical in its operations, and in each case specially adapted to the particular business to be served. The Balance Sheet System, as adjusted for one department store, would not necessarily be entirely adequate nor, in all respects, the best for some other department store. In each case the skill of an accountant of long practice, or of an expert in designing and adapting systems, more correctly designated by the term accounting engineer, is called into play, just the same as in erecting a building or constructing the machinery for a factory, an architect or mechanical engineer, as the case may be, is brought into requisition for plans and specifications.

"No" the Correct Word

"My son," said the graybeard, "you are about to go forth to do battle with the world."

"Yes, father," answered the young man.

"One of the first things you should learn, my boy," the old man continued, "is to learn to say 'no.'"

"I think I understand."

"I dunno whether you do or not. The point I am trying to get at is that the habit of saying 'naw' and 'nit' was all right while you were in college, but it ain't the correct thing for a business man."—Cincinnati Enquirer.

Wealth brings noble opportunities, and competence is a proper object of pursuit; but wealth, and even competence, may be bought at too high a price. Wealth itself has no moral attribute. It is not money, but the love of money, which is the root of all evil. It is the relation between wealth and the mind and the character of its possessor which is the essential thing.—Hillard.

---

he begins to speak a little louder: people think him more sensible, and soon he thinks himself so.—Cecil.

Extra interest signifies extra risk.
—Wellington.

Accountics

The Office Magazine.

A. O. KITTREDGE, F. I. A., C. P. A., Editor.
E. R. KITTREDGE, Associate.

Accountics is devoted to the Science of Accounting, to the Art of Bookkeeping and to the advocacy of Improved Office Methods.

Subscription.—One dollar a year, payable in advance.

Postage is prepaid by the publishers in the United States, Canada and Mexico. For all other countries in the Postal Union, subscribers must add 50 cents a year.

Discontinuances.—In the absence of specific orders to discontinue at the end of the subscription term the magazine will be continued and a bill sent.

Remittances should be by Draft, P. O. Order or Express Order, payable to the order of the ACCOUNTICS ASSOCIATION. Money and postage stamps are at the risk of the sender, unless sent by express or in registered letters. Add 10 cents each to checks on local banks to defray collection charges.

Advertising Rates will be quoted on application.

Official Journal.—This publication, by resolutions duly passed, has been made the official publication of the following organizations:—

THE INSTITUTE OF ACCOUNTS.
THE NEW YORK CHAPTER of the Institute of Accounts.
THE WASHINGTON CHAPTER of the Institute of Accounts.
THE HARTFORD CHAPTER of the Institute of Accounts.

ACCOUNTICS is the accredited medium of intercommunication between members of the Institute of Accounts wherever located.

ACCOUNTICS ASSOCIATION, Publishers,

Lancashire Bldg., Pine St., near Nassau,
New York.

Publishers' Desk

Wesley Farrington, C. P. A., is again at his desk at No. 203 Broadway, New York, having just returned after an extended sojourn in the Western States. Mr. Farrington's trip West was for the purpose of examining and auditing the accounts of a number of concerns which had been absorbed into the carriage and billiard-table trusts, respectively.

Did you notice the paper clip a facsimile of which is printed on our outside covers? It will hold a package of letters or papers one-fourth of an inch thick or less, with the grip of grim death. Send 20 cents to the Niagara Clip Co., 30 Broadway, New York, and they will mail you 250 of them. You will not regret the investment. Incidentally tell them what you think of their advertisement in this magazine.

It may not be generally known that there is now a board of Certified Public Accountants employed at 280 Broadway, New York, as special advisers to Comptroller Bird S. Coler. This board is officially known as the Commission on Revision of City Bookkeeping, and consists of John R. Sparrow, C. P. A., chairman; Daniel C. Tate, C. P. A. and Arthur W. Teele, C. P. A. This commission has been quietly and industriously at work since March, 1898. It was appointed during that month by Comptroller Coler to revise the methods of city bookkeeping and to state the accounts of Greater New York as constituted on Janury 1, 1898.

Immutable inks are a commercial rara avis. The manufacturers of one of the latest and best advertise in ACCOUNTICS this month. Send $1 to the Bankers' Safety Ink Co., 7 Cedar street, New York, and they will deliver a full pint bottle to you free, anywhere. This ink, of blue-black color, flows freely, neither eats paper nor corrodes pens, and cannot be removed by any known chemicals. A sample of writing done with the immutable ink advertised, which had been immersed in a bottle of pure water for a week, on removal was as live, clear and plain as the day it was written. Manuscript written with other inks subjected to the same test had faded somewhat.

Good typewriters are hard to get, and after you have got them, they are difficult to keep in perfect alignment and in repair. D. A. Gorman, of 79 Nassau st., New York, whose advertisement we print elsewhere, keeps all makes of typewriters, and sells, repairs and rents them. Those interested will do well to write for his special offers and circulars.

Among our book advertisements in this issue is that of Goodwin's Improved Bookkeeping and Business Manual, published by J. H. Goodwin, 1215 Broadway, New York. Among the many publications of "Every-ManHis-Own-Bookkeeper" type which have passed through our hands for review, we have rarely noted one of more merit than Mr. Goodwin's compilation. He offers "three dollars to any purchaser who will send to him a valuable point which he has discovered in his own experience, and which is not already covered in this book." In commendation of the book we would say that we think the prize would be a very difficult one indeed to win.

Paper clips are now being used by the business man more extensively than ever. Their price is down so low that they are about as cheap as pins. Clinch Paper Clip, which is advertised in this issue by G. D. A. Gorman, 79 Nassau st., New York, has a host of friends, and is making new ones every day. A box containing 250 will be mailed you postpaid on receipt of 20 cents.

Upon receipt of $2.50 ACCOUNTICS will deliver to you free an ideal Draft Record of 120 pages, printed on L. L. Brown Ledger paper and bound in a first-class manner, size $8\frac{1}{2}$x14, with capacity for recording 2,400 drafts. A book of this character will enable you to systematically record all data regarding draft collection (beginning with notification to drawee), in a form involving but little labor and showing at a glance the dates upon which drafts are to be made, as well as all subsequent details. This book is a great labor saver and an invaluable aid toward making prompt collections.

Noticeable is the gradual disappearance from office outfits of the ordinary press letter book. The perfection of carbon paper, the universal use of the typewriter and the advent of ball-pointed pens have probably contributed much to bring about this change. The newest and latest letter book which has been called to our attention is the one manufactured by the Pen-Carbon Manifold Co., of 221 Canal Street, New York, advertised elsewhere in this issue. They call it the Pen-Carbon Letter Book. It is a 200 page book, full indexed and well bound. The carbon sheet is attached to a clip which also holds the letter paper firmly while writing, and at the same time acts as a "handle" to the carbon sheet, which is never touched with the hands, and which prevents the possibility of soiling them. In the use of this book the simple act of writing the letter produces a beautiful copy at the same time, and this is accomplished with simply the users' own paper, pen and ordinary writing inks or pencil, so that the book can be used in the office, home, on the road, in the mountains, or anywhere. The manufacturers will send samples free on request, mentioning this notice.

Everybody nowadays uses fountain pens. We print in this issue the advertisement of the Soper Fountain Pen, which is manufactured at 89 Fulton street, New York. Those of our readers wanting a perfect fountain pen or desirous of having their fountain pen repaired will do well to write for Mr. Soper's special circular.

We are in receipt of the current issues of the Public Accountant, a monthly journal published in Philadelphia, and devoted to the interests of professional accountants. The latest issue of the the journal named contains interesting biographical sketches of the personnel of the Pennsylvania Board of Examiners of Public Accountants, a resume of the evidence required from Pennsylvania candidates for the C. P. A. certificate, and an account of the legislative death and burial of the proposed Wisconsin act to regulate the profession of public accountants in that State. The Public Accountant also makes editorial promises which are worthy of attention. "The Settlement of Fire Insurance Losses" (when the actual amount of money to be paid by the insurer can only be calculated from receipts for goods purchased and receipts for goods sent from the factory to the store of the burned out firm), the auditing of accounts of Masonic lodges and papers on "Vouchers" and "Expert Testimony" are all subjects to be touched upon and discussed in coming issues.

A unique advertising novelty to which our attention was called recently is a regulation No. 6 envelope made in Japan of a very thin sheet of wood pasted on a very thin sheet of paper. The paper has printed on it a variety of Japanese figures and designs. The envelope will probably never have any commercial value, except, perhaps, as an advertising medium. Its odd outward appearance and peculiar effect on the sense of touch, when handled, will at once strike the curiosity of the recipient and cause him to inquire further into its contents, etc. It is being imported by C. G. Davison & Co., 337 Broadway, New York.

Standard makes of typewriters at bargain prices are rare as oases in a desert. Nevertheless, we publish an opportunity of buying eight Elliott & Hatch Book Typewriters cheap from Frederick Loeser & Co., Brooklyn, N. Y. Prospective purchasers should write them for further particulars.

Volume V, Nos. 1 to 6
July 1899 to December 1899

Accountics

VOL. V JULY 1899 No 1

The Monthly Statement

In that portion of Bernard Dale's essay relating to the ascertainment of the profits for the year, which appears in another part of this issue, the author shows that permanency is not the certain test of fixed capital and that marketability is not an infallible indication of circulating capital. He shows that articles classed as "circulating" capital agrec in no one respect save that of being destined by their owner to be made profitable by parting with them, and that articles classed as "fixed" capital agree in no one respect save that of being destined to be made profitable by their owner retaining them. These fundamental distinctions are then illustrated and enforced by references to certain court decisions. English law on questions of this sort is perhaps clearer than anything that we have in this country, and yet the business done here, and the conditions affecting that business, are not unlike what prevails in the United Kingdom. Further, we use terms and names of our own, and therefore the words and phrases of our English cousins sometimes confuse us, or fail to produce a clear idea of the matter indicated. It is only by close study or very careful reading that we are able in many cases to perceive the likeness to our own affairs and to express the idea in our own words. The author's argument concerns every business man, and more especially every one who invests in a manufacturing plant, in a railway line, in a steamship company, or in any enterprise whatever in which a considerable part of the capital is expended for the machinery, equipment and facilities necessary for doing the business and in which another part is retained and used for the operation of the business, whatever it is. There certainly is a very important distinction between these two natural and inevitable divisions, but it is something that is very frequently overlooked by the management of the business and more especially in the way in which the books of account are laid out and conducted.

Almost every issue of the daily papers of late contains a list of recently formed trusts. To the casual observer it would seem that the country is trust mad at the present time. Already there looms up the trust as one of the leading issues of the next political campaign. There are trusts and trusts, some no doubt organized in defiance of law, for the purpose of monopolizing business and crushing out competition and raising prices, and others far more in number we believe than those of the first class,—which have for their object only legitimate business economies. A so-called trust to-day, of average capital, it may be asserted exercises no more influence in the community, and is relatively no stronger politically than was the individual or firm of a generation or two ago, with a cash capital of $100,000 to $500,000; considerations of this nature serve to put the trust in its proper light.

The conditions that the country faces at the present time demand business conducted upon a much larger scale than ever before. The disastrous competition of the last few years and the lack of profits in almost every line of trade have driven men to consider various propositions of reorganization and consolidation, which they never before have been willing to face. Circumstances are forcing them to throw aside the small clothes of childhood and to dress themselves as mature adults according to their positions in the world. Again the amount of executive ability in existence to-day is divided among for less men than there are business establishments to direct, and for this reason alone many concerns can profit by consolidation, for thereby they would secure a share at least of some able man's executive ability.

The trust is very much in the public eye to-day everywhere. It has its enemies and it has apologists as well. It is being discussed by almost every one. Accountants and business men are studying the trust—using the name now in a general sense and not in the least as a term of reproach—as a feature of the business situation and as a development in the general process of business evolution. What precedes the formation of a trust is the subject of an article presented on another page of this issue. It shows in an entertaining way the nature of the investigation that must be made by the promoter or projector of a trust and the facts of the situation that must be collected before capital will give the project any consideration. We commend it to the consideration of our readers as being a readable contribution to the business literature of the period. It may suggest to some of the young men among our readers the nature of an undertaking in which they may profitably engage, either now or at some future time. Opportunities of the kind cited exist in various directions. It is to be remembered in reading the article that it is only a study and not the announcement of a fact nor yet any part of the history of a corporation that has been formed.

The regents of the University of the State of New York have appointed as examiners for the degree C. P. A., for the year July, 1889, to June, 1900, inclusive, the following: C. W. Haskins, of the accounting firm Haskins & Sells, 30 Broad street, New York; John R. Loomis, 30 Broad street, New York, and A. O. Kittredge, President of the Account, Audit and Assurance Co., 25 Pine street, New York. All of these gentlemen are members of both the Institute of Accounts and the N. Y. State Society of Certified Public Accountants.

A moot question at the last convention of the Street Railway Accountants' Association was the disposition of taxes. Should taxes be considered an expense of operation, or something to be deducted from income? The meeting was divided on this point, and when the question was fairly before the house a considerable number of delegates were found ready to express their opinions. The younger element—we mean younger in railway accounting experience, not necessarily younger in years—soon indicated its preference for considering taxes an expense, regarding it as being something of the nature of a license, varying in amount from time to time according to valuations and rate of assessment, but under all circumstances of the nature of an expense necessary to be defrayed before any profits could be declared.

The older and more conservative element preferred to treat taxes as a deduction to be made from net income, although it seemed like a contradiction in terms to have a net income that should be subject to deductions of any sort. The men of this class argued that taxes, in amount, being something entirely beyond the control or influence of the management, was an item that the management could be in no wise responsible for, and that therefore it had no place among expenses of operation, for all of which, under proper restrictions, the management is justly responsible. Still other arguments that were presented included the fact that the steam railways are treating taxes as a deduction from earnings and also that the laws of various States require taxes to be so reported. The other side was quite ready to reply to these arguments. It was shown that mercantile and manufacturing corporations, as well as private firms generally, treat taxes of all kinds as an expense, and that from a proper accounting point of view it is quite right that they should do so. There would seem to be no proper exception to the general rule in the case of street railways.

So far as concerns the precedent set by the steam railways of the country, it was pointed out that in various respects steam railway accounting practice is not what it should be, owing in the main to the fact that the traditions of railway accounting were established, so far as the United States is concerned, during a period when accounting was less well understood than at present. On the other hand, street railways, as operations and investments, have come forward when times are propitious for doing things right. Without the incumbrances of incorrect and illogical precedents, the accountants in charge of street railway ventures ought to secure for them that which is strictly correct in principle and best in practice, the steam roads to the contrary notwithstanding.

So far as concerns the form of reports demanded by the different States, it was pointed out that proper accounting is one thing and the form in which a report is required to be made out quite another, and that accounts should be correctly kept irrespective of the rules that may be made by legislatures or boards of railway commissioners with respect to annual statements. With accounts showing actual results correctly, any form of statement, it was shown, can be made up that is demanded. Further, legislative committees that frame laws for the regulation of railway reports, and boards of railway commissioners charged with enforcing the regulations, are not accountants, and seldom, if ever, do they consult accountants in matters that come under their charge. Is it not strange, therefore, that some of their requirements are foolish if not unreasonable? They meant well when they acted, but they did not know, and they did not take the trouble to find out. Accordingly, as successive legislatures and boards of railway commissioners review the work of their predecessors, and by contact with practical accountants become acquainted with the real needs of the case, laws and rules are modified. Hence it appears that whatever may be the requirements of the law at present, these requirements are subject to change at any time, and are likely to be modified first and last, until that which is really correct has been finally spread upon the statute book. The modification in the ruling of the treasury department of the national government in the matter of the reports of condition of national banks which occurred some eighteen months or two years since, was referred to by way of illustration, and the argument was still further strengthened by brief reference to the modifications of treasury department regulations yet needed to bring them into line with logical and correct accounting practice.

Much more was said on both sides, but we have reported enough to indicate the trend of the discussion. The radical or younger element, as we have described it, it was soon admitted, had the best of the argument, and several who had at first espoused the cause of taxes as a deduction from income, indicated a change of heart. The question, however, was not formally decided. It was, at the suggestion of several, allowed to remain open pending such consultations with other bodies during the year as then appeared to be imminent. What has been done recently in this matter is recounted upon another page of this issue.

We are pleased to be assured that the representatives of the Street Railway Accountants' Association present at the conference reported finally assented to taxes as a deduction only because it seemed expedient so to do. They were not convinced of the correctness of the ruling, by any manner of means, but were of the opinion that some future occasion would be better than the present for a division on this point. We are disposed to commend their discretion in the matter, for oftentimes a compromise is very advantageous merely as a stay, being far better than prolonged dissension and discussion when more important matters are in hand.

It should not be lost sight of, however, that what has been done is nothing more than a compromise, good, no doubt, for a period of time, more or less extended according to circumstances, but in effect only a postponement of the inevitable. The item of taxes in itself is relatively unimportant. As a fact, it is a principle in accounting practice that is at stake and not merely the disposition of an expenditure.

When the Street Railway Accountants' Association of America has got through with mere bookkeeping details, such as the classification of expenses, and really begins to give attention to accounting as applied to street railways, we dare say it will perceive the bearing of such questions as this much more clearly than at present. By that time it will have secured a support among managers, stockholders, bondholders and financial men in general, which, as a relatively new organization, it cannot command. It will then be in position, by reason of the knowledge of its members and the following that it will command, to declare for accounting principles according to its convictions, no matter what the precedents may be and no matter what State boards of railway commissions may require in way of reports. Until that time arrives the compromise now agreed to should prevail.

The National Association of Credit Men

By A. O. Kittredge, F. I. A.

It is the midst of the vacation season. Office absentees are numbered by the score. There is no office that has its complete force at the present time. Those who are making a pretense of attending to business are either just back from a vacation, and therefore not yet down to work, or getting ready for a vacation, therefore hurrying matters, or doing two men's work for the sake of letting some other fellow have a vacation. Withal, the weather is the most trying of the year, and for these reasons, and others that might be mentioned, matters in credit circles are quiet, at least so far as they are manifested in the organizations, national and local.

* * *

Secretary W. H Prendergast assumed his official duties the first of the month, and in the short time that he has been in office has had opportunity to do little more than to become acquainted with the routine work and the requirements of the position. He has, however, conducted a somewhat extensive correspondence, and has had interviews with various prominent credit men, thereby getting into close contact with the opinions of the more active workers in the field. He has given particular attention to the planning of committee work and is co-operating with the chairmen of the several committees.

* * *

The formal annual meeting of the National Association was held according to appointment, and the proxies which had been accumulated for the occasion were duly voted, in accordance with the program agreed upon at the Buffalo convention. The National Association of Credit Men is a New York corporation, with its central office located in the city of New York. Accordingly, it is essential to transact its routine business at that point. The convention from year to year expresses its will, the individual members and the delegates appointed by local associations file their proxies, and then the meeting is held by a select few, in a way to comply with the law. President John Field came over from Philadelphia, and there were likewise present at the meeting James G. Cannon, ex-President, and F. R. Boocock, ex-Secretary. All that was transacted in a business way was merely routine.

* * *

President Field is giving the most careful consideration to the program to be mapped out for the work of the association for the current year, as well also as to matters of general policy. He has laid it down as a rule, from which there shall be no deviation, that the expenditures shall not exceed the income. While fully realizing that the income, even with the increase in dues that has been agreed upon, is still inadequate for as much work as it will be desirable for the association to accomplish during the year, at the same time he is firmly of the opinion that there is no other safe plan than to hold the effort strictly within the limits of the cash in hand. In this he will be sustained by the rank and file of the members everywhere. Just what the policy will be in various matters left largely to the discretion of the executive it is yet too soon to announce, but Mr. Field has taken hold of the work in a way to give all those who know his business-like methods and are acquainted with the aggressive and persistent efforts that he always puts forth the assurance that there will be no lack of success.

* * *

The news from local associations throughout the country is meager, and with few exceptions is of no particular interest or importance. Various organizations are giving careful attention to the program for the Fall and Winter months, and in no direction is there any indication of an abatement of interest.

Instead, all seem fired with enthusiasm and ready to take up work energetically as soon as the approach of Autumn makes conditions propitious for such effort.

'Tis true; for those that she makes fair, she scarce makes honest, and those she makes honest, she makes very ill-favoredly.—Shakespeare.

Meeting of Railway Accountants

The following account of an important meeting of railway accountants is from the Street Railway Journal, weeklyn news edition, of July 15. Our comments on the same appear upon one of the editorial pages of this issue.

At the request of William O. Seymour, engineer in charge for the Board of Railroad Commissioners of the State of Connecticut, and chairman of the special committee on standardization of accounts of the National Association of State Railroad Commissioners, a meeting was held in New York on July 11 to consider certain final questions of accounting practice preliminary to a final report to several national organizations of a standard system of steam and street railway accounting. There were present at the meeting, in addition to Mr. Seymour, Ashley W. Cole, chairman of the New York State Board of Railroad Commissioners; H. T. Billings, clerk of the Connecticut Railroad Commissioners; H. M. Kocherspergen, comptroller of the New York, New Haven & Hartford Railroad Company; J. D. Greene, auditor of disbursements of the Pennsylvania Railroad Company; C. N. Duffy, secretary and treasurer of the Citizens' Railway Company of St. Louis, and William F. Ham, auditor of the Brooklyn Rapid Transit Company. Messrs. Kocherspergen and Greene represented a committee appointed by the Association of American Railway Accounting Officers to assist the committee of the National Association of Railroad Commissioners, and Messrs. Duffy and Ham represented a committee of the Street Railway Accountants' Association of America, appointed to formulate a standard system of street railway accounting. High compliments were paid in the meeting to Messrs. Duffy and Ham upon the work of their committee, and the standard classification formulated by that committee was adopted substantially in its entirety for recommendation to the National Association of Railroad Commissioners as a general standard throughout the country. At the earnest request of Mr. Seymour and the railroad representatives at the meeting, based upon the almost universal practice in steam railroading, Messrs. Duffy and Ham consented to advise the Street Railway Accountants' Association to reverse its ruling that taxes should be included in operating expenses, and to class taxes as "deductions from earnings," although the basis for the present ruling was fully recognized and appreciated by all. As the matter stands now, it seems certain that the Railroad Commissioners of the country will, within a comparatively short time, establish a uniform system of accounting for steam and street railroading, by means of which comparisons between the results in different parts of the country can be readily obtained.

Value of a Stock Book

A large element in the success of any business is the ability to purchase goods properly. This is as true in the drug store as in any place else. There are several kinds of buyers: First, the plunger, who buys in large quantities simply because by so doing he can save a few cents a pound or dozen, not taking into consideration his reasonable wants at all; then the man who is interested in mere cheapness of price, losing sight of quality entirely in his endeavor to get a low quotation; next we have the buyer who is afraid to buy enough goods to supply his wants for fear he will overstock. It is plain to everybody that neither of these can be called a good buyer. A good buyer will not sacrifice quality for price, but will seek to buy goods as cheaply as possible; he will not buy in quantities in excess of his legitimate wants in order to save a few cents a pound, while he loses twice the amount saved in having the excess over his wants as dead stock.

In order to buy intelligently one must know how goods sell, what is a reasonable price to pay for them, and what grade of goods are best suited to his wants. Nothing gives a merchant so much information in regard to just what he wants to know as a well-kept stock book. Such a book will give just such information as is necessary to enable the buyer to have a complete record, not only of prices paid, but when and from whom purchased, and also the quantity purchased. In other words, such a book, if properly kept, is a complete history of purchases made, and as such is an indispensable aid to the intelligent purchasing of goods.

How are the Profits of the Year to be Ascertained?

By Bernard Dale

(Continued from page 107 of the May number.)

The examples given of "fixed" and "circulating" capital show (1) that permanency or durability is not the criterion of "fixed" capital, for the masquerade dresses and the funeral furniture let out on hire, to which Adam Smith refers, would be "fixed" capital, and yet one should hesitate to speak of them as assets of a durable and permanent nature; while, on the other hand, many of the assets used as "circulating" capital are extremely durable such as the hardware of an iron manufacturer and the land and buildings in the hands of a land-jobber; (2) that being marketable or readily saleable is not the criterion of "circulating" capital, for what is so readily salable as consols? And yet, as Macleod shows, consols in the hands of a permanent investor are a fixed capital.

The articles classed as "circulating" capital agree in no one respect save that of being destined by their owner to be made profitable by his parting with them, and the articles classed as "fixed" capital agree in no one respect save that of being destined to be made profitable by their owner retaining them. It is in these points of agreement between the constituents of each species of capital that we find its distinctive characteristic, and as on examination these characteristics appear to be the negatives or opposites of each other, we may be sure that we are dealing with a real division, and that every item of the genus capital will be found in one or other of its two species, "fixed" and "circulating"

Accepting the principle of division as above indicated, we are in a position to recognize, in addition to the instances cited above, the following assets of a company as "fixed" capital: The lands, patents, concessions or mining rights of a company formed to work them; the stocks forming the reserve of a bank (for these the company do not intend to make profitable by selling them, but by means of the increased business which a substantial reserve is calculated to attract); the factory, plant, machinery and trade implements of a manufacturing company; the raw materials and partly manufactured goods in the hands of a manufacturing company, for these the company do not intend to make profitable by selling them in their then state, but by retaining and using them in manufacturing operations until they emerge as finished goods; when, and not before, it can be said that their owner intends to make them profitable by selling them. Of this class of goods it may be affirmed that at one point of their career they are a "fixed" and at another a "circulating" capital, if, indeed, they have not entirely lost their identity in the course of their transformation into the finished product.

It must be borne in mind that any one of the above assets would have been a "circulating" capital in the hands of an owner who intended to make a profit by selling it; and also that frequently the intention of the owner toward an article used as "fixed" capital, say, machinery which has become obsolete, changes, and he determines to sell it, in which case it loses its character of a "fixed" and becomes a "circulating" capital. Then, again, as on the conclusion of a venture all the assets have to be sold, the assets used during the currency of the venture as "fixed" capital, become "circulating" capital.

The following are some cases in which the distinction drawn by economists between fixed and circulating capital appears to have been adopted by the courts as the ground of their decisions.

In the case of Salisbury v. Metropolitan Railway Company, 22 L. T. 839, the railway was a "fixed" capital, as the company were intending to make an income, not by its sale, but by its use. The company had not sufficient net receipts, including the rent of their surplus lands, to pay the year's dividend; but the surplus lands had greatly increased in value, and this increase the railway company sought to treat as profit, citing in support of their contention the practice of traders to value their assets for the purpose of the balance-sheet. V. C. James, however, after saying "that he had no doubt in valuing partnership assets an increase or decrease in the value of an article is treated, and properly treated, as part of the profit or loss at the end of the year," declined to allow the increase in value of the surplus lands to be treated as profit.

In the case of Midland Land and Investment Corporation, Limited, 8th November, 1866, the business of the company consisted of the purchase and sale of land. The company was therefore a land jobber or dealer. The revenue arising from the rents of the company's land, after payment of working expenses, was not sufficient to pay a dividend, but from valuations it appeared that there was an increase of value in the company's properties, and this increase the directors treated as profit. In the liquidation of the company it was sought to make the directors liable for the dividends paid out of this increase of value on the ground that their payment was ultra vires and Salisbury v. The Metropolitan Railway Company was relied on as showing that the estimated increase in the value of lands should not be taken into account in declaring dividends. Mr. Justice Chitty, however, distinguished the two cases on the ground that the railway was a "fixed undertaking," whereas the land of the Land Company was part of their ordinary stock-in-trade, and he held that the valuations having been made bona fide and by competent valuers, the dividends had been properly declared and paid.

Next consider the case of Verner v. General and Commercial Investment Trust, Limited. "Times" Law Reports, 7th March, 1894. Here the income from this company's investments, after payment of the year's expenses, amounted to several thousands of pounds; but on the other hand, during the year some of the investments had depreciated in value to an extent which more than counterbalanced the net revenue. Mr. Justice Sterling, after ascertaining from the articles that the business of the company was not to job in its investments, but to retain them permanently with the view of dividing annually the net income, held that a dividend might be declared, at the same time intimating that his decision would have been different "if he had been dealing with an ordinary trading company, e. g., if the object of the company had been to carry on a stockbroker's business and the investments had been ordinary stock-in-trade." In delivering the judgment of the Court of Appeal confirming this decision, Lord Justice Lindley said (L. R. Ch. Div., 1894, vol. 2, p. 239), "If the income of any year arises from a consumption in that year of what may be called circulating capital, the division of such income as dividend without replacing the capital consumed in producing it, will be a payment of a dividend out of capital within the meaning of the prohibition which I have endeavored to explain. Perhaps the shortest way of expressing the distinction which I am endeavoring to explain is to say that fixed capital may be sunk and lost, and yet that the excess of current receipts over current payments may be divided, but that floating or circulating capital must be kept up, as otherwise it will enter into and form part of such excess, in which case to divide such excess without deducting the capital which forms part of it will be contrary to law." And Lord Justice Kay in the same case said: "If the company were formed for the purpose of buying stocks, shares and the like for sale again, and their business was to make profit on such resale, it is obvious that any profit or loss on such transactions must be estimated in the way I have stated. But this is not their business. They buy stocks, shares and the like, and they have power to sell and change them. But they buy as investments, and do not look to the sale as a source of their profit."

Difficulties of Classification of Accounts

"It's hard work," declared the Filipino General. "I have taken an inventory and now I am making up the balance sheet. I don't know whether to put down this lot of left-over Spanish prisoners among the assets or liabilities."

His uncertainty was no greater than that of many a business man in some of the everyday details of business. Liabilities or expenses they really are, and yet he would fain consider them assets for the time being. He does this, trusting to the alchemy of events to change their nature, but they don't change. The last end of that man is worse than the first.

Dame Nature gave him comeliness and health; and Fortune, for a passport, gave him wealth.—Walter Harte.

What Precedes the Formation of a Trust.

By Rollin Jeffries

If it were necessary to this article to present a satisfactory definition of the word "trust," I might have to occupy so much space in explanation as would leave little or no room for anything else. Suffice it, therefore, to say, by way of introduction, that the word "trust,"—whatever may have been its original significance—has come to mean, of late, any business enterprise of unusual dimensions. Any corporation that takes over several small businesses—whether previously owned by other corporations or by private individuals or firms—is, in the common acceptation of the term, a trust. The term is usually applied as a reproach or as an insinuation that the enterprise is something intrinsically wrong. There may be excellent business reasons for the consolidation of several small businesses into one large enterprise. For example, the community may thereby be benefited by the ability of the consolidation to render better service or to turn out better product, or the business may be bettered in itself by the advent or more abundant capital and the services of abler managers. Whatever the reasons for change the temper of the public at present is such that the stigma of "trust" is almost invariably applied. With the assertion, therefore, that there are trusts and trusts, so far as concerns in the way in which the term is employed, we may drop the definition part of the present inquiry.

I take it that no man starts into business except he perceives a fair chance for profit. The abler business man he is, the more likely are his plans to be correct. The more knowledge he possesses of business conditions the more likely he is to plan intelligently. His enterprise may be either of several general kinds. It may be that of tilling the soil, or opening a mine, or building a factory, or entering upon some line of business not thoroughly developed in his community, and the absence of competition in which seems to afford him a special opportunity for profit. Whatever the line of business selected the governing principles are the same.

Wherever the individual, with large or small capital, starts in to improve a business opportunity and serve the community by increasing the supply of either the necessaries or the luxuries of life, thereby giving employment to more or less labor, and profitably using capital, he is looked upon as a benefactor; and yet the individual does nothing, in matters of this kind, that is different from what most of the so-called trusts do, save only in degree. The trust is an aggregation of capital usually many times stronger than any individual could be, but the conditions which prevail in the selection of a business for the trust, or in other words for the employment of extremely large capital, are exactly the same as govern the selection of a business for the individual, or for the use of moderate capital.

I shall use the term "trust" in this article, not in the sense of a corporation that by its management is a reproach, but, rather, by way of indicating the relative size of the business enterprise. A trust, I believe, may be just as honorable as an individual, and in turn an individual may have all the bad qualities and do all that is wrong and unjust in a business sense that is usually attributed by the opponents of progress to those aggregations of capital commonly called trusts.

At the outset some one must perceive the opportunity of profitable business in a certain direction before the organization of the corporation or trust is undertaken. In many lines of trade all the usual opportunities are already improved. Openings apparently do not exist. It is impossible, for example, to engage in trade to-day, in any of the common lines, with capital of the ordinary amount without entering into direct competition with some persons, firm or corporation already in that line, and who is thoroughly established. Any one investigating in this direction, therefore, would at once conclude there was little chance for a profitable trade in staple lines with average capital and average ability. The opportunities that existed in these channels in the past were seized upon according to the capital and business strength of the men then in the management of affairs, and have ever since been retained. To go into business to-day, therefore, one must proceed upon an altogether different plan. He must base his calculations of profit upon some improvement in the arts, or upon economies which were impossible on the old plan of doing business, or upon an output or turn-over many times larger than was possible upon the old plan, with corresponding advantages in buying and in expense of handling.

The so-called trust to-day, with a capital anywhere from a million to ten million dollars, is a no more important force in the community relatively than was the individual business man of a century ago, with a capital of one hundred thousand to five hundred thousand dollars. In itself, therefore, a trust cannot be declared to be evil, save only as all business is believed to be evil. That trusts do abuse their power is something that every one must admit, but that individual business men have likewise abused their power and influence ever since business was begun is also true.

What I want to get before the reader in this article is a study of the situation in a certain line of trade, which might afford the foundation of a so-called trust—that is, afford profitable employment to a large amount of capital by taking over a business which is now handled by a number of small operators, at a considerable cost to the community and at an apparent disadvantage to all concerned. What we shall do in this case is only what is usually done in what precedes the formation of a trust, so called.

Our investigation, which I again remark is only a study, is the coal distribution of a large city—for example, New York. Up to the present time the distribution of coal to factories, office buildings, stores, hotels and dwellings in the metropolis has been at the hands of a large number of small dealers employing their quota of teams and wagons, drivers, carriers, etc., and each of whom must maintain his own office and stand the general expenses of conducting a business. An examination of the situation reveals in this trade an opportunity for the employment of capital in one amount adequate for the purpose, and under one direction, that might prove advantageous. In other words there are apparently excellent opportunities in retailing coal on a large scale for making handsome profits on a considerable investment, while at the same time reducing prices to the consumer. There would also be the result ultimately of increasing the use of anthracite, both for domestic and manufacturing purposes.

The typical retailer of coal, as almost every one knows, is a man of comparatively small means, running a meagre plant, or acting merely as agent. As a fact, in the retail coal business in Greater New York there are upwards of five hundred dealers, not counting grocery stores and hucksters who are also engaged in the business. Adding the members of these branches of the trade, it would be within the limits of probability to say that as many as twelve hundred concerns are interested, in one way or another, in retailing coal. Of these careful investigation shows that two hundred and fifty yards do most of the business. It may be conceded, however, that every retailer concerned makes some profit out of the coal he handles.

There are variations from time to time in the retail prices of coal, but these are brought about for the most part by changes of wholesale rates, and accordingly there is always about the same margin between the price which the dealer pays for the coal and the price which he gets for it from his customers. The difference between buying and selling may be taken to average about $1.10 per ton, making a gross profit of from say 25 to 30 per cent. on cost. The net profit, of course, depends upon what it costs the dealer for handling. For the average yard and with fair operating facilities in a normal location, it costs to unload from the barges to the coal pockets, 10 cents per ton; for storing, 4 cents; for loss by screening, 10 cents; for cartage and distribution, 32 cents, and for miscellaneous expenses, including clerical work, rents and losses, 19 cents; making a total of 75 cents per ton for what may be termed operating expenses and necessary charges. The difference between this and the sales profit leaves a net profit of 35 cents per ton. For a dealer with a moderate trade ten thousand tons per annum is a fair year's business, and therefore nets him say $3,500.

Further study shows that it is the man who runs a small business in this way, handling nine thousand to ten thousand tons a year, at a profit of about 35 cents a ton, who sets the price. Economically speaking, it is to be inferred that his power to do this results from his personal acquaintance in his immediate district and from the absence of competition among large dealers not dependent upon direct association with their customers.

Engineers estimate that a moderate size coal plant, capable of handling say 500,000 tons per annum, would cost about $250,000. From this it appears that a profit of only 5 cents per ton would pay 10 per cent. on the cost of the plant. Dealers who tried to keep on making 35 cents a ton, or even 25 cents a ton profit, after such a plant was in operation would therefore have to move to another neighborhood. With all the distributors combined, serving the city from a few well located and large yards, and doing business not only with heavy trucks but with hucksters' wagons for small buyers, experts in the business say a handsome profit could be made, with a material reduction in price to the consumer.

With these facts developed by careful study and investigation, the promoter of the trust is ready to get out a prospectus. When this is ready capitalists are invited to investigate the figures which it contains. Noses are counted, and practical men for conducting the business are looked up and their records investigated. The plans are finally formed, and then on some bright morning the community wakes up to the fact that business has made another giant stride of progress, that old things have passed way and all has become new in the coal business. The Metropolitan Coal and Supply Company, if that be the name that is given the trust, has bought the necessary docks, has taken over by purchase the business of a considerable number of the the largest coal distributors, has started to build well designed, eligibly located coal plants, has contracted with certain coal mining companies for all their product, and has promised the community clean coal, prompt service, honest weights and low prices. So much for what precedes the formation of the trust. Next a word about what follows.

A howl at once goes up from the hucksters and the grocers and the small dealers that honest labor is being crushed by capital. So it was when the stage-coach men protested against the railway train, and when the tailors cried out against the sewing machine. Progress, however, was not stayed by their feeble opposition, nor is progress being stayed now by populistic opposition to business development and economical administration. The study as we have presented it is only a specimen of what thousands of bright men all over the country are doing.

The present period is one that perhaps in the future will be designated as the trust-forming period. Some so-called trusts are being established that are legitimate in conception, honest in purpose, capable in management and serviceable to the community, while also profitable to their stockholders. Other trusts there are, it must be admitted, that have no excuse for existence, and which are dishonest in their methods and therefore an absolute hurt to the community. Time undoubtedly will right the wrongs that are thus being done by crowding to the wall all those which are false to the community, and on the other hand will reward those which are honest in organization and management.

The formation of so-called trusts is likely to increase in the near future rather than diminish. The country in the last few years, in its natural growth, has forged far ahead of its business facilities. Business, of necessity, must hurry forward or lose its place in the race. The nation needs what so-called trusts are alone able to furnish just as much as it needs railways, which individuals are never able to build single-handed. We can no more endure business conducted in a small, expensive and unsatisfactory way, at the hands of men of mediocre ability and limited capital, than we can endure the stage-coach for transportation or the tallow dip for illumination.

A tutor, who tooted the flute,
Tried to teach two young tooters to toot;
Said the two to the tutor,
"Is it harder to toot or
To tutor two tooters to toot?"

One man pursues power in order to possess wealth, and another pursues wealth in order to possess power; which last is the safer way, and generally followed.
—South.

Whereas they have sacrificed to themselves, they become sacrificers to the inconstancy of Fortune, whose wings they thought, by their self-wisdom, to have pinioned.—Bacon.

Accountants' Associations

New York Chapter of Institute of Accounts

According to the precedent established several years ago no meetings of the New York Chapter of the Institute of Accounts are held in the summer months. This year the vacation period was commenced a month earlier than usual, and was made to include June. The first autumn meeting will be in September, the program of which, however, has not yet been announced.

Hartford Chapter

The June meeting of the Hartford Chapter of the Institute of Accounts was held on the evening of the 27th of that month. It was open to the public, and there was a large attendance of both members and guests. Gershom Smith, president, presided.

The speaker of the evening was the Hon. Jas. G. Batterson, President of the Travelers' Insurance Company, who delivered a most interesting address on the topic, "Are Corporations Beneficial to Society?" His arguments were in the affirmative of this question. Mr. Batterson stated at the outset that he would deal with the practical side of the question—a question of fact. He then defined a corporation to be a union of many persons with a common purpose, in an undertaking too extensive for a single individual or even for a common partnership. Commercial or business corporations, he declared, though organized primarily for profit, are ostensibly for the benefit of the public at large, and as a fact they do serve the public.

The Standard Oil Company is commonly quoted as a great monopoly which is not beneficial to society. Dr. J. B. Terry, a Hartford man, was the first to distill "kerosene oil" from petroleum, but the process was very expensive. Later a young man applied to a Cleveland bank for a loan of $2,000 to enable him to experiment in the production of kerosene. The bank declined the loan on the ground that the risk was too great. The President of the bank, however, saw possibilities and advanced the money from his private funds. The young experimenter was successful. His name was John Rockefeller. The manufacture of kerosene oil was thus begun, and it gradually became the illuminant of the world. It was at first transported in large tank cars. Later the Standard Oil Company was organized and smaller companies were combined with it. Pipe lines were built, through which the oil could be made to flow in a steady stream to the centres of distribution, thereby largely reducing the expense of transportation and thus lessening the cost to consumers.

This consolidation of companies is called a "trust." In what way has the public been harmed by the Standard Oil Trust? The Standard Oil Company, by its resources and economies, was enabled to supply the oil at a lower cost than prevailed before its organization, and still make a profit. It was prospering without the small dealers who did not enter the combination. The small dealers, however, could not compete with it, and the public would not help the small producers, but preferred instead to buy where it could buy the cheapest, and thereby reap the benefits conferred by the trust.

Mr. Batterson next called attention to the great railway corporations of the country, and stated that the so-called Vanderbilt System—the greatest of all the combinations in the field—has done more for the development and expansion of the United States than all the others taken together. The inconvenience to the traveling public in changing cars frequently upon what would now be considered only a short trip was overcome by a combination of several connecting lines, making possible the running of through trains long distances. Expenses were thus diminished, and the value of the shares of stock of the several roads rose, so that the many small holders as well as those owning larger blocks of stock, were benefited. The speaker declared that the phenomenal fortunes of many of those interested in the great corporations has needlessly excited the criticism of the people. He paid his respects to General Master Sovereign, of the Knights of Labor, quoting an extract from his pen to the effect that corporations are inimical to public interests (Page 95 of "Labor and Capital"). These views were combatted by Mr. Batterson by the assertion that a State is not wealthy by reason of the cash balance in its treasury, but rather by the wealth in property of its citizens upon which revenue may be raised by taxation.

The New York Central, he pointed out, has about 23,000 owners, or stockholders, and the beneficial result to them is trifling compared with that to the public.

The speaker supported his arguments by reading many statistics.

The address was profoundly interesting and instructive, and was listened to with careful attention from beginning to end. The comments of the daily papers in reporting this meeting clearly indicated that the Chapter secured a star speaker when Mr. Batterson agreed to address it. These accounts also indicate that the Hartford Chapter in the comparatively short time it has been in the field has become one of the prominent and extremely useful technical institutions of Connecticut's capital city.

No meetings of this body will be held in July and August. The September meeting is to be devoted to a discussion of savings banks and their methods.

A Valuable Catalogue

A catalogue just received from the Globe Company, Cincinnati, with branch offices in New York, Boston and Chicago, is No. 29 in series, and is entitled "Globe-Wernicke Elastic Cabinets." The subtitle is "A System of Units." Our readers are already familiar with the Globe-Wernicke system, which is so thoroughly adapted to business men's wants, that they may begin with a single unit and end with a complete office equipment, and yet during the time the articles were accumulating never have bought a single item in advance of actual requirements. The units are arranged to fill almost any shape of available space, to build up in all kinds of combinations, and in every respect to be adjusted to suit the exigencies of the business. The illustrations in the catalogue are a special feature, and show various adaptations and combinations of the greatest interest to business men. It is the most complete and satisfactory exposition of the unit system that has yet been put before the public. Many of the cuts are in half-tone, and the book, from beginning to end, is full of such information as business men will be glad to have at hand, whenever considering the question of a change in or addition to their office equipment. It will be sent to all applicants who mention this notice in ACCOUNTICS.

Self-Made Men.

By Walton Day.

Somebody has said in regard to self-made men that "he made himself and didn't quite finish the job." This may not be exactly true, but certainly, to use a carpenter's illustration, "the man who works on himself can very rarely see whether he is out of wind or not." In other words, his weak points, which are those of humanity in general, are not likely to be apparent to him. Consequently he has a large supply of the faults which teachers usually correct in their scholars. These weaknesses are not easily corrected later in life.

There is one leading fact that stands out to prevent the progress of the self-made man. He cannot learn anything as other men do. Lack of discipline in youth prevents him from assimilating or understanding experiments or truths which other men have made or discovered. He may read in books that a certain amount of nitric acid is capable of dissolving a given quantity of silver, but that fact is of no use to him until he has weighed out his silver, measured his acid, put the two together and submitted them to heat until solution has taken place. In a word, he does not know anything until he has learned it experimentally.

Another weakness is his unlimited faith in science, provided always that the science is wild enough. Downright, hard-fisted science, maxims of which are to be found in books and the calculations of which are based upon consecutive reasoning, does not appeal to him. He is incapable, as a rule, of following such a line of deductive reasoning or being convinced by it; but he is willing to put half the chemicals in a drug store into all the liquids he can think of, set them in bottles on his shelves and wait for their solution with the expectation that some new wonder may grow out of them, very much as corn might sprout. Scientific deduction of cause from an effect is out of the question. His early training has been already too diffuse, and he has not had sufficient drilling in downright mental hard work to enable him to see the scientific relation of fundamental facts or even to grasp them. Even the ability to study has often been denied him, and while he is capable of long-continued exertion, he does not find his mind fitted for the hard application which is necessary in acquiring modern scientific facts.

Globe Post Binder.

The accompanying ilustration shows a new form of Post Binder recently introduced to office men by the Globe Company, with factory at Cincinnati and sales departments in Chicago, New York and Boston. The binder is made in all standard sizes, and is distinguished from those heretofore in the market by its simplicity of parts, neatness of finish and ready adjustment. The contained sheets are clamped in place by mechanism which is operated by the small stud which is seen projecting through a slot in the casing. Pushed to the right, the cover may be readily removed. Pushed to the left the cover is clamped upon the posts in such a way that it may be forced downward, but cannot by any ordinary effort be forced upward. Accordingly, the papers may be put in place and the cover tightly compressed with the assurance that the mechanism will hold all securely in place. The parts are extremely simple, and there is absolutely

THE GLOBE POST BINDER.

nothing to get out of order. The operation of the device, being by the stud already referred to, is very much easier and quicker than that of binders using a key, either at the end or side. The contained mechanism is far preferable to that which is exposed, whether in the form of springs or grips. The Globe Post Binders are made with heavy board covers, encased in duck, and reinforced at the corners with leather. Those who have used this device are well pleased with it, and readily give it a preference over others with which they are acquainted.

Pocket Time Stamp.

Yankee ingenuity is "to the front" again with a compact, complete "time stamp," with a height of only 4½ inches and a weight of 10 oz. It is small enough and light enough, it will be observed, to be carried in the coat pocket, if necessary. S. H. Hoggson & Co., of the Thames Building, New York, have just put before the public the time stamp shown in the

NEW TIME STAMP.

accompanying cut, which they sell for $12 net. It is not much larger than the ordinary rubber desk hand stamp, and prints, after the manner of the rubber dating hand-stamp, year, month, day, hour and minute. It is adapted to use in the receipt or delivery of goods and telegrams, and may be employed in the cancellation of revenue stamps. It is useful in recording rentals of billiard tables, employes' time, watchman's doings, etc. It is admirably adapted for use on mail trains, steamships and trolley cars, since, as the manufacturers claim, shaking or jarring does not interfere with its operation. The device requires no electric batteries, wires or connections, air tubes or other complicated mechanism that gets out of order. It prints directly from its own die, on a rubber air cushion, in any colored ink desired, and gives a clear, clean impression. It is now employed by many leading concerns, who express great satisfaction with its operation.

How Should Accounts Payable be Treated? *

Frank W. Hawley, M. I. A.

Probably the most common method among mercantile houses of treating invoices or bills to be paid, is to enter them in a journal or substitute book of original entry and post them from there into a ledger. When the bills are paid the cash is posted to the opposite side of the account and the transaction closed. This system has its advantages but it does not seem to me to be in keeping with the progress made in other branches of accounting.

The system that I shall attempt to describe is one which involves no posting of individual items, but the entire record is kept in one book, the original entry for each invoice being the final one. This book, which I shall call Purchase Record, is ruled as shown in the front of the accompanying diagrams. First, there is a space for the name of firm billing goods, and the address, following which are columns for date, amount of bill, total, rebates and allowances, cash discount and transportation. All of which need no explanation. Next is a column for any charges which may be in the ledger against the firms represented in the Pur-

NAME	ADDRESS	Date	Amount of Bill	Total	Rebates and Allowances		Cash]
					Explan.	Amount	Rate

FO

DEPOSITS			Number of Check	FAVOR	ACCOUNT
Date	Amount				

FO

*Read before the Hartford Chapter of the Institute of Accounts, May 23, 1899.

chase Record. These amounts are deducted in settlement the same as discount, transportation and other items, and posted direct from the Purchase Record to the Ledger, balancing the charges there. The columns following are "Net amount to be paid" and "Date of payment." If nothing but merchandise bills are entered in the Purchase Record and the merchandise all of one class, there need be no further ruling. If, however, it is necessary for the invoices to be apportioned over a number of accounts, as many more columns may be added as desired and the amount of each invoice charged to its proper account in the column which represents that account.

The first pages of each month's record should be preserved for cash bills. These bills may be entered as often as desired and if the deductions are placed in that proper columns at the time of entering no further reference to the invoice is necessary. I think it preferable to make out remittance sheets after each lot of invoices are entered, and as each sheet is completed, take the net amount of same and enter in the "Net amount" column in the Purchase Record. After the remittance sheets have all been made out, the book may be footed and if the "Net amount" column plus the amounts of columns containing the deductions equal the total of the column containing the gross amount of invoices your work on the book is shown to be correct, as well as the correctness of the remittance sheets proved.

isportation	Ledger Charges		Net Amount Payable	Date Paid	DISTRIBUTION OF ACCOUNT						
									SUNDRIES		
	Page	Amount							Name of Account	Ledger Page	Amount

ICHASE RECORD.

CREDIT				DEBIT						
					LEDGERS					
er Oak Bank 't of Check	Ledger Page	Chk	SUNDRIES General Ledger	Accounts Payable	Page	Chk	General	Out of Town	City	OFFICE CASH

IK CASH BOOK.

These remittance sheets may be arranged in the order that they become due so that each day the remittance sheets for the bills due that day will be on top. I think this method of keeping tabs on the maturity of bills preferable to having a column in the Purchase Record for each day in the month, owing to the large amount of space saved and other reasons which I think are apparent. Time bills may be entered at stated periods during the month or held until the end of the month. It is desirable, however, where there are a number of bills due one concern, that they be grouped together, in order that they may be footed and show the total amount due that concern for the month.

After all the invoices for the month have been entered the several columns may be footed and posted to the debit or credit of the ledger as is proper. The net amount of invoices being credited to Accounts Payable.

It is desirable, though not necessary, where this system is in use to have two cash books, one for office or safe cash and one for bank cash. On the payment side of the Bank Cash Book are columns for check numbers, name of party check is in favor of and amount. There is also a column headed "Accounts Payable," in which should be placed the amounts of checks drawn for accounts in the "Purchase Record." The other columns in the Bank Cash Book need not be described as they are not concerned in this subject.

Checks are drawn directly from this book, no stubs being necessary. At the end of each month when the Bank Cash Book is footed the total of the "Accounts Payable" column is charged to the Accounts Payable account in the Ledger. The difference between the two sides of the account will show the total of the invoices remaining unpaid in the "Purchase Record."

With this system should be used a specially ruled index divided on the second or third letter. A column at the left should contain names and if desired, addresses, and the balance of each page ruled for page numbers. Each invoice should be indexed according to the page on which it appears in the "Purchase Record." By providing an index of large capacity and leaving sufficient space for each firm the index will show in one place the pages of the "Purchase Record" on which appears the name of any firm for a number of years, if desired.

If preferred, the entry for each invoice may be numbered and these numbers indexed instead of page numbers, but in a large business it takes but a very little while for the invoice numbers to reach four figures, while it will take as much longer for pages to reach that point as there are lines on a page, and for all practical purposes the page number is sufficient. This system may be varied in many ways to satisfy individual preferences or provide for the particular requirements of any business, without affecting the main principle. Also any form of remittance sheet or voucher desired, may be used in connection with it, as may also any system of filing invoices.

I have carefully compared this system with that which involves posting into the ledger and have failed to find any question regarding the condition of any individual account or Accounts Payable as a whole, which could be answered by a ledger any more fully than by the "Purchase Record" book. Probably the most formidable objection which would arise in the mind of any one not acquainted with this system would be that the volume of business with any particular firm for a year or period of years could not be easily arrived at. This objection is for the largest part overcome by the index by which the location of the bills of any firm can be easily found. The other part, I think, is of very little consequence, as after an account is settled the occasion for looking up same is not of frequent occurrence.

It will be seen that by the use of this method of treating Accounts Payable, not only the labor of posting is obviated, but it also does away with the labor incident to carrying a Purchase Ledger with from one hundred to perhaps many thousand accounts and drawing off a trial balance every month.

In accounting, the object is not to take a procession of figures and demonstrate how beautifully, accurately and scientifically we can put them through the mazes of many manipulations and bring them out again without losing their identity, but to get at results by the shortest cut consistent with leaving behind us tracks which may be easily traced by the auditor or any one who has occasion to follow us.

Interest and Discount—VI

By Charles W. Rohne

Present Values.

The present value of a specified rate of $1, due at the end of a specified number of years, is a sum which improved at the specified rate would at the end of the term amount to $1. Thus the present value at 3 per cent., of $1,000, due in ten years, would be $744.09, this being the sum which would, at 3 per cent, amount to $1,000 in ten years.

The present value at a specified rate of an annuity of $1 for a specified number of years, is a sum which, improved at a specified rate during the term, would provide for the annual payments as they severally became due. Thus, $853.02, being the present value at 3 per cent. of an annuity of $1000 during the next ten years, is the sum which, invested now and improved at 3 per cent, would just provide at their maturity for the ten annual payments of $100 each.

Every Sum of Money is Equivalent to the Sum of the Present Values of an Infinite Series of Future Payments.

The investigation of the theory of the value of land demonstrates a proposition of great importance in economics. It is seen that $100,000 given to purchase an estate in land expected to produce $3,000 a year, is in reality the sum of the rights to its future products forever. Each annual product has a present value, and the value of the land is simply the sum of this infinite series of present values. But the same is evidently true of every sum of money. Hence, every sum of money is not only equal in value to a certain quantity of material goods, or to a certain quantity of services, but also to a perpetual annuity. The lowest form of an annuity is the right to receive a single future payment, such as a bank note, a check, or a bill of exchange. The highest form is the right to receive an infinite series of future payments, such as the land or the funds. And there may also be the right to receive a limited number of future payments intermediate between the two, which is called a terminable annuity. Hence, an annuity or the right to receive a series of future payments is an economic quantity, which may be bought or sold or exchanged, or whose value may be measured in money, like any material chattel. As when a sum of money is given to purchase land or the funds or municipal or other obligations, such as railway debentures. So an annuity may be paid to secure a certain sum of money at a given time, or on a given contingency, such as a life or fire insurance.

It is thus seen that economics comprehends three great departments: (1) Material things, (2) personal qualities, (3) annuities.

The first school of economists restricted their attention to the first of these departments, and refused to take any notice of the other two. Adam Smith, J. B. Say and J. S. Mill have given much attention to the second, and treated labor as a marketable commodity. They have also noticed the existence of the third department, but they never made any attempt to exhibit the commerce in rights. And yet, at the present day, it is the most extensive of any, because it comprehends the whole theory of the value of land, the funds, mercantile credit, banking, the foreign exchanges, shares in commercial companies and all other incorporeal wealth.

Interest Tables.

Formulas, by means of which all the values to be found in interest tables can be independently calculated as required, are usually given in complete algebras and in text books on the subject of life insurance, but it is evident that such a process would be tedious, and that the convenience is great of having those values that will be commonly wanted ready prepared and presented in tabular form.

The solution of many problems, too—such, for instance, as finding the rate of interest involved in a term of annuity—is rendered very much more easy by a reference to tables, and to the skilful actuary they are at all times invaluable auxiliaries in his work. It will be frequently noticed that where a novice goes through an intricate calculation in answering a question, the adept produces the same result seemingly without thought or effort, and on inquiry it will usually be discovered that tables are the tools he used to shorten his labor and save his time.

An intimate acquaintance with the nature of the tables he may find in his hands is essential to the actuary, for without that knowledge he cannot turn them to the best account. It is therefore very desirable for the student to practice the construction of the tables for himself, although those he may require may already be in print, as by actual experience in their manufacture he will much more readily obtain a clear knowledge of the properties of his tools than by any theoretical study.

In interest tables the functions most commonly tabulated for each rate of interest are the following:

1. The amount of 1 in any number of intervals.
2. The present value of 1 due at the end of any number of intervals.
3. The amount of annuity of 1 for any number of intervals.
4. The present value of an annuity of 1 for any number of intervals.
5. The sinking fund which will redeem a debt of 1 in any number of intervals; or, in other words, an annuity which will accumulate to 1 in any number of intervals.
6. The annuity for any number of intervals which 1 will purchase.

The values under each heading are arranged in columns commencing with the value of one interval and finishing generally with that for 100 intervals.

The following is an example of the form the interest table sometimes assumes:

the columns, one to six, for each rate of interest, rising by ¼ per cent., from 3 per cent. to 6 per cent., and not only does he do so, but for each rate of interest he also gives the values of all the functions when interest is convertible either yearly, half yearly or quarterly.

Some tables, instead of supplying the values for interest convertible half yearly or quarterly, very minutely subdivide the rate of interest and also being with very small rates. In this way they answer the same purpose as Corbaux's tables. Thus, an annuity of 111 per annum, payable quarterly for 20 years, at 4½ per cent., interest convertible quarterly, is equivalent to an annuity of 25 per annum for 80 years at 1⅛ per cent. interest convertible yearly. We therefore see that in speaking of interest tables it is more appropriate to name intervals, as we have done, rather than years.

The tables of Col. Oakes, published in 1877, are of the last named description. They furnish columns one to four at each rate of interest, rising ⅛ per cent. from ¾ per cent. to 10 per cent.

We have said that it is usual to tabulate functions of all values from 1 to 100, but for ordinary purposes a table to such an extent is not essential, and it is not often in practice that the values and amounts of annuities are required for so long a period as 100 years. A table, too, may be effectually used for longer terms of years than it actually includes. Thus, suppose there is a table which goes up to 50 years only, and it is required to find the value of the functions for 60 years. We have $(1+1)^{60} = (1+1)^{50} \times (1+i)^{10}$, $V^{60} = V^{50} \times V^{10}$, etc., etc. It is, however, convenient to possess extensive tables, especially if they are of the description of those of Oakes and not of Corbaux, and we must use them for intervals instead of years; because, for example, an annuity

n.	1.	2.	3.	4.	5.	6.
1	1.050000	.952381	1.00000	.95238	1.000000	1.050000
2	1.102500	.907029	2.05000	1.85941	.487805	.537805
3	1.157625	.863838	3.15250	2.72325	.317209	.367209
4	1.215506	.822702	4.31013	3.54595	.232012	.282012
5	1.276282	.783526	5.52563	4.32948	.180975	.230975
6	1.340096	.746215	6.80191	5.07569	.147017	.197017
7	1.407100	.710681	8.14201	5.78637	.122820	.172820
8	1.477455	.676839	9.54911	6.46321	.104722	.154722
9	1.551328	.644609	11.02656	7.10782	.090690	.140690
10	1.628895	.613913	12.57789	7.72173	.079505	.129505
etc.	etc.	etc.	etc.	etc.	etc.	etc.

FORM OF AN INTEREST TABLE.

Corbaux, in his work published in 1825, "Doctrine of Compound Interest," supplies very complete tables. He gives all

for 25 years at 5 per cent. payable quarterly, is eqivalent to one at 1¼ per cent. for 100 intervals.

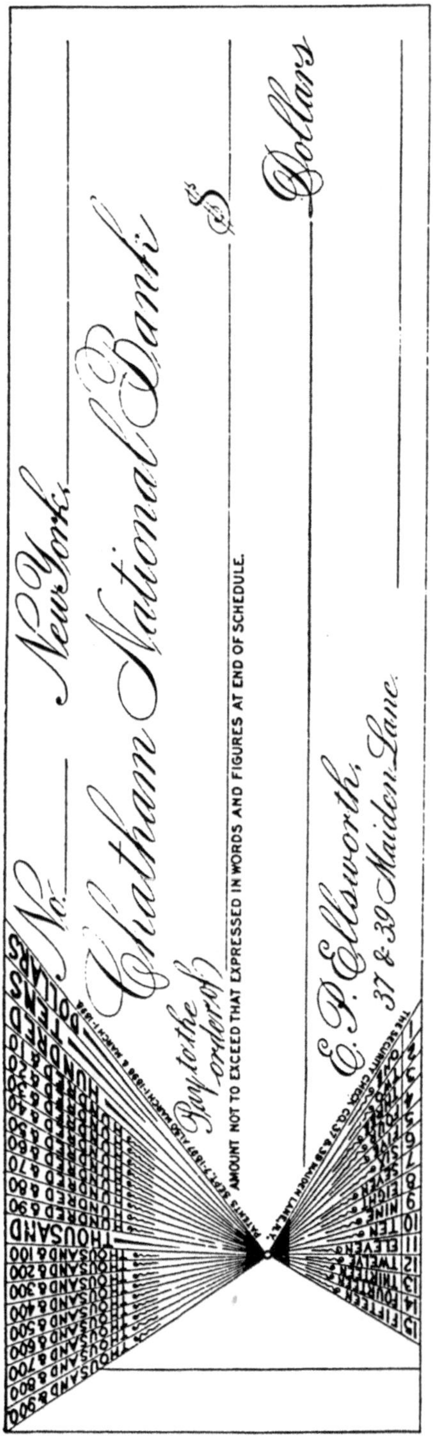

Safeguard Against Alteration of Checks and Drafts.

The very latest device for safeguarding against the alteration, mutilation and forging of checks, drafts, notes and other monetary papers is shown in the cut printed below. The rapidity and ease with which it finds favor among all classes of business men indicate that it has come upon the market to stay, and perhaps to crowd out the numerous perforating devices, check-punchers, safety papers and inks which are now in very general use.

The need for absolute safeguarding devices is urgent. According to clippings furnished by a clipping bureau and collated by the manufacturers of this device, the newspapers throughout the United States report from three to four hundred instances weekly of bank check and promissory note frauds, an average of fully three hundred and fifty a week. These figures, the manufacturers believe, represent only a percentage of such frauds, because many banks and depositors when hit accept their loss and suppress the facts.

Inks designed to resist the action of acids and alkalies have been repeatedly put upon the market, but it is claimed so far no ink has proved its title to safety. For example, a manufacturer recently put an ink upon the market containing a carbon that neither acid nor the ordinary bleaches would touch; good chemists using chemicals which their experience suggested failed to remove it from the paper, but finally it was discovered that a damp sponge would wash it off, leaving scarcely a trace on the paper.

Instead of depending upon something placed upon the paper, which can be removed or placed at pleasure, this new device takes away a part of the paper itself, which cannot be replaced.

Defalcations such as that which a few weeks ago wrecked the Middlesex County Bank at Perth Amboy, N. J., would also be rendered impossible by this device. In the case of the Middlesex County Bank, its embezzling cashier, George M. Valentine, pursued the method of filling out a draft on the National Park Bank, the New York correspondent of the Middlesex Bank, for a large amount and filling in the stub in the draft book for a smaller amount. The result was, when the crash came, that the Middlesex Bank books showed that the National Park owed it $80,000, while the National Park Bank's books showed the Middlesex Bank $30,000 overdrawn — a state of affairs which would never have been possible had this latest safeguarding system been in use by the Middlesex Bank. For the most casual inspection of the Middlesex County draft book would have shown that drafts had been drawn for a larger amount than were entered in the stubs.

The ordinary check is printed from 1½ to 2 inches longer than usual, and on the left of the check, within the additional space thus gained, is printed the safeguarding device or schedule shown in the cut. Further than this, the words directing the payment of money are qualified by the following printed into the body of the paper: "Amount not to exceed that expressed in words and figures at the end of the schedule."

After the drawer has properly written in the amount of money directed by the paper to be paid, he adjusts a small, sharp-edged ruler or paper cutter to that line of the upper half of the schedule which bounds the maximum amount to be paid in dollars, tens, hundreds or thousands, and tears off the check down as far as the small ring in the centre of the schedule. Then he revolves his ruler, as though upon a pivot, and adjusts it to that line of the lower half of the schedule which bounds the number of dollars, tens of dollars, hundreds or thousands to be paid, and then completes the tearing of the check from the stub along that line. The lower or left hand division of the schedule becomes the numerator of a fraction showing how many units, tens, hundreds or thousands are taken, while the upper portion determines the value, whether ones, tens, hundreds or thousands.

This one act of tearing automatically accomplishes a twofold result. It leaves in the hand of the check-drawer, the customary check absolutely safeguarded against alteration, for the left-hand margin expresses in words and figures the amount "not exceeding" for which it has been drawn, and it leaves in the checkbook the customary stub, which also shows by the left-hand margin, by simple process of subtraction, the amount for which the removed check has been drawn.

When it is considered that the drawer of a check is chargeable with the amount paid on it, provided his signature be proved genuine, no matter for what amunt he has previously filled it in, the value of the device can hardly be overestimated.

Although this ingenious device has only been on the market a few months, it is already in active use by upward of 150 banks and trust companies. Several railroad companies are using the device upon their "pay-checks," and banks are using it upon their cashiers' checks.

The company introducing the device is the Security Check Co., 37 and 39 Maiden Lane, New York, and has on its directorate the names of Maurice L. Muhleman, Deputy Assistant Treasurer of the United States at New York, and Alvah Trowbridge, President of the North American Trust Co., New York—sufficient guarantee of the merit of the novelty.

Passbooks vs. Certificates of Deposit.

Certificates of deposit are rapidly becoming unpopular, and almost all trust companies have discontinued giving them, furnishing in their place a passbook, like a bank passbook, containing simple deposit entries, and against which the depositor can draw his checks. The explanation for the change is this: The new United States Internal Revenue law provides that stamps to the amount of two cents upon each $100 shall be affixed to every certificate of deposit drawing interest, such as were formerly issued by trust companies for money deposited with them. The interest usually allowed by the companies being only 2 per cent. per annum, or $2 on the $100, the tax of two cents per $100 amounted to the interest for nearly four days and greatly discouraged the making of deposits. Hence the change of business methods on the part of the trust companies.

"Who would a-thought it?" exclaimed the old man, rapturously; "here's John turned out to be a writer fer the papers."

"Do tell!"

"Hit's a fact! Here's a paper what says he sells bacon cheaper an' cheaper, an' they jest can't beat him on flour, an' his name signed to the whole piece!"—Atlanta Constitution.

There is but one good throw upon the dice, which is, to throw them away.

—Chatfield.

Questions and Answers
Concerning the
BALANCE-SHEET SYSTEM OF ACCOUNTS
Conducted by the
Account Audit and Assurance Co., Ltd.
25 Pine Street, New York

Special Account Books.

From J. W. C. Wheeling:

Does the Balance Sheet System of accounts require an equipment of special books? Can ordinary account books be used? If special books are required, do you furnish them? Are they many or few in number?

Answer: We have installed the Balance Sheet System of Accounts without employing any special books save only the Balance Sheet Ledger, and this book we always furnish. It is included in the price of the installation. In other cases we have employed special books throughout. It depends upon the nature of the business, the departments into which it is divided, the number of the daily transactions and various other conditions essentially special to each and every enterprise. What we aim to secure in every case is that which is best for the business in hand. Where books of special ruling will save labor or secure a better analysis than ordinary books, we do not hesitate to recommend their use. In fact, we practically insist upon them by making such special rulings an essential part of the specification.

We design all the books that may be required in use with the system, as a part of our specification work, but do not include the cost of making the books in our prices on installations. Sometimes the special books required are very few. In other cases they run into a considerable amount of money. We do the designing and specifying, leaving the purchase of the books to the discretion of our client.

What is the Balance Sheet Method?

From S. W. V., Elizabeth, Pa.:

I have carefully perused your advertisements and circulars and have determined to make a change in my bookkeeping system. July 1 will be a convenient date. I would like, however, in advance, more of an idea of what the Balance Sheet Method is and how the results it promises are accomplished.

Answer: We are quite willing to contribute as much as we are able to your conception of the method or system we offer you and the manner of its operation. Allow us to state at the outset, however, that you are more interested in the results accomplished by our plans than you are in the details of those plans. While it is comparatively easy to tell you just what the Balance Sheet System of Accounts will do for your business in the way of showings, it is difficult, through the medium of correspondence at least, to explain just how the results are reached. It is for still another reason that we put the results first. We are proceeding upon the idea that the object of all accounting is to produce a perfect balance sheet. A perfect balance sheet must be a correct showing of the conditions of the business. A correct showing of the business is the best foundation upon which to base plans of management. With a clear conception of what the managing business man requires in this regard we first chart what the Balance Sheet Ledger is to be made to show, and then proceed to adjust the bookkeeping details in accordance therewith.

While accounting principles are inflexible, bookkeeping details can be adjusted to suit any and every requirement. The bookkeeping details usually employed with the Balance Sheet System of Accounts are simpler and more economical of labor than those in common use. In many cases we retain much of what is already in use. In any event we never make a change merely for the sake of a change.

There are two possible points of view in all accounting work. These may be described as prospective and retrospective. The usual plan occupies the latter. A given fiscal period, six months or a year, is reviewed and a statement or balance sheet made up to embody the results of the business as they are found to be. The Balance Sheet System occupies the former. A skeleton balance sheet is made out in advance and the accounts are so managed that the transactions of every day take their place in proper order in it, thus producing a going or perpetual balance sheet. The changes in the bookkeeping details are only those necessary to this change in point of view.

The Balance Sheet System of Accounts is sometimes described as double entry rounded out and perfected. It embodies a rigid enforcement of a classification of accounts on balance sheet principles, and the employment of the Balance Sheet Ledger, which is merely a convenient means to the end in view. The only accounts in the Balance Sheet Ledger are those which would appear in a complete balance sheet of the conventional kind, made up at the end of a fiscal period. The daily transactions as the business proceeds are classified upon the same plan and are posted in like order. Starting with a balance sheet and adding daily thereto the transactions of the business, the result is a balance sheet at all dates.

The Balance Sheet System in addition to many other valuable showings keeps constantly before the merchant a comparison of his expenses and his income. By income we mean the difference between the cost of the goods and the selling price. He is therefore afforded by it the exact information that he needs in making his plans and in giving directions to his subordinates.

Wide Applicability.

From R. J. C., Detroit:

Kindly send me your advertising matter. I am in search of a bookkeeping scheme particularly applicable to a manufacturing business. I also want a bookkeeping scheme for the care of an estate which involves various investments in stocks and bonds, mortgages, rental properties and in unsecured loans. I suppose, however, it is hardly fair to expect any given system to work with correspondingly satisfactory results in such diverse lines.

Answer: The Balance Sheet System of Accounts is equally applicable to all lines of business in which profit and loss statements and balance sheet showings are usual and proper exhibits. As the first step there is established the desired balance sheet showing, and its accompanying presentation of profits and losses. This is accomplished through the medium of the chart of the accounts, which may be described as the skeleton of the plan, or in other words, the frame work. The next thing is to clothe this frame work with proper bookkeeping details which, continuing the figure, are the flesh and muscle. As the frame work of different undertakings differs in plan, so will the completed systems differ in appearance, and as bookkeeping details differ from time to time to meet requirements, so will also the appearance of the finished work differ. In every case, however, there will be a Balance Sheet Ledger, which is only a going summary of the business scientifically arranged, and in every instance the bookkeeping details will be arranged to contribute to that summary. The Balance Sheet System of Accounts is adaptable to all lines of trade, and may be as safely relied upon in one case as in another.

The Balance Sheet System applied to a manufacturing business includes an adequate system of cost accounts, described in some of our advertising matter as the Proof-by-Balance System of Cost Accounts. As a final result of this important adjunct there is kept constantly before the management a complete balance sheet of the enterprise, including the factory accounts as well as the office accounts, and also a complete profit and loss statement. These features are made going parts of the books, and are not, as is usual, something derived from and made up outside of the books at stated intervals. The long fiscal period is done away with, the books are always closed and are likewise always open. All this, however, you will gain in a general way from the advertising matter, which we have mailed you.

The Balance Sheet System, applied to the accounts of an estate, would be altogether different in bookkeeping details, and yet exactly the same in principle. There would be produced as the final result of the system, a going statement, showing the exact condition of the estate in all divisions at all times.

Accounting Engineers.

From G. W. Y., Cleveland:

I have seen your advertisement. If the Balance Sheet System of Accounts will do what you say it will do, it will be of value to our establishment. I am not clear, however, that a proprietary system can be made to meet the requirements of an extensive and somewhat complicated business such as we are transacting. Please send me such literature as will give me an insight into the matter, and in reply such additional particulars as you think are appropriate.

Kindly give an indication of your prices. Answer: We are in receipt of your letter and in reply have pleasure in sending you by even mail several of our advertising circulars. None of these relates to a manufacturing enterprise of the exact character that you are conducting, but, nevertheless, we have had wide experience in installing our system in factories not only in your general line, but in various others, wherein quite as difficult problems have arisen as would obtain in your case. We unhesitatingly guarantee all the results which our literature sets forth.

Ours is not a ready-made, proprietary system, sold on the "hand-me-down" plan. Instead, what we offer is in each instance a carefully worked out plan, with special reference to the requirements of the case. If you will kindly think of us as accounting engineers, doing for the office, in the way of invention, adaptation and arrangement, what a mechanical engineer does in laying out a factory and designing machinery, or an architect in preparing the plans and specifications for a building, you will have a correct conception of our work.

We bring to bear upon the accounting problems presented by different business enterprises the wide experience and careful training of a large corps of able accountants, who have made a specialty of such engineering work as is above described. In addition, we have certain specialties in accounting methods and facilities essentially our own, which have grown out of the experience above referred to, and which help to accomplish the results we guarantee, in an efficient and very economical manner.

Our usual plan, after surveying the situation and becoming familiar with what is required, including the size of the operation, etc., is to name a lump sum for the installation. We have work in progress at the present time that figures, per installation, all the way from $300 up into the thousands. We attempt to make our prices reasonable in view of what is required and to ask only what the work is worth, in view of its cost to us.

Local Expressmen Not Common Carriers.

The Commissioner of Internal Revenue has decided that local baggage expressmen are not common carriers, and consequently not affected by the provisions of the new United States Internal Revenue act, which requires every common carrier to give a receipt for goods accepted by him for transportation, and to affix to it a one-cent stamp. This relieves local baggage carriers from paying a tax of one cent for each trunk or article of baggage transported by them.

Accountants in South Africa.

We are indebted to Mr. Henry Gibson, the Secretary of the Society of Accountants and Auditors at Cape Town, South Africa, for a list of members of that organization, arranged both alphabetically and geographically, and supplemented by extracts from the by-laws. Fifty-four of our professional brethren doing business in South Africa are on the rolls, divided pretty evenly in business location and residence between Cape Town, Johannesburg, Balawayo, Kimberley, Pietermaritzburg, East London, Beira, Pretoria, Durban, Port Elizabeth and Salisbury—all geographical names which our daily journals have kept us pretty familiar with during the past three or four years. Arranged by colonies, we find two practicing their profession in the Orange Free State, three in Matabeleland, twenty-two in Cape Colony, nine in Natal and twenty-one in the South African Republic. This South African Society of Accountants is an offshoot or branch of the Society of Accountants and Auditors at London, England, which parent society has on its rolls upward of 1,000 members, residing in various parts of the world. Notable are the facts, that the question of what the society will accept as evidence of fitness on the part of a professional accountant, is determined by its Legal Examiner in London; the degree of associates admitted to practice is qualified by the addition of the place where they are examined, e. g., Melbourne, and they are not deemed qualified to practice elsewhere without sitting for an additional examination.

Death of the Foreign Bill of Exchange.

The new United States Internal Revenue act, which has been in operation a year, has caused the disappearance from commercial circles of the familiar "foreign bill of exchange." The reason for this is that while the law requires only a two cent stamp for bank checks and orders for money payable at sight, foreign bills of exchange are made subject to a stamp tax of two cents for each $100 of their amount. Bankers, therefore, promptly stopped drawing sight bills of exchange, and in their place began drawing checks, putting only a two-cent stamp on each check. The Internal Revenue Commissioner has conceded, with reluctance, that this is not a violation of the act, and thus the new practice has become established.

Accountics

The Office Magazine.

A. O. KITTREDGE, F. I. A., C. P. A., Editor.
E. R. KITTREDGE, Associate.

Accountics is devoted to the Science of Accounting, to the Art of Bookkeeping and to the advocacy of Improved Office Methods.

Subscription.—One dollar a year, payable in advance.

Postage is prepaid by the publishers in the United States, Canada and Mexico. For all other countries in the Postal Union, subscribers must add 50 cents a year.

Discontinuances.—In the absence of specific orders to discontinue at the end of the subscription term the magazine will be continued and a bill sent.

Remittances should be by Draft, P. O. Order or Express Order, payable to the order of the ACCOUNTICS ASSOCIATION. Money and postage stamps are at the risk of the sender, unless sent by express or in registered letters. Add 10 cents each to checks on local banks to defray collection charges.

Advertising Rates will be quoted on application.

Official Journal.—This publication, by resolutions duly passed, has been made the official publication of the following organizations :—

THE INSTITUTE OF ACCOUNTS.
THE NEW YORK CHAPTER of the Institute of Accounts.
THE WASHINGTON CHAPTER of the Institute of Accounts.
THE HARTFORD CHAPTER of the Institute of Accounts.

ACCOUNTICS is the accredited medium of intercommunication between members of the Institute of Accounts wherever located.

ACCOUNTICS ASSOCIATION,
Publishers,
Lancashire Bldg., Pine St., near Nassau,
New York.

Publisher's Desk.

A very attractive little pamphlet issued by Philip Hano & Co., 808-918 Greenwich street, New York, is entitled "Light on a Dark Subject." The dark subject is carbon papers, of which this firm is one of the largest manufacturers in the world. It is pregnant with suggesticns concerning labor-saving methods. Other circulars issued by this firm are also of interest and value to the business man. Send for a full file and mention this notice in THE OFFICE MAGAZINE.

What business man is not unconsciously impressed either for or against his correspondent by the "get-up" of a letter—its heading, the paper upon which it is written, the manner in which it has been folded, etc.—even before he reads it? "Modern business stationery" is a subject to which our readers can not give too much attention. Elsewhere in this issue we print the ad. of the American Embossing Company, of 73 Lock Street, Buffalo, N. Y. Their specialty is embossing business stationery, in color, from steel dies. They turn out 50,000 sheets daily, of the very best and highest grade. Write them for samples and quotations.

It has seldom been ACCOUNTICS' privilege to turn over the pages of a better edited and prepared monthly than the June issue of "Profitable Advertising and Art in Advertising," published by Kate E. Griswold, at 227 Washington St., Boston, Mass. The self-confidence of many business men in their ability to draft an advertisement which will be a "puller" will oftentimes provoke a smile when it is recalled the moment of looking over the effort which is the product of that self-confidence. Such men, as well as all others interested in giving their goods profitable publicity, will absorb many ideas of inestimable value to them in making up "ads" by examining the pages of "Profitable Advertising and Art in Advertising."

9,999,999. The Bates Numbering Machine will noiselessly, accurately, consecutively and automatically number from 1 up to 9,999,999, and it is guaranteed that even an office boy can't get poor work out of it. Turn the dial to the first point, and it will number in duplicate. Turn the dial to "repeat" and it will reprint the same number right along. ACCOUNTICS advertises the Bates machine in this issue. Write to the Bates Mfg. Co., 135 Fifth Avenue, corner of 20th Street, New York, for their descriptive booklet No. 11, and for their series of letters from banks, insurance companies and manufacturing corporations, telling of their satisfaction with the Bates numbering machine.

"The Klip with the Grip" can be obtained postpaid by addressing H. H. Ballard, 403 Pittsfield, Mass. ACCOUNTICS advertisers this solver of the binding problem in another page of this issue. It is a cheap and lasting device by which libraries, colleges and reading rooms, lawyers, doctors, scientists, clergymen, clerks, banks and everybody else who has papers to keep, binds them together, one sheet or 300 sheets, in ten seconds. You will find it a great convenience in your office.

If time is money and money is time, and you use automatic paper fasteners in any way, how much money do you lose and fritter away each year while you are punching holes or hunting for fasteners that cannot be found, or do not fasten? Mr. Alex. H. Irvin, of Curwensville, Clearfield Co., Pa., will answer this question if you will write him. Further, he will send you, on order, the "Star" automatic paper fastener which ACCOUNTICS advertises elsewhere, a device which is absolutely certain, ever ready, always loaded and cannot hang fire.

Accountics

VOL. V AUGUST 1899 No. 2

The Monthly Statement

One of our readers, who describes himself as particularly interested in the new accounting and in advanced office methods of all kinds, raises the question of the expediency of devoting any of the space in ACCOUNTICS to such subjects as advertising. We have replied to him privately, expressing our views at length, but, in the belief that others may have similar interrogatories in their minds, it seems only appropriate that we should give the substance of our answer as wide circulation as the magazine itself. Accounting and office work are so intimately associated that it is hard to consider one without giving attention to the other. A very important subdivision of office work at the present time is that of advertising, whether it be the preparation of catalogues, or the formulating of announcements to appear in stated newspaper spaces. Take it far and by over the country, many secretaries, treasurers and even bookkeepers and accountants find it necessary, as a subdivision of their duties, to give attention to the announcements of their respective establishments. Comparatively few concerns are able to maintain separate advertising departments or to employ special talent in this direction. Hence it is that many who are nominally accountants, and many who apparently subscribe to ACCOUNTICS only because it treats of advanced accounting, are at the same time interested in advertising and in all the methods of obtaining publicity.

It should not be forgotten also that the sub-title of this periodical is "The Office Magazine," a term introduced to better define its place among technical and class journals in general. So far as we can judge from the responses to questions which we occasionally put to our subscribers we are pleasing them best with those numbers which more nearly reflect the office in all its departments than by those which are held strictly to what is commonly termed higher accounting. "Accounting is the vital element of business," and accounting, in the sense of recording facts and ascertaining results, applies to advertising in a very particular manner. Or, to put it otherwise, advertising divested of the accounting by which its results are correctly shown is a risky undertaking. Good accountants, in the broad meaning of the term, are in many respects the best advertising managers that can be secured. Again, no accountant, be he more or less eminent in the profession, can entirely neglect the question of publicity. With the fact staring him in the face that a very considerable part of the money which in the past has been expended for advertising, by whomsoever the advertising was conducted, has been wasted, he is particularly interested in a presentation of those principles underlying advertising which will guide him in the expenditure of whatever amount of money he may appropriate for the purpose of obtaining publicity. Accountants, as a professional class, are neither bound by tradition nor yet by current practice to avoid publicity, or advertising in various appropriate mediums, as apparently are the members of certain other professions—notably those of law and medicine. The lawyers, however, are fast learning the necessity of legitimate advertising, and many of them are manifesting commendable enterprise in getting themselves before prospective clients. Accountants have appreciated the advantage of appropriate advertising from the beginning, and doctors, in spite of the code, are of late learning to do a little advertising to their material benefit. Accountants are not likely to forego their present advantages out of respect for any antiquated code that may be sprung upon them now or in the future. They are in too close touch with real business to make such a mistake. Still other reasons for occasional reference to advertising in these columns might be supplied, but quite enough has been stated to justify all that we have done in this field or are likely to do in the near future.

Accountants and auditors are being well employed at the present time. There are comparatively few practitioners of standing and repute who are not full of business and calling to their aid all the skilled help that they can secure. Further, it would seem from the trend of events that there is abundant business ahead of them to keep them fully employed for a considerable time to come. Not a few have had more or less to do with examinations and reports such as must necessarily precede consolidations and amalgamations, and some are already engaged on the work of unsnarling some of the tangles in business affairs caused by the disruption of consolidations which have failed of the expected measure of success. Brokers in Wall Street profit by an active market or one with many fluctuations rather than by a market showing simply a rise. They stand to win, their commissions at least, whether stocks go up or down. To a certain extent accountants and auditors are in the same position. Business consolidations and the dissolution of trusts are both likely to afford considerable business for the profession, and for some time to come, apparently, there will be both kinds of business in abundance.

As the summer season closes, the immense volume that the fall trade promises to measure becomes apparent. The business man now more fully than ever before realizes that he is in the midst of an active campaign and that he is doing business in an era of unexampled prosperity. The resources of general business, as well as of transportation in particular, are being taxed to the utmost. Factories in many lines are not only behind orders, but in some cases great embarrassment is being experienced for lack of raw materials. The railroads are doing a phenomenal amount of business. Where a single train of comparatively few cars sufficed a short time since to transport all the passengers offering, now many roads are not only running very long trains, but very frequently send out their trains in several sections. It is no longer possible for the commercial traveler to secure "a lower berth in the middle of the car" as a matter of course, making application just before the train starts. Instead, unless he has engaged his sleeping-car accommodations somewhat in advance, he is liable to be told that there is "nothing but an upper berth at the end of the car," or else that "everything is full." From different sources the statement reaches us that the travel for business alone at the present time is larger in volume than the travel that was induced by the Columbian Exposition in 1893. It is a good adage which advises one to "make hay while the sun shines." Business men generally are quick to act upon advice of this kind, and surely it would seem that the present is good (business) haying weather. Every effort, well considered and ably made, promises to result in a business advantage.

This issue of ACCOUNTICS goes forth with a larger assortment of valuable matter for office men, business managers and accountants than perhaps any other issue we have ever put forth. The cover also presents a slight change in design, and "The Office Magazine," which is truly descriptive of this publication, is given greater prominence than ever before. The changes that we have made in this periodical from time to time have been carefully considered in the light of expressed wishes and opinions of our readers, and in the past we seem to have been able, as a rule, to meet the ideas of our constituency. We flatter ourselves that the slight changes now made, as well as the general direction in which we are driving, will likewise please our readers. We take this occasion to say, however, that at present and in the future, as in the past, letters of criticism, as well as of commendation, are in order, and will always have careful attention.

"Can you lend me 105 marks?"

"That's a singular amount to ask for. What do you want of the odd five?"

"I wish to demonstrate my honest intentions by paying to you at once five marks on account."—Fliegende Blaetter.

The Baltimore and Ohio Receivership

There has nothing occurred in the financial and transportation worlds for a long time of greater interest to observing business men, or more pregnant with useful business lessons, than the Baltimore and Ohio receivership. The circumstances leading up to the receivership were almost dramatic in character. The contest over certain details at the beginning of the receivership served to attract public attention to the matter, and the reports of different accountants, which were published and given wide circulation, still further riveted attention upon the special management of this important property. Finally, the receivership came to an end, the property was restored to the stockholders, and by a fortunate change in the general business conditions of the country, the road was turned over to its owners at a time that it could be used advantageously up to the limit of its capacity. An advance in prices of railway equipment which took place shortly after the receivers had purchased a large amount of rolling stock and general supplies demonstrated the wisdom of their management.

At the convention of the Maryland Bar Association, held late in July, a paper was read by President John K. Cowen, of the road in question, entitled "The Baltimore and Ohio Receivership." The following epitome of his remarks will be read with interest by accountants and business men everywhere. The speaker announced at the outset that he could say nothing new, because the press had given at one time or another an account of the various orders of the Court, whether entered by consent or after full argument at the bar. He then reviewed the receivership, step by step, from the time the property was thrown into the Courts on February 29, 1896. At that time the company owed for material and supplies and for operating indebtedness generally $4,325,447. The receivers found the property, he said, notably its equipment and track, greatly in need of repairs. There being no money with which to make these repairs, the Court on May 21, 1896, authorized the issue of $5,000,000 receivers' certificates. The effects of the issue of these certificates, he said, were to prevent a further disastrous decline in the price of the company's mortgage bonds and to enable the receivers to make the repairs and improvements to track and equipment, essential to take care of the business, and at the same time pay off some indebtedness to shippers along the line of the road who had furnished material to the company. On the same date, May 21, 1896, the receivers asked and received authority to issue $3,400,000 equipment bonds with which to pay for 75 locomotives and 5,000 freight cars. This arrangement, he continued, secured for the road a large addition to its equipment without requiring any cash payment.

Mr. Cowen reviewed the work on the Belt Line Railroad Company, which built the rail connection between the main line of the Baltimore and Ohio and the Philadelphia branch at Bay View, including the tunnel under Baltimore City. In order to complete this connecting link, receivers' certificates for $956,000 were issued on December 1, 1896, secured by a special lien upon the properties of the Maryland Construction Company, including a portion of Camden station.

The Pittsburg and Connellsville Railroad, extending from Cumberland, Md., to Pittsburg, Pa., with several branches, is one of the leased lines of the Baltimore and Ohio. The receivers found it necessary to issue $650,000 receivers' certificates, secured specially upon the Pittsburg and Connellsville for the purpose of completing certain terminals at Pittsburg, and to improve the roadway and trackage.

Receivers' certificates were issued on July 1, 1897, for $680,000 to pay for 40,000 tons of new rails, and for $2,383,050 with which to acquire 3,000 box cars, 750 hopper gondola cars, and 40 locomotives. In January, 1898, the receivers were given authority to lease for ten years or to purchase 3,250 box cars and 1,900 coal cars.

Under date of June 22, 1898, said Mr. Cowen, the various parties in interest agreed upon a plan for the reorganization of the Baltimore and Ohio Railroad Company, and since that date the receivers have acquired equipment under car trust leases made by the railroad company, to which the receivers were parties only to the extent of agreeing to comply during the receivership with the obligations the company had made. All of these arrangements were made under authority of the Court, and, of course, without any opposition, but with the approval of all parties in interest. The amount of the equipment so acquired was 6,000 box cars, 2,500 coal cars, 5,000 steel coal cars, and 80 locomotives.

There were sundry other orders of Court, authorizing the acquisition of small lots of passenger, freight and marine equipment, which I have not thought it necessary to go into the details of.

During the receivership of three years and four months the railroad earned $92,899,546.89, including $3,127,827.64 miscellaneous income, and there were spent for operating expenses, including large extraordinary outlays for maintenance of road and equipment $68,162,583.50, leaving a net balance of $24,736,963.39.

In addition to the extraordinary sums spent for maintenance and charged to operating expenses, there were improvements and additions made to the road costing $4,018,652.85.

And now what have been the results of this administration of a great trust by the United States Circuit Court for the District of Maryland?

(1) Every bondholder of the Baltimore and Ohio Railroad has received new securities which substantially pay his full debt. In other words, the bondholders have been paid in full.

(2) The floating debt creditors have received every cent of their indebtedness.

(3) The first preferred stockholders have received in cash 75 per cent. of the par value of their stock, the Court overruling their claim of preference over the bondholders and creditors. The second preferred stockholders have received securities which, after payment of this assessment, net about $70 per share, at the present market, and at times over $80 net could have been realized.

(4) The common stockholders, instead of being wiped out, have received their common stock in the new company, upon paying an assessment, the net amount of which (because of the value of the securities received for such assessment) would not exceed five or six dollars.

(5) The company saves its old charter for whatever value may attach to it.

It is true that although this paper deals with the judicial administration of a great trust, it does not present any fine hair-splitting legal questions, but it shows that in American jurisprudence there has been evolved a method whereby the Courts can take a great property whose administration is full of difficulty, and they can so rehabilitate it that substantial justice may be done to bondholders, floating debt creditors, and stockholders, that this can be done without violating any of the well-defined rights of any creditor, and that it is the duty of the Courts in administering these great trusts to place the property in the position where its possible earning capacity can be shown, and consequently a fair and just reorganization can be made.

When the Court had done its work and put the property into the position where its fair earning capacity could be shown it became evident that no one interest need be sacrificed, and then was brought into play that wonderful and delicate machinery of modern commerce, a part of what Mr. Bagehot calls the "lending apparatus of the world," whereby the distribution of more than $200,000,000 of securities was secured by great banking houses—Speyer Brothers, Speyer & Co., and Kuhn, Loeb & Co. They placed their names on a reorganization agreement, concluded Mr. Cowen, and at once the "loan and investment fund" and the "speculative fund" of two continents was drawn on to make the plan a success.

The enterprise of the Saturday Evening Post, Philadelphia, the advertisements of which appear at the present time in every part of the country, is certainly commendable. It seems to be exploring every field of inquiry. Recent issues particularly have appealed to business men. The series dealing with municipal affairs of great American cities has deservedly excited marked attention. The article entitled "New York Under Tammany Rule," by Frank Moss, counsel for the Mazet Investigating Committee, received special consideration at the hands of various citizens of the metropolis.

Endless

The longest lane must have a turning,
  The rock wears out where drippings fall,
Yet man may daily keep on learning,
  And never get to know it all.

—S. E. Kiser.

Lawful Money Reserve of National Banks*

By Edwin Brower, M. I. A.

"How Is the Reserve in a Bank (required by law) Estimated?" is the question, as assigned. As my experience has been entirely with National Banks, I shall treat the subject as applying to such banks.

The reserve is regulated by law and is defined, both as to amount required and of what it shall consist, in the Revised Statutes of the United States in sections known as the National Bank Act and amendments thereto. There is no excuse for estimating the same, as it can be accurately figured according to rules adopted by the Comptroller of the Currency under whose supervision all National Banks are operated.

The reserve of a bank is a certain percentage of its deposits which the bank shall at all times have on hand in lawful money of the United States.

In the early days of the present national banking system, banks were required to hold a reserve upon the amount of their circulation as well as on deposits, but were relieved of that liability by act of June 20, 1874, so that now only deposits are liable. Nowhere in the statutes have I been able to discover in actual words for what purpose the reserve is required but assume that it is to compel banks to have on hand at all times enough funds to enable them to meet on demand all drafts of their depositors against moneys deposited, and the percentage fixed is deemed adequate for all withdrawals until the bank can realize upon its assets, which may consist of loans both demand and time.

The statutes originally named certain cities as reserve cities and banks located therein are accorded the privilege of having on deposit a portion of the lawful money reserve of national banks located in other places. New York City was further named wherein its national banks could hold a portion of the reserve of banks located in reserve cities as well as all others. The act of March, 1887, authorizes the Comptroller of the Currency, upon written application of three-fourths of the national banks located in any city of the United States having a poulation of 50,000 people to designate such city as a reserve city in addition to those already named by the statutes. This act goes further and allows the Comptroller, upon application of three-fourths of the national banks in a city having a population of 200,000 people, to designate, with the approval of the Secretary of the Treasury, such city as a central reserve city, in which national banks are accorded the same privileges as those located in New York City. Under this act the list of reserve cities has been slightly increased, Indianapolis being designated only recently as a reserve city, and Chicago and St. Louis have been made central reserve cities.

National banks located in any place, except central reserve cities, may select, subject to the approval of the Comptroller of the Currency, one or more national banks located in any of the reserve cities with which a portion of the reserve may be kept, either in open account or as a special deposit, and banks so designated and approved are known as "Approved Reserve Agents," and there appears to be no limit as to the number of such agents a bank may have.

National banks located in all reserve cities are required to keep on hand 25 per cent. of their deposits, and in central reserve cities this amount must be kept in the bank itself, while banks located in other reserve cities may keep one-half of their lawful money reserve in cash deposits with its approved reserve agents in central reserve cities.

National banks located in all other places, outside of reserve cities, are required to keep on hand 15 per cent. of their deposits, three-fifths of which may consist of balances on deposit with their approved reserve agents in any of the reserve cities.

National banks in reserve cities must therefore keep at least one-half, and those in other places two-fifths of their reserve actually in the bank, but if they do not care to avail themselves of the privilege of keeping a portion with their reserve

---

*Paper read before Hartford Chapter of Accounts May 23, 1899.

agents they must keep the entire amount on hand in the bank.

It will have been noticed that the reserve must consist of lawful money, and in order to ascertain whether a bank reserve is sufficient it will be necessary to understand just what lawful money is, as available for reserve purposes.

From the opinions of Attorneys-General of the United States "the term 'lawful money' is understood to apply to every form of money which is endowed by law with the legal-tender quality." Lawful money, therefore, may consist of:

1. Gold coin of the United States at its nominal value when not below the limit of tolerance in weight.
2. Standard silver dollars of the United States.
3. Legal-tender notes of the United States and Treasury notes of July 14, 1890.
4. Fractional silver coin (while legal tender to the extent of $10 only), is held to be available for reserve in any amount.
5. Clearing house certificates representing specie or lawful money specially deposited for the purpose, of any clearing house association, is also deemed to be lawful money in the possession of any association belonging to such clearing house and holding and owning such certificates (Section 5192 Revised Statutes).
6. United States Gold Certificates (under act of July 12, 1889).
7. United States Silver Certificates (under same act).
8. Certificates for legal tender notes deposited with the Treasurer of the United States (Section 5193 R. S.).

The act of June 20, 1874, exempting circulation from reserve requirements, provided that each bank shall keep on deposit with the Treasurer of the United States a sum equal to 5 per cent. of its circulation, to be held and used for the redemption of such circulation, which sum shall be counted as a part of the lawful reserve of the bank making the deposit.

It is also necessary to know how deposits, subject to reserve required by law, shall be determined. Embraced in the term are:

1. Individual deposits subject to check, consisting of all deposits standing to the credit of individuals, firms, corporations, towns, cities, counties and States, in fact all deposits except those made by the United States and balances due to other national banks and to State and private banks and bankers.
2. Demand certificates of deposit.
3. Time certificates of deposit.
4. Certified checks.
5. Cashiers' checks outstanding.
6. Dividends unpaid.
7. United States deposits.
8. Deposits by United States disbursing officers.
9. Balances due to other national banks and to State and private banks and bankers in excess of balances due from other national and State banks and bankers. But if the balances due from banks is in excess of balances due to banks, such excess cannot be applied in reduction of liability on other deposits.

The Comptroller of the currency has ruled that certain assets of the bank may be allowed to reduce the amount of deposits liable for reserve, and these are:

1. Exchanges for the clearing house, i. e., checks on other banks in the same place on hand awaiting time of clearing.
2. Checks on other banks in the same place which may refer to checks on banks not members of the clearing house; also in places where there are no clearing house fecilities.
3. Bills of other national banks held by the bank.

Having the requirements before us, we are now ready to take up the computation, which is a very simple matter unless complicated by the division into amount in bank and amount with reserve agents.

Let us take for examples a bank in a central reserve city where the whole reserve is kept in the bank, and one located outside of a reserve city where three-fifths of the reserve may be kept with reserve agents.

Example A. Computation of Reserve of a National Bank located in a Central Reserve City.

Due to other National Deposits	$7,500,000	
Due to State Banks and Bankers	5,420,000	$12,920,000
Due from other National Banks..	1,800,000	
Due from State Banks and Bankers	120,000	$1,920,000
Balances due to Banks in excess of balances due from Banks		$11,000,000
Individual Deposits, Certificates of Deposit, Certified		

Checks and Cashiers' Checks		18,000,000
Dividends unpaid		5,000
United States Deposits		1,000,000
Total Deposits		$30,005,000

DEDUCTIONS.

Exchanges for Clearing House	$4,780,000	
Checks on other Banks in the City..	15,000	
Notes of other National Banks	110,000	4,905,000
Net deposits subect to reserve..... ...		$25,100,000
Deduct 4 x ($22,500, amount of 5 per cent. Redemption Fund.)		90,000
Amount upon which Reserve is to be kept in Bank........		$25,010,000
25 per cent. of which is the Reserve required, and is		6,252,500

LAWFUL MONEY ON HAND.

Specie — Embracing gold and silver coin, and gold and silver certificates	$4,500,000	
Legal tender notes and certificates for same	3,200,000	$7,700,000
Excess of Reserve held		$1,447,500

Example B. Computation of Reserve of a National Bank located outside of a Reserve City.

DEPOSITS.

Balances due to Banks in Excess of Balances due from Banks........		$65,890
Individual deposits, Dividends unpaid, etc.... ...		498,266
Total Deposits		$564,156

DEDUCTIONS.

Exchanges for Clearing House, Notes of other Banks, etc.............		11,900
		$552,256
Deduct 6 2-3 x ($2,250 amount of 5 per cent. Redemption Fund.)		15,000
		$537,256
15 per cent. Reserve required is		80,588
Two-fifths of Reserve must be kept in Bank...		32,235
Three-fifths of Reserve may be kept with Reserve Agents	$48,353	

LAWFUL MONEY ON HAND.

Specie and Legal Tenders		$40,000
On deposit with approved Reserve Agents	$196,000	
Apparent Excess in Bank		7,765
Apparent Excess with Agents	147,647	

The amount with Reserve Agents being in excess of the three-fifths which may be kept with them, such excess can be applied to reduce the balance due to Banks and in this case is sufficient to offset the whole amount, so that the amount upon which Reserve is to be computed is reduced by $65,890, and is $471,366

15 per cent. required upon this amount is..........		70,705
Two-fifths of which is...		28,282
The actual Excess in Bank therefore is.......		11,718
Three-fifths of which may be kept with Agents...		42,423
Amount with Reserve Agents	$196,000	
Is reduced by amount applied as above........	65,890	130,110
Actual Excess with Agents...		$87,687

Four times the amount of the 5 per cent. Redemption Fund is deducted from deposits before computing, because in Reserve Cities, the fund will protect that much deposits, and in 15 per cent. banks deposits to the extent of 6 2-3 times the 5 per cent. Fund are protected. The Revised Statutes allowing the 5 per cent. Redemption Fund to be counted as a part of the lawful-money reserve, do not specify whether it shall be applied to offset a like amount of the reserve required to be kept in the bank or with Reserve Agents, and this method of handling same, by reducing deposits by the amount protected, divides it proportionately between the two.

It may be held, however, that inasmuch as the Statutes specifically provide that three-fifths of the required reserve may be kept with Approved Reserve Agents, the 5 per cent. Redemption Fund might be considered a portion of the remaining two-fifths, and therefore counted as being in the Bank; in which case the computation of the percentage required will be upon the net deposits subject to reserve, and the lawful money in bank increased by including the amount of the 5 per cent. Redemption Fund. The figuring of the ratio between reserve on hand and Deposits will also be made more simple.

These examples will suffice for usual cases, but there are occasionally times when the amount in the bank (in other than Central Reserve Cities) is quite close to the amount required and then a more careful figuring must be done in order to determine the exact excess with Re-

serve Agents, which excess can be applied to reduce the amount of difference due to banks over that due from banks, and thereby reduce amount of deposits upon which reserve is required and so change the reserve in bank to an actual excess.
the Reserve in Bank to an actual excess.

There are liable to be several conditions whereby one of many rules for the computation of reserve may be used as a short method of arriving at the amount required, which might if figured out require a long mathematical computation, but I believe I have sufficiently answered the question as far as it may interest all save those who are obliged to compute a complicated case.

Whenever the Lawful Money Reserve of any National Banking Association is below the amount required, the law provides that such association shall not increase its liabilities by making anw new loans or discounts otherwise than by discounting or purchasing bills of exchange payableat sight, nor make any dividend of its profits until the required proportion between the deposits and its lawful money has been restored, and if the Association fail to make good its lawful money reserve within 30 days after being notified to do so, the Comptroller of the Currency may with the concurrence of the Secretary of the Treasury, appoint a receiver to wind up the business of the Association.

Curiosities of the Calendar

The following are some of the curiosities of the Gregorian calendar, as recounted by a writer in one of the French magazines: Since the reform of the calendar by Pope Gregory XIII., in 1582, no century can begin with a Wednesday, a Friday or a Sunday. Also, the same calendar can be used every twenty years. January and October of the same year always begin with the same day. So do April and July, also September and December. February, March and November also begin with the same day. New Year's Day and St. Sylvester's Day also fall on the same day, except, of course, in leap years. Each day of the week has served as a day of rest somewhere; Sunday among Christians, Monday with the Greeks, Tuesday with the Persians, Wednesday with the Assyrians, Thursday with the Egyptians, Friday with the Turks and Saturday with the Jews. Finally, the error of the Gregorian calendar, compared with the actual course of the sun, does not exceed one day in 4,000 years. As it is quite probable that neither you nor I shall every verify this, we shall not risk very much by believing the statement.

The Treatment of Good Will

The matter of good will as an asset is receiving more and more attention as the months go by, from public accountants and auditors, both at home and abroad. From time to time definitions of good will are found in various trade papers, which betrays the fact that the general question is up for consideration in many different directions at the present time. With the multitude of reorganizations and consolidations now in progress, the matter of good will as an asset is being brought to the attention of many men who perhaps have never before given it adequate consideration. That good will is an asset, something that can be bought and sold, and even mortgaged, is fully sustained by the courts, but frequently, in the preparation of the schedules of companies, the term good will is employed where something else would be better. Certain discrepancies between the capitalization of a company and the difference between its tangible assets and its real liabilities are termed good will, when some other word or phrase would better express the nature of the account.

However, it is not the purpose of this article to enter into a discussion of this phase of the subject, but instead to present for the consideration of our readers the results of an investigation into the subject of good will, made a short time since by a British accountant:

Though usually included with the other business assets, a good will has long been recognized by the law of England as a distinct property, liable to be dealt with by the owner like any other kind of property. It can be sold, it can be mortgaged, it can be bequeathed by will.

In various cases which have come before the courts, judges have essayed to give definitions of what good will really is, but it must be confessed that their lordships have not attained to any remarkable lucidity in these efforts.

The celebrated Lord Eldon defines a good will thus: "Good will is nothing more than the probability that the old customers will resort to the old place," but years afterwards this definition was discussed by Lord Justice Cotton, in the Court of Appeal, who said: "If the language of Lord Eldon is apt to be taken as a definition of good will of general application, I think it is far too narrow, and I am not satisfied that it was intended by Lord Eldon as an exhaustive definition."

The question of a good will has generally arisen in cases where a business has been sold, and the vendor has attempted to set up in opposition to his old business or play some trick of that sort. In such circumstances when there is no restraining clause in the agreement of transfer the point naturally arises, What exactly did the vendor sell when he sold his "good will?"

Said Vice-Chancellor Wood on this subject: "Good will, I apprehend, must mean every advantage, every positive advantage, that has been acquired by the old firm in carrying on its business, whether connected with the premises in which the business was previously carried on, or with the name of the late firm, or with any other matter carrying with it the benefit of the business."

The recently deceased Lord Herschell gave a fair explanation of the meaning of the word "good will," in a case argued before the House of Lords in 1895, in which he said: "Attracting customers to a business is a matter connected with the carrying of it on. It is the formation of that connection which has made the value of the thing sold. . . . It is the connection thus formed, together with the circumstances, whether of habit or otherwise, which tend to make it permanent, that constitutes the good will of a business. It is this which constitutes the difference between a business just started and one which has acquired a good will. The former trader has to seek out his customers from among the community as best he can. The latter has a custom ready made."

It was decided a hundred years ago that the seller of a good will (in the absence of express stipulation) did not sell anything which prevented his opening another business in the same line, so long as he did not solicit orders from his old customers. In 1817, Vice-Chancellor Plumer said: "A person not a lawyer would not imagine that when the good will and trade of a retail shop were sold the vendor might, the next day, set up a shop within a few doors. The authorities, however, show that a person selling the good will of a business for however large a consideration is not prevented from setting up in trade."

In the case of a dissolution of partnership, the partner who is to retain the good will can prevent the other partners from soliciting orders from customers of the firm, just as a purchaser of the good will might do so. In the case of Trego vs. Hunt, the courts even interfered before a partnership was dissolved, where one of the partners was copying the names and addresses from the firm's ledger with the object of afterwards trading with them, the injunction granted against him being as follows: "Restraining the defendant, his servants and agents from applying privately, by letter, personally, or by a traveler, to any person who was, prior to the dissolution, a customer of the firm of T. & Co., asking such customer to continue after the dissolution to deal with him, or not to deal with the plaintiff'—an injunction which he would find it rather hard to get around.

Modes of Address

Custom prefixes Honorable to almost every holder of public office; yet, so far as we know, continues the Sun, no citizen, not even an official or the past or present, is styled Honorable by legal authority. In the old Commonwealth of Massachusetts the Governor is His Excellency, and the Lieutenant-Governor is His Honor, by the Constitution. He might, perhaps, be addressed as Hon. All other Honorables are so by impulsive courtesy.

It is harsh to charge caddishness against the use of the suffix Esquire, after it has spread so universally among English-speaking people; but it ought to be stopped, as caddish, as unnecessary, and as contrary to the genius of the future. Originally it denoted a certain one of the many social ranks among the Enlish, which was higher than some and lower than others. That distinction has gone out, but it is still used in English to denote a "gentleman" as contrasted with a "tradesman." A gentleman is Esq., and Mr. is a tradesman. Roscoe Conkling, by way of condemning this sort of caddishness, and perhaps of throwing a higher light on his own individuality, once struck off the Esq. which the printer of one of his speeches had placed at the end of the author's name. Mr. has still the usefulness of enabling married women to be known as Mrs., but Esq. is a piece of social frippery and should be abolished.

John Smith is the best form of title for every citizen of the United States, whether President, ex-President, Judge, Governor, Alderman, or only plain John Smith.

How are the Profits of the Year to be Ascertained?

BY BERNARD DALE

(Continued from page 7 of the July number.)

Since the owner of "fixed" capital does not seek to make it profitable to him by its market or selling value, but by its use, any increase or diminution in its market or selling value may be disregarded in arriving at the year's profits. This is the reason why it is not customary to value "fixed" capital for the purpose of the annual balance sheet, although, curiously enough, the reason is sometimes overlooked.

In his paper, "What Is Profit of a Company?" page 24, Mr. Ernest Cooper, an able and experienced accountant, says: "But when the asset is of a marketable nature and can be readily sold and replaced by purchase, the fall in value, although temporary, should, I think, appear in the account, and be charged to profit and loss."

Now, plant and other "fixed" capital, save perhaps that of a specialized nature, are generally of a marketable character, and can be readily sold and replaced; but, as Mr. Cooper himself admits, it is not usual to value plant, and this custom, he says, is based on reason. The reason, however, is not grounded on the non-marketability of plant, but on the circumstance that the owner of plant intends to employ it as a "fixed" and not as a "circulating" capital, that is to say, to make it profitable to him by its use and not by its sale. As the owner of "fixed" capital is not a seller, the market price at the date of the annual balance sheet should not be taken into account. On the other hand, in the case of an asset used as "circulating" capital, the owner being a seller, the market value must be regarded, since it is upon that value that the owner is dependent for his profit.

As some of the examples given by economists of "fixed" capital and cited above show, not being marketable is no more the criterion of "fixed" capital than being marketable is of "circulating" capital.

Mr. Cooper quotes as supporting his view Sir G. Jessel's dictum in Robinson v. Ashton (20 Eq. 28), that "the rise or fall in value of fixed plant or real estate belonging to a partnership was as much profit or loss of the partnership as anything else;" but Sir G. Jessel did not decide that during the partnership, and for the purpose of determining the annual profit the rise or fall in value of fixed plant should be taken into account. The partnership having terminated, it was for the purpose of the final balance sheet that his lordship decided that the excess of price over cost was as much profit of the partnership as anything else. This decision is in perfect accord with the principles above stated, for the partnership having ended, and the plant having to be turned into money, it had ceased to be a "fixed" and had become a "circulating" capital.

Another writer who does not seem to have adopted the rationale of the division of capital into "fixed" and "circulating" is the eminent counsel, Mr. Buckley, Q. C. In the sixth edition of his work on the Companies' Acts, Mr. Buckley puts the following question: "Suppose I buy £100 consols at 97, and at the expiration of a year they have fallen to 94. Is my income £3 or nothing? If nothing, then, if at the expiration of a year they had risen to par, my income would be parity of reason have been £6, not £3. Is the result affected by the question whether at the end of the year I am or am not about to sell the consols?"

The circumstance of the investor in the case supposed by Mr. Buckley being a seller, is of course an all-important one, having regard to the considerations above stated. The consols, if their owner became a seller, would no longer be a "fixed" but a "circulating" capital, and it would be to the price to be realized on resale that the investor must look for his income. On the other hand, if the owner remained an investor, then, as the example quoted from Macleon shows, the consols would remain "fixed" capital, and the fluctuations in market price might be disregarded.

In a paper read at a meeting of the Chartered Accountants' Students' Society of London, Mr. Thos. A. A. Welton, the well-known chartered accountant, while drawing a distinction between "permanent assets" and "floating assets," includes among permanent assets the ship of a manufacturing company as well as the ship of a ship-owning company, and states that in neither case "do I find that the proper conduct of a company's affairs demands that they should be revalued." However, as some of the examples given above show, the ship of a manufacturing company stands on a different footing to the ship of a ship-owning company. In the former case the ship is a "circulating capital," and since the company do not intend to make their profit out of its market value, that value is an all-important ingredient for the purpose of the balance sheet. In the latter case the ship is a "fixed capital," and since the company do not intend to make their profit from the market value, there is no need to take that value into account; indeed, to do so would be a proceeding as void of purpose as taking the chairman's temperature, or feeling the secretary's pulse; and Mr. Welton would be quite right in thinking that the conduct of the company's business would not demand that such an asset should be revalued, and that only deterioration from use need be considered. Later on, Mr. Welton says "as to investments not necessary for that purpose (i. e., carrying on business), the usual practice is to value them at cost, or at a less figure, but there is no real reason why marketable investments, such as railway stocks and consols, should not be valued at every balancing date, provided the thing is done systematically; and all investments not currently saleable are valued low."

Let us now apply the definition by economists of capital as wealth used as a source of income, as opposed to a source of present enjoyment, to the assets of some given company, say a railway company. If we take the assets of such a company in the order in which they come into existence, we shall have the following list:

(1) The monies received from the shareholders.

(2) The monies received from the debenture holders.

(3) The railway itself.

(4) The rolling stock and station furniture.

(5) The monies received from the public for the use of the railway.

As to items 1 and 2, these are capital, as they are to be productively expended, the one in the construction of the railway and the other in the purchase of rolling stock, and they are "circulating" capital, because they are to fulfil their mission of income-making by changing masters. If, therefore, the company were to return any of the monies received from the shareholders, say as interest during construction, they would be returning capital. As to items 3 and 4, these are capital also, since they, too, are to be used by the company to earn an income, and they are "fixed" capital, because they are to earn this income without changing masters. If, therefore, the company were to divide among the shareholders, in specie, any portion of the railway and rolling stock, they would be dividing capital. As to item 5, the result is slightly different. So much of the money received from the public for the use of the railway, as is required to be used each year for the working of the railway, and so to produce the net receipts would, by reason of that user, be capital; but, as to any surplus remaining after the payment of the working expenses, including the maintenance of the road and the rolling stock, this would not be capital, because it is not intended to be used any further to earn income, but to be distributed among the shareholders as a fund for their present enjoyment.

Let us now take a different class of company, say a banking company, and as in the last case deal with its assets in the order in which they come into existence. We shall have the following list:

(1) The monies received from the shareholders.

(2) The reserve represented by the investments, into which say the monies (item 1) have been converted.

(3) The dividends on the last mentioned investments.

(4) The bank premises.

(5) The monies received from customers on deposit or current account.

(6) The bills and other obligations to pay money into which, say the monies (item 5) have been converted.

As to items 1 and 4, these are covered by the preceding example. They are all capital, and items 2 and 4 would be a "fixed" capital, since the company intended to make them profitable by retaining and not by selling them. As to item 3, these dividends would also be capital, since the company intended to make their divisible profit out of their banking operations and not out of dividends on investments. These dividends, therefore, together with the other receipts during the year, would have to be turned over as capital in the company's business. As to item 5, these monies, when received, become as much the absolute property of the bank as items 1, 2, 3 and 4; and, as they are intended to be made profitable by employment in the company's business, they also would be capital to the company.

Interest and Discount—VII

BY CHARLES W. ROHNE

Constructing Interest Tables

To construct a table, the most obvious course is to calculate independently each value that is to be tabulated, but that course would very seldom be the best to pursue. It would usually be very laborious, and besides, in order to insure accuracy, the whole work would have to be done in duplicate. It is generally much preferable to take some formula connecting the consecutive values of the functions, and by means of it to compute them one from the other in succession. In this way each value is made to depend on all that goes before it, with the consequence that if an error occur in one it is carried on to those that follow, and we can therefore feel confident that if any particular value be correct, all those that go before it are also correct. This method of constructing tables is called the "continued method," and when it is used, a periodical check, say at every tenth step, is all that is required.

To employ the continued method, three things are necessary. We must have a convenient working formula connecting the value of the functions for any number of years with that for the next highest number; we must know the initial value on which all the others are to be built, and we must have a verification formula by which to apply periodical checks. In interest tables these three requisites are simple and easily obtained.

When (i) consists of but one significant figure, for instance when i = .04, the work of making the table is very easy. A type of the operation is given below. The number of decimal places will go on increasing indefinitely unless the increase be checked. When we have obtained as many as we require, we must, as in the example, cease to allow them to extend, merely taking account of the proper carriage from the neglected figures to the figures which we retain. Thus, in the example below, the result of multiplying the last two figures of (1+i)by .04 is 256, we neglect the 56, and as the figures neglected are greater than 49, we increase the next figure by unity, carrying three instead of two. In order to insure accuracy in the last decimal place of the tables, we must work to two places more than we mean finally to keep, and when the work is finished we must note down the results to the required limit, taking care always, when the value of the rejected figures is greater than 49, to increase by unity the last place retained. Thus, if we wish to cut down 2.4647155 to five places of decimals, we should write 2.46472, whereas to cut down 2.46477145, we should write 2.46471.

Where (i) is such a number that multiplying becomes burdensome, recourse must be had to logarithms.

INTEREST TABLE 1.04.

		(1+1) 4 per cent.
1.	....	1.04
	....	416
2.	....	1.0816
	....	43264
3.	....	1.124864
	....	44995
4.	....	1.169859
	....	46794
5.	....	1.216653
..		.. ..

The biomial theorem of expanding (a+b) is applicable to compound interest by substituting one, or unity, in place of a, and the rate of interest in place of b. I will give an illustration, using 4 per cent. as the interest rate:

Expanding a+b to the tenth power, we have $a + 10a^9b+45a^8b^2 + 120a^7b^3 + 210a^6b^4 + 252a^5b^5 + 210a^4b^6 + 120a^3b^7 + 45a^2b^8 + 10ab^9 + b^{10}$.

By substituting one, or unity, in place of a, and .04 in place of b, we have:

	1.	×	1	=	1.
$.04^1$	.04	×	10	=	.40
$.04^2$	.0016,	×	45	=	720,
$.04^3$	0,64	×	120	=	76,80
$.04^4$	,0256,	×	210	=	5,3760,
$.04^5$	10,24	×	252	=	,2580,48
$.04^6$	,4096,	×	210	=	86,0160,
$.04^7$	163,84	×	120	=	1,9660,80
$.04^8$	6,5536,	×	45	=	294,9120
$.04^9$	,2621,44	×	10	=	2,6214,40
$.04^{10}$	104,8576	×	1	=	104,8576
Adding, we have......	1.04^{10}			=	1.4802,4428,4918,3439,2576

The result obtained above shows the interest on $1 compounded annually for ten years and correct to twenty places of decimals. Ordinarily, it is not necessary to have a table extending farther than five places of decimals. The amount given in the compound interest table of Lieut.-Col. W. H. Oakes as the compound interest of $1 for ten years at 4 per cent. per annum, annual compound, is 1.48024, which agrees exactly with the above result so far as it goes.

Compound interest tables can be computed by continuous multiplications, but the ordinary method used by actuaries is to employ the use of logarithms. By this method calculations are very materially shortened. In using logarithms addition is substituted for multiplication, subtraction for division, multiplication for involution, or raising a number to any power, and division for evolution, commonly called extraction of roots. The logarithm given in Von Vega's seven-place tables for $1.04 is .0170333; multiplying this amount by ten gives a result of .170333; finding the natural number in the table of logarithms we find the interest to be $1.4802, with a remainder of 126, which gives us 4 as the next figure and a remainder; therefore we may be safe in designating the interest as $1.48024.

French Commercial Schools

All who give attention in the slightest degree to the status of business education in this country are interested in what is being done in the same general field abroad. Particularly are inquirers interested in the educational work of those countries which produce the ablest men. It has been very generally recognized in this country that the commercial schools of Paris afford a broad curriculum which prepares the student for an active business career. A writer in the columns of our contemporary, Success, recently described these schools, from whom we quote as follows:

Paris has celebrated commercial schools which are well worthy of study. The French, says Director Belfield, of the Chicago Manual Training School, practice the old Greek maxim of "teaching the boy what the man needs," and they broaden it to include the girl. Not only schools of law, medicine, pedagogy, engineering and art are found in France, as with us, but trade schools, technical schools, schools of the domestic arts, supported wholly or in part at public expense, sometimes wholly by associations of private persons.

Among the most interesting and important schools of Europe are the commercial schools of the Paris Chamber of Commerce, a body composed of many of the prominent business men of that city. These commercial schools are organized in four general divisions, as follows: 1. The Commercial School. 2. Free Evening Commercial Schools for Men and Women. 3. The Higher School of Commerce (Ecole Superior de Commerce de Paris). 4. The School for High Commercial Studies (Ecole des Hautes Etudes Commerciales).

The Commercial School, founded by the Paris Chamber of Commerce in 1863, has two courses, "preparatory" and "normal" (equivalent to our word professional). To the preparatory course children of ten years are admitted; to the normal course, none under twelve and a half years of age.

The curriculum includes the French language and literature; a practical knowledge of English, German and Spanish; arithmetic, bookkeeping, penmanship, stenography, lectures on commercial law and political economy; a general knowledge of geometry, drawing, and the physical sciences, history and geography "in their immediate relation to trade; that is to say, from the point of view of the raw material or of the manufactured products of different countries, their relations, and the various means of communication between them." In 1863 there were eighty pupils; in 1893, five hundred and eight. Tuition is forty-four dollars a year, but there are forty competitive scholarships.

The free evening classes in bookkeeping were opened to women in 1874, three evenings in the week. In 1875 classes for men were formed, occupying the other three evenings. In 1893 the women pupils numbered two hundred, the men eight hundred. The object is stated to enable women to become, either to their husbands or to their employers, efficient aids. This is declared to be also useful to the wife, as a housekeeper, and to the widow in business. Tuition is free. Pupils are admitted at twelve years of age.

The Higher Commercial School was the first institution in France created with the object of imparting exclusive commercial instruction. It trains youths to become merchants, bankers, managers and directors of industrial and commercial establishments. The course of study likewise fits young men for diplomatic and consular careers. It was founded in 1820 by two Paris merchants, MM. Brodard and Legret.

Criticisms and Reviews

Modern Bookkeeping

The Art of Modern Bookkeeping: By Enos Spencer. Large octavo. 230 pages, bound in cloth; stamped side title. Price, $2.

Mr. Spencer is at the head of the Spencerian Business College of Louisville, Ky., an institution which exerts an important influence over the business habits and methods of the young men of a considerable territory naturally centering in that city. As a teacher, he has experienced the need of a text-book for use in his school, different from any heretofore to be had in the market, and, accordingly, some time since he set out to supply the want, resulting in the volume which is now issued.

The book appeals to the public in a double character. While it is primarily a text-book, it is also a manual of bookkeeping which will be more or less consulted by business men and those directly engaged in office work. It is, perhaps, on the side of its instruction addressed to practical office men that we are most interested, and to these features we naturally address ourselves in this review.

At the outset we should compliment the author upon the character of the illustrations employed. He has used red ink sparingly and appropriately. He has not hesitated to give a fragmentary example when a fragment would answer the purpose, and, accordingly, the illustrations are relatively small, a feature that will be regarded as a pleasing contrast to much that has preceded in the same line. One, for example, will be devoted to footing lines and another to a head; still another to a fragment of a bill, and another to a section of a statement, and so on. In this regard the book will be found to be far more acceptable to the business man than most of the volumes relating to bookkeeping that have been issued in the past.

In the author's statement to us concerning the work he calls special attention to the classification of accounts, which he presents at the very begining of the book. We feel bound, therefore, to notice this feature, even though we do not agree with him in all particulars. We quote from page 6: "Cash, bills receivable and personal accounts due the business are known as resource accounts. . . . These accounts represent all the resources of the business except those shown by the inventories of the speculative accounts or the value of the property on hand." While this definition is literally true from the standpoint of the author, and many other teachers and authors, there is no business man who will not quarrel with it and strenuously object to having his expensive stock of goods, amounting to perhaps a million dollars, either by insinuation or otherwise, crowded out of his resources. If the author had taken the trouble to consult with any managing credit man, whether of a mercantile institution or of a bank, thereby obtaining from him a statement form such as is usually filled by those desiring credit, he would have found that the practical business man always includes under resources such items as merchandise and real estate, because they represent that upon which money can be realized.

In the definition quoted above the author uses the term "speculative," which leads us to investigate his definition of that term. We find it on page 24, as follows: "All accounts which represent the operations of the business in buying, selling and exchanging property, the expenses incident thereto, and those for services rendered, either for or by the business, show a loss or gain, and are known as speculative." Perceive, dear reader, in the light of the foregoing, into what peculiar company the merchandise account is thrust! It is being ranked with the expenses of the business.

Evidently there is something wrong in the definition, or in the way business is being done. The only explanation that can be offered is that this author, as well as those who have preceded him, has failed to see that whereas, possibly, in the earlier days, the merchandise account was merely a trading account, no great quantity of goods being carried on hand modern business demands such an arrangement of accounts as will permit the carrying of immense stocks. The merchandise on hand is certainly a resource. On the other hand, buying and trading or exchanging values is something else. There is evidently the need of two accounts. With only one account to represent two things, or to put it otherwise, with one account having two sets of values included in its records, the confusion becomes great, and that is the trouble in this book as in many others that have been published in the past.

In discussing factory operations. reference is made to cost accounts and, casually, the author lays down excellent principles which it would have been greatly to his credit had he still further exploited. We should say this with a reservation, however, for we must not forget that his primary object has been to produce a text-book for school use and not to issue a treatise on higher accounting for the edification of professionals. Referring now to the features alluded to, it is suggested that a stock card (or account) be kept on every lot of goods, and that when the job is completed and turned into stock, merchandise cost be debited for the total cost, material account credited for the cost of the material used, the wages account credited for the wages paid on the lot, factory expense account credited for the per cent. of factory expense chargeable to the cost of the goods, and depreciation account credited for the per cent. necessary to cover wear and depreciation of plant. When sales are made merchandise sales account is to be credited for the selling price obtained. At the end of every month the merchandise sales account is to be debited and merchandise cost account credited for the cost price of the goods sold. All this we are pleased to say is good doctrine, and it is to be regretted that it was not more prominently in the author's mind when he was discussing the definitions of terms and classification of accounts in earlier pages, to which allusion has been made.

To sum it all up, the volume before us has much in it to commend and comparatively little to criticise. It really occupies advanced lines, so far as current practice in commercial schools is concerned, and is not nearly so far behind the practice in the business world as many of the volumes of its class with which it might be compared.

Interest Tables

We are indebted to Frank Wittenberg, of Little Rock, Ark., for a copy of his "Interest Tables," which show the interest at every rate from 1 to 2½ per cent. for a period of one day, on amounts from $100 to $9,000,000, calculated on the basis of 360 days per annum and also of 365 days per annum. These tables have been arranged for banks and for general use, and are in exceedingly convenient form for finding the interest on daily balances. It may interest the reader to know that according to these tables the difference in interest, as between the 360-days-per-annum plan and the 365-days-per-annum plan, on $1,000,000 at 2 per cent. is a little over 76 cents per day.

Business Correspondence

How to Write a Business Letter: By C. R. Wiers. Pamphlet, 48 pages.

The author of this little work, which, by the preface, we are informed, has been designed for use in schools, offices and as a general reference book, is instructor in penmanship and bookkeeping in a business college. In the preface the author says: "The average person enters business life with but a vague understanding of the importance of becoming a good correspondent. A clear knowledge of business correspondence and a fair degree of ability in conducting correspondence would be strong contributors to business success."

At the outset the author describes materials, giving data about quality of paper and envelopes, including dimensions, weights and colors, and the same information concerning pens and ink. Under the head of Construction of Letters there are sub-chapters bearing such titles as Clearness, Spelling, Neatness, Penmanship, Abbreviations, Quotations, Directness, Truthfulness, etc. Under the head of General Information are remarks upon the courtesy of inclosing a stamp where the reply is entirely in the interest of the applicant; the care of letters; filing of letters and the preparation of letters for mailing.

A number of succinct and carefully phrased rules comprise the chapter under the head of Capitalization and Punctuation. Each of these rules is illustrated by examples taken from actual practice. In the same way the parts of a letter are discussed, with specimen headings, introductions and complimentary closings. Finally there is given a skeleton letter wherein is embodied much of what has preceded. Several pages are devoted to Superscriptions, with examples. Various forms of letters are discussed, embracing those of Introduction, Recommendation, Application, etc., together with Commercial Letters inclosing invoices, orders, remittances, etc. A few pages on general postal information brings the little book to a close.

The author's recommendations are excellent throughout. He conforms for the most part to the practice of the best business concerns, and there is much less of the pedantic and far more of the practical in this book than is ordinarily encountered in volumes of its general class.

The 3-A Loose-Leaf Ledger

The Globe-Wernicke Company, of Cincinnati, with sales offices corner of Fulton and Pearl Streets, New York, 226 and 228 Wabash Avenue, Chicago, 64 and 66 Pearl Street, Boston, has just announced a new loose-leaf ledger, which they are introducing under the trade designation of "3-A." It possesses such features of construction and adjustment as to insure for it a cordial reception wherever it is examined.

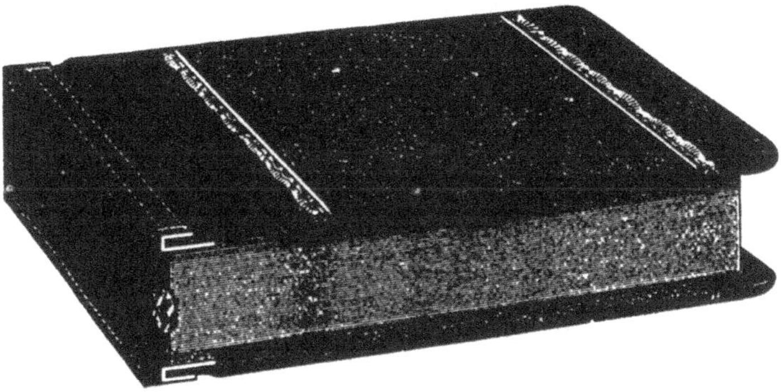

THE 3-A LOOSE-LEAF LEDGER. FIG. 1—GENERAL APPEARANCE OF THE BOOK CLOSED.

In the first place, the removal of a leaf when the ledger is closed is impossible without actually tearing the leaf. This insures the integrity of the book in a way to merit the approval of users generally. The binding holes are not slotted; instead the sheets are pierced and the binding posts of the ledger penetrate the sheets—all as clearly shown in the cut. Four b'nding posts are provided, there being two on each side of the binding. The leaves have four corresponding perforations or binding holes. When the ledger is shut and locked, all four posts penetrate the leaves. The length of the binding posts is the same as the thickness of the book. Accordingly all the leaves, when the ledger is open, can be put on either one or the other of the two sets of binding posts. This makes it possible to readily reach any required position among the leaves for taking out or inserting.

The 3-A Loose Leaf Ledger is provided at one end with a key, clearly shown in the engraving. The use of this key is not to open and close the ledger, but instead to lock the ledger shut against the possibility of opening without again using the key. The mechanism for releasing the posts so as to permit the covers to be pulled apart, as shown in the engraving, is controlled by a stud which is shown projecting through the back near the top, or at the end of the back opposite the key. The key may or may not be employed, according to the preference of the user. Unlocking the ledger and putting the key away, leaves it to be controlled solely by the movement of the stud already referred to. On the other hand, if it is desired to lock the ledger securely against any opening, all that is

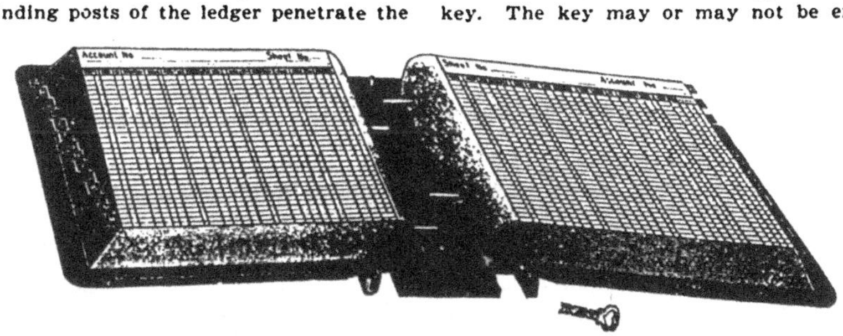

FIG. 2—BOOK OPEN, AND BINDING RELEASED FOR REMOVING AND INSERTING LEAVES.

necessary to do is to bring the key into use.

The construction of the ledger is such that there are no loose parts, the only exception being the key. All the parts are attached together and in correct relationship, whether the ledger is open or shut. The covers are never removed for any cause and in making changes none of the leaves need be disturbed except those which are removed. The method of binding is such that there is no need of reinforcing the edges of the leaves with muslin where the holes are punched, nor yet is there any need of muslin hinging. Instead the leaves are slightly crimped at the angle, thus forming a hinge or binding portion in the leaf itself. The index leaves, which are used with this ledger, are similarly crimped—a fact which still further adds to the general utility of the book. The mechanical features of the book are such that there is less shank space required than usual with books of its class. This is an important economy in the use of the book, since it enables a larger fraction of a leaf, whatever its dimensions may be, to be employed for the record than has heretofore been the rule with books of its class.

The finish given this ledger is up to the usual high standard of the company making it, and is not only attractive to the eye, but is of a character to be extremely durable in use. The back is flat rather than rounded, and is covered with Russia leather with gilt-embellished margins. There is space for any lettering that may be required. The sides of the ledger have Russia bands at each end, which are also gilt-embellished, while the panels are covered in imitation seal. Two sizes of the 3-A Loose Leaf Ledger are ready, one taking leaves of 8½x11 inches and the other 9¼x13 inches. A very convenient and neatly finished transfer binder has also been prepared to go with this ledger.

The Pen Carbon Letter Book

The Pen Carbon Letter Book is a most useful article recently put upon the market by The Pen Carbon Letter Book Company, of 221 Canal Street, New York. It seems destined to become popular in that it very satisfactorily supplies a long-felt want. The use of the book enable a writer, by the simple act of writing, to produce at the same time a fac-simile copy of his work. This he may accomplish, using his own special stationery and pen and employing ordinary writing ink, or even a pencil, if it is preferred. The book can be used in the office, at home, on the road, or anywhere else that it may be required.

The Pen Carbon Letter Book is made in two sizes; letter size, 8¼x12 inches, and note size, 6x10½ inches. Each book contains 200 leaves of good quality Manila paper, clearly numbered. The leaves are preceded by an index. The binding is of a durable character and is re-fillable or

THE PEN CARBON LETTER BOOK.

not, as the purchaser may desire. The leaves for re-filling are attached by a substantial cardboard flap, which fits snugly into a pocket which is provided in the cover.

Every Pen Carbon Letter Book is furnished with a metal clamp, of the same width as the book, to which a very sensitive sheet of carbon paper is attached by means of a gummed tip. This clamp is supplied with three clips operated by a rod. Turning the rod opens the clips. The top edge of the writing paper is then placed under the clips and the rod is turned back. The clips spring into place and hold the paper fast. The metal clamp then holds both the writing paper and the carbon and is to be inserted in the jaws of the book by gently pressing with the thumbs on the clips.

The correspondent may now commence

his letter. He may use any kind of ink, and any grade of pen will do, although a stiff nibbed pen will make a better copy than a flexible one. A thin writing paper also makes a sharper copy than one that is heavier, but a heavy paper does very well if he writes a steady, firm hand. Each book as sent out is supplied with four sheets of carbon.

The accompanying cut shows the Pen Carbon Letter Book open and ready for work. The upper sheet is the letter. The lower sheet, a portion of which is shown by turning over the lower corner of the original, is the copy, made by the pressure of the pen point on the manifold or carbon sheet and paper below. The complete outfit weighs no more, is no more cumbersome and but little more expensive, than the every-day commercial letter book.

Leg and Back Rest

An article that may be considered a boon to business men, tourists, invalids, and others, has just been put upon the market by the Ideal Leg Rest Company, of 65 West Broadway, New York. It is

THE IDEAL LEG REST IN USE.

called a "leg rest," although its usefulness is not by any means confined to easing the lower limbs. It can be helpfully employed as well to prop up an invalid in bed, and to support the head of one who is disposed to recline upon the grassy sward or upon the sands of the seashore.

This leg rest is a substantial, well-seasoned quarter-inch board of appropriate wood. It is three feet long, a foot wide at one end and eight inches at the other. By means of a pair of hinges, which, by the way, can be readily disjointed, the leg rest may be attached, at its widest end, to the seat edge of any chair as shown in the cut. When in use in this form, it is supported by a 10x16 inch part hinged to its under side, much as ironing boards in laundries and typewriter stands in offices are held up. When not in use, the rest can be instantly detached from the chair, folded up and put away in very small space until needed.

When separated from the chair, the rest can be employed to support a sick person in bed or one lying upon a lounge or upon the ground, by simply turning it around, firmly fixing the broad end beneath or upon the mattress or on the floor, as the case may be, and elevating and supporting the narrow end by the hinged board on the under side.

The "Perfect" Mucilage Cup

A mucilage bottle that will take care of itself, keep mucilage or paste from drying up and from clogging the mouth of the bottle, has long been desired by office men the world over. Such a bottle is being placed on the market by the Perfect Mucilage Bottle Co., of 6,600 Wentworth Avenue, Chicago, Ill. This bottle is handsomely made of satin-finished aluminum and is provided with two walls between which is a water reservoir which, it is said, requires replenishing only once a year. The evaporation from this reservoir keeps the air in the bottle and cap always moist and prevents the contents from thickening or clogging. It is described as being always ready for immediate use and cannot get out of order. The cap has a flat top to rest upon, which prevents it from rolling about on the desk. The cap fits clear over the mouth of the bottle and rests on its shoulder.

The Rochester Time Recorder

The accompanying illustrations represent a form of time recorder put upon the market by the Willard Frick Mfg. Co., of Rochester, N. Y., and known as the Rochester Time Recorder. The first illustration shows the mechanism and the second, one of the cards used in the system. There is a clock, which, in addition to indicating the hour of the day, also has a connected mechanism which prints the time upon a card when the card is inserted for the purpose. The card shown in the illustration indicates that on Monday morning the holder entered the shop at 6.58 and left at 12 noon. It also shows that in the afternoon he returned at 12.55 and left at 6 in the evening. He is credited, therefore, with 5 fours for each of the two fractions of the day. The reader

THE ROCHESTER TIME RECORDER. FIG. 1—GENERAL VIEW OF CLOCK.

will readily perceive how the time on other days has been recorded, and how the calculations have been made at the bottom.

In use the time recorder is provided with two racks with numbered pockets or holders for retaining the cards. One of these is known as the "In" and the other as the "Out." A workman on entering the shop takes his card from the "Out" rack, inserts it in the slot for printing and then puts it in the "In" file. Again, on leaving the shop he withdraws his card from the "In" file, has it printed by the mechanism in connection with the clock, and puts it in place, according to its number, in the "Out" file.

This plan saves the chance of loss of cards as well as the spoiling of the stamp by the workmen carrying them about, and in addition gives exact information to the office management at any time as to the presence or absence of any workman. In many cases where this system is employed the convenience in the latter regard is held to be worth so much that its use is extended to the clerks in the office and to the officers as well. While it is obvious that the time-recording part would not be employed in figuring the salary of the officers, yet the presence

FIG. 2—FAC SIMILE OF TIME CARD.

of an officer's card in the "In" or "Out" file as the case may be instantly informs any one who is searching for the information whether or not the officer is on the premises. There are many other features about this device to recommend it for use, which appear in careful detail in the catalogue that has been issued by the manufacturers, and which they send upon application. In writing for it please mention this article in ACCOUNTICS.

Accountics

The Office Magazine.

A. O. KITTREDGE, F. I. A., C. P. A., Editor.

E. R. KITTREDGE, Associate.

Accountics is devoted to the Science of Accounting, to the Art of Bookkeeping and to the advocacy of Improved Office Methods.

Subscription.—One dollar a year, payable in advance.

Postage is prepaid by the publishers in the United States, Canada and Mexico. For all other countries in the Postal Union, subscribers must add 50 cents a year.

Discontinuances.—In the absence of specific orders to discontinue at the end of the subscription term the magazine will be continued and a bill sent.

Remittances should be by Draft, P. O. Order or Express Order, payable to the order of the ACCOUNTICS ASSOCIATION. Money and postage stamps are at the risk of the sender, unless sent by express or in registered letters. Add 10 cents each to checks on local banks to defray collection charges.

Advertising Rates will be quoted on application.

Official Journal.—This publication, by resolutions duly passed, has been made the official publication of the following organizations:—

THE INSTITUTE OF ACCOUNTS.

THE NEW YORK CHAPTER of the Institute of Accounts.

THE WASHINGTON CHAPTER of the Institute of Accounts.

THE HARTFORD CHAPTER of the Institute of Accounts.

ACCOUNTICS is the accredited medium of intercommunication between members of the Institute of Accounts wherever located.

ACCOUNTICS ASSOCIATION,
Publishers,

Lancashire Bldg., Pine St., near Nassau,
New York.

Entered at the Post Office New York as Second Class Matter.

Publisher's Desk.

Among the attractive things in an advertising line that have come floating toward this office lately is a collection of letters in loose cover, entitled "The Proof," issued by the Virginia Business College, Richmond, Va. It is by all odds the most attractive piece of advertising that we have seen issued by any business college in a long time. The letters are of the form of testimonials addressed to the institution named by different business men in Richmond and Washington and other cities, concerning the writers' satisfaction with the course of instruction or with the services of the employees that they have engaged from among the graduates of the school. The letters are in fac-simile with respect to head and style of paper and also with respect to the body of the letter, whether written by pen or typewritten. The signatures are likewise in fac-simile. As already intimated, it is an exceedingly attractive pamphlet, and one that is likely to carry conviction as to the thoroughness of the school wherever examined.

Soper, of 89 Fulton Street, New York, the veteran manufacturer of Soper's Keystone Fountain Pen, announces that hereafter with each pen ordered by a reader of ACCOUNTICS he will supply without extra charge a two-part pen and pencil pocket. The pocket as described will be 5 inches long by 1⅞ inches wide, and will be made of tan-color sheepskin, furnished with a nickel-plated safety pin for attaching to the pocket of vest or coat. This simple and effective device insures against the loss of pen or pencil, and in the event of accident to the pen prevents the staining of the clothing. All of our readers will profit by a good fountain pen, and this special offer of Mr. Soper's ought to warrant their ordering the Keystone, mentioning therewith this notice, thereby securing the premium offered.

A very handsome catalogue entitled "The Manufacture of Pianoforte Action; its Rise and Development," reaches us with the compliments of Strauch Brothers, New York City. The book is a reprint from articles that appeared some time since in the American Musician. The illustrations are in part in colors and the technique of the subject is very carefully worked out. Near the close of the book are views of the offices, stock-rooms, shops and various departments of the firm who issued it. The cuts in this part are half-tones of excellent quality. The binding of the book, which is in imitation seal, is in keeping with its excellent features in other respects and will cause it to be treasured by those to whom it is sent.

"Mens sana in corpore sano," sang Horace 2,000 years ago. Business men everywhere are alive to the aptness of the Horatian suggestion, and do much, and ought to do more, to put and keep their digestive and excretory organs in good working order. A great aid to the stomach under trying conditions is the Kutnow Effervescent Powder, something that is greatly favored by all who have tried it. Our readers can have a free sample of Kutnow's Effervescent Powder sent them by dropping a card to Kutnow Bros., Ltd., Domestic Building, Union Square, New York. A remittance of $1 will bring you a large bottle of the same powder, postpaid. Kutnow's powder is a mild aperient and harmless in after effect.

The Edison Chemical Co., of 7 Cedar Street, New York, are putting upon the ink market, an ink tablet which they call Edison's Ink Concentrates; or, the Wizard's Powder. Each tablet when dissolved in water, it is asserted, will make one ounce of blue-black ink, warranted to be indelible, and not to be removed by any known chemical. Other colors—jet black, blue, purple and carmine, are also supplied, all but the last named being immutable.

Accountics

VOL. V SEPTEMBER 1899 NO. 3

The Monthly Statement

The third annual convention of the Street Railway Accountants' Association of America is to be held in Chicago October 17th and days following. It will be attended by representatives of nearly all the companies who hold membership in the organization named. An attractive and comprehensive programme has been arranged for the occasion. Several papers are to be presented, discussing topics of more than passing interest to those concerned in the accounts of street railway corporations. The collection of blanks and forms, the gathering of which has been in progress under the auspices of the secretary for some time past, is to be on exhibition, and it is supposed will afford a basis of considerable discussion, as well as also being the means of much information to those who are considering readjustment in their general routine. The reports of several important committees will also be presented.

This organization, which is just completing the third year of its existence, has for its chief object the systematizing of street railway accounting. The immediate object in view is to secure uniformity of statement, so that investors may have a basis of comparisons when considering the results of different companies, and so also that managing men may be able to judge relative of the success of their efforts in the conduct of the enterprises with which they are connected. So far, the work of the organization has resulted in little more than an agreement upon certain schemes of classification of expense accounts. The broad features of accounting have not been discussed, and methods of bookkeeping, the conduct of accounts, the direction of the office force, and various other collateral and cognate subjects have not received any attention whatsoever. It is to be supposed that after a full agreement has been reached in the matter of expense classifications that some of these other subjects will come up for consideration.

An article of considerable length might be written at this time upon the opportunities of the Institute of Accounts, and if written as it might be written, it would, we fancy, be of interest to the members of the Institute, wherever located. In no period since the formation of the Institute has there been such general interest manifested in accounting and improved office routine as prevails at the present time in almost every direction. It would seem that the floods of the panic of 1893 swept away much of the old-fogyism and general apathy which covered almost out of sight the real importance of accounting in all business undertakings. It would seem also as though the floods of the disastrous period referred to also swept out of the ranks of business many of those who, by nominal conservatism but in fact actual inertia, stood opposed to progress in accountancy, and that more progressive men had risen up to take their places.

Whatever may be the reason for the change, the community at the present time seems alive to improvements in all office work. Business men are ready for labor-saving appliances and for advanced methods as well. Their eagerness to obtain that which is best naturally stimulates the accountants and bookkeepers of their establishments to renewed exertions, and even causes them to feel that they ought to study and thereby learn more about their chosen calling. It is not strange, therefore, that inquiries should be coming in from different directions with respect to membership in the Institute and the advantages which follow therefrom. It is recognized as an educational institution that can be of special service at this particular time.

As our readers are already informed, the Institute of Accounts is a federation of chapters. Its fundamental law is such as to permit and encourage the formation of local bodies throughout the country, and these local bodies collectively constitute the Institute or the national organization. The local bodies in turn elect delegates who assemble as a convention once a year and transact such general business as may come before that body, including the election of the National officers. With the exception of this annual gathering, the meetings and general activities of the Institute are restricted to what the chapters do. At these local gatherings technical papers are presented, questions are asked and answered, addresses are delivered by specialists, both in and out of the membership, and discussions are conducted. All the advantages that follow from men of a kindred calling and like ideas getting together and talking over the interests which they have in common follow upon these meetings.

The fundamental law of the Institute is so extremely liberal that the several chapters have practically as much liberty of choice concerning the character of their meetings and entertainments as though they had no connection with the central or national body whatever. Accordingly, the surveyor of the general field will discover chapters in various stages of development and manifesting varying degrees of activity. New ideas are from time to time projected by the different chapters, and special efforts are being made by some of them by way of being serviceable to the community. For example, the chapter at Hartford, Conn., has recently added to its other features a study course, intended to benefit and assist prospective members. New members, of course, are to be recruited out of the ranks of those who are at present clerks and subordinates, and in order to enable them to qualify for the necessary examination, the Hartford Chapter has undertaken to conduct this course of study. A more commendable piece of work could scarcely be named.

The opportunitites of the Institute, referred to above, grow out of the interest that the business public is at present manifesting in all matters relating to accounts, and the experience which it has had to date in the formation of chapters. The Institute has a large number of what may be called members at large, actually members of the New York Chapter, because it was the parent chapter organized, and therefore included in its membership all the members at large then existing, but in fact living in various portions of the country remote from New York. To give the addresses of all these members would be to include in our account the names of numerous large cities and towns throughout the length and breadth of the land. It has no doubt one time or another entered into the mind of each of these members to do something toward the formation of a chapter in the place in which he is residing. It is also entering the minds of many of the daily associates in business of these members to inquire into the workings of the Institute, with a view to secure membership therein. The opportunity then exists for the formation of a large number of chapters by bringing these two elements together. The consummation of such a result—that is, the establishment of many new chapters—requires only a small amount of effort, and the work is well worth undertaking.

We do not intend to intimate by what has preceded that there are members of the Institute in every city and town in the country. There are some important centers in which at present there is no member of the Institute. In such cases the opportunity is before the enterprising accountants of that city to organize a chapter independent of any assistance that might be rendered by one who is already a member. This is not a difficult undertaking, either, and it will repay amply the effort that may be put forth. We understand that the National Secretary is at present ready with blanks and forms to co-operate with all who are disposed to undertake the formation of local chapters. His address will be found in connection with the stated card of the Institute on another page. The long evenings of the year are just at hand, and to what better use could a few of them be put than to the formation of a chapter of the Institute of Accounts, thereby securing locally the same advantages to its members that the gentlemen of the New York Chapter have for so many years enjoyed?

Prevention Versus Sympathetic Nursing

It gives us pleasure to bring to the attention of the readers of The Office Magazine those bright things which we see in our exchanges from time to time which otherwise might be forever lost. The accompanying cut is an instance in point and is borrowed from our esteemed contemporary, The Financial Record. It tells in a pictorial way a truth which should be brought to the attention of every business man. After perceiving the facts of the case, and possibly comprehending the irony of our contemporary's remarks, the business man may take heed to his own advantage.

Under the cut, as published in the periodical above mentioned, a dialogue was printed. The citizen who has stopped the policeman, who, as will be seen, poses as a public accountant, says to him: "Why don't you stop those fellows? They intend to go through that man." To this the policeman or public accountant replies: "Well, he could save lots of money, and some people are beginning to appreciate that it is better to employ an accountant to watch out for them than to be robbed—but we can't be too forceful in offering our services. After the robbery we are engaged to find out the extent and how it was done." Our contemporary evidently thinks that the public accountant is not blameless for this state of affairs.

This incident reminds us of something that occurred at a dinner some time since, at which several prominent accountants were present. One of them, addressing a colleague across the table, said: "Mr. X, we think you are doing too much for the business man." "Why so?" asked X in response. "Well, you see, it is not professional to do what you are doing. You are giving the business man too much instruction. You give him helps in accounting systems that really make his position very secure, and therefore there is less need of the professional services of our class. Now, what we like is to be called in, at a good round rate per diem, of course, whenever the business man is in trouble, or when he has occasion to make up a statement, as, for example, at the end of a year. We like to be treated the same as lawyers and doctors." "If I understand you," said X in reply, "you expect to render your services only when there is a crisis, when there is some particular emergency, or an actual disaster,

PUZZLE PICTURE—FIND THE PUBLIC ACCOUNTANT.

just as the physician is called in when there is a case of fever." "Well," said No. 1, "that is about the situation." To this X said: "I have often thought that the cupidity of physicians might cause them to wish in their secret hearts that an epidemic would prevail, so as to make lots of business for them, and since accountants are quite as fallible as doctors, it might be thought that they would secretly wish for business disasters in a considerable number, in order to make business lively for them. Summing it all up," said X, in conclusion, "for my part I would rather not be a doctor in the accounting sense. I would greatly prefer to be a board of health, helping the business man to avoid disaster and keeping his affairs in such shape that outside help is needed as seldom as possible."

It is evident that the editor of the Financial Record and Mr. X, whom we have quoted above, view matters from essentially the same standpoint.

Stuck With "We-Stic-It"

We are in receipt of a neat cardboard box containing 500 "We-Stic-It" Adhesive Wafers, made by M. C. Robbins, of 132 Grace street, Syracuse, N. Y. They are in four sizes, ranging from ½x½ to ½x 1½ inches and sell at a very low price. These wafers, if we may so designate them, are made of very thin, transparent and tough parchment paper, mucilaged on both sides. They will be found to be of great value to any one having occasion to mend correspondence, repair bank notes or piece together documents of any kind which have been torn or mutilated. They are also convenient for fastening together two or more sheets of paper. Mr. Robbins' trade cry is "Stuck With We-Stic-It." His letter-heads are sent out with a paper leaflet stuck in place by a "We-Stic-It" wafer. The wafers, we find by test, stick and hold with a tenacity hard to overcome.

Adjustable Index Tags

Charles C. Smith, of Exeter, Neb., calls attention to his adjustable index tags as a device which, it is asserted, will save 20 per cent. of a bookkeeper's time in posting and one that is adapted to a wide variety of uses. This invention consists of a thin, flat clip enclosed in leather and finished. The clip is made of tempered clock-spring steel and with proper use will not lose its grip. The covering is made from kid-finished leather, lined with muslin, which gives it firmness and durability; it is stitched with silk and fastened to the clip by a strong adhesive.

These adjustable tags are supplied either plain or printed with names of ledger accounts, cities, States, letters of alphabet, months, etc., or they can be furnished with a facing, on each side, of linen ledger paper, on which inscriptions may be written with ink or pencil and erased at will. They can be attached anywhere to any leaf of an account book simply by starting the clip on at the upper corner of the leaf and pushing it inward and downward along the margin to the desired place. On the other hand, a quick movement will pull the tag off.

A plain tag of this variety enables the bookkeeper to put any reference required at just the page wanted. A numbered tag for every twenty-fifth page enables him to open within a few leaves of any page wanted or to readily find items or accounts entered numerically.

It Made a Difference

A working man with a dinner pail in his hand came out of a little shop and was met by a fellow working man, who said:

"Why, Jim, you're working over time now, aren't you?"

"No," was the reply, "I'm not."

"Aren't you putting in more than eight hours a day?"

"Yes."

"I thought eight hours was the union schedule?" remarked the outsider.

"Yes, but you see, I have just bought the shop."

Confidence in Oneself

Suppose Grant had said to himself, "It is not reasonable to think that a tanner-boy can perform what Sherman, Meade, or Halleck have failed to do!"

What if McKinley had pictured himself as a failure, or as possessing only mediocre ability when a boy!

What if Wanamaker had pronounced himself a failure when working in a store at a dollar and a quarter a week, and walking four miles every day to Philadelphia! Would he have succeeded as a merchant?

Form of Voucher.

A collection of voucher forms, remittance blanks, checks and other matters relating to payments would form a most interesting contribution to the business literature of the period. Every one who has to do with the receipts of a business encounters from time to time voucher forms and checks that are of special interest. In our own experience we are no exception to the general rule, as witness the fac-simile herewith.

As likely to interest our readers on lines above suggested, we present a reproduction of a combined check and voucher received some time since from the Cambria Steel Company, of Philadelphia. From the phrasing of the form it is to be supposed that the one object in making the voucher itself payable in bank, was to secure the prompt return of the voucher. We fear that our handling of this paper has been an exception to the rule and likewise an annoyance to the auditor of the company, for, truth to be stated, it was lodged with our engraver much longer than was really necessary. Finally, however, the cut was made and the check or voucher, whichever it is to be called, took its course in regular line. It has been "cashed in" long since, but its shadow still remains to be examined for the edification of the reader.

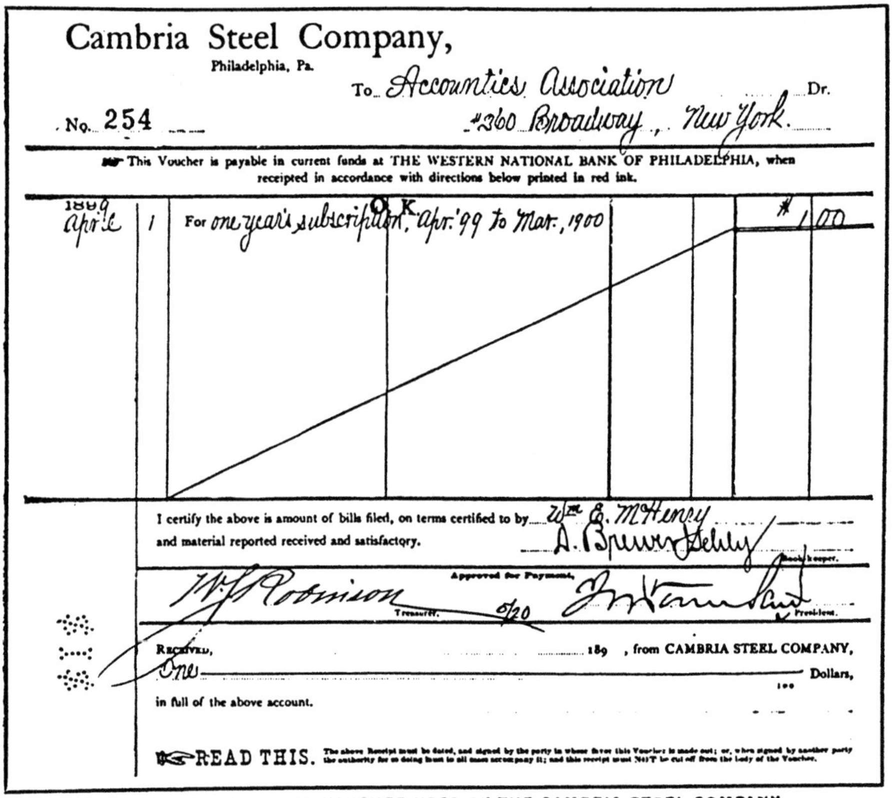

Cambria Steel Company,
Philadelphia, Pa.

To Accountics Association Dr.
No. 254 #260 Broadway, New York.

This Voucher is payable in current funds at THE WESTERN NATIONAL BANK OF PHILADELPHIA, when receipted in accordance with directions below printed in red ink.

1899 April 1 For one year's subscription, Apr. '99 to Mar., 1900 O.K. $1.00

I certify the above is amount of bills filed, on terms certified to by Wm. E. McHenry
and material reported received and satisfactory. A. Brewer Selby Book-keeper.

Approved for Payment,
W. J. Robinson Treasurer. 5/20 President.

Received, 189 , from CAMBRIA STEEL COMPANY,
One Dollars, 100
in full of the above account.

READ THIS. The above Receipt must be dated, and signed by the party in whose favor this Voucher is made out; or, when signed by another party the authority for so doing must in all cases accompany it; and this receipt must NOT be cut off from the body of the Voucher.

COMBINED CHECK AND VOUCHER USED BY THE CAMBRIA STEEL COMPANY.

Let not one look of Fortune cast you down; she were not Fortune if she did not frown.—Earl of Orrery.

Fortune is like a coquette; if you don't run after her, she will run after you.
—H. W Shaw.

If wealth come, beware of him, the smooth, false friend! There is treachery in his proffered hand; his tongue is eloquent to tempt; lust of many harms is lurking in his eye; he hath a hollow heart; use him cautiously.—Tupper.

Accountant's Associations

New York Chapter of the Institute of Accounts

The opening meeting of the autumn and winter season of the New York Chapter of the Institute of Accounts was held at the Waldorf-Astoria on the evening of September 21. There was a good attendance of members, and several visitors were also present. The subject, as had been announced for discussion, was that of "Inventories." President Frederick W. Child, having called Mr. Dillon to the chair, opened the discussion with a few pertinent remarks, of which the following is a running summary:

There are many and diverse opinions, even among accountants, with reference to the method of placing proper values on the inventory of, for example, the completed goods and raw materials of a manufacturing establishment. A careful examination of numerous publications on the subject of bookkeeping shows that none of them presents a clear idea on this point, and some of them afford no information upon it whatsoever.

The efforts of competent accountants are often made practically useless by the illogical and loose way in which inventories are priced or valued. Everything else connected with accounts may be left to the judgment of the accountant, but before inventories can be entered up to the several accounts, the prices, as a rule, must be revised by the proprietor or some one in authority, who often knows little or nothing of the plan upon which the books have been constructed and are being conducted. The scale of prices which are thus put upon inventories not infrequently depends upon the state of mind of the person who fixes them. If business has been dull and sales slow during the period, it is often thought wise to augment the inventory prices so that a respectable showing can be made. If large profits have been made, the opportunity is sometimes seized upon to mark down some of the stock, which on previous inventories may have been carried at too high figures.

Some manufacturers carry their ideas of conservatism to the point of charging all purchases of tools and machinery directly into Expense.

The market value of whatever raw material may happen to be on hand at the time of taking the inventory has a powerful influence with some in determining the figures of the inventory. This, the speaker believed, is going entirely outside of the question, for the goods which the concern manufactures will cost, so far as materials are concerned, just what was paid for them. What they cost is the important item of information that is to be obtained, and not what they would have cost if better judgment had been used in purchasing materials.

The speaker declared that he was not denying the proprietory right of the owner of a business to order these things to be done as he sees fit, but he did hold that literal compliance with such directions often destroys the value of the accounts as records of the business. The results shown reflect the wishes of the owners rather than embody a statement of actual facts.

Continuing, the speaker said that in every well-ordered set of books there should be clearly shown what profits and losses are due to trading and what are due to management or other causes. To accomplish this, the inventories in a going mercantile concern should be figured at exactly cost prices to the concern and credited to the several accounts at these prices. In manufacturing concerns completed stock and work in progress should be taken at the ascertained cost. This cost, the speaker stated, should include an allowance for depreciation of plant. To facilitate the calculations in this respect, the speaker stated that the plants should be valued at cost and that the allowance for depreciation should be kept in a proper reserve account. In other words, the value of the inventory should be the book value or the amount of the capital of the concern that has gone into the stock on hand. By this provision the trading profit or loss in the several sub-accounts may be shown apart from any other profits or losses. With a showing of this kind, it becomes possible to determine what percentage of profit or loss on the investment has been made.

With respect to the treatment of depreciation, so far as it concerned inventosies, the speaker said: A rate of probable yearly depreciation should be fixed on the different classes of plant account and included in the manufacturing expenses. This cost is to be added in with the other costs of the product in proper proportions. Of course, this will increase the cost of the goods manufactured and will proportionately increase the inventory value of such goods on hand and of work in progress.

In cases of stock of goods on hand, which goods have for any reason depreciated beyond recovery, the inventory should first be calculated at actual cost prices and in this form credited to the several accounts. Then the amount of depreciation should be ascertained and it should be made the subject of a separate entry, distinctly stating the course of the loss. The speaker here pointed out that many of such losses are exceptional and are often so serious as to materially affect the legitimate trading profits. For these reasons they should always appear as separate items.

With respect to revaluations, the speaker recorded his views as follows: Revaluations are sometimes rendered imperative, as, for example, in changing the form of copartnership by the admission of a new partner, or by the death or retirement of an old partner. Revaluations are also necessary where the business is to be reorganized in the form of a corporation. Revaluations are also required in the light of various other contingencies which may arise. Unless revaluations are absolutely necessary, they are in most cases undesirable. One reason for holding this view, the speaker declared, is that expert valuers, who may be called in to establish the figures on machinery and other items of plant, are by no means a unit in their ideas of value. Different men of this class are governed by entirely different rules of procedure. Accordingly, frequent revaluations have a tendency to interrupt the continuity of the accounts and destroy their value for purposes of comparison. On the other hand, if the plant accounts are kept at their original cost, and reserve accounts for depreciation are maintained with good judgment, these abnormal fluctuations are avoided. In case revaluations are made and accepted, the speaker continued, the reserve accounts should be closed out to the different property accounts, and the difference between the book values thus shown and the values established should be charged or credited, as the case may be, to the profit and loss account, with a full statement of the reason for making the entry.

At this point the general subject was thrown open for discussion, with the statement that the speaker would be glad to answer such questions as might be proposed to him. Mr. Cheney inquired concerning the advantages of maintaining reserve acounts, as opposed to credits for depreciation directly to plant account. To this Mr. Child replied in substance as follows: Depreciation of plant is due to many causes, among which is the wear by more or less constant use, and which can only be partially restored by repairs. Another cause is accidents, which may render a machine worthless, and a still more potent cause is the activity of inventors, who are constantly making improved machinery, which causes the old to become obsolete. The actual amount of depreciation, therefore, is an uncertain quantity. It may be more or less, according to circumstances, which may or may not arise. For this reason the depreciation should be held in abeyance until the actual loss is ascertained, so that the assumed or anticipated loss may be adjusted in the light of ascertained facts. Again, the plant account ought to show the amount of the company's capital invested therein, but if these uncertain amounts are deducted periodically, the plant accounts will soon be in a condition to show neither the amount of capital invested, nor yet the amount of the value on hand. When handled in this way, the plant accounts soon get into such a condition as to show nothing in particular.

Mr. Dutton, after complimenting the speaker upon the excellent points that he had made in his address, dwelt upon a missing element in inventories and asserted that it was the accountant, rather than the proprietor, who ought to fix the inventory prices whenever any important question arose.

Mr. Kittredge took exception to the statement of the last speaker by inquiring if any one present was willing to put the accountant, however able a man he might be in his own profession, above the proprietors of a business and all others who have devoted their lives to learning the intricacies of a given line of trade? He declared that for his part he believed that the function of the accountant was that of an expert assistant, skillfully applying the information that the proprietor might have with respect to costs and the condition of the work in progress, which the inventory must include, but that in no case was it expedient for the accountant to arrogate to himself, by reason of his profession and his technical attainments, however great, a knowledge of a given business, beyond that of those who had spent the whole of their lives in it.

Next referring to the remarks of Mr. Child with respect to revaluation of plant, Mr. Kittredge directed the attention of the meeting to English practice in this regard, making the point that, judging by decisions of the English courts, which had been more or less extensively published in this country of late, it would seem that it was coming to be understood among English accountants that it is just as wrong to sustain or make whole capital, at the expense of dividends, as it is to pay dividends out of capital. If this theory prevails, then reserves of the kind recommended by Mr. Child are not in order. Instead, plant must be run until it is worn out, and when it is used up or destroyed, it is to be replaced by a further contribution of capital. In the mean time, dividends must be paid to the limit of the earnings.

The speaker said that he only presented these views, being the result of somewhat careful reading of decisions of the English courts and of addresses and essays by prominent English accountants, as matters of collateral interest. For himself, he did not agree with the British idea as here outlined. Instead, he was quite in sympathy with the speaker's contention, that plant should be kept good out of earnings, or, in other words, that the depreciation of plant was a legitimate element of the cost of the goods produced. He also stated that he was in full sympathy with the proposed scheme of reserve accounts, as outlined by the first speaker, and which allows plant account to represent the actual investment in plant, regardless of its condition. The reserve accounts accumulate that which has been charged into cost of product and what is kept in hand to make good the depreciation of plant, whenever the opportunity occurs.

E. A. Washburn, a visitor who declared himself a business man and not an accountant, gave in a few well-turned sentences his opinion of the arbitrary way in which accountants sometimes attempt to manage those matters which, while effecting the accounts, still seem to be in the particular domain of the business manager. He said: "From the business man's standpoint, an accountant should be an assistant to the manager and proprietor, pointing out what is proper to be done and assisting in doing it, instead of arbitrarily putting himself in the position of dictator and proceeding alone, without the help of the manager or proprietor in respect to matters concerning which, as a rule, he greatly needs their knowledge."

Remarks were also made by Messrs. Stratton, Dillon, McNeal and others.

At the close of the public meeting the members of the Chapter were invited to a conference with reference to various matters pertaining to the welfare of the organization. In this conference informal reports were presented by the officers. Considerable discussion followed as to the programme of the winter meetings and the means that may be advantageously employed for making them entertaining and profitable. It was at a late hour that the conference was adjourned.

Hartford Chapter of the Institute of Accounts

The Hartford Chapter, after a vacation during the months of July and August, resumed its monthly meetings in September. The date fixed was Tuesday evening, the 26th, and the meeting then held had a fair attendance. Two registrants for membership were admitted to the privileges of the Chapter for a course of study upon the stipulation that they prepare themselves for membership in the Institute and apply for the same within three years.

The applicants in this case are the first to take advantage of an opportunity offered by this Chapter to those who desire to specially advance themselves in the science and practice of accounting, thereby increasing their usefulness to their employers and incidentally benefiting their salary accounts, while also fitting themselves for membership in the organization. Speaking on this point, an officer of the Hartford Chapter expressed himself recently in the following terms: "We believe that there is a considerable number of young men occupying junior positions in the business institutions in this community, who, with a fair opportunity and with favorable surroundings, might become good accountants. To such as care to avail themselves of the privileges under our plan, we grant the use of our library and allow them to attend our meetings and participate in discussions, and, in fact, to enjoy generally the privileges of the Institute. They are to take part in all we do, save in the general business of the Chapter."

President Gershom Smith, after opening the meeting, announced with much feeling the death of one of the members of the organization, Daniel P. Colton, secretary of the Hartford Electric Light Company, and one who had been active in the formation of the Chapter. Mr. Colton died on the morning of September 25. The Chapter took formal notice of Mr. Colton's death by sending to his house a floral tribute in the shape of a pillow of flowers, upon which was worked the emblem of the Institute, namely, a triangle within a circle, with the letters "I. of A."

The Topic Committee had provided as the special exercises of this meeting an address by Gilbert W. Chapin, savings bank actuary, who was then introduced. Mr. Chapin first explained and illustrated methods of keeping accounts in the bank with which he is associated. The system outlined it appeared is so perfectly adjusted that everything seems to move like clockwork. As explained by the speaker, accuracy is secured by proofs at every point, and, as it might be described, by proof upon proof. In the ten years since the plan was adopted not an error of even a single cent, it was stated, has passed without detection. This is a record that would be impossible under the old system of proving work, by having one man check what another has done.

Mr. Chapin then traced a deposit from its receipt through the regular channels until it was credited on the ledger to the proper account. He next described the different records employed with deposits. Drafts go through the same process, except that the slips are of a different color. This change in color makes it impossible to mistake a debit for a credit. The manner of balancing each day's cash receipts and withdrawals was also carefully described, and likewise how the monthly balance of each ledger, of which no less than seventeen are in use, is obtained.

The system employed for computing interest on the accounts, or, rather, how the amounts upon which interest is to be allowed and figured, was next explained in detail. A duplicate or skeleton ledger, having first a column for the balance of each account at the beginning of six months, then pairs of columns for each of the six months, namely, a debit and a credit column, in which drafts and deposits are posted in proper monthly order, is employed. Following the monthly columns, the speaker said, there are four specially ruled columns, the first three of which represent the balances at the end of six months before interest is added, in the following order: First, a six months' column, in which is entered all amounts entitled to six months' interest. All balances that have not changed are carried into this column, as well as such portions of those which have changed as are entitled to six months' interest. Second, a three months' column, in which are carried all deposits made during the first part of the six months which remain on the books for at least three months immediately preceding interest date, or, in other words, those amounts which are entitled to three months' interest. Third, a no-interest column, the title of which is self-explanatory. It will be readily seen, as the speaker pointed out, that the footings of these three columns combined represent the total amount on deposit, and further that by the form of the book each page is self-proving.

The speaker directed particular attention to the ease with which interest is figured. If the calculations are at 4 per cent., which is the usual rate in the State of Connecticut, 2 per cent. would apply to the amounts in the first column and 1 per cent. to the amounts in the second column, while, as before explained, those in the third column receive no interest whatsoever. The amount of interest is entered in the fourth column mentioned and the footings of this are proved by computing interest on the totals of the six months and three months' columns. By this plan errors either in figuring interest or footing the columns are always revealed. The interest is finally added to the principal and the amount compared with the balances of each account in the several ledgers, to which the interest has been added by independent computations. The daily balance of the bank was explained, as was also the monthly statistical statement.

Mr. Chapin's address was quite informal and was all the more interesting on this account. The forms which he brought with him for illustrating his remarks were very carefully examined by all who were present.

3-A Time Books and Pay Rolls

We present on this and the page following several illustrations of 3-A Pay Rolls and Time Books recently brought out by the Globe-Wernicke Co., Cincinnati, with sales offices in New York, Boston and Chicago. The 3-A Pay Rolls and Time Books are special adaptations of the long and short leaf construction which this company has been applying to books for various purposes for some time past. By this special construction a space for writing the names of workmen is provided on the projecting margin of the wide leaf, leaving the narrow leaves for the time and rate columns and for extensions. By increasing the number of narrow leaves, a single writing of the names may be made to answer for a very considerable period of time.

The Pay Rolls here illustrated have several features peculiar to them beyond that of the construction to which reference has already been made. It will be noticed that in forms A and B, for example, there are some columns for "distribution." These provide a convenient means for the paymaster to determine the exact number of bills of each of the several denominations, and number of pieces of fractional currency as well, required to liquidate a given pay roll. Form B differs from form A in that the former is adapted for recording two weeks' time.

PAY ROLL

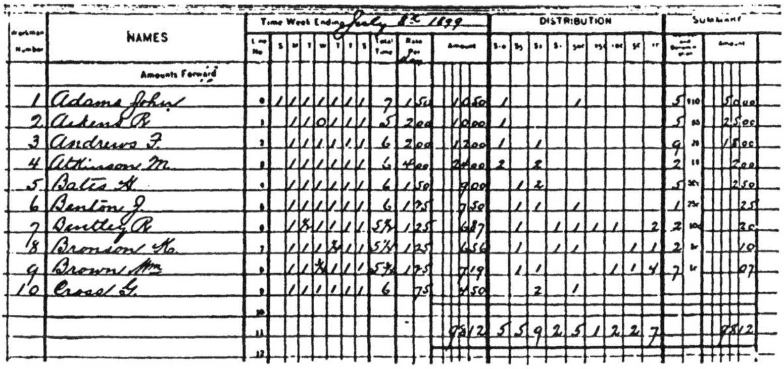

Time Week Ending July 8th 1899

Workman Number	Names	Total Time	Rate Per Day	Amount
	Amounts Forward			
1	Adams John	7	1.50	10.50
2	Aikens R.	5	2.00	10.00
3	Andrews F.	6	2.00	12.00
4	Atkinson M.	6	4.00	24.00
5	Bates H.	6	1.50	9.00
6	Benton J.	6	1.25	7.50
7	Bentley R.	5½	1.25	6.87
8	Bronson H.	5¼	1.25	6.56
9	Brown Wm.	5¾	1.25	7.19
10	Cross G.	6	.75	4.50
				98.12

3-A PAY ROLLS AND TIME BOOKS.

Fig. 1, Form A.—Weekly. Names written once in six weeks.

PAY ROLL

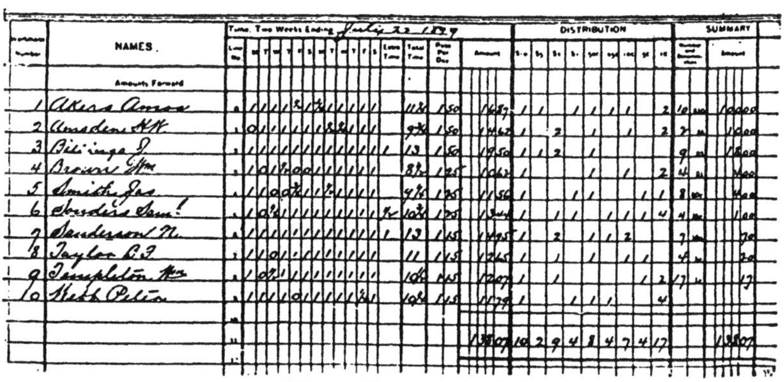

Time, Two Weeks Ending July 22 1899

Workman Number	Names	Total Time	Rate Per Day	Amount
	Amounts Forward			
1	Akers Amos	11¼	1.50	16.87
2	Amsden H.H.	9¾	1.50	14.62
3	Billings J.	13	1.50	19.50
4	Brown Wm.	8½	1.25	10.62
5	Smith Jas.	9¼	1.25	11.56
6	Sanders Saml.	10¾	1.25	13.44
7	Sanderson N.	13	1.15	14.95
8	Taylor C.J.	11	1.15	12.65
9	Templeton Wm.	10½	1.15	12.07
10	Webb Peter	10¼	1.15	11.79
				138.07

Fig. 2, Form B.—Bi-Weekly. Names written once in eight weeks.

The description under the several cuts is explanatory and will indicate the usefulness of these forms in all cases where pay rolls are to be made out.

The company announce that they are ready to make special pay rolls to order

PAY ROLL

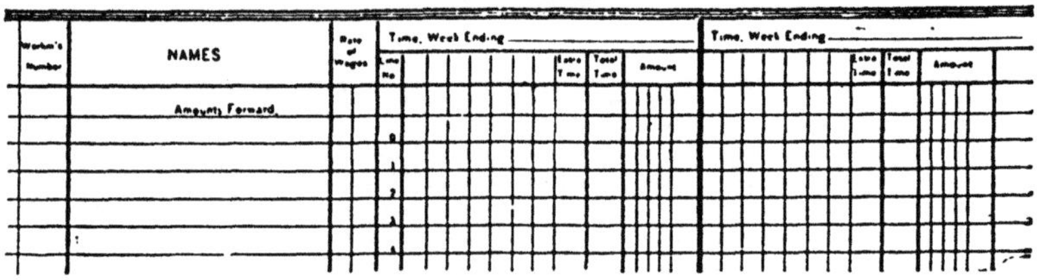

Fig. 3, Form C.—Weekly. Names written once in eight weeks.

where these stock rulings do not answer, and also mention that the sizes of the books may be varied from demy to very small dimensions, or that they may be extended above demy. A pamphlet con-

PAY ROLL

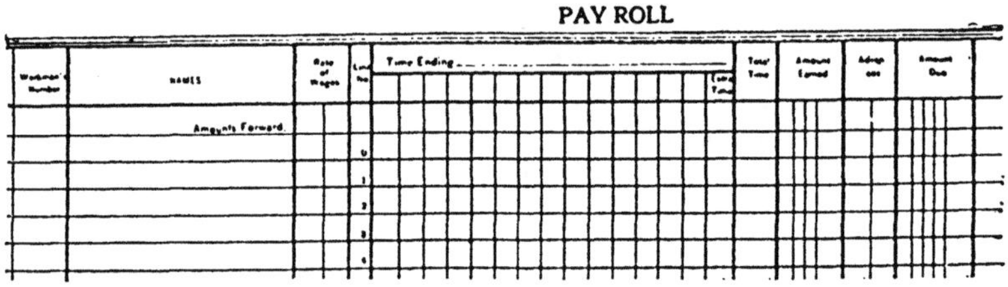

Fig. 4, Form D.—Bi-Weekly or Semi-Monthly. Names written once in eight weeks.

taining interesting particulars concerning these goods has been prepared, a copy of which will be sent to any of our readers who apply for the same. We also understand that the company is willing to send sample sheets to prospective buyers.

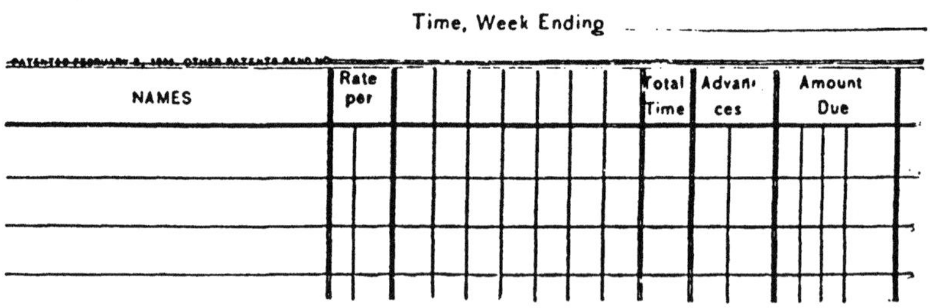

Fig. 5 —Weekly. Names written once in six weeks.

Unique Advertising

The Livermore & Knight Co. have long been famous throughout the country for their unique advertising designs, which are patronized by leading houses everywhere. A sample which has recently come to hand, employed by the John Hancock Mutual Life Insurance Co., is entitled "The Book of Knowledge." It represents, by embossing, a book of antique design on a desk. The sub-title is "Open and things that are hidden from thee shall be revealed." Underneath this attractive title, and projecting from a packet made by the embossing in a way to attract attention, was the circular of the company mentioned.

Interest and Discount—VIII

By Charles W. Rohne

Repayment of Loans by Installments

The principle of annuities can be and often is applied to the repayment of loans by installments. A numerical example will enable us to understand more clearly the application of the principle referred to: The sum of $5,000 is to be advanced at 5 per cent. interest, to be repaid in fifteen years by equal annual installments, including principal and interest. It is required to separate each year's payment into principal and interest.

By referring to a table showing the present value of $1.00 per annum, we find that the present value of fifteen annual payments at 5 per cent. is $10.37966. Therefore we find that the amount per annum necessary to accomplish the repayment in fifteen years is $481.711. Deducting from this amount the interest on $5,000 at 5 per cent. for one year, or $250, we find that the sinking fund contained in the first payment is $231.711.

1 Year. (Mth.)	2 Interest Contained in Mth. Payment.	3 Principal Contained in Mth. Payment.	4 Principal Repaid to Date.	5 Principal still Outstanding.
1	$250.000	$231.711	$231.711	$4,768.289
2	238.414	243.297	475.008	4,524.992
3	226.249	255.462	730 470	4,269.530
4	213.476	268.235	998.705	4.001.295
5	200.064	281.647	1,280.352	3,719.548
6	185.982	295.729	1,576.081	3,423.919
7	171.196	310.515	1,886.596	3,113.404
8	155.670	326.041	2,212.637	2,787.363
9	139.368	342.343	2,554.980	2,445 020
10	122.251	359.460	2,914.440	2,085 560
11	104.277	377.434	3,291.874	1,708.126
12	85.406	496.405	3,688.179	1,311.821
13	65.590	416.121	4,104.300	895.700
14	44.784	436 927	4,541.227	458.773
15	22.938	458.773	5,000.000	0.000

Table illustrating the redemption of $5,000 in 15 years by equal annual installments of $481.711, including principal and interest at 5%.

In the accompanying schedule, or table, the transaction is worked out at length. The amount of principal opposite any year in column three is obtained by multiplying by (1+i), or $1.05, the amount opposite the previous year, and it will further be found that the amount opposite any year may be ascertained without making the intermediate calculations. The amount of principal in the 10th payment could be ascertained by applying the expression $481.711v^{n-m+1}$. or $481.711v^{16-m}$. Thus for the 10th year, v^6 = .7462154, and $v^6 \times 481.711 = 359.460$.

Reducing the expression above to an arithmetical expression, the amount of principal in the tenth payment is ascertained by taking the total number of years that the loan has to run, plus one, deducting therefrom the number of years which have expired, and using the present worth of $1.00 for the difference, which in this instance is six years, then multiplying by the amount paid yearly will produce the sinking fund, or principal contained in that payment.

The principal repaid to date given in column four is simply a progressive footings of column three. It will also be found to be the amount of an annuity of the sinking fund for the period elapsed. Thus the amount of an annuity of $1.00 for ten years is $12.578, as shown by any compound interest table giving the amount of $1.00 per annum at 5 per cent. Now, multiplying $12,578 by the sinking fund contained in the first payment, or $231.711, we find the product to be $2,914.440, which is also the amount opposite ten in column four of the table. The principal outstanding as given in column five is obtained by taking all the previous repayments of principal as given in column four from the original $5,000.

It sometimes happens that in consideration of a terminable annuity, a lender grants an advance at a higher rate of interest than he can secure from other investments, and that he wishes to realize the higher rate on the whole of the capital during the entire term of the annuity, although, as we have seen, part of his capital is repaid to him year by year. He must, therefore, so fix the price he pays for the annuity that he may realize interest at the higher rate, called the remunerative rate.

These terms are very onerous to the borrower, as he is not only to pay the higher rate of interest on the capital which remains in his possession, but also to make up to that higher rate during the whole period for which the annuity has to run, the interest on the accumulations of the sinking fund which are in the hands of the lender.

A numerical illustration will be useful, and for this purpose it is convenient to repeat with the necessary modifications the one already given. By this means a comparison can be instituted between the ordinary annuity and the special annuity now under consideration.

Suppose a lender to advance $5,000, and we are asked to find the annuity for fifteen years, which will pay him 7 per cent. on his capital and replace that capital at 5 per cent.

The annuity for fifteen years which $1 will purchase at 5 per cent. is $.0963423. Add to this 02 (the difference between 7 per cent. and 5 per cent. expressed decimally), and multiplying by $5,000. we have $581.711. This is greater than in the previous illustration by $100, or 2 per cent. on $5,000.

outstanding, and also interest at 2 per cent. on the capital already repaid, so as to raise to 7 per cent. the interest on that portion of capital also.

The operation of the fund is shown in the accompanying schedule, or table, by which it is seen that all of these requirements are fulfilled. Columns three, four and five are identical with the columns bearing the same headings in the previous examples, but interest in column six in the present table is always 2 per cent. more than that in the corresponding column (i. e., column two) of the preceding example, while we have added column eight, showing the balance of interest on the principal already paid. It will be seen that the sum of the amounts opposite any year in columns three, six and eight is always equal to the annual rent

1	2	3	4	5	6	7	8	9
Year, (M.)	Annual Rent of Annuity.	Principal Included in Mth. Payment.	Principal Repaid to Date.	Principal Still Outstanding	Interest at 7% on Outstanding Principal at End of Previous Year Provided by Annuity.	Interest at 5% Earned on Repaid Principal at End of Previous Year.	Balance of Interest on Repaid Principal at End of Previous Year, Being Difference Between 7% and 5% (Provided by Annuity.)	Redemption Money. (Formula a,)
1	$581.711	$231.711	$ 231.711	$4,768.289	$350 000	$ 0.000	$ 0.000	$4,708.289
2		243 297	475.008	4,524.992	333 780	11.586	4.634	4,524.992
3		255.462	730 470	4,269.530	316.749	23.751	9.500	4,269.530
4		268.235	998.705	4,001.295	298 867	36 524	14.609	4,001.295
5		281.647	1,280.352	3,719.648	280.090	48.936	19.974	8,719.648
6		295.729	1,576.081	3,423.919	260 375	64.018	25.607	3,423.919
7		310.515	1,886.596	3,113 404	239.674	78 804	31.522	3,113.404
8		326.041	2,212.637	2,787.363	217 938	94 330	37.732	2,787.363
9		242.343	2,554.980	2,445.020	195.115	110.632	44.253	2,445.020
10		359.460	2,914.440	2,085.560	171.151	127.749	51.100	2,085.560
11		377.434	3,291 874	1,708.126	145.989	145.723	58.2-8	1,708.126
12		396.305	3,688.179	1,311.821	119 569	164.594	65.837	1,311.821
13		416.121	4,104 300	895.700	91 827	184.410	73.763	895.700
14		436.927	4,541.227	458.773	62.699	205.216	82.085	458.773
15		458.773	5,000.000	0.000	32 114	227.062	90.824	0.000

Table illustrating the operation of an annuity to repay $5,000 in 15 years at 7% interest, Sinking Fund accumulating at 5%.

The sinking fund is to be taken simply at 5 per cent., and therefore must be the same as in the illustration already given, or $231.711. The annual payment, or as it is sometimes expressed, the rent of the annuity, is, as above, $581.711, which is equal to the sinking fund, together with $350, or 7 per cent. on $5,000. The lender may, therefore, treat the $350 as income during the whole of the fifteen years, if he invests annually the sinking fund at 5 per cent. to replace his capital. But we may consider that part of the capital is repaid year by year and that on the repaid portions of the capital the lender only realizes 5 per cent. interest.

The annual rent of the annuity must then supply an installment of capital, interest at 7 per cent., on the capital still of the annuity, and that the sum of the amounts in columns six, seven and eight is always $350, or 7 per cent. of the total capital advanced. Column nine in this example is exactly the same as column five in the previous example.

The principal outstanding may be looked upon as the redemption money payable by the borrower to the lender if the contract is to be determined, i. e., ended. If the contract is to be prematurely determined at the request and for the convenience of the lender, he cannot expect to receive at the cost of the borrower interest on his capital at the remunerative rate for the remainder of the original term. The contract being at an end, the borrower must be freed from this obligation and he must be called upon to pay only the bare amount required to liquidate the debt. If, on the other hand, the contract is to be determined at the request and for the convenience of the borrower, the lender must not be prejudiced, but he must be placed in as good a position as if the contract was to be allowed to run on. He must, therefore, be paid such a sum as will enable him to purchase elsewhere an annuity for the remainder of the term.

Lastly, if it is desired by both parties to terminate the contract, if it is for their mutual convenience that the debt be liquidated, then justice will be met by carrying out the transaction on the same principles as were adopted at the commencement.

Under the first illustration the redemption money may for some years be greater than the original advance, but this need not excite surprise. The borrower had entered into a contract, and if he seek to cancel it, that cannot be done without cost.

Discount Tables

Child's Tables of the Net of Any Amount, With Trade Discounts Deducted. Compiled and published by Frederick W. Child, Accountant and Auditor. 6x8 inches, oblong. Bound in cloth. Price $10.

The special object in view in the preparation of this book was to produce something that would fill an often-expressed want in the steam-fitting trade and other allied branches of business, wherein list prices with discounts are the rule. The book before us is declared to embrace all the discounts on wrought iron pipe, brass and iron pipe fittings, valves, cocks, gauges, plumbers' supplies and other similar goods. The work, with the exception of the title page, is in fac-simille typewriter. Two colors of ink are employed—red for the amounts from which discounts are deducted, and black for the net amounts. The pages are provided with a cut index, so arranged as to make easy the instant turning to any rate that is wanted.

The rates are arranges in what may be called two classed: The basal rates, which are ordinary single discounts, (as, for example, 5 per cent., 10 per cent., 33 1-3 per cent., etc.) are those to which the first page in each section is devoted, and are those in turn which appear upon the index tabs. The collateral rates are those which follow in regular order after the pages devoted to the basal rates. For example, the page to which the marginal index 55 is attached indicates the net amounts with the basal discount of 55 per cent. deducted. The following pages are devoted to collateral rates and contain the net amounts with 55 and 2½ per cent., 55 and 5 per cent., 55 and 7½ per cent., 55 and 10 per cent. and 55 and 10 per cent., and 10 per cent., etc., deducted. The figures representing the amounts from which the discounts are deducted are in the same relative position in each of the tables, and are arranged in sections of five. Each table gives the net of $1, with the stated discount deducted, and then, advancing by single dollars, the same for other amounts up to $100.

The manner of using the tables will be gained from the following illustrations: Suppose the amount from which the discount to be subtracted is $95; and suppose further that the discount is 45 and 10 per cent. and 10 per cent. By turning to the page carrying the nets of this discount, and referring to 95, we find the net to be $42.32. If the gross amount had been $950, the result, $423.22, would have been read from the same page, simply changing, mentally, the place of the decimal.

If the net value is wanted of an amount containing odd dollars and cents, the user is obliged to resort to a combination of figures, which, however, are very easily obtained. Suppose that the net value of $19,797,97 is required, the discount being 55 and 7-10ths. The amount is analyzed by the table devoted to the net figures with this discount deducted. Set down first the net of 10,000, then the net of 9,700, then of 97, and then of 97. Added together, these give $4,261.19, the net of the amount named.

While these tables were designed particularly for the trades mentioned, they are just as useful in various other lines of business. One reason for printing them in the peculiar manner above mentioned, namely, fac-simille typewriter, is to keep them in shape for special combinations. The author states at the conclusion of his preface that he is ready on short notice to make up books containing any classification of discounts that may be desired, thus giving each trade and line of business that which is especially adapted to it in the most convenient form.

Weis Brush Tube Mucilage.

Every desk should have its supply of good mucilage. Convenient means for replacing the mucilage on the back of a postage stamp or for supplying the deficiency on the flap of an envelope or for attaching one piece of paper to another are always in demand. The big pot of

THE WEIS BRUSH TUBE MUCILAGE.

mucilage with a swab within it almost the size of a whitewash brush is no longer favored. At best it was a dirty, unsightly device when in general use, and little by little its place has come to be occupied by devices much more in keeping with good desk equipment.

The accompanying cut is a miniature reproduction of what is called the Weis Brush Tube Mucilage. The mucilage or paste is held in a collapsible tube, very much the same as artists' pigments are put up. There is this special condition, however, that the mouth of the mucilage tube is supplied with a brush. The brush is hollow, and as the mucilage exudes, under pressure, it passes through the brush. The brush is small in diameter and, therefore, in spreading the mucilage is applied just where it is needed and nowhere else. The device may be characterized as cleanliness and neatness personified. The manufacturers, the Weis Binder Co., of Toledo, Ohio, declare that mucilage in this form is cheaper than when it is bought by the pint or quart, in the usual form, which is an assertion our readers in general will feel a lively interest in. We have used this device ourselves for a long time past and have no hesitation in saying that we have been greatly pleased with it.

We make our fortunes, and we call them "fate."—Beaconsfield.

Globe Loose Sheet Holder

The accompanying illustration shows a new form of loose sheet holder recently brought out by the Globe Company, with factory at Cincinnati, and sales departments in Chicago, New York and Boston. The lower cover is rigid. The upper cover is provided with a flexible hinge, as shown in the cut. To open the holder, the upper cover is thrown back over the clamping jaw, and in that position becomes a lever for spreading the jaws. The clamp, when thus raised, is automatically held open, facilitating the insertion of whatever blanks it is desired to place in it. When all is ready, the clamp is shut down by simply touching a trigger, as shown in the engraving. The trigger is at the top of the binder, and is constructed of a form to be conveniently operated by the thumb, and the parts are so sunk below the surface as to be free from the annoyance of scratching the desk or tripping the trigger when not required. The Globe loose sheet holder is provided with very stout clamping

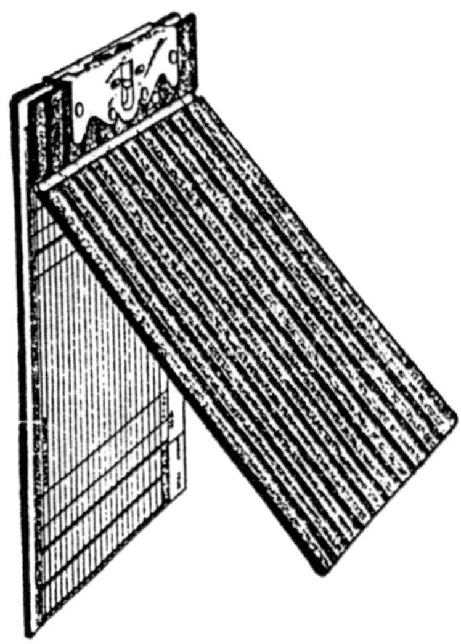

THE GLOBE LOOSE SHEET HOLDER.

jaws, and is adapted to hold anything that may be put in it, from a single sheet up to forty to sixty sheets, or even more, according to the thickness of the paper.

Gambling is a mode of transferring property without producing any intermediate good.—Dr. Johnson.

A New Envelope and Stamp Moistener

Below is printed a cut of a very neat, new and compact envelope and stamp moistener, manufactured by The Weis Binder Company, of 314 Jackson Street, Toledo, Ohio. They are reported to give splendid satisfaction and find ready sale. The use of this simple article does away with the necessity for the disagreeable, disgusting and dangerous practice of moistening with the tongue.

The moistener is made entirely of nickel-plated metal. It is four inches long, three-quarters of an inch wide, and weighs about three ounces. In the cup, at the end of the cylinder, is a small sponge. To use the moistener, unscrew the cup containing the sponge, and draw water into the cylinder. Then replace the cup and sponge, and press the valve slightly from time to time, forcing enough water into the sponge to keep it moist.

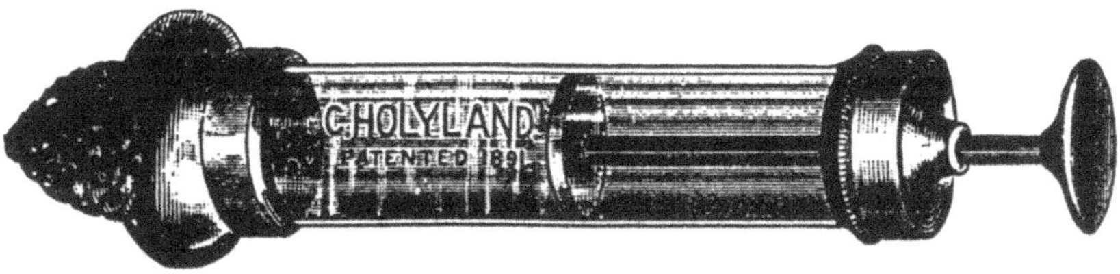

ENVELOPE AND STAMP MOISTENER.

Globe-Wernicke Unit Furniture

We have in these columns on repeated occasions referred to the unit system of office furniture known as the Globe-Wernicke. We now have the opportunity of laying before our readers several handsome cuts, showing in a very satisfactory manner the wide applicability of the idea which this system embodies.

Individual units, comprising letter files, catalogue files, document files, card index cabinets, legal blank drawers, and a host of others, are made in uniform size, so constructed and adjusted as to be combined in any desired order. Bases and cornices are provided by which a single unit, or any number of units in combination, can be appropriately finished, both top and bottom. The advantages are that the purchaser of this furniture may buy as little or as much at the outset as he sees fit, with the assurance that, as he needs more, additions of just what he requires can be made. If he starts with a letter file too small, additional units may be added. If he starts with a card index cabinet, the capacity of which is soon outgrown, he can add another section to it, and so on in all the other units. The units are so small that they can be taken through the narrowest door with which an office is likely to be provided, and further, they are so light that they can be readily handled. If, as the furniture is combined at the outset, it is not satisfactory in arrangement, it can be readily changed, for example, putting the letter files at the top, or at the bottom, as the case may be. All these facts and many others are set forth in a very happy manner, in a special catalogue which the Globe-Wernicke Co., with factory at Cincinnati, and sales offices in Chicago, New York and Boston, has recently issued. It

The Globe-Wernicke Unit System of Office Furnitu
Fig. 1—A single unit with flat top and base placed above

Fig. 2—General view in office showing Globe-Wernicke Units arranged for use back of desks and also as pedestals in the middle of the floor.

will pay the reader to send for it, whether he desires furniture immediately, or anticipates a purchase at a later date.

Fig. 1 of the illustrations presented herewith shows a single unit finished with a flat top and flat base, set on the top of a roll front desk. This may be the nucleus with which the general furnishing of an office is commenced, or it may be a special piece of equipment desired for permanent use in the place named. Fig. 2 is a general view in an office, showing Globe-Wernicke units arranged for use at the back of the desks, and also stacked in the form of pedestals near the middle of the floor. The wonderful economy of space and general utility secured by this arrangement will be perceived without argument.

The third illustration shows the case with which Globe-Wernicke units may be handled in putting them in position in the office for the first time, or readjusting them for the sake of better accomodations. This cut also illustrates the special line of bases with cupboards and drawers which are also provided to go with the unit furniture.

Fig. 3—Putting Globe-Wernicke Units in position.

Accountics

The Office Magazine.

A. O. KITTREDGE, F. I. A., C. P. A., Editor.
E. R. KITTREDGE, Associate

Accountics is devoted to the Science of Accounting, to the Art of Bookkeeping and to the advocacy of Improved Office Methods.

Subscription.—One dollar a year, payable in advance.

Postage is prepaid by the publishers in the United States, Canada and Mexico. For all other countries in the Postal Union, subscribers must add 50 cents a year.

Discontinuances.—In the absence of specific orders to discontinue at the end of the subscription term the magazine will be continued and a bill sent.

Remittances should be by Draft, P. O. Order or Express Order, payable to the order of the ACCOUNTICS ASSOCIATION. Money and postage stamps are at the risk of the sender, unless sent by express or in registered letters. Add 10 cents each to checks on local banks to defray collection charges.

Advertising Rates will be quoted on application.

Official Journal.—This publication, by resolutions duly passed, has been made the official publication of the following organizations:—

THE INSTITUTE OF ACCOUNTS.
THE NEW YORK CHAPTER of the Institute of Accounts.
THE WASHINGTON CHAPTER of the Institute of Accounts.
THE HARTFORD CHAPTER of the Institute of Accounts.

ACCOUNTICS is the accredited medium of intercommunication between members of the Institute of Accounts wherever located.

ACCOUNTICS ASSOCIATION,
Publishers,
Lancashire Bldg., Pine St., near Nassau,
New York.

Publisher's Desk.

Much delay has occurred in reaching a decision in the Card Index Competition proposed some time since by The Globe Company, Cincinnati, an announcement of which was presented in these columns in several issues early in the year. The result, which is now made public by judges in the contest, we regret to say, is likely to be a disappointment to our readers. After mature deliberation, a report to the effect that none of the studies submitted has complied in all particulars with the conditions named in the announcement has been rendered. Accordingly, there has been no course left for the company except to return to the contestants all of the studies submitted, without an award of prizes. This, as it will be recalled, is in accordance with a stipulation in the original advertisement. It is possible that the contest may be readvertised, in which case those who have in the first instance failed to comply with the reasonable conditions stipulated in the announcement, will have the opportunity of re-entering their work in correct form.

The advertising of the Acme White Lead and Color Works, Detroit, Mich., has always been on a very high plain, both as to character of statement and manner of dress. Not a little of the success of this establishment, which at present enjoys a national reputation, has been due to the shrewdly intelligent management of its advertising department. We are in receipt of recent samples of cards that this company has distributed. One of them has for its leading head, "Hollering." This is illustrated by a picture of a man who, with his hands to his mouth as if to form a speaking trumpet, is making himself heard over a wide area. There is an apology to the reader to the effect that "Hollering is an inartistic word, but nevertheless it expresses the thought." The other card in a similar way takes for its thought the word "Reflect," following which is an argument with respect to the goods that are offered. In the lower right hand corner of the card is a list of rapid sellers which this company is putting out. The company has been in the habit of "Hollering" for many years past, and these cards are characteristic specimens of the kind of "hollering" that it does.

A very attractive catalogue issued by the Sadler-Rowe Company, Publishers, Baltimore, Md., has reached us. It is embellished by some very handsome halftones printed in brown ink, and also by fac-similies of the binding and other features of some of the books described.

On another page in this number is an advertisement of the American Photo Furniture Co. of Schoolcraft, Mich. The company designs and manufactures office chairs, baskets, and desk trays for special uses, also photographic accessories of superior quality. The factory buildings of the company, which are eligibly located in the beautiful village named, contain upwards of five thousand square feet of floor space. The manager of the company, J. H. Pratt, is of Eastern birth, but a Western man by adoption, and now, after twenty years of hard labor in building up the business, begins to see the fruits of his labor. His success verifies the old adage that he who keeps constantly at it will win. Mr. Pratt says: "If there were only three words I might use in advising a young man in starting business, they would be: 'Never give up.' I would counsel him to have confidence in himself, concentrate all his forces upon the one object that he has in view and to be willing at all times to sacrifice comfort, amusement, and even self, if need be, for that object, and then I would add, 'Never give up.'"

Irving P. Fox, 8 Oliver street, Boston, is drawing the attention of the public to what is called "Fox's Complete Draft Book." The book is arranged very much like the conventional check book, but in place of checks attached to the stub there is first a finely engraved form of letter, and below that a draft for signature. The stub is devoted to a record of the date, on whom the draft is made and the place and name of bank to which it is sent for collection. An appendix contains some extra drafts printed the other way of the page and also a list of the banks in all the cities and towns of the United States.

The same publisher is also putting out two forms of what he calls the "Daily Cash Balance Slip." This is a collection of slips in paper covers, so arranged as to be easily detached therefrom, on which are printed various data that the average business manager would like to see when the cash books is made up for the day. There is a place for recording the total receipts, total payments, and for indicating the amount on hand in items of bills, gold, silver, nickels, pennies, money orders, postage stamps, checks, etc.

A new line of rubber-stamp ink is being put upon the market by Walter Sparks, 70 S. Sixth street, Brooklyn, N. Y. Red, blue, green, purple and black are offered. The packages range from one-half ounce to eight ounces and also include pints and quarts. The price list states that these inks are sent out in original packages only.

The indexed coupon books which are manufactured and sold by J. P. Forbes, Drawer B, Coshocton, Ohio, are calculated to overcome many of the perils and annoyances of retail trade. The general scheme is to secure a promissory note from the retail customer in payment for the coupons. Or the cost of the book in lump may be charged to the customers' book account. The coupons then pass as currency in purchases. This plan saves all bookkeeping and puts an account in most excellent shape for collection. There can be no disputes about items. If household supplies are to be sold upon a credit basis, this would seem to be one of the least objectionable plans that could be used. Various styles of books are manufactured, some containing coupons to the amount of five dollars and others to the amount of ten dollars. The coupons in all of the individual books are of different values, running from one cent to fifty cents each. The different values are printed on different colors of paper in one case, and in other cases are printed upon the same color of paper, but on coupons of different lengths, and then are put into the covers in a way to index them, thus making it possible to readily take out a coupon of any amount. A circular descriptive of these goods will be sent to any of our readers who see fit to apply for the same and who mentions this notice.

E. St. Elmo Lewis, advertising specialist, 1,524 Chestnut street, Philadelphia, sends us a copy of his booklet, entitled "The Advertising Specialist." It is clean in its typography, attractive in its paper and ink, and bound in a cover that will command attention wherever it is sent. The text in the book is devoted to those arguments which support the proposition that merchants can well afford to pay a specialist to write their advertising as compared with undertaking to do it themselves. It is something that will be of interest to every one who will take the trouble to write for a copy. Please mention ACCOUNTICS.

The Robert F. Rose School for Shorthand, Unity Building, Chicago, are issuing a booklet entitled "Shorthand as a Home Study." In it there are discussed the broad questions of the practicability and expediency of undertaking to acquire stenography by home study. The argument is well sustained and it becomes very clear upon reading the book that any one who is competent to study away from the constant supervision of an instructor can aspire to shorthand at home. The system taught—a modified Graham—certainly recommends the general undertaking. Some of the best shorthand writers with whom we are acquainted secured their knowledge of their art by unassisted effort, and surely if they were successful others may expect to succeed, particularly if their work is constantly watched through correspondence by some one who has their interests at heart. Send for a copy of the pamphlet and mention ACCOUNTICS.

Business cards in a form to suggest wedding invitations are very popular at the present time in various directions. We received a few days since, in stylish garb, a notice issued by Messrs. Niles & Niles, public accountants and auditors, being the announcement of the removal of their New York offices to No. 40 Wall street. Putting the announcement in the form which was given it was no doubt done in the thought that thereby it would command special attention. This firm, who are advertising themselves as Certified Public Accountants, both Henry A. and Charles E. Niles holding regent certificates, are now comfortably situated in the Manhattan and Merchants' Bank Building at the address above given.

A new mailing envelope named the "Eureka" is being put upon the market by Walter Sparks, 70 S. Sixth street, Brooklyn, N. Y. A price list of no less than twenty-two sizes is issued by the manufacturer. This mailing envelope, unlike many with which it is in competition, has no metal parts. There is a stiff manilla clasp, one attached to the flap of the envelope and the other to the body, and so arranged as to be easily brought into locking contact in a way to form a satisfactory fastening and yet be within the law concerning unsealed packages. A sample will be mailed to any reader of this notice, who, in applying for the same, mentions ACCOUNTICS.

Accountics

VOL. V OCTOBER 1899 No. 4

The Monthly Statement

If there is any one matter upon which professional accountants are fully agreed, and concerning the right of which it will be impossible to start a controversy, it is that of professional secrecy. The accountant, like the lawyer and the doctor, becomes the repository of various confidential facts, the making known of which to the public would be of serious embarrassment, if not of actual injury, to the interests of his client. The one thing, therefore, upon which accountants are fully agreed, as we have already stated, is that confidence should be maintained at all hazards, and that every client should be made to feel that whatever he intrusts to his accountant will be as sacredly guarded as would be his confidential communications to professional men of other classes.

Strange as it may seem, there is very little law relating to the subject of professional secrecy. Not even in the domains of law and medicine have special statutes been passed. On the other hand, the ethics of the several professions, written and unwritten, are very pronounced upon this subject. Very little can be obtained from a witness that is of the nature of what an accountant would consider the betrayal of a confidential communication. The law is only fairly clear upon this point. It would appear from the wording of it that information which might have come to a professional man during the course of his professional visits to or conversation with his clients, which was not distinctly necessary to enable him to act in that capacity, was not privileged and that its disclosure might be properly forced by the courts. On this matter, however, the ruling has been a broad one, and, after all, the professional man himself must be the judge of what is necessary to enable him to act in his professional capacity, and, therefore, he has broad reasons, which the judges, as a rule, sustain, for declining to answer all dubious questions.

When doctors disagree who shall decide, or, rather, what interest have laymen in the quarrels of professionals? A long while ago a somewhat obscure individual connected with a branch of commercial instruction and located in the far West, conceived the idea of home instruction of those aspiring to positions as bookkeepers and office employes. His scheme embodied the use of a case or box, from which lessons could be withdrawn seriatim and by which the pupil would have successfully concealed from him the lessons in the latter part of the course while he was giving attention to those in the earlier part. A little later this pioneer in a somewhat novel field moved to the central part of the country, and by his aggressiveness in pushing his radical ideas of commercial instruction, which in the mean time had broadened to include the use of his novelty in the schools, attracted the attention of the leaders in the field of commercial instruction. Quite numerous were the discussions of this man's methods in the annual and semi-annual sessions of the national organization, not to mention the meetings between the various local societies in which are enrolled the teachers in and proprietors of commercial schools. He was denounced right and left and held up to scorn by those who represented what may be called the old lines of instruction.

Still later in the history of this development, a prominent firm of publishers in the eastern part of the country brought out something which, though differing in detail, was manifestly founded on the lines of this pioneer. By great advertising ability, as well as large financial resources, the new interpretation was pushed before the attention of commercial teachers to such an extent that the original was practically lost sight of. Evidently, this concern met with financial success, for more recently still another firm of publishers have brought out something in competition therewith. Of late they have been calling attention to their goods with such success by way of results that the other firm—the one who first copied—has begun to shout "plagiarism," "imitation," and other words of a similar nature. It might be likened to a tournament, the two contestants being carefully watched by the commercial educators of the country who compose the audience. The whole squabble, as the reader must perceive, turns on the proprietorship of certain interpretations of a special method of instructing the young business man. But of what interest is this to the said young man, or more particularly to the business managers who are the readers of this paragraph? The answer is, none at all. We risk nothing in the assertion that whoever may be the original Jacobs, all of these tables and budgets and boxes, call them by what name we may, contain a large amount of first-class misinformation in prime condition. It is of a character that may be safely warranted to confuse and bother the student who is unfortunate enough to have it meted out to him through the larger part of his business career. Half of his business life will be spent in the necessary unlearning.

❧ ❧

The publication in these columns of the article by Bernard Dale, entitled "How Are the Profits of the Year to Be Ascertained?" being, as we have previously explained to our readers, a reprint of a pamphlet issued in England some time since, is attracting marked attention in various directions. Those who have followed the installments so far presented have no doubt apprehended the drift of the argument to be that it is just as wrong for the depreciation of capital to be made up at the expense of dividends as it is for dividends to be paid out of capital. There may be a loss of capital, but capital lost cannot be replaced at the expense of dividends. Not a few of our readers have been surprised at the trend of the argument produced, and also by the numerous decisions of the English courts cited in support of the proposition. The theory, it would seem, is at variance with American ideas and undoubtedly is directly opposed to what is current in the various States of the Union. In this connection it is to be stated that, notwithstanding the citations made of English decisions in support of this theory, the English courts as a fact are by no means unanimous on this point. Other decisions could be cited which would show that ideas more nearly in keeping with those of this country on the points named are current to at least a limited extent in Great Britain.

❧

American accountants, and some business men as well, have for a long time past been in the habit of reverently respecting English precedents. The first large industrial organizations in this country were formed by British capital under the direction of British accountants, and to a certain extent under the advice of British lawyers. Some of these enterprises were actually incorporated in Great Britain, although operating in this country, and in all such cases, of course, English ideas prevailed throughout. The beginning of accountancy in this country, as a profession, was made by accountants who came here from England. For these reasons and others, Americans have been in the habit of taking from their English cousins more or less of their ideas of accounting. These conceptions of course were obtained altogether at second-hand, but nevertheless they have been accepted as correct. But sufficient time has elapsed since accountancy became a recognized profession in this country for the American idea to develop and assert itself, and wherein lies the difference in the situation in certain legal directions these articles serve to show. However willingly accountants accepted English precedents a short time ago, now it would seem there are quite enough distinctively American precedents on record to establish an American practice on American lines.

The laws of our several States, relating to corporations and to business matters in general, have been enacted for the most part without the active assistance of accountants, whether of British or American antecedents. Various matters upon which accountants are called upon to pass must of necessity conform to the law as it is written. Therefore in this country we are governed by our laws as we find them and not by such laws as English accounting theorists would like to have. While our lawmakers undoubtedly entertain a proper respect for English precedents, they did not have precedents of any kind to consult when they were doing this work. They therefore provided in respect to corporations just what they thought best, regardless, and in thus acting, unrestrained by musty and illogical precedents, they worked out what to Americans appear a far more rational plan than commonly prevails in Great Britain, if Mr. Dale's essay properly reflects the situation in that country.

The differentiation of American from English accounting is something in which every accountant is deeply interested. It is something which as yet is only a little more than begun, but which, as the years roll by, is likely to become a well-defined and clearly recognized progress. America in various developments has from the beginning been a rule unto itself. Her pioneers have been influenced by the special circumstances prevailing and the general environment to be encountered, rather than by precedents. So original have our methods been in various directions that we have to a certain extent come to disregard all precedents. American development has been characterized by what may be described as an eye to the main chance. For the most part our engineers, our business managers and our various specialists have amply succeeded in accomplishing that to which they set themselves. From the present point of view it would seem that in accounting matters, not only with respect to the law, but more particularly in methods of practice and in those matters which may be called mere routine, we are likely to have our own rules and methods, and that these are likely to differ in material features from the practice of our English cousins in corresponding lines.

Criticisms and Reviews

Legal Reference Book

Johnson's Handy Reference Book of Law and Fact, containing the National Bankruptcy Act of 1898; an epitome of the Rules in Bankruptcy, promulgated by the Supreme Court of the United States in November, 1898; and the Commercial Laws of the several States, tabulated, including important legal forms. By Walter Johnson. 206 pages; ordinary octavo; bound in cloth. Printed by the Nonpareil Company.

This book is so thoroughly described in the title page, which we have reproduced above, that further description can add very little to it. There is within its covers a considerable fund of legal information, covering such points as arise in ordinary business practice and bearing upon questions that are constantly coming before the business man for attention. The arrangement of the information is in a form to be readily accessible, and the book is supplemented by a fairly satisfactory index. The author is a member of the Iowa Bar and has gone at the preparation of this volume painstakingly and with a desire to make it generally useful.

Window Dressing

Window Dressing for Grocers, arranged by professional window trimmers, including Harry Harman, of Chicago. Pamphlet, 80 pages. Published by E. N. Root & Bro. Price, $1.

The prefactory chapter of this little pamphlet gives some general directions about the dressing of show windows, and also points out the properties that can be advantageously employed in arranging displays. How to make puffs and rosettes in drapery and how to secure monumental effects over proper forms, all are clearly set forth. Succeeding chapters are devoted to descriptions of specific displays in the grocery line. These are both illustrated and described. The work cannot fail to be of value to retail merchants everywhere.

Credit Men's Affairs

BY A. O. KITTREDGE

The credit men of the country, as represented by their local organizations, would seem to be among the last to recover from the interruptions from business incident to the hot weather or vacation period, as it is coming to be called. Even at the date at which this letter is written, a number of the organizations have not yet announced their first meetings for the autumn season. The National Secretary has found it difficult to secure prompt answers to his letters until very recently, on account of the large number of absentees. In all directions it would seem that the vacation period this year has been prolonged beyond ordinary limits.

* * *

An exception to the general rule was the opening fall meeting of the New York Credit Men's Association, which occurred on the evening of Thursday, September 21. According to the custom established by this organization, the meeting took the form of a dinner, to which were invited various guests, including Hon. John Field, of Philadelphia, President of the National Association. The dinner was given in the rooms of the Commercial Club, and altogether there were present about one hundred members and guests. By way of introduction to the speaking, which followed the dinner, ex-President Fessenden, of the New York Association, gave a synopsis of the transactions of the year.

* * *

He first called attention to the fact that the organization was four years old and that in this time it had made substantial progress, evidenced particularly by the continued enthusiasm of the present meeting and the effort that was made at the first gathering preliminary to the organization, at which there were only about a dozen credit men. With twelve members in 1895, the organization has over four hundred in 1899. Not alone in numbers has it become strong, for in its progress it has come to be recognized in the city and the State as a factor necessary to be consulted in all laws affecting mercantile credits. The speaker next pointed out the special work that has been done by sub-committees and outlined in some respects what is now in hand and about to be undertaken. He was disposed to be pleased with the operation of the bankruptcy law to date, although he admitted that in the eyes of credit men it was not without its blemishes. He strongly favored amendment of the law in various particulars, thereby putting it into better shape to accomplish the object for which it is primarily intended. He closed his address by citing an instance of how the law as it stands at present can be defeated by fraudulent debtors taking advantage of certain State exemption laws.

* * *

An address was also delivered by T. H. Bartindale, the President-elect of the organization. After recounting his view of some of the early pages of the history of the organization, Mr. Bartindale gave expression to the objects of the Association as follows: It is organized for protection and educational purposes; to combine the intelligence and influence of members for protection against imposition and fraud; to agitate and effect changes in the laws of the various States and of the United States, to the end of securing uniformity of statutes and protection of creditors against abuses now prevalent; to banish commercial fraud whenever legally possible, and to establish closer ties of business association, to the end that the welfare of all may be more highly conserved. Mr. Bartindale's remarks were brief, and at their conclusion he introduced Hon. John Field, of Philadelphia, President of the National Association, who then addressed the meeting.

* * *

Mr. Field's remarks were very happily apropos of the occasion, and, referring to the commercial rivalry between the different large cities, he said: "France has her Paris, Austria her Vienna, Germany her Berlin, Italy her Rome, and Russia her St. Peterburg. We might as well acknowledge it candidly on this side of the water that the United States have this one great metropolitan city, the City of

New York." The speaker continued by referring to the various issues that have engaged the thought and attention of men. To-day, he declared, business and business interests are receiving more thought and more brain power than anything else that exists among men. He thought it remarkable, therefore, that so much attention has been given to the production of raw materials and their development into useful articles of commerce, and so little attention has been given to the saving of results. The failures in 1898, for example, aggregated the enormous sum of $130,622,899. The real object of the Credit Men's Association is to reduce the amount of failures to the minimum, and by concentrating attention to the matter of preventing losses, to secure better and more satisfactory results.

* * *

Alluding to the fact that the number of failures and the amounts of the failures are at present smaller than for some time past, which, to a degree, might be accounted for by the new era of prosperity that has set in, the speaker declared that he was fully satisfied in his own mind that a part of the reduction in losses comes from the increased care that is being exercised in credit departments and which has been promoted by the efforts of the Association of Credit Men.

* * *

The only feature of the work of the National Association for the current year to which the speaker devoted attention was that relating to the prosecution of dishonest debtors and the inauguration of such measures as will render the perpetration of fraud upon creditors a hazardous undertaking. He said: "Let the dishonest man realize that there is a fund under the control of this organization for the criminal prosecution of all dishonest merchants and it will have a salutary effect upon those contemplating fraud and robbery." Mr. Field's idea is to establish a fund of not less than $10,000, to be used in the prosecution of fraud. He would have the fact that this fund had been provided made known throughout the length and breadth of the land. At the same time, he would let it be understood that no case of prosecution for fraud would be undertaken by the National organization until it has been carefully examined by a committee of competent credit men in the locality where the wrong has been done. He would also have each case passed upon by a competent attorney under the supervision of the General Committee. When a case has been so examined, and the facts clearly show that a fraud has been committed, and the action has the approval of the attorney of the organization, the dishonest debtor should be prosecuted to the limit of the law without mercy. In conclusion, the speaker said that the credit men's organization and its work is only in its infancy. He believed it destined, if properly supported by the business community, to exert a most powerful and salutary influence upon the business interests of the country.

* * *

The good work recently accomplished by Secretary Prendergast in the organization of a local association in Cleveland is only an earnest of what is likely to follow. Various other points prominent as distributing centers, in which the credit men at present are unorganized, are giving indications of their willingness, and, in fact, their active desire to co-operate with the National organization, which, it is evident, is doing a large amount of good. Various calls are being made upon the national secretary for help in organization, to which undoubtedly he will respond to the limit of his ability. Cleveland starts out with a well-manned and well-officered association and will no doubt contribute its fair quota of influence and good works to the general cause.

* * *

While speaking of Cleveland, it is a pleasure to mention a credit incident that occurred in that city a few weeks since in connection with the annual convention of the American Bankers' Association. Jas. G. Cannon, ex-President of the National Association of Credit Men, delivered an address before the bankers, in which he discussed the expediency of every bank organizing and maintaining a credit department. Mr. Cannon was not content to present mere verbal arguments in support of the proposition, nor yet to leave the working out of the plan which he advocated to inexperienced men. Instead, he accompanied his address by a most instructive and interesting series of object lessons. The address itself was illustrated by enlarged fac-sim-files of the various blanks and forms required in the operation of a bank's credit department. These were of such liberal dimensions as to be of the nature of maps or diagrams, and were displayed from the stage and referred to as his address proceeded. In addition, there were equipped in working order in a room adjacent to the convention room, three full-fledged credit departments, thereby illustrating the furniture and appliances in general that would be required for the credit departments for banks, ranging from the smallest, through those of middle class, up to those of the largest capital that are in existence. Full sets of blanks, including cards for every required use, were put up in neat sets in envelopes in convenient form for the members to take home with them.

* * *

The furniture and other appliances used in illustrating these credit departments were loaned for the purpose by the Globe Wernicke Company of Cincinnati. Among the conveniences and facilities illustrated by samples in this exhibit were Bradstreet reports, Trow city directories, leading banking directories, Poor's Manual, and files of various commercial and financial periodicals. Altogether, the undertaking was on a most liberal scale and was greatly appreciated by the bankers in whose interest the exhibits were organized. By this work Mr. Cannon has undoubtedly given a new impulse to organized credit departments. His argument was one the force of which will be felt for a long time to come.

State Vice-Presidents of the N. A. C. M.

The following is a list of names, business connection and addresses of the State Vice-Presidents of the National Association of Credit Men, whose selection has been recently announced by National Secretary Wm. A. Prendergast:

ALABAMA—A. D. Bellamy, Florence Wagon Works, Florence, Ala.

CALIFORNIA—J. J. Schutz, Haas Bros., San Francisco, Cal.

COLORADO—C. F. Best, J. D. Best & Sons, Denver, Colo.

CONNECTICUT—F. H. Bosson, Pope Mfg. Co., Hartford, Conn.

INDIANA—Geo. B. Caldwell, Merchants' National Bank, Indianapolis, Ind.

ILLINOIS—Harry T. Smith, Bradner, Smith & Co., Chicago, Ill.

IOWA—W. H. Robbins, Letts, Fletcher Co, Marshalltown, Iowa.

KANSAS—Wm. C. Chaves, Symns Grocer Co., Atchison, Kan.

KENTUCKY—Philo Laib, The Ahrens & Ott Mfg. Co, Louisville, Ky.

LOUISIANA—T. H. Ferguson, New Orleans, La.

MARYLAND—J. Harry Tregoe, Carroll, Adams & Co., Baltimore, Md.

MASSACHUSETTS—Chas. L. Lewando, National Shoe & Leather Exchange, Boston, Mass.

MICHIGAN—Geo. B. Pulfer, Acme White Lead and Color Works, Detroit, Mich.

MINNESOTA—F. G. Hopkins, Janney, Semple & Co., Minneapolis, Minn.

MISSISSIPPI—H. H. Threefoot, Threefoot, Bros. & Co., Meridian, Miss.

MISSOURI—J. R. Barclay, Simmons Hardware Co., St. Louis, Mo.

NEBRASKA—Ed. Baum, Omaha, Neb.

NEW HAMPSHIRE—B. F. Strand, C. B. Lancaster Shoe Co., Keene, N. H.

NEW JERSEY—J. W. Herbert, Jr., Geo. Holm Co., Helmetta, N. J.

NEW YORK—Frank Sibley, Sibley & Holmwood, Buffalo, N. Y.

NORTH CAROLINA—H. P. Richardson, Jr., H. P. Richardson, Jr., & Co., Reidsville, N. C.

OHIO—W. A. Hopple, The John Shillito Co., Cincinnati, Ohio.

OREGON—W. B. Struble, Union Meat Co., Portland, Ore.

PENNSYLVANIA—J. H. Ritter, Biddle Hardware Co., Phila., Pa.

RHODE ISLAND—C. S. Sisson, C. S. Sisson & Co., Providence, R. I.

SOUTH CAROLINA—Geo. A. Wagoner, Geo. A. Wagoner & Co., Charleston, S. C.

TENNESSEE—Geo. C. Mason, Oliver-Finnie Grocer Co., Memphis, Tenn.

TEXAS—W. O. Connor, Sanger Bros., Dallas, Tex.

VIRGINIA—W. B. Roper, John L. Roper Lumber Co., Norfolk, Va.

WASHINGTON—Thos. S. Griffith, Benham & Griffith, Spokane, Wash.

WEST VIRGINIA—J. C. Brady, Wheel-Hinge Co., Wheeling, W. Va.

WISCONSIN—O. C. Hanson, Cream City Hat Co., Milwaukee, Wis.

How are the Profits of the Year to be Ascertained?

By Bernard Dale

(Continued from page 35 August number.)

The statement in the Memorandum and Articles of Association that the capital of a company is a certain sum divided into shares of a certain fixed amount throws at the best only a side light as to what assets are intended to be used as capital of a company.

In order to arrive at a definite conclusion on this point, it is always necessary to study closely the nature of the venture in which the company is engaged. In the case of the railway company just given as an example, the whole of the paid-up share and debenture capital having, by the supposition, disappeared in the construction and equipment of the road, it was clearly the intention of the company that the capital for the working of the railway should consist of the monies received from the public who use the road. So, in the example given of a banking company, the whole of the paid-up share capital having, by the supposition, been converted into the stocks representing the reserve, it was equally the intention that the capital for carrying on the business was to consist of the monies received on deposit or current account. Again, suppose a company formed to sink the whole of its paid-up share capital in the purchase of a particular asset of a wasting nature, say, a coal mine, after the coal had been exhausted, the business of the company was to cease, and, consequently, that no part of the net revenue arising from the working of the mine was intended to be set aside to form a capital for use after that exhaustion. If, then, the company were to distribute the whole of the net revenue as dividend, they would not be dividing "capital," for it could not be predicated of the fund thus divided that it was wealth intended to be used by its owner as a source of income.

It is not, however, necessary to resort to imaginary cases to establish our conclusions. The decisions of the law courts show the principle in the clearer light. In the case of McDougall v. Jersey Imperial Hotel Company, in which instance the question at issue was the return of capital as interest during construction, Wood, V. C., said: "The bill avers that there are no profits, and that interest has been paid, or is about to be paid, out of the capital; that the shareholders have paid £4 per share and are discharged to that extent, and that they are now about to take back sums equal to 5 per cent. of that very capital in the shape of interest. On the ground of public policy, and on every principle, not only of honesty as regards the public generally, but of the interests of this company itself, I feel bound to prevent this proceeding. This is not in accordance with the contract entered into with the legislature on behalf of the public whereby it was determined that the shareholders should be liable to a certain defined amount, and no more, to the creditors of the company, and not in accordance with the contract between the parties, whereby each of the shareholders was protected against creditors to the extent of the contributive liability of all the others."

This passage was referred to with approval by Fry, J., in re Alexandra Palace Company, where the question raised was the payment of dividends out of borrowed monies.

Although Wood, V. C., partly bases his judgment on a contract supposed to have been entered into by the legislature on behalf of the public, whereby it was determined that the shareholders should be liable to a certain defined amount, the decision would have been the same if the interest had been paid to the shareholders out of borrowed monies; Lord Chief Justice Lindley said, in re Verner v. The General and Commercial Investment Trust, infra, to pay a dividend out of borrowed money "would be as unjustifiable, in point of law, as it would be reckless and blameworthy in the eyes of business men."

In the case of Davison v. Gillies, the point at issue being the payment of dividend out of gross receipts, it transpired that the London Tramways Co. had for several years paid dividends to its ordinary shareholders out of its gross receipts without making good the annual wear and tear of its tramway. Sir George

Jessel, on the application of a shareholder, held that the dividends had been improperly paid. The point to be noted in this case is, that the payment of the dividend was held to be ultra vires of the company, although it was not paid either out of the paid-up share capital, which, of course, had disappeared in the construction and equipment of the tramway, or out of the capital asset represented by the tramway itself, but out of a third fund, namely, the receipts arising from the working of the tramway. That annual receipts are capital, within the meaning of the rule that dividends may not be paid out of capital, also follows from the judgment of Lord Justice Lindley in Verner v. General Commercial and Investment Trust, Limited, infra, in which he said: "A dividend presupposes a profit in some shape and to divide, as dividend, the receipts say, for a year, without deducting the expenses incurred in that year in producing the receipts would be as unjustifiable in point of law as it would be reckless and blameworthy in the eyes of business men. * * * The law is much more accurately expressed by saying that dividends cannot be paid out of capital than by saying that they can only be paid out of profits."

In the case of Lee v. Neuchatel Asphalt Company, the payment of dividends without making good annual waste of a terminable asset, being the issue, it was shown that the company was an amalgamation of certain other companies, and that its principal asset consisted of a certain concession which it had been formed to work and which would expire in 1904.

There was a provision in the articles that it would not be necessary to set aside a reserve fund against the wasting of the concession. At the end of a given year, the company had some income in hand after paying all the expenses for the year of getting the asphalt, and out of this net income they proposed to pay a dividend. It was sought to restrain them on the ground that the value of the capital asset represented by the concession had depreciated from effluxion of time and exhaustion by working, and that this depreciation should be provided against by setting aside a portion of the net reserve fund before the proposed dividend was paid. In delivering judgment, confirming the decision of Mr. Justice Sterling refusing the injunction, Lord Justice Lindley said: "It is obvious with respect to such property, as with respect to various other properties of a like kind, mines and quarries, and so on, every ton of stuff which you get out of that which you have bought with your capital may from one point of view be considered as embodying and containing a small portion of your capital, and that if you sell and divide the proceeds you divide some portion of that which you have spent your capital in acquiring. It may be represented that that is a return of capital. All I can say is, if that is a return of capital, it appears to me not to be such as is prohibited by law."

In the above extract Lord Justice Lindley was dealing with an argument addressed to the court to the effect that, as the mine had been purchased with the paid-up capital it must be capital, a conclusion which of course by no means follows, seeing that many things, such as the dividends on Consols, may be purchased with capital and yet are not capital.

In the case of Wilmer v. McNamara & Co., Limited, it was shown that the company had been formed to purchase and carry on an existing business, and the question arose whether depreciation of the good will purchased should be taken into account in arriving at the annual profits. Mr. Justice Sterling, after referring to the cases above cited, decided that the good will was "fixed" capital, and that the proposed dividend might lawfully be paid without taking into account the depreciation of good will.

In commenting upon the decision in Lee v. Neuchatel Asphalt Copany. Mr. Palmer, the eminent company lawyer, in his well-known "Company Precedents," says: "It must be admitted that the system propounded by the Court of Appeal is not unlikely to mislead the public, and especially those who deal with the company in reliance on its having its paid-up capital as a fund undiminished by dividend among its shareholders. It goes to render the protection, supposed to be afforded by the Act, a delusion and a trap. Assuming the system to be legal, it follows that a company which has some surplus capital, say £200,000, and bona fide, desires to pay extra dividends, can invest it in a short leasehold intertest, say three years, returning, say, £8,000 per annum, and then divide the whole income, less outgoings, as profit;

thus, in effect, returning the capital to the shareholders and withdrawing it from the limited fund, to which the creditors have a right to look; and it may do this without the sanction of the court, and without any of the formalities prescribed by the 'Companies' Acts, 1867 and 1877,' and without any notice to the creditors or the public." This criticism, takes without conferring any compensating advantage on the community at large..

In the particular case which drew forth Mr. Palmer's criticism, such an imposition would have been worse than useless, for the venture not being intended to continue after the concession had run out, the only object of forming a reserve would have been its eventual distribution amongst the undertakers, that is to say, the doing in the lump on the termination of the concession, of the very thing to which exception was taken, when done by instalments during its continuance.

(To be continued.)

Wernicke Bookcases

Our readers are already familiar with a style of business furniture built upon the "elastic" plan, known as Globe-Wernicke units. What we present now is something very similar in construction, but adapted to library uses, instead of being restricted to office purposes. Various styles and sizes of bookcase units are made, finished in styles from an average grade up to the most elaborate desired. The units may be superimposed in a single width, or in several adjacent widths, as clearly shown in the illustrations. Different styles of bases are provided and also different styles of cornices and tops. Each individual unit is provided with its own glass door, arranged to raise and slip into the case above the books, whenever a volume is to be removed. These doors are dust-proof and, in addition, give the completed bookcase a very handsome and artistic appearance. Wernicke bookcases are manufactured by the Globe-Wernicke Co., Cincinnati, with salesrooms in New York, Chicago and Boston. A special catalogue has been recently issued which will be sent to any one on request who mentions this notice.

Census Director Asks Farmers to Keep Books

Director of the Census Merriam, Washington, D. C., says that he would like to see the 22,000 newspapers and periodicals published in the United Utates urge the farmers now, while harvesting and marketing are in progress and census-taking is pending, to make a record of the acreage, quantity and value of all crops and products. The resulting benefit, he adds, would be immeasurable. If everybody would keep accurate accounts of their operations the work of gathering census statistics would be lessened more than one-half and their value would be more than doubled.

Fig. 1—A Wernicke Bookcase two units wide and five units high, exclusive of base and top.

Fig. 2—A Wernicke Bookcase three units wide and six units high, not counting base and cornice.

Questions and Answers

Concerning the

BALANCE-SHEET SYSTEM OF ACCOUNTS

Conducted by the

Account Audit and Assurance Co., Ltd.
25 Pine Street, New York

Distinctive Features

From F. A. L., Cleveland.

I have given careful attention to all that has been presented concerning the Balance Sheet System of Accounts, and I am impressed by reading what has been published that it contains only that which the business man usually wants, and that in general terms it may be declared that its final results are no different from those produced by ordinary bookkeeping plan. If the Balance Sheet System gives only what the business man really wants and what has heretofore been secured to him by ordinary bookkeeping methods, then it would seem to me that the features of the Balance Sheet System which distinguish it from other plans must relate to the process by which the results are achieved. They certainly do not seem to appear in the results. Will you, for my enlightenment, give me in the briefest space possible, a conception of what distinguishes the Balance Sheet System from other bookkeeping plans?

ANSWER.—We think it scarcely fair to compare an accounting system with a plan of bookkeeping, but perhaps our correspondent did not intend, even in the language he uses, to compare things with each other that are essentially different by nature. However, it is only proper to remark, before proceeding to answer the question asked, that an accounting system is something that can be evolved, charted and described without ever a reference being made to the bookkeeping dress that may be given to that system. For example, it is entirely competent to discuss ledger accounts, with respect to the classes into which the accounts divide, etc., without any reference to the ruling that the ledger is to have, and also without allusions to the methods by which the items shall be got into the ledger. It is entirely competent to lay down an accounting system, discussing its details in a way to make sure that the scheme outlined meets the requirements of the business man and the kind of business the transactions of which are to be recorded before giving any attention whatsoever to the bookkeeping dress that is to be applied to that system. These remarks are quite enough to indicate that accounting is the science, while bookkeeping is the art, and that the science is possible of various interpretations, as manifested in the art.

We may have our ledger of the conventional ruling, of the progressive form, or on cards. All this relates to bookkeeping, whereas the accounting system simply goes so far as to decide that certain ledger accounts are necessary, and that it is necessary to arrange them in certain classes, according to the nature of the transactions to be recorded and other considerations.

Our correspondent wants in a sentence some indication of the distinctive features of the Balance Sheet System. He argues because the final product (if we may use manufacturing terms) is the same as that produced by ordinary accounting methods, that the destinations cannot be in the results which the system accomplishes. He contends that therefore it is only different from others in the process by which those results are accomplished.

We can scarcely subscribe to his conclusions, at least as a total. In part he is right, but he also omits much that is very important. While the output or product of a factory and a small shop may be the same nominally, there is possible a vast difference in quality, which alone would distinguish the results. A pair of shoes made by a cobbler and a pair of shoes being a part of the product of a well-equipped, up-to-date shoe factory may be asserted to be equivalents, so far as product is concerned, and the argument therefore might follow that the difference between the two depends entirely upon the processes. The latter assertion would be correct as far as it goes, but those who wear shoes are quite willing to bear testimony to the great satisfaction experienced with modern machine-made shoes as compared with the rough work formerly current of unintelligent cobblers, who were compelled to use poor tools and put up with inadequate manufacturing appliances, to say nothing of struggling with an imperfect knowledge.

The Balance Sheet System is distinguished from other systems by the character of its product quite as much as by the processes by which the product is produced . There is a quality to the results that does not appertain to the product of ordinary bookkeeping plans. There is so much difference between the two that, with the statement that no offense is intended, we may declare that the ordinary product is comparable to the rough and clumsy shoes produced by cobblers, while the product of the Balance Sheet System is equivalent to the best machine-finished article that can be turned out by a modern, thoroughly equipped factory employing operators of the highest skill.

And yet there is a difference in the processes, as our correspondent asserts. In this regard the advantage is quite as much on the side of the Balance Sheet System as it is on the side of the modern up-to-date factory in the illustrations previously discussed. To give an idea of these in a single sentence is practically impossible, but several sentences may serve to convey an idea of at least a part of the theory upon which the Balance Sheet System of Accounts is founded:

There is always left behind a balance corresponding to the inventory. The ordinary plan in a manufacturing concern, for example, is to charge the factory with all the materials that are bought. The Balance Sheet System charges into Manufacturing Operations only so much of the materials as are consumed. There is as stated, an inventory balance left behind.

It is the usual plan to credit Merchandise Account with sales. In the Balance Sheet System Merchandise Account is credited, not with sales; but with the amount of goods disposed of taken at cost, thus always leaving in Merchandise a representative of inventory balance.

By the ordinary plan an inventory is necessary to find out what goods or materials there are on hand. By the Balance Sheet System inventorying is resorted to only to prove the correctness of the balances shown by the book accounts. The cashier counts his cash not to discover how much is to be written into the credit side of his Cash Book to produce a balance, but to verify the balance that is shown by the figures of his Cash Book. In the same way, all the inventorying that is done under the Balance Sheet System is for the purpose of verifying amounts which the books show should be on hand.

An Easy Experiment

The public is a gentle joy
 To any crafty man;
Just fix it up some little toy
 As simple as you can.
Then to its operations join
 A mystery profound,
And we will gladly pay our coin
 To see the wheels go 'round.

Don't waste your time on useful things
 To benefit your race;
Procure a lot of cogs and strings
 And set them into place.
And men will come from miles away
 Your praises they will sound,
And cheerfully their money pay
 To see the wheels go 'round.

'Tis not required that you shall know
 Mechanics and the like.
If into statesmanship you go
 Success you'll often strike
By fitting empty phrases in
 And letting noise abound.
And making people pay their tin
 To see the wheels go 'round.

His Conscience

"No," said the old shopkeeper, sternly, "I will not do it. Never have I sold anything by false representations, and I will not begin now."

For a moment he was silent, and the clerk who stood before him could see that the better nature of his employer was fighting strongly for the right.

"No," the old man cried again, "I will not do it. It is an inferior grade of shoe, and I will never pass it off as anything better. Mark it 'A Shoe fit for a Queen,' and put it in the window. A queen does not have to do much walking."—Tid Bits.

Adjustable Punch

The accompanying illustration represents an adjustable punch for office use, adapted for perforating order blanks, invoices, and other sheets for filing in post binders and arch files, which has been put upon the market recently by the Saml. C. Tatum Co., Northeast corner John and Water Streets, Cincinnati, Ohio. The device consists of two levers, coupled together in a way to punch two holes simultaneously. The special feature to which attention is directed is the adjustability of the punches. The distance between centers may be varied from two inches minimum to eight inches maximum.

Almost every office at the present time employs more or less post binders and arch files, the sheets for which in many instances are punched in advance by the stationers who supply them. It frequently occurs, however, that it is desired to punch odd sheets or to attach stationery to a post binder which was originally intended for some other purpose; hence the utility of a device like that here illustrated, which will accomplish the work speedily and efficiently, and which is adapted to all the various sizes of binders in use. The manufacturers direct special attention to the care that has been exercised in the construction of this machine to features of design and durability. It is also a model of neatness in the office. The two cups set over the punches, one of which in the cut is shown with the lid removed, catch all the perforations and avoid what otherwise would be a very annoying litter in using the device.

Appreciative

From E. P. A., Holyoke.

I used to think ACCOUNTICS was too deep to help me very much, but I changed my mind some time since. It is deep, but it is not dry, and it is ahead of anything published. It is very interesting and helpful.

The Ledgerette

One of the hard problems which confronts the bookkeeper is the handling of small accounts, accounts which are of so transient a nature that to enter them on the regular ledger hardly pays. Many a bookkeeper has longed for some device to fill this want, and, with this idea in view, what is called the Ledgerette was designed. How well it has filled the bill the large number already sold will best testify. In this file all accounts are kept alphabetically, so that they can be located instantly. At the end of the month, if such is the wish, those not yet paid may be transferred to the regular ledger. The makers of the Ledgerette are also extensive manufacturers of trade checks in aluminum, brass and cardboard, circulars, samples and prices of which will be sent on request. Write direct to W. R. Adams & Co., 31 Congress street, W., Detroit, Mich., mentioning the source of your information.

The Founder of Spencerian Penmanship

The style of copper-plate penmanship that was almost invariably taught when the present generation of business men were boys has suffered various modifications, and in the severeness of its hair lines and carefully proportioned shades is no longer the universal standard. Business utility has greatly modified ideas in this regard. Nevertheless, the world honors the name of the father of Spencerian penmanship, over whose grave in the Geneva (Ohio) Cemetery, a monument was erected some time since bearing the following inscription, attesting the gratitude of at least one of his pupils who had attained conspicuous success in life.

PLATT ROGERS SPENCER

1800-1864.

Poet, Penman, Educator.

Author of Spencerian Penmanship,

Reformer, Benefactor.

Erected by His Grateful Pupil,

MAHLON J. WOODRUFF,

New York City.

There is now on foot a project to erect, in Geneva, the scene of this educator's labors, a memorial library. The building is to be of stone, is to cost some $20,000 and in addition to housing an extensive library, is to shelter the historical collections of Ashtabula County. A correspondent of the Philadelphia Record gives the following interesting particulars in a letter recently addressed to that journal:

In this town (Geneva), now of some 2,000 inhabitants, Spencer lived in the early days of the Western Reserve, and in the little log school house, which was also his residence, first taught writing. This little log house is fresh in the memories of hundreds of the most successful men and women of the United States, who in early days came from all sections of the country to attend this school, which was commonly known as "Jericho" or the "Log Seminary."

Spencer's life was filled with hardships, and all that he attained was gained by hard study, persevering work and strength of purpose. He could, therefore, as a teacher, appreciate the hardships of his pupils in their struggles for an education. It was as much Spencer's attitude toward his pupils as his capabilities that made him famous as an instructor. Although Spencer was a teacher of many branches, his specialty, as is well known, was penmanship.

When his penmanship characters first took form it was not upon carefully prepared paper, but in the sands by the water's edge, on the bark of trees and upon the framework forming the cabin of a lake steamer. Long before he had attained the age of eight years his great desire was to write or draw.

Even at this early age his hardships in pursuing his chosen work are noticeable, for up to that time he had never seen a piece of writing paper. He had heard of writing paper and its uses, however, and it was his great desire to secure, if possible, a single sheet. He then lived at East Fishkill, N. Y., his native town. This point was a Mecca for lumbermen in those days, who often traversed a distance of many miles to the nearest town of any size.

To one of these lumbermen the ambitious boy intrusted what was probably his first penny, instructing him to buy him a sheet of paper before his return. It was nearly midnight when the lumberman got back, but the boy was waiting for him, and with the precious sheet before him in his room he began to write.

While in school at Conneaut his penmanship was so noticeably fine that he was levied upon to write copies for the entire writing class. These copies were usually of his own composition, and many times were verses containing some gem of thought.

When he became a teacher he gave no countenance to the pupil who was inclined to waste his time. He would, however, stay hours after school to assist the willing student, and a parent could have taken no more heart-felt interest in his welfare.

Bets at first were fool-traps, where the wise like spiders lay in ambush for the flies.—Dryden.

It is a law of the gods which is never broken, to sell somewhat dearly the great benefits which they confer on us.—Corneille.

Commercial Law

Representations in the Sale of Merchandise.

By B. R. Price.

The legal effect of representations in the sale of chattels is alike interesting to the seller and the purchaser. The "butcher, the baker and the candlestick-maker" all make representations, either expressly or by implication. The matter of representation was simpler in the days when goods were passed from hand to hand, as is yet the case with the ordinary retailer; but with the expansion of trade, advertising, sending samples, or selling through correspondence and traveling salesmen, render it more complicated, and its elucidation by the courts has in many instances proven a costly one to both the tradesman and his customer. The citation of a few principles, deduced from recent decisions, may put both classes on their guard, and save some of our readers from being deceived, or innocently, perhaps, misleading others and becoming liable for damages.

A representation that will render one liable to another in case of sale of personal property must amount to fraud: Fraud is either actual or constructive. Actual or positive fraud consists in deception practiced in order to induce one to buy goods, and which actually accomplishes that result. Constructive fraud is given by the law where such effect is produced indirectly. In order to render it actionable, the following facts must appear: First, that the representations were made as alleged. Second, that they were made in order to influence the sale. Third, that relying upon them, the party made the purchase. Fourth, that the representations were untrue. Fifth, that the party suffered damage. Sixth, that this damage followed proximately from the deception.

Fraud is never presumed, and the party alleging and relying upon it must prove it. That is, a transaction, honest and lawful on its face, must be treated as such until it is proven otherwise. This may be shown positively, or be deduced from the circumstances surrounding the sale. Whatever evidence satisfies the mind that fraud has been committed is sufficient.

In general a mere silence, a mere failure to apprise the party with whom one is dealing of facts important for him to know, is no fraud. Caveat emptor (let the buyer beware) is the motto of commercial law; and every person is expected to look after his own interest, and is not at liberty to rely upon the other party to protect him against the consequences of his own blunders or heedlessness. Therefore, when the sources of information are equally open to both parties to any dealing, and the one obtains an advantage of the other, without resort to any trick or artifice of concealment calculated to throw the other off his guard, or to any false presentation of facts, the advantage he gains is deemed legitimate, and the losing party must bear such loss as has resulted from his own want of vigilance or prudence. This is true not merely as to quality or value, but extends to all those facts and circumstances likely to influence a buyer if known to him at that time.

It is not essential, in order to render one liable for deception, that the false assertions should be made in words. A nod, a wink, a shake of the head, or a smile artfully contrived to induce the buyer to believe in a non-existent fact which might influence the negotiations, may have all the effect of false assertions, and be equally deceptive and fraudulent. Silence, however, is fraudulent, when it amounts to an affirmation that a state of things exists which does not, and the party is deceived to the same extent as he would have been by positive assertion. Where one is making a purchase for a specific purpose, which is disclosed to the seller, and the latter knows that what he offers is wholly unfit for that purpose by reason of some defect not manifest, it is his duty to make known that fact. For if the applicant were suffered to buy, supposing it were suitable for the purpose, the fraud would be as gross, if no words were uttered, as it would be if the sale were accompanied by the most positive assertions of its adaptability to the purchaser's wants. Independently of any express and formal stipulation, the relation of the seller to the buyer may be of such a character as to impose a duty upon the former differing very little from warranty. Silence in such a case would be a deceit.

Mere expressions of opinion, however strongly or positively made, though they are false, are no fraud, because these are matters in respect to which many men will be of many minds, and judgments are often governed by whim or caprice. So for a salesman to assert that the goods he is selling are of a particular value, greatly above their real worth, or to exaggerate their good qualities, etc., is no fraud. Nor do some of the courts deem it a fraud for one to assert that he paid more for an article than he really did. But where one is purchasing goods, the value of which can be only known to experts, and he is relying upon the seller's opinion as such, the dealer must give him accurate information, or be liable as for a misrepresentation.

Where ordinary care and prudence are sufficient for all protection, it is the duty of the buyer to make use of them. If representations be made, with opportunity of investigation, and the buyer sees fit to take the assertions on trust, the law in general will leave him where he placed himself.

No one has a right to accept and rely upon the representations of others but those to influence whom they were made. It is then assumed that they were made for the express purpose of influencing the action of such party, and it is assumed that they were made deliberately and after due inquiry, and it is no hardship to hold the party making them to their truth. But he is accountable to no one else but the one he seeks to influence. The representation must be of a decided and apparently reliable character, and productive of the desired result, for fraud does not consist of mere intention, but intention carried out by hurtful act.

A Choice Offered.

"Is the boss in?" he asked of the bookkeeper.

"Which one do you wish to see," replied the bookkeeper, "the office boy or the typewriter?"—Life.

How Fortune plies her sports when she begins to practice them!—Ben Jonson.

The Scotch Cash Credit System.

"Every facility and accommodation which their balances, business and responsibility warrant," is about as definite a promise as an intending depositor can obtain from an American bank or banker. In contrast to this, attention is called to the "Cash Credit System" of Scotch banks, which, up to the present time, has been confined to Scotland only, although it has always been recommended as a desirable innovation by economists. It enables a man of honor, integrity and industry to have a bank account, although he may not in reality have the cash, to maintain a balance, conduct an established business, have a commercial rating, or possess, in fact, any means beyond a capital of honesty and a capacity and ability for work. The fact is that in Scotland their cash credit system has been the foundation stone of many fortunes and Scotch banks and bankers have been, and are, most liberal in extending these credits to any one who can supply the requisite guarantors. This cash system suggests the idea whether or not something of a similar kind could not be adopted in this country in such shape as to work advantageously both to banks and their customers.

The system is briefly described as follows: An individual is permitted to open an account with a bank, not with a deposit or a discount, but an actual credit for a certain amount, which the bank loans to him, charging him the customary interest on his daily debits. This account the individual can operate with and check against, as if he had so much cash on deposit. This loan, it must be understood, is not a time loan, but is permitted to remain as a loan just as long as the bank and its customer are mutually satisfied. These cash credits in amount usually range from $500 to $5,000. A man may desire to start in business. He has no cash and no capital, and both are necessary. He applies to some convenient bank for a cash credit of, say, $2,500. He gets some of his friends "to become bound" to the bank as guarantors for him, and the bank opens an account with him, giving him a credit of $2,500. The guarantors, of course, are very careful to watch the operations of the depositor, and they maintain a careful lookout over his account. The bank, on its part, expects the account to be a reasonably live one, and that deposits and withdrawals be made with frequency. Statistics have demonstrated that in some instances the total transactions based upon a very small cash credit are enormous; as much, sometimes, as $200 to $300 for a single dollar in a year.

The Depreciation of Goods

By Rollin Jeffries

Nothing in the line of merchandise escapes the loss of value entailed by exposure, handling and the lapse of time. Goods become shelfworn, more or less soiled, and last but not least, in many cases, out of style. Whatever may be the effort of the salesman to dispose of goods promptly, even when resort is had to such expedients as reduction of prices, still at the end of the season it will be found that a considerable amount of value is locked up in some form or another that is practically worthless. There is therefore a loss from depreciation of goods which must be taken into account in planning a business campaign for a mercantile establishment, the same as the loss growing out of the depreciation of factory equipment, which obviously must be taken into account in establishing the cost of goods made. That is to say, out of the gross profits made upon the goods sold there must be paid on the one hand, the depreciations of value in goods left on hand, and on the other hand the depreciation in the value of the factory plant.

In conversation with a wholesale dealer in a staple line of goods a short time since I learned that his firm for several years past had written off on the occasion of each annual inventory a sum varying from $30,000 to $60,000, averaging perhaps $45,000 a year for depreciation in value. The inventory of course ran into figures of considerable magnitude; but to face a loss in the nature of depreciation in value of stock on hand to the extent of $40,000 or upwards, was that which particularly commanded my attention. The gross profits of the enterprise must manifestly be enough to stand this loss in addition to all the expenses of the business, in order to show a profit at the close of the year.

How to treat this loss from depreciation, in accounting, is a question of considerable interest, and one which has been carefully considered by accountants in various parts of the world for time out of mind. While comparatively few concerns face the loss from depreciation of goods in amount anything like the instance above mentioned, yet the principle is the same even though the figures be but one-tenth of the size.

I am disposed to regard the loss from depreciation as being of the nature of an expense. It is one of the costs of doing business. Therefore if I were calculating the loading of my prices in the sense of adding to the cost of the goods purchased enough to cover the expenses of selling, bad accounts and other losses and finally a profit, I should certainly figure in to that loading an ample allowance for depreciation of goods on hand.

If this plan is agreed to, the next question that comes up for consideration is the basis upon which the calculation is to be made. If the cost of the goods sold by a given establishment is $250,000 per year, and if the reduction that is to be made in the inventory of the goods remaining on hand at the close of the season amounts to $10,000; or in other words, if $10,000 a year must be figured as the amount of loss by depreciation, then 4 per cent. of the cost value of the goods purchased must be added in the process of loading, in order to provide this amount. Manifestly the basis of calculation must be on the cost of the goods. It would not do to figure it against the selling price, which fluctuates from time to time. If this plan were followed the calculation would be sure to lead us astray.

Another plan that is possible to pursue, assuming that the management is willing to consider the loss by depreciation as being in the nature of a cost of doing business, would be to charge up arbitrarily to expenses a fraction of this cost each month, carrying the credit which offsets the charge to a reserve account. For example, suppose that the loss from depreciation is estimated to be $9,000 a year, and that the fiscal period of the business is twelve months: Then one-twelfth of $9,000 is the amount to be charged into the expenses of doing business each month. The same amount is to be posted each month to the credit of the reserve account for depreciation on merchandise. When the inventory comes to be taken at the close of the year there will have been accumulated $9,000 to offset a like amount written off from it. Carrying $750 per month into expenses on one side and to the credit of the reserve account, on the other side, would bring the gross profits of the business into proper contrast with the expenses. Further, by this plan the allowance would be calculated in a way to give the management all proper data for direction and planning. It is certainly better than disregarding the matter entirely as the months roll on, leaving the actual shrinkage to be "deducted from profits."

One thought that I would like to leave with the reader in closing, if up to this point he has felt an interest in these remarks, is this: Depreciation of merchandise is something that cannot safely be disregarded, whatever may be the view point as to its disposition. It is a fact; and since bookkeepers deal with facts, this fact among others must be taken into account by bookkeepers or at least their official superiors, the auditors, who direct their work.

Thoughts are Things.

By Walton Day

The suggestive foot line to the pages of a little pamphlet that has recently come to my attention, entitled "How to Push Your Business," written by Prentice Mulford, and being No. 29 of the White Cross Library, is "Thoughts Are Things." The assertion, it seems to me, is pregnant with suggestions, and the more one dwells on the statement the more impressed he is with the fact of its correctness. The further he pursues his investigation in the sense of discovering illustrations that bear out the assertion the more he becomes assured of the commercial value of thoughts.

The argument throughout the pamphlet turns upon the sentence that "Thoughts Are Things." The introductory sentence contains in a measure the keynote of the entire work: "No matter what position you are in, be it clerk, typewriter, porter, bookkeeper, car conductor, an employee in a factory or elsewhere, if you make up your mind or fall into the way of thinking that you are always to remain where you are and never rise any higher or receive more for your services, the chances are very largely against your rising."

A little further along we find this: "The pushing of any kind of business always commences first in the mind. The man who is to-day controlling a dozen railroads, commenced in some relatively humble position; but in mind he was always aiming higher. When he gained this step ahead he did not in mind stop there; in imagination he was on the next step."

A little further along is this: "If a man for years a rag picker and scavenger has never looked or aimed any higher, he sees himself always a rag picker. In his thoughts he never gets beyond the rag picker's limits. He may envy people who are better off and wish for some of the things they enjoy; but he never says in thought, 'I am going to get out of this occupation. I am going into something higher, cleaner and more remunerative.' So he remains always a rag picker."

I shall not attempt to reproduce the whole pamphlet. The advice that is contained in the book will be satisfactorily exemplified by one or two more brief extracts: "Dare to think of yourself now as a leader in business and as a handler of great sums of money. So to dare in your own secret mind exposes you to no ridicule from others. It is as cheap so to see yourself as to imagine yourself always at the foot of the ladder. Cultivate the art of expecting success. Confident expectation of success is the most useful habit of mind, or method of using your thought force you can cultivate. Constant expectation of misfortune, disaster and bad luck is the most ruinous method of using your thought force, and is a sure road to poverty."

Again we have the following: "The world gets better things than it ever had before; better houses, better food, better amusement, new recreations, new devices in art. It is constantly wanting and paying well for the best. Do not say in your mind you cannot devise and push something before it. You can. To say in your heart you cannot is to put an impassable barrier between you and your possibilities. To say 'I can' and 'I will' is to put yourself within reach of the thought current, which will bring wealth to you."

From these brief quotations the drift of the author's argument is plain. Thoughts are things. They are things that are of commercial value. And last but not least they are valuable in the extreme as incentives to work.

Whatever fortune has raised to a height, she has raised only that it may fall.—Seneca.

A Suggested Form of Postal Currency

Every one who is doing a business, any part of which comes under the designation of a mail order business, and every one, as well, who has occasion to make small remittances by mail, is brought face to face with the lack, in our present currency system, of something which is convenient for use in making small remittances. Post-office orders and express orders are excellent in their way, but they are attended with considerable bother. There is the necessity of filling out a tedious blank, and, last but not least, waiting to have the money order completed and handed to you for inclosure in the letter. The charge which the government exacts for drawing the order is the least part of the difficulty. The time and the trouble are the more important items.

Thirty-odd years ago the country had a paper fractional currency. Irrespective of the objections that it was subject to, it served a most useful purpose for transmission by mail, and while it was in vogue the mail order business thrived as it has not done since. Long after the paper fractional currency was withdrawn from use odd pieces continued to come to hand from time to time, being transmitted by those who were induced to part with keepsakes because there was no other plan of sending money by mail that was so convenient and satisfactory.

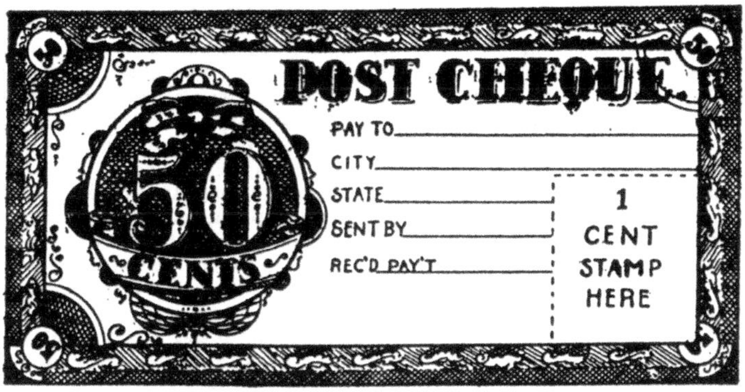

SUGGESTED FORM OF POSTAL CURRENCY.
FIG. 1—Blank Postal Check to pass current or for all purposes.

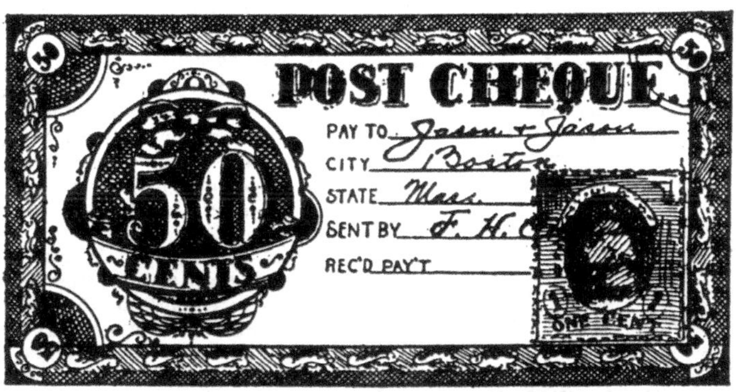

FIG. 2—Postal Check withdrawn from general circulation by the holder and by him made payable to a certain party only. In this condition it is redeemable upon proper identification at a designated place.

Stamps are frequently resorted to for inclosures. They are objectionable on account of the sticky condition of the mucilage with which their backs are covered; and to be received in large quantities by any one in business except possibly a publisher, would be altogether inconvenient. Stamps are discriminated against as a medium of remittance by both sender and receiver for these reasons and others. It is unnecessary to say that coins cannot be satisfactorily transmitted by mail, even with the forms of coin cards that are more or less in evidence in almost every office. The presence of a coin in a letter is easily detected, if the packet happens to fall into the hands of a dishonest person, and further the weight of the coin itself frequently works destruction to the envelope.

The session of Congress that is approaching is likely to be characterized by several efforts towards amendment of the currency laws, each seeking to solve the problem of providing the business community with a form of fractional currency convenient for transmission by mail. Among the suggestions to which attention has reeently been called, looking to the accomplishment of this object, is one offered by C. W. Post, chairman of the Postum Cereal Company, Ltd., of Battle Creek, Mich. We present herewith two electrotypes of the form of postal check suggested by Mr. Post. What is accomplished is a paper fractional currency which on occasion can readily be converted into a remittance to order by the mere attachment of a stamp and the filling in of a name and address. When so filled in the currency is redeemable only at the post office or other designated governmental agency. Before the filling in of the name the currency may pass from hand to hand in the usual transactions of business. There are many arguments in favor of this device. Certainly business men generally would welcome it, or something equally as good, particularly in view of the great stimulus it would give at the present time to the mail order business.

The Institute of Chartered Accountants of England and Wales.

Some idea of the development of the profession of Accountancy in Great Britain may be gathered by even a casual examination of the annual volume that is issued by the Institute of Chartered Accountants of England and Wales. When it is recalled that this organization is only one of several bodies of considerable size and importance in the United Kingdom, some of which can show a membership nearly as large as that of the organization named, it becomes still more manifest that accounting is fairly well recognized by our English cousins.

The book before us contains some 400 pages. At the outset there is a list of the past presidents and vice-presidents of the Institute. The Institute was organized in 1880 and was incorporated by royal charter on the 11th of May of that year. During its existence it has had eleven presidents. The general rule, it would seem, has been to re-elect, sometimes to the fourth term. The charter and by-laws, including forms, occupy nearly seventy pages. The list of members, which is presented first alphabetically and afterwards topographically, fills the balance of the book, the membership total of which is 2,478, divided as follows: Fellows, 729; associates in practice, 1,164; associates not in practice, 496, and members practicing or resident out of England and Wales, 89.

By What Shall We Judge a Man?

How true it is that when a man is at a distance from us, says a writer in one of our exchanges, we are governed by his penmanship, and when he is before us by his words; and how often we are made to suffer, yet we repeat the same mistake. In the years gone by men did not seek an education as they do now. They were then given too little, as now the boys and girls are given too much, for their own good or the good of the community.

I am reminded of all this by the following extract from a letter just received from a good, faithful workman: "I was sorry and supprised when you stated In your letter that a manufactu Judged a man by is writing I consider it a very poor way of Judging a mans qualities I have known men that could nither reed nor write that Where as good a workman As ever took a wrence or Tool in hand."

"By their works ye shall know them," and not by their penmanship or by their words, for of both an ambush can be made behind which a poor workman can hide himself.

Accountics

The Office Magazine.

A. O. KITTREDGE, F. I. A., C. P. A., Editor.

E. R. KITTREDGE, Associate.

Accountics is devoted to the Science of Accounting, to the Art of Bookkeeping and to the advocacy of Improved Office Methods.

Subscription.—One dollar a year, payable in advance.

Postage is prepaid by the publishers in the United States, Canada and Mexico. For all other countries in the Postal Union, subscribers must add 50 cents a year.

Discontinuances.—In the absence of specific orders to discontinue at the end of the subscription term the magazine will be continued and a bill sent.

Remittances should be by Draft, P. O. Order or Express Order, payable to the order of the ACCOUNTICS ASSOCIATION. Money and postage stamps are at the risk of the sender, unless sent by express or in registered letters. Add 10 cents each to checks on local banks to defray collection charges.

Advertising Rates will be quoted on application.

Official Journal.—This publication, by resolutions duly passed, has been made the official publication of the following organizations :—

THE INSTITUTE OF ACCOUNTS.

THE NEW YORK CHAPTER of the Institute of Accounts.

THE WASHINGTON CHAPTER of the Institute of Accounts.

THE HARTFORD CHAPTER of the Institute of Accounts.

ACCOUNTICS is the accredited medium of intercommunication between members of the Institute of Accounts wherever located.

ACCOUNTICS ASSOCIATION,
Publishers,

Lancashire Bldg., Pine St., near Nassau,
New York.

Publisher's Desk.

We are indebited to W. M. Reid, Morris, Ill., for a copy of his little work entitled "Points on Advertising." It is a clearly printed little pamphlet, 3½x5 inches in size, containing a collection of ideas and suggestions, with remarks concerning methods. The booklet is one that may be perused with advantage by every advertiser, whether experienced or otherwise.

We are indebted to Mr. William G. Mowat, C. P. A., Buffalo, N. Y., for a copy of a pamphlet entitled "The Cost Question," being a paper read before the American Malleable Castings Association, at their meeting April 19th, 1899, by E. G. Felthousen, of Buffalo. The cost question, as viewed by this author, is restricted to foundry practice. He approaches the question from the standpoint of estimates to be verified by records, and deals with castings of the smallest kind, rather than with castings of considerable size. In the course of his remarks he pays a deserved tribute to accounting experience by saying that he knows that it is necessary to place the making up of a cost sheet in the hands of an expert accountant. Reference is made in the pamphlet to a cost sheet which the author evidently displayed with his address, but a reproduction of the sheet does not accompany the pamphlet.

We are indebted to Powhattan Windham Robertson, of Washington, D. C., for a copy of the chart which he issued sometime since entitled the Bookkeeper's Compendium, or Bookkeeping in a Nutshell. The chart purports to show how to open, keep and close any set of books by double entry, and is printed in several colors. The effort is made by means of lines of different characters to show the relationship, not only in general but specifically, with respect to entries, of day-book to journal, cash-book to journal, day-book to invoice-book and sales-book, and likewise the relationship of journal to ledger.

A considerable portion of the chart is devoted to directions and definitions. Among the latter we find the following with regard to the classification of accounts: "Accounts may be classified under two distinct heads—Real or Financial, and Representative or Business—and may be shown thus: Real, those which represent resources or liabilities, as cash, notes receivable and personal accounts; representative, those which represent gains or losses, as merchandise, real estate, interest, discount, commission, shipments, consignments and other property accounts." We fancy that accountants in general will question the correctness of this definition in various particulars. To exclude from resources such accounts as merchandise and real estate is somewhat surprising. This author, like many another, it would seem, is up against the missing link in double-entry bookkeeping, and does not know just what to do. Recognizing the trading feature, or exchange feature, of merchandise and real estate, he yet has failed to provide means for taking care of the resources that are ordinarily included in these accounts, unless, indeed, the annual inventory is relied upon. But merchants carrying stocks of hundreds of thousands of dollars in value, which stocks are a recognized basis of credit, do not like to depend upon inventories alone for statements of value of goods on hand.

The chart, considered as a whole, is a somewhat attractive embodiment of the usual instruction that is imparted to students with respect to the double-entry system. The balance sheet that is presented is a combination of a trial balance sheet; in other words, the conventional business school favorite, and that which is, on general principles, the least satisfactory to the business man. Here real estate and merchandise are recognized as resources, creeping into the statement through the inventory door.

Accountics

VOL. V | NOVEMBER 1899 | NO. 5

The Monthly Statement

That all accountants are good fellows, able to enjoy the pleasant things of life and to appreciate each others' society on occasion, even though they are members of opposing organizations between which strong rivalry exists, was strikingly illustrated by a dinner party on November 6, of which C. W. Haskins was host and the Manhattan Club of New York the place of gathering. There were present representatives from all the accounting societies of New York. At the same time the gathering was limited to certified public accountants. After the good things with which the tables were bountifully supplied had been disposed of, short addresses were made by a number of the guests, all informal in character and proceeding without prearranged program. The desire to secure co-operation in the best and broadest sense of the term and of a character to be of the greatest benefit to the profession was the thought most commonly expressed. Consideration was also given to steps that might be taken by the present generation of accountants to help young men, accountants' assistants and others, to qualify for the C. P. A. examination. Various educational measures were suggested. It was at a late hour that the guests dispersed, all having thanked their host for a most enjoyable occasion and one which they firmly believed would be fruitful in results.

The necessity of greater accuracy and more business-like methods in keeping the records of financial affairs of cities, towns and other public or semi-public corporations is often felt by those who come into close relations with those organizations. Frequently the office of treasurer is filled by men unskilled in the duties pertaining to their position, whose political "pull" has put them in the place they hold. This subject received much discussion at the meeting of the Municipal League of Iowa, held at Des Moines on the 12th of October. It was proposed that there be a uniform system of accounts for cities and towns, and it was recommended that a law be passed providing for a state examiner for accounts of municipalities. We hope the agitation of the subject will extend to other States where a too loose system prevails and result in the legislation necessary to put some such law in operation.

Every one knows something of the extent to which manufacturing and industrial enterprises are based upon patents. In a measure the hard times checked the issue of patents, although the general average prior to the period of stringency may not have been materially reduced. Since the return of prosperity, invention has been marked by the same activity which has characterized all the business interests of the country, and the number of applications by inventors for governmental protection not only breaks all records, but is in itself phenomenal. A recent number of the Patent Office Gazette, which is the official weekly publication of the Government, shows this clearly. It is the largest ever sent out, having no less than 322 pages of illustrations and containing the record of 535 patents. The work of getting this issue out was so heavy that an extra force of men was required to prepare it within the schedule time. Other recent numbers have also been very large.

Credit Men's Affairs

By A. O. Kittredge

Among the recent activities of Secretary Prendergast may be mentioned a new issue of the constitution and by-laws of the National Association of Credit Men, a little pamphlet of convenient pocket size and very handy in form for consultation. It is accompanied by a list of the officers, board of directors, State vice-presidents, and the several standing committees.

* * *

The Philadelphia Credit Men's Association held its anual meeting for the election of officers on October 24. The annual address, delivered by President John Field, on "The Objects and Aims of the Association," was a masterly effort and commanded attention not only upon the part of those present, but was also very favorably referred to in the daily papers. Secretary Prendergast was present on the occasion and spoke on "The Value of Credit Men's Association Work."

* * *

A very strong effort is being made by the Secretary to increase the membership of the Association, particularly in the class known as individual members. A circular was issued early in October relating to this matter, and soliciting the co-operation of those who are at present individual members, to induce their friends to join. The argument is the need that the Association experiences for larger income and the good work that could be accomplished if funds were at hand for the purpose.

* * *

Secretary Prendergast has lately made a second visit to Cleveland, in connection with the organization of the Cleveland Credit Men's Association. This body starts out under most favorable auspices, with a membership that is entirely representative of the mercantile and manufacturing establishments of the Forest City. The prospect of the national convention of the credit men being held in Cleveland in June next has given special impetus to this movement.

On the 16th of October Secretary Prendergast addressed the opening meeting of the season of the Detroit Credit Men's Association. His address was confined to a survey of the work that credit men can do in their organized capacity, and to a consideration of the general scope of what may be designated as the association movement.

* * *

The steady stream of complaint against the political jobbery, fraud and trickery practiced in our municipalities is broken now and then by a suggestion from some practical citizen that measures be taken for conducting municipal affairs with the same degree of care and foresight as the average man carries into his private business. Why, he argues, do we allow these public matters, covering such large interests and touching us so closely, to be managed so loosely and unscientifically, while among ourselves we subject the credit of private firms and corporations to close scrutiny for the protection of each other? The credit department of business institutions, both mercantile and manufacturing, has been so thoroughly exploited of late that it is hardly necessary to discuss it here, but a credit department for municipalities seems to be a brand-new thought. This idea was brought forward in an address by Comptroller Bird S. Coler, of New York City, at a banquet of the New York Credit Men's Association, November 22. Coming from one so intimately connected with the financial affairs of a large city, the words have great weight.

Mr. Coler said: "If all business men would talk about public affairs as much as you credit men are supposed to discuss the affairs of business men, the result would be a better knowledge of public business, a clearer understanding of the principles and purposes of politics and government, and a better political situation all around. In fact, I think it would be a good plan to have a Credit Men's Association in politics, and the business men of the city should constitute the membership of such an organization. Then we should have no more boodle Boards of Aldermen and no more Ramapo water contract jobs."

Who Shall Write the Advertisements?

By Ziba B. Cranford

Every business man, and every professional man as well, is interested in advertising. Advertising is a necessity in all business enterprises, large or small, and is recognized as such by every one. Advertising mediums are abundant and are to be found on every hand. New ones, of the nature of circulars and catalogues, are being constantly created. There is ever present the opportunity to advertise and every incentive to advertise, but fundamental to all schemes of publicity there is the question, who shall write the advertising, or who shall shape the announcements?

The novice, who first attempts to phrase an advertisement, whether it is to occupy a stated space in a periodical or the back of a postal card, or to constitute the body of a circular, seldom acquits himself in a way that is entirely satisfactory. When afterwards he compares his work with something that has proved to be so successful as to be a needed piece of work, he realizes the difference between the product of a trained and skillful hand and that of one who has not had the benefit of experience and discipline.

For a number of years past the business public has been overrun with the offers of so-called advertising specialists to write advertisements, to prepare catalogues, to get up booklets, and in general to voice whatever schemes of publicity are under contemplation. Ready-made advertisements, syndicate advertisements and stock work of various kinds and descriptions have been hawked by the same class of energetic venders from one end of the country to the other, until it would seem that for a fact a new industry had been established.

There are comparatively few large advertisers—and this term is used in a relative sense, for some small concerns are large advertisers and some large concerns are, comparatively speaking, only small advertisers—who have not first or last employed one or the other of these advertisement writers in the preparation of some special line of advertising. But there are few, we are persuaded, who have continued their patronage for any considerable length of time. For reasons that are too numerous to mention in detail, the experiment has seldom proved profitable. The results in one sense, perhaps, have been satisfactory, but in various other respects they have been quite unsatisfactory.

This condition of affairs very naturally has had its effect upon the advertisement writers. That they have failed in their efforts to build up a regular demand and to secure an established clientage is evidenced by their own utterances, which of late begin to reflect their disappointments. For example, some of the more prominent apostles of the new dispensation have recently altered their addresses to the business public in a way to clearly indicate that they are sensible of their failure, or, rather, in a way to admit that what they have attempted to do, in establishing a staple industry, has met with far less success than they first anticipated. We do not mean by this that they admit defeat, nor do we assert that they have been entirely defeated. The real facts of the case are that the development of advertisement writing has not moved along the lines that apparently these men thought would prevail as long ago as they began their careers. What they have done has promoted the cause of advertising broadly, even though it has not served to build up for them a special industry in advertisement writing.

One of the oldest and most widely known advertising experts is reported to have declared before a prominent convention of manufacturers some months since that no one could write advertising for those manufacturers nearly so well as they could do it themselves; and that he, and even the expert, could not not do it for them as well as they could get it done in their own establishments. This assertion, which has been variously reported and discussed in the trade papers, has caused no small sensation, for it is in effect a contradiction of all that the said expert has been printing and doing for many years past. That he had such a feeling in his heart, although he has put a different interpretation upon his words, upon being asked for further particulars, became evident in one respect at least by a radical change in his scheme of business, as more recently announced to the public. He turned his attention to a school for advertising writers, at the same time virtually relinquishing the writing of advertisements.

Still later another very prominent advertisement writer has announced through the advertising periodicals that advertisement writing cannot be as successfully done at long range as in close contact, and that, therefore, he has made special arrangements for the instruction of those who are on the ground and who, therefore, are better situated for writing advertisements. He argues very justly that mere arrangement of words, rhetorical flourishes and display type do not make up all there is of an advertisement, and that much depends upon a knowledge of the goods and of the market in which the goods are sold, and the real wants of the customers to whom sales are to be made. Going further, this writer illustrates his position by citing the case of a physician. If a man requires the services of an ordinary physician, he writes, he would do well to employ one close at home. If there is any thing serious the matter with him he would probably consult a New York physician, or, at a pinch, would even go as far as London to obtain the services of the best specialist.

During the time that a few men of conspicuous and acknowledged ability have been serving the public as advertisement writers, there has sprung up all over the country a generation of so-called advertisement writers, whose qualifications are for the most part undemonstrated qualities. The papers abound in their announcements. The mails are loaded with their circulars. In many cases their work soon shows that they are men of mediocre ability, and yet very frequently they are fair imitators. In some cases they are graduates from local printing offices and, therefore, know a little something about typographical dress. In other cases they are offshoots from the reportorial departments of the daily papers and accordingly have a certain familiarity with advertisers and advertisers' usual requirements. These men have been quick to seize upon the livery of acknowledged leaders in the new crusade, and to obtrude themselves upon the public in season and out. It has been difficult for some time past for the public to readily distinguish between advertisement writers of real ability and of established reputations and some of these upstarts, all of whom have been perfectly willing to pocket the fees gullible business men have been willing to pay. This fact no doubt has had much to do in the evolution of advertisement writing which is in progress, and no doubt it has been a potent influence in driving the writers of real ability from the position which they formerly occupied to that which at present seems to be their stand.

Our question is, who shall write the advertisements? We are disposed to say in reply that the conclusions reached by the leaders in the advertising profession seem to us to be as nearly correct as any answer that can be given to the conundrum at present. Advertisements should be written by men thoroughly familiar with the business, experimentally acquainted with the trade addressed, and well up in the technical terms that are employed in describing the goods referred to. Borrowing the phraseology of the illustration quoted above, there should be an advertising doctor (family physician) in every business concern, but all these local practitioners should be in direct correspondence with or in other appropriate relationship to the more eminent experts and specialists to be found only in the large cities. There can be no possible objection to the local advertising men standing in the relationship of pupils of the specialists.

Advertising is an art dependent upon a science which is gradually being formulated. Practice makes perfect and experience is absolutely necessary. Intelligent co-operation between the specialist on the one hand and the local man on the other is likely to produce better results than ever could be accomplished by any system of ready-made advertisements, or by the establishment of great advertisement-writing mills, warranted to produce a saleable output, each piece of which is suitably labeled and duly trade-marked.

Why, Hal, 'tis my vocation, Hal; 'tis no sin for a man to labor in his vocation.
—Shakespeare.

Usury is the land-shark and devil-fish of commerce.—J. L. Basford.

The synonyme of usury is ruin.—Dr. Johnson.

Accountant's Associations

New York Chapter Institute of Accounts

The regular monthly meeting of this organization was held at the Waldorf-Astoria, on Thursday evening, November 23. There was a large attendance of both members and visitors. The address of the evening was delivered by Charles Dutton, supervising auditor of the Account, Audit & Assurance Co., Limited. His subject was "Industrial Combinations." A condensed abstract of his remarks appears on another page of this issue.

Mr. Dutton's address was prefaced by a brief account of the United States Industrial Commission, upon some of the sessions of which he had been in attendance a short time since. He alluded to the fact that many otherwise well-informed persons in the business community seemed to know little or nothing concerning the purpose of the commission. Questions asked him, from time to time, he said, betrayed this. For example, several have inquired: "What are they trying to prove?" The answer to this, he declared, is "Nothing." The purpose of the commission, as the speaker proceeded to explain, is to ascertain the nature of the existing legislation of the several states and of the United States bearing upon industrial conditions; the actual operation of that legislation in its relation to the working man, to the manufacturer and business man, and to the consumer; the character and effects of similar legislation in foreign countries, and how far it is applicable or desirable in the United States, and what legislation, if any, along new lines is practicable or desirable for the improvement of industrial conditions, with a view to determining how far it is possible to frame uniform industrial laws, the adoption of which can be recommended to Congress and to the legislatures of the several states.

The main work of the commission may be said to be to study and compare existing laws bearing upon industrial conditions here and elsewhere; to ascertain by competent testimony wherein they are deficient, defective, inoperative, or oppressive, and to recommend such remedial statutes as will tend not only to make the conditions of industry more uniform as between the several states, but to remove such existing sources or causes of discontent, inequality and injustice as can be reached and regulated through legislation.

The speaker referred to the personnel of the commission and to the sub-commissions that have been organized for investigating certain special phases of the situation. The sub-commissions include one on agriculture and agricultural labor, another on conditions of labor and capital employed in manufacturing and general business, a third on conditions of labor and capital employed in mining, another on transportation, and still another on statistics.

At the conclusion of Mr. Dutton's address, various phases of the subject presented were discussed by Messrs. Jaudon, McNeal, Gedney, Child, Dillon, Ott, Kittredge and others.

Before adjourning the meeting, President Child called attention to the fact that the fourth Thursday in each month had been fixed upon as the regular meeting night for the chapter and requested all to bear the fact in mind and keep that evening free from other engagements. He also extended a cordial invitation to the visitors who were present to attend regularly and to come prepared to participate in the debate.

Illinois Institute of Accountants

In response to the requests of a number of our readers, we have secured, at the hands of W. S. McKinley, Secretary of the Illinois Institute of Accountants, 113 Adams Street, Chicago, the following particulars concerning this organization, its past history and its prospects:

The Illinois Institute of Accountants was incorporated in 1896, and in the interval since that date has passed through varied experiences with more or less prosperity. Quite recently its growth and development have been very satisfactory, and there is manifestly a promise of still better things for the future. In evidence of this it is pointed out that interest in the meetings was sustained through the Summer months, and as the cooler weather has come on it has greatly increased. The attendance in the past, though not extremely large numerically, has been of an excellent character. Various visiting friends have contributed to the interest of recent meetings by practical talks on live topics. The membership is constantly growing.

A short time since, the board of managers, deeming it an opportune time for the investigation and discussion of corporation accounting, made special arrangements therefor. Their plans were not confined to formal papers on the subject, but extended to the discussion and solution of practical problems submitted by the members. In several instances the method of treating these questions was portrayed on charts, which were placed on the wall in full view of the audience. L. L. Abbott, president of the Institute, and J. B. Chamberlain, chairman of the board of directors, have been especially active in arranging meetings, and adding new names to the membership list. Similar remarks might be made with respect to the rank and file of the members and the other officers.

At the September meeting J. Hoefman, of the accounting department of the Republic Iron and Steel Company, gave the Institute an impromptu talk on accounting matters. At the October meeting A. Stauffer discussed the treatment of treasury stock. There were developed at this meeting various differences on the legal phases of the subject. The discussion was both entertaining and instructive. Frank E. Webner, manager of the Chicago office of the Account, Audit & Assurance Company, Ltd., New York, was a visitor to the Institute at one of its recent gatherings. The November meeting was addressed by Norman H. Camp, a corporation lawyer of ability and standing, whose subject was the "Initiatory Steps of Incorporating."

The Street Railway Accountants' Association

As noticed in our September number, the third annual convention of the Street Railway Accountants' Association of America was held in Chicago, the 17th of October. The papers read and the discussions upon the same developed the want of a common unit or basis for the stating expense and earning result. Mr. Mackay, of Milwaukee, contended that this unit of comparison should be the motor-car-hour, meaning thereby, car-miles divided by the average rate of speed. This unit he advocated using for both earnings and expenses.

Mr. Vreeland, of the Metropolitan Street Railway Company of New York, contended that this system was not adapted to street railways operated under conditions in which speeds differ not only between different lines, but as between different sections of the same line and as between different hours of the day or a given section of any of several lines. He maintained that the car-mile was the only satisfactory unit of comparison or basis of statement of results.

Col. Heft, of the New York, New Haven and Hartford Railroad, held that all such questions must be settled in the light of the conditions on each of the several lines and that no fixed or stereotyped rule is possible. This view was also taken by many of the speakers.

A prominent street railway president, speaking outside of the convention, but nevertheless continuing the discussion, asserted that the proposition of a single unit is preposterous. "I can readily see," he said, "how a conference might result in fixing a unit for the car, and one for the track, another for the power and one for receipts, and still another for time and wages of the operation, and no doubt as many more as are necessary, but to get an expression that shall include all these in one, and be fair in all cases, seems to me not only impossible, but an absurdity on its face. The variations in the underlying conditions, impossible of expression, would render comparison on such a basis of no value whatever."

After all it must be said that nothing really was accomplished by the convention in the direction of accounting as applied to street railway operations. What was said only touched on details of bookkeeping in the various departments and the basis of arranging statistical results. The opportunity which the association offers for a scientific discussion of the principles of an accounting system, which shall put in the hands of the executive departments of railway companies an analytical statement of the facts so arranged in simple, yet logical form, that it can be easily comprehended and become a working basis, was wholly neglected. The fundamental principle of the relation of the profit and loss statement to the balance sheet of a street railway company did not once come up for consideration. Further than this, the expediency of adapting those aids to street railway office work, which modern scientific accounting has found so labor-saving in other directions, was not even broached.

Industrial Combinations*

BY CHARLES DUTTON, F. I. A.

Organizations with large capital are one of the striking features of the present day. In many instances, these organizations are in effect the consolidation of numerous smaller enterprises. The newspapers are filled with articles about trusts. Political demagogues delight in haranguing their audiences upon the evils of trusts. Hunting the octopus has become a feature of rare sport in some of the state legislatures. So much has the current of public opinion turned against large corporations, indiscriminately but erroneously called trusts, and so great is the misinformation concerning these organizations, that from several points of view it were presumptuous to talk about them.

Many years ago, when the noted temperance orator, John B. Gough visited London, he was waited upon by a committee that urged upon him the expediency of a subject that would not necessarily offend the fine sensibilities of his audience. The committee contended that in London it would not do to talk upon temperance in the way that Gough had been talking upon temperance in America. It was argued that the people wanted to listen to Gough rather than to a temperance lecture by Gough, and so the wily orator, consenting to the suggestion of the committee, announced for his subject, "Man." One of the largest halls in London was filled to the utmost, and before that audience the orator unfolded his theme, but that portion of his subject which received the largest part of his attention was drunken man.

The particular man which Gough discussed was numerous relatively. On the other hand, trusts, using the term in the correct meaning, are very few relatively. Industrial combinations, which are numerous, are not necessarily trusts. As a fact, there are very few trusts in existence at present and a very much smaller number has ever been organized than is commonly supposed to be the case.

At the outset, let me declare frankly that I am in favor of industrial combinations. I look upon them as legitimate developments under well defined business conditions. They are the embodiments of efforts to solve certain economic problems. There are good reasons for their existence in themselves and, on the other hand, the public at large is benefited by them.

Those who stand opposed to industrial combinations are comprised in three classes. The first class includes ignorant people, many of them undoubtedly honest, who set themselves against all progress because they cannot perceive the advantages of progress. The second class comprises those who have been stranded in their business for reasons which they may or may not perceive, and who are prone to cast the blame upon what they call trusts, or who have seen their friends similarly distressed in business and who justly or unjustly lay the blame for the situation to the so-called trusts. The third class comprises those who are chronic objectors and who on principle are opposed to everything. This class is strikingly illustrated by the story of the Irish juror in a case wherein a corporation was the defendant. Shutting his eyes to all the evidence and disregarding the charge of the judge, his answer to every inquiry was, "I am agin corporations."

What does "trust" mean? What is a trust in the correct sense of the term, and wherein does a trust differ from an industrial combination? The difference can be stated in a very few words. An industrial combination proceeds upon the basis of ownership. A trust means trusteeship. There is no ownership about a trust, but trustees manage the property or sales, as the case may be, as to them seems best. A trust is opposed to the law, by the very nature of its organization and the purposes to which it is devoted, but an industrial combination is not necessarily opposed to the law. A large corporation is no more opposed to the law than a small corporation. There are very few

---

* A condensed abstract of an address by Charles Dutton, F. I. A., Supervising Auditor of the Account, Audit & Assurance Co., Limited, delivered before the New York Chapter of the Institute of Accounts, Thursday evening, November 23, 1899.

cases among the large number of gigantic corporations that exist to which the term "trust" can be correctly applied. Some of the most notable instances of trusts in the past have since discovered the illegal nature of their operations, have thereupon changed their form of organization, and of late have become actual owners of the property which they operate, thus purging themselves of offense.

Centralization, in business especially, is the order of the day. Instances of growth and increased strength and development on broader lines are to be seen on every side. That business equipment which answered a good purpose when the nation was younger and the volume of business was smaller, and the population of the country was less, is no longer adequate.

The department store is a good illustration in point. A little while ago there were to be found in every city a number of shops side by side, each managed by its individual owner. All that has passed away, and now, in almost every business center, is to be found one or more gigantic caravansaries, selling under a single roof almost everything that the individual or the family may require. The department store exists because on the one hand economy of administration is secured and expenses are reduced, while on the other hand, the convenience of the public is served and prices are lowered.

Another illustration is afforded by the railway systems of the present day. Few, perhaps, have had their attention called to the change that has been wrought in this direction in the span of a single generation. In the history of English railways the longest road in existence in the United Kingdom was at one time only fifteen miles. In 1847, there were 5,000 miles of railroad in Great Britain managed by 123 corporations. In 1892, there were 13,000 miles of railway in Great Britain controlled by 12 corporations. Only a little while ago, in our own country, to go from the Hudson River to Lake Erie one had to pass over sixteen different roads. Now the traveller not only may go from New York to Lake Erie without change of cars, but he may go double the distance without leaving the coach that he first entered. In fact, transcontinental trains are being run. All this is natural development. It is an example of economic evolution, and following in natural order are the industrial combinations of the present day.

It is not a condition that is forced upon the people, but it is a condition of the people that demands these stronger and larger business facilities and the greater economies which they secure.

In 1898, when the country was shaken from center to circumference by war and the news of war; when Dewey was sinking a Spanish fleet in the harbor of Manila, and Sampson or Schley (which was it?) had made a prisoner of Cervera in Santiago Harbor; when Shafter's army was fighting on San Juan Hill, when the nation in its new-found strength was carrying on a war that attracted the attention of the world and compelled for it a respect of the great powers which had never existed before, this country incorporated industrial combinations to the extent of nine hundred millions of dollars. In 1899, up to the present date—say ten months—the amount of the capitalization of incorporation in the United States is no less than three thousand, two hundred millions of dollars.

There have been various attempts to state the reasons for the existence of industrial combinations. Mr. Havemeyer, of the American Sugar Company, on a certain occasion answering a question, gave as the reason the protective tariff. This reason is certainly inadequate, for a tariff, like any other law, does not discriminate. It favors the small as well as the large, the individual as well as the corporation. Many other reasons have been given, to only one of which I shall give attention in passing. The purpose of business is two-fold—first, the safe investment of capital, and second, the making of a profit. The financial object and the industrial object, go hand in hand. Prior to the advent of industrial combinations, manufacturing was conducted under localized conditions. Each little factory was managed by the owner, who was unknown outside of his own community and who was therefore deprived of the advantages and the resources actually needed to develop his business in a way to meet the demands made upon it.

In the last twenty-five years, the investing public has become acquainted with railroads. Railroads, in turn, have been managed in such a way as to be understood by investors. The development of our railway system has depended not so much upon the co-operation of the communities through which the roads run, as upon the investment of money in them by people at a distance. For example, it was asserted a very short time ago that ninety-seven per cent. of the stock of all the railway companies in Iowa was owned by people outside of that state.

Before the entrance of industrial combinations upon the board, manufacturing establishments were scattered all over the country, which were unknown outside of the several communities in which they existed. They had no ability to sell their bonds or to otherwise raise the capital necessary for the extension of the business required to meet the demands of a growing country. They were, therefore, faced by the sheer necessity of doing something. The demands of the people called for it. Following the excellent example of the department store, to which allusion has already been made and the work being facilitated by the able and industrious promoter, these establishments in various instances have got together in a community of interest, or in other words, in the form of industrial combinations.

There have been various fads and fashions in investments. A little while ago it was Western land; a little later it was farm mortgages, and then came the era of railways. All the available Western land has been taken up; farm mortgages have become a staple business, with much of the humbug and speculation weeded out; railways have been built up to the limit of the country's need and perhaps beyond it. Something new, therefore, is needed. Just at present the fad is industrials. As Western land was overdone, and as farm mortgages were mismanaged in a way to result in losses; and as many railways were built in advance of the demand for them and therefore resulted in loss, so, perhaps, will industrials be overdone in time. But there is less danger in that regard than in the other instances, because of the experience of the past, and because as a nation we are abler business men and more practical financiers than we have been in the past.

The advent of industrial combinations has changed our ideas with respect to business in many directions, as well also as regards methods of conducting business. The old adage had it that competition is the life of trade. Experience has shown that competition is a very expensive luxury. The saving of the cost of competition is in itself so large a gain that capital may reserve to itself a very large dividend, and still have enough remaining to materially reduce prices to consumers.

Who are there specially objecting to industrial combinations? Among others, there are the travelling men, who of late are meeting in conventions and loudly protesting against the trend of events, simply because it happens to interfere with their occupation. They cannot see that what they may be called upon to sacrifice individually is greatly to the benefit of the community at large. Because they have been employed as travelling men in the past, therefore they should always be employed as travelling men and never be called upon to adapt themselves to new conditions. Yet every one of them knows that three to five of them will be covering the same territory in competition when one of them could do all the business. Here is an unnecessary expense to which they are active parties. The costs of travelling men, which are heavy, must be paid by the consumer. Whatever is saved by reducing the necessity of travelling men, therefore, is an advantage to the consumer. The hotel men likewise protest, and also the livery stable men, simply following in the wake of the travelling men who are their patrons and seconding their objections.

The purveyors of advertising object to industrial combinations. I will mention the figures of a single instance that has come under my observation that will clearly explain the situation in this regard. In a certain manufacturing concern having sales of $750,000 per year, the advertising costs over $100,000.

Two concerns making the same line of goods, and of substantially of the same character and grade but with one located in Michigan and the other in Massachusetts, sell in each other's territory. Massachusetts ships to Michigan, and incidental to its shipments is the usual complement of travelling men, and advertising almost without stint. Michigan ships to Massachusetts and likewise supports its goods by all legitimate means. The public would have been as well served in each instance if the goods had been locally distributed, instead of being sent so far away from the respective factories at such heavy expense.

In the popular estimation, single interests or practically single owners dominate each great industrial combination. The public seems to lose sight of the fact that the shares in corporations are purposely made small, so that every one may be accomodated, according to the size of his pocketbook. Instead of single individuals owning the stock of large industrial corporations, the stock as a fact is very widely distributed. An examination of the stock ledgers of any one of the conspicuous industrial combinations now in the public eye will show a share distribution that will surprise those who are not already aware of the facts. The shareholders in these organizations are frequently numbered by the tens of thousands. They are to be found in every part of the country. They embrace members of every class in the community, from the workmen employed in the factories, to estates, widows and orphans, and people of moderate circumstances, who occasionally put by a penny for a rainy day.

The common objection to an industrial combination that is urged by those who do not stop to think, is that it has the power to raise prices, and that therefore it is or may become a grinding monopoly. Admit that it has the power in the abstract, still an industrial combination like an individual is controlled by business and natural laws that cannot be disregarded. It must always have an eye single to its prosperity and continuous existence. The best results at the present time are not obtained by exacting the highest possible prices, but instead by offering goods at popular or reasonable prices. The history of every industrial combination is that it has reduced prices. It must reduce prices in its own interest and therein the community is benefited by what it does. A little while ago it was heralded far and wide that it was possible to buy seven and a half pounds of sugar for one dollar. Since then, the so-called trust has come in and we are now able to buy twenty pounds of sugar for a dollar, and I expect to see the time when I can buy twenty-five pounds for a dollar. Watches, a little while ago, were ten cents a box, and were not very good matches at that. To-day you can buy a dozen boxes of good matches for ten cents. The saving in each instance has been the result of a combination. The profits of combinations are made out of savings and not at the expense of the public. The public gets the larger part of the savings.

I do not propose on this occasion to touch upon the question of labor in connection with industrial combinations. If labor is capital, as it is generally asserted to be, then there can be no possible conflict at this point because the underlying principles are the same in the two cases and the application of them is the same. Combinations regulate production. They avoid over-production. The very strength of a combination enables it to dispose of its goods in foreign markets, when the home market could not absorb all that it can produce. It is financially able to send its surplus product across the ocean whereas the local manufacturer could do nothing but sit in idleness until times improved.

And now in conclusion, let me draw your attention to certain legal decisions which bear upon the subject that we have been discussing. The courts are carefully scrutinizing all that is being done in industrial combinations. Decisions from time to time have been rendered, and at the present date we have decisions both for and against industrial combinations, not against them in principle, or as being opposed to the law broadly, but as against certain special provisions of the law, the constitutionality of which, perhaps, is yet to be determined. The first that I shall read you is one that is opposed to industrial combinations, and I offer it in advance of the others because thereby I shall be demonstrating my intention to deal fairly and impartially with the question. I refer to the decision of the Supreme Court of Illinois against the Glucose Sugar Refining Company. I read from a report:

"The Glucose Company is a New Jersey corporation, and it seems to have done nothing more than its charter and the corporation law of New Jersey permitted. That fact, however, the Illinois Supreme Court held, was immaterial. The question was whether the Glucose Company had violated the law of Illinois by purchasing the property of several corporations engaged in making glucose. The court held that such a violation had taken place, and expressed very pronounced views on the subject of monopoly. It laid it down that no sale of its property by one corporation to another is valid, if the transaction has the effect of regulating prices, of limiting competition, or of controlling production. Glucose, it seems, can be successfully manufactured only within what is known as the 'corn belt,' which consists of an ellipse about 950 miles in length from east to west, and 700 miles in width. All of this belt is within 1,000 miles of Chicago, and, by the terms of sale, the parties conveying their property agreed not to manufacture glucose within 1,500 miles of that city. Hence, their agreement was in effect a total or general restraint of trade, void not only by statute but at common law.

"Moreover, the evidence showed that the Glucose Refining Company intended to acquire all the concerns engaged in the manufacture of glucose. Such a proposition vitiated all purchases embodying it. On this point the court said: 'The material consideration in the case of such a combination is, as a general thing, not that prices are raised, but that it rests in the power and discretion of the trust or corporation taking all the plants of the several corporations, to raise prices at any time, if it sees fit to do so. It does not relieve the trust of its objectionable features that it may reduce the price of the articles which it manufactures, because such reduction may be brought about for the express purpose of crushing out some competitor or competitors. * * * It makes no difference whether the combination is effected through the instrumentality of trustees and trust certificates, or whether it is effected by creating a new corporation and conveying to it all the property of the competing corporations. The test is whether the necessary consequence of the combination is the controlling of prices, or limiting of production, or suppressing of competition, in such a way as to thereby create a monopoly. Necessarily, when corporations thus situated unite together all their properties in one new organization, and permit the latter to operate their properties, competition will be suppressed, and the new corporation will possess the power to limit production and control prices.' "

And now something on the other side. What I shall next read you is an extract from a decision by Vice-Chancellor Pitney in a recent case in New Jersey, brought to restrain a mining company from purchasing the mines of rival companies and consolidating their interests in settlement of a long litigation:

"Now I am unable to find any foundation either in law or in morals, for the notion that the public have any right to have the private owners of this sort of property continue to do business in competition with each other. No doubt the public has a reasonable ground to entertain the hope and expectation that its individual members will generally in their several struggles to acquire the means of comfortable existence, compete with each other. But such expectation is based entirely upon the exercise of the free will and choice of the individual and not upon any moral duty to compete and can never from the nature of things, become a matter of right on the part of the public against the individual. In fact, the essential quality of that series of acts or course of conduct which we call competition is that it shall be the result of free choice of the individual and not of any legal or moral obligation or duty." This decision was affirmed by the Court of Errors for the reasons given by the Vice-Chancellor.

Let me next call your attention to the case of the Mogul Steamship Company. In this case it was admitted that a combination among ship owners to crush out competition by lowering prices and discriminating against shippers who dealt with rival companies might be unenforceable if in general restraint of trade, but it was held that it was not illegal and was not a criminal offense, nor an actionable wrong, and the Judges in the House of Lords maintained in the strongest language the right of combination for the purpose of acquiring property and controlling business.

As a matter of fact, the combination of business concerns in large corporations has been unchallenged in England, and has reached enormous proportions. The English opinion was expressed some time since by the London Economist, when it said: "It is absurd to keep going a hundred inefficient competing agencies to do badly what one efficient consolidated agency can do well."

An eminent writer, in discussing industrial corporations and trusts a short time since, expressed himself as follows: "The trusts are with us to stay. The fight against them may possibly wage never so fiercely, but their oncoming was as inevitable as was that of railways, sewing machines and electricity. Legislation to prevent abuses of their power will stand; but such as is aimed at their destruction will be as futile as were the protests against labor-saving machinery."

And now another quotation to show the opinion in which industrial combinations are held by thinkers and political economists in general: "If they serve a useful purpose and are in accordance with the laws of social development, they will go on and the courts will be powerless to stop them."

In conclusion, let me say that there are some bad combinations, but the exceptions prove the rule, for there was never yet anything in this world so good that its quality was not made the more apparent by something of the same class spoiled or otherwise bad. All combinations may be divided into three general classes: First, those which may be defined as good, conferring benefits upon the public and working economies of administration; second, those which are burdensome, lacking strength, financially and otherwise, and which eke out an uncertain existence and are unable, by lack of strength to demonstrate their right to live; and third, and finally, those which are actually bad. It is of the last that we hear far more than of either of the other two. It is of the good that we hear the least, because they offend no one and no one attacks them. I might illustrate this by referring to history. Those great warriors who, for the purpose of accomplishing their ambitions, have plunged their nations into war after war, ruining homes, destroying business, and wrecking everything, have page after page of history devoted to the record of their deeds, while men of peace and industry who mend and repair, and law makers, who adjust burdens and conserve public interests, are dismissed with a sentence, or perhaps their names are never mentioned at all. We hear much of the bad, but we hear little or nothing of the good.

And now, just one more extract. Here is something that was written by Henry Wood and published as far back as 1887:

"The menace to government and citizens by great business combinations is much overrated. Without regard to legislation, natural law hedges them in on every side. Its pressure also against all artificial rings and combinations is steady and strong, and it is with difficulty they can be maintained for any length of time. While great aggregations of capital, in their operations, are subject to many abuses, they are great forces in production, and have an important place in the economic functions of society. Our safety consists in the fact that the natural laws of supply and demand are sovereign and that there is no danger of their repeal or suspense."

A Blow to the Commission Business

The condition of affairs in Minnesota is such that the commission merchants for the future are likely to become merchants. The St. Paul Pioneer Press, of recent date, referring to the fact that the appeal to the Federal courts from the Grindeland law, so far as it relates to consignments from without the state, was dismissed by Judge Lochren, in the United States Circuit Court, continues as follows:

Two cases were originally brought against commission men, and it was decided by the State Supreme Court that the law requiring commission men to give bonds and take out licenses was a valid exercise of the police power of the state. The state court, however, declined to pass on the question whether the law was in conflict with the power reserved to Congress to regulate interstate commerce, where consignments were made from other states to Minnesota commission men.

It is held by Judge Lochren that the law is not primarily concerned with interstate commerce, but incidentally at most. It was intended simply to protect persons who send goods for sale through commission men, and as such makes no inequality between states, imposes no tax on business between states and does not regulate business between states except and in the same measure as it regulates domestic business. The courts will not hold that to be an interference with interstate commerce which is an incidental application of the regulation of domestic commerce.

It has not yet been decided whether the commission men will take an appeal from this decision, but it is thought likely they will not. In domestic commerce they have already decided not to comply with the law, but to avoid liability under it by refusing to do a commission business. They propose buying and selling farm produce the same as any other commodity. And having this decision against them in the lower Federal court, it is likely they will apply the same practice to business originating in another state.

Confidence imparts a wonderful inspiration to its possessor.—Milton.

The Department Store

By Walton Day

The controversy with respect to the department stores still goes on. The smaller merchants throughout the world seem to be convinced that the department store is an evil that should be remedied and a menace to their welfare which should be removed without delay. Political demagogues, socialists, populists and what-not chime in, with the result that department stores are receiving an immense amount of advertising for which they are paying nothing. The public, through the press, by speeches at political gatherings and in State legislatures, and through the medium of pamphlets and circulars almost without number, is being regaled by a discussion of the right and wrong of the matter, to an extent that is unparalleled. To a casual observer it would seem that there are far more who assail the department stores by pen and by voice than there are those who venture to defend it. Now and then there appears in a public journal a word or two going to show the reason of the existence of the department store, and occasionally some brave writer goes so far as to show wherein the public is benefited by the large store departmentized, even though admitting at the same time that its presence is somewhat hard on the small merchant. Some have ventured to say that the department store exists by reason of the law commonly described as "survival of the fittest." This, however, is merely a truism. A department store could not exist if it did not have the strength to exist, and the fact that it does exist where others fail is evidence that for some reason or other it is fit, or, what is the same thing, able to exist.

We are free to say that from our point of view the department store seems to be an important advantage to the community at large. It appears to be only a legitimate development in the process of business evolution, and a something which has the right to exist by reason of its usefulness to the community. On the other hand, we hold that although in some cases the small merchant, irreproachable in character and a useful citizen in the community, is being crowded to the wall by the department store, yet as a rule the ruin of the small merchant comes about because he has not within himself proper reason for existence and because he is not serving the community well enough and in a way that is satisfactory or entirely meets requirements. His service is such that there is good reason for desiring better things. Hence the opportunity of the well organized, ably managed store of large growth.

The department store is fairly comparable to the modern railway train, in which case the small merchant is to be likened to the old-time stage coach. There are people to this day who deplore the fact that the stage coach has been driven out of existence and that it is no longer available to those who prefer a trip in a pokey, jerky stage coach to going across the country seated in a palace car. Yet to the majority of people the modern railway train is a necessity. According to their way of thinking the stage coach has been relegated to the lumber room, as something that we have entirely grown and altogether passed beyond.

The majority of department stores have grown out of small retail stores. This fact is often overlooked in the discussion. It is an important consideration, however, because it presents a reason for the existence of the present quota of department stores and also for the advent of the thousands upon thousands of others, which in the near future are sure to be added to the list. The small merchant who really perceives his opportunities at once introduces those elements of business management which put him abreast of the demands of his trade and abreast of the times. Fundamentally, there is put into operation a good accounting system; next means are taken to fix the proper measure of responsibility upon each employee. The store force is classified and organized. Lines and boundaries are established. Instead of the old order of things under which every one did everything, the rule is established wherein each person discharges one special line of duties and becomes responsible for some one particular class of things. The business is departmentized, in fact, long before this condition becomes evident to the public, but hence it is thus well organized and well managed, the public appreciates it and gives it patronage. It grows, and as it grows the system which gives it reason for growing gradually becomes apparent. Finally there is the large measure of success which very usually attends department stores.

The object of this reference to the usual rule of growth and development of department stores is simply to emphasize the part which good accounting plays in the combination. A remark made many years since by a shrewd and observant business man, referring not only to department stores, but also to other large business enterprises, may be pertinently quoted in this connection. He said: "Show me a large, successful, well-managed business, whatever may be the line of trade, and I will show you fundamentally an adequate accounting system and in connection therewith a man presiding over the enterprise who is in daily touch with the results which the accounts show."

It is impossible to conceive of a successful department store without forming some conception of the merits of the accounting system which enables the enterprise to exist and which makes it possible for one man, or a small group of men to successfully manage, what in fact is an aggregation of minute details. The promoters and organizers of department stores have simply improved their legitimate business opportunities. They have seen in advance the advantages which follow upon good system in business, when it is reinforced by good system in accounting. The foundations thus laid, the department store, like "Topsy," has simply "growed." It has carried with it its right to existence. Meanwhile the demagogues attack the department store, for the same reasons that footpads waylay travelers with money. They are on the make.

The Chicago ordinance, intended to break up department stores, to which the attention of the whole country has been drawn, was a few days since declared invalid. The judge of the Superior Court has very reasonably decided that the proprietor of a department store was not guilty of violating any law in selling meats, fruits, vegetables and other provisions under the same roof with dry goods, jewelry and other merchandise. Inferentially, we may add he was not violating any law or proper principle of business when he arranged to accommodate the public by bringing various lines of goods into one store and sustain his enterprise by an accounting system which would show his profits in each separate division of his business, thus enabling him to direct the enterprise intelligently.

The German Government, in an effort to please the small storekeepers and the socialistic party of the empire, it is reported, has undertaken of late a remarkable experiment in the way of discouraging department stores. A bill has been introduced in the Reichstag, which if it becomes a law will compel the larger establishments to contribute a larger proportion than the small stores to Germany's revenue. It proposes to tax department stores out of existence. The bill provides that three factors are to determine the taxation—namely, the number of departments or branches, the number of employees and the amount of rent. Stores with branch establishments are to be treated as if all were under the same roof. On the other hand, co-operative stores are not to be taxed under this law.

All this is interesting, because it shows the nature of the attempts that are being made to discourage and counteract business development along lines which mark legitimate growth. That the effort in Germany will be as futile as the effort in Chicago, which has just come to naught may be presumed from the outset. The courts of final resort are likely to decide that such a measure as is being proposed is arbitrary and senseless.

The blindness of those who fight the department store to the principles of business and the conditions that go to make an enterprise profitable is another fact that should be considered in this connection. A method which has been suggested of meeting the competition of the department stores is the combination of retail dealers in different lines to carry on a department store of their own. In this they seem to entirely overlook the economies of the department store, owned and controlled by a single interest. They apparently assume that all that the public wants is an aggregat'on of merchandise under a single roof. It is no doubt true that the public is attracted by the fact that various kinds of goods can be bought at one store, but this fact alone would not sustain a department store. There must be, in addition, ample reasons in price, in quality of goods, in character of service, and in a dozen other minor particulars to warrant all the patronage that a department store receives. An aggregation of small merchants, each managing his own special line of goods, could never equal a department store controlled by a single interest, because such a combination leaves out the discipline of the clerical force, the unity of management, and all the economies to be conserved by a large business directed by a single head. So long as ordinary accounting and business methods prevail among the small merchants thus associated there is omitted the usefulness of the refinement of bookkeeping which alone makes possible intelligent direction down to the smallest detail. For such a combination to succeed against the department store, each of the small merchants entering it would have to become merely the head clerk or department managers in the specialty to which he has heretofore devoted his time. He would have to work cheerfully and industriously under the general management of a head man—one to be selected for the place on account of his special ability as director of affairs. But to this arrangement none of them would consent, and the root of the whole difficulty would thereby at once become apparent. All want to be head boss, and none is willing to serve in the capacity of assistant or even specialist in a given department.

Few are born to command and lead. The many are only able to obey orders and follow. Wherever there is a born general there will be an army or a following, and before the ablest general with the largest force all small opponents must go down. Small stores did very well a while ago. They were, however, only the creations of corporals and sargeants, each with a medium of ability and only a handful of men. Time has progressed. Business has advanced in development. The day of large business armies with tried and experienced generals in command is at hand. The war that is on is one that reveals the fittest to survive, the elements of endurance being, in the order of their importance, as follows: First, the convenience afforded to buyers; second, the ability to organize and manage, and third the amount of capital. We put capital last, for most of the department stores in existence today had little or nothing of this element until they had demonstrated the possession of an ample stock of the other two, and also because it alone cannot do anything.

Syndicate Advertising

We have received from the Chas. Austen Bates Syndicate, Vanderbilt Building, New York, a little pamphlet prepared by Chas Austen Bates, entitled "Practical Helps for Retail Advertisers." It is an announcement of a series of books—twenty in number—on the advertising and management of stores in various retail lines. These lines include all the common trades that the buying public is familiar with, ranging from clothing, drugs, groceries and dry goods on the one hand, to coal, bicycles, jewelry and pianos on the other. Each book, it is stated, is to be devoted exclusively to the proper advertising of the line of trade to which it is devoted. Each book is to be a volume of about 400 pages. Each book is to contain a large number of ready-made advertisements. These are available for use with no greater alteration than writing in the name and address of the merchant, together with prices, where prices are demanded. These advertisements are to be printed on one side of the sheet, so that all the pages will be available for clipping. The cuts used in these advertisements are to be furnished by the Syndicate at a very low price. Additional to the ready-made advertisements are prints of cuts which are available for the advertising which the local man may prepare on his own account. For the purpose of promoting the sale of these books, we are informed, each will be accompanied by a lot of coupons, by which the cuts and electrotypes of advertisements, etc., are to be secured at extremely low figures, and by which still additional information and technical instruction may be obtained. From the pages of the circular we gather that the introductory portion of each book is to give the theoretical side of advertising, while the ready-made advertisements will give the practical part. The ready-made advertisements focus the whole matter right down to the advertising, and the cut coupons give the privilege of buying a most attractive lot of cuts at a very low price. We understand that these books are to be distributed in a way to allow only one in each business center to a given line of trade. This will avoid duplication of advertising in local mediums. By the business plan of the syndicate it is even made possible for one man to take the entire set of books for a given section, thereby putting into his hands the opportunity of syndicating this particular line of advertising for the commuuity. We regard this as one of the most aggressive strokes in the advertisement writing and advertisement teaching line that has come to our attention.

Reviews and Criticisms

Bank Bookkeeping

Bank Bookkeeping. A text-book for business schools and private students. By S. S. Parkard. 88 pages, 8¼x11 inches. Bound in cloth, with gold side title. Published by S. S. Packard. Price $1.25.

This volume represents one of the latest works of importance of the late S. S. Packard, for his death occurred only a short time after the book had been issued from the press. It may be regarded as his last contribution to the text-book literature of business, and, therefore, entitled to more than casual examination. No one knows better than the writer of these lines the high ambition of Mr. Packard in all his various works, and his constant endeavor, as well, to elevate the standard of business education, thereby to better qualify young men for the responsibilities of active life. In justice, however, it should be said that he originated comparatively little in imparting the art of bookkeeping, and recorded quite little of what was new in accounting science. In all his years of business school work (and they were many), and in all his text-books (and they were numerous as well), he introduced no radical changes in system nor in method, and finally he left business education, at least when viewed from a practical standpoint, very little advanced from the condition in which he found it. And yet there are numerous men, many of them quite conspicuous in the business world, who attribute much of their success to their training in the Packard School.

This author was content in all the text-books he put out to reflect bookkeeping and business routine as he found them, without either criticism or amendment. His mission, as he frequently described it, was to reduce to a teaching basis, so far as he was able, that which he encountered in practical use by business men. Nor was he always fortunate in discovering the best examples and the highest types. He seldom, if ever, undertook to say that the practice he reflected was or was not up to the highest standard of excellence, nor that it was or was not in strict accordance with well defined accounting principles.

His latest book was no exception to the general rule. Accordingly, we find it essentially a transcript or summary of the banking routine of certain large and well known institutions. Defined thus, we have little to criticise in the work before us, for undoubtedly it correctly portrays what it undertakes to describe, and as a reflection of the practice of certain leading banks, it is a most acceptable and exceedingly valuable addition to business literature. Certain matters, which the volume presents, however, and certain lessons conveyed, are open to objection, when viewed from a different standpoint. A rigid enforcement of the principles of accounting would, we believe, lead the student away from certain cumbersome methods and irrational, as well as illogical, statements of conditions which are included in this book, for no better reason than that they are generally current in banking practice.

At the outset we are informed that the material gathered as the foundation for this text-book on bank bookkeeping has been obtained from leading banks of New York and Chicago, and that their methods of doing business have been followed as closely as possible, the purpose being to give to schools and private learners the readiest and surest means of acquiring a practical knowledge of the subject. This at once rules out banks of small to average size. The routine of any one of the large banks of New York is very different from that of a bank of one hundred thousand dollars to two hundred and fifty thousand dollars capital in one of the interior cities of the country, but in number there are perhaps a thousand small banks for each of the large banks.

Our author proceeds with a description of the machinery of the bank, as though all banks had a complete corps of employes, ranging from president, vice-president and cashier, down through a long list, including assistant cashier, chief clerk, check clerk, collection clerk, credit bookkeeper, dealers' bookkeeper, ledger keepers, discount clerks, note teller, receiving teller, paying teller, general bookkeeper, runners, messengers and general utility men. The book would more nearly have met the wants of business schools and more satisfactorily have answered the questions of private students—the asserted objects for which it was published—if banking routine had been discussed broadly, independent of the size of the bank, making the lessons applicable to the small bank as well as the large bank. Evidently the author has left this conception of a text-book on bank accounting to be worked by another. That such a book will ultimately be put forth we have faith to believe, for until the text-books are constructed upon this principle, whether relating to banking or to other divisions of business activity, there will be comparatively little progress made in the methods of commercial education.

Adhering strictly to what is found in practice, the author is led into the somewhat absurd position in presenting a statement of resources and liabilities of a bank, to include in the former "current expenses," "taxes paid" and "interest paid." Items which, as resources, would certainly go but a very short way in liquidating liabilities. When it comes to the formulation of the statement which periodically National banks are required to file with the Treasury Department, the form that is at present in use is adhered to, wherein "current expenses" and "taxes paid" are subtracted from undivided profits. It was the rule of the Treasury Department, until a comparatively short time since, that reports should be made out, and sworn to by the proper officers, with "current expenses" and "taxes paid" set forth as resources. The present position of the Treasury Department, in requiring "current expenses" and "taxes paid" to be subtracted from undivided profits, is about as ridiculous and unreasonable in method as the former. Neither is good accounting. However, as we have before stated, the author set out to reflect current practice in bank bookkeeping, and in no part of the work does he undertake to criticise methods nor point out correct principles. Therefore it is unfair to take him to task for what, in the estimation of all good accountants, has been ridiculous in the practice of the Treasury Department for many years past.

The book is one that deserves a place in every accountant's library. As a description of the practice that prevails in several large and prominent banking institutions, it is of great value. The style of the text is lucid, the matter is well arranged, the illustrations are pertinent, and for the most part are in fac simile, and, aside from the facts that it does not attempt to present an exposition of the principles of bank accounting, nor yet does not show current practice adapted to the use of small banks, nor yet to banks of average size, it is entitled to a wide circulation outside of the school limits for which it was especially designed by the author. In the preface obligations are expressed to several prominent bankers, who were freely consulted in the preparation of this work. Special credit is given to James G. Cannon, Vice-President of the Fourth National Bank, New York, the routine of which institution is clearly presented in various parts, and to H. H. Swasey, Secretary of the Fifth Avenue Trust Company, New York.

Newspaper Men Novelists

The old idea that newspaper life unfits a man for the higher pursuits of literature is false, as is shown by the experiences of a number of the brilliant lights in the book world.

Rudyard Kipling, who is, perhaps, in many respects the greatest writer of the day, was once an every-day reporter, and afterwards the editor of a newspaper published in India. W. D. Howells, the novelist; John Hay, the present Secretary of State; Charles Dudley Warner, Harold Frederic, and a score of others all have at some time in their lives been engaged in the drudgery of newspaper work.

It is true, however, that journalism disqualifies many men for literary work. The daily grind of reporting, when followed year in and year out, has a depressing effect upon literary style. It is destructive of continued effort along any line of work. Men become so accustomed to finishing up a task in a day or in a week, perhaps, that they cannot bring themselves to engage upon a work which cannot be finished in months.

Of course, there are minds which cannot be hampered by such surroundings. They become stronger as the years go by, and, when backed up by determination and will, accomplish tasks in the way of literary production that astonish the world.—Fourth Estate.

The Bartindale Dinner

The complimentary dinner given by the stockholders of Morse & Rogers to T. H. Bartindale was an occasion to be remembered by all who were so fortunate as to be participants. Mr. Bartindale, who has been for the past ten years the credit manager for Morse & Rogers, recently resigned that position to accept the first vice-presidency of the Mutual Mercantile Agency, of New York, and as a partial expression of the appreciation felt by the stockholders of the corporation, a dinner was tendered him at the Arkwright Club, on Tuesday, the 31st of October. At the close of the repast Mr. Morse arose and in a happily turned speech presented Mr. Bartindale with a solid silver loving cup bearing an appropriate inscription. Mr. Bartindale had hardly recovered from this pleasant surprise, when Mr. Erastus Wiman, representing friends "outside of Morse & Rogers," presented him with a solitaire diamond ring. Then followed speeches by well known business men of New York and Boston, among whom were William B. Rice, of Rice & Hutchins, and Nathaniel C. Fowler, Jr., of Boston, and Chas. S. Young, cashier of the Central National Bank, New York, and Geo. E. Moulton, of "Bradstreets." Mr. Bartindale's position as first vice-president of the Mutual Mercantile Agency is one of importance and large responsibility and the good wishes of his numerous friends attend him in his new connections.

S. & T. Loose Sheet Holder

The illustrations presented herewith show a form of loose sheet holder, known as the S. & T., that is being introduced by Sieber & Trussell Manufacturing Co., of St. Louis, Mo. Its features will be

Inserting Sheets.

readily gained by an examination of the cuts. In general form it is not so much distinguished from others that have preceded it as it is in style and mechanism. It is much lighter than various loose sheet holders which we have heretofore examined, and the pinch or bite on the sheet is obtained in a somewhat different manner. The grip of the holder has a sharper edge than is common to most loose sheet holders, and the mechanism employed is such that a very small shank to the sheet answers every requirement. How the sheets are inserted is clearly indicated by the first of the cuts, and the appearance of the book with the sheets in place is shown in the second illustration. This holder, as we gain from the sample before us and the statements of the manufacturers, is finished in various styles, to meet the numerous requirements that exist for a device of this kind. It is also made in a larger number of sizes than usually prevails. The price list before us indicates holders of some twenty dimensions, ranging from 3½x5½ inches, with a binding side of 3½ inches,

Sheets Inserted. Holder Open Like a Book.

up to 17x22 inches, with a binding side of 17 inches. The finish in which this binder is sent out is described as being either brown, green, red or straw colored art canvas, or black cloth, as preferences may be. Among the uses mentioned in the circular before us to which the binder may be devoted, we note general office purposes, warehouse work and shipping, private use, for schools and colleges, and for catalogue sheets.

How You May Write It

Some one has noted that the year "1888" was one of the hardest to write in Roman numerals. It took thirteen letters—thus, MDCCCLXXXVIII. Next year we are to get on much easier—thus, MCM.

Father—Well, my son, what did you study about in school to-day?
Johnny—Fractions, pa.
Father—Well, my boy, what is a fraction?
Johnny—A part of anything, pa.
Father—Can you give me an example of a fraction?
Johnny—Yes, sir—the Fourth of July.

If thou art rich, thou art poor; for, like an ass whose back with ingots bows, thou bearest thy heavy riches but a journey, and death unloads thee.—Shakespeare.

Pocket Knife Hone

Who does not appreciate the convenience of a pocket knife with a clean cutting edge? Here is a simple device by which every man can give his pocketknife and other edge tools just the degree of sharpness they require. It is Pike's Quick Edge Pocket-Knife Hone, which more particularly described, is a very quick cutting stone mounted on a hard wood handle with a strip of horse hide leather on the back. The superiority as an abrasive or sharpening material of the natural stone to any composition or contrivance of steel or iron will commend itself to those who have ruined good knives in using such substitutes. The materials employed in the manufacture of this hone are of the best quality and accordingly it can be used in sharpening scissors, ink-erasers and any other small tools. Each hone is put up in a neat folding paper box or sheath, so that it can be carried in the pocket if desired or be conveniently kept in the pigeon hole of a desk. It is supplied by The Universal Speciality Company, of Pike Station, N. H., and 153 Chambers Street, New York. In writing for circulars please mention ACCOUNTICS.

Pocket Knife Hone.

Combination Rule and Blotter

A blotter is an indispensable adjunct of every desk. A rule is something that is frequently required either for measuring or for guiding a pen in special markings. A rule and a blotter combined constitute an article of equipment serviceable on the desk of every business man and clerk. When the combination consists of the very best of each article, something exceedingly satisfactory is provided. The accompanying illustration represents a combiration rule and blotter which is being sent out by Baldwin, Tuthill & Bolton, of Grand Rapids, Mich. The rule is made of polished aluminum graduated into fractions of an inch. It has a protractor at one end, from which any desired angle can be laid out. The blotter, which is clearly shown in the cut, can be instantly removed when desired to permit of the insertion of a new one. No special grade in the latter respect is required, for any ordinary blotter can be readily utilized. The rule, which is approximately nine inches in length, is of a character to be specially convenient for balancing accounts and ruling lines for whatever purpcse.

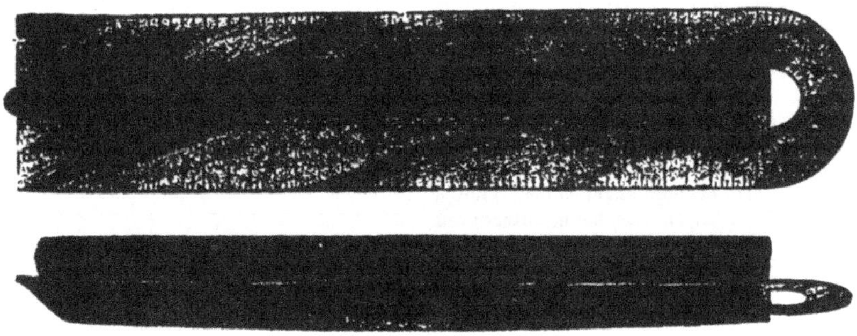

Combination Rule and Blotter.

Accountics

The Office Magazine.

A. O. KITTREDGE, F. I. A., C. P. A., Editor.

E. R. KITTREDGE, Associate.

Accountics is devoted to the Science of Accounting, to the Art of Bookkeeping and to the advocacy of Improved Office Methods.

Subscription.—One dollar a year, payable in advance.

Postage is prepaid by the publishers in the United States, Canada and Mexico. For all other countries in the Postal Union, subscribers must add 50 cents a year.

Discontinuances.—In the absence of specific orders to discontinue at the end of the subscription term the magazine will be continued and a bill sent.

Remittances should be by Draft, P. O. Order or Express Order, payable to the order of the ACCOUNTICS ASSOCIATION. Money and postage stamps are at the risk of the sender, unless sent by express or in registered letters. Add 10 cents each to checks on local banks to defray collection charges.

Advertising Rates will be quoted on application.

Official Journal.—This publication, by resolutions duly passed, has been made the official publication of the following organizations:—

THE INSTITUTE OF ACCOUNTS.

THE NEW YORK CHAPTER of the Institute of Accounts.

THE WASHINGTON CHAPTER of the Institute of Accounts.

THE HARTFORD CHAPTER of the Institute of Accounts.

ACCOUNTICS is the accredited medium of intercommunication between members of the Institute of Accounts wherever located.

ACCOUNTICS ASSOCIATION,
Publishers,

Lancashire Bldg., Pine St., near Nassau,
New York.

Publisher's Desk.

A thoroughly up-to-date and useful advertising novelty is the packet or folder with contents which the Globe-Wernicke Company, of Cincinnati, is distributing at the present time. It goes out for one cent postage and yet has more real force about it than several letters ordinarily carry. On the address cover is the legend, "Expansion—A Vital Question." On what would ordinarily be the title-page of the pamphlet to which we next note is a little chapter entitled "Expansion," which we quote in full: "We may differ on this policy as applied to the nation's possessions, but as applied to business we are a unit." There is a play on words in this that becomes apparent when the following pages are examined. The first of these is entitled "Business Expansion" and the second "Cabinet Expansion." The illustrations show applications of the Globe-Wernicke unit system of furniture, including cabinets arranged for indefinite expansion. Several pages following are illustrative of the different features of this elastic cabinet system presented without any allusion to prices. At the last there is a description of catalogue No. 29, which we learn tells about elastic cabinets. This the reader is invited to send for. Attached to the end of the back cover, and perforated for easy removal, and so arranged as to fold in when the packet is closed, is a private mailing card. This is printed with the address of the company on the outside, and with a request for catalogue No. 29 on the inside, requiring only the signature of the applicant and the attachment of a stamp to complete it. As said at the outset, there is much more in this little circular than is ordinarily contained in a long letter with several enclosures, and therefore it is to be commended.

Mr. B. W. Murray, Accountant in the Supreme Court of Judicature for Ontario, has recently issued a revised edition of his Interest Tables. These tables cover rates from 2½% to 8% by ⅛% rates, thereby containing, in addition to the usual even rates, the fractional rates. Mr. Murray has presented to the public a work which is the result of years of careful computation and those who have frequent occasion to use such labor-saving devices will find much in his book to interest them.

Notwithstanding the lack of success generally attending juvenile publications, and in the face of a large number of actual failures in this field, the Sprague Publishing Company, of Detroit, have launched in the recent past a new twenty-four page, illustrated monthly, called The American Boy. This magazine is edited by Wm. C. Sprague, widely known by reason of his connection with the Sprague Correspondence School of Law. Editor Sprague proceeds upon the assumption that while there is sufficient literature for men, women and children, there is none for boys. He is impressed with the idea that what a boy really needs is the literature of achievement, and that boys want to know what other boys are doing. The departments of the magazine include, "Successful Boys of To-day," "What Boys Are Doing," "The World Through a Boy's Eyes," "Talks on Business," "Boys as Money-Makers and Money-Savers," "Boys in Office, Store and Factory," "Boys in Home, Church and School," "Boys in Games, and in Sports," etc. We shall watch the development of this effort with great interest and shall hope that the editor's conspicuous ability as manager and writer may enable him to put out a paper which the boy will cherish after he ceases to be a boy, and thus do his part in continuing the subscription list. The trouble with juvenile papers in the past has been the necessity of continual rebuilding the subscription list. The magazines have been like children's clothes—soon outgrown and thrown aside. May this one have better luck.

Accountics

VOL. V DECEMBER 1899 No. 6

The Monthly Statement

The recent change in the head of Yale University has attracted general attention and the public look for important results to flow from the administration of President Hadley. That our Universities are no longer devoted chiefly to the study of dead languages and abstruse philosophy of which the man of affairs knows little and cares still less is apparent to any one who will examine the curriculum of any of our leading institutions. The active interest in the great commercial movements of the day shown by the heads of educational centers is a hopeful sign that the student will find instruction in matters pertaining to the life before him. The part which Yale will take along lines which touch the business of the country is foreshadowed in the words spoken by President Hadley at the annual dinner given by the New Haven Chamber of Commerce on November 15. In reply to the toast "Yale University" he said:

"Of all universities there is, I think, none which has given so much to commerce as Yale. She had her birth in commerce. On one of my trips through England I visited the home of the man I know of as the founder of Yale. My guide book informed me that the local church yard was the burial place of Elihu Yale, who was celebrated as the inventor of auctions. Yale was the first college to introduce political economy as a regular part of the curriculum. If industry is organized as trusts there must be trained people who will take it as a trust and who will recognize their rights and their responsibilities as leaders of the people. If the college can make its students realize the moral basis of modern business, it will perform its greatest service to mankind."

The State clerks and civil employes of the State of New York, as well as those of Greater New York and other cities in the State, are said to have organized themselves, for mutual benefit and to obtain, if possible, the enactment of laws granting them a pension. Members' dues are to be graduated according to the amount of wages earned. In the event of death, sickness or disability, certain specified benefits will be paid. Uniformed policemen and firemen, and all appointed and elective officers, are ineligible for active membership, because pensions are already provided for the first-named, and the last-named hold office for a definite period. This new organization, in the main, consists of those who hold civil service positions. Few persons have any idea of what an army of these are at work. In New York State there are between 50,000 and 60,000. Greater New York alone employs 16,000 of them. Yet the law offers no reward to them for faithful and efficient service, in the way of pensions or otherwise. Up to the present time we believe there has not been any similar organization.

We wish to express our disagreement with the opinions advanced by Prof. Robert Ellis Thompson in his address befor the Bookkeepers' Beneficial Association as reported in another column of this issue. Prof. Thompson tells us that combinations of capitalists were patterned after the trades unions, and later goes on to say that trusts are really a form of socialism and that trades unions are the great agency warding off socialism. By attempting to follow the learned doctor's position, we find ourselves traveling in a circle. A grave danger lurks in loose statements like the above. As a fact the combinations referred to are not (many of them) trusts at all. He fails to discriminate between a large business organization and a trusteeship. If the would-be teachers of political economy would candidly and with scholarly carefulness trace back our industrial situation to its beginnings, they would find the so-called trust an inevitable growth from pre-existent conditions. Instead of an excrescence upon the body politic, it is a natural development, holding within itself the power of good or evil as it may be wielded by just and upright men, or by selfish and unscrupulous, but always subject to the sovereign laws of supply and demand. The thoughtful man will pause before he condemns as a positive evil an economic situation which has given opportunities for employment to hundreds of thousands of workers, and has cheapened commodities so as to bring to the home of the laborer comforts undreamed of in past generations. But perhaps Prof. Thompson likes the roll of political agitator better than that of an impartial investigator, or were his remarks colored to suit the known or assumed tendencies of his audience?

One of the conspicuous, even though minor virtues, in which the young people of the day are more or less carefully drilled, is that of saving things and caring for the various articles which pass through their hands. The string with which a bundle is tied is to be carefully preserved for future use. The paper wrapped about a package is likewise to be saved for a future occasion. It is not necessary, however, to enumerate in detail what is included in the art of saving, for the principle is universally recognized and the applications are as numerous as the occasions which arise. There is, however, another art that is not so conspicuously taught, but which, by reason of its importance in modern every-day affairs, deserves far more attention than it at present receives, and that is the art of discarding or throwing away, the very opposite of the art of saving.

The average office is lumbered with numerous things, the keeping of which is attended with expense, that in themselves are of no use to the business and which in fact are actually dertimental to the business. They are kept year after year, and sometimes moved from place to place, for no other reason than that the man in charge and who is responsible for matters of this kind has not learned the art of discarding or throwing away. The average manufacturing establishment is similarly encumbered with tools and machines, useless because out of date or because of wear, which occupy places among the useful equipment of the shop, when, in fact, on their merits, they should be in the scrap heap. In such an establishment there will be found, under benches and in dark corners, a woeful accumulation of bits of material, lost tools, scrap and dirt simply because the foreman or superintendent has not learned the art of throwing away. The same condition of affairs will be found in the household. It is true of the wardrobe of many a business man. He hangs on to articles of apparel that he does not wear and cannot afford to be seen wearing, to the crowding of closet space, because he has not acquired the art of discarding or throwing away.

Some things are worth keeping, but many things are not worth keeping. Time is money, but also, where rent is being paid, space is money. The art of discarding, rejecting, throwing away, ridding oneself of encumbrances, is therefore a very important one. Coming closer to the office, the defect in training by which men fail to discriminate between that which is useful and that which is useless will be found in the way in which papers are filed, and in which desks are managed. It is not uncommon among clerks to find those who apparently cannot discriminate between a piece of paper that should go into the waste-basket and thus be permanently disposed of as useless, and another piece of paper that should be put away in the letter-file or elsewhere carefully preserved. Items of this kind are in one indiscriminate mass on the desk or in the drawers of the desk. Self-training is the rule of the day. We therefore appeal to as many teachers as there are readers of this article to work for a reform. In training yourselves, be careful to discriminate between that which is worth keeping and that which is absolutely useless and which therefore should be got out of the way to make room for that which is useful.

Accountant's Associations

Hartford Chapter

The regular monthly meeting of the Hartford Chapter of the Institute of Accounts was held, as per announcement, on Tuesday evening, November 28. The address of the evening was delivered by A. O. Kittredge, F. I. A., C. P. A., of New York, his subject being "A Scientific Analysis of Business Accounts."

At the outset the speaker expressed his pleasure in being permitted to meet with the Hartford Chapter, and also stated that he bore in most pleasant recollection the occasion of the first or inaugural meeting of the organization. Good reports, he said, had gone abroad of the work of the Hartford Chapter. Its success in the way of lectures, addresses and debates, as evidenced by the reports which have been published of the same from time to time, was appreciated by the members of the Institute everywhere, and its more recent enterprise in establishing a study course for young men, including office assistants and students who aspired to higher work in accounting as they get further along, including membership in the Institute, was commendable in the extreme. Continuing, the speaker said that he brought to the Hartford Chapter the cordial greetings of the New York Chapter. Its good will, he asserted, goes without saying, but there is more than that to it: There is a fraternity of sentiment and interest among Institute members wherever situated. The Institute of Accounts, the speaker continued, stands for much more than is commonly understood. It is the only organization in the whole country that has for its object the advancement of the science of accounts and the improvement of the art of bookkeeping. The only possible exceptions that might be noted are one or two societies which were organized and in the past have been officered more or less by Institute members living in cities remote from New York, and which are being conducted upon independent lines and not as chapters. All other organizations, which convey by their titles the suggestion of accounts, accounting, or accountants, are in effect class or trade organizations. Their avowed object is to advance the craftsman or practitioner by all legitimate means, and more particularly to serve the pecuniary interests of their members. The general uplifting of the science and the art of accounting is very generally lost sight of in the work that they attempt to do for the individual.

Much of the responsibility for the unsatisfactory condition of accounting science and bookkeeping art at the present day, the speaker asserted, is due to the selfishness of members of the profession. They are disposed to practice what they know, and, as a rule, they are unwilling to exert themselves to any great extent to acquire a broader knowledge. They do not attempt to advance the methods of the average office into which they are called professionally for fear, apparently, that in case improved plans are adopted they will not be able to keep up with the procession and make as large an income under the new conditions as is possible under present conditions.

Accounting to-day, the speaker continued, seems to many observers to be in very much the same position as was electrical science before Brush and Edison and Thompson and many others, each of them a man of genius and progressive ideas, forced upon the attention of the schools and the authors of text-books various applications of principles and numerous facts which the professors of the day had entirely overlooked. That is to say, the average accountant would seem to regard accountancy as something completed and finished, in which there is no progress to be made, save only as one advances from a position of comparative inexperience to a full acquaintance with all that accountants as a class are acquainted with. The idea of development, evolution, or invention, applied to accounting, seems to have very little lodgment in his brain. It would seem, therefore, the speaker asserted, that there is the opportunity for genius to drive new stakes and to establish new and enlarged boundary lines about accounting, the same as genius has surveyed new fields in other branches of applied science. To this high ideal, he suggested, every accountant and every student of accountancy ought to aspire.

Following this general introductory, the speaker proceeded to a consideration of the subject which had been announced in the invitation slips. A report of the address will be presented in a later issue. At the conclusion of the address a considerable number of questions were proposed by the members and guests present. For the purpose of facilitating this part of the evening's exercises blank cards had been distributed, upon which all were invited to write such queries as they would like to have answered by the speaker. These cards were gathered up, and no less than an hour's time was necessary to answer the questions thus proposed, all of which were pertinent and served to indicate the special interest of the audience in the ideas advanced. It was an unusually late hour at which the chapter adjourned, its course in this matter being very much like Institute proceedings in other parts of the country. Interest in the discussion was so great that no one was aware of the passage of time.

Bookkeepers' Beneficial Association

A regular monthly meeting of the Bookkeepers' Beneficial Association of Philadelphia was held on the 2d of October at Odd Fellows' Temple. After the usual business meeting, at which fourteen new members were admitted, an address was delivered by G. H. Davis, a well-known lawyer of Philadelphia, on "The Destiny of America and Her Influence on Other Nations." The meeting was also rendered enjoyable by a number of musical selections rendered by the Y. M. C. A. Mandolin Club.

At the regular meeting of the Association, held on the 6th of November, Dr. Robert Ellis Thompson, Principal of the Boys' High School, of Philadelphia, delivered an address on "Trusts and Their Injurious Influence on the Commercial Interests of the Country." Dr. Thompson traced the development of modern industry after the introduction of Watts' invention of the steam engine and the consequent breakdown of the guild system in 1820. He said in substance that while this country was benefited by the change, in England the capitalist grew richer while the laboring man grew poorer, till in 1860 trades unions were legalized. Capitalists in their first combinations patterned after the trades unions, but such combinations, the speaker contended, are a source of dangerous social and political power. Trusts up to the present time have avoided coming into collision with trades unions when possible, but a struggle is approaching and probably a social war will arise in the future. These trades unions have in the past been the great agency warding off socialism.

State legislation, the speaker said, furnishes no remedy for trusts, but an ammendment of the constitution giving the National Government power over corporations may be a solution of the difficulty.

"Trusts have become a grave problem in our national politics," he declared. "We want industrial liberty, but by endless combinations of capital industrial liberty will disappear, and with it social and political liberty."

The Results of Prosperity

S. S. Conover, of the National Association of Credit Men, in discussing some of the results of the present prosperity of the country, says:

The year 1899, which is rapidly drawing to a close, has been most unique in its freedom from business failures. In the memory of the oldest merchants no year in mercantile life compares favorably with it. This is all the more remarkable, in view of the increased volume of business transacted, attended by substantial increases in prices.

A canvass of some of the principal lines of trade indicates that the amount of losses sustained this year through bad debts is only trivial; and the credit man who had so much to contend with in the tempestuous periods of 1893 and 1896 has recently experienced the pleasure of the summer sea.

The bankruptcy law has also had the effect of checking questionable embarrassments on the part of the smaller traders, who were in the habit of failing over night. Every one now knows that in case of business suspension the law gives all of the creditors an equal chance, and this acts as a deterrent to those who are in any way inclined in the direction of making fraudulent assignments.

Another pleasing feature that has characterized the present year is the numerous credits entered to profit and loss accounts, previously charged with losses made in former years. Verily, prosperity is a boon to the credit man.

Trial Balances and the Localization of Errors*

By H. Portlock, A. S. A. A.

I think everybody present will agree with me that the agreement of the books of a financial concern is a matter of the very utmost importance. Anything short of an absolute balance provides a possibility of the existence of serious discrepancies, and though a small difference probably only consists of an unimportant oversight, it may conceal several grave errors. It is true that arithmetical accuracy is only one of many qualities essential to a professional accountant, and that the more laborious detail work is generally left to clerks occupying a subordinate position, but clerical accuracy is undoubtedly of supreme importance and forms the foundation upon which all after requirements rest. Looking back myself I can recollect many undiscovered differences, and many weary hours spent in discovering others, but I admit of no single instance where by the adoption of a system suitable to the occasion, and the exercise of diligence, an exact balance cannot invariably be arrived at.

Personally I submit that the object of the trial balances is simply to test the agreement of the books, and should be taken advantage of as frequently as circumstances permit in order to locate as far as possible the periods during which a difference occurs. It is true that a trial balance may serve to indicate the result of the business operations and the financial position, and is often not resorted to until all necessary adjustments have been made, but except in cases where the scope of the accounts is very limited I do not recommend this, and I am strongly of opinion that in the majority of cases it is advisable to extract the balances of all the accounts and test the same before any of the closing entries are made. I would, therefore, recommend that so soon as the everyday transactions have been recorded and posted, the balances should be taken out, but with a view to a saving of labor at a later stage the balances should be taken out under the following headings, viz.:

1. Balance-sheet Items, such as Cash, Bills Receivable and Payable, Plant, &c.

2. Profit and Loss Items, such as Sales, Purchases, Trade Expenses, &c.

3. Creditors, which may be sub-divided into Trade Creditors, Loan Accounts, &c.

4. Debtors.

As the balances are taken out, all accounts requiring further consideration can be marked, and all doubtful accounts queried. Then the clerical accuracy of the books having been denoted by the double entry system, the balances must be carefully scrutinized and critically examined, the necessary reserves made, all bad debts written off, and all liabilities taken into consideration. It will then probably be found that the original lists of debtors and creditors will stand subject to some alterations, the profit and loss items will be extinguished, and a fresh list of balance-sheet items and summary of balances can be made to indicate the final agreement of the books.

As you are all probably aware there are other opinions as to the time when it is advisable to have recourse to the Trial Balance, and I would ask you to consider them briefly. Let me criticise for a moment the opinion held by many that it is not necessary to resort to the Trial Balance until all requisite adjustments have been made. This I submit is practicable in businesses presenting few difficulties, and where the entries and accounts are comparatively few, but in large and difficult cases, if it is not impossible, it complicates the mere agreement of the books a great deal, and except in the case of a very able accountant it does not in the long run save time.

As regards the system of making such entries as can easily be made before using your Trial Balance, I see no harm in this, but on the other hand I fail to find any advantage. The discovery of an error — and errors always unfortunately occur in most unlikely places—may entail several alterations.

Therefore I suggest, take out the Trial Balance as soon as the ordinary commercial entries are made, agree the figures, and then having considered them, decide upon and make all the adjusting entries possible.

Now as to the localization of errors.

*Portions of a paper read at a meeting of the Incorporated Accountants' Students' Society of London, January, 1899.

It will generally be admitted that the difficulty of balancing books increases in proportion to the number of recording entries. Of course, granting that certain audits always present exceptional difficulties, by reason of the circumstances under which they are conducted, or illegible writing and bad figures. Just let me lay down as a principle that some distinctive tick be used to denote the checking done. All alterations must be carefully examined, and the figures as they finally stand repeated in colored ink in the margin by the auditor. I think it will also be found advisable to deal with one book at a time, for instance, completing the cash book before touching other subsidiary books, and if possible retaining the book under your control until done with. Generally speaking, all postings should be checked before a book is cast, and then as the castings are checked it can be seen that everything is ticked and all alterations and erasures repeated. It will be found a great assistance to use a different colored ink for checking each year or successive audit, as the color of the ink supplies the date of an item more readily than a single figure at the head of a column might.

With care no difficulty will be found in balancing ordinary small traders' books, and I will confine myself to cases where the magnitude of the work makes it impossible or difficult to check everything in detail, and makes it desirable to agree the books sectionally. In different firms various methods of dividing up the trade and customers will exist, and the accountant will base his system on these. For instance, there will probably be town, country, and export ledgers, and the customers of these different departments may be subdivided alphabetically. The object of the accountant will be to make each ledger or set of ledgers self-balancing. One way is to make each each ledger contain a complete system of double entry by means of an adjustment account. Tabular cash books, journals, day books, credits and debits books will become necessary. It will be found advisable not to multiply the number of books more than absolutely necessary, and to obviate this the subsidary books must have a separate column ruled for postings to each ledger or set of ledgers desired to be balanced separately. The totals of these columns should be posted to the various adjustment accounts which will give from time to time the net total of the debit or credit balances existing on the ledger. These adjustment accounts, quite apart from their use as a means of balancing the ledgers, are extremely useful if at any time it is necessary to hurriedly ascertain the extent of the liabilities and book debts, and moreover form a very valuable check on the ledger keeper.

You will all probably understand what I mean by an adjustment account, but for the sake of an example let us presume that we wish to balance the sales ledger of a firm by itself. In the sales ledger, we shall have a private ledger adjustment account, in the private ledger a sales ledger adjustment account. The items in these two accounts will be identical, save that the debit and credit sides will be reversed. Briefly the private ledger adjustment account will be as follows, viz.:

Dr.	
To Cash received from customers..	£5,200
To Allowances and Discounts......	260
To Returns..........................	100
To Bad Debts........................	15
To Balance..........................	3,425
	£9,000
Cr.	
The initial starting Balance of (say)	£3,000
By Sales..............................	6,000
	£9,000
By Balance....................	£3,425

This balance of £3,425 will represent the sum total of the book debts existing on the sales ledger, and the enormous advantage of being able to roughly arrive at the book debts and liabilities of a business by means of such an adjustment account cannot be overrated. There is only one objection that may be urged against adjustment account, viz.: that the account in the sales ledger may afford a ledger keeper a chance of falsifying his books. To avoid this let the head of the counting-house keep memorandum adjustment accounts, and dispense with the same in the personal ledgers. The ledger keepers will then only be in a position to tell whether their ledgers balance on submitting the balances to the accountant.

Mr. Norton, in his work, "Balancing for Expert Bookkeepers," provides a somewhat elaborately ruled test journal to prove the arithmetical accurary of the books, and to any who want to go very fully into the subject I would recommend his book, but the method practically amounts to the same as the one I have gone into.

I have seen some bookkeepers go even further than agreeing ledgers sectionally, and endeavor to locate errors to the debit or credit side of the ledger, as the case may be. To do this, it is necessary to extract the balances in the following way, the balances paper being ruled with folio, detail, and four cash columns, in which must be extracted the total of the debit side, casts of the ledger since the date of the last agreement, the total of the credit side, and the balance between the two, either debit or credit, as the case may be.

Supposing we are now balancing the bought ledger. It will be seen that the casts of the credit side of the bought ledger as appearing in the second column should agree with the credit balances at the commencement of the period plus the purchases during the period. If the two agree, then it will be obvious that the error is on the debit side, which can in turn be agreed with the total of cash payments made during the period, and the returns, allowances, etc. By this means, errors can often be localised to one side or the other of the ledger, and the ground to be covered in looking for a difference very materially lessened. Of course, this involves a good deal of extra work, but where differences are frequent it is time well spent, and in the long run will be found an economy both of time and temper. There are a certain class of entries, which somewhat complicate the agreement of books sectionally, and which perhaps I should refer to, viz.: transfer entries. It is the custom in many businesses where good are bought from and sold to the same person, to set the one against the other, or to adjust the accounts by the way of contra. Care must be taken, if a system of balancing sectionally is in vogue, to pass all such contra entries through a subsidiary book, and it is usual to have a book kept and ruled expressly for this purpose, generally called a transfer book.

I envy none the gilding of their woe.
—Young.

In goodness, rich men should transcend the poor, as clouds the earth; raised by the comfort of the sun to water dry and barren grounds.—Tourneur.

Reviews

Bankers' Time Tables

Time Tables for Every Month in the Year, Showing Due Dates of Notes and Bills, Time by Days or Time by Months, etc. By Frank Wittenberg. Published by the author. Bound in cloth. Embossed with gilt side title. Price, 75 cents.

This book contains twenty-four tables, each a full page in extent. Each table is thirty-one lines in depth and seven columns in width. Referring to the latter there is first the date from which the calculation is to be made, following which are in the first of each pair of tables referring to a calendar month, columns respectively for one month, two months, etc., up to six months, inclusive, and in the second of each pair of tables, from seven months up to twelve months, inclusive. Under each monthly head are the dates representing the termination of the interval between the date in the first column and the period expressed by the heads. Thus, for example, take it in the month of January and the last day of the month. One month from January 31, we find, expires on February 28, two months on March 31, three months on April 30, five months on June 30, and so on. Interspersed with the monthly columns are what are called by the author "index figures." Thus, opposite February 1 is 32, being a continuation of the numerals beyond the month of February and indicating the number of days that have expired since January 1. Opposite March 1 is 60, and opposite March 31 is 90, and so on. These index figures are continued thirty-one days beyond a calendar year, thus affording every necessary reference within a given twelve months. The directions contain the following: "To time notes and bills by days, refer to the table for the month of the given date, then add the number of days the note has to run to the given date. The result will be the index number of the due date, which is shown by the table. Thus, for example, take a note dated March 15 at 90 days. Refer to the March table and say mentally, 15 and 90 is 105. The index number 105 is found to be opposite June 13, which is the due date." In a similar manner calculations may be made on notes and bills by months, and there may be also determined the difference in time between dates. The only exception to be made in the rules laid down is in the case of leap year.

Letters from Readers

Where Should Taxes Be Placed?

From Fundamental, New York.

I was very much interested in the paragraph published in the July number of ACCOUNTICS, referring to the argument presented at the last convention of the Street Railway Accountants, concerning the place that the charge for taxes should occupy. Should taxes be considered an expense of operation or something to be deducted from income? Not to take up too much of your valuable space, I beg to offer the suggestion that taxes are an inherent charge or expense. Let it be assumed that it is intended to organize a railway plant. Land is purchased, buildings are erected and construction is commenced. On assuming title of the land and constructing buildings, the town or city finds occasion for assessment of a tax. Before actual operation of the railway is begun, the tax bill is presented and paid. Earnings then begin and actual operating expenses are charged. The remainder shows net income from operating. The net income inherits a fixed charge, whether of taxes or bond interest—not necessarily dividends. Out of this net income there should remain enough to pay the inherited tax. It seems to me, therefore, that taxes should not be considered in any sense as an operating expense, but as something to be deducted from net income.

In the case of manufacturing industries, one wants to know what it costs to manufacture. Again, what are the factory expenses and the cost of supplies? And again, what does it cost to place the product on the market? After all these factors are obtained, then what is left goes to pay office expenses, and such other charges as there may be, including taxes, office supplies and salaries, and finally dividends. It seems to me that there need be no argument as to the classification of the charge for taxes, since the net income inherits taxes and has to pay for the same.

NOTE.—Our correspondent's arguments will scarcely bear a critical analysis. First, let it be said that terms are frequently used by the different parties to an argument with various understandings of their meanings. Our correspondent, for example, presents "operating expenses" in a restricted sense, whereas the same term, in so much as has preceded in this matter, has been used in the broad sense. Some of those who argued on this subject at the convention at Boston last year objected to taxes being included among expenses, for the reason that expenses at large are subject to control and modification by good management whereas taxes are a quantity, fixed beyond peradventure. This was replied to in part by one of the delegates, who mentioned that taxes were frequently reduced by the judicious management of the officer in charge of such matters.

The real point under discussion excludes the term "operating expenses" in the restricted sense, and therefore the question becomes simply this: Shall taxes be regarded as an expense or something to be deducted from income?

Our correspondent argues that taxes should be deducted from "net income." We have another letter before us, much in the same line, wherein the statement is presented that taxes should be deducted from "surplus net income." The adjectives are interesting, to say the least. What is net income? Evidently net income, from the standpoint of this correspondent, is one thing, while net income from the standpoint of a stockholder, would be something else.

There are no objections to be offered to arranging a system of accounts in such a way as to show income in various stages of application or derived from various sources, but "net" income, we submit, using the term as the dictionaries define it, must be that which is left after all charges have been taken into account. What "surplus net income" is we do not pretend to guess, although we recognize the term as one frequently employed by the legal fraternity, and one which is honored by prominent position in the statutes of a certain State regarding corporations.

Our correspondent cites the case of a manufacturing company, and therewith presents a peculiar idea of account classification applied to such an industry. He apparently brings into the cost of manufacture the expense of placing the product on the market. We think he is scarcely prepared to stand by this, for certainly commercial expenses are no part of the cost of goods. He says that after providing for factory expenses, supplies, and the cost of placing the product on the market, what is left goes to pay office expenses and other charges such as taxes, office salaries and dividends. Is not this a little mixed as a statement? A part of the office expenses, in a factory conducted by a corporation that markets its own goods, belongs to the cost of goods produced, covering such matters as keeping the cost records in the factory, making out the pay rolls, the clerical labor in connection with the buying of materials, etc. Another part belongs to commercial expenses, and these prevail whether a profit results or not. Salaries of clerks and other employes must be paid regardless of profits, the same as labor in the factory. In the event of the failure of the company they are, under the laws of many States, as much of a preferred lien against the assets of the company as is the manual labor that is employed. Therefore our correspondent's assertion that these are paid out of what is left is hardly accurate.

We are prepared to admit that upon the loose classification that this correspondent advocates, taxes might with propriety appear where he places them, but on a strict and scientific classification, taxes on factory plant are a part of the cost of the goods produced. Goods cannot be manufactured without the factory; the factory cannot exist without paying to the State its proper tax. After the goods are produced, there is the expense of selling, or what we have called above, the commercial expenses. The goods are sold at the highest possible price in the market. The selling price, less the cost of goods, makes gross profit. Gross profit, diminished by commercial expenses, makes net profit. But the profits are not "net" so long as there are deductions to be made from them. Net profits, at the discretion of the directors of the company, are carried to the surplus account, and out of surplus dividends are paid.

We apprehend that the whole discussion of the matter of where taxes should be placed grows out of the lack of a comprehension of the principles of classification of accounts in general, or from a mistaken or inadequate basis of classification. We shall welcome other communications upon this subject.

Management of Petty Cash

From W. G. Mowat, C. P. A., Buffalo, N. Y.

In your June issue, I have read with great interest the article on handling Petty Cash, and would say that whenever I am called upon to investigate the dealings of the "bookkeeper" of the ordinary business concern, Petty Cash is very seldom found to have been guarded with the care that its importance demands.

It is a very useful device, when properly handled, and a very difficult leak to detect when it is not so. In the first place it is a good general principle to follow, to enter all transactions in their chronological order, and date them only on the day of their occurrence. One good record of a transaction, made as, when, and where it should be, is enough, and more than enough is too much. The rewriting of the disbursements made through Petty Cash in the General Cash Book at the end of the month may lead to duplications, and it is bad accounting, because the exact date of many, otherwise unimportant payments, may be the turning point in some very expensive litigation, and the production of the General Cash Book with a record of such payment having been made upon the last day of the month, whereas it was really paid upon the tenth of the month, furnishes evidence for the other side. No business man should ever make evidence for the enemy. They can usually make enough of it for themselves. It is well known that both courts and juries come to very extraordinary conclusions at times. A payment made through Petty Cash should not be entered in the General Cash Book, either on the date that it occurred or any other date, but at the end of the balance period a Journal entry should be made debiting the various accounts to which the disbursements belong, and crediting Petty Cash. The object should be to have as small a balance on hand as possible. It is well to remove from employees the temptation to float a little I. O. U. in Petty Cash. It is always a suspicious circumstance to find a larger balance of "Cash on Hand" than the amount of the next day's deposit. In that case it is fair to suppose that "Cash on Hand" comprised a good deal of non-bankable material.

From F. J. R., Pittsburgh.

I was very much interested in reading the very clear and explicit article entitled the "Imprest System of Handling Petty Cash," published in the June issue of Accountics. Possibly some such suggestion as the following might have been advantageously added to the description given of the system as practised in this country, especially in those cases where the total cash received each day is deposited and every expenditure is evidenced by check, and presumably also by voucher.

No voucher should be paid from the money in the imprest cash box, but all vouchers should be paid by check. In such cases the check drawn to replenish the imprest cash box will equal the amounts withdrawn therefrom from the cashier in charge and which have been duly examined, approved and vouchered. Thus each check has to be indorsed by the party in whose favor the voucher is drawn. If the custom of many large business houses is followed, namely that of filing all indorsed and canceled checks with the vouchers, it will greatly facilitate the work of the auditor, who may be called upon to examine the books.

NOTE.—We have read our correspondent's letter repeatedly without feeling sure that we correctly apprehend his meaning. It would seem to turn upon the definition of the word "voucher." The very object of imprest cash is to take care of small disbursements like street-car fare, unimportant office supplies, telegrams, express charges, etc. If no voucher is to be paid from the money in the imprest cash box, we do not see how it is going to require replenishing.

It would seem from this correspondent that the evidences of petty disbursements are not to be considered vouchers. Now we are under the impression that anything that evidences a disbursement is a voucher, whether large or small, including everything from a check to a receipted bill, and from a formal acknowledgment of payment to any writing which shows that money has been paid out for a given purpose upon certain authority.

Our own preferred plan of managing imprest cash is to provide what perhaps in contradistinction to the usual voucher form should be called "petty vouchers." Each disbursement, whether of five cents or five dollars or some other amount, is to be evidenced by one of these petty vouchers, signed by the person receiving the money, where it is possible to obtain such a signature, and in other cases to be signed by the one disbursing the money. These petty vouchers in the course of time are gathered together and a check is drawn to replenish the imprest fund, the record on the stub of the check being "In payment of vouchers Nos. —— to ——, inclusive."

The letter printed above indicates, as many others in the past have done, the difficulty of intelligently discussing accounting and office methods, for the lack of an agreement as to the significance of terms. And this reminds us to say once more what we have given expression to in the past, namely, that if at the beginning of a controversy the parties thereto would agree as to the precise meaning of the terms to be employed, all chances of dispute or disagreement would be removed.

Treatment of Good Will

From E. Layton Bennett, Chartered Accountant, London, Eng.

I am much obliged for the copy of The Office Magazine, which has been sent me. It appears to be a very interesting journal and well written, although American. The articles on "The Treatment of Good Will" is remarkably good and deals with a very important question so far as accountants are concerned. Unfortunately no reference appears to be made to the possibility of depreciation. In my opinion this question is one that ought to be settled once for all. Although good will may be a tangible asset, it is in no better position than a leasehold building or plant and machinery, and should, therefore, in the ordinary course be subject to some scale of depreciation.

Note.—Our accountant readers generally will fully agree with Mr. Bennett's conclusions, namely that good will is subject to depreciation. Whether they will agree with him that this question can be settled once for all is entirely another matter. The scale or rate of depreciation in one case we imagine would be very different from that applying in some other. While the principle that good will should be gradually written off may be accepted as sound, it will still remain with the accountants in each individual case to determine the rate at which it should be retired.

A Play on Words

Good Words.

This inscription is to be found in Lynford Church, on the borders of Dartmoor, over the grave of a watchmaker:

Here lies in horizontal position
The outside case of
George Routledge . . Watchmaker.

Whose abilities in that line were an honour to his profession. Integrity was the mainspring and prudence the regulator of all the actions of his life. Humane, generous, and liberal, his hand never stopped till it relieved distress. So nicely regulated were all his motions that he never went wrong, except when set agoing by people who did not know his key; even then, he was easily set right again. He had the art of disposing his time so well that his hours glided away in one continued round of pleasure and delight till an unlucky minute put a period to its existence.

He departed this life
Nov. 14, 1802. Aged 57,

Wound up in hopes of being taken in hand by his Maker, and being thoroughly cleaned, repaired, and set going in the world to come.

Credit Men's Affairs

By A. O. Kittredge

The machinery of the Secretary's office is in active motion, and various matters are being ground out that are of special interest to credit men, and which by their nature will go far toward proving the advantages of the organization to the business world. The commercial agencies are to be watched by credit men everywhere, for the purpose of recording their delinquencies and to the end that the credit men, in convention assembled, shall be able to point to chapter and verse sustaining their demand for change in and improvement of service, the Secretary has prepared a book which is entitled "Record of Commercial Agency Service." It is a volume to be added to the ordinary records of the offices making annual subscriptions to the Dun and Bradstreet agencies. It is proposed by means of this record to demonstrate their comparative efficiency.

* * *

The pages of the book are ruled in a way to record, first, the average time intervening between the application for reports and their receipt; second, as to the average age of the reports received, expressed in months; third, as to the percentage of reports containing signed statements, not more than one year old; fourth, as to the percentage of reports containing only general information; without a signed statement, or one older than a year; fifth, as to which of the agencies furnishes information the more promptly with regard to changes; sixth, as to which of the two agencies furnishes reports arranged and tabulated in the better form; and seventh, as to which particular district or local association receives service inferior to that of other local associations. A circular was issued by the Secretary a short time since, enclosing sample sheet of the book which embody the items of record above mentioned, and in addition two leaves, detachable, for the reports to be sent in to the National Secretary.

* * *

Secretary Prendergast has recently sent out a neat pamphlet, entitled "Suggestions for a Model Credit Department." It is issued under the auspices of the Credit Department Methods Committee of the National Association. By way of preface, it has a page devoted to the personnel of the committee, of which Green Benton, of J. C. Reeves & Co., Nashville, Tenn., is the chairman. Then follow a few sentences relating to the advantages of a well organized credit department and the useful part that it plays in business administration. The essay or description which the book contains describes the credit department, "from the time of the receipt of a new order until the account is finally given up as a hopeless loss." This quotation is from the first sentence and would lead outsiders to suppose, inferentially at least, that all accounts ultimately result in a loss. The first illustration is a reduced fac-simile of the salesman's information blank. Other blanks shown include the attorney's report blank, attorney's card and credit reference card. There are also reductions of the report folder, maturity slips, collection cards, ruling for a suspended ledger, judgment book and card, etc. The pamphlet is supplemented by samples and price list of the different property statement blanks, styles A to G, inclusive, which have been endorsed and recommended by the National Association.

* * *

A circular has been issued by the National Secretary embodying the opinion of a prominent firm of lawyers located in Texas as to the constitutionality and effect of the Texas Anti-Trust Law. An epitome of this opinion is as follows: (1) The law will be held by the Texas courts to be constitutional; but (2) it will probably be held unconstitutional by the Federal courts; (3) the statute can have no extra-territorial effect, and consequently insurance companies foreign to Texas may enter into combinations outside of that State to fix the rate of insurance, and such act cannot be punished by a Texas court; (4) a foreign corporation, even having an office and doing business in Texas, will not be subject to the statute for entering into a combination outside of Texas to fix rates outside of that State; (5) but such company would be subject to the statute in so far as the combination affected policies upon property in Texas. In this connection it is to be remarked that the Texas courts have not yet passed upon the statute, but on the other hand the courts in Arkansas, which State has laws very similar to the Texas law referred to, have passed upon the question and it is upon their decisions that the opinion above epitomized is based.

* * *

Business Topics, the editorial clipping sheet which was started some time since by the National Association as a means of making known to the business world sional men he serves place confidence, but something of the Association's work and of getting before the business public short practical articles on credit subjects, and which was suspended some time since for lack of funds, has been recently revived. The first number of the new series appeared in Octol· . While the pages have been slightly reduced in number and various internal changes have been made in the paper, still the general appearance is much the same and the good work which the former series did is likely to be continued and fully sustained. Business Topics in its circulation was originally restricted to a selected list of trade papers. At present it is being sent to every member of the National Association. With this extension of circulation it becomes a medium of communication between the officials of the organization and the membership at large. Therein it somewhat resembles an organ or official publication, something which, it is to be remarked, the association has in the past strenuously set its face against.

* * *

At the dinner of the Boston Association of Credit Men, on the evening of November 10, the speakers were Hon. John Field, president of the National Association of Credit Men; T. H. Bartindale, vice-president of the Mutual Mercantile Agency; Hon. Thos. N. Hart, president of the Mt. Vernon Bank of Boston, and W. A. Prendergast, secretary of the National Association of Credit Men. Mr. Bartindale discussed the bankruptcy law; Mr. Hart spoke on the desirability of securing reliable property statements; and Mr. Prendergast spoke on the work of the National Association. Mr. Field's address included a brief survey of the work of the organization from the inception of the movement to the present time. The membership, as he pointed out, is at present composed of 2,700 leading mercantile establishments, representing business interests, the aggregate capital of which is over $1,000,000,000. Passing from a consideration of the historical features of the organization, he next referred to the statistics of failures, and showed that in 1898 there were over 10,000 failures in this country, with losses aggregating upwards of $130,000,000. In concluding his address Mr. Field said that in the past the purchasing and selling departments of mercantile houses have absorbed nearly all the time and attention of the proprietors and managing men, with the result that the credit department to a degree has been overlooked. Its importance is at present being emphasized and brought to the front by the Credit Men's Association. "We may purchase our goods at the lowest market prices and sell them at a fair profit; yet if we fail to collect our accounts, all other efforts will be fruitless and may be disastrous."

* * *

Quite a ripple in the otherwise placid affairs of the Credit Men's Association has been caused by the publication of the fact that prominent credit men have identified themselves with a recently organized mercantile agency, and are using their influence to promote its interests. A circular letter sent out by the agency a short time since was addressed particularly to credit men and was worded in a way that was intended to secure their favorable opinion of the effort and their co-operation as subscribers and patrons. The presence of such names as that of Mr. Bartindale, in the capacity of vice-president; and of Mr. Boocock, Mr. Bannin, and others in the Board of Directors, seems to have been interpreted by some as being an effort to commit the National Association of Credit Men to the support of this new enterprise, or at least to identify the National Association with it. All this obtained, notwithstanding an expressed declaration that was in the body of the letter, that nothing of the kind is intended and that these gentlemen are acting simply in their private capacities. Secretary Prendergast has been in receipt of many protesting letters, as well also of numerous protests delivered in person. So far as can be seen, nothing has been done by the gentlemen who are held to have offended, that they did not have a perfect right to do.

It is not unnatural, however, that their confreres and associates should have some feeling in the matter. Meanwhile the new agency is well under way and will soon be an active competitor for business in the general field.

Interest and Discount—IX

By Charles W. Rohne

Bond Values

When a bond is bought as an investment its present worth or value, as usually computed, supposes the interest received from it to be reinvested at the same rate as that of the proposed investment of the purchase money, and in the following examples a like supposition is made. The present worth of a bond is made up of two items: (1) The present worth of the maturity value of the bond and (2) the present value of its installments of interest.

Example 1. What is the present worth (as a 5% per annum investment) of a $100 6% bond, paying interest annually and having 30 years to run? The present worth of $100 due in 30 years is shown by the table to be $23.14; the present value of an annuity or one for 30 years is $15.37245, which multiplied by $6.00, the interest due at the end of each year, produces $92.23. Adding the two items we have the present worth, $115.37.

Example 2. What is the present worth of a $1000 4% bond, interest payable semi-anually and having 56 half years to run, that will yield a 3% semi-annual rate on the investment? By the table we find the present worth of a $1000 due at the end of 56 half years at a semi-annual rate of 3% to be $191.04. By the table we find the present value of an annuity of one for 56 periods to be 26.96546. As the semi-annual interest is $20.00, we multiply this amount by 20, which gives a result of $539.31, adding the two we find the present worth of the bond to be $730.35.

The values of bonds, as ordinarily given in printed tables, are their values taken at a period of time immediately after one of the semi-annual installments of interest has become due and been paid. Although all bonds are named after the annual rates of interest they pay, the interest on them is nevertheless almost invariably paid semi-annually. For instance, a 4% bond (so-called) pays 2% semi-annually, and most bond tables are computed on this basis.

The present worth of value of a bond (as an investment at a given rate) depends, all other things being equal, upon the rate at which reinvestment of interest may be made, i. e., upon the rate which money will be worth at the time of such re-investments. Now it is well known that when a bond is bought (as an investment) at a premium, a certain portion of the interest money received therefrom must, as soon as received, be re-invested at compound interest, and be kept so re-invested until the bond matures, at a rate which will make its accumulations during the time it has to run amount exactly to the premium paid, so that the face value of the bond added to the accumulations and re-invested interest will amount, when the bond matures, to exactly what has been paid for the bond; and when a bond has been bought at a discount (as an investment at a given rate) the interest received semi-annually from the bond will not be as great as the amount yielded for the same period by the investment. Hence, an amount equal to this difference may be semi-annually expended, and the holder still have at maturity the amount he has paid out for the bond. Thus, he practically anticipates the payment of so much of the bond as is equal to the discount at which it is bought, by using each half year, in addition to the interest received, such an amount as would (if placed successively each year at compound interest at the semi-annual rate of 2% during the time the bond has to run) exactly amount to the discount.

It needs no argument to prove that on the same day and under the same circumstances, money received from any one source may be invested at the same rate as that received from any other source, and yet all the books within my knowledge, with one exception, that profess to give the present worth or value of bonds, assume the contrary, that is to say, they assume that interest received from a bond, yielding a 10% investment for instance, will be reinvested at 10%; whilst interest received from a bond yielding a 3% investment will be reinvested at 3%; and this, notwithstanding the fact that that interest from both bonds may be received in the same day. The assumption is an absurdity, and yet some of our apparently wisest financiers seem to have accepted the principle as finality.

The Robinsonian bond and investment tables assume a rate of 4% on reinvestment, whatever the rate of interest may be on the bond, and while it is true that it is impossible to predict with certainty the rate of interest which will be obtainable in the future, it is nevertheless generally conceded that the average rate at which investments may be expected to be safely made is about 4% per annum, i.e., 2% semi-annually. It is for these reasons that the values given by J. Watts Robinson in his bond tables differ from those in other tables in all cases except that where the rate of investment is the same as that of the bond, or where other authors assume the rate of investment to be 4%, that is, 2% semi-annually.

In using the expresison "where the rate of interest is the same as that of the bond," it should be qualified as follows:

Where the rate of interest is the same as that of the bond (which will always be the case where the bond is bought at par) there is no necessity for reinvestments of interest, as there is no premium or discount to be taken care of at maturity, the bond itself in such cases repaying the amount invested. Hence, the holder will retain (as the yield of his investment) the whole interest received from the bond, and as the face value of the bond and the amount of his investment are the same, the rate yielded by the bond and by the investment must necessarily be the same. Thus, a 4% bond bought at par is always a 4% investment, and a 4% bond to be a 4% investment must be bought at par.

The difference between these two methods of computation may be simply illustrated as follows:

According to the tables of the Mutual Life Insurance Company of New York, a 5% bond, having 16 years to run, if purchased at 129, would produce 2¾%, provided the bond was held at maturity. Under the method used by Robinson, a 5% bond having 16 years to maturity, purchased at $130.94, would exactly produce 2¾%. According to the Mutual Life tables, the same bond purchased at 77 would produce 7.49%, whereas by the Robinsonian table, if the purchase price was $79.20, the rate of interest realized would be 7½%.

The illustration given above is on a bond in excess of 4%; if the opposite illustration should be given, the variation would be the other way. One illustration will answer: By the Mutual Life table a 3% bond having 16 years to run, and purchased at 69, would produce 6.05%; whereas by the valuation given by Robinson, it would produce 6¾%.

Municipal Accounts

At the convention of the National Municipal League which assembled in Columbus, Ohio, the middle of November, considerable attention was given to accounting and to the forms of public financial statements.

Professor L. S. Rowe, of the University of Pennsylvania, in the course of an address, said:

In the management of public as well as private corporations the determination of official responsibility is largely dependent upon the accuracy, ready intelligibility and unequivocal character of the financial statements. The hopelessly complex reports of such cities as New York make it impossible for any one except an expert to ascertain the financial situation of the city. In order to remedy this evil the proposed constitutional amendment and municipal corporations act provides for regular financial reports arranged in accordance with forms prescribed by the fiscal office of the state.

The provisions for financial control over receipts and expenditures are intended to prevent collusion between two or more officials in defrauding the city. It is important to note that the controller is given indefinite tenure and stands but second to the mayor in importance.

The system of accounting in municipal industrial enterprises is a matter of the very greatest importance. Failure to provide for such fixed charges as sinking fund, depreciation and repairs leads to the deterioration of the city's public works and paves the way for the periodical raids by private corporations, from which Philadelphia has had recently to suffer.

On the question of the accounting of grantees of municipal franchises your committee has been anxious to secure to the city the most complete data concerning the franchises of public-service corporations. To this end the controller is required to keep a separate record for each grantee, which shall contain every item of information necessary to form an estimate of the value of the franchise.

The grantees of such franchises are required, furthermore, to keep books of account, which must conform to the standards formulated in the act. From the information thus made readily accessible it will be possible to treat intelligently with such corporations when the question of a revaluation of their franchises arises.

Professor Charles W. Tooke, of the University of Illinois, spoke on "The Accounting of Public Service Industries." He maintained that an essential to obtaining successful financial administration of cities is to have municipal bookkeeping so designed as to give the public thoroughly reliable and intelligible information of the financial standing of the city's enterprises, from a business point of view. A separate account should be kept for each public service industry. All expenditures should be charged to the department for which they are incurred. Professor Tooke holds that city bonds issued for construction or operation of a municipal enterprise should be secured by mortgages on the enterprise for which they are issued and should not become a general claim against the municipality.

A. L. Crosby, formerly deputy auditor of Cleveland, O., spoke on "The Financial Control Over Receipts and Expenditures." He argued that there is needed an absolute standard authority of financial control, based on a fixed quantity and subjected to no fear of supersession or overthrow so long as such authority is executed within proper and legitimate limits, and that such authority can be conferred only by state law.

Walter S. Allen, of New Bedford, Mass., read a paper on "Accounts of Grantees of Municipal Franchises." He said in part:

A prime essential of public control of franchise companies is an accurate system of bookkeeping which shall show every detail in such a way as to enable a true value to be placed at any time upon the business. One of the features which the financial statement of the company should show would be the exact cost of construction, including the cost of equipment. The whole object of accurate methods of bookkeeping and of public supervision and control of the accounts of franchise companies is to secure an equitable division of profits among the three parties in interest; that is, the users of the service, the investors of the capital employed and the community at large.

By securing accurate returns from franchise companies, and by careful analysis of these returns, the relative proportion of the net profits due to each of the parties interested—the users, the investors and the whole community—can be ascertained. In this way only may reasonable charges for service, fair dividends and a return to the community of interest on that part of the capital which it supplies, namely, the franchise, be secured.

Some New Words

Owing to the war which has arisen between England and the Boers, a number of words, new to English-speaking people are coming into use. It may be interesting to follow them back a little in their history.

"Boer," which now means a Cape Colonist, is of German or Dutch descent and meant originally husbandman. We have the same word in a modified sense as boor. It may be on account of this relationship that the Cape Colonists prefer to call themselves Africanders. "Veld" in its various combinations means prairie; "kloof," which suggests our "cleft," means a hollow between two hills. "Dorp," which has also done service as an English word, but is now obsolete, means village or hamlet. "Spruit" a small stream, "reim" a leather thong, and "dissel-boom," the pole of an ox-wagon, are not so familiar in their sound.

"Voortrekkers" means pioneers, the voor, fore, first, foremost people to go to a new country. "Kraal" means a collection of huts and is credited to the Spanish. "Sjambock," which has a queer sound to Anglo-Saxon ears, was caught from the Malays who were imported into Cape Colony as slaves in the seventeenth century. It means a strip of rhinocerous hide used as a whip.

Poverty is the only burden which is not lightened by being shared with others.—Richter.

We have now learned that rashness and imprudence will not be deterred from taking credit; let us try whether fraud and avarice may be more easily restrained from giving it.—Dr. Johnson.

Fortune is painted blind in order to show her impartiality; but when she cheers the needy with hope, and depresses the wealthy with distrust, methinks she confers the richest boon on the poorest man, and injures those on whom she bestows her favors.—Chatfield.

How are the Profits of the Year to be Ascertained?

By Bernard Dale

(Continued from page 73 October number.)

One might take a case presenting more extreme features than those of the Neuchatel Company. Suppose a company formed for the sole object of sinking its paid-up share capital in the purchase of a concession, and selling it at a profit. Say, the company, in due course, having purchased the concession, sell it for £10,000, and, after paying all creditors, have a balance of £9,000. The business which the company was formed to transact having now ceased, this £9,000 would not be capital, for it would be a fund intended to be used as a source of income, but, on the contrary, a fund intended to be distributed amongst the shareholders as a source of present, it is conceived, can only be accepted with considerable qualification. It is surely going too far to suggest that the ratio decidendi of Lee v. Neuchatel Asphalt Company would sanction a company, say a land jobbing company, to expend any of its capital in acquiring a terminable lease and then dividing the rent as dividend. In their hands the lease would be part of their ordinary stock in trade. It is perfectly true, however, to say that the principle of the decision sanctions the expenditure of the whole of the paid-up share capital of a company in the acquisition of a particular patent which, say, it has been formed to work, and the distribution of the whole of the net income arising from the working of the patent as dividend, so that, say, by the time the patent has run out there is no asset of the company to represent the paid-up share capital. But can there be any valid objection to such a proceeding? If a number of persons choose to associate for purchasing and working a patent or other terminable property, agreeing among themselves and announcing, by the registration of their regulations, to those with whom they deal the nature of the operation in which they are engaged, and the conditions under which they propose to carry it into effect, is there any reason that the law should raise objections to this proceeding and impose on them restrictions which they disclaim? For whose sake? Not for that of the members themselves; for it is they who selected the venture as best calculated to promote their interests without restriction, and, if they should find that they are wrong in this respect, the remedy will be in their own hands. It must, therefore, be for the sake of third parties, namely, those who may have transactions with the company beyond what the gross income arising from the working of the patent suffices to pay. But nobody is obliged to deal with the company; still less is any one obliged to persons with whom such companies have give it unlimited credit. The class of dealings are, in general, persons quite capable of taking care of themselves, and there seems no reason why the law should be more careful of their interest than they themselves will be; provided, of course, no false representation is held out, and they are aware from the first what they have to trust to. To compel a company, under such circumstances, to set aside out of net revenue, a fund to meet the depreciation of their patent or other terminable property by lapse of time, would, it is conceived, in the majority of cases, entail serious inconvenience on the undertaking.

The terms "profit," "income," and "revenue," are frequently used by economists as synonymous terms. It is not until economists come to deal with the question, what are profits of a trade or business that we find clearly stated the notion of a surplus of returns over advances which is so closely associated in the mind of the mercantile community with the idea of profit.

In its strict sense the term "profit" is not synonymous with "income."

"It is undoubtedly true," said Bronson J., in People v. Supervisors of Niagara, 4 Hill, 20, "that 'profits' and 'income' are sometimes used as synonymous terms; but strictly speaking 'income' means that which comes in or is received from any business or investment of capital, without reference to the outgoing expenditure; while 'profits' generally means the gain which is made upon any business or investment when both receipts and payments are taken into account. 'Income' when applied to the affairs of individuals expresses the same idea that revenue does when applied to the affairs of a State or nation, and no one would think of denying that our government has any revenue because the expenditure for a given period may exceed the amount of receipts." As to the meaning of the term "profits" in the Income-Tax Acts, see Coltness Iron Co. v. Black, 6 Appeal Cases, 329.

The following are some definitions of profit by leading writers: John Stuart Mill says: "The capitalist, then, may be assumed to make all the advances and receive all the produce. His profit consists of the excess of the produce above the advances; his rate of profit is the ratio which that excess bears to the amount advanced." ("Principles of Political Economy," Book II., Chap. XV.)

Senior also defines profit as the difference between the value of the advances and the value of the returns; he says: "And the capitalists' profit depends on the difference between the value of the advance and the value of the return. In producing the return the wages and materials are necessarily consumed; they are parted with by the capitalist, and therefore termed circulating capital. The implements are not necessarily consumed; so far as they are unconsumed they remain the property of the capitalist, and are therefore termed fixed capital. The value of that portion of them which remains unconsumed must be added to that of the other returns before the profit can be estimated. * * * The profit in every case consists, as we have already stated, of the difference between the value of the advance and the value of the return." ("Political Economy," p. 86.)

Macleod says: "Profit is the difference between the cost of production of any goods and their price or value. This difference may be in excess of the cost of production, then the profit is positive and is termed a gain; but it may be in defect of the cost of production, and then profit is negative and is termed a loss." ("Elements of Economics," Vol. II.)

In his great work on the "Law of Partnership," Lord Justice Lindley says: "Profits are the excess of returns over advances; the excess of what is obtained over the cost of obtaining it. Losses on the other hand are the excess of advances over returns; the excess of the cost of obtaining over what is obtained." (5th Edition, p. 7.)

Professor Marshall in his "Economics of Industry," p. 68, says: "When a man is engaged in business, his profits for the year are the excess of his receipts from his business during the year over his outlay for his business; the difference between the value of his stock and plant at the end and at the beginning of the year being taken as part of his receipts, or as part of his outlay, according as there has been an increase or decrease of value."

It is to be noticed that, of the definitions above given, that of Professor Marshall is the only one which deals with what are "profits for the year."

There is, however, as we shall see hereafter, an all-important difference between the profits of an "entire venture," that is, a venture the profits of which are not to be ascertainel until its conclusion, and "profits for the year" of a continuing venture.

In Dent v. London Tramways Co., 16 Ch. Div., 344, Sir George Jessel, whose knowledge of the details of commercial business has, perhaps, never been surpassed on the Bench, said: "Profits for the year, of course, mean the surplus in receipts after paying expenses, and restoring the capital to the position it was in on the 1st of January in that year."

In that case the company had issued preference shares, the holders of which were entitled to a dividend "dependent on the profits of the particular year only," and the regulations contained a provision for the taking of yearly accounts. It was argued that before there was profit in any year to pay the preference dividend, all depreciation of the tramway from its start must be made good, and not merely the wear and tear for the year in question; but it was held by Sir George Jessel that the preference shareholders were entitled to a dividend out of the profits of any year, after providing for depreciation of the tramway in that year, but without making good depreciation in preceding years, that is to say, that for the purpose of ascertaining whether there were profits for any year, the capital asset represented by the tramway was to be restored to the condition it was in on the 1st of January of that year, and not to the condition it was in on the opening of the tramway.

The sole object of inserting in the regulations of joint-stock companies a provision for an annual balance sheet and profit and loss account is, it is conceived, to make the trading of each year a venture separate from that of other years.

Such a provision will be found in the regulations of ninety-nine companies out of a hundred. In its absence, and until some direction be given by the shareholders in general meeting, there would, it is surmised, be no alternative but to treat the business of the company as constituting one "entire venture" and to wait until the liquidation of the company before ascertaining the profit. Obvious, however, as the object of such a provision is, it has been strangely ignored by the two competing systems for ascertaining profit of a company, known respectively as the "Single Account System" and the "Double Account System."

(To be continued.)

To have nothing is not poverty.—Martial.

Public credit is suspicion asleep.—Thomas Paine.

Star Paper Fastener

The cut on this page represents a form of paper fastener that has many features that recommend it for use. It is handy to employ. The fasteners are in such shape that they do not become detached or lost, and the efficiency of the instrument is beyond dispute. The paper fastener shown in the center of the cut is twice actual size. The loading of the machine is shown by the fasteners attached together in a strip and placed in the spiral which extends from the back of the machine. This device is being put upon the market by A. H. Irwin, Curwensville, Pa.

General View of the Star Paper Fastener.

The following jingle would be amusing if the same ideas were not gravely put forward in more pretentious phrases as economic truths:

Rags make paper,
Paper makes money,
Money makes banks,
Banks make trusts,
Trusts make poverty,
Poverty makes rags.

There is at least one untruth in every line.

The Haine Suspended Ink-Well

What busy office man does not appreciate any device which will increase the working surface of his desk? Modern invention has tried to accomplish this in various ways, but nevertheless much valuable room has always been occupied by the receptacles for holding ink. At last we have a space-economizing device in the form of a suspended ink-well. The advantages of the Haine Ink-well are so obvious that we hardly need the suggestions of the manufacturers that in addition to economy of space, its suspended position prevents spattering or spilling of ink and that it is in the easiest and most

Fig. 1—Ink-Well attached to bottom shelf of pigeon holes of roll-top desk.

natural position for use. The ink bottles cannot be upset and their construction is such that the pen can only be submerged to a certain depth. The Haine Ink-well holds two kinds of ink, a neat sponge cup and a convenient pen rack. It can be put on or taken from the desk in a

Fig. 2—Ink-Well attached to rack above a bookkeeper's desk.

moment, no screws or nails, only a pair of small spring clips being used. Fig. 1 shows the ink-well attached to the bottom shelf of the pigeon holes of a roll-top desk, and Fig. 2 to the rack above a bookkeeper's desk. The third illustration shows more clearly the manner in which the attachment is made and affords a better idea of the ink-well itself. The ink bottles are fitted with hard rubber tubes, which render them air tight and dust proof. The frame is made from heavy stamped brass and is offered in four styles of finish. It presents a very handsome appearance. This article is put upon the market by the Universal Specialty Company, No. 151 Chambers Street, New York.

The Braham Pen

The general introduction of fountain pens has got people into the habit of depending upon the pen itself for a supply of ink, as opposed to the old plan of constantly dipping the pen in the ink-well. At the same time there is still a need for pens of the ordinary kind, and particularly is this the case among bookkeepers and other clerical men who do writing more or less constantly. To supply an ordinary pen with a sufficient quantity of ink to write from three to five times the space that could be covered with a single dipping is in the direction of labor-saving improvement. A form of pen being introduced by G. H. Ander, 241 East Forty-sixth Street, New York, called the Braham pen, is calculated to afford the advantages above described.

Fig. 3—Showing manner of attachment.

The pen itself may be of any desired variety, ranging from the finest to the coarsest, and from the smallest to the largest. Inside of the pen, and so located as to hold the fluid in proper position for feeding down as used, is a supplementary bit of metal, so put in place as to be entirely out of the way and yet to be very effective in use. These pens are offered at a remarkably low price Those of our readers who see fit to mention this notice in writing to Mr. Ander, and enclosing fifteen cents, will receive a dozen pens in response.

Accountics

The Office Magazine.

A. O. KITTREDGE, F. I. A., C. P. A., Editor.

E. R. KITTREDGE, Associate.

Accountics is devoted to the Science of Accounting, to the Art of Bookkeeping and to the advocacy of Improved Office Methods.

Subscription.—One dollar a year, payable in advance.

Postage is prepaid by the publishers in the United States, Canada and Mexico. For all other countries in the Postal Union, subscribers must add 50 cents a year.

Discontinuances.—In the absence of specific orders to discontinue at the end of the subscription term the magazine will be continued and a bill sent.

Remittances should be by Draft, P. O. Order or Express Order, payable to the order of the ACCOUNTICS ASSOCIATION. Money and postage stamps are at the risk of the sender, unless sent by express or in registered letters. Add 10 cents each to checks on local banks to defray collection charges.

Advertising Rates will be quoted on application.

Official Journal.—This publication, by resolutions duly passed, has been made the official publication of the following organizations:—

THE INSTITUTE OF ACCOUNTS.

THE NEW YORK CHAPTER of the Institute of Accounts.

THE WASHINGTON CHAPTER of the Institute of Accounts.

THE HARTFORD CHAPTER of the Institute of Accounts.

ACCOUNTICS is the accredited medium of intercommunication between members of the Institute of Accounts wherever located.

ACCOUNTICS ASSOCIATION,
Publishers,

Lancashire Bldg., Pine St., near Nassau,

New York.

Publisher's Desk.

A series of cards issued by the John Hancock Mutual Life Insurance Company, of Boston, Mass., and prepared for them by the Livermore & Knight Company, of Providence, to some of which we have referred in the past, continue to be sent out to the business public. The originality of the design cannot fail to attract the attention of the curious and critical. The one that has just come to hand is merely addressed on the face, while the back shows a picture of a youth carrying a well-filled bag over his shoulder. The bag is realistic in the extreme, being actually present. It is of manila paper and is tied at the top with a cotton string. This string passes through the hand of the boy and is knotted on the opposite side of the card. Protruding from the bag are the feet of what may be supposed to be a turkey. Opening the bag, however, one finds instead of the conventional Thanksgiving fowl a neat little circular advertising the advantages of a policy in the company named.

The Youth's Companion sends its subscribers for the year 1900 another of its artistic calenders. This, like some others in the past, is made up of three panels, the two outer ones square and the center one round. On the first, above the calender for half the year, is a picture in colors of a maiden seated on a grassy hillside, her lap full of roses; on the last panel above the remainder of the calender is the picture of another maiden gracefully poised, being the principal feature of a summer landscape. Looking from its center panel is a beautiful dark-eyed girl with brown curls escaping from beneath an old-fashioned bonnet. Her rosy cheeks and pink gown give tone and expression to the combined pictures. On the reverse side of the panels we have the dates 1827-1900, reminding us that this is the seventy-fourth year of the publication which sends this pleasant greeting to its friends.

"The Experience of 187 Advertisers" is the title of a very attractive pamphlet issued some time since by Charles D. Lanier, Business Manager of the American Monthly Review of Reviews. The pamphlet consists of fac-simile reproductions of letters addressed to the periodical named, by its general advertisers, setting forth the opinion in which the service is regarded. It is needless to say that no one, so far as these letters go, speaks adversely of the medium. We doubt very much if any one ever entertained such an opinion, much less ever put it into letter form. In addition to the letters presented in fac-simile, there are extracts from other letters, given in ordinary type. The pamphlet is divided into several distinct divisions, according to the different departments in the periodical named. In general get-up, whether considered as a whole or in the care with which the several letters are reproduced, the pamphlet is one of the finest that has come to our attention. The cover is dark-green, bound with a silken cord, and the side-title is in bronze.

Accountics: The Office Magazine FOR 1900

GENERAL PROGRAM

There are various good things prepared and in store for the readers of ACCOUNTICS during the new year. There are some decided innovations upon the established order to be introduced which will tend to make the magazine more valuable because more practically useful.

In the first place, commencing with the issue for January, the page is to be enlarged to better admit the display of forms and illustrations of office furnishings and specialties.

In the second place, while relinquishing none of the features of higher accounting which have characterized the magazine in the past, certain new departments are to be added which will tend to popularize the work and render it useful to a still larger class in the business community.

A few of the more prominent articles which will appear in the new volume are mentioned below:

Information for Office Men

By reference to our premium subscription coupon plan, described upon another page, it will be noticed that every subscriber is entitled to answers to any two practical office or accounting questions which he may see fit to propose. The many thousands of queries which we expect to receive through this means, will no doubt include a large number which, if presented in the printed pages of ACCOUNTICS along with the answers made thereto, would be helpful to all our readers. Judicious selection is to be made and just as many of the question and answers as our columns can conveniently accommodate, are to be treated in this manner. By this plan not only will each subscriber have the benefit of answers to his own questions but also of many others.

The Clearing House

Every business man knows at least a little about a clearing house and the important part which it plays in the financial transactions of the period, but it is safe to say he would like to know more. The daily papers abound with clearing-house statements and references to clearing-house statistics as indications of the nation's prosperity. In seasons of financial distress and panic clearing-house loan certificates are used to settle balances between banks. All this the average business man sees day by day, but the questions "why" and "how" remain unanswered.

How a clearing house is administered, what it does for the financial and business public, why clearing-house loan certificates are issued, and what is accomplished thereby, and many other points about clearing houses are to be explained to readers of ACCOUNTICS during the new

(*Continued on page D*)

Cash Premium Subscription Canvass

Acknowledgments

Wherever Accountics, The Office Magazine, has been presented, it has made friends and subscribers. Every reader, so far, has helped in extending its circulation and many have done a considerable amount of labor in this regard without any other reward than the consciousness of having helped a good thing along. We have seldom known whom to thank or recompense. Hereafter it will be different.

Double Reward for Effort Made

By the cash premium coupon plan explained below, every one who does a little work for Accountics will not only be paid for what he does but he will also be putting into the hands of each of his friends who subscribes through his instrumentality the chance of being similarly rewarded for any efforts they may see fit to make.

Further, each one who subscribes upon this coupon plan is to be accorded certain special rights and privileges, all as mentioned in the body of the coupon.

What You Will Get for $1

The scheme may look intricate, and one hard to work out, and still harder to correctly record in an accounting way. Just read the coupon and see what you will get for a dollar:

1. A year's subscription to Accountics.

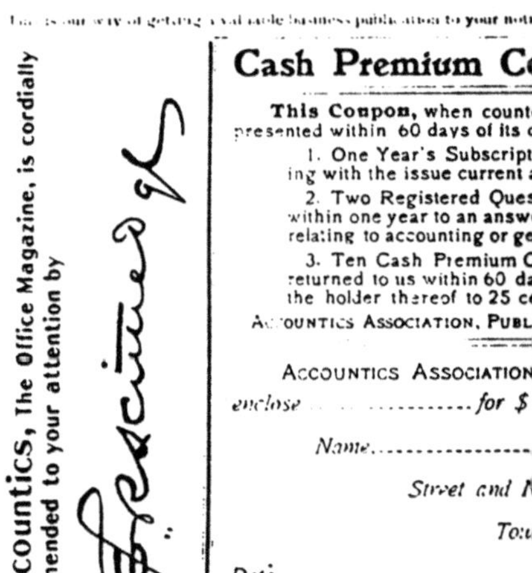
Accountics, The Office Magazine, is cordially commended to your attention by

Cash Premium C

This Coupon, when count
presented within 60 days of its d
1. One Year's Subscript
ing with the issue current a
2. Two Registered Ques
within one year to an answ
relating to accounting or ge
3. Ten Cash Premium C
returned to us within 60 da
the holder thereof to 25 ce
Accountics Association, Publ

Accountics Association
enclose .... for $
Name..................
Street and N
To
Date..................

THIS COUPON IS C

2. Answers (by mail, if postage is enclosed) to any two questions that may be proposed relating to accounting or general office practice.

3. Ten premium coupons for distribu-

tion, each of which, if returned to us accompanied by one dollar, will entitle you to twenty-five cents cash and the new subscriber to the same advantages that are herein offered to you.

How It Works

The successful working out of this scheme depends in part upon an adequate accounting plan and its proper bookkeeping equipment. All this has been furnished us by the Account, Audit and Assurance Co., Ltd., of New York. It also depends in part upon the proper equipment of office furniture and appliances, and these have been supplied by The Globe-Wernicke Co., of Cincinnati. The whole thing is so simple and easy that

ng, push it along.—*The Publishers*

...e, JANUARY 31, 1900.

by a subscriber of record, and
, entitles the holder to
: OFFICE MAGAZINE, commenced.
...titling the holder at any time
sent) to any practical question
...t he may propose.
distribution, each of which if
...anied by one dollar, will entitle

...ilding, Pine St., New York.

...eptance of the above offer, I
...azine addressed as follows:

No. 13119

...istered letter. *We do not pay ...*
...s If there is a collection expense
...ways at sender's risk.

Subscriber's Voucher.

The subscriber is requested to fill out this stub and to detach it before mailing the coupon

Countersigned by

....

Form of remittance.

....

Remarks ....

Date sent..............

No. 13119

Keep this for reference. If correspondence becomes necessary, use this number for identification.

Accountics Association,
New York.

...T OUT AND USE IT.

just how it is done may make one of the interesting special articles to be published a few months hence.

Our Delivery

For your dollar you will get (1) your name on our mailing list for a year; (2) a receipt for your remittance and a number which will be the key to your questions, and (3) the ten premium coupons mentioned, all numbered and recorded in your name, and each providing a space for your signature, by which you, as the sender, will be identified to your friend.

What You Can Do

Enclosing these coupons in your private letters, or even slipping them into occasional business letters, will cost you very little trouble and will have the effect of bringing the best office and accounting publication to the notice of your correspondents, while earning you a liberal reward for your effort. You have the chance of geting $3.50 value for an investment of $1. At the outset you get the magazine, which cannot be estimated as worth less than a dollar, so you have your money's worth anyhow. Then each subscriber secured through your effort gives you 25 cents or the whole ten the sum of $2.50, making $3.50 in all.

Time Limit

It would be manifestly impracticable to keep this offer open indefinitely, and therefore the coupons are stamped with a date and are limited to the period of time thereafter that is mentioned.

New and Old Subscribers on the Same Plane

This offer is open to new and old subscribers alike. It will not be extended to any one for remittances already made, but will be conceded to any one already on ACCOUNTICS mailing list who remits a dollar (accompanied by a numbered coupon) for extending his subsbcription a year in advance of present date of expiration.

Make all remittances payable to the order of ACCOUNTICS ASSOCIATION, Lancashire Building, New York.

Continued from page A

year by one of New York's most eminent bankers. This series of papers will be amply and attractively illustrated.

The Application of Advanced Accounting Methods to Modern Business Enterprises

By A. O. Kittredge, F. I. A., C. P. A.

A series of studies based upon actual installations.

The first paper of this important series will be published early in the year, and the others will appear thereafter in order about as follows:

1—Introductory, embodying a general statement of principles.
2—The Machine Shop.
3—The Cotton Mill.
4—The Foundry.
5—The Street Railway.
6—The Department Store.
7—Stationery and Job Printing.
8—Instalment Payments.
9—Periodical Publishing.
10—General Manufacturing.

Business Science

Charles Dutton, who stands prominent among the accounting specialists of the metropolis, always commands the earnest attention of the audience he addresses, while the reader of the reports of his lectures, as well as of the special articles that he writes, is both edified and instructed. In connection with work for the Institute of Accounts, of which he is the national secretary, Mr. Dutton will contribute to ACCOUNTICS during the year several papers, the title of one of which we are able to announce at this time: "The Duality of Business," a study in practical economics, will appear in one of the early issues of the new year. Mere mention of this title in connection with the author's name is to all those who are acquainted with Mr. Dutton a promise of new ideas and an incentive to better and more thorough work.

Business Half-Facts

By Pierson Peale.

There are so many things in business that are not so, so many conceptions of facts that are false, so many rules that have to be unlearned, and so much that is not true because it is grossly misstated, that we risk nothing in saying that the author who has engaged to give us a series of sketches under the general title "Business Half-Facts" would not exhaust his subject, if he were allowed to fill many columns of each number of ACCOUNTICS during the entire year. We can only give him occasional space, taking his turn with others, but from an examination of the manuscript now in hand, we are of the opinion that our readers will wish we could allow him far more than is our plan at present.

Letters from Practical Office Men

We have already mentioned that the proposed change in the dimensions of the page is for the purpose of better accommodating diagrams and other illustrations that are important to the text. This has been done particularly to help along a new department, in the conduct of which we are promised the help and co-operation of many of our old subscribers. A prominent feature of the new volume will be letters from practical office men describing how they conduct certain parts of their regular work, and illustrated by reproductions of their blanks and forms.

Old Saws Reset for Business Purposes

By Myron MacLean.

It is far easier to ask questions than it is to answer them. One function of a question is to provoke thought and that is the principal object in view in the series of queries which Mr. MacLean has arranged for our readers. He does not attempt to present answers to his interrogatories, possibly because he could not satisfactorily reply to all of them if he were to try; but he does undertake to ask pertinent questions about accounting, office work, and business in general, in a way to stimulate inquiry and investigation.

Questions and Answers Concerning the Balance Sheet System of Accounts

Selections from the correspondence of the Account, Audit and Assurance Co., Ltd., concerning their accounting methods, have characterized these pages in the past and will be continued for some time to come. The wide interest manifested in the novel but eminently successful plans of the company mentioned, is a wholesome sign of the times. Business men are beginning to appreciate perfect accounting and scientific office methods, as in the past they have learned to appreciate the best machinery in their factories and high-grade furniture in their stores and offices. The object in presenting these extracts from inquiries and the replies made thereto, is to meet a well-defined want for information concerning the very best.

Accountics

The Office Magazine.

A. O. KITTREDGE, F. I. A., C. P. A., Editor.
CLARENCE F. CHATFIELD, Associate.

Accountics is devoted to the Science of Accounting, to the Art of Bookkeeping and to the advocacy of Improved Office Methods.

Subscription.—One dollar a year, payable in advance.

Postage is prepaid by the publishers in the United States, Canada and Mexico. For all other countries in the Postal Union, subscribers must add 50 cents a year.

Discontinuances.—In the absence of specific orders to discontinue at the end of the subscription term the magazine will be continued and a bill sent.

Remittances should be by Draft, P. O. Order or Express Order, payable to the order of the ACCOUNTICS ASSOCIATION. Money and postage stamps are at the risk of the sender, unless sent by express or in registered letters. Add 10 cents each to checks on local banks to defray collection charges.

Advertising Rates will be quoted on application.

Official Journal.—This publication, by resolutions duly passed, has been made the official publication of the following organizations:—

THE INSTITUTE OF ACCOUNTS.
THE NEW YORK CHAPTER of the Institute of Accounts.
THE WASHINGTON CHAPTER of the Institute of Accounts.
THE HARTFORD CHAPTER of the Institute of Accounts.

ACCOUNTICS is the accredited medium of intercommunication between members of the Institute of Accounts wherever located.

ACCOUNTICS ASSOCIATION,
Publishers,
Wool Exchange, New York.

Entered at the Post Office New York as Second Class Matter.

Publishers' Desk

Albert B. King & Co., 105 William St., New York, are sending out samples of the new form of promissory notes, which they are prepared to supply in books of fifty each. Since October 1, 1898, attorney's fees and a confession of judgment may be included in a negotiable or promissory note in the State of New York.

The King Safety Tint Paper, which affords protection against alterations of checks and other valuable papers, is also offered by this firm.

The American Graphophone Company of New York is introducing an improved talking machine, which is called the Graphaphone Grand. An exhibition was given before a large audience in the Astor Gallery of the Waldorf-Astoria Hotel, Tuesday, January 10. The reproductions upon this machine are better in volume and more accurate than those of any former production of this company.

"Banking Helps" is the title of a very attractive pamphlet recently issued by The Globe Company, of Cincinnati, with salesrooms in New York, Chicago and Boston. The articles described include the Globe Card Index File, the Globe Bank Check File, the Globe Deposit Ticket File, the Globe-Wernicke Sectional Cabinet, and the Globe Banker's Note Case. The book is printed in two colors, with the illustrations, which are partly line cuts and partly half-tones, in happy contrast with the text. The initial sentence in the introductory is the keynote of the whole work: "Any device that will improve service, lessen labor and increase safety in the conduct of a banking business is a banking help and worthy the consideration of all bankers." While the pamphlet is specially addressed to bankers, it contains much that is of interest in every business office. Particularly is this true in what is shown of the Globe-Wernicke Sectional Cabinet.

The Age of Steel, St. Louis, Mo., celebrates its forty-first anniversary in its issue of January 7. This number is handsomely printed and ilustrated, and contains letters and descriptive articles from all parts of the world setting forth the advantages and possibilities of foreign markets for American products.

An article, "On the Necessity for a Higher Commercial Education for Business Men Engaged in Foreign Commerce," by J. B. Johnson, Professor of Civil Engineering in Washington University, St. Louis, is interesting and pointedly suggestive of various possible advancements in this direction.

The first number of Machinery Review, published by D. T. Mullett, at 89 Chambers street, New York, was issued in January. It is a quarterly illustrated review of machinery and tools, with forty-four pages and cover, 10¼x13¾ inches in size. The contents consist chiefly of descriptive matter and illustrations of machinery and tools, such as will be found in various manufacturers' catalogues. The subscription price is 50 cents a year.

It is proposed to introduce a new law into the Connecticut Legislature at an early day, providing for an annual accounting of combines and insolvent estates by trustees. Attention has been recently called to the number of outstanding Connecticut receiverships on which no report has been made for years, and the new law is intended to hit cases of this kind.

The year which has just closed was a remarkable one in the iron and steel trade, not only from its having been the year of greatest tonnage, but for many other reasons as well. The year closed stronger than any year since 1879, while there is no probability of any collapse like the disastrous one which followed the boom in 1879-80.

Accountics

The Office Magazine.

A. O. KITTREDGE, F. I. A., C. P. A., Editor.
E. R. KITTREDGE, Associate.

Accountics is devoted to the Science of Accounting, to the Art of Bookkeeping and to the advocacy of Improved Office Methods.

Subscription.—One dollar a year, payable in advance.

Postage is prepaid by the publishers in the United States, Canada and Mexico. For all other countries in the Postal Union, subscribers must add 50 cents a year.

Discontinuances.—In the absence of specific orders to discontinue at the end of the [illegible] the magazine will be continued and a bill sent.

Remittances should be by [illegible] P. O. Order or [illegible] Draft, payable to the order of the Ac[illegible] [illegible] banks [illegible]

Advertising Rates [illegible]

Official Journal. [illegible]

[illegible]

[illegible] ASSOCIATION.

[illegible]

[illegible] and [illegible]

[illegible]

[illegible] This company [illegible] the [illegible] in the building [illegible] Insurance Company, [illegible] five offices which have been fitted up in excellent shape for the purpose. A large force is busily engaged in the rapidly growing business of the organization.

Frank J. Sager, an occasional contributer to the columns of ACCOUNTICS, but with whose writings our readers are well acquainted, resigned his position as cashier of the Exchange Bank, White Oaks, New Mexico, a short time since, and is now installed as manager of the accounting specialty department of the Globe Company, Cincinnati. Mr. Sager's wide experience in business affairs, and his practical ideas concerning bookkeeping equipment and accessories render him a valuable man for the position named.

The Ladies Home Journal for 1899 promises to be better than ever before. The management, with characteristic energy, is keeping the publication well at the front, while the brightest writers of the day are numbered among the contributors.

Charles Dutton, one of the best known public accountants and auditors in New York, and an expert who has for many years made a specialty of surrogate practice, municipal investigations and corporation work, has recently accepted the position of supervising auditor of the [illegible] Audit and Assurance Co., Limited, [illegible] direction to the auditing department of this organization. Mr. [illegible] will still serve his old clients and [illegible] under the auspices of the [illegible] so long [illegible]

"Soft Soaps."

[illegible] for [illegible] don't like [illegible]

[illegible] is started along with him and [illegible] his failure in life to his laziness. It is a fault or peculiarity of human beings to look outside of themselves for reasons for their failure. They never think about turning the light upon their own imperfections and studying themselves, and that is really the only place they ought to look, and the only place it will do any good to look."

"Take life too seriously, and what is it worth?" asks Goethe. "If the morning wakes us to no new joys, if the evening brings us not the hope of new pleasures, is it worth while to dress and undress? Does the sun shine on me to-day that I may reflect on yesterday?—that I may endeavor to foresee and to control what can neither be foreseen nor controlled,—the destiny of to-morrow?"

FOR YOUR CONVENIENCE.

Notice that the panel below contains a Subscription Order, that it is at the bottom of a page, with a line of perforations above for detaching, and arranged in various other respects in a way to save your time and labor in forwarding your order.

This is our way of soliciting subscriptions. May we not hear from you at once?

ACCOUNTICS ASSOCIATION,
260 West Broadway, New York.

SUBSCRIPTION ORDER.

(23)

ACCOUNTICS ASSOCIATION,
260 West Broadway, New York. Date, 189

Gentlemen: –

Enclosed please find one dollar, for which mail Accountics for one year, addressed as follows:

(Name)_

(Full Address)_

Remit by draft on New York, express or postal money order or currency in registered letter. Currency or stamps not registered at the risk of sender.

Accountics

The Office Magazine.

A. O. KITTREDGE, F. I. A., C. P. A., Editor.
E. R. KITTREDGE, Associate.

Accountics is devoted to the Science of Accounting, to the Art of Bookkeeping and to the advocacy of Improved Office Methods.

Subscription.—One dollar a year, payable in advance.

Postage is prepaid by the publishers in the United States, Canada and Mexico. For all other countries in the Postal Union, subscribers must add 50 cents a year.

Discontinuances.—In the absence of specific orders to discontinue at the end of the subscription term the magazine will be continued and a bill sent.

Remittances should be by Draft, P. O. Order or Express Order, payable to the order of the ACCOUNTICS ASSOCIATION. Money and postage stamps are at the risk of the sender, unless sent by express or in registered letters. Add 10 cents each to checks on local banks to defray collection charges.

Advertising Rates will be quoted on application.

Official Journal.—This publication, by resolutions duly passed, has been made the official publication of the following organizations:—

THE INSTITUTE OF ACCOUNTS.
THE NEW YORK CHAPTER of the Institute of Accounts.
THE WASHINGTON CHAPTER of the Institute of Accounts.
THE HARTFORD CHAPTER of the Institute of Accounts.

ACCOUNTICS is the accredited medium of intercommunication between members of the Institute of Accounts wherever located.

ACCOUNTICS ASSOCIATION,
Publishers,
Lancashire Bldg., Pine St., near Nassau.
New York.

Entered at the Post Office New York as Second Class Matter.

Publishers' Desk

Our advertisers and correspondents generally are informed that Clarence F. Chatfield, who for a very short time was employed upon this periodical, is no longer connected with it in any capacity. All communications, whether relating to business or editorial matters, should be addressed to ACCOUNTICS ASSOCIATION.

Circulation

The circulation of ACCOUNTICS is steadily and rapidly growing. The magazine seems to be appreciated wherever it is introduced and our old readers are doing not a little to help along the development of its subscription list. In each issue there is printed on one of the advertising pages a subscription blank with a line of perforations for convenient detaching. This serves as a gentle reminder to those who see the paper for the first time that a subscription is desired, and it also proves a convenience for those who desire to direct the attention of their fellow business men to the usefulness of the publication. We are always glad to send sample copies on request and take this occasion to thank various correspondents for the lists of names which they have recently forwarded to us, requesting that samples be mailed them. Those who are disposed to benefit their friends by calling attention to a helpful, practical, office journal, are requested to send in additional lists. Where we are permitted to do so, we write a letter to each person named in the list saying that a sample copy has been sent at the request of the one who has sent us the list, thus directly connecting the receipt of the paper with the name of their friend or acquaintance.

Change of Date

Attention is directed to the advertisement of The Globe Company in another page of this issue, wherein they announce a postponement of date in the card index competition. So many of those who have signified their desire to take part in this contest have requested a little longer time for preparation, that it has been deemed wise to extend the time two months from the original date. If, by any accident, those who at once set about preparing their exhibits when the announcement of this contest was first made, should not see this postponement and should send in their work at the original date, their entries will remain unopened until the final date. If, in turn, they should desire to withdraw them for additional consideration, they will be returned on request accompanied by proper identification.

Curiosities of the Calendar

The "Westminster Gazette" publishes the following interesting item:

"These little curiosities of the Gregorian calendar are recalled by the fact that we have entered upon a new year:

"Since the calendar was reformed by Pope Gregory no century has ever begun on a Wednesday, a Friday or a Sunday; and the same order of days is repeated every twenty years. January and October of each year always begin with the same day; so with April and July; so with September and December; so with February, March and November. Strangely enough, there is no single day of the week which is not accepted by some portion of the human race as the 'day of rest.' For example: Christians, Sunday; Greeks, Monday; Persians, Tuesday; Assyrians, Wednesday; Egyptians, Thursday; Turks, Friday; Jews, Saturday. As measured by the unerring sun, the errors in the Gregorian calendar amount to one day in every 4,000 years."

For Your Convenience.

Notice that the panel below contains a Subscription Order, that it is at the bottom of a page, with a line of perforations above for detaching, and arranged in various other respects in a way to save your time and labor in forwarding your order.

This is our way of soliciting subscriptions. May we not hear from you at once?

ACCOUNTICS ASSOCIATION, Publishers,

Lancashire Building, Pine St., near Nassau, New York.

SUBSCRIPTION ORDER.

(24)

ACCOUNTICS ASSOCIATION,

Lancashire Bldg., Pine Street near Nassau, New York. 189

Gentlemen: –

Enclosed please find one dollar, for which mail Accountics for one year, addressed as follows:

(Name

(Full Address)

Remit by draft on New York, express or postal money order or currency in registered letter. Currency or stamps not registered at the risk of sender.

Accountics

The Office Magazine.

A. O. KITTREDGE, F. I. A., C. P. A., Editor.
E. R. KITTREDGE, Associate.

Accountics is devoted to the Science of Accounting, to the Art of Bookkeeping and to the advocacy of Improved Office Methods.

Subscription.—One dollar a year, payable in advance.

Postage is prepaid by the publishers in the United States, Canada and Mexico. For all other countries in the Postal Union, subscribers must add 50 cents a year.

Discontinuances.—In the absence of specific orders to discontinue at the end of the subscription term the magazine will be continued and a bill sent.

Remittances should be by Draft, P. O. Order or Express Order, payable to the order of the Accountics Association. Money and postage stamps are at the risk of the sender, unless sent by express or in registered letters. Add 10 cents each to checks on local banks to defray collection charges.

Advertising Rates will be quoted on application.

Official Journal.—This publication, by resolutions duly passed, has been made the official publication of the following organizations:—
The Institute of Accounts.
The New York Chapter of the Institute of Accounts.
The Washington Chapter of the Institute of Accounts.
The Hartford Chapter of the Institute of Accounts.

Accountics is the accredited medium of intercommunication between members of the Institute of Accounts wherever located.

ACCOUNTICS ASSOCIATION,
Publishers,
; Lancashire Bldg., Pine St., near Nassau,
New York.

Entered at the Post Office New York as Second Class Matter.

Publishers' Desk

The attention of all our readers and advertisers is called to our change of address. Accountics is now very comfortably and eligibly located in the Lancashire Building, Pine Street, less than a half block from the corner of Nassau Street, and directly east of the Sub-Treasury Building. We shall be pleased to have all our friends and patrons visit us in our new quarters as often as it may be convenient for them to do so.

Circulation

The circulation of Accountics is steadily and rapidly growing. The magazine seems to be appreciated wherever it is introduced and our old readers are doing not a little to help along the development of its subscription list. In each issue there is printed on one of the advertising pages a subscription blank with a line of perforations for convenient detaching. This serves as a gentle reminder to those who see the paper for the first time that a subscription is desired, and it also proves a convenience for those who desire to direct the attention of their fellow business men to the usefulness of the publication. We are always glad to send sample copies on request and take this occasion to thank various correspondents for the lists of names which they have recently forwarded to us, requesting that samples be mailed them. Those who are disposed to benefit their friends by calling attention to a helpful, practical office journal, are requested to send in additional lists. Where we are permitted to do so, we write a letter to each person named in the list saying that a simple copy has been sent at the request of the one who has sent us the list, thus directly connecting the receipt of the paper with the name of their friend or acquaintance.

Change of Date

Attention is directed to the advertisement of The Globe Company in another page of this issue, wherein they announce a postponement of date in the card index competition. So many of those who have signified their desire to take part in this contest have requested a little longer time for preparation that it has been deemed wise to extend the time two months from the original date. If, by any accident, those who at once set about preparing their exhibits when the announcement of this contest was first made, should not see this postponement and should send in their work at the original date, their entries will remain unopened until the final date. If, in turn, they should desire to withdraw them for additional consideration, they will be returned on request accompanied by proper identification.

The Office Boy Balances the Books.

For Your Convenience.

Notice that the panel below contains a Subscription Order, that it is at the bottom of a page, with a line of perforations above for detaching, and arranged in various other respects in a way to save your time and labor in forwarding your order.

This is our way of soliciting subscriptions. May we not hear from you at once?

ACCOUNTICS ASSOCIATION, Publishers,
Lancashire Building, Pine St., near Nassau, New York.

SUBSCRIPTION ORDER.

(25)

ACCOUNTICS ASSOCIATION,
Lancashire Bldg., Pine Street near Nassau, New York. 189..

Gentlemen:—

Enclosed please find one dollar, for which mail Accountics for one year, addressed as follows:

(Name) ....

(Full Address) ....

Remit by draft on New York, express or postal money order or currency in registered letter. Currency or stamps not registered at the risk of sender.

Addition, Multiplication and Division

Are performed on the Comptometer at a great saving of time and worry. Used in bookkeeping in the offices of thousands of large firms. Used by mechanical and civil engineers. Once used becomes indispensable. Many after trying one have purchased two, three and four.

Scott & Williams, Builders of Knitting Machinery, Philadelphia, write: "We perform by its use all the office calculations incident to an extended business with great rapidity and absolute correctness."

The American Glucose Co., Peoria, Ill., writes: "We have two of your Comptometers in use in our office and are pleased to say that they are giving us the best of satisfaction; in fact, we would hardly know how to get along without them."

Write for full description and sixty days' trial offer.

Felt & Tarrant Mfg. Co., 52 to 56 Illinois Street, CHICAGO

SEE THAT CLIP?

The Niagara Clip holds securely from the thinnest sheet of paper up to ⅜ inch in thickness, and can be used over and over again. Better than pins for filing letters, records, cards, etc. Avoid unsightly pin holes in attaching second letters, business cards, checks, drafts, invoices, etc. Put up in boxes of 100 especially for desk convenience. Sample box 20 cts. postpaid.

NIAGARA CLIP CO., 30 Broadway, N. Y. City.

FAC SIMILE.

Agents Wanted.

MURRAY'S INTEREST TABLES.

The only Table Showing 2½ Per Cent. Rates. Price $10.

Revised Edition.
Most complete Tables in the market—2½, 3, 3½, 4, 4½, 5, 5½, 6, 6½, 7, 7½ and 8 per cent. From 1 day to 368. On $1 to $10,000. **B. W. MURRAY.** Accountant's Office, Supreme Court of Ontario, Toronto, Ontario.

Has a Loose Cap.

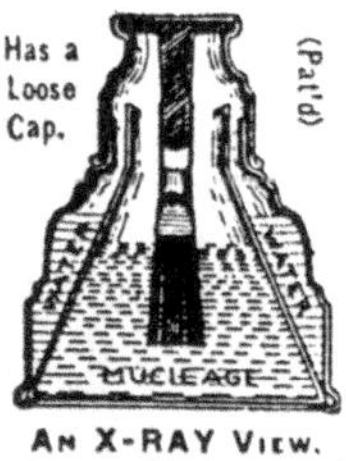

(Pat'd)

AN X-RAY VIEW.

NO DRIED-UP MUCILAGE

Just when you need it, if you use

Lindsay's "Perfect" Mucilage and Paste Fount
Satisfies Everybody—Always Ready—Takes Care of Itself.
Has a Water Reservoir, which keeps air moist.
Can't Dry-up or Clog.
Made of Aluminum.
Lighter, stronger, prettier than glass. Its Simplicity and Handiness will surprise you. Price 50 cts., post paid

Sent on 30 days' trial to responsible parties.

If you don't like it, your money back.

PERFECT MUCILAGE BOTTLE CO.,
6600 Wentworth Ave., CHICAGO, ILL.

Just What You Want!

$2. per set, cash with order, 500 letterheads, 500 envelopes, 500 cards, neatly printed. A trial order will show you the value of this offer.

$3.50 per set, cash with order, 1000 letterheads, 1000 envelopes, 1000 cards printed.

Parker Co., Box 2799, Boston, Mass.

ABOUT a Pay Roll which proves itself, corrects all mistakes in figuring, divides up Pay Roll into several amounts needed to pay each person.

But let us send you a sample leaf, with circular, which tells the whole story.

BARLOW BROS.
GRAND RAPIDS, MICHIGAN.

STATIONERY

For business use Embossed in Color from Steel Dies—Nothing else. Capacity, 50,000 sheets daily. Samples and quotations gladly furnished.

The American Embossing Co. 73 Lock St Buffalo N. Y

SEE THAT CLIP?

Pages IV, VIII and IX.

Your CREDIT SYSTEM

is incomplete without a device for keeping all reports on each customer in one place convenient for instant reference. Such a device saves delays, embarrassing alike to yourself and to your customer, permits prompt and judicious action and increases in value in proportion to added records of credit information gained through years of business engagement.

The Globe Mercantile Report Cabinet

IS the ideal device for keeping in a convenient, compact and orderly manner all credit information

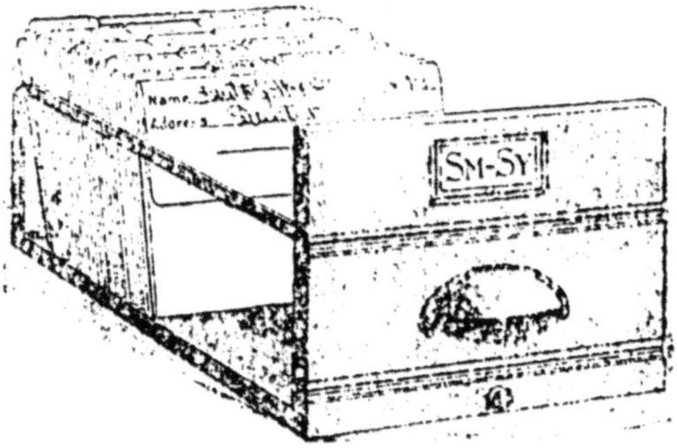

IT is substantial, attractive, simple in operation, and perfect in arrangement. It consists of

FOLDERS FOR HOLDING REPORTS.
FILES FOR HOLDING FOLDERS.
CABINETS FOR HOLDING FILES.

Folders of heavy Manilla paper, with printed form for memoranda, to which reports are attached.

Files fitted with removable partitions, alphabetically indexed or numbered as wanted, between which folders are placed, all held together in upright position by an adjustable follower.

Cabinets furnished, with or without roll front, in sizes ranging from six to thirty-six files, with capacity of from 1,500 to 8,000 folders with contents.

Shipped on approval, freight prepaid.

For particulars, address

The Globe-Wernicke Co.

1224-1248 W. 8th St., Cincinnati.
Fulton & Pearl Sts., New York
64-66 Pearl Street, Boston
226-228 Wabash Ave., Chicago

For Product Safety Concerns and Information please contact our EU representative GPSR@taylorandfrancis.com Taylor & Francis Verlag GmbH, Kaufingerstraße 24, 80331 München, Germany

Batch number: 10725933

Printed by Printforce, the Netherlands